TENTH EDITION

DELINQUENCY

IN SOCIETY

Robert M. Regoli, PhD

PROFESSOR EMERITUS
UNIVERSITY OF COLORADO AT BOULDER

John D. Hewitt, PhD

PROFESSOR
GRAND VALLEY STATE UNIVERSITY

Matt DeLisi, PhD

PROFESSOR AND COORDINATOR
IOWA STATE UNIVERSITY

JONES & BARTLETT
LEARNING

World Headquarters
Jones & Bartlett Learning
5 Wall Street
Burlington, MA 01803
978-443-5000
info@jblearning.com
www.jblearning.com

Jones & Bartlett Learning books and products are available through most bookstores and online booksellers. To contact Jones & Bartlett Learning directly, call 800-832-0034, fax 978-443-8000, or visit our website, www.jblearning.com.

11360-0

Production Credits
VP, Executive Publisher: David D. Cella
Executive Editor: Matthew Kane
Associate Acquisitions Editor: Marisa A. Hines
Director of Production: Jenny L. Corriveau
Production Editor: Lori Mortimer
Director of Marketing: Andrea DeFronzo
Marketing Manager: Lindsay White
Cover and Text Design: Kristin E. Parker

Director of Rights & Media: Joanna Gallant
Rights & Media Specialist: Robert Boder
Media Development Editor: Shannon Sheehan
Cover Image: ©Banana Republic images/Shutterstock.
Manufacturing and Inventory Control Supervisor: Amy Bacus
Composition: S4Carlisle Publishing Services
Printing and Binding: LSC Communications
Cover Printing: LSC Communications

Library of Congress Cataloging-in-Publication Data
Names: Regoli, Robert M., author. | Hewitt, John D., 1945- author. | DeLisi, Matt, author.
Title: Delinquency in society / Robert M. Regoli, John D. Hewitt, Matt DeLisi.
Description: Tenth edition. | Burlington, MA : Jones & Bartlett Learning,
    [2017] | Includes bibliographical references and index.
Identifiers: LCCN 2016019287 | ISBN 9781284112955 (pbk.)
Subjects: LCSH: Juvenile delinquency—United States. | Juvenile justice,
    Administration of—United States.
Classification: LCC HV9104 .R43 2017 | DDC 364.360973—dc23
LC record available at https://lccn.loc.gov/2016019287

6048

Printed in the United States of America
21 20 19 18 17   10 9 8 7 6 5 4 3 2

Dedication

To Debbie, *I still do.* Love U, Bob.
—RMR

To Carl Keener, Civics Teacher, Burris Laboratory
School, and Eliot Benowitz, Professor of Chinese
and East Asian History, Western Washington State College.
Thank you for being my teachers.
—JDH

To my students, who are exploring their intellectual and
applied interests in criminal justice and criminology.
—MD

Contents in Brief

References

Complete references to this title are available in an
appendix located in Navigate 2 Advantage Access.

Contents

© AlexandreNunes/Shutterstock.

© edfuentesg/E+/Getty.

© Rob Marmion/Shutterstock.

CHAPTER 14

Complete references to this title are available in an
appendix located in Navigate 2 Advantage Access.

© ejwhite/Shutterstock.

SECTION 4

CHAPTER 13

Acknowledgments

We would like to thank our team at Jones & Bartlett Learning for their support in developing the *Tenth Edition* of *Delinquency in Society*. We also would like to thank our colleagues and students for their solicited and unsolicited insights, guidance, criticism, and assistance. Other colleagues who were selected by Jones & Bartlett to review the text helped improve this *Tenth Edition* in innumerable ways. We extend our sincere gratitude to those reviewers. In addition, many researchers have shared their papers and provided diverse feedback on this text over the years. We would like to acknowledge Mike Baglivio, Kevin Beaver, Monic Behnken, Mark Berg, Mark Pogrebin, Brian Boutwell, Chet Britt, Kyle Burgason, Jon Caudill, Pete Conis, Heith Copes, Ray Corrado, Frank Cullen, Alan Drury, Angela Glosser, Michael Gottfredson, Darin Haerle, Karen Heimer, George Higgins, Travis Hirschi, Andy Hochstetler, Wesley Jennings, Kareem Jordan, Jerome Kagan, Chris Kierkus, Anna Kosloski, Eric Lacourse, Mike Leiber, Evan McCuish, Matt Moore, Anthony Peguero, Alex Piquero, Nicole Piquero, Chad Posick, Travis Pratt, Eric Primm, Dave Pyrooz, Nick Recker, Mike Rocque, Chris Salas-Wright, Jukka Savolainen, Molly Sween, Chad Trulson, Michael Vaughn, Tom Winfree, Kevin Wolff, and John Wright. And finally, special thanks to Debbie, Georgia, and Melissa, who have inspired, encouraged, and supported us through this project.

Preface

If it is true that in teaching we learn, we have had the good fortune to do quite a bit of both since the first edition of *Delinquency in Society* was published in 1991. Its continued success is a reflection of what we learn from the comments and suggestions of our students, our colleagues, and their students around the country who read the book. We do enjoy hearing compliments, but we pay very careful attention to the suggestions for improvements. Such suggestions have resulted in a number of changes to the *Tenth Edition*, which we detail here.

Chapter Updates

Chapter 1
- Updated box feature on delinquency worldwide
- New discussion of Flourishing Children project
- Updated box feature on parent liability laws
- Updated box feature on violent video games and delinquency
- New box feature on the National Center for Missing and Exploited Children

Chapter 2
- New box feature on erroneous arrest in the United States
- Redesigned box feature on National Incident-Based Reporting System
- New coverage of the changes in the Uniform Crime Reporting index offenses
- New discussion of the Uniform Crime Reporting Redevelopment Project
- New section on National Survey of Children's Exposure to Violence I and II
- New box feature on the long shadow of delinquent victimization
- Revised box feature on the code of the street
- New section on Pathways to Desistance Study

Chapter 3
- Revised box feature on rational choice theory and predatory offending
- Revised box feature on ADHD
- New box feature on the teenage brain
- New discussion of the biosocial implications of the Flint, Michigan water contamination

- New box feature on sleep and delinquency
- Expanded discussion of neuroscience of adolescent brain development and implications for juvenile justice policy

Chapter 4
- Expanded discussion of psychoanalytic theory and attachment theory
- Revised box feature on attachment and delinquency
- Expanded discussion of the Dark Triad of personality
- New box feature on enduring effects of personality and personality disorder
- New discussion of behavioral disorders consistent with DSM-5
- New box feature on psychopathy at birth and early childhood

Chapter 5
- New discussion of street efficacy
- Expanded discussion of collective efficacy
- Revised box feature on delinquent peer effects
- Expanded discussion of general strain theory
- Expanded discussion of Cloward and Ohlin
- Revised box feature on the popularity of self-control theory

Chapter 6
- New box feature on defiance theory and a general theory of African American offending
- New box feature on adverse childhood experiences
- Revised box feature on reducing social inequality through mentoring

Chapter 7
- Expanded discussion of worldwide research on developmental theory
- New box feature on protective factors against delinquency and youth violence
- Revised box feature on delinquency abstainers
- New box feature on temperament and delinquency
- New discussion of DeLisi and Vaughn's temperament theory

Opener image: Shutterstock / Jason Stitt: Spray icon: © sabri deniz kikil/ShutterStock, Inc.; Texture: © kasha_malasha/Shutterstock.

Chapter 8

- Revised box feature on gendered legacies of crime
- Revised box feature on gender socialization
- Expanded discussion of gendered pathways to offending
- Revised box feature on delinquency programming for girls

Chapter 9

- New box feature on violent delinquency and abuse running in families
- Revised box feature on parents and delinquency
- Expanded discussion of child maltreatment

Chapter 10

- New discussion of the school-to-prison pipeline
- New box feature on schools, behavioral functioning, and life chances
- Expanded discussion of bullying
- New box feature on school-to-prison pipeline

Chapter 11

- New discussion of Keepin' it REAL program
- New box feature on youth violence in global context
- Revised box feature on the murder of very young children
- New box feature on armed juveniles
- New box feature on the legal marijuana, marijuana smoking, and its effects
- New box feature on drug use, drug selling, and delinquency

Chapter 12

- Revised box feature on why people are group oriented
- Expanded discussion of delinquent groups
- Revised box feature on comparing gang and non-gang youth
- Revised box feature on MS-13
- Expanded discussion of gangs and gang violence
- Expanded discussion of anti-gang policies and initiatives

Chapter 13

- New discussion of *Miller v. Alabama*
- New discussion of *Montgomery v. Louisiana*
- Greatly expanded discussion of changes in juvenile justice law and policy
- Revised box feature on the relationship between police and race/ethnicity
- Expanded discussion of correlates of police contact
- Expanded discussion of juvenile justice procedures
- New box feature on the perils of juvenile detention
- Expanded discussion of confinement facilities and youth therein

Chapter 14

- New box feature on saving children from a life of crime
- New discussion of Stop Now and Plan (SNAP) program
- New box feature on cost savings of prevention programs
- Revised and expanded box feature on the success of mentoring programs

The Student Experience

Every chapter opens with a succinct list of objectives. Students should review this list prior to diving into the chapter to help guide their focus. As they progress through the chapter, they should periodically flip back to the objectives to ensure they are fully grasping the chapter's key concepts. This practice will encourage students to think critically about the field of delinquency in criminal justice.

Feature boxes abound in all chapters. There are seven types of boxes: *A Window on Delinquency, Delinquency Around the Globe, Delinquency Controversy, Delinquency Prevention, From the Bench, The Face of Delinquency,* and *Theory in a Nutshell.* Each box type is identified by a colorful and distinctive logo placed near the title of the box.

A Window on Delinquency offers a glimpse into various statistics from sources such as the National Incident-Based Reporting System data, the Uniform Crime Reporting offenses, and the National Crime Victimization Survey. Supportive cases are often discussed in a concise manner designed to demonstrate statistical findings in a manner that will resonate with the reader.

Delinquency Around the Globe discusses up-to-date case examples from around the world that best exemplify current-day issues and aim to open the reader's mind to large-scale phenomena experienced across the globe.

Delinquency Controversy dives into topics surrounded by varying levels of discourse. Topics such as usage of the term "ADHD" as well as the concept of "super-predators" are explored in an objective manner, allowing the reader to attain a nonbiased view on controversial topics.

BOX 8.5

Delinquency Controversy

Sexual Labeling and Control of Girls

Although adolescent girls and boys frequently engage in harmless bantering, kidding, and joking with each other, all too often the informal verbal interactions take on an insidious, demeaning, and manipulative flavor designed to facilitate boys' control of girls. Mark Fleisher suggests that the use of insulting terms in the verbal dueling of girls and boys in the Freemont area in Kansas City helps to establish social hierarchies, allows for the release of tensions without violence, and defines group membership and friendships: "Boys call girls by the standard list of insulting terms, including 'bitch,' 'rotten bitch,' 'stank bitch,' 'pussy,' 'cunt,' and 'slut,' among others. Girls retaliate with a vengeance, shouting, 'bastard,' 'prick,' 'pussy,' 'bitch,' 'little dick,' . . . among others. Girls call one another by the standard list of insults." The seeming equality of insults, however, masks the actual inequalities in the relationships. According to Fleisher:

> Girls think about relationships as moral contracts; boys don't. Beyond the street rhetoric of the gang, girls' implicit construction of relationships, especially with boys, includes fairness, reciprocity, and equality. . . . In what they perceive to be long-term relationships, girls feel an inherent responsibility toward the boys with whom they are involved, but the boys feel neither reciprocity nor fairness nor equality.

Elijah Anderson's study of the informal street code that guides interactions between boys and girls in the inner city of Philadelphia reflects a similar pattern of control in relationships. Whereas many girls "offer sex as a gift" in their attempt to gain a boy's attention, boys define the exchange as only a means to enhance their self-esteem. According to Anderson, "The girls have a dream, the boys a desire. The girls dream of being carried off by a Prince Charming who will love them. . . . The boys often desire either sex without commitment or babies without responsibility for them." The boys want to "score" with as many girls as possible—the more girls a boy has sex with, the higher his esteem in the eyes of his male peers. "But the young man not only must 'get some'; he also must prove he is getting it. This leads him to talk about girls and sex with any other young man who will listen." Labels may also be used to control boys. If his peers suspect him of becoming too committed to a girl, they are likely to sanction him with "demeaning labels such as 'pussy,' 'pussy whipped,' or 'house husband.'"

Many of the interviews Mark Totten conducted with 90 Canadian boys ages 13 to 17 in Ottawa, Ontario, reflected the boys' willingness to use demeaning labels to control girls. Steve, a 15-year-old, responded to Totten's question. "Do you like girls?:"

> No, not really . . . I think most of them are stupid bitches. I'll call them bitch, slut, whore all the time. They're always trying to show me up—make me look stupid, like a goof. . . . It's all about knowing your place in society. Some girls do, but most girls don't know what they're supposed to do. . . . We all think that girls should do what we want them to. And it pisses us off when they don't. So I've seen some of them when they've hit girls. And all the time we are just joking around, calling them names—slut, cunt, whore, bitch, fat cow—we all do it.

When boys label girls in this manner as part of their oppression and control of girls, it should not be surprising that boys also express an attitude of negative fatalism with regard to future generations of girls. Philippe Bourgois spent 5 years studying the neighborhood culture of the crack trade in East Harlem. Getting girls pregnant seemingly produced some ambivalence. Many boys took pride in noting how many girls they had impregnated. Luis, for example, bragged about getting a number of girls pregnant in just a 9-month period, but then referred to them as "holes out there." The ambivalence came from thinking about the possibility of the pregnancy producing a daughter. According to one youth, "That's why I would never want to have a daughter, if I was to get my girl pregnant. I couldn't handle the fact of having a baby, and then I have to see her being a 'ho.'" And an 11-year-old commented about his mother's pregnancy: "He told us he hoped his mother would give birth to a boy 'because girls are too easy to rape.'"

Elijah Anderson, *Code of the Street: Decency, Violence, and the Moral Life of the Inner City* (New York: W. W. Norton, 1999); Philippe Bourgois, *In Search of Respect: Selling Crack in El Barrio* (New York: Cambridge University Press, 1995); Mark Fleisher, *Dead End Kids: Gang Girls and the Boys They Know* (Madison, WI: University of Wisconsin Press, 1998); Mark Totten, *Guys, Gangs, and Girlfriend Abuse* (Peterborough, Ontario: Broadview Press, 2000); Deborah Prothrow-Stith and Howard Spivak, *Sugar and Spice and No Longer Nice: How We Can Stop Girls' Violence* (San Francisco: Jossey-Bass, 2005); Kelly King, Dexter Voisin, and Ralph DiClemente, "The Relationship between Male Gang Involvement and Psychosocial Risks for their Female Juvenile Justice Partners with Non-Gang Involvement Histories," *Journal of Child and Family Studies* 24:2555–2559 (2015).

The Face of Delinquency guides the reader through historical concepts of delinquency modified into modern-day theories. An advanced developmental theory with supporting evidence is examined and discussed with an eye to future studies.

BOX 7.12

The Face of Delinquency

Temperament: The Raw Ingredients of Delinquency and Problems Across Life

Temperament is the stable, largely innate tendency with which an individual experiences the environment and regulates his or her responses to that environment. Temperament reflects core differences in central nervous system reactivity that manifest in differential activity level, emotionality and mood, approach and withdrawal behavior, and self-regulation among individuals. It is likely that one's parents mentioned positive and negative aspects about their temperament.

Temperament is a very old scientific concept. Hippocrates developed the four humors model of distinct temperaments. These comprise the *melancholic* person, who was described as moody and anxious, with a predominance of black bile; the *sanguine* person who was described as cheerful, spirited, and good natured, with a predominance of blood; the *choleric* person, who was angry and irritable, with a predominance of yellow bile; and the *phlegmatic* person, who is slow to arouse and possesses substantial phlegm. In terms of relationship to delinquency, the choleric person would be most likely to be delinquent.

Drawing on this rich heritage, Matt DeLisi and Michael Vaughn advanced a developmental theory that uses temperament as its explanatory focus. They suggest that two temperamental constructs—effortful control and negative emotionality—are significantly predictive of self-regulation deficits and behavioral problems in infancy, toddlerhood, childhood, adolescence, and across adulthood. In addition, their theory asserts that people with poor self-regulation and generally negative moods also tend to have problematic interactions with others, such as parents, peers, and juvenile and criminal justice practitioners. Thus, their theory not only explains delinquency, but also the often negative consequences that delinquents face in their interactions with the legal system.

Unlike most theories of delinquency, which are heavily and often exclusively rooted in criminology, DeLisi and Vaughn's work is multidisciplinary and draws on studies of research subjects as young as infants and as old as octogenarians. There is considerable evidence supporting their work. Michelle Horner and her colleagues, for instance, found that temperament disturbances in infancy, specifically low self-regulation and poor negative emotional regulation, predict substance use disorders 20 years later. Other researchers have found stable evidence of people with particularly difficult temperaments relating to effortful control (self-control) and negative emotions, and these features are consistently associated with behavioral problems across life.

Criminologists have provided supporting evidence as well. Kevin Wolff and his colleagues found that adolescents with low effortful control and high negative emotionality are more likely to engage in delinquency and recidivate after release from juvenile custody compared to youth without these temperamental features. Similarly, Glenn Walters reported that temperamental features consistent with this theory are associated with parenting problems and are the origin of the self-control problems that are so strongly associated with delinquency.

The theory is likely to inspire additional tests, in part because so many academic disciplines draw on temperament as a foundational method of understanding behavior.

Matt DeLisi and Michael Vaughn, "Foundation for a Temperament-Based Theory of Antisocial Behavior and Criminal Justice System Involvement," *Journal of Criminal Justice* 42:10–25 (2014); Michelle Horner, Maureen Reynolds, Betty Braxter, Levent Kirisci, and Ralph Tarter, "Temperament Disturbances Measured in Infancy Progress to Substance Use Disorder 20 Years Later," *Personality and Individual Differences* 82:96–101 (2015); Charles Beekman, Jenae Neiderhiser, Kristin Buss, Eric Loken, Ginger Moore, Leslie Leve, Jody Ganiban, Daniel Shaw, and David Reiss, "The Development of Early Profiles of Temperament: Characterization, Continuity, and Etiology," *Child Development* 86:1794–1811 (2015); Hannah Snyder, Lauren Gulley, Patricia Bijttebier, Catharina Hartman, Albertine Oldehinkel, Amy Mezulis, Jami Young, and Benjamin Hankin, "Adolescent Emotionality and Effortful Control: Core Latent Constructs and Links to Psychopathology and Functioning," *Journal of Personality and Social Psychology* 109:1132–1149 (2015); Soo Jin Lee, C. Robert Cloninger, Soo Hyun Park, and Han Chae, "The Association of Parental Temperament and Character on Their Children's Behavior Problems," *PeerJ* 3:e1464 (2015); Kevin Wolff, Michael Baglivio, Alex Piquero, Michael Vaughn, and Matt DeLisi, "The Triple Crown of Antisocial Behavior: Effortful Control, Negative Emotionality, and Community Disadvantage," *Youth Violence and Juvenile Justice*, in press (2016); Glenn Walters, "Early Childhood Temperament, Maternal Monitoring, Reactive Criminal Thinking, and the Origin(s) of Low Self-Control," *Journal of Criminal Justice* 43:369–376 (2015).

Delinquency Prevention spotlights various laws, studies, historical events, and current-day movements that serve to reduce delinquency in our society.

BOX 7.4

Delinquency Prevention

The Wonderful People: Moffitt's Abstainer Subgroup

Moffitt's developmental taxonomy offers three general types of individuals: a large group of normative adolescents who flirt with delinquency during their teen years, a small pathological group whose conduct problems are essentially lifelong, and another small group who abstain from antisociality altogether. The latter group has not received much research attention because they do not commit delinquency, and for this reason criminologists have viewed them as somewhat unimportant. In addition, there is also the idea that abstainers are isolated teenagers who lack the peer networks and opportunities to commit delinquency. In this way, their abstention is viewed as more the result of social ineptitude than prosocial characteristics they might have.

Research indicates such a cynical view is incorrect. Individuals who never commit delinquency have characteristics that suggest that they are simply better than the majority of people who do. Two studies based on nationally representative data sets from the United States indicate that delinquency abstainers have many characteristics that suggest they "have their act together" at an early age. In the National Longitudinal Survey of Youth, investigators found that abstainers have high levels of attachment to their teachers, high interaction and monitoring with parents, high involvement with prosocial peers, and low levels of internalizing symptoms, such as depression. In addition, there was no evidence that abstainers were socially alienated from their peers who happened to commit some delinquency. In the National Epidemiologic Survey on Alcohol and Related Conditions, which is a massive sample of more than 43,000 Americans, Michael Vaughn and his colleagues found that abstainers are significantly less likely than nonabstainers to experience mood, anxiety, or personality disorders over their lifetime.

The beneficial features of abstainers are also found elsewhere. Researchers in Sweden found that abstainers have the most prosocial family backgrounds and are psychologically healthier than youths who follow the adolescence-limited and life-course persistent pathways. A major explanation for the positive profile of abstainers is personality, especially the facet conscientiousness. People who are high scoring on conscientiousness, which is a central component of structural models of personality, are less likely to use drugs, less likely to drink alcohol, less likely to have unhealthy eating habits, less likely to have psychiatric disturbance, less likely to smoke, and less likely to engage in any form of deviant behavior. Using data from the Cambridge Study in Delinquent Development, Wesley Jennings and his colleagues found that abstainers were the most well-adjusted across various life domains and had the best functioning through age 56 compared to those who had been adolescence-limited or life-course persistent offenders. Using the same data, Natalie Mercer and her associates reported that abstainers were honest and conforming in their behavior.

Given this profile, it is likely that delinquency abstainers will receive increased research attention from criminologists who are looking for protective factors that guard against delinquency. In this way, abstainers are a naturally occurring experiment of delinquency prevention.

Alex Piquero, Timothy Brezina, and Michael Turner, "Testing Moffitt's of Delinquency Abstention," *Journal of Research in Crime and Delinquency* 42:27–54 (2005); Michael Vaughn, Qiang Fu, Stephen Wernet, Matt DeLisi, Kevin Beaver, Brian Perron, and Matthew Howard, "Characteristics of Abstainers from Substance Use and Antisocial Behavior in the United States," *Journal of Criminal Justice* 39:212–217 (2011); Håkan Stattin, Margaret Kerr, and Lars Bergman, "On the Utility of Moffitt's Typology Trajectories in Long-Term Perspective," *European Journal of Criminology* 7:1–25 (2010); Tom Bogg and Brent Roberts, "Conscientiousness and Health-Related Behaviors: A Meta-Analysis of the Leading Behavioral Contributors to Morality," *Psychological Bulletin* 130:887–919 (2004); Wesley Jennings, Michael Rocque, Bryanna Hahn Fox, Alex Piquero, and David Farrington, "Can They Recover? An Assessment of Adult Adjustment Problems among Males in the Abstainer, Recovery, Life-Course Persistent, and Adolescence-Limited Pathways Followed up to Age 56 in the Cambridge Study in Delinquent Development," *Development and Psychopathology*, 28:537–549 (2016); Natalie Mercer, David Farrington, Maria Ttofi, Loes Keijsers, Susan Branje, and Wim Meeus, "Childhood Predictors and Adult Life Success of Adolescent Delinquency Abstainers," *Journal of Abnormal Child Psychology*, 44:613–624 (2016).

From the Bench offers insightful discussions on select court rulings. This feature walks the reader through the case, from background information to the court's final decision, all in a brief and succinct manner.

Theory in a Nutshell highlights various theories discussed within the realm of delinquency through the use of real life examples. These boxes also highlight various theories in a concise manner in order to stress key theories and concepts to the student.

BOX 11.7
From the Bench
Board of Education of Pottawatomie County v. Earls et al.

Lindsay Earls, a 16-year-old girl, objected to her school's policy requiring warrantless random drug testing as a condition for any student to participate in any school-sponsored extracurricular activity. The school board believed that a drug problem existed in the school and that it was not limited to students involved in athletics. The U.S. Supreme Court, in a 5-to-4 decision following its earlier ruling in *Vernonia* in 1995, cited the "special needs" of public schools that permit school searches without the traditional Fourth Amendment requirement of individualized suspicion before a search. The Court ruled that:

A student's privacy interest is limited in a public school environment where the State is responsible for maintaining discipline, health, and safety. Schoolchildren are routinely required to submit to physical examinations and vaccinations against disease. . . . Students who participate in competitive extracurricular activities voluntarily subject themselves to many of the same intrusions on their privacy as do athletes. Some of these clubs and activities require occasional off-campus travel and communal undress. All of them have their own rules and requirements for participating students that

do not apply to the student body as a whole. . . . We therefore conclude that the students affected by this Policy have a limited expectation of privacy.

The court went on to say that:

In this context, the Fourth Amendment does not require a finding of individualized suspicion and we decline to impose such a requirement on schools attempting to prevent and detect drug use by students. Moreover, we question whether testing based on individualized suspicion in fact would be less intrusive. Such a regime would place an additional burden on public school teachers who are already tasked with the difficult job of maintaining order and discipline. A program of individualized suspicion might unfairly target members of unpopular groups. The fear of lawsuits resulting from such targeted searches may chill enforcement of the program, rendering it ineffective in combating drug use. . . . Finally, we find that testing students who participate in extracurricular activities is a reasonably effective means of addressing the School District's legitimate concerns in preventing, deterring, and detecting drug use.

Board of Education of Pottawatomie County v. Earls et al., 536 U.S. 822 (2002).

BOX 5.4
Theory in a Nutshell
Walter Miller

Miller blames delinquency on two structural features associated with the lower class: focal concerns and female-based households. Together, they produce sex-role problems for boys. Boys, who need to learn to become men, must learn from women. This learning is inadequate, so they join together and form a gang. Status is achieved in the gang by living up to focal concerns, some of which lead to delinquency.

WRAP UP
THINKING ABOUT JUVENILE DELINQUENCY: CONCLUSIONS

This chapter reviewed theories from three schools of sociological thought. Cultural deviance theory was the first school of thought to reject biological and psychological theories. It shifted attention to considering the role of the environment in delinquency, particularly the child's neighborhood.

Strain theory distinguished itself by claiming that there is no unique lower-class culture. In the United States, the dominant culture emphasizes wealth and status—but not every person can achieve success because the legitimate means to do so are more broadly available to the middle and upper classes.

Thus lower-class children are more likely to give up chasing these goals or go about achieving them in illegal ways.

According to social control theory, children are amoral; without controls on their behavior, they will commit crime. The theories put forth by proponents of this school of thought ask, "Why do some children conform?" They answer the question in a variety of ways. For example, delinquency might be explained in terms of a child's self-concept; bond to his or her parents, school, or peers; or the quality of parenting that the child has received.

CHAPTER SPOTLIGHT

- Social disorganization theory suggests that neighborhoods characterized by poverty, residential turnover, renters, and ethnicity heterogeneity create social disorganization, which fosters cultural conflicts that then allow delinquency to flourish.
- Cultural deviance theories suggest that socially disorganized neighborhoods engender an oppositional subculture that lends itself to failure at conventional social institutions and delinquency.
- Social inequality contributes to anomie or strain, which—according to the theories of Merton,

Cloward and Ohlin, Agnew, and Messner and Rosenfeld—leads to financial and emotional stresses that result in delinquency.
- Differential association theory showcases how delinquency is learned from social relationships with family and friends in primary groups.
- Social control theory assumes that people are naturally self-interested and prone to delinquency.
- Two of the most important control theories are social bond theory (advanced by Hirschi) and self-control theory (advanced by Gottfredson and Hirschi).

CRITICAL THINKING

1. Even in the worst neighborhoods in the United States, the majority of residents are law abiding, suggesting that individual flaws explain delinquency. How might sociologists, psychologists, and biologists differ in the ways they address this issue?
2. Many crimes are not committed for financial reasons—that is, to alleviate strain. For example, some armed robbers commit crimes to obtain drugs, but rarely do they commit crimes to pay their rent. Are most juveniles who commit property crimes *really* economically motivated?
3. Is it wasteful to channel resources to retreatists, such as transients, drug addicts, and alcoholics?

4. Is it inevitable that some people will not succeed in life?
5. Some criminologists believe that children with low self-control are more likely to commit crime. What does this perspective suggest about the chances of rehabilitation or positive change for delinquents?
6. In West Palm Beach, Florida, police installed stereo systems that play classical music 24 hours per day in high-crime neighborhoods. Since the policy was implemented, crime has decreased in the area. Does this example demonstrate that neighborhoods and their delinquency rates can be altered by ecological change?

Teaching Tools

To assist you in teaching this course and supplying your students with the best in teaching aids, Jones & Bartlett Learning has prepared a complete supplemental package available to all adopters. Additional information and review copies for qualified instructors are available through your Jones & Bartlett sales representative.

The **Slides in PowerPoint Format** presentations package provides lecture notes, graphs, and images for each chapter of *Delinquency in Society*. Instructors with Microsoft PowerPoint software can customize the outlines, images, and order of presentations.

The **Lecture Outlines** provided as a text file include chapter outlines, teaching tips, learning objectives, and additional concept and essay questions.

The **Test Bank** questions are available as text files and as files formatted to be ready for Angel, Blackboard, Desire2Learn, and Moodle.

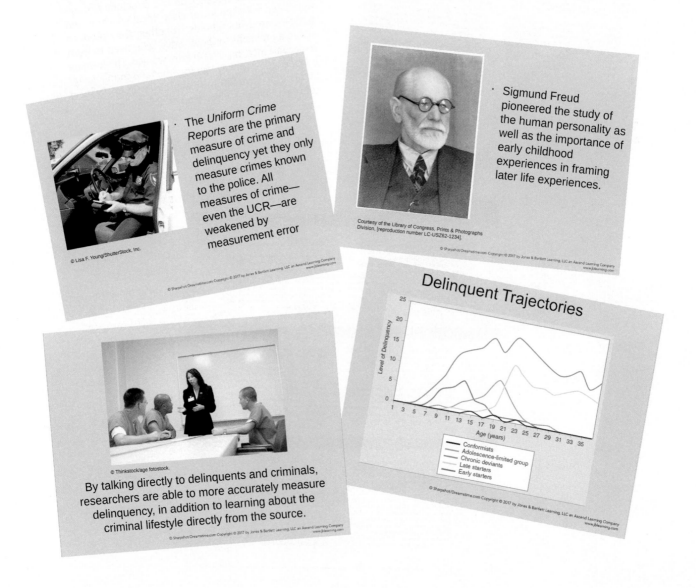

· The *Uniform Crime Reports* are the primary measure of crime and delinquency yet they only measure crimes known to the police. All measures of crime—even the UCR—are weakened by measurement error

© Lisa F. Young/ShutterStock, Inc.

· Sigmund Freud pioneered the study of the human personality as well as the importance of early childhood experiences in framing later life experiences.

Courtesy of the Library of Congress, Prints & Photographs Division, [reproduction number LC-USZ62-1234].

© Thinkstock/age fotostock.

By talking directly to delinquents and criminals, researchers are able to more accurately measure delinquency, in addition to learning about the criminal lifestyle directly from the source.

Delinquent Trajectories

- Conformists
- Adolescence-limited group
- Chronic deviants
- Late starters
- Early starters

About the Authors

Robert M. Regoli is professor emeritus of sociology at the University of Colorado. In 1975, he received his PhD in sociology from Washington State University. Professor Regoli has found himself in an assortment of roles in the criminal justice system. In addition to having published more than 100 scholarly papers and authoring more than 10 books on topics ranging from police cynicism and causes of delinquency to unreported rule infractions in prisons, he also has been a crime victim, misdemeanor offender, criminal complainant and witness, jury member, and legal consultant. Dr. Regoli is also a past-president and fellow of the Academy of Criminal Justice Sciences, former executive editor of *The Social Science Journal*, recipient of two William J. Fulbright senior specialist awards, and member of Phi Beta Kappa. Today, Dr. Regoli's research is focused on the social organization of the fast-growing sport of pickleball, with an eye toward understanding the evolution of the game's norms, roles, hierarchies, and mechanisms of social control that affect its play.

John D. Hewitt recently retired as professor of criminal justice at Grand Valley State University. He was born in Carmel, California, grew up in Indiana, and then completed his undergraduate work at Western Washington State College and his PhD at Washington State University. He has taught for more 30 years at small and large state colleges and universities, as well as in small liberal arts colleges in the Midwest and West. During his career, Dr. Hewitt was a member of the Board of Directors of the Delaware County Youth Services Bureau, president of the Board of Directors at Bethel Place for Boys, and testified as an expert witness in Arizona on the identification of youth gangs in schools. He has written extensively about issues of crime, criminal justice, and delinquency, including co-authoring *Exploring Criminal Justice; Exploring Criminal Justice: The Essentials*; and *The Impact of Sentencing Reform*, as well as numerous articles on issues ranging from the oppression of children and adolescent risk taking, to youth gangs and violence and juvenile justice policy in The People's Republic of China.

Matt DeLisi is coordinator of criminal justice studies, professor in the department of sociology, and faculty affiliate with the Center for the Study of Violence at Iowa State University. Professor DeLisi has published nearly 350 scholarly works and his research interests are juvenile delinquency, criminal careers, psychopathy and psychopathology, molecular and behavioral genetics, inmate behavior, and testing criminological theories. Professor DeLisi is the editor-in-chief of the *Journal of Criminal Justice* and is fellow of the Academy of Criminal Justice Sciences.

Reviewer List

Other colleagues who were selected by Jones & Bartlett Learning to review the text helped improve this *Tenth Edition* in enumerable ways. We extend our sincere gratitude to those reviewers listed here.

LeAnn Cabage
Iowa State University
Ames, Iowa

S. E. Costanza
University of South Alabama
Mobile, Alabama

Mitch Darnell, MS, OSM, CRC
Los Rios Community College District
Sacramento, California

Aric W. Dutelle
University of Wisconsin-Oshkosh
Oshkosh, Wisconsin

David Ellis
Northwest Vista College
San Antonio, Texas

Mandi Fowler
The University of Alabama
Tuscaloosa, Alabama

Jennifer Innerarity
Louisiana State University at Alexandria
Alexandria, Louisiana

Jason Jolicoeur, PhD
Zane State College
Zanesville, Ohio

Steven C. Kempisty, Esq.
Bryant & Stratton College
Liverpool, New York

E. Jay Kolick, III
Rosemont College
Rosemont, Pennsylvania

Jon Maskaly
University of Illinois at Chicago
Chicago, Illinois

Rafael Rojas, Jr.
Southern New Hampshire University
Manchester, New Hampshire

Ken Salmon
University of Phoenix
Phoenix, Arizona

Jill Sturges
Penn State Fayette, the Eberly Campus
LeMont Furnace, Pennsylvania

James Windell
Wayne State University
Detroit, Michigan

Stephen Wofsey, PhD
Northern Virginia Community College—
    Annandale Campus
Annandale, Virginia

Valerie Wright
Cleveland State University
Cleveland, Ohio

Dominic D. Yin, MS, JD.
City College of San Francisco
San Francisco, California

Nature and Extent of Delinquency

Section 1 introduces you to the problem of defining and measuring juvenile delinquency. Experts have struggled for more than 100 years to define delinquency, yet it remains a complex problem that makes measurement even more difficult.

Chapter 1 reports on the status of children in American society. It also reviews past and present definitions of delinquency and defines legal definitions of delinquency that regulated the behavior of children in the American colonies, legal reforms inspired by the child-saving movement at the end of the 19th century, status offenses, and more recent changes in state and federal laws.

Chapter 2 examines the extent and nature of delinquency in an attempt to understand how much delinquency there is. Determining the amount and kind of delinquent acts that juveniles commit, the characteristics of these acts, the neighborhoods in which these children live, the kinds of social networks available, and the styles of lives they lead is vital to understanding where the problem of juvenile crime exists in U.S. society. Such knowledge also helps us to understand the problem more completely. Is delinquency only a problem of lower-class males who live in the inner city? Or does it also include females, middle-class children who attend high-quality schools, troubled children from good families, and "nice" children experimenting with drugs, alcohol, and sex?

SECTION OUTLINE

Defining Delinquency

OBJECTIVES

+ Understand why juvenile delinquency is difficult to explain.

+ Know what the status of children is relative to adults.

+ Explain the role of the Child Savers during the 19th-century delinquency prevention movement.

+ Grasp the distinction between what defines juvenile delinquency and who a juvenile delinquent is.

+ Comprehend how the media contribute to the social definition of juvenile delinquency.

KEY TERMS

Approximately 2400 years ago, Plato expressed concern about the state of young people in society. He noted that children and adolescents seemed to have lost respect for their elders, were disobedient toward their parents, and seemed more immoral than young people were during previous eras. Children and adolescents were viewed as having lost their way, and the state of society held in the balance. In other words, there was concern among the citizenry that youth behavior and misbehavior was a problem. Even Plato noticed.

Fast forward to today where there is evidence for similar concern. Across the United States, adolescents use social networking sites on the Internet to plan "flash mobs," where dozens of teenagers arrive at a store or public place in order to commit theft, robbery, assault, or create a public disturbance. Adolescent flash mobs are so problematic that they have sparked public policy. For instance, Philadelphia Mayor Michael Nutter instituted strict curfews to reduce the incidence of flash mobs after several high-profile incidents in the city. Youthful behavior not only affects others, but many times negatively affects children as well. A survey of university students found that nearly one in five has played the "choking game," where children choke themselves or others to cut off blood flow to the brain and induce a feeling of intoxication or euphoria. The choking game has resulted in deaths

Sixteen-year-old Ethan Couch drove while intoxicated and killed four people. His defense team argued that he suffered from "affluenza," saying that his wealthy upbringing contributed to feelings of entitlement.

© LM Otero/AP Photo.

across the county, and is the latest of behaviors among youth that cause public concern. And then there is the case of Ethan Couch and his "affluenza." At age 16, Couch was convicted of four counts of intoxication manslaughter and two counts of intoxication assault causing serious bodily injury. After brazenly driving into a crowd that resulted in four deaths, Couch attempted to flee the scene. Despite the seriousness of his crimes, Couch was sentenced to just 10 years of probation, in part because his defense counsel asserted that his wealthy upbringing contributed to feelings of entitlement and irresponsibility, or that he suffered from "affluenza." The case generated international outrage and was consistent with public fears that wealthier delinquents are afforded a more lenient form of justice than impoverished youth. In 2016, Couch fled to Mexico along with his mother where he visited strip clubs and continued his life of leisure. After serving time in a detention facility in Mexico City, Couch was extradited back to the United States, and ordered to serve 180 days for each count against him.[1]

Juvenile delinquency is a complex phenomenon that is difficult to define, measure, explain, and prevent. One reason for this challenging nature is because juvenile delinquency shares a relationship with social institutions such as families, schools, media, law enforcement agencies, and juvenile and adult courts. Perhaps the biggest mistake anyone can make is to think that juvenile delinquency exists in a vacuum, stands alone, and has no connection to other parts of society. Because of its complexity, many theories of delinquency have evolved that place the blame on targets ranging from a child's embryonic development to dysfunctional families, dilapidated schools, abject poverty, peer relations, low self-control, or any combination of these and other factors.

The delinquency of children is often a sign of countless and usually unknown problems they face, which are interrelated in complex and multifaceted ways. In recent years, juveniles have committed many serious crimes that have affected how people think about crime, its causes, and its solutions. The most recent data show that U.S. law enforcement agencies arrested more than 804,000 **juveniles** or persons younger than age 18. Juveniles accounted for nearly 11% of all violent crime arrests and 15% of all property crime arrests in the United States in 2014. The substantial growth in juvenile violent crime arrests that began in the late 1980s and peaked in 1993–1994 has been followed by an unprecedented decline in youth violence. In the decade after the peak of juvenile crime, juvenile arrests for serious violent crime fell 49%, reaching its lowest level since the late 1980s. In the decade between 2001 and 2010, the number of juveniles who were arrested declined by nearly 24%. In the decade between 2005 and 2014, the juvenile arrests for violent crime declined 43% and juvenile arrests for property crime fell 46%. In addition, between 2005 and 2014, juvenile murders dropped 45%, juvenile rapes declined 16%, juvenile robberies dropped 34%, and juvenile aggravated assaults dropped 49%.[2]

The majority of juveniles who commit delinquent acts, including first-time juvenile offenders, are likely to be informally processed or diverted from the juvenile justice system. Relatively few juveniles are *chronic offenders*. Most juvenile offenders commit only a few offenses and tend to commit a variety of crimes. In other words, whereas it was once thought that juveniles specialized in a particular type of crime—theft or drug sales, for example—research has found that they do not.[3] Juvenile offenders are "garden variety offenders," who are inclined to commit an assortment of offenses, although some may favor a particular type of crime more than others. The majority of juvenile offenders commit relatively minor offenses and only a small percentage commit occasional serious crimes.[4]

Some of the crimes that juveniles commit are so serious they gain national attention. These "sensational" crimes include one committed by 15-year-old Evan Savoie, whose juvenile record contained 19 court referrals beginning at age 12 and who ultimately stabbed a playmate to death, and another by 14-year-old Michael Hernandez, who slit the throat of 14-year-old classmate Jaime Gough in a school bathroom and then calmly returned to class with bloodstained clothing. In November 2015 in Birmingham, Alabama, an 8-year old boy was charged with murder for killing a 1-year-old girl who "would not stop crying" while he babysat the girl. The childrens' mothers were partying at a nightclub when the murder

KEY TERMS

juvenile
A person younger than age 18.

occurred. Crimes such as these shake the conscience of law-abiding citizens across the nation.[5]

As shocking as these crimes are, few crimes committed by juveniles have caused as much fury and concern as that of Dedrick Owens. Six-year-old Dedrick found a .32-caliber semiautomatic pistol in his uncle's home and took it to school. During a class-changing period, in the presence of a teacher and 22 students, Dedrick yelled at Kayla Rolland, also age 6, "I don't like you," before pulling a gun from his pants and shooting her. The bullet entered Kayla's right arm and traveled through her vital organs. She grabbed her stomach, then her neck, gasping for air. Kayla died soon after being shot, despite the teacher's call for emergency services. After firing the shot, Dedrick threw the handgun into a wastebasket and fled to a nearby restroom, where he was found by a teacher and taken into police custody. Because of his age, Dedrick could not be charged with murdering Kayla (but would go on to become a violent criminal). In 1893, the U.S. Supreme Court ruled in *Allen v. United States* that any child younger than age 7 could not be guilty of a felony or punished for a capital offense because he or she is presumed to be incapable of forming criminal intent.[6]

Juvenile crime is not only a problem in the United States, but also around the world (see **Box 1.1**, the "Delinquency Around the Globe" feature). A large-scale study of nearly 30,000 children selected from 21 societies including China, Croatia, Denmark, Finland, France, Greece, Hong Kong, Iran, Italy, Jamaica, Lithuania, Netherlands, Poland, Portugal, Puerto Rico, Romania, Serbia, Singapore, Thailand, Turkey, and the United States found remarkable agreement among teachers and parents in terms of identifying and rating mild, moderate, and serious forms of conduct problems and delinquency. As in the United States, serious juvenile crime constitutes only a small fraction of the offenses youths commit across the globe. Most juvenile crimes involve relatively less serious offenses, such as larceny-theft, liquor law violations, use of fake IDs, and petty drug offenses. But even minor forms of delinquency can have deadly consequences. Consider that in recent years many youths have smoked *K2*—an herbal-blend home

incense—that is sometimes marketed as synthetic marijuana but with 10 times the intensity. Ingestion of *K2*, also known as spice, blaze, demon, crazy clown, scene, smoke, skunk, and others, can contribute to serious physical and psychiatric problems, and has been linked to overdoses and suicides. *K2* is banned in many cities across the United States and in other countries, including Austria, France, and Germany.[7] Thus, even innocuous household items, such as laundry dryer sheets, magic markers, highlighters, glue, and household cleaners, can contribute to violations of law among juveniles.

Regardless of the seriousness of their offenses, when children commit crimes, people ask questions: Why do they do it? What can be done to prevent it? These questions, in turn, invite others: Who is responsible? What is the child's family like? Does the mother work outside the home? Where is the father? Who are the child's friends? Did the child play violent video games? Should young offenders be rehabilitated or punished severely? How should juvenile offenders be rehabilitated or punished?

Status of Children

Status describes a socially defined position within a group, characterized by certain rights, expectations, and duties. Who someone is in relation to others affects how he or she interacts with them and how others interact with him or her. There are two types of statuses: achieved and ascribed. **Achieved status**

Dedrick Owens was 6 years old when he took a gun to school and shot and killed Kayla Roland, his 6-year-old classmate. Dedrick was not prosecuted for the crime because in 1893, in *Allen v. United States*, the U.S. Supreme Court ruled that children under age 7 could not be held criminally responsible for crimes they committed.

© Paul Sancya/AP Photo.

BOX 1.1

Delinquency Around the Globe

Children and Crime

Juveniles worldwide commit serious crimes. Sometimes their crimes are violent, and sometimes not. The vignettes provided here involve crimes committed for a variety of reasons ranging from needing shopping money, to retaliation, to racism. As you see from these examples, juvenile crime is not restricted to any particular age, location, race, or sex.

- In St. Petersburg, Russia, a group of 10 to 12 drunken teenagers beat and stabbed a 9-year-old Tajik girl to death and severely wounded her father and 11-year-old cousin. The attackers were armed with knives, brass knuckles, chains, and bats, and assaulted the three Central Asians in a courtyard in the city center. Many Tajiks come to Russia in hopes of making a living and are often targeted in such attacks.

- In Darwin, Australia, two teenage boys murdered two female Thai prostitutes. The boys tied the women up and tossed them alive into a crocodile-infested river. They were convicted and sentenced to life imprisonment with nonparole periods set at 25 years. During his police interview, one of the boys stated that he killed the prostitutes because "just suddenly something really irritated me, can't remember [what] but it just ticked me off really bad."

- In London, England, police arrested four teenagers for the killing of a 10-year-old immigrant from Nigeria. The stabbing death, which took place in the stairwell of a housing project, caused revulsion on account of evidence that showed passers-by had let the boy bleed to death. The boy, Damilola Taylor, was attacked in the early evening as he returned from an after-school computer class. Stabbed in the leg, he dragged himself to the open stairwell where he died from loss of blood.

- In Ahmedabad, India, a 15-year-old Indian boy died after setting himself ablaze upon hearing that his parents were infected with HIV. Reports claimed that the boy was worried about his future and being ostracized from society. In India, schools will turn away children whose parents have HIV.

- In Accra, Ghana, hundreds of youths, upon returning from a funeral for Muslims killed in Africa's worst soccer disaster, vented their anger by attacking a police station and destroying kiosks in a working-class neighborhood. The youths had come from a funeral service for 30 people who were killed in a mass stampede at the Accra sports stadium. A total of 126 people died in the crush.

- In Okayama, Japan, a teenager was arrested for pushing a 28-year-old man off a platform at a railway station, causing him to be killed by a train.

- In Tuusula, Finland, an 18-year-old student shot and killed five boys, two girls, and the female principal at Jokela High School; at least 10 others were injured. The gunman shot himself and died from his wounds in the hospital.

In addition to these media items, cross-cultural studies show remarkable consistency in the mechanisms that push juveniles into delinquency. For example, the Second International Self-Report of Delinquency study is an examination of delinquency among 67,883 juveniles in 31 countries. The data include nations as diverse as Antilles, Aruba, Cyprus, Estonia, Iceland, Russia, Surinam, Switzerland, and the United States of America. Despite this diversity, studies show that delinquency is more common and severe among boys than girls, is commonly an outcome of parenting deficits and family problems, and is importantly related to self-regulation deficits. In other words, a look at delinquency around the globe tends to tell a very similar and familiar story.

Spiro Doukas, "Crowd Management: Past and Contemporary Issues," *The Sports Journal*, retrieved April 15, 2012 from http://www.thesport journal.org/article/crowd-management-past-and-contemporary-issues; "New Damilola Trial Is Considered," BBC News, retrieved January 14, 2016 from http://news.bbc.co.uk/2/hi/uk_news/england/london/4874872.stm; "Racist Violence on the Rise," World Press, retrieved January 14, 2016 from http://www.worldpress.org/Europe/2375.cfm; "Teen Held in Deadly Train Platform Push," retrieved January 14, 2016 from http://search.japantimes.co.jp/cgi-bin/nn20080327a2.html; "Man Kills Eight at Finnish School," BBC News, retrieved January 14, 2016 from http://news.bbc.co.uk/2/hi/europe/7082795 .stm; Ekaterina Botchkovar, Ineke Marshall, Michael Rocque, and Chad Posick, "The Importance of Parenting in the Development of Self-Control in Boys and Girls: Results from a Multinational Study of Youth," *Journal of Criminal Justice* 43:133–141 (2015); Alexander Vazsonyi and Li Huang, "Hirschi's Reconceptualization of Self-Control: Is Truth Truly the Daughter of Time? Evidence from Eleven Cultures," *Journal of Criminal Justice* 43: 59–68 (2015).

is based on merit, achievement, or accomplishments, such as being a college student or being a juvenile delinquent. **Ascribed status** is based on innate characteristics that describe who a person is, not what they do; some examples include being born Asian American or female. Typically, status involves a mixture of ascription and achievement: Ascribed status influences achieved status.

KEY TERMS

ascribed status

A status that is received at birth; it partly determines what opportunities are available and, thus, what can be achieved.

Of all statuses in American society, the status of a child is the least privileged. Throughout history, children have been treated as chattel or as the property of their parents. At other times, children have been mistreated based on their status. The 1874 case of Mary Ellen Wilson is generally regarded as the first documented child abuse case in the United States. Mary Ellen, who was badly abused by her adoptive mother, was removed from her home and placed in a state child protective facility. Her adoptive mother was criminally prosecuted and convicted of felonious assault (see **Box 1.2**, the "A Window on Delinquency" feature).

There are many other more horrific incidents of parents harming their children.[8] Nicole Beecroft stabbed her newborn baby 135 times and then put the child in a garbage can outside her home.[9] Debra Liberman beat her 7-year-old daughter with a dog chain and keys, burned her wrists on a stove, doused her naked body with bleach, and then locked the girl inside a closet in a coal cellar with a burning furnace filter.[10] In addition, no fewer than 4450 Catholic priests have been accused of molesting more than 11,000 minors.[11] The issue of sexual abuse became even more pronounced in 2012 when Jerry Sandusky, the former defense coordinator of the Penn State University football team was convicted of multiple counts of sexual abuse of children over a period of many years.

In addition to Catholic priests, other religious leaders sometimes mistreat children. For example, Atlanta police arrested Pastor Arthur Allen and five members of his 130-member church, who had whipped children as a form of discipline. The leader of the House of Prayer and several other church members were charged with cruelty to children. Even though they had been arrested, church members said they would continue to whip unruly children. They believe parents have an absolute right to discipline their children however they see fit. These persons think that what parents do to their children is no business of the state or federal government.

BOX 1.2

A Window on Delinquency

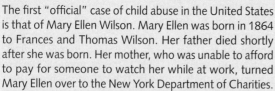

The Story of Mary Ellen Wilson

The first "official" case of child abuse in the United States is that of Mary Ellen Wilson. Mary Ellen was born in 1864 to Frances and Thomas Wilson. Her father died shortly after she was born. Her mother, who was unable to afford to pay for someone to watch her while at work, turned Mary Ellen over to the New York Department of Charities.

Mary Ellen was sent to Blackwell's Island for orphaned and abandoned children. When she was 4 years old, she was taken from the facility by Mary and Thomas McCormack who, without any legal documentation proving a relationship, claimed that Mary Ellen was Thomas's child from a prior relationship.

In her new home, Mary Ellen was poorly treated by her new mother. Neighbors in the apartment building quickly became aware of the girl's suffering. One neighbor told Etta Wheeler, a Methodist social caseworker who visited the impoverished residents of the public housing community regularly, the terrible tale of child abuse and asked her to check on Mary Ellen. When she did, she encountered a 10-year-old girl who was dirty and thin. Mary Ellen was dressed in threadbare clothing and had bruises and scars along her bare arms and legs. It was then that Etta Wheeler began to pursue legal redress and protection for her.

To help Mary Ellen, Etta Wheeler turned to Henry Bergh, founder of the American Society for the Prevention of Cruelty to Animals. Bergh told Wheeler that he needed a good, strong testimony of child maltreatment. Soon thereafter Wheeler provided Bergh with the information he requested. Bergh then had his lawyers present Judge Abraham Lawrence, of the New York Supreme Court, with a petition on behalf of Mary Ellen, showing she was being held illegally and being physically abused. The lawyers requested the judge to issue a warrant to remove Mary Ellen from the home and place her in the protective custody of the state and that Mary Connolly (her adoptive mother) be brought before the court on charges of felonious assault. Judge Lawrence honored the attorney's request and issued the warrant.

When Mary Ellen appeared in court, she was dressed in ragged clothing and had bruises all over her body and a gash over her left eye and cheek where Mary Connelly had struck her with a pair of scissors. On April 10, 1874, Mary Ellen testified before the court:

> Mamma has been in the habit of whipping and beating me almost every day. . . . The whip always left a black and blue mark on my body. I have now the black and blue marks on my head where they were made by mamma, and also a cut on the left side of my forehead which was made by a pair of scissors. . . .

Judge Lawrence then issued a court order to bring Mary Ellen under court control. Shortly thereafter, Mary Connolly was charged, prosecuted, and convicted of felonious assault and sentenced to one year of hard labor in prison.

Eric Shelman and Stephen Lazoritz, *Out of the Darkness* (Baltimore: Dolphin Moon, 2003); Lloyd deMause, *The History of Childhood* (New York: Peter Bedrick, 1988).

The beatings were done at the church, administered by parents and other adults with belts and switches, and under the supervision of Pastor Allen, who advised them on how severe the beatings should be. Allen based his decision on the seriousness of the offense considering how old the child was and whether the child had expressed remorse for his or her wrongdoing. For example, teenage girls who had sexual intercourse were whipped during church services, after having their skirts or dresses removed. Children who misbehaved in school were later beaten at the church. Three adults held one 7-year-old boy in the air while his uncle whipped him with a switch as Allen stood by giving instructions. A 16-year-old girl was beaten with belts for 30 minutes. Police photographs showed 3-inch-long welts on some children, and a boy, age 10, had open wounds on his stomach and side.

In 2002, a court found Allen guilty of cruelty to children and sentenced him to 90 days in jail and 10 years of probation. Allen violated his probation and eluded authorities for 5 months before being found by U.S. park police in a parked car. He was arrested and returned to prison. Allen served a 2-year prison term and was released. Four other church members also were convicted and sentenced in connection with the beatings.[12]

These are just a few examples of child abuse in the United States. In fact, in 2012, each day more than 1,836 children were confirmed by state child protection agencies as having been abused or neglected by their adult caretakers. More tragically, each day four children are killed as a result of abuse or neglect.[13]

There is good, strong evidence to suggest that child maltreatment adversely affects children. In a carefully crafted study conducted over a 25-year period by Cathy Widom and Michael Maxfield, 908 mistreated and victimized children were matched by age, race and ethnicity, sex, and socioeconomic status with a comparison group of 667 children not officially recorded as being abused or neglected. Among these researchers' findings were the following:[14]

- Being abused or neglected increased the likelihood of being arrested as a juvenile by 59%.
- Maltreated children were younger at the time of their first arrest, committed nearly twice as many offenses, and were arrested more frequently than their peers who did not suffer maltreatment.
- Physically abused and neglected children (versus sexually abused children) were the most likely to be arrested for a violent crime.
- Abused and neglected girls were at an increased risk of arrests for violence when compared to juvenile and adult women.

Today, child maltreatment continues to be a serious social problem. If there is good news to report it is that David Finkelhor and his colleagues recently uncovered data revealing there is much less child maltreatment today

Mary Ellen Wilson was the victim in the first recorded child abuse case in the United States. Laws preventing cruelty to animals were used to remove her from the home. This photo shows Mary Ellen at her court appearance in 1874.

Courtesy of the George Sim Johnston Archives of the New York Society for the Prevention of Cruelty to Children.

than there was in the recent past. Among 50 trends in exposure to crime, violence, abuse, and maltreatment, 27 showed significant declines between 2003 and 2011 and no form of exposure showed a significant increase. Indeed, there has been such improvement in the social and behavioral health of children that Child Trends, a nonprofit research organization, has initiated the Flourishing Children Project that focuses on positive characteristics of children and adolescents that are associated with conventional behaviors and negatively associated with delinquency and other problem behaviors. The flourishing constructs include gratitude, forgiveness, hope, life satisfaction, purpose, diligence and reliability, educational engagement, trustworthiness, integrity, thrift, empathy, and social competence, among others.[15]

Early Prohibitions of Juvenile Behavior

The systematic denial of privileges and subsequent maltreatment of children are not a new phenomenon. Throughout history, children have commonly been viewed as different from and inferior to adults. In the process, societies have constructed legal prohibitions aimed at regulating the behavior of juveniles.[16]

The Code of Hammurabi

The **Code of Hammurabi** is one of the earliest and most complete legal codes, originally proclaimed by Babylonian king Hammurabi in 1750 BCE. The collection of 282 laws and standards stipulated rules for commercial interactions and set fines and punishments to meet the requirements of justice. Many of the rules prescribed severe penalties, applying the dictum "An eye for an eye, a tooth for a tooth." Rule 195 was specifically aimed at children who disobeyed their parents: "If a son strikes his father, his hands shall be cut off." The Code of Hammurabi also established a special set of rules for adopted children. Rule 192 stated, "If an adopted child says to his father or mother 'You are not my father or my mother,' his tongue shall be cut off" and Rule 193 added that if an adopted son returned to his biological parents, then his eyes would be plucked out.[17]

The Greek Empire

The Greek Empire spanned the years between the sixth and third centuries BCE, when juvenile misbehavior was considered to be a serious problem. The Greeks responded to delinquency by creating laws holding parents responsible for the behavior of their children. These were likely the first parental-liability laws (see **Box 1.3**, the "Delinquency Prevention" feature).

If today's definition of assault was applied to the behavior of ancient Greek children, Greek society would have been filled with children who were "psychopathic delinquents." Many Greek children were so unruly that a law was passed specifically prohibiting them from beating up their parents. Some historians blame this aggressive behavior on the values of the larger society. Young Greeks were exposed to violence from an early age. Their heads were filled with stories of psychopathic gods and humans such as Kronos, who castrated his father; Hephaestus, who chained up his mother; and reprobate humans such as Oedipus, who killed his father and married his mother. Many Greek stories also gave vivid examples of what parents might do to their children:

- Heracles slaughtered his children in a fit of madness.
- Agave killed and dismembered her son, Pentheus.
- Tantalus chopped up his son, Pelops, to be eaten at a banquet held in honor of the gods.
- Laius nailed together the ankles of his infant son, Oedipus, before leaving the child to perish on a mountain.

KEY TERMS

Code of Hammurabi
One of the earliest and most complete legal codes, originally proclaimed by Babylonian king Hammurabi in 1750 BCE.

secular law
A body of legal statutes developed separately from church or canon law.

- Medea murdered her children to punish her husband for abandoning her for another woman.

These and other related stories helped create a society where (1) violent and destructive relations between children and adults were not uncommon and (2) the propensity toward delinquency was in part rooted in one's relationship with one's parents.[18]

The Middle Ages

There is very little documentation describing adult–child relations during the Middle Ages (500–1500 CE). Those writings that do exist suggest that children were treated badly. It was not uncommon for mothers to suffocate their children and leave their dead bodies on the streets. Despite their poor treatment, children living in the Middle Ages were viewed more like miniature adults than they are today. Children were permitted to curse, openly engage in sex, drink (both in taverns and at home), and wear firearms; also, they were not required to attend school.[19]

Laws regulating the problem behaviors of children began to emerge in the 10th century, when King Aethelstane pronounced that any thief older than age 12 should receive the death penalty if he or she stole more than eight pence (a very small amount of money). This declaration was later modified to provide that a person younger than age 16 could not be put to death unless he or she resisted arrest or ran away.[20] These laws recognized that a child younger than a minimum age, typically 12 years, was exempt from prosecution and punishment; they provided little distinction between older juveniles and adults.

The 16th and 17th Centuries

One of the best accounts of juvenile delinquency in the 1500s and 1600s is found in Mary Perry's *Crime and Society in Early Modern Seville*. The youths of Seville, Spain, committed many unlawful acts, including theft, gambling, prostitution, and homosexual solicitation. As Perry noted, boys and girls alike were arrested:

> Prostitution also offered a livelihood for boys. Some became pimps for their sisters or girlfriends, but others became prostitutes themselves. Some boys involved in homosexual acts in Seville were as young as eight years, but it is likely that the younger boys were victims rather than working prostitutes. Children growing up in the streets learned the tricks of gambling very early . . . They learned to mark cards with pin pricks, scratches, and watermarks.[21]

Most of the juveniles arrested were street children. Many were part of the underworld organization of Seville; they received protection for a price and were required to share their goods with the organization.

The legal regulation of juveniles in Seville came about through **secular law**, which defines a body of

BOX 1.3

Delinquency Prevention

Parental-Liability Laws

Increased juvenile violence and the horrified reaction by the U.S. public have caused state legislatures to increasingly hold parents responsible for some of their children's damage. Parental-liability laws are now on the books in almost every state. Some states hold parents responsible for their child's mistakes when they damage property or hurt someone. Although specific parental-liability laws vary, in eight states, parents may be held responsible only for crimes committed by their children. State parental-liability laws typically cover such behaviors as vandalism of government or school property; defacement or destruction of national and state flags, cemetery headstones, public monuments, or historical markers; and destruction of property as part of a hate crime. Personal injury in connection with any of these acts may also be included under the rubric of parental liability.

As early as 1846, Hawaii established a parental-liability law designed to punish, deter, or reform parents of juveniles who harmed others. Under early common law, parents could not be held liable for damages done by their children unless the damage was caused by action or inaction on the part of the parent. By the late 1950s, some states had enacted statutes similar to those found in Hawaii. Today, all states except New Hampshire and the District of Columbia allow victims to seek compensation from parents as a result of damages caused by their children.

Legislatures in some states have passed laws that impose criminal sanctions on parents whose children do not attend school. In 2008, in DeKalb County (Atlanta), Georgia, nine parents spent the night in jail, snared in a truancy crackdown. The jailed parents were locked up as authorities began arresting 59 people who had not complied with a court order to get their children to school. In DeKalb County, parents may be charged with educational neglect when their child has more than five unexcused absences in a school year. Also in 2008, an Ohio man was jailed for 6 months because his daughter failed her GED exam. In 2006, the court ordered Brian Gegner to make sure his daughter Brittany, then age 16, received her high school diploma. Soon thereafter, Brittany went to live with her mother, Gegner's ex-wife. When Brittany failed her GED test, however, her father was sent to jail.

Under an Oregon law, parents of second-time violators of the juvenile code may be fined as much as $1,000 or be required to attend parenting classes. Mississippi has a school truancy law that sends parents to jail for up to 1 year and levies fines of as much as $1,000 if their school-age children are habitually truant. In Florida, parents may be imprisoned for 5 years and receive a $5,000 fine if their children kill or injure someone with a weapon. In 1988, California passed the Street Terrorism Enforcement and Prevention Act, which includes provisions for punishment of parents for the gang-related activities of their children. Parents may be arrested and imprisoned for 1 year if their children are suspects in a crime and the parents then knowingly fail to control or supervise them.

The general rule regarding parental liability is that the mere relationship between parent and child does not impose any legal liability on the parent for the bad acts or carelessness of the child. Rather, parents are held liable only when the child is acting as an agent of the parent or when some carelessness of the parent made the bad act possible. Some examples regarding parental liability as an agent include harm resulting from a car accident caused by the negligence of a child when the child was running an errand for a parent, or when a parent encourages a child to physically attack another person. Parents also can be held liable when their own negligence contributes to a child causing injury to another. For instance, if a parent serves a child alcohol and then permits the child to drive a car, the parent may be liable for damages. Thus, for a parent to be found liable for the behavior of his or her child, the child must be acting on behalf of the parent or the parent must have made the harm possible through his or her own carelessness or negligence.

Although it might seem that the public supports parental-liability laws because of their concerns about delinquency, there is little research on the topic. A recent study, however, reported unexpected findings. Eve Brank and Victoria Weisz surveyed nearly 1000 adults and found relatively low support for holding parents legally responsible for their children's misconduct even though there was general acknowledgement that parents were morally responsible. More conservative individuals, however, were significantly more likely to believe in the value of parental-liability laws.

Regardless of its public support, parental-liability laws are one way that the criminal law can mandate accountability among parents. This is important because a significant portion of delinquency is explicitly related to children and adolescents who act out in order to strike back or gain revenge against their parents. For instance, a survey of more than 5000 youth in Finland reported that half of assaults perpetrated by youth are motivated by feelings of revenge against parents and peers. In addition, up to 20% of instances of running away from home and vandalism reflect a revenge motivation against one's parent(s). If parental liability laws help to improve parent–child relations, then reduced delinquency is a likely outcome.

Eve Brank and Leroy Scott, "The Historical, Jurisprudential, and Empirical Wisdom of Parental Responsibility Laws," *Social Issues and Policy Review* 6:2653 (2012); "Ga. Parents Jailed in Truancy Crackdown," *USA Today*, September 18, 2008, p. 3A; "Only in America," *The Week*, May 23, 2008, p. 4; Joan Lisante, "Blaming Mom and Dad," retrieved January 15, 2016 from http://www.consumeraffairs.com/parenting/blaming_mom_and_dad.htm; Eve Brank and Victoria Weisz, "Paying for the Crimes of Their Children: Public Support of Parental Responsibility," *Journal of Criminal Justice* 32:465–476 (2004); Janne Kivivuori, Jukka Savolainen, and Mikko Aaltonen, "The Revenge Motive in Delinquency: Prevalence and Predictors," *Acta Sociologica* 59:69-84 (2016).

legal statutes developed separately from church or canon law. All children had a legal identity and were taken care of by their parents or another member of the community. Unfortunately, the law did not provide for dependent and neglected children as it does today. In early Seville, children had to fend for themselves, and because no law prohibited adults from beating them, their best defense was a pair of fast legs and a place to hide.[22]

The 18th and 19th Centuries

By the end of the 17th century, concern about juvenile delinquency had become widespread throughout England. Although most juvenile crime involved theft, violent crime was also common among youths. Wiley Sanders reports on some of the children's cases that were tried in the Old Bailey (the primary criminal court in London) between 1681 and 1758:[23]

- On January 17, 1684, John Atkins, a little boy, was indicted for stealing a silver tankard valued at 10 pounds. He was found guilty, sentenced, and sent out of the country.
- On April 16, 1735, John Smith, a young boy, was indicted for stealing four yards of printed linen valued at five shillings. He was found guilty and exiled from the country.
- On December 7, 1758, Thomas Lyon, age 12, was sentenced to be transported for 7 years for stealing a watch.

At a time when juveniles were commonly sentenced to prison or transported to a prison colony for theft, the penalties these children received could have been much more severe. In 1733, for instance, Elizabeth Ran, a little girl, was sentenced to death for stealing from Stephen Freeman—to whom she was apprenticed. Prison, however, was the usual punishment for delinquency at this time. Between 1813 and 1815, 208 boys and 40 girls younger than age 15 were committed to Newgate prison in London. The next year, 429 boys and 85 girls were incarcerated.[24]

As an alternative to prison, many English children were banished along with adults. Two ships, the *Leviathan* and the *Retribution*, each carried between 30 and 40 juveniles on their trips to Australia. In 1829, 4000 convicts were placed on board the *Euryalus* to make the same trip, nearly 300 of whom were juveniles and 72 of whom were younger than age 13.[25]

Juvenile delinquency had become a serious problem in England by the mid-1800s. In London, the greatly feared criminal class, with its large numbers of children, was linked to the related problems of poverty, internal migration, and population growth. John Wade's book, *A Treatise on the Police and Crimes of the Metropolis*, reports on a theory of delinquency that was popular at the time:

There are, probably, 70,000 persons in the Metropolis [London] who regularly live by theft and fraud; most of these have women, with whom they cohabit, and their offspring, as a matter of course, follow the example of their parents, and recruit the general mass of mendicancy, prostitution, and delinquency. This is the chief source of juvenile delinquents, who are also augmented by children, abandoned by the profligate among the working classes, by those of poor debtors confined, of paupers without settlement, and by a few wayward spirits from reputable families, who leave their homes without cause, either from the neglect or misfortune of their natural protectors. Children of this description are found in every part of the metropolis, especially in the vicinity of the theaters, the marketplace, the parks, fields, and outskirts of the town. Many of them belong to organized gangs of predators, and are in the regular employ and training of older thieves; others obtain a precarious subsistence by begging, running errands, selling playbills, picking pockets, and pilfering from shops and stalls. Some of them never knew what it is to be in a bed, taking refuge in sheds, under stalls, piazzas, and about brick-kilns; they have no homes; others have homes, either with their parents, or in obscure lodging-houses, but to which they cannot return unless the day's industry of crime has produced a stipulated sum.[26]

As reported in the writings of Wade and others, juvenile delinquents were seen as thieves or prostitutes, frequently employed by older criminals, living in urban poverty, often orphaned or deserted, and likely to end up in prison.[27]

Under the existing laws of the time, children younger than age 7 were presumed to be incapable of harboring criminal intent. Therefore, they were exempt from criminal penalties. Children between the ages of 7 and 14 also were presumed to lack the intellectual ability to produce criminal intent. However, the law did not always limit prosecutors in charging these youths with crimes. Indeed, historical records reveal that in the early 1800s, a child of 13 was hanged for the theft of a spoon, and a 9-year-old boy was executed for minor theft from a printer.[28]

American Delinquency

Children in the American colonies were often treated badly by both adults and the law. The treatment children received during this time closely resembled the way children were cared for during the Colonial era, which was very similar to the treatment they received years earlier in England. The English who settled the colonies saw children as a source of labor and service, but little more. As such, until approximately

1880, child labor was widespread in America and the apprenticeship system was widely practiced. It was normal for the poor to give their children to farmers or craftsmen who would teach them a trade. Orphaned children were sold into apprenticeship, where they were often poorly treated. Corporal punishment was the rule, not the exception.[29]

American Colonies

It was not just apprenticed children who faced strict regulations on their behaviors; all children did. In 1641, the General Court of Massachusetts Bay Colony passed the **Stubborn Child Law**, which stated that children who disobeyed their parents could be put to death.[30] The text of the statute was drawn almost verbatim from the Book of Deuteronomy, the fifth book of the Old Testament (21:18–21). The Stubborn Child Law descended from the Puritans' belief that unacknowledged social evils would bring the wrath of God down upon the entire colony. The Puritans believed they had no choice except to react to juvenile misbehavior in a severe and calculated manner. Not all colonies adopted the Stubborn Child Law, however. Outside Massachusetts, children found guilty of serious crimes were frequently whipped and caned.

It was more than just the activity of children that concerned the colonists; children's inactivity bothered them as well. In 1646, the Virginia General Assembly passed legislation to prevent "sloth and idleness where young children are easily corrupted."[31] In 1672, the General Court of Massachusetts Bay Colony prohibited an adult from luring a young person from his or her studies or work. In addition, "rude, stubborn, and unruly" children were to be separated from their parents and placed with masters who would "correct" the misbehavior of boys until they were 21 years old and girls until they reached the age of 18. Children younger than age 14 who were found guilty of lying would be punished with a monetary fine for the first offense and higher fines thereafter.[32]

The Puritans were ambivalent about children. Although they believed children were born in sin and should submit to adult authority and hard work, they also thought children required separate legal provisions. For instance, in 1660 the laws of the Massachusetts Bay Colony provided that for sodomy. . . . children under fourteen were to be "severely punished" but not executed; for cursing and smiting parents,. . . . only those "above sixteen years old, and of sufficient understanding" could be put to death; for being stubborn or rebellious sons. . . . only those "of sufficient years and understanding [sixteen years of age]" were liable; for arson,. . . . the law also applied only to those "of the age of sixteen years and upward" for "denying the Scriptures to be the infallible word of

God," again the minimum age was sixteen for those who were liable to the death penalty.[33]

The Puritans made no distinction between delinquency and sin. The laws of the colony were the laws of God, so children who misbehaved were considered to have violated God's law.

The Puritans were not the only people concerned about children. By the 18th century, childhood was considered a special period of life when children needed thoughtful guidance and discipline. Children were seen as "fragile, innocent, and sacred, on one hand, but corruptible, trying, and arrogant on the other hand."[34] Members of the upper class believed that children demanded close supervision and needed discipline rather than coddling, modesty was of great importance, and strict obedience to authority was essential.

Postcolonial Patterns of Delinquency

Whereas humanitarian control motivated early interest in children, the actual purpose of many reforms, such as compulsory or required education, was to control the children of poor immigrants. Their swarming, ragged presence on city streets made these youngsters highly visible to a worried and fearful public. For the first time, Americans were forced to confront large numbers of children who had no home or who lived an undisciplined existence. Thus the new concern for children was paradoxically tied to the fear that many of them threatened the well-being of society.

The fear of children was based on personal experiences. In the early 19th century, America was in the midst of a massive economic depression. Crime rates soared, and lawlessness spread like wildfire. Particularly worrisome was the harassing and assaulting behavior of juvenile gangs. An editorial in a Philadelphia newspaper expressed both fear and outrage over the "new" street gangs:

> A few nights ago, a number of boys assembled on Fifth-street, between Market and Chestnut-streets to divert themselves with firing squibs. A gentleman and a servant [were] driving a carriage, with a pair of horses [that] had broken loose. The boys [saw this as] a fine opportunity for sport and mischief, and eagerly seized the moment to light a squib and fling it towards the horses. Luckily . . . the beasts were in good hands and, though frightened, were prevented from [running off]. Had not this been

KEY TERMS

Stubborn Child Law
A law passed in 1641 stating that children who disobeyed their parents could be put to death.

the case, the newspapers might [be reporting] a list of five or six persons killed or wounded.[35]

By the early 1800s, juvenile gangs had become an unwanted fixture in the big cities. They hung out on street corners, verbally abused pedestrians, and pelted citizens with rocks and snowballs—and these were among the least threatening of their behaviors. The more serious behaviors of these violent gangs of juveniles included robbing and aggravated assault of innocent citizens. Something needed to be done—but what?

The Child Savers

In the first quarter of the 19th century, the United States underwent rapid social change in response to the Industrial Revolution. Meanwhile, leisure time increased for wealthy people, opportunities for public education burgeoned, and communal life in the cities began to break down. Although simultaneously fearful and worried about the changes occurring around them, affluent people needed something to fill their lives. They turned their attention to saving other people's children, reasoning that in the long run, they would in turn be saving themselves. Many of those who joined this movement formed a group called the Child Savers.

Like other Americans, the **Child Savers** believed in the goodness of children. They saw children as being born good and only becoming bad over time. Juvenile crime was blamed on external factors such as exposure to poverty, overcrowding, immigration, and lack of parental guidance. The solution to youth crime was to remove problem children from bad homes and place them in good, rehabilitating environments.[36]

Early History of Institutional Control

The Child Savers actively pursued the passage of legislation that would allow children, especially juvenile paupers, to be placed in reformatories. The goal of removing children from extreme poverty was admirable, but ultimately resulted in transforming children into nonpersons (that is, people without legal rights). Children were shunted into factories, poorhouses, orphanages, and houses of refuge, where they were treated poorly with almost no attention being given to their individual needs. All too often, the legal system hid these problems from public view, taking away children's freedoms and occasionally their lives in the process.

Under the guise of providing children with better preparation for life, the new institutions sometimes did children more harm than good. A case involving the Children's Aid Society illustrates this point: The society originally wanted to place "unwanted" children in good homes in the countryside where they would learn to value hard work and love nature, but what evolved was a profit-making organization that drafted nearly 200,000 children into indentured servitude until age 18 (see **Box 1.4**, the "Delinquency Prevention" feature).

Some of the first recorded attempts to formally control delinquency in the United States took place in the 1800s. By that time, childhood was regarded as a period of life that deserved the care and attention its innocent nature demanded. In cities such as Boston, New York, and Philadelphia, conflicting aspects of juvenile behavior gained public notice. In big cities, the young delinquent stood in sharp contrast to notions about the purity of childhood. Child Savers launched interventionist efforts to save delinquents, rectify the circumstances that had hampered their development,

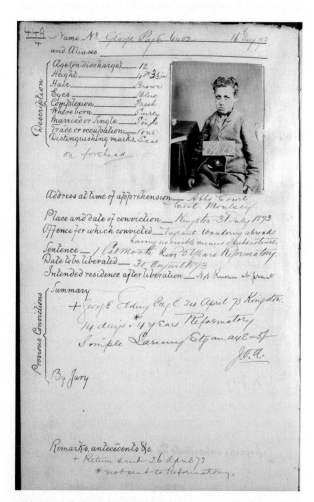

In the early 19th century, children of any age could be brought before the court. Here, a 12-year-old boy was convicted of being a vagrant with no visible means of subsistence.

KEY TERMS

Child Savers
Reformers in the 19th century who believed children were basically good and blamed delinquency on a bad environment.

BOX 1.4

Delinquency Prevention

The Orphan Trains

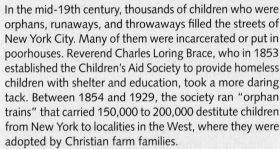

In the mid-19th century, thousands of children who were orphans, runaways, and throwaways filled the streets of New York City. Many of them were incarcerated or put in poorhouses. Reverend Charles Loring Brace, who in 1853 established the Children's Aid Society to provide homeless children with shelter and education, took a more daring tack. Between 1854 and 1929, the society ran "orphan trains" that carried 150,000 to 200,000 destitute children from New York to localities in the West, where they were adopted by Christian farm families.

The process of finding new homes for the children was haphazard at best. At town meetings across the country, farming families took their pick of the orphan train riders. Children who were not selected got back on board the train and continued to the next town. The children who were selected, and their new adopted parents, had 1 year to decide whether they would stay together. If either party decided not to continue the arrangement, the child would be returned to the Children's Aid Society, board the next train out of town, and be offered to another family.

Although approximately 40% of the orphan train riders were female, Brace referred to his passengers almost exclusively as "lads." Female orphan train riders were treated decidedly different than the males. Brace felt that street-girls were less salvageable and "hopeless" after the age of 14 because he thought them to be "weak in flesh" and prematurely "womanly." The Children's Aid Society did, however, continue to send girls to the underdeveloped West, where overworked farm wives were in dire need of relief. Orphan train girls were often treated harshly by their host families and considered cheap domestic help. It was assumed that getting married was the best outcome that could be expected for the female orphans.

The impact of Brace's efforts on children's lives was variable. Some children thrived. Two boys became the governors of Alaska and North Dakota, another became a Supreme Court justice, and many other "lads" became mayors, congressmen, local representatives, lawyers, and doctors. Unfortunately, thousands of other children did not fare so well. They became drifters and thieves; at least one became a murderer. The vast majority of the children, however, led ordinary lives.

The Children's Aid Society, *The Orphan Trains*, retrieved January 14, 2016 from http://www.childrensaidsociety.org/about/history/orphan-trains; Rachel Bandy, Robert Regoli, and John Hewitt, "Farmed-Out: A Case Study of Differential Oppression Theory and Female Child Farm Labor in the Early 20th Century," *Free Inquiry in Creative Sociology* 33:3–19 (2005); Stephen O'Connor, *Orphan Trains* (Boston: Houghton Mifflin, 2001).

and guide them firmly toward the path of righteousness. This path, however, was often a winding one because of these well-meaning reformers' anxieties. To them, delinquents were not just innocent children gone wrong; they were "bad seeds" capable of wreaking havoc and causing substantial harm on society. Therefore, reformers believed delinquents had to be restrained from activities that violated social norms, and these restraints sometimes reached astonishing proportions. Some interventionists went so far as to claim that the parents of delinquents should be sterilized to prevent further members of the "dangerous class" from ever being born.

It was during this political climate that the doctrine of *parens patriae* was adopted from earlier English common law. This doctrine defined the state as a kind and caring parent, and as "the supreme guardian of every child." As the "super-parent," the state enjoyed wide latitude in its efforts to redeem delinquent children. One of the earliest judicial expressions of *parens patriae* in the United States was fought vigorously in 1838 by a distraught father whose child fell victim to the "compassion" of the Philadelphia House of Refuge. Mary Ann Crouse was committed to the house of refuge by her mother, who alleged she was incorrigible (meaning that her mother believed she was hopeless).[37] Mary Ann's father disagreed, arguing that the commitment procedures were unfair, and that Mary Ann was accused of committing what later became known as a **status offense**—an act illegal only for children, such as truancy, curfew violations, and running away. The child herself was allowed neither defense nor trial. The court accepted the mother's charge and committed Mary Ann to the state for guidance.[38]

The New York House of Refuge

The first house of refuge opened in 1825 in New York State; it represented another example of the mixture of concerns underlying the philosophy of *parens*

KEY TERMS

parens patriae
A doctrine that defines the state as the ultimate guardian of every child.

status offense
An act considered illegal *only* for children, such as drinking alcohol, running away, truancy, curfew violations, and smoking cigarettes.

Status offenses are acts that are *only* illegal for juveniles, such as drinking alcohol, running away, curfew violations, and smoking cigarettes. Relatively few juveniles who only commit status offenses are adjudicated delinquent by the juvenile court.

© Alexandra Dudkina/EyeEm/Getty.

patriae. In 1824, nearly 10,000 children younger than age 14 were living in poverty in New York City. The New York House of Refuge served as one of the main instruments to remedy this problem. Designed to "save children from a life of crime," the house soon revealed its real orientation toward "saving society from children."

The reformers' attitudes toward delinquency were rooted in their beliefs about poverty and delinquency. Poverty was linked with idleness, which was seen as a reprehensible moral quality that led to crime. The managers of the New York House of Refuge translated this equation into a severely regimented boot camp type of existence for house inmates, where "children were marched from one activity to the next, were put on a rigid time schedule . . . and were corporally punished for being uncooperative."[39] Children suffered terribly at the hands of adults, whose mixture of hostility and kindness produced a peculiar atmosphere. There was an emphasis on remorse and punishment, which was common to most houses of refuge. Children accused of crimes were not only persuaded to see the error of their ways, but also made to suffer for their crimes. Retribution in the form of punishment provided the most convenient method of conversion.

The Juvenile Court

Progressive reformers continued looking for new solutions to prevent the growing problem of juvenile delinquency. Their most significant remedy was the creation of the first juvenile court in Cook County (Chicago), Illinois, in 1899. Just as in the earlier houses of refuge, the purpose of the juvenile court was to supervise problem children closely. Unlike in the houses of refuge, however, this new form of supervision would likely occur within the child's own home and community—not in institutions.

As mentioned earlier, the Child Savers were outraged by the plight of and the potential threat posed by so many needy children. In response, they joined hands with lawyers and penologists to establish the Illinois juvenile court, beginning with the 1899 legislative act "to regulate the treatment and control of dependent, neglected, and delinquent children." This act defined a delinquent child as someone "under the age of 16 years who violates any law of the State or any City or Village ordinance." A *dependent* or *neglected* child was one:

> . . . who for any reason is destitute or homeless or abandoned; or dependent upon the public for support; or has not proper parental care or guardianship; or who habitually begs or receives alms; or who is found living in any house of ill fame or with any vicious or disreputable person; or whose home . . . is an unfit place for such a child; or [one] under the age of 8 years who is found peddling or selling any article or singing or playing any musical instrument upon the street or giving any public entertainment.[40]

These court proceedings were established as *civil*—not criminal—procedures, perhaps because social workers spearheaded the court movement. They believed that children must be *treated*, not punished, and that the judge should act as a wise and kind parent. The new court segregated juvenile offenders from adult criminals at all procedural stages. Furthermore, the court hired probation officers to exercise friendly supervision over children involved in informal court proceedings.

The juvenile court reaffirmed and extended the doctrine of *parens patriae.* The paternalistic philosophy meant that reformers gave more attention to the "needs" of children than to their rights. In their campaign to meet the needs of children, the Child Savers enlarged the role of the state to include the handling of children in the judicial system. Because of its innovative approach, the juvenile court movement spread quickly. Less than a decade after Illinois established its juvenile court, 10 more states and the District of Columbia had followed suit. By 1925, all but two states had passed juvenile codes. When Wyoming finally established its juvenile court in 1945, the list of U.S. states with such courts was complete.[41]

In spite of the speedy embrace of this concept by jurists and legislatures, creating the juvenile court proved much easier than making it work over the longer term.[42] The promise of the all-encompassing child-caring role envisaged by court personnel crumbled as municipal officials, who had rushed to establish their own juvenile courts, quickly discovered that the new institution frequently failed to live up to its goals. In many cities, juvenile courts simply could not function with their prescribed tasks. In almost all states, reformatories and penal institutions were still filled with hundreds of children, and in many jurisdictions where detention homes had not been provided for court use, children were still confined in jails, often with adult criminals, to await hearings.[43] Responses to a 1918 Children's Bureau questionnaire seeking information on the workings of the new court system suggested that in most jurisdictions, special provisions were not yet made to handle children coming before the courts. A report on punishments meted out to children by one court provided commentary on the blending of old and new ways: "65 were sent to jail; 40 were placed in a chain gang; 12 were sent to a reformatory and one to an orphanage; 156 were placed on probation."[44] This report was not atypical; many judges still clung to their old attitudes and handed out the old punishments. Moreover, the Children's Bureau study reported countless other deficits in the courts' operation: inadequate probation service, general unavailability of treatment facilities, inept record keeping and a failure to use those data that did exist, and unqualified judges who lacked either proper legal training or an understanding of children.

These problems were made more acute by staffing and financial deficits. Ideally, court officers were to be trained, experienced, and sympathetic; in practice, the courts neither attracted nor retained highly qualified people. Top-flight judges increasingly avoided the juvenile court bench, and as time passed, enthusiasm for the courts waned.[45] In many jurisdictions, but particularly in large cities, a system of rotation was put in place where judges sat in a specific court no longer than 3 months at a time. Unfortunately, this system hindered the ability of judges to thoroughly grasp individual cases and ensured that the fate of a child was often passed from one judge at the court to another—a situation that paralleled that in the outside world, where the child was shunted from an inadequate home to a foster home, then perhaps to another foster home, and finally to an institution before the cycle began again.

Part of the dilemma facing the early juvenile court had to do with who its clients should be—that is, which children and which behaviors constituted juvenile delinquency?

Definitions of Juvenile Delinquency

As noted at the beginning of this chapter, delinquency is difficult to define. Criminologists, policymakers, and social reformers have all struggled to identify those behaviors that qualify as "delinquency" and determine exactly who is a "delinquent." What defines delinquency in a legal sense may be very different from how delinquency and the delinquent are defined by the general public. In the next section, we review some definitions of delinquency and delinquents that have emerged during different time periods from legal scholars, criminologists, the public, and the media.

Legal Definitions

Juvenile delinquency is a broad, generic term that includes diverse forms of antisocial behavior by a child. In most states, **juvenile delinquency** is defined as behavior that is a violation of the criminal code and committed by a youth who has not reached adult age, which typically is age 18. The specific acts constituting juvenile delinquency differ from state to state. One definition of juvenile delinquency that is widely accepted by criminologists is:

> Juvenile delinquency cases . . . are acts defined in the statutes of the State as the violation of a state law or municipal ordinance by children . . . of juvenile court age, or for conduct so seriously antisocial as to interfere with the rights of others or to menace the welfare of the delinquent himself [or herself] or of the community.[46]

Other juvenile justice agencies may define a delinquent as any juvenile arrested or contacted by law enforcement agencies, even though many of these children are merely reprimanded by the officer or have their parents called to come and pick them up at the police station. In reality, fewer than 50% of juveniles handled by law enforcement agencies are referred to the juvenile court system.

The legal definition of juvenile delinquency is found in state juvenile codes and statutes. Generally, the criminal law definition of a **juvenile delinquent** is a person, usually younger than age 18, who commits an illegal act, and is considered a delinquent when he or she is officially processed through juvenile or family court. A juvenile does not become a delinquent until he or she is officially adjudicated (labeled) as such by the juvenile court. In Ohio, for instance, a delinquent child is one who (1) violates any law of the state, any law of the United States, or any ordinance or regulation of a political subdivision of the state, which would be a crime if committed by an adult or (2) violates any lawful order of the court.

KEY TERMS

juvenile delinquency
Behavior that violates the criminal code and is committed by a youth who has not reached the specified adult age.

juvenile delinquent
A person younger than age 18 who commits an illegal act and is officially processed through the juvenile or family court.

In contrast, in Montana, a juvenile delinquent is a child who has either committed a crime or violated the terms of his or her probation. In Mississippi, a juvenile delinquent includes a child who is age 10 or older and "who is habitually disobedient, whose associations are injurious to the welfare of other children."[47] As a result of differing definitions, a child who could be defined in many situations as "delinquent" in Mississippi would not be considered "delinquent" in either Montana or Ohio.

Throughout the first six decades of the 20th century, the juvenile court failed to make clear distinctions between dependent and neglected children, status offenders, and delinquents. For the most part, the period between the 1930s and the early 1960s was marked by little change in how juvenile delinquency was defined and which activities constituted delinquent conduct. As the decades wore on, however, juveniles became increasingly involved in more serious crimes, such as motor vehicle theft, vandalism, and gang-related incidents. In addition, research began to show that more middle- and upper-class juveniles were engaging in crime.

In the 1960s, legal and public concern with juvenile delinquency took a sharp turn. During the first part of the decade, **baby boomers** (persons born between 1946 and 1964) were reaching their teenage years and delinquency rates began to soar to alarming levels. Not only were juveniles being arrested for traditional minor property crimes, mischief, and status offenses, but many young people also were being arrested for murder, forcible rape, aggravated assault, and robbery. As violent juvenile crime rates increased, so, too, did adults' fear of juveniles, widening the ever-increasing divide between parents and children.

Some states responded with new policies whereby juveniles who posed a serious threat to the community would be treated as adults. New York, for instance, is one of several states where juveniles between the ages of 16 and 18 are presumed to be adults for the purpose of criminal prosecution. However, New York's Youthful Offender Statute allows judges to grant youthful-offender status to "worthy" children between the ages of 16 and 18. This statute enables the court to legally process such youths as juveniles and consequently spare them from the stigma and severity of a criminal conviction.[48] Youths convicted of certain offenses—including murder, arson, and kidnapping—are not eligible for the more lenient classification, however.

By the early 1970s, many states had adopted legislation that redefined the noncriminal behavior of juveniles. New statutes were written to change the previously vague distinctions made among status offenses, dependency, and neglect. In 1976, the National Advisory Committee on Criminal Justice Standards and Goals recommended that status offenses be limited to only five specific categories:[49]

1. *School truancy.* This category encompasses a pattern of a repeated or habitual unauthorized absence from school by any juvenile subject to compulsory education laws. The court's power to intervene in cases of truancy should be limited to situations where the child's continued absence from school clearly indicates the need for services.
2. *Repeated disregard for or misuses of lawful parental authority.* Family court jurisdiction under this category should be restricted to circumstances where a pattern of repeated disobedient behavior by the juvenile or unreasonable demands on the part of the parent(s) creates a situation of family conflict clearly evidencing a need for services.
3. *Repeatedly running away from home.* "Running away" is defined as a juvenile's unauthorized absence from home for more than 24 hours. Family court jurisdiction in this category should be the last resort for dealing with a juvenile who repeatedly runs away from home, refuses or has not benefited from voluntary services, and is incapable of self-support.
4. *Repeated use of intoxicating beverages.* This pattern is defined as the repeated possession and/or consumption of intoxicating beverages by a juvenile. In this category, the family court should have the power to intervene and provide services where a juvenile's serious, repeated use of alcohol clearly indicates a need for these services.
5. *Delinquent acts committed by a juvenile younger than 10 years of age.* A "delinquent act" is defined as an act that would be a violation of a federal or state criminal law or of a local ordinance if it were committed by an adult. Family court delinquency jurisdiction covers juveniles ages 10 and older. This category is intended to cover the situation where a juvenile younger than 10 years repeatedly commits acts that would support a delinquency for an older child, or where the "delinquent acts" committed are of a serious nature.

Similarly, the International Association of Chiefs of Police (IACP) held that the term "juvenile delinquent" should be reserved for children who commit criminal offenses and who are in need of supervision or treatment. By contrast, the IACP suggested that the term "unruly child" be applied to children who commit status offenses, are ungovernable or habitually truant from school, and are in need of treatment for those problems.[50]

The idea that noncriminal juvenile delinquents are in need of special treatment and supervision by the state—whether they are status offenders, neglected youths, or dependent youths—has spawned a variety of legal designations. Although Georgia, Ohio, and North Dakota joined the IACP in using the term "unruly child," many other states have adopted one or more of the following categorizations:

- MINS: minor in need of supervision
- CHINS: child in need of supervision
- PINS: person in need of supervision
- JINS: juvenile in need of supervision
- YINS: youth in need of supervision
- CHINA: children in need of assistance

Unfortunately, even in the 1980s, many status offenders were still being sent to institutions. One report found that of the more than 25,000 juveniles being held in long-term, state-operated correctional institutions, slightly more than 2% were in custody for status offenses such as truancy, running away, and incorrigible behavior.[51] It would be misleading, however, to conclude that the remaining 98% were in custody for serious criminal offenses. Many of these juveniles were **chronic status offenders** or children who continued to commit status offenses despite repeated interventions by family, school, social service, or law enforcement agencies. Chronic status offenders typically commit new status offenses, such as running away from home while on probation. Consequently, these children are charged with the criminal offense of violating a formal court order specifying the particular conditions of their probation, a process known as **bootstrapping**.

Fortunately, the days of placing status offenders in detention or confinement are largely over. There has been unanimous national compliance by the states and U.S. territories in terms of removing nonoffenders and status offenders from secure placements in the juvenile justice system. In the 21st century, there are fewer than 5000 status offenders in custody; however, most of these are chronic status offenders with additional delinquent offenses or they are seriously at-risk youth who are ultimately placed with human service providers to provide treatment and tertiary prevention.[52]

Social Definitions

Just as legal definitions of juvenile delinquency have varied, social definitions have evolved as well. As Norval Morris and Gordon Hawkins so aptly put it:

Juvenile delinquency is not a simple term. It means different things to different individuals, and it means different things to different groups. It has meant different things in the same group at different times. . . . In popular usage, the term juvenile delinquency is used to describe a large number of disapproved behaviors of children and youth. In this sense, almost anything the youth does that others do not like is called juvenile delinquency.[53]

For example, a juvenile's parents, siblings, or relatives may call a certain behavior "delinquent" even though no law was violated. The youngster who refuses to do household chores, fights with siblings, associates with "bad" friends, talks back, or listens to the "wrong" music may be called delinquent by parents, although the juvenile court would likely ignore the problem.

It is not unusual for parents to complain to their local probation department that their child is a juvenile delinquent and beyond their control. Once parents discuss the matter in detail with a probation officer, they may redefine their youngster as a problem child or a person in need of supervision (PINS), but not as a delinquent. Parents also may find family counseling more appropriate than the juvenile court for addressing many adolescent problems.

In the public's mind, a few juveniles hanging out together on a street corner elicits the image of a delinquent gang. Although these juveniles may not belong to any formal gang, it is their appearance that decides a person's view. When juveniles use obscene language, pose in "threatening" ways, listen to explicit music, or wear clothing to set them apart from the adults watching them, it is not surprising that they are labeled delinquent. However, their actual behavior does not need to be legally defined as delinquent for the public definition to be applied.

In each of the previously mentioned settings, juvenile misbehaviors provoke public reactions. On some occasions and in some settings, their misbehaviors may be tolerated; in others, they may not. When the legal definition of delinquency applies to a juvenile's behavior, it suggests that what he or she did exceeded the limits of public tolerance and further suggests that the behavior would be considered inappropriate for adults as well as for children.

The variety of legal and nonlegal definitions of juvenile delinquency suggests that there is a level of subjectivity in definitions and societal images of delinquency. These images frequently originate in literature, film, television, music, and video games. When art accurately reflects society, there is little doubt that some degree of reality is being represented. From

KEY TERMS

chronic status offender
Children who continue to commit status offenses despite repeated interventions by the family, school, social service, and law enforcement agencies.

bootstrapping
A practice in which a chronic status offender who commits a new status offense while on probation is charged with the criminal offense of violating a formal court order that specified the conditions of that child's probation.

the youthful pickpockets of Dickens' 19th-century London to the neglected and tormented youth in *Rebel Without a Cause*, novels and films have been known to vividly capture aspects of juvenile delinquency. However, these images of delinquency leave no room for the more subtle shadings of behavior, and they overemphasize the more dramatic facets. Unfortunately, for much of society, juvenile delinquency and the delinquent exist exactly as portrayed by text, in film, or, more recently, in video games.

Literature

In *Oliver Twist*, Charles Dickens describes urban slum life and the corrupting effects of adults like Fagin on innocent youths.[54] Stephen Crane depicts the tribulations of children with his portrayal of a young girl forced into prostitution in *Maggie: A Girl of the Streets*.[55] There is little doubt that their descriptions are reasonably reflective of the times. Similarly, Mark Twain's *The Adventures of Tom Sawyer* and *The Adventures of Huckleberry Finn* seemingly reflect youthful adventure and misbehavior in the rural Midwest during the late 1800s.[56] Indeed, Twain may have been the first to identify a link between child maltreatment and delinquency when he wrote about Huck running away after being beaten by Pap.[57] For Dickens, Crane, and Twain, juvenile delinquents are seen as being led astray by either corrupt adults or their own benign failures. Portrayals of juvenile delinquency in early 20th-century American literature often focus on the effects of the pursuit of wealth, as in Theodore Dreiser's *An American Tragedy*.[58] In addition, the teenage drinking, gang fighting, and sexual pursuits of Studs Lonigan in a trilogy of novels written by James Farrell in the 1930s suggest juvenile delinquency is generally a product of ethnic and lower-class socialization. In the novels, such activities are considered a normal part of life for a young boy growing up on the South Side of Chicago.

Another book written in the 1920s emphasizes the contribution of poverty and racial discrimination in the creation of juvenile delinquency. Richard Wright's *Black Boy*, an autobiographical account of Wright's childhood in the South, suggests that lying, drinking, torturing and killing animals, and stealing are all adaptive mechanisms used to distract one from the painful conditions imposed by the formal and informal rules of the Jim Crow South.[59]

The images of juvenile delinquency in literature of the 1940s and 1950s also reflect public concerns of the period. Novels such as *The Amboy Dukes*, *The Golden Spike*, and *The Cool World* represent new concerns over urban gangs and youthful drug addiction.[60] Evan Hunter's *The Blackboard Jungle* describes a growing loss of control in inner-city high schools,[61] and the notion of middle-class delinquency was introduced in J. D. Salinger's *The Catcher in the Rye*.[62] The novels written in these two decades suggest an increased concern with the problems of youth in general, not just with the social and economic conditions that foster delinquency.[63]

In the late 20th and early 21st centuries, in a series of seven books, J. K. Rowling introduced readers to the prodigal delinquent Harry Potter, who stirred fear among many adults with his use of witchcraft to fight evil, which they believed would have a negative effect on their children.[64] Opponents of Rowling's books feared that they would lead children to believe that the occult and witchcraft were acceptable and legitimate means of dealing with adversity. Many of those opposed to the *Harry Potter* series tried to ban these books from school classrooms and libraries; legal challenges to their placement in schools have occurred in at least 13 states.[65] Ultimately, each of these attempts failed when lower courts cited the earlier ruling of the U.S. Supreme Court in *Island Trees School District v. Pico* (1982), stating that it is a violation of the First Amendment to ban books from school libraries.[66]

Clearly, as time has passed, not only has literature painted a picture of delinquency that reflected the beliefs of the public at large, but it also has proved instrumental in molding, shaping, and creating those beliefs.

Movies

Film was perhaps even more important than the novel in reflecting 20th-century concerns about juvenile delinquency, and it continues to shape our attitudes today. By the early 1930s, movies reached audiences numbering in the millions. Delinquency and adult crime were frequent film subjects. Like the early novels dealing with wayward youth, films such as *The Dead End Kids* and *Boys' Town* emphasized the influence of slum life and urban poverty on juvenile delinquency. The juvenile delinquent was portrayed as a good boy gone bad—a "misunderstood victim of official ignorance, indifference, or corruption."[67]

In the 1930s and 1940s, audiences were given two or three alternative portrayals of adolescents. On the one hand, they saw Andy Hardy, an innocent, middle-class, Midwestern child with an understanding father and a wonderful mother and sister. Any misbehavior on Andy's part was always viewed as a youthful prank or a consequence of some misunderstanding. On the other hand, movies such as *Wild Boys of the Road*, *Mayor of Hell*, *Angels with Dirty Faces*, *Where Are Your Children*, *Youth Run Wild*, and *I Accuse My Parents* were essentially indictments of parental neglect.

Films produced between 1955 and 1970 emphasized the many faces of juvenile delinquency. Rebellion, dropping out of school, terrorizing innocents, and teenage alienation were all delinquency-related behaviors portrayed in films of this period. Members of society were presented with such films as *The Wild Ones*, *High School Confidential*, and *The Bad*

Seed during this era. James Dean became a teenage idol by representing the ambiguity and alienation of youths unable to bridge the gap with their "uncaring and materialistic" parents. Unlike in the films of previous decades, delinquency was portrayed as much more violent and threatening to community stability during the late 1950s and 1960s. In depicting youth-related issues of the day ranging from gangs and drugs in schools to rock-and-roll music, hot rods, and drag strips, these films showed adults an image of adolescence very alien to their own.

In the 1960s, youths were portrayed in various—and often contradictory—lights. They were shown as good hearted and fun loving in numerous beach movies such as *Beach Blanket Bingo, How to Stuff a Wild Bikini, Beach Party*, and *Muscle Beach Party*; as romantically involved gang members in *West Side Story*; as subjects of adult misunderstanding in Dick Clark's *Because They're Young*; and as drug-using, motorcycle-riding adolescents looking for thrills in *Easy Rider, The Wild Angels, The Trip*, and *The Love-Ins*. In the 1970s, many films focused on "the good old days," exemplified by *American Graffiti, The Lords of Flatbush*, and *Grease*, where the delinquent was just "one of the guys" and not a "real" threat to anyone. The characters in these films would smoke, drink, experiment with sex (and often get caught), and drive high-powered cars. These activities produce an image of nice adolescents misbehaving, not juveniles bound for reform school.

By contrast, films since the 1980s, such as *The River's Edge, The Outsiders, Bad Boys, Close Range, Colors, Over the Edge, The Lost Boys, Menace II Society, Boys N' the Hood, New Jack City*, and *Juice*, portray alienated, defiant, and ultimately violent juveniles, willing—even anxious—to challenge the established order. Several more recent movies have continued to help define delinquency, including Larry Clark's *Kids* and *Bully*, which paint a world of children divorced from adults. The "rave" scenes portrayed in *Go, Heavy Traffic*, and *Groove* illustrate teenagers in their own element, living an essentially parent-free life. More recent films that focus on young people and delinquency include *Pineapple Express, Project X, In a Better World, Twelve*, and *Holy Rollers*.

Television

Perhaps because television brings the same characters to audiences week after week, individual roles (and their actors) need to elicit more sympathy. Weekly shows aim to establish attractive and interesting characters. A juvenile who uses drugs, steals, or assaults vulnerable strangers is unlikely to generate the desired audience reaction. Consequently, very few television series hint at serious juvenile delinquency, with rare exceptions like *South Park* and *Jackass*. The standard portrayal of delinquency is one of "innocent" rebellion or youthful pranks, such as those depicted in shows like *90210*, *The Secret Life of the American Teenager, Weeds, Friday Night Lights*, and *Gossip Girl*.

In addition, television programmers often air movie reruns or made-for-TV movies. Whereas reruns contain the images of delinquency already discussed, television film specials often focus on more controversial material. For example, *Born Innocent* shows the ordeal faced by a 14-year-old girl in a juvenile detention center and raises the specter of uncaring parents, but also describes how the brutality of the detention center staff and the other inmates destroys the girl's innocence. Ultimately, the audience is asked to judge a juvenile justice system that degrades even the most minor offender. In a very different vein, *Go Ask Alice* portrays a middle-class teenage drug abuser who, after running away from home, falls into prostitution and eventually dies of a drug overdose.

Music

One of the oldest elements of popular culture is music. By the Middle Ages, songs and ballads were widely used to comment on life situations. Popular music today, however, finds itself in a relatively unique position. It appears as though no other medium is as generational, compartmentalized, or specific. In other words, specific genres of music are produced and consumed by particular audiences, and the age of the consumer is an important factor in deciding one's tastes.

Rock music and rap songs portray perhaps the most widely shared images of juvenile delinquency. Not coincidentally, these styles of music are largely youth oriented. Young people not only constitute the vast majority of consumers, but also make up a large number of the acts and artists producing the music. Robert Pielke suggests that rock music challenges conventional morality and law[68] in songs ranging from the Beatles' *Maxwell's Silver Hammer*, Bob Marley's *I Shot the Sheriff*, and Bobby Fuller's *I Fought the Law and the Law Won*, to songs that reflect acceptance of illegal drugs such as *Because I Got High* by Joseph "Afroman" Foreman, *Lit Up* by Buckcherry, *Rehab* by Amy Winehouse, and *We Are All on Drugs* by Weezer. These songs, along with heavy metal music, are widely associated with delinquency and youth gangs.

Gangsta rap music may present an even greater challenge to authority. Songs of sexual exploitation, rape, murder, robbery, and drugs are interspersed with songs attacking the police and politicians, such as *Murder for the Mission; Execution of a Chump; Street Killer; Famous When You're Dead; Nobody Move, Nobody Get Hurt*; and *G Code*—all of which reflect an acceptance of interpersonal violence. Meanwhile songs such as *F—the Police* and *Cop Killer* express serious threats to law enforcement, and Eminem's *Cleanin' Out My Closet* and *Janie's Got a Gun* by Aerosmith discuss the

rebellion of juveniles in reaction to serious maltreatment. Pearl Jam's *Jeremy* is based on the true story of a child who committed suicide with a firearm in his classroom and whose depression was based in part on parental neglect and disinterest and the alienation of suburban life.

To what extent does gangsta rap music reflect widely held values among youth that are in conflict with the views of conventional society? Do the images of criminal and delinquent acts portrayed in gangsta rap reflect real social conditions, or is the delinquency greatly exaggerated for the "benefit" of the larger society? Does this musical genre influence the attitudes and behaviors of youths? To the extent that artistic expressions generally reveal something about the culture in which they exist, gangsta rap music may present some of the most disturbing images of adolescence in the popular culture. Furthermore, regardless of the accuracy of the depictions, the music is instrumental to the formation of beliefs about delinquency in the minds of the public and even law enforcement officials.[69]

Video Games

As shown in the "Delinquency Controversy" feature (see **Box 1.5**), a large body of research is now identifying a connection between violent video games, such as *Call of Duty, Carmageddon, Postal 2, MadWorld, Manhunt, Gears of War 2, Thrill Kill, Splatterhouse, Grand Theft Auto V, Soldier of Fortune, Mortal Kombat X*, and *Dead Space*, and aggressive behavior in children. One reason is that children and adolescents play video games often. On average, children ages 8 to 12 spend 4 to 5 hours each day in front of screens, mostly playing video games. Older adolescents spend more than 6 hours each day in front of media screens, again, often playing video games on their phone, tablet, or television.[70] Because video games are interactive, the

players often identify with and model the behavior of a specific character. Two aspects of this relationship may be harmful for children: (1) what they see in video games shapes their definition of what constitutes delinquent and criminal behavior and (2) more directly related to the game itself, what the child often sees in the game is a violent world, where he or she is required to shoot, rape, harm, and kill people, including prostitutes, innocent pedestrians, and police, to be successful. In addition, the sound effects in many of the video games manufactured in the 21st century are frightfully similar to reality; the shotgun reloads, the car swerves, and bodies fall.

Craig Anderson and his colleagues have studied this topic extensively. They have concluded that when children play violent video games, it increases their physiological arousal—for example, resulting in higher systolic blood pressure and aggressive cognitions. Children who play regularly are more likely to be socially maladjusted and express aggressive emotions and behavior, including aggressive play with objects and with peers. As a result of these social stigmas, the child may experience intense frustration. Playing violent video games affect children in at least five ways:

1. *Identification with an aggressor increases imitation.* In these games, children must take on the role of an aggressive character. Children most often take on this role in "first-person shooter" games, where players "see" what their character would see if they were inside the video game themselves. These games force children to identify with a violent character, which may increase the likelihood that they will imitate these aggressive acts in the future.

2. *Active participation increases learning.* When children are enthusiastically involved in an activity, they learn more than when they are passively drawn in (e.g., watching television). By their very nature, violent video games force children to engage in committing violent acts.

3. *Practicing an entire behavioral sequence is more effective than practicing only a portion of it.* There are many steps when learning how to complete a task successfully. To be successful in a violent video game, the child must decide to kill someone; choose the weapon to use; decide how to attain the weapon; if the weapon is a gun, figure out how to attain ammunition and load the weapon; stalk the victim; aim the weapon; and ultimately use the weapon. In these games, children continuously repeat these steps. This sequence of events teaches some children the technique(s) for attempting to commit crime.

4. *Violence is continuous.* The impact of violence on children is greater when the violence is unrelieved and uninterrupted. In video games, the violence is reoccurring. Children must constantly be on

Criminologists have determined that children who regularly play violent video games are more likely to be socially maladjusted and exhibit aggressive behavior toward their peers.

© Alex Segre/Alamy.

BOX 1.5

Delinquency Controversy

Violent Video Games and Delinquency

Playing video games is a pervasive aspect of recent American adolescence. Millions of children and adolescents spend time in video arcades playing video games, and the experience is fun and seemingly innocent. From this vantage point, video games are harmless even if the content contains violence and other noxious stimuli. Over time, however, video games have become more violent and because of technological advances, more realistically violent. Does such violence translate into increased aggression among youth?

The answer is *yes*. Violent video gaming is associated with increased aggression in a variety of contexts. Persons who just played violent video games have been shown to be less likely to assist persons in need of assistance and generally numb to the pain and suffering of others. In a large-scale meta-analysis, violent video games were significantly associated with aggressive behavior, aggression affect, aggressive cognition, reduced empathy, and decreased prosocial behavior. To put it differently, violent video games affect day-to-day aggression.

This area of research often engenders debate, with much of it heated up by a recent U.S. Supreme Court decision that focused on a California law restricting the sale of violent video games to children without parent permission (*Brown v. EMA*, 2011). In a 7-2 decision, the Court ruled that the government does not have the authority to "restrict the ideas to which children may be exposed." In the case, two *Amicus Curiae* briefs were submitted to the court by teams of researchers. One argued that research was fairly strong showing that violent video games are related to aggression, and one argued that the research was weak. Why do proponents and critics of the research seem to disagree on what should be a fairly clear distinction? What makes them seem so different is that they focus on different outcomes. The critics of the aggression literature tend to focus on "violence." That is, they care most about criminal-level physical violence. In contrast, the proponents of the research tend to focus on "aggression." That is, they care most about day-to-day low-level aggression, such as verbal aggression, relational aggression, and minor physical aggression—the types that are seen daily in any eighth-grade classroom.

In the *Brown v. EMA* case, the Justices were divided on how strong they believed the scientific evidence to be. The majority opinion stated that the accumulated studies did not "prove that violent video games *cause* minors to *act* aggressively (which would at least be a beginning)" (pp. 12–13). Note the standard that is required—"proving" (a word scientists almost never use) that games cause children to immediately act aggressive would only be a "beginning" and would still not be sufficient. Although there is strong evidence that violent video games (and violent media in general) can change the way people think, this psychological cognitive level of effect is clearly not compelling to the court. Although thoughts are related to actions, they are neither necessary nor sufficient. In fact, even if violent games *did* necessarily change children's actions every time, such as by making them bully their siblings, the court admits that it would only be a start. The court is not an arbiter of scientific truth, which they admit directly—"We have no business passing judgment on the view . . . that violent video games . . . corrupt the young or harm their moral development" (p. 17). Instead, the court is an arbiter of legal precedent, and as such, it is concerned with the types of issues that the legal system deals with. That means that it cares about *criminal-level aggression*, not low-level aggression. This appears to be why the majority opinion of the court agrees with the critics of the literature—they both care about criminal aggression rather than low-level daily aggression.

More recently, studies have shown that violent video games are associated with delinquency and violence, even among serious delinquents who are in confinement facilities and even while controlling for important confounds such as demographic characteristics, delinquent career measures, and psychopathic personality traits. In psychology, both "sides" of the debate—those who believe that violent video games are a risk factor and those who do not—have conducted meta-analyses and both show significant relationships between violent video games and increased aggression and antisocial conduct and reduced prosocial conduct. In the end, it is important to observe that violent video games, like all cultural and media effects described in this chapter, are one of many risk factors for delinquency. Even when their effects are significant, they are just one piece of the puzzle in terms of understanding the causes of delinquency.

Christopher Ferguson, "Do Angry Birds Make for Angry Children? A Meta-Analysis of Video Game Influences on Children's and Adolescents' Aggression, Mental Health, Prosocial Behavior, and Academic Performance," *Perspectives on Psychological Science* 10:646–666 (2015); Douglas Gentile, "What is a Good Skeptic to Do? The Case for Skepticism in the Media Violence Discussion," *Perspectives on Psychological Science* 10:674–676 (2015); Hannah Rothstein and Brad Bushman, "Methodological and Reporting Errors in Meta-Analytic Reviews Make Other Meta-Analysts Angry: A Commentary on Ferguson (2015)," *Perspectives on Psychological Science* 10:677–679; Christopher Ferguson, "Pay No Attention to that Data Behind the Curtain: On Angry Birds, Happy Children, Scholarly Squabbles, Publication Bias, and Why Betas Rule Metas," *Perspectives on Psychological Science* 10:683–691 (2015); Matt DeLisi, Michael Vaughn, Douglas Gentile, Craig Anderson, and Jeffrey Shook, "Violent Video Games, Delinquency, and Youth Violence: New Evidence," *Youth Violence and Juvenile Justice* 11:132–142 (2013); Brad Bushman and Craig Anderson, "Comfortably Numb: Desensitizing Effects of Violent Media on Helping Others," *Psychological Science* 20:273–277 (2009); Craig Anderson, Akiko Shibuya, Nobuko Ihori, Edward Swing, Brad Bushman, Akira Sakamoto, Hannah Rothstein, and Muniba Saleem, "Violent Video Game Effects on Aggression, Empathy, and Prosocial Behavior in Eastern and Western Countries: A Meta-Analytic Review," *Psychological Bulletin* 136:151–173 (2010); *Brown v. Entertainment Merchants Association*, 564 U.S. 08-1448. Washington, DC: U.S. Supreme Court, retrieved January 15, 2016 from http://www.supremecourt.gov/opinions/10pdf/08-1448.pdf.

alert for hostile enemies and then select and execute aggressive behaviors.

5. *Repetition increases learning.* The most effective way to learn any behavior is to repeat it ("Practice makes perfect"). If you want to learn a new telephone number, you should constantly repeat it to yourself to place the number in your memory. Some children play video games many hours of the day, during which they repeat violent acts again and again. Doing so increases the likelihood that children will learn violence from the games—with some of what they learn potentially becoming habitual to the point of being automatic.

Finally, in a study that tracked more than 4000 adolescents as they grew up, Brian Primack and his colleagues found that for every extra hour a teenager spends playing video games (or watching television) on an average day, he or she is 8% more likely to develop depression as an adult. What Primack and his associates observed is that teens' experiences shape their developing brains, and sitting playing video games or watching television replace positive academic, athletic, and social activities that give young people a sense of mastery and self-respect. Video games and television teach children to be passive and to judge themselves against characters whose looks and accomplishments are out of reach except for only a few.[71]

Ultimately, parents and guardians play a crucial role in supervising the games that their children play. Unfortunately, although many parents may lay down ground rules for how long their children may play video games, they are often shocked when they witness the content of the game. Even though manufacturers are required to attach "ratings" to their products to help guide parents in their purchases, the rating system does not always accurately reflect the true content of the games. Some games rated by the industry as appropriate for "everyone" ("E" rating) contain harmful content; many games designed for teens contain violent content. For example, cartoons are rarely perceived as dangerous, yet young children may still be affected by their violent nature. Extremely violent video games are now forced to include labels stating they are for mature audiences only ("M" rating). Although the effect of playing violent video games is likely to vary among children, those persons most likely to be adversely affected are young children who have lax supervision and a history of aggression and violence.

KEY TERMS

adolescence-limited offenders
A term applied to the overwhelming majority of children who commit a few minor acts of delinquency on an inconsistent basis during their teenage years.

Regardless of the effects of violent video games on some children, the courts have consistently ruled in favor of the video game industry's right to continue producing such games. In 2006, for example, Federal District Court Judge James Brady overruled Louisiana's violent video game law, arguing that video games are protected under the First Amendment; regardless of whether the games are violent or not, they are protected by free speech provisions in the U.S. Constitution.[72]

What Is Delinquency? Who Is a Delinquent?

It is difficult to decide just which behaviors constitute juvenile delinquency and who juvenile delinquents are. The reason for this confusion is that societal views of children change over time and vary from place to place. Actually, beyond defining a juvenile delinquent as a child who has violated a state's penal code, there is little uniformity among the 50 U.S. states regarding who is a delinquent. The age of the offender is what separates "crime" from "delinquency." In short, delinquency refers to criminal acts committed by juveniles.

When deciding who is delinquent, criminologists often do not adopt a strict legal definition because nearly all children have broken the law and, had they been caught, arrested, charged, prosecuted, convicted, and sentenced could have been institutionalized for one or more years. However, differences in the behavior of children are measurable, and it is not instructive to argue all children are delinquent. Most children only sporadically act in a delinquent manner, and only a small percentage of them are chronic offenders.

One way to characterize juvenile delinquency is to locate the behavior of children on a series of four continua representing (1) duration, (2) frequency, (3) priority, and (4) seriousness of the behavior. As shown in **Figure 1.1**, each factor forms its own continuum, with children falling at different points on each one.

The overwhelming majority of delinquents commit a few minor acts of delinquency on an inconsistent basis during their teenage years.

Some children may commit minor delinquencies and only one or two more serious crimes as teenagers. These juveniles are called **adolescence-limited offenders**. These individuals usually demonstrate delinquent or antisocial behavior only during their teen years, but then stop offending during the adult years. Even while they are delinquent, their antisocial behaviors are generally unserious and relate to the tenuous transition from child to adult. As a result, delinquency such as underage drinking, fist fighting, harassment, shoplifting, and marijuana use are typical acts of the adolescence-limited offender.

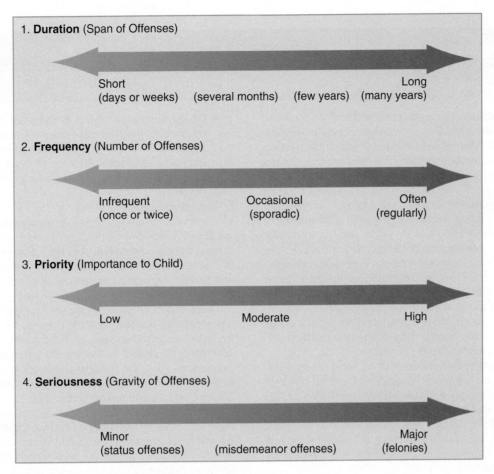

Figure 1.1 Continua of Juvenile Delinquency

© Jones & Bartlett Learning.

In contrast, the most serious delinquents are **life-course persistent offenders**. They represent a small group of individuals who engage in antisocial behavior of one sort or another at every stage of life. Life-course persistent offenders are deeply committed (priority) to problem behavior and have committed many (frequency) serious offenses (seriousness) over an extended period (duration). In addition to their extensive involvement in delinquency, life-course persistent offenders are also more likely to have extremely disadvantaged family backgrounds and to have experienced multiple forms of abuse, neglect, and exposure to drugs and violence (see **Box 1.6** for a look at an organization that attempts to help these troubled youth). When a life-course persistent offender's antisocial tendencies continue into adulthood, he or she is considered a "chronic offender" and placed on the extreme right side of the continua.

The middle of the continua is reserved for adolescent-limited offenders, whose involvement in delinquency is generally minor, inconsistent, and restricted to their teenage years.[73] If no one intervenes to help chronic delinquent offenders, however, their delinquency may worsen. Still another group of youths, called **abstainers**, do not engage in delinquency at all. There is evidence that abstainers

are psychologically healthier than youths who do commit delinquency.

Determining whether a child is an adolescence-limited offender, a life-course-persistent offender, or an abstainer depends in part on several factors. Studies consistently show that males are more delinquent than females in terms of the severity of bad conduct and also the frequency with which it is committed. There are also several forms of nondelinquent conduct problems that often predate actual delinquency. These include showing a lack of guilt, breaking household rules, lying, cheating, using profanity, hanging out with older kids, and hanging out with kids who already engage in delinquency. Alexandra Burt and her colleagues found these behaviors often occur before true delinquency, and that the most severely delinquent youth commit nondelinquent conduct problems at very high levels relative to other youth.[74]

KEY TERMS

life-course persistent offenders
The most serious juvenile delinquents; a small group of children who engage in antisocial behavior of one sort or another at every stage of life.

abstainers
Youth who do not commit delinquency.

BOX 1.6

A Window on Delinquency

The National Center for Missing and Exploited Children

One of the most important organizations dedicated to the welfare of children and adolescents is the National Center for Missing and Exploited Children, the national clearinghouse for information on missing and exploited children in the United States. In its 31 years of existence, the National Center for Missing and Exploited Children has assisted law enforcement in the recovery of more than 211,000 missing children and engaged in the training of more than 314,000 juvenile justice and human service providers. The National Center for Missing and Exploited Children performs several functions. For example, the organization is authorized by Congress to operate CyberTipline, a national mechanism for public and electronic service providers to report suspected child sexual exploitation. In 2014, CyberTipline received 1.1 million reports, mostly relating to child pornography, online sexual enticement, and the sexual trafficking of children.

According to the most recent report from year-end 2014, the National Center for Missing and Exploited Children:

- Assisted law enforcement with more than 12,000 cases of missing children
- Of those children, 84% were endangered runaways, 12% were family abductions, 2% were lost, injured, or otherwise missing, and 1% were nonfamily abductions.

- Of the more than 10,000 endangered runaways reported to the National Center for Missing and Exploited Children, one in six children were likely victims of child sex trafficking; of those children, 68% were in the care of social services when they ran away.

The National Center for Missing and Exploited Children offers several programs. Team Adam provides rapid, on-site assistance to law enforcement in cases of critically missing children and, to date, has been deployed nearly 900 times. Project ALERT provides technical assistance and outreach regarding long-term missing child cases and has been deployed more than 8800 times.

The National Center for Missing and Exploited Children is a secondary provider of AMBER Alerts, which have led to the successful recovery of 772 children, including 20 recoveries credited to the wireless emergency alert program. In 2014, the National Center for Missing and Exploited Children launched the AMBER Alert Twitter account, and thus 49 million Twitter users in the United States receive AMBER Alerts. The many programs of the National Center for Missing and Exploited Children show the tremendous progress the United States has made in its advocacy and care for the well-being, health, and safety of children.

The National Center for Missing and Exploited Children, *Key Facts*, retrieved January 15, 2016 from http://www.missingkids.com/home.

WRAP UP

THINKING ABOUT JUVENILE DELINQUENCY: CONCLUSIONS

The way a society defines delinquency reflects its view of children. As society's beliefs about children change, the society's formal response to delinquency also changes. For instance, during the period when juveniles were viewed as miniature adults, the legal codes that applied to adults were presumed to be adequate to control children. However, with the changes in social roles and relationships brought about by the Industrial Revolution, juveniles began to be seen as different from adults, and their violations of the law became defined as more problematic challenges to the social order.

Although the legal codes of the 17th and 18th centuries equated delinquency with sin, the 19th century replaced this view with one that forged a connection between urban poverty and crime. During this era, juveniles were increasingly involved in crimes (mainly thefts) that resulted in them being sent to reform institutions or houses of refuge. To a large extent, the plight of the urban adolescent, poverty, and exposure to the corrupting influences of adult criminals were responsible for many of the reforms that took place at the end of the 19th century and the beginning of the 20th century. The most significant reform was the creation of the juvenile court system. The juvenile court and codes that followed carved out special areas of misbehavior and conditions that allowed for court intervention and the designation of a child as delinquent.

CHAPTER SPOTLIGHT

- Juvenile delinquency is a complex phenomenon that is difficult to define, measure, explain, and prevent.
- Throughout history, from the Code of Hammurabi to the 18th and 19th centuries in Europe, children were treated badly. Although some societies proved to have harsher treatments toward children than others, throughout time children have widely been considered property of their adult guardians and often forced to lead cruel and unsympathetic lives.
- In the 19th-century United States, a group called the Child Savers promoted the notion of the basic goodness of children. The Child Savers blamed delinquency on the child's exposure to poverty, overcrowding, immigration, and lack of parental guidance. Their solution to youth crime was to remove problem children from bad homes and place them in rehabilitating environments.

- The Child Savers were responsible for the creation of the juvenile court system and houses of refuge.
- Criminologists who subscribe to a legalistic definition define juvenile delinquency as behavior that is committed by a youth who has not reached adult age and that is a violation of the criminal code.
- Criminologists who adopt a social definition of delinquency define juvenile delinquency broadly and recognize the possibility that it means different things to different individuals and groups.
- A large body of scientific studies has concluded that when children play violent video games, the games increase their physiological arousal, as evidenced by higher systolic blood pressure and aggressive cognitions. Children who regularly play violent video games are more likely to be socially maladjusted and express aggressive emotions and behavior, including aggressive play with objects and with peers.

CRITICAL THINKING

1. Should a child ever be sentenced to life in prison without parole?
2. Is the status of a child the least privileged? Are some children more privileged than others? If so, how and in what ways?
3. Were the orphan trains a viable solution for preventing delinquency? How does society today manage orphaned and unwanted children?

4. Why do we designate some behaviors as status offenses? Should chronic status offenders be punished or treated? What should their punishment or treatment be?
5. Should violent video games such as *Call of Duty* and *Mortal Kombat X* be illegal? Is it a person's right to choose whether to play them?

OBJECTIVES

- Understand the ways that law enforcement agencies have measured crime.

- Explore victimization surveys and the ways victimization data overlap with official statistics.

- Examine self-reports from delinquents as a way to measure delinquency.

- Identify trends in terms of how much delinquency exists and which social groups are involved.

- Understand the special characteristics of serious, violent, and chronic juvenile offenders and major research initiatives that study them.

KEY TERMS

Historically, it has been difficult to measure juvenile delinquency. Years ago, the economist Sir Josiah Stamp said about crime statistics that they "come in the first instance from the village watchman, who just puts down what he damn pleases."[1] Criminologists have drawn the same conclusion. In 1947, Edwin Sutherland wrote that "the statistics of crime and criminals are the most unreliable of all statistics."[2] Twenty years later, Albert Biderman and Albert Reiss concluded that crime statistics involve "institutional processing of people's reports. . .the data are not some objectively observable universe of 'criminal acts,' but rather those events defined, captured, and processed by some institutional mechanism."[3] It is even difficult to measure the most severe forms of delinquent and antisocial behavior, such as murder. For example, a review of the various types of law enforcement data, death certificate data, and coroner/medical examiner data used in the National Violent Death Reporting System, found that approximately 70% of the time, these assorted data sources matched. Of course, this also means that there were discrepancies in the measurement of roughly 30% of violent deaths.[4]

Measuring crime and delinquency is also not something on which most people focus. As a result, citizen perceptions of delinquency can be wildly off base—including estimates made by students in juvenile delinquency and criminology courses. For proof of this notion, consider the work of Margaret Vandiver and David Giacopassi, who administered questionnaires to nearly 400 students in an introductory criminology course and to seniors majoring in criminal justice to determine how well they grasped the magnitude of the crime problem relative to other mortality conditions. They found that almost 50% of the introductory-level students believed that more than 250,000 murders were committed annually in the United States (there were actually some 17,000 murders and fewer than 1000 murders committed by juveniles during the year of their study). Fifteen percent of the students estimated that more than 1 million people were murdered each year.[5]

One explanation for the "mismeasure" of crime is that single incidents of delinquency and violence affect people's subjective assessment of the crime problem. Usually, subjective assessments are very different from larger trends in crime data. The United States, for example, is currently enjoying one of its safest eras in terms of delinquency and violence. The overall declines in delinquency, crime, and violence in the United States are so apparent that in 2012, for the first time in nearly a half century, homicide dropped off of the list of the 15 most common causes of death. The top two causes of death, heart disease and cancer, account for more than half of all deaths annually.[6] For many reasons, but perhaps most notably because of the extensive media focus on crime, students overestimated the likelihood of being murdered but underestimated the prevalence of other causes of death that were less sensationalistic, such as accidents.

There are other reasons why gathering and verifying crime data have proven problematic. For example, crime is both *context* and *time* specific. Behavior is evaluated differently depending on where and when it takes place. For instance, in the United States, sexual promiscuity was judged differently in the Victorian period of the 19th century than it was during the 1950s, the 1960s, and today. Behavioral norms that exist in Los Angeles and New York might be less accepted in other regions of the country. Additionally, some adolescents may commit crimes at relatively high levels but are never "caught" and punished for their misdeeds, whereas other youths are arrested on their first offense. Thus, arrest records do not necessarily always reflect actual delinquent behavior.

Today, to overcome these data-related problems, criminologists measure delinquency in different ways. When these different measures are put together, they provide a respectable *approximation* of the extent and nature of delinquency (for an example of the potential pitfalls of "counting crime," see **Box 2.1**, the "A Window on Delinquency" feature). The most popular sources of data for estimating delinquency are the *Uniform Crime Reports*, victimization surveys, and self-report studies.

Uniform Crime Reports

The *Uniform Crime Reporting Program* is a nationwide, cooperative effort of more than 18,000 city, county, and state law enforcement agencies that voluntarily report, to the Federal Bureau of Investigation (FBI), data on crimes brought to their attention. The data are published in an annual report titled *Crime in the United States*, also known as the **Uniform Crime Reports (UCR)**. The UCR contains data on the following items:

1. *Crimes known to the police.* These are crimes that police know about, either because the crimes were reported to police or because the police discovered the crimes on their own.
2. *Number of arrests.* The UCR reports the number of arrests police made in the past calendar year. The number of arrests is not the same as the number of people arrested because some people are arrested more than once during the year. Nor does the number of arrests indicate how many crimes the people who were arrested committed, because multiple crimes committed by one person might produce a single arrest, or a single crime might result in the arrest of multiple persons.
3. *Persons arrested.* The third section of the UCR reports the number of persons arrested, the crimes for which they were arrested, and the age, sex, and race of those arrested. A large number of the nation's law enforcement agencies participate in the UCR Program, representing nearly 98% of the total U.S. population, which presently stands at roughly 325 million people and is steadily growing.

Since 1930, the FBI has administered the UCR Program. Its primary objective is to generate reliable information for use in law enforcement administration, operation, and management; however, over the years, the UCR data have become one of the country's leading social indicators. The American public looks to the UCR for information on fluctuations in the level of crime, and criminologists, sociologists, legislators, municipal planners, the media, and other students of criminal justice use the statistics for varied research and planning purposes.

KEY TERMS

Uniform Crime Reports (UCR)
The annual publication from the Federal Bureau of Investigation that provides data on crimes reported to the police, number of arrests, and number of persons arrested in the United States.

BOX 2.1

A Window on Delinquency

Getting a "Bum Rap": False Accusations and Erroneous Arrest in the United States

The usual concern about official estimates of crime, such as arrest, is that they underestimate the true amount of crime and delinquency that an individual commits. It is normative to engage in some level of delinquency, especially during the teenage years, but most people are able to avoid ever being arrested. As a result, even "normal," nondelinquent people understand that arrests are a fallible measure of delinquency.

But additional concerns are raised when an individual is falsely accused of delinquent behavior or worse, arrested erroneously. The former is offensive and the latter is a miscarriage of justice. How prevalent are false accusations of crime and erroneous arrest? Wendi Pollock and Scott Menard provided estimates of these examples of getting a "bum rap" using data from the National Youth Survey Family Study (NYSFS), which is described fully later in this chapter. The NYSFS is a nationally representative sample that contains self-reports on a host of delinquent and problem behaviors. The survey guarantees confidentiality, thus participants have nothing to gain or lose by telling the truth about their delinquency, whether the delinquent behavior did not result in arrest, whether it did result in arrest, and whether they were erroneously arrested.

In their analyses, Menard and Pollock found that 11% of the original survey respondents, 27% of the adult offspring, and 23% of the young offspring of the original survey participants had been falsely accused of criminal

behavior. Risk factors for actual delinquency were the best predictors of being falsely accused of delinquency. For example, being male, showing low academic achievement, having many delinquent friends, and having previous involvement in delinquency were significantly associated with subsequently being falsely accused.

In terms of erroneous arrest, Pollock and Menard found that the prevalence is exceedingly low. Only 26 participants experienced one erroneous arrest. One individual experienced two erroneous arrests and one other individual had three erroneous arrests. The prevalence of erroneous arrest was 0.3%. They also found that social status affected the likelihood of erroneous arrest. Males, persons with poor academic achievement, those with friends who were involved in delinquency, minorities, and those who were actually engaging in crime and delinquency were more likely to be erroneously arrested. Thus, being falsely accused and being erroneously arrested are essentially functions of being a usual suspect or an individual who associates with known delinquents. In this way, inaccurate police contacts largely stem from guilt by association or prior bad acts.

Fortunately, the agreement between self-reported delinquency and official arrests is over 80% and most of the error relates to chronic offenders, who are less reliable in self-reports of crime. For those who have never been arrested, there is greater convergence between self-reports and official tallies of delinquency.

Scott Menard and Wendi Pollock, "Self-Reports of Being Falsely Accused of Criminal Behavior," *Deviant Behavior* 35:378–393 (2014); Wendi Pollock and Scott Menard, "'It Was a Bum Rap': Self-Reports of Being Erroneously Arrested in a National Sample," *Criminal Justice Review* 39:325–338 (2014); Wendi Pollock, Scott Menard, Delbert Elliott, and David Huizinga, "It's Official: Predictors of Self-Reported vs. Officially Recorded Arrests," *Journal of Criminal Justice* 43:69–79 (2015).

Historical Background

Recognizing a need for national crime statistics, the International Association of Chiefs of Police (IACP) formed the Committee on *UCR* in 1927 to develop a system of uniform crime statistics.

Establishing offenses known to law enforcement as the appropriate measure, the committee evaluated various crimes on the basis of their seriousness, frequency of occurrence, pervasiveness in all geographic areas of the country, and likelihood of being reported to law enforcement. After studying state criminal codes and making an evaluation of the record-keeping

KEY TERMS

Crime Index
A statistical indicator consisting of eight offenses that was used to gauge the amount of crime reported to the police. The Index was discontinued in 2004.

practices in use, the committee completed a plan for crime reporting that became the foundation of the *UCR* Program in 1929.

Seven main offense classifications, called Part I crimes, were selected to gauge the state of crime in the United States. These offense classifications, which eventually became known as the **Crime Index**, included the violent crimes of murder and non-manslaughter death, forcible rape, robbery, aggravated assault, and the property crimes of burglary, larceny, and motor vehicle theft. By congressional mandate in 1979, arson was added as the eighth Crime Index offense. In 2013, human trafficking/commercial sex acts and human trafficking/involuntary servitude were added to Part I offenses.

During the early planning of the *UCR* Program, it was recognized that the differences among criminal codes in the various states precluded a mere aggregation of state statistics to arrive at a national total of crimes.

The *Uniform Crime Reports* are the primary measure of crime and delinquency, yet they only measure crimes known to the police. All measures of crime—even the *UCR*—are weakened by measurement error.

© Lisa F. Young/Shutterstock.

Further, because of variances in punishment for the same offenses in different state codes, no distinction between felony and misdemeanor crimes was possible. To avoid these problems and to provide nationwide uniformity in crime reporting, standardized offense definitions by which law enforcement agencies were to submit data without regard for local statutes were formulated.

In January 1930, 400 cities representing 20 million persons in 43 states began participating in the *UCR* Program. For more than 85 years, the *UCR* Program has relied on police agencies to forward information to the FBI, either directly or through a state-level crime-recording program. Police tabulate the number of offenses committed each month based on records of all reports of crime received from victims, from officers who discover violations, and from other sources. The data are forwarded to the FBI regardless of whether anyone was arrested, property was recovered, or prosecution was undertaken.[7] The FBI audits each agency report for arithmetical accuracy and for deviations from previous submissions. An agency's monthly report is also compared with its earlier submissions to identify unusual fluctuations in crime trends. Large variations from one month to the next might indicate changes in the volume of crime being committed, or they might be because of changes in an agency's recording practices, incomplete reporting, or changes in the jurisdiction's geopolitical structure (e.g., land might have been annexed).

Recent Developments

Although *UCR* data collection had originally been conceived as a tool for law enforcement administration,

by the 1980s the data were widely used by other entities involved in various forms of social planning. Recognizing the need for more detailed crime statistics, U.S. law enforcement agencies called for a thorough evaluative analysis that would modernize the *UCR* Program. These studies led to the creation and implementation of the *National Incident-Based Reporting System (NIBRS)* in 1989.

The *NIBRS* collects data on victims, known offenders, and relationships for 23 offense categories comprising 49 offenses (see **Box 2.2**, the "A Window on Delinquency" feature). The NIBRS also contains arrest data for 11 more offenses for which only arrest data are collected. The detailed, accurate, and meaningful data produced by *NIBRS* benefit local agencies. Armed with comprehensive crime data, these agencies can make a stronger case when it comes time to acquire and effectively allocate the resources needed to fight crime.

Currently, 6520 law enforcement agencies contribute *NIBRS* data to the national *UCR* Program. The data submitted by the agencies represent more than 29% of the U.S. population and 35% of the crime statistics collected by the *UCR* Program. The current timetable calls for all U.S. law enforcement agencies to be participating in the *NIBRS* Program by 2020. Sixteen states are currently 100% NIBRS-reporting, which means that all agencies in the state participate in the program. Thirty-three additional states are certified and working toward 100% NIBRS-reporting.[8]

The *NIBRS* has several advantages over the *UCR* Program:

1. *NIBRS* contains incident- and victim-level analysis disaggregated to local jurisdictions and aggregated to intermediate levels of analysis. By comparison, the *UCR* is a summary-based system.
2. *NIBRS* provides full incident details, which permits the analysis of ancillary offenses and crime situations. By comparison, the *UCR* hierarchy rule (discussed later) counts only the most serious offenses.
3. *NIBRS* data permit separation of individual, household, commercial, and business victimizations.
4. *NIBRS* offers data on incidents involving victims younger than age 12. By comparison, the *National Crime Victimization Survey (NCVS*—discussed later in this chapter) covers only victims 12 and older.
5. *NIBRS* offers a broader range of offense categories.
6. *NIBRS* contains victimization information beyond that which the NCVS provides.
7. *NIBRS* yields individual-level information about offenders based on arrest records and victim reports, thereby yielding residual information on victims and offenders.

Additional reforms have improved the quality of *UCR* data. In 1988, to increase participation in the *UCR* Program, Congress passed the *Uniform Federal*

BOX 2.2

A Window on Delinquency

National Incident-Based Reporting System

NIBRS records the following information for Group A.

Incident Report

Administrative Segment
Originated agency identifier number
Incident number
Cargo theft
Incident date/report date indicator/hour
Cleared exceptionally
Exceptional clearance date
Exceptional clearance offense code

Offense Segment
UCR Offense Code
Offense attempted/completed
Offender suspected of using
Bias motivation
Location type
Number of premises entered
Method of entry
Type criminal activity/gang information
Type weapon/force involved
Automatic weapon indicator

Property Segment
Type property loss/etc.
Property description
Value of property
Date recovered
Number of stolen motor vehicles
Number of recovered motor vehicles
Suspected drug type
Estimated drug quantity
Type drug measurement

Victim Segment
Victim sequence number
Victim connected to UCR offense code
Type of victim
Type of officer activity/circumstance
Officer assignment type
Officer-ORI other jurisdiction
Age, sex, race, and ethnicity of victim
Resident status of victim
Aggravated assault/homicide circumstances
Additional justifiable homicide circumstances
Type injury
Offender number to be related
Relationship of victim to offender

Offender Segment
Offender sequence number
Age, sex, race, and ethnicity of offender

Arrestee Segment
Arrestee sequence number
Arrestee transition number
Arrest date
Type of arrest
Multiple arrestee segments indicator
UCR arrest offense code
Arrestee was armed with automatic weapon
Indicator
Age, sex, race, and ethnicity of arrestee
Resident status of arrestee
Disposition of arrestee under 18
Clearance indicator
Clearance offense code

Group B Arrest Report

ORI
Arrestee sequence number
Arrestee transition number
Arrest date
Type of arrest
Multiple arrestee segments indicator
UCR arrest offense code
Arrestee was armed with automatic weapon indicator
Age, sex, race, and ethnicity of arrestee
Resident status of arrestee
Disposition of arrestee under 18

Federal Bureau of Investigation, *National Incident-Based Reporting System* (Washington, DC: U.S. Department of Justice, 2015).

Reporting Act. This legislation mandated that all federal law enforcement agencies submit crime data to the *UCR* Program. In 1990, to facilitate the collection of data on a wider range of crimes, Congress passed the *Hate Crime Statistics Act.* In its annual *Hate Crime Statistics* report, the FBI now publishes data on the number of crimes motivated by religious, ethnic, racial, or sexual-orientation prejudice.

In 1990, in response to increasing crime on college and university campuses across the nation, Congress passed the *Crime Awareness and Campus Security Act.* This law requires colleges to tally and report campus crime data to the *UCR* Program. It was passed after Jeanne Clery, a 19-year-old freshman at Lehigh University (Pennsylvania), was raped and murdered while asleep in her residence hall on April 5, 1986. When Jeanne's parents, Connie and Howard, investigated the crime, they discovered that Lehigh University had not told students about 38 violent crimes on the Lehigh campus in the 3 years before Jeanne's murder. The Clerys joined with other campus crime victims and persuaded Congress to pass this law.[9] Today, every college in its annual campus security report publishes crime data that are available to all students, parents, and the public.

An important change to the *UCR* Program was implemented in 2004, when it was decided that the Crime Index would be discontinued. However, the FBI will continue to publish in the *UCR* a serious *violent* crime total and a serious *property* crime total until a more viable index is developed. The serious violent crime total includes the offenses of murder and non-negligent manslaughter, forcible rape, robbery, and aggravated assault; the crimes included in the serious property crime total are burglary, larceny-theft, motor vehicle theft, and arson (see **Box 2.3**, the "A Window on Delinquency" feature).

Although the Crime Index was first published in 1960, it has never been a true indicator of the degree of criminality in the larger society. The Crime Index was simply the title used for an aggregation of offense classifications, known as Part I crimes, for which data have been collected since the *UCR* Program's implementation. The Crime Index was driven upward by the offense with the highest number of occurrences—specifically, larceny-thefts. This methodology created a bias against jurisdictions with high numbers of larceny-thefts, but low numbers of other serious crimes, such as murder and forcible rape.

Currently, larceny-theft accounts for nearly 60% of all reported crime in the United States; thus the sheer volume of those offenses overshadows more serious, but less frequently committed offenses.

The most recent, substantive, and long overdue change in the *UCR* occurred in 2012 when the crime of forcible rape was refined to capture a truer sense of victims of sexual assault. Based on the recommendation from an FBI advisory panel, Attorney General Eric Holder announced that any kind of nonconsensual penetration regardless of the gender of the attacker or victim would constitute rape (the redundant and somewhat insensitive adjective "forcible" has been dropped). Today, the crime of rape is defined as "penetration, no matter how slight, of the vagina or anus with any body part or object, or oral penetration by a sex organ of another person, without the consent of the victim." The improved definition encompasses the full extent of types of sexual assault as well as consideration of all victims of the crime, not just female victims of male rapists.

In response to the *William Wilberforce Trafficking Victims Protection Reauthorization Act of 2008*, the FBI began collecting data in 2013 on human trafficking, which is now considered a Part I offense. In 2016, the FBI will begin tracking animal cruelty cases and dividing this form of crime into four categories: animal neglect, animal torture, organized abuse (e.g., illegal dogfighting rings), and animal sexual abuse. Previously, various forms of animal abuse were collected but lumped together in a residual "other" category.

Finally, the *UCR* went digital in 2013 when the FBI no longer accepted hard copy submissions to its program. The *UCR Redevelopment Project* is currently aimed toward improving the overall speed, accuracy, and public accessibility of *UCR* data.

Criticisms of *UCR* Data

Criminologists disagree on whether the *UCR* is a valid measure of crime. Walter Gove and his associates suggest that the *UCR* is "a valid indicator of crime as defined by the citizenry."[10] Other criminologists believe that because the *UCR* reports only "crime known to the police," it grossly underestimates the number of delinquent acts committed (incidence) and the number of juveniles who engage in delinquency (prevalence). A report published by the U.S. Department of Justice, for instance, found that only 42% of all crime was reported to the police. Victims did not report crime for a variety of reasons, including that they considered the crime to be a private or personal matter, that it was not important enough, or that they feared reprisal.[11]

More recently, criminologists examined the statistical accuracy of the *UCR* using data from 12 large municipal police departments. There was evidence of undercounting of more serious index and violent crimes, and there was evidence of overcounting of less serious forms of delinquency. However, the overall

KEY TERMS

incidence
The number of delinquent acts committed.

prevalence
The number of juveniles committing delinquent acts.

BOX 2.3

A Window on Delinquency

Uniform Crime Reports Offenses

The *UCR* is divided into 10 "serious" violent and property crimes and 21 "other" offenses. Law enforcement agencies report data on the number of serious violent and property offenses known to them and the number of people arrested monthly to the FBI.

Serious Violent and Property Offenses

1. *Murder and nonnegligent manslaughter*: The willful killing of one human being by another.
2. *Rape:* Penetration, no matter how slight, of the vagina or anus with any body part or object, or oral penetration by a sex organ of another person, without the consent of the victim.
3. *Robbery*: The taking or attempting to take anything of value from the care, custody, or control of a person or persons by force or threat of force or violence and/or by putting the victim in fear.
4. *Aggravated assault*: The unlawful attack by one person upon another for the purpose of inflicting severe or aggravated bodily injury.
5. *Burglary*: The unlawful entry of a structure to commit a felony or theft.
6. *Larceny-theft*: The unlawful taking, carrying, leading, or riding away of property from the possession or constructive possession of others. Examples include thefts of bicycles or automobile accessories, shoplifting, and pocket-picking.
7. *Motor vehicle theft*: The theft or attempted theft of a motor vehicle.
8. *Arson*: Any willful or malicious burning or attempt to burn, with or without intent to defraud, a dwelling house, public building, motor vehicle or aircraft, or the personal property of another.

9. *Human trafficking/commercial sex acts*: Inducing a person by force, fraud, or coercion to participate in commercial sex acts, or in which the person induced to perform such act(s) has not attained 18 years of age.
10. *Human trafficking/involuntary servitude*: The obtaining of a person(s) through recruitment, harboring, transportation, or provision, and subjecting such persons by force, fraud, or coercion into involuntary servitude, peonage, debt bondage, or slavery (not to include commercial sex acts).

Other Offenses

1. Other assaults
2. Forgery and counterfeiting
3. Fraud
4. Embezzlement
5. Stolen property—buying, receiving, possessing
6. Vandalism
7. Weapons—carrying, possessing
8. Prostitution and commercialized vice
9. Sex offenses (except rape and prostitution)
10. Drug abuse violations
11. Gambling
12. Offenses against the family and children
13. Driving under the influence
14. Breaking liquor laws
15. Drunkenness
16. Disorderly conduct
17. Vagrancy
18. All other offenses (except traffic)
19. Suspicion
20. Curfew and loitering violations
21. Runaways

error rate in the *UCR* data was less than 1%, which suggests these data are representative measures of the crime problem. Errors in official estimates of crime are important because people with arrests are less likely to otherwise divulge criminal activity or consent to record searches. Walter Forrest and his colleagues found that individuals who were dishonest, delinquent, impulsive, negatively reactive, less attentive, and less trusting were less likely to consent to record searches or honestly reveal their delinquent history.[12]

Because most crime is not reported, there exists an extremely large **dark figure of crime**, which is the gap

KEY TERMS

dark figure of crime
The gap between the actual amount of crime committed and the amount of crime reported to the police.

between the actual amount of crime committed and the amount of crime reported to the police. One early criminologist who had observed the so-called dark figure was the 19th-century scholar Adolphe Quetelet, who wrote, "All we possess of statistics of crime and misdemeanors would have no utility at all if we did not tacitly assume that there is a nearly invariable relationship between offenses known and adjudicated and the total unknown sum of offenses committed.[13] A century later, Edwin Sutherland suggested that the *UCR* was invalid because it did not include data on "white-collar criminals."[14] In his work on female criminality, Otto Pollack reported that females were underrepresented in the *UCR* because police treated them more leniently.[15] From certain perspectives, it is fair to draw the conclusion that the *UCR* might have more to say about police behavior as it responds to criminality than it does about criminality itself.

Another major limitation of the *UCR* is its reliance on the **hierarchy rule** whereby in a multiple-offense situation police record only the most serious crime in the incident. If someone robs a person at gunpoint, rapes the victim, and then steals the victim's car, only the rape is reported in the *UCR* totals; the less serious offenses of robbery and motor vehicle theft are not counted. The hierarchy rule does have an exception: It does not apply to arson, which is reported in all situations.

Its limitations aside, the *UCR* statistics are widely used. The *UCR* Program is one of only two sources of data that provide a *national* estimate of the nature and extent of delinquency in the United States. Criminologists who use *UCR* data assume that the inaccuracies are consistent over time and, therefore, that the data accurately depict delinquency trends. In other words, although *UCR* data might be flawed, they may be stable enough to show year-to-year changes.

In fact, recent research supports the validity of the *UCR* and of official crime data generally. Ramona Rantala, a statistician with the Bureau of Justice Statistics, and Thomas Edwards, an FBI systems analyst, recently compared the *UCR* and *NIBRS* systems to determine if they produced similar estimates of crime. They concluded that they do. Rantala and Edwards found that when comparing data from the same year, *NIBRS* rates differed only slightly from summary *UCR* rates. Murder rates were the same. Rape, robbery, and aggravated assault rates were approximately 1% higher in the *NIBRS* than in the *UCR*. The *NIBRS* burglary rate was a mere 0.5% lower than the *UCR* rate. Differences in crime rates amounted to slightly more than 3% for theft and just 4% motor vehicle theft. The convergence of *NIBRS* and *UCR* data suggests that both programs produce reasonable estimates of crime in the United States.[16]

Victimization Surveys

Research focusing on crime victims was developed in the late 1960s in response to the weaknesses of the *UCR*, particularly in regard to the "dark figure of crime." One popular measure of crime from victims' perspective is the **victimization survey**. Instead of asking police about delinquency, victimization surveys ask people about their experiences as crime victims.

National crime surveys have several advantages over the *UCR*. Specifically, they are a more direct measure of criminal behavior. In addition, victim surveys provide more detailed information about situational factors surrounding a crime—for example, the physical location of the crime event, the time of day when the crime occurred, the weapon (if any) used, and the relationship (if any) between the victim and the offender.

National Opinion Research Center Survey

In 1967, the **National Opinion Research Center (NORC)** completed the first nationwide victimization survey in the United States. Interviews were conducted with 10,000 households, which included approximately 33,000 people. In each household, a knowledgeable person was asked a few short "screening" questions—for example, "Were you or was anyone in the household in a fist fight or attacked in any way by another person—including another household member—within the past 12 months?" If the respondent answered "yes" to the question, the victim was interviewed. What director Philip Ennis found was that the victimization rate for Crime Index offenses as reported through the NORC survey was more than double the rate reported in the *UCR*.[17] This finding triggered both surprise and alarm, and interest in victimization surveys soared, prompting the development of a much larger effort, the National Crime Victimization Survey (NCVS), a few years later.

National Crime Victimization Survey

In 1972, the U.S. Bureau of Justice Statistics launched the *National Crime Survey*. In 1990, this effort was renamed the **National Crime Victimization Survey (NCVS)**, to emphasize more clearly the measurement of victimizations experienced by U.S. citizens. The NCVS was redesigned in 1992, making it problematic to compare results from surveys conducted in 1992 and later with those conducted from 1972 to 1991.[18]

The NCVS is the most comprehensive and systematic survey of victims in the United States, producing data on both *personal* and *household* crimes. The personal crimes are divided into two categories: crimes of

KEY TERMS

hierarchy rule
The guideline for reporting data in the *Uniform Crime Reports*, in which police record only the most serious crime incident.

victimization survey
A method of producing crime data in which people are asked about their experiences as crime victims.

National Opinion Research Center (NORC)
The organization that conducted the first nationwide victimization survey in the United States.

National Crime Victimization Survey (NCVS)
An annual nationwide survey of criminal victimization conducted by the U.S. Bureau of Justice Statistics.

violence (rape/sexual assault, robbery, and aggravated assault, and simple assault) and personal theft. Murder is *not* measured by the NCVS because the victim cannot be interviewed. Household crimes targeted by the survey include burglary, household larceny, and motor vehicle theft. These eight offenses, which are known as the **crimes of interest**, were selected because victims are likely to report them to police and victims are typically able to recall the incidents when Census Bureau interviewers question them.

NCVS data are obtained from interviews with nearly 169,000 people who represent more than 90,000 households. Households remain in the sample for 3.5 years and new households rotate into the sample on an ongoing basis. Only people age 12 and older are interviewed. Each interviewee is asked a few screening questions to determine whether he or she was a victim of one or more of the crimes of interest (see **Box 2.4**, the "A Window on Delinquency" feature). Respondents who answer "yes" to any of the screening questions are asked additional questions that further probe the nature of the crime incident. On the basis of the responses received, the interviewer classifies the crime incident as falling into one of the crimes of interest categories. In the most recent wave of data collection for the NCVS, the response rate was over 84% of households and 87% of eligible individuals.[19]

Households are selected for inclusion using a rotated panel design. Every household—whether urban or rural, whether living in a detached single-family house or an efficiency apartment, whether consisting of a family or unrelated people—has the same chance of being selected. Once chosen for inclusion, the household remains in the survey for 3 years. If

Often seen as the forgotten part of the criminal justice system, victims of crime provide another important way to measure delinquency.

© Design Pics/age fotostock.

KEY TERMS

crimes of interest
The crimes that are the focus of the National Crime Victimization Survey.

BOX 2.4
A Window on Delinquency
The National Crime Victimization Survey

The NCVS asks juveniles directly about crimes committed against them during a specific time period. The questions children are asked are similar to those presented here:

1. Did you have your (pocket picked/purse snatched)?
2. Did anyone try to rob you by using force or threatening to harm you?
3. Did anyone beat you up, attack you, or hit you with something, such as a rock or bottle?
4. Were you knifed, shot at, or attacked with some other weapon by anyone at all?
5. Did anyone steal things that belonged to you from inside any car or truck, such as packages or clothing?
6. Was anything stolen from you while you were away from home—for instance, at work, in a theatre or restaurant, or while traveling?
7. Did you call the police during the last six months to report something that happened to you that you thought was a crime? If yes, how many times?

Jennifer Truman and Lynn Langton, *Criminal Victimization in the United States, 2014* (Washington, DC: U.S. Department of Justice, 2015).

members of the household move during this period, that address remains part of the survey and the new occupants enter the sample. No attempt is made to follow past occupants who move to new addresses. After 3 years, a participating household is replaced with a new one, so new households are always entering the sample.

NCVS data are a very useful source of information, particularly in terms of increasing our understanding of the dark figure of crime. For instance, NCVS data:

- Confirm that a considerable amount of delinquency is unknown to police.
- Uncover some reasons why victims do not report crime incidents to police.
- Demonstrate that the amount of variation in the official reporting of delinquency changes across type of offenses, victim–offender relationships, situational factors, and characteristics.
- Focus theoretical attention to delinquency often being the result of social interaction between a victim and an offender.

Like any measuring tool, the NCVS has some flaws. Obviously, the small number of crimes of interest is problematic, particularly since the most severe criminal offense—murder—cannot be measured. Although it is important to collect data on the crimes of interest, those offenses represent only a small fraction of all crimes committed in the United States. Most arrests are for crimes involving alcohol and illegal drugs, and many robberies, burglaries, and larcenies are committed against businesses, rather than against individuals. Because it excludes these and other crimes, the NCVS provides data on just a small subset of all crime incidents in this country.

As mentioned previously, the NCVS is based on answers people give to questions regarding past and sometimes troublesome events. At least five known problems might affect the reliability of data for that reason:

1. *Memory errors.* People forget, and some will have difficulty recalling when or how many times an event occurred.
2. *Telescoping.* Interviewees might "remember" a crime of interest as occurring more recently than it did because the event remains vivid in their memories.
3. *Errors of deception.* It may be difficult for victims to report events that are embarrassing or otherwise unpleasant to talk about or events that might incriminate them. In addition, some people might potentially fabricate crime incidents.
4. *Juvenile victimizations.* Adolescents might be less likely to discuss their victimizations with an adult stranger, particularly if their victimizations involve peers or family members.
5. *Sampling error.* When samples are used to represent populations, there always is the possibility of a discrepancy between sample estimates of behavior and the actual amount of behavior. For instance, because the sampling unit in the NCVS is the household, homeless children—who are at greater risk of victimization—are excluded from the sample.

The NCVS is an essential tool for quantifying the delinquency and violence problem in the United States. Although it continues to be the primary victimization measure of crime, other victimization surveys have also been developed. One of the most comprehensive and important is the Developmental Victimization Survey that is explored next.

Developmental Victimization Survey

The **Developmental Victimization Survey (DVS)** is a telephone interview survey of a nationally representative sample of 2030 children ages 2 to 17 years. The interviews are conducted with the primary caregiver (usually a parent) of the children below age 10. Children older than age 10 participate in the interview. The sample is equally split in terms of sex and age range of the children (51% were age 2 to 9 and 49% were age 10 to 17). About 34% of the sample had household incomes between $20,000 and $50,000

and 10% of the sample reported household incomes below $10,000. In terms of race and ethnicity, the sample is 76% white, 11% African American, 9% Hispanic, and 4% from other races including Asian Americans and American Indians.

The DVS measures 34 forms of victimization that occurred in the prior year. The victimizations are grouped into five areas. *Conventional crimes* include robbery, personal theft, vandalism, assault with weapon, assault without weapon, attempted assault, kidnapping, and bias attack. *Child maltreatment* includes physical abuse by caregiver, emotional abuse, neglect, and custodial interference or family abduction. *Peer and sibling victimization* includes gang or group assault, peer or sibling assault, nonsexual genital assault, bullying, emotional bullying, and dating violence. *Sexual victimization* includes sexual assault by a known adult, nonspecific sexual assault, sexual assault by a peer, rape, flashing or sexual exposure, verbal sexual harassment, and statutory rape. *Witnessing and indirect victimization* includes a host of indirect and vicarious exposures. These are witnessing domestic violence, witnessing parent assault of a sibling, witness to assault with a weapon (and without), burglary of family household, murder of a family member or friend, witness to murder, exposure to random shooting, and exposure to war or ethnic conflict.

The DVS indicates that 71% of children had experienced some form of victimization in the prior year. Certain forms of victimization especially relating to assault and bullying are exceedingly common with about half of children in various age ranges incurring these forms. Overall, the DVS provides an important lesson about the need for multiple measures of delinquency. According to David Finkelhor and his colleagues, "The findings from this survey of youth and parents do not support the impression that might be drawn from police statistics: a greatly accelerating rate of victimization in the teenage years. The aggregated burden of victimizations is high across the full span of childhood."[20]

National Survey of Children's Exposure to Violence (NatSCEV I and NatSCEV II)

The success of the DVS motivated the Office of Juvenile Justice and Delinquency Prevention and the Centers for Disease Control and Prevention to

KEY TERMS

Developmental Victimization Survey (DVS)
A telephone interview survey of a nationally representative sample of 2030 children ages 2 to 17 years that examines 34 types of victimization.

create a greater initiative to measure the incidence and prevalence of children's exposure to violence across multiple ages, settings, and timeframes. Spearheaded by the researchers who led the DVS, the **National Survey of Children's Exposure to Violence I (NatSCEV I)** was launched in 2008 and its successor, **NatSCEV II**, in 2011. The NatSCEV II is a nationally representative telephone survey of 4503 children and youth ages 1 month to 17 years (or their caregivers for children younger than age 10 years). The average cooperation rate was 60%, and the average response rate was 40%. The NatSCEV II contained items on 54 forms of offenses against youth that included conventional crime, child maltreatment and neglect, peer and sibling victimization, Internet and cell phone victimization, assault and bullying, sexual victimization, property victimization, and witnessed and indirect victimization.

The NatSCEV II has produced many important findings to better understand the extent and magnitude of diverse forms of child maltreatment among the nation's youth. Among the key findings:

- In the past year, 41% have experienced a physical assault, and 55% have experienced a physical assault over their lifetime.
- Nearly 6% have experienced any sexual victimization in the past year, and 10% have over their lifetime.
- Nearly 14% have experienced any child maltreatment in the past year, and 26% have over their lifetime.
- In the past year, 24% have experienced any property victimization, and 40% have over their lifetime.
- In the past year, 22% have witnessed violence, and 39% have over their lifetime.
- In the past year, 3% have experienced indirect exposure to violence, and 10% have over their lifetime.

While trend data show important declines across the board, the NatSCEV II nevertheless demonstrates the common reality of abuse and violence in the lives of American children.[21]

Do Official Crime Data and Victimization Data Match?

To what degree do official and victimization data paint the same picture about the extent of crime in the United States? This question is important. If official and victimization reports conflict widely, then we would have little confidence in our understanding of the true magnitude of crime. If official and victimization data converge, then we are likely measuring the crime problem with confidence, validity, and reliability.

Fortunately, official and victimization data generally match. For example, Janet Lauritsen and Robin Schaum compared *UCR* and NCVS data for robbery, burglary, and aggravated assault in Chicago, Los Angeles, and New York over a two-decade span. Given that these three locales are the three largest cities in the country, this sampling method represents the bulk of crime that is committed in the United States. Lauritsen and Schaum found that for burglary and robbery, *UCR* crime rates were generally similar to NCVS estimates over the study period. Police and victim survey data were more likely to show discrepancies in levels of and trends related to aggravated assault. Lauritsen and Schaum also found that even when *UCR* and NCVS data were different, the differences were not statistically significant. Substantively, the *UCR* and NCVS tell the same story about the extent of these three serious crimes in the nation's three biggest metropolitan areas. Indeed, for decades, criminologists have found that official and victimization data generally tell a like story about the incidence of crime and delinquency in the United States.[22]

Official ways to measure delinquency, such as the *UCR*, *NIBRS*, and victimization surveys (e.g., the NCVS), paint a very broad picture of the amount of delinquency occurring in the United States. But there is another way to evaluate whether official and victimization measures of delinquency overlap: We can evaluate at the individual level whether there is convergence of data. In other words, are the adolescents who are at the greatest risk for committing delinquency also at the greatest risk for being victims of delinquent acts? Similarly, are youths who have many protective factors and who are not involved in delinquency less likely to be victimized as well? The answer to both of these questions is "yes." The youths who are most involved in committing delinquency also are, generally speaking, the youths most likely to be victimized. Put simply, being antisocial increases the odds of all forms of antisocial interactions. The same logic applies to youths who are prosocial and engaged in conventional activities, such as going to school, playing sports, working, and associating with their friends. Researchers have found that both prosocial and antisocial behaviors seem to cluster in the same youths. Whereas most youths lead lives that are relatively free from delinquent offending and victimization, others have multiple problems and are troubled on both fronts.

For decades, criminologists have noted the overlap between being a perpetrator and being a victim of delinquency. Albert Cohen and James Short, Jr. have observed that:

> Any act—delinquent or otherwise—depends on "something about the actor," that is, something about his values, his goals, his interests, his temperament, or, speaking inclusively, his personality, and it depends also on "something about the situation" in which he finds himself. Change either actor or situation and you get a different act for delinquent acts always depend on appropriate combinations of actor and situation.[23]

Delinquency and victimization coincide for two reasons. First, the most serious delinquents (discussed later in this chapter) are so immersed in antisocial behaviors that they have increased opportunities to both offend and to be targeted by offenders. This link segues into the second reason for overlap between offending and victimization, which pertains to lifestyle factors. Adolescents who commit delinquency are more likely to associate with peers who commit delinquency, more likely to abuse alcohol and other drugs, more likely to have their "misbehavior" interfere with school success, and overall more likely to engage in diverse forms of crime.[24] Juvenile delinquents and victims of delinquency are basically drawn from the same population pool. Using data from the NYSFS (described later in this chapter), several criminologists found that delinquency was the strongest predictor of being the victim of assault, robbery, larceny, and vandalism. The effect of a youth's involvement in a delinquent lifestyle even accounted for significant effects of other important correlates of delinquency, such as gender. Indeed, in a systematic review of the delinquent-victimization overlap, Mark Berg observed, "Individuals who perpetrate violence and those who suffer from it share a similar demographic and social profile. In fact, victims and offenders are not always drawn from distinct groups; they are one in the same."[25]

The overlap between delinquency and victimization (and by extension, the overlap between official and victimization measures of delinquency) is not limited to an American context. Robert Svennson and Lieven Pauwels compared the risky lifestyles of nearly 3500 adolescents selected from Antwerp, Belgium, and Halmstad, Sweden. They found that both delinquent propensity and involvement in a risky lifestyle characterized by substance use, having many delinquent peers, and socializing late at night predicted delinquent interactions. Youths with the greatest delinquent propensity were particularly likely to get into trouble when they engaged in a risky lifestyle.[26]

Wesley Jennings and his colleagues recently examined 50 years of research on the offending-victimization overlap to examine to what degree they converge. Of the 37 studies reviewed, 31 studies showed dramatically supportive evidence that offenders and victims were essentially the same individuals. The remaining six studies also showed support, although the findings were more modest. In other words, none of the studies in their review found evidence that offending and victimization do not match. The two most frequent explanations for why offenders and victims overlap relate to antisocial traits, such as those implicated in self-control theory and risky, deviant situations that are associated with an antisocial lifestyle.[27]

The same overlap is also found with repeat offending and repeat victimization. Based on data from a longitudinal study of young people in Brisbane, Australia, Abigail Fagan and Paul Mazerolle found that adolescents who were repeat victims of delinquency also engaged in repeated, serious forms of delinquency. In fact, more than half of all youths who had been victimized during two separate periods of data collection also were serious delinquents at both phases.[28] To reiterate a point made earlier, the importance of the behavioral overlap between offending and victimization is that it reinforces the notion that official and victimization data are measuring the same phenomenon.

Self Report Studies

A third source of information on the nature and extent of delinquency comes from **self-report studies**, which ask juveniles directly about their law-violating behavior (see **Box 2.5**, the "A Window on Delinquency" feature). The advantage of self-report studies is that the information criminologists receive from juveniles regarding their involvement in crime has not been filtered through the police or through any other criminal or juvenile justice officials; rather, it consists of raw data.

This strength, however, is also the principal weakness of self-reports. The reports of crimes that adolescents say they have committed may not be accurate for some of the same reasons that victimization surveys are flawed: memory errors, telescoping, and lying.

Historical Background

In 1946, Austin Porterfield published the first self-report study of delinquent behavior. He compared the self-reported delinquency of 337 college students with that of 2049 youths who had appeared before the juvenile court. Porterfield found that more than

KEY TERMS

self-report study
A study that yields an unofficial measure of crime, and in which juveniles are asked about their law-breaking behavior.

BOX 2.5

A Window on Delinquency

Self-Report Delinquency Survey

A self-report survey asks juveniles directly about their participation in delinquent and criminal behavior during a specific time period. In the following example, respondents are asked to indicate how many times in the past 12 months they have committed each offense in the list by checking the best answer.

Offense	Never	1	2–5	6–9	10 or more
1. Petty theft	_____	_____	_____	_____	_____
2. Forgery	_____	_____	_____	_____	_____
3. Used cocaine	_____	_____	_____	_____	_____
4. Used marijuana	_____	_____	_____	_____	_____
5. Gambling	_____	_____	_____	_____	_____
6. Weapon violation	_____	_____	_____	_____	_____
7. Burglary	_____	_____	_____	_____	_____
8. Fighting	_____	_____	_____	_____	_____
9. Used fake ID	_____	_____	_____	_____	_____
10. Vandalism	_____	_____	_____	_____	_____
11. Truancy	_____	_____	_____	_____	_____
12. Runaway	_____	_____	_____	_____	_____
13. Curfew	_____	_____	_____	_____	_____
14. Liquor violation	_____	_____	_____	_____	_____
15. Drunk driving	_____	_____	_____	_____	_____

90% of the college students surveyed admitted to at least one felony.[29] The next year James Wallerstein and J. C. Wyle conducted a survey of self-reported delinquent behavior using a sample of 1698 adult men and women, focusing on behavior the survey respondents had committed when they were juveniles. They discovered that 99% of the sample admitted to committing at least one offense they could have been arrested for had they been caught.[30] In 1954, James Short, Jr. reported findings from the first self-report study to include institutionalized juvenile delinquents.[31] In 1958, Short and F. Ivan Nye published a study of (1) juveniles in three Washington communities, (2) students in three Midwestern towns, and (3) a sample of delinquents in training schools. They found that delinquency was widespread across these social groups.[32]

KEY TERMS

National Youth Survey Family Study (NYSFS)

A nationwide self-report survey of approximately 1700 people who were between the ages of 11 and 17 in 1976.

These findings inspired more systematic research. In 1963, Maynard Erickson and LaMar Empey interviewed boys between the ages of 15 to 17 and included four subsamples: (1) 50 boys who had not appeared in court, (2) 30 boys who had one court appearance, (3) 50 boys who were on probation, and (4) 50 boys who were incarcerated. They found that there was a tremendous amount of hidden or undetected delinquency, and those who had been officially labeled "delinquent" admitted to committing many more offenses than those who had not been so labeled.[33] Some years later, Jay Williams and Martin Gold conducted the first nationwide self-report study of delinquency in 1967. Using interviews and official records of 847 13- to 16-year-old boys and girls, they discovered that 88% of the teenagers admitted to committing at least one chargeable offense in the prior 3 years.[34]

The most comprehensive and systematic self-report study conducted in the United States is the **National Youth Survey Family Study (NYSFS)**, which was begun in 1976 by Delbert Elliott. The NYSFS is a nationwide survey of more than 1700 youths who were between the ages of 11 and 17 at the time of their first interview. Coming from more than 100 cities and towns, the respondents represented every socioeconomic, racial, and ethnic group. For nearly 40 years, this original group of respondents (now approaching middle adulthood) has reported to Elliott how often during the past 12 months (from one Christmas to the next) they have committed certain criminal acts, ranging from felony assaults to minor thefts.[35] The survey was known as the National Youth Survey for three decades but is now called the National Youth Survey Family Study (NYSFS) and includes DNA data to examine the biosocial underpinnings of delinquency. The name change is also important because the NYSFS data allow researchers to study the intergenerational transmission of behaviors and explore the degree to which environmental and biological factors contribute to them.

Strengths and Weaknesses of Self-Report Studies

Criminologists have learned much about delinquency from self-report surveys. It is now widely accepted that more than 90% of juveniles have committed an act that, if they had been caught, arrested, charged, prosecuted, convicted, and sentenced to the full extent of the law, could have had them incarcerated. Self-report studies have also made criminologists more aware of how large the dark figure of crime might be: The amount of delinquency hidden from the criminal justice officials is between 4 and 10 times greater than the amount reported in the *UCR*. Finally, and perhaps most importantly, self-report research has produced consistent evidence that is suggestive of a racial and ethnic bias in the processing of juveniles who enter the juvenile justice system.[36]

The criticisms of the self-report method are similar to the ones leveled at survey methodology generally. One complaint focuses on how the data are collected. Another concern is whether it is reasonable to expect that juveniles would admit their illegal acts to strangers. Why should they? Other problems pointed out by critics of the self-report method include the same concerns that are raised regarding victimization surveys. When juveniles are asked about their involvement in delinquency, they may forget, misunderstand, distort, or lie about what happened. Some teenagers may exaggerate their crimes, whereas others may minimize theirs.

These concerns have caused criminologists to design methods to validate the findings from self-report studies. One approach is to compare each youth's responses with official police records. Studies using this technique have found a high correlation between reported delinquency and official delinquency. Other techniques criminologists have used to validate self-reports include having friends verify the honesty of the juvenile's answers, testing subjects more than once to see if their answers remain the same, and asking subjects to submit to a polygraph test.[37]

Findings from studies implementing one or more of these validity checks have provided general support for the self-report method as a means to accurately characterize juvenile delinquency. In a comprehensive review of the reliability and validity of self-reports, Michael Hindelang and his colleagues concluded:

> The difficulties in self-report instruments currently in use would appear to be surmountable; the method of self-reports does not appear from these studies to be fundamentally flawed. Reliability measures are impressive and the majority of studies produce validity coefficients in the moderate to strong range.[38]

Despite the strong support for the self-report method, it has one glaring weakness—namely, the worst delinquents rarely participate in these surveys. For instance, Stephen Cernkovich and his colleagues suggest that self-report studies might exclude the most serious chronic offenders and, therefore, provide a gauge of delinquency among only the less serious, occasional offenders. They reached this conclusion after comparing the self-reported behavior of incarcerated and nonincarcerated youths. The researchers detected significant differences in the offending patterns of the two groups, leading them to make the following statement: "Institutionalized youth are not only more delinquent than the 'average youth' in the general population, but also considerably more delinquent than the most delinquent youth identified in the typical self-report."[39]

The potential omission of the most serious and chronic delinquents is a critical issue for two reasons. First, surveys that lack the most active delinquent offenders, by definition, do not produce valid estimates of delinquency. Second, the failure to include the worst delinquents results in a mischaracterization of delinquency trends because the behavior of chronic delinquents is significantly different from that of "normal" delinquents. The importance of chronic delinquents is discussed later in this chapter.

Despite its shortcomings, the self-report method provides "expert" perspective because no one is more familiar with the ways that delinquency occurs than delinquents themselves. Scott Decker has examined how tapping into the antisocial expertise of criminal offenders can yield payoffs as to how the criminal justice system combats crime. Decker's research has produced a wealth of information about crimes, motives, and techniques among active criminals. For example, serious delinquents are versatile in that they commit lots of different types of offenses. Drug offenders, in particular, are likely to commit violent, property, and drug crimes. Serious offenders also commit delinquency in "peak and valley" patterns and are often unpredictable. Partying, status maintenance, group dynamics, self-protection, and retaliation are the primary motives for committing crimes; according to Decker, few delinquents commit

crimes to meet rational economic needs, such as the need to pay the rent or buy groceries.

A delinquent's lifestyle plays an important role in offending. The rate of victimization is extremely high among offenders, and incidents of victimization often motivate further offending. In a certain sense, crimes can be understood as a series of advances and retaliations between criminals and victims. Although delinquents respond to specific criminal justice policies such as concentrated police stings, they are largely unfazed by the deterrent effects of the criminal justice system.[40] In sum, the self-report method provides a complementary perspective to official and victim accounts of crime to arrive at the most valid and reliable way to measure delinquency.

Delinquency Correlates

Approximately 325 million people live in the United States and 23% are **juveniles**, or persons younger than age 18.[41] Also in the United States, a violent crime is committed every 21 seconds, a rape every 2 minutes, and a murder roughly every 31 minutes. Who is primarily responsible for this crime? Are the offenders more likely to be adults or juveniles? Are offenders more often males or females? Wealthy or poor? African American, white, Asian, or Hispanic? When the offender is a child, adults ask a lot of questions. Are more children committing crime today than years ago? Is the criminal behavior of girls becoming more like that of boys? Do African Americans commit

By talking directly to delinquents and criminals, researchers are able to more accurately measure delinquency, in addition to learning about the criminal lifestyle directly from the source.

© Thinkstock/Stockbyte/Getty.

KEY TERMS

juvenile
A person younger than age 18.

status offenses
Behaviors that are unlawful only for children—for example, truancy, curfew violations, and running away.

more crimes than whites? Are age and delinquency related? How does social class influence involvement in delinquency? These and other important questions are answered in this section.

In the most recent *Crime in the United States* report, police made more than 11 million arrests and approximately 9% of *all* persons arrested were juveniles. Among both adults and juveniles who were arrested, most persons were arrested for relatively minor crimes. For instance, juveniles were most commonly arrested for larceny-theft. The most recent data indicate that young people were arrested for 9% of *all* crimes and for 10% and 15% of serious *violent* and *property* offenses, respectively. Juveniles were most likely to be arrested for **status offenses**, or behaviors that are deemed unlawful only for children, such as underage drinking and running away.[42] As is the case with adults, the United States has experienced dramatic declines in delinquency and violence for the past two decades. Nevertheless, youth are still exposed to considerable victimization, and these experiences often present lifelong consequences (see **Box 2.6**, the "A Window on Delinquency" feature). Yet despite the unprecedented downturn in crime and violence, the basic correlates of delinquency have remained stable and are discussed next.

Sex/Gender

Delinquency is primarily a male phenomenon. Boys are arrested more often than girls for *all* crimes, with the exception of prostitution and running away. Nine out of every 10 persons arrested for murder, rape, robbery, carrying and possessing weapons, sex offenses (except prostitution) and gambling are boys. Gender is so strongly related to delinquency that sociologist Anthony Harris concluded:

> That the sex variable in some form has not provided the starting point of all theories of criminal deviance has been the major failure of deviance theorizing in the century. It appears to provide the single most powerful predictor of officially and unofficially known criminal deviance in this society and almost certainly in all others.[43]

That delinquency and antisocial behavior are much more common among boys than girls sometimes gets lost in discussions of crime trends that are associated with the measures of crime discussed in this chapter. For example, there is evidence that the arrest gap between the sexes is closing. On the surface, girls seem to be catching up. Since 1960, the difference in the juvenile sex-arrest ratios for serious violent and property offenses has steadily declined. In 1960, the juvenile sex-arrest ratio for violent offenses was 14 to 1; that is, 14 boys were arrested for each female arrested. By 1970, the ratio had declined to 10 to 1, and by 1980 it had dropped to 9 to 1. By 2000, the

BOX 2.6

A Window on Delinquency

The Long Shadow of Delinquent Victimization

The good news is that delinquency and adolescent victimization have impressively declined since their peak in 1993–1994. However, as the official, victimization, and self-report data in this chapter indicate, children and adolescents continue to be exposed to a litany of abuse and delinquent acts, and many of these experiences wreak havoc on children's development. According to the most recent data from the National Crime Victimization Survey (NCVS), youth ages 12 to 17 years experienced more than 422,000 criminal victimizations and the violent crime victimization rate for youth ages 12 to 17 years (30.1 per 1000 persons) is the highest of any age range in the survey.

Delinquent victimization can result in a variety of emotional and physical problems, including anxiety, depression, emotional distress, anger, hostility, stressful hypervigilance, insomnia, hypertension, disordered eating, and others. About 51% of adolescents who experienced violent victimization reported that they suffered from emotional or physical problems in the wake of the crime. For crimes such as robbery (74%), rape (65%), and aggravated assault (61%), the prevalence of negative health problems is even higher. These victimization experiences spill over into other aspects of the child's life, and also can have negative effects on school attendance, school performance, school functioning, peer relations, and involvement in extracurricular activities.

In addition to direct victimization, children suffer from violence that occurs around them at home and at school. Some of this is lethal violence. Uxoricide, or spousal homicide, often produces the loss of both parents because one parent is murdered and the other is usually imprisoned. As a result, the children must be raised by family, guardians, or become wards of the state. These changes necessitate major life changes in terms of the child's socioeconomic status and residency. The loss of both parents often means attending a new school and having to make new friends—major changes for most children.

Children who survive mass shootings at school experience many negative effects. Some experience extraordinary trauma, such as being shot, directly witnessing the murder of other people who may be family or friends, and seeing dead bodies. These experiences often result in increased psychological distress, Post-Traumatic Stress Disorder (PTSD), depression, and anxiety. Other survivors of lethal violence have difficulty adjusting to life and experience dissociation, avoidance behaviors, and problems with emotional regulation. About 30 to 40% of children who are exposed to life-threatening violence will meet criteria for PTSD, and the severity and prevalence is even higher if the proximity to the violence is closer. Children who are shot can experience a range of medical problems that negatively impact their functioning, their livelihood, and their mental health status. In sum, direct or indirect victimization casts a long shadow on the lives of children and adolescents.

Jennifer Truman and Lynn Langton, *Criminal Victimization, 2014* (Washington, DC: U.S. Department of Justice, 2015); Lynn Langton and Jennifer Truman, *Socio-Emotional Impact of Violent Crime* (Washington, DC: U.S. Department of Justice, 2014); Barbara Parker, Richard Steeves, Sarah Anderson, and Barbara Moran, "Uxoricide: A Phenomenological Study of Adult Survivors," *Issues in Mental Health Nursing* 25:133–145 (2004); James Shultz, Siri Thoresen, Brian Flynn, Glenn Muschert, Jon Shaw, Zelde Espinel, Frank Walter, Joshua Gaither, Yanira Garcia-Barcena, Kaitlin O'Keefe, and Alyssa Cohen, "Multiple Vantage Points on the Mental Health Effects of Mass Shootings," *Current Psychiatry Reports* 16:1–17 (2014); Matt DeLisi, *Homicide* (Dubuque, IA: Kendall/Hunt, 2015); Helen Fisher, Avshalom Caspi, Terrie Moffitt, Jason Wertz, Jasmin Wertz, Rebecca Gray, Joanne Newbury, Antony Ambler, Helena Zavos, Andrea Danese, Jonathan Mill, Candice Odgers, Carmine Pariante, Chloe Wong, and Louise Arseneault, "Measuring Adolescents' Exposure to Victimization: The Environmental Risk (E-Risk) Longitudinal Study," *Development and Psychopathology* 27:1399–1416 (2015).

juvenile sex-arrest ratio for serious violent offenses dropped to 4 to 1, one-third of what it was in 1960. Today it is less than 5 to 1.

Self-report studies confirm the *UCR* arrest data: Boys admit to committing more delinquency, and more boys commit delinquency than do girls. Studies also report a higher sex-arrest ratio for serious rather than less-serious crimes.[44]

Yet, even though there is consistent support for the idea that the behavior of boys and girls is becoming more similar, we must caution against misunderstanding gender differences in delinquency. Even though girls are "catching up" to boys in terms of delinquent involvement, arrest rates for males are *still several hundred percent higher* than for girls. Gender differences are even more pronounced for the most violent crimes. Joycelyn Pollock and Sareta Davis suggest that the

idea that females are becoming increasingly more violent than (or as violent as) males is a myth, and note that statistical increases for girls are relatively small when considering the total perspective of gender differences in crime.[45] There is also recent evidence that girls' involvement in violent delinquency is often dependent on exposure to violent boys and peer networks where girls have a larger proportion of friends who are boys.[46]

A major explanation for the gender differences in delinquency centers on the assumptions about the different ways children are socialized according to gender expectations. It is assumed that boys are allowed to engage in "rough and tumble" play, are encouraged to be active, engaging, and assertive, and are given a pass on misbehavior. On the other hand, it is also assumed that girls are expected to behave in

more refined and controlled ways, and parents are less tolerant of their lack of self-control. In a landmark study, Hugh Lytton and David Romney found that overall, boys and girls are parented very similarly and that evidence of gender socialization is modest at best.[47] Many other advantages that girls have over boys, such as greater self-regulation, greater effortful control, less direct aggression, more empathy, and other factors contribute to their lower involvement in delinquency.

Still another explanation for a narrowing of the gender gap of delinquency relates to how closely the police are monitoring crime among females. If the police are either more stringently monitoring female crime or if women have become more antisocial, then there should be differences between official and self-report measures of female crime.

Jennifer Schwartz and Bryan Rookey evaluated 25 years of crime data, taking a particular interest in drunk-driving behavior among men and women. They found that women of all ages were making arrest gains on men for the crime of drunk driving or driving under the influence (DUI). However, self-reported and supplementary traffic data indicated little to no systematic change in the drunk-driving behavior of women. This finding suggests that a narrowing gender gap for DUI is not reflective of increased female delinquency, but rather illustrative of the social control of drunk driving among women.[48]

A final consideration of the sex/gender and delinquency relationship relates to seriousness of the behavior. Boys and girls might engage in similar amounts of low-level and often trivial forms of misbehavior. When the behavior in question becomes more serious; so too does the sex gap. For example, girls are dramatically less likely than boys to commit predatory forms of delinquency and these differences are seen across the life-course. According to the most recent correctional data provided by the U.S. Department of Justice, in the United States there are 3173 people on death row. These are individuals who have been convicted of the most extreme forms of crime, most commonly multiple homicides or murders committed along with other serious felonies. Indeed, aggravating conditions are required for persons to be sentenced to death. Of the 3173 condemned offenders, 3113 are men and 60 are women. This is a sex ratio of more than 50 to 1![49]

Race

The study of race and delinquency has traditionally reflected larger social concerns. Throughout history, one or more oppressed groups have been assigned the brunt of the responsibility for crime. Today, much of the delinquency problem is blamed on young African American and increasingly, Hispanic, males. A recent study attributes this perception to the news media's

For a variety of reasons, including gender socialization, differential treatment by the juvenile justice system, and biological differences between males and females, girls account for significantly less delinquency than boys. But in recent years, female delinquency rates have been increasing.

© Shane Hansen/Daxus/iStock/Getty.

routine portrayal of young African American males as disproportionate perpetrators of crime. This negative characterization has made many whites fearful of being victimized by African American or Hispanic juveniles even though all racial groups are more likely to be victimized by their own racial group (crime is mostly *intra*racial [same race] instead of *inter*racial [different race]).

These stereotypes are not limited to whites, however. Research conducted by Robert Sampson and Stephen Raudenbush evaluated racial and ethnic differences in opinions about race, disorder, and crime. They found that whites, African Americans, and Hispanic Americans perceived that as the populations of neighborhoods changed to include a larger proportion of African Americans, they were also increasingly characterized by disorder and crime, when controlling for the effects of the respondent's individual characteristics and actual neighborhood conditions. In other words, *all people*—at least among the three largest racial and ethnic groups in the United States—perceive disorder, vice, and crime as being greater threats when they see that the composition of a neighborhood mostly consists of African Americans.[50]

Cultural values that are deeply rooted in years of history contribute to many of our beliefs. From the early colonial period to the mid-20th century in the United States, whites have oppressed African Americans. Along with oppression came the presumption by whites that African Americans are lazy, aggressive, inferior, subordinate, and troublemakers. The transmission of such a racist ideology, which is passed from one generation to the next, has contributed to myriad negative effects on African American children. For instance, the percentage of African American children living in poverty is three times greater than the corresponding percentage of white children. The effects of living in poverty go far beyond malnourishment and the ruinous consequences of poor nutrition; they also mean that many of these children are more likely to endure family stress and depression, have access to fewer resources for learning, and experience severe housing problems.

The unique racial history of the United States persists to the present day in terms of beliefs about the causes of delinquency and violence. Shaun Gabbidon and Danielle Boisvert conducted a public opinion survey about crime causation and uncovered across the board differences between whites and African Americans about the factors that contribute to crime. African Americans were more likely to believe that stressful events, social inequality, and poverty were important causes of crime. Whites were more likely than African Americans to believe that genetic factors, psychological traits, neighborhood factors, social learning and peer effects, negative labeling, and social control best explained crime. In this way, perceptions about delinquency as it relates to race and ethnicity reflects a long history that is informed by official data, victimization data, media images, prejudice, and denial.[51] This leads to another important conclusion about the relationship between race and delinquency: African American youths *are* more delinquent than youths from other racial groups. This effect is strongest for the most serious forms of delinquency, including armed robbery and murder. For example, Brendan O'Flaherty and Rajiv Sethi pointed to staggering data about race differences in homicide offending and victimization:

African Americans are roughly six times as likely as white Americans to die at the hands of a murderer, and roughly seven times as likely to murder someone; their victims are black 82% of the time. Homicide is the second most important reason for the racial gap in life expectancy: eliminating homicide would do more to equalize black and white life expectancy than eliminating any other cause of death except heart disease.[52]

In another study that demonstrated this relationship, James Alan Fox and Morris Zawitz examined race differences in homicide offending and victimization among various age groups from 1976 to 2004. Across three decades of data, African American males between the ages of 14 and 24 accounted for approximately 1% of the U.S. population during that period, but represented between 10 and 18% of the murder victims. In terms of offending, African American males ages 14–24 constituted between 15 and 35% of the homicide offender population! By contrast, white males between ages 14–24 accounted for between 5 and 10% of the population but were overrepresented as both murderers and murder victims, but not nearly to the extent of African Americans.[53]

Unlike official estimates, such as homicide data, self-report data offer a "mixed bag" of findings regarding the relationship between race and delinquency. Some studies have reported that African American juveniles and white juveniles are equally involved in delinquency, but early studies generally focused on trivial forms of misbehavior and did not validate the truthfulness of self-reports with information from other perspectives, such as the youth's mother, father, siblings, teachers, or peers. Self-report studies based on large-scale samples indicate significant race differences in terms of total delinquency and predatory crimes that are most likely to result in arrest.[54] Terence Thornberry and Marvin Krohn discovered that African American males substantially underreport their involvement in delinquency, a finding consistent with the work of Barbara Mensch and Denise Kandel, who detected differences among races in terms of their level of truthfulness when answering survey questionnaires.[55] If these researchers are correct, African Americans are likely to appear *less* delinquent than they actually are.

Findings from the NCVS complement both *UCR* data and self-report survey results. Recent analyses of NCVS data for 1980 through 1998 have compared the rates of offending for African American and white juveniles as reported by crime victims. One study focused on the serious violent crimes of aggravated assault, robbery, and rape—all crimes in which victims have face-to-face contact with offenders. Data from victims indicate that the serious violent offending rate for African American juveniles is higher than the corresponding rate for white juveniles.[56] Over a two-decade span, the offending rate for African American juveniles was, on average, more than four times the offending rate for white juveniles. In comparison, the African American-to-white ratio of arrest rates reported in the *UCR* for these same offenses shows greater disparity than was found in victim surveys. The average arrest rate was almost 6 times higher for African American juveniles than for white juveniles. For both offending rates and arrest rates, though, the ratios of African American-to-white rates have declined slightly in recent years. From 1992 to 1998, the African American-to-white rates were very similar for arrests and offending. On average, African American juveniles had arrest and offending rates that were five times greater than the corresponding rates for white juveniles.

What do these data suggest about race and delinquency? Why are African American juveniles and, to a certain degree, Hispanic juveniles, more involved in crime than whites as both offenders and victims? Three interrelated theoretical explanations have been advanced to explain the disproportionate involvement in delinquency among African Americans specifically, and among racial minorities generally: economic deprivation, family breakdown, and cultural factors.

Economic Deprivation

In a series of landmark books, sociologist William Julius Wilson argued that African Americans—more than whites or any other minority group—face an acute shortage of economic opportunities as the result of the inequitable distribution of services and wealth. During the latter part of the 20th century, as the U.S. economy shifted from manufacturing to service-oriented jobs, those workers without the necessary credentials or skills were left behind. Over time, middle-class citizens left urban centers and migrated to the suburbs. At first, whites moved from the cities because of the new job opportunities found there and also because of their prejudice against African Americans. Soon, however, middle-class minorities relocated to the suburbs for many of the same reasons.[57]

The economic problems and residential segregation created **concentrated disadvantage**—that is, small areas characterized by extreme poverty and high-crime rates in largely African American neighborhoods in cities. This situation has caused frustration, stress, and a sense of fatalism among many African Americans in their pursuit of cultural goals through legitimate means, which contributes to higher delinquency rates among African Americans.[58] The social problems caused by concentrated disadvantage affect all African American youths residing in troubled neighborhoods. For instance, Jennifer Cobbina, Jody Miller, and Rod Brunson found high levels of fear of crime and perceptions of danger among adolescents living in high-risk areas of Saint Louis, Missouri. The various risks associated with exposure to concentrated disadvantage also contribute to delinquency, which may be perceived as a means of protecting oneself against the hostile environment.[59]

Family Breakdown

Economic deprivation creates a host of strains that contribute to family breakdown in the African American community, resulting in approximately 70% of African American children being born to unmarried parents, many of whom are still teenagers. Other characteristics of family breakdown include the availability of few positive male role models, absentee fathers, overworked single mothers, children who must largely raise themselves, and children who associate with friends who often share their family background.[60] Disruptions in family structure negatively affect school performance, which in turn contributes to the seemingly endless cycle of poverty. As a result, children raised in neighborhoods of concentrated disadvantage are poorly equipped to succeed in American society.[61]

Karen Parker and Tracy Johns have found that family disruption is a significant predictor of homicide, particularly among racial minorities living in large American cities. Conversely, greater stability in the family can serve as a buffer against delinquency. For example, Parker and Amy Reckdenwald found that the presence of a traditional male role model—or father figure—reduced rates of youth violence among African Americans.[62]

Family breakdown is often viewed as a "big city" problem, but researchers have also shown that family variables are related in important ways to delinquency everywhere. For instance, Alexander Vazsonyi and his colleagues studied nearly 1000 African American adolescents living in either rural or urban settings in an attempt to evaluate the ways that parenting and neighborhood factors influence delinquency. They found that parenting measures relating to the ways that parents monitored, supported, and communicated with their children were stronger predictors of delinquency and maladaptive behaviors than were neighborhood characteristics.[63]

Cultural Factors

The *culture of poverty* also contributes to serious and violent forms of delinquency. John MacDonald and Angela Gover found that economic and cultural problems were particularly closely related to homicide committed by adolescents and young adults.[64] In fact, criminologists have provided compelling evidence to support the idea that concentrated disadvantage—that is, life in the most economically impoverished, racially segregated neighborhoods—is related to delinquency. Far from being a pervasive problem, serious delinquency and violence among African Americans are overwhelmingly limited to the "worst" neighborhoods in the United States, the very places that define concentrated disadvantage.[65]

Another explanation for why African Americans are proportionately more likely to commit crime suggests that their life experiences have contributed to the development of a hostile view of larger society and its values. According to this perspective, African Americans have constructed a culture with distinctive modes of dress, speech, and conduct that are at

KEY TERMS

concentrated disadvantage
Economically impoverished, racially segregated neighborhoods with high-crime rates.

BOX 2.7

A Window on Delinquency

Code of the Street

For many years, explanations for the disproportionately high levels of delinquency and violence among African Americans, especially males, were convoluted, difficult to empirically examine, and also shrouded in political correctness. Elijah Anderson's code of the street thesis advanced that poverty, social dislocation, and racial discrimination contribute to antisocial attitudes, thought patterns, and behaviors that are oppositional to mainstream society and instead adhere to a street code. Those who subscribe to the street code are known as "street." Conversely, most African Americans who live in conditions of poverty not only do not subscribe to the street code, but also behave in ways that are consistent with conventional norms. Anderson referred to the nondelinquent citizens as "decent." In moral terms, decent people are conventional whereas street people are delinquent.

The code of the street is an important opportunity to shed light on the alarmingly high levels of violence. Eric Stewart and Ronald Simons found that decent families are less likely to engage in violent conduct. However, they found that street youth were not more violent until 2 years after they internalized the street code. This suggests that many African American males posture a "street" persona perhaps to protect themselves from conflicts, but over time this leads to violence. Similarly, Susan McNeeley

and Yue Yuan found that youth who adopt the street code are more likely to be violently victimized and also experience greater fear of crime. What was theorized to be a protective mechanism to look tough actually results in greater fear and proneness to be victimized.

Holli Drummond and her colleagues found that hopelessness was an important emotion in the street code process. Adolescents who report greater feelings of hopelessness in their life are more likely to subsequently identify with street code attitudes. In turn, this contributes to higher involvement in violent delinquency. This is an important finding because it is compatible with the fatalism inherent in the "kill or be killed" culture that typifies crime-ridden neighborhoods.

The code of the street is a classic sociological explanation for disproportionately high delinquency and violence in the African American community, but it is important to recognize that individual differentiation characterizes all groups. Thus, in recent years, criminologists have begun to explore the antisocial traits that underlie the street code as well as different trajectories that African American youth take along the street code, some of whom are deeply enmeshed in delinquency and others who are more superficially antisocial.

Eric Stewart and Ronald Simons, *The Code of the Street and African American Adolescent Violence* (Washington, DC: U.S. Department of Justice, 2009); Susan McNeeley and Yue Yuan, "A Multilevel Examination of the Code of the Street's Relationship with Fear of Crime," *Crime and Delinquency*, in press (2016); Holli Drummond, John Bolland, and Waverly Harris, "Becoming Violent: Evaluating the Mediating Effect of Hopelessness on the Code of the Street Thesis," *Deviant Behavior* 32:191–223 (2011); Richard Moule, Callie Burt, Eric Stewart, and Ronald Simons, "Developmental Trajectories of Individuals' Code of the Street Beliefs through Emerging Adulthood," *Journal of Research in Crime and Delinquency* 52:342–372 (2015); Matt DeLisi, "Antisocial Traits Murdered the Code of the Street in a Battle for Respect," *Journal of Criminal Justice* 42:431–432 (2014).

---

odds with the cultural trappings of the larger society. Crime, then, is the result of African Americans not respecting the values of the larger society and being more willing to flaunt social norms.

Some criminologists suggest that the culture of poverty may place tremendous importance on personal appearance and self-respect because economic deprivation is so pronounced. Consequently, youths interpret signs of disrespect or other seemingly trivial affronts as serious threats. Elijah Anderson calls this concept the "code of the street," in which violence—even murder—is viewed as a normative response to signs of disrespect (see **Box 2.7**, the "A Window on Delinquency" feature).[66] Arguments, fights, and even homicides stemming from trivial confrontations, such as bumping into another person or staring at another person in a threatening manner, are likely to lead many youths to subscribe to a subcultural code of the streets. Research by Eric Stewart, Christopher Schreck, and their colleagues

suggests that youths who adopt the code of the street set themselves up for greater involvement in both violent delinquency and victimization as the targets of violence.[67]

An alternative theory proposes that the race-arrest differences are a function of differential law enforcement—namely, that more police patrolling African American neighborhoods and more calls for service from residents of African American neighborhoods result in more police–citizen interactions.[68] This police bias results in **racial profiling**, a practice where police use race as an explicit factor in creating "profiles" that then guide their decision making.

KEY TERMS

racial profiling
A practice in which police use race as an explicit factor to create "profiles" that then guide their decision making.

Approximately half of all African American men say they have been victims of racial profiling. Police justify racial profiling on the basis of arrest statistics that suggest African Americans are more likely than whites to commit crime. Studies of racial profiling, however, indicate this is not necessarily the case. For example, in Maryland, 73% of those drivers stopped and searched on a section of Interstate 95 were African American, yet state police reported that equal percentages of the whites and African Americans who were searched, statewide, had drugs or other contraband. Other research also supports the contention that police use racial profiling on a routine basis. Nationally, citizens report that police make traffic stops of African American male drivers more frequently than traffic stops of drivers from other ethnic groups. African American drivers are more likely to report the police did not have legitimate reasons for stopping them and that police acted improperly during the traffic stop. In addition, African Americans are significantly more likely than whites to be searched after a traffic stop. Many studies of racial profiling have concluded that police actions are discriminatory and reflect the racial prejudice of individual officers or organizational racism found in police departments.[69]

Even when legally relevant variables, such as the seriousness of the current offenses or the youth's delinquent history are taken into account, a young person's race still matters when determining his or her treatment within the juvenile justice system. Specifically, when that person is African American, male, and young, the odds are significantly higher that those statuses will influence his legal treatment.[70] Indeed, the notion that African Americans are more greatly involved in delinquency and, therefore, subject to greater social control can even affect non-African Americans. For example, Kenneth Novak and Mitchell Chamlin reported that in neighborhoods where the racial composition is mostly African American, the police tend to conduct more searches of all citizens. This effect was observed only for white motorists who were driving in mostly African American neighborhoods; the logic was that police perceived that those whites were engaged in delinquency, such as buying drugs, when they were in neighborhoods where they were the minority.[71]

In sum, the relationship between race and delinquency is complex. The existing data tell a mixed story. Based on data produced for the *UCR*, from self-report studies, and from the NCVS, the conclusion that more African American juveniles are involved in delinquency than are whites is warranted. By contrast, studies of racial profiling, although not directly studying police–juvenile interactions, are strongly suggestive of the possibility that a juvenile's race influences the decision by an officer regarding whether to arrest. At the same time, profiling by officers would not account

Elijah Anderson's "Code of the Street" describes the delinquent subculture where violence—even murder—is viewed as a normative response to signs of disrespect.

© Tom Antos/Shutterstock.

for the race-offense differences found in self-report studies and the NCVS.

Social Class

Unsurprisingly, studies reporting on delinquency and social class have produced mixed results. Some studies report a direct relationship between social class and delinquency, whereas others have found no relationship or, at best, a very weak one. Research based on official data (e.g., the *UCR*) has typically found that lower-class youths are arrested and incarcerated more often than middle- and upper-class adolescents. A landmark study examining the relationship between delinquency and social class was published in 1942. Clifford Shaw and Henry McKay observed a very strong relationship among delinquency rates, rates of families on relief, and median rental costs in 140 neighborhoods.[72] Follow-up research reported similar findings for a variety of measures of social class.

Of course, relationships at the neighborhood level do not mean those factors are related at the individual level. To assume that they are is to commit the

ecological fallacy, which could occur for a variety of reasons:

1. Police could be biased, arresting juveniles in lower-class neighborhoods for behavior (e.g., loitering) that they would ignore in other neighborhoods.
2. People could leave their middle- and upper-class neighborhoods and go to lower-class neighborhoods to commit crimes (e.g., illegal drug sales).
3. Only a small number of juveniles might be committing most of the offenses in a lower-class neighborhood.

For these reasons, in the 1960s criminologists started to use self-report surveys to evaluate the relationship between delinquency and social class. These early studies revealed there was *no* relationship between the two conditions. This conclusion stirred considerable controversy. Some criminologists contended that the self-report method was not a reliable or valid tool. Other criminologists were sufficiently intrigued to conduct their own research, using other samples, to see if they would find the same thing. Often they did: Delinquency was as common among middle- and upper-class juveniles as it was among lower-class teenagers.[73]

The debate surrounding delinquency and social class has not been resolved. Charles Tittle and his colleagues report that the relationship between delinquency and social class depends on *when* and *how* the research was conducted. Not only did the relationship vary from decade to decade, but use of a self-report data collection methodology yielded different results than did collection of official data. Official data in the 1940s showed a strong correlation between delinquency and social class, but the correlation weakened in later decades and fell to practically zero in the 1970s. In self-report studies, the average correlation between social class and delinquency was never high. Before 1950, there were no self-report studies examining this relationship, and afterward, the correlation was only very weak.[74]

These findings lend themselves to different interpretations. Perhaps the official data of the 1940s and 1950s are invalid and should be rejected. Or maybe the official data are accurate, and lower-class juveniles during those eras did have a monopoly on delinquency, but middle- and upper-class teenagers have now caught up.

Tittle and his colleagues reject both of these possibilities. They think self-report data are probably correct in showing that the relationship between delinquency and social class has not changed very much over the years and that lower-class adolescents are only slightly more likely than others to commit crime. They also suggest that the official data reflect bias. According to these researchers, police and court officials have frequently discriminated against lower-class juveniles, arresting and referring them to court more often—

particularly in the 1940s and 1950s—than was the case for other children. Tittle and his colleagues' contention has been supported by research conducted by Robert Sampson, who examined arrest decisions and found that for most offenses committed by teenagers, official police records and court referrals were structured not just by the act, but also by the juvenile's social class.[75] Similarly, John Hagan found that police characterize lower-class neighborhoods as having more criminal behavior than other areas.[76] Douglas Smith perhaps captured the dynamic of the ecological fallacy "in action" best when he noted:

> Based on a set of internalized expectations derived from past experience, police divide the population and physical territory they must patrol into readily understandable categories. The result is a process of ecological contamination in which all persons encountered in bad neighborhoods are viewed as possessing the moral liability of the area itself.[77]

The conclusions of Tittle and his colleagues and those researchers whose work supports their claims have been soundly criticized. Michael Hindelang and his associates observed a rather consistent relationship between delinquency and social class for serious crimes.[78] John Braithwaite wonders whether Tittle and his associates really take their conclusion of no relationship between delinquency and social class seriously. He has questioned whether they "adopt no [more] extra precautions when moving about the slums of the world's great cities than they do when walking in the middle class areas of such cities." Braithwaite contends that the evidence overwhelmingly supports the notion that delinquency and social class are related.[79] Even though the connection between delinquency and social class is sometimes inconsistent, more research has identified the presence of a significant class difference than would be expected by chance. When you consider that self-report studies exaggerate the proportion of delinquency committed by middle-class juveniles by paying too much attention to minor infractions, the "true" relationship between delinquency and social class begins to emerge. Studies of delinquency and social class based on official records, for example, have consistently found sizable class differences.

One study examining the relationship between delinquency and social class was able to test the conflicting opinions by using such a large sample that it could include serious offenses. Delbert Elliott and Suzanne Ageton compared the self-report data of more

KEY TERMS

ecological fallacy
The mistake of assuming relationships found at the neighborhood level mean those factors are related at the individual level.

than 1700 juveniles from lower-class, working-class, and middle-class backgrounds. They concluded that the self-reported behavior of adolescents was similar, *except for predatory crimes against persons* (robbery and aggravated assault). For these crimes, the differences observed across the social classes were profound. For every such crime reported by middle-class juveniles, three of these crimes were committed by working-class youths and four of the crimes were reported by lower-class juveniles. This finding led Elliott and Ageton to conclude that the behavior of lower-class teenagers is similar to the behavior of adolescents for "run-of-the-mill offenses" but that lower-class juveniles commit many more serious crimes.[80]

Anthony Walsh effectively summarized the decades of dispute over the social class and delinquency relationship:

> The issue of the connection between social class and delinquent and criminal activity has been bedeviled by semantic and methodological deceit. Semantically, researchers have examined trivial misbehaviors and called it criminality, delinquency, and crime. Methodologically, they have searched for a type of subject in places where they are not likely to find them and substitute another type simply because they are readily available. Those who deny the class-crime relationship ignore official statistics and ecological studies . . .[81]

The take-home message is that although all people can engage, do engage, and have engaged in delinquent conduct at some point in their lives, it does nothing to destroy the inverse social class-delinquency relationship. When the most severe forms of delinquency are considered, such as murder, armed robbery, rape, and burglary, the delinquents are overwhelmingly more likely to come from impoverished backgrounds.

Age

Age and delinquency are strongly and negatively related. This means that involvement in delinquency is generally higher during adolescence and early adulthood and then sharply declines across life. The association between them was originally observed by the 19th-century French criminologist, Adolphe Quetelet, who noted that crime peaks in the late teens through the mid-20s. Nearly two centuries later, the basic observation from Quetelet stands. Patrick Lussier and Jay Healy examined recidivism among convicted sex offenders and found that measures relating to age were the strongest determinants of whether offenders would recidivate. In fact, an offender's age at release from prison was as strong a predictor of recidivism as a sex offender classification tool.[82] Today, the **age–crime curve** is a well-established fact. It states that crime rates increase during preadolescence, peak in late adolescence, and steadily decline thereafter.[83] The high point of the curve is slightly different for serious violent and property offenses. Arrests for serious violent crimes peak at age 18 and then steadily decline. By comparison, arrests for serious property crimes top out at age 16 and decrease consistently thereafter. Juveniles whose behavior fits this pattern are called **adolescence-limited offenders** because their delinquency is restricted to the teenage years.[84]

The general age–crime curve does not apply to all juveniles. Some children begin and end their involvement in delinquency at earlier and later ages. Variation in offending patterns among juveniles has been observed across offense type, by sex, and by race. For instance, (1) violent offending by girls peaks earlier than violent offending by boys and (2) African American children are more likely than whites to continue offending into early adulthood.[85] What is constant across all categories of juveniles is that they commit fewer crimes as they grow older—a process criminologists call the **aging-out phenomenon**.

Several competing explanations have been put forth regarding why crime diminishes with age:

- Personalities change as juveniles mature. Once-rebellious adolescents often become adults who exercise self-control over their impulses.
- Adolescents become aware of the costs of crime. They start to realize they have too much to lose if they are caught and too little to gain.
- Peer influences over behavior weaken with age. As juveniles grow older, the importance of their peers' opinions of them decreases.
- For males—inasmuch as aggression is linked to levels of testosterone, a male sex hormone—as they grow older, the level of testosterone in their body decreases, as does their aggressiveness.
- Some crimes, such as strong-arm robbery and burglary, decline with age because older people lack the physical strength or agility to commit them.
- The need for money decreases. It is much more difficult for juveniles to get money than adults. As adolescents grow older, their prospects for full-time employment increase.

KEY TERMS

age–crime curve
The empirical trend that crime rates increase during preadolescence, peak in late adolescence, and steadily decline thereafter.

adolescence-limited offenders
Juveniles whose law-breaking behavior is restricted to their teenage years.

aging-out phenomenon
The gradual decline of participation in crime after the teenage years.

Of course, the most likely explanation for the age–delinquency relationship is one that combines many of these factors. For instance, personality is a stable, individual-level characteristic that also is adaptable to environmental conditions. This means that one's personality develops over the life course in response to biological and social changes that also occur across life. One of the most adaptable components is conscientiousness or constraint, which is characterized by self-discipline and the ability to regulate one's emotional and behavioral responses. Daniel Blonigen reviewed personality development as it relates to the age–crime relationship and found that studies show that between 10 and 34% of individuals experience increases in constraint and conscientiousness as they enter adulthood. This suggests that the age–crime curve represents a host of biological, psychological, and social changes that bear on personality.[86]

Although most children age out of delinquency, some do not. The latter group of children often become **chronic offenders**, also known as serious, violent, and chronic juvenile offenders. Typically, chronic offenders are juveniles who begin offending at a very young age and continue to offend as adults.

Serious, Violent, and Chronic Juvenile Offenders

The first juvenile court in the United States was established in 1899 in Cook County (Chicago), Illinois. Judge Merritt Pinckney, one of the judges who presided over this court, had the following to say about some of the youths he met:

> A child, a boy especially, sometimes becomes so thoroughly vicious and is so repeatedly an offender that it would not be fair to the other children in a delinquent institution who have not arrived at his age of depravity and delinquency to have to associate with him. On very rare and special occasions, therefore, children are held over on a *mittimus* to the criminal court.[87]

Now consider this assessment from criminologist Terrie Moffitt, who developed the developmental taxonomy consisting of "adolescence-limited offenders" and "life-course persistent offenders" (LCPs):

> Longitudinal research consistently points to a very small group of males who display high rates of antisocial behavior across time and in diverse situations. The professional nomenclature may change, but the faces remain the same as they drift through successive systems aimed at curbing their deviance: schools, juvenile justice programs, psychiatric treatment centers, and prisons. The topography of their behavior may change with changing opportunities, but the underlying disposition persists throughout the life course.[88]

Although nearly a century separates these two quotations, both address the same recurrent problem in delinquency: *chronic offenders*. Today these persons are referred to as serious, violent, and chronic juvenile offenders. In fact, it has always been the case that a small group of serious violent youths are responsible for the overwhelming majority of serious violent crime occurring in a population. These youth have lengthy delinquent careers (duration), commit crimes at very high rates (frequency), are deeply committed to antisocial behavior (priority), and are most likely to commit crimes such as murder, rape, robbery, and aggravated assault (seriousness).

Major Delinquent Career Research

From very early in life, chronic offenders separate themselves from others based on their recurrent maladaptive, antisocial, and, later, delinquent behaviors. The childhood and adolescence of the average chronic offender are typically characterized by a host of risk factors that have important implications for antisocial behavior:[89]

- Underresponsive autonomic nervous system
- Extreme fussiness
- General irritability
- Difficult to soothe
- Less parental bonding during infancy
- Hyperactivity
- Impulsivity
- Rejection by peers
- Negative emotionality
- Language difficulty
- Reading problems
- Physical aggression
- Lying and stealing during childhood
- Limited impulse control
- Failure at school
- Poor relationship quality
- Deviant peers
- Hostility or aggressive bias against others
- Use of alcohol and drugs
- Manipulation of others
- Juvenile justice system involvement during adolescence

Chronic offenders often commit their first serious crime before age 10 and by age 18 have achieved a lengthy police record. (See **Box 2.8**, the "A Window on Delinquency" feature for a profile of chronic

KEY TERMS

chronic offenders
Youths who continue to engage in law-breaking behavior as adults. They are responsible for the most serious forms of delinquency and violent crime.

BOX 2.8

A Window on Delinquency

State Delinquents

Serious, violent, and chronic juvenile offenders are unlike most juveniles in that their conduct problems emerge at remarkably early ages, such as during the preschool years, their delinquency includes violent and more serious behaviors; their delinquency generally disrupts their social development at school, with peers, and within their families; and they recurrently are contacted by police and the juvenile court. Along with their extreme antisocial behavior, juvenile chronic offenders also have breathtakingly severe victimization histories characterized by multiple forms of abuse (e.g., physical, sexual, and emotional), neglect, poverty, and exposure to unhealthy lifestyles and role models (e.g., parents involved in gangs, criminal activity, or substance abuse). Because of these overlapping risk factors, chronic offending juveniles frequently are committed to detention centers and, in the most serious cases, confinement facilities for their delinquency.

Chad Trulson has referred to serious, violent, and chronic juvenile offenders as "state delinquents," because their antisociality has resulted in them becoming wards of the state. Using data from 2520 incarcerated juvenile offenders, Trulson and his colleagues have demonstrated the seriousness of the behaviors of state delinquents and how their psychopathology negatively affects their development even when under juvenile justice system supervision. For instance:

- During this cohort's time in confinement facilities, they committed more than 200,000 incidents of minor misconduct and nearly 19,000 incidents of major misconduct. Youths who had more extensive juvenile records were more likely to be repeatedly noncompliant during confinement.
- Along with other indicators of the delinquent career, youths who continued to misbehave behind bars were more likely to have the adult component of their blended sentence invoked. Blended sentencing allows juveniles the opportunity to serve part of their sentence in the juvenile justice system, and if there is improvement, avoid a harsher adult sentence.
- On average, state delinquents were released from confinement facilities at age 19, and 50% of them were rearrested for a felony offense. This means, of course, that 50% of former state delinquents were not arrested again at follow-up.

Trulson and his colleagues recently examined a cohort of 3300 serious and violent delinquents in Texas who were sentenced first in the Texas Youth Commission and then either transferred to adult prisons at age 18 or released from custody. Contrary to the law and order reputation of Texas, Trulson found that 70% of these state delinquents were released to the community after relatively brief confinement in juvenile facilities, and most engaged in significant misconduct while in custody and continued recidivism after release. In sum, a serious, violent, and chronic delinquent history is often the forerunner of a lifetime of antisocial behavior and criminal justice system involvement. Despite their youth, state delinquents represent the extreme of individual-level behavioral risk and family background disadvantage.

Chad Trulson, Darin Haerle, Jonathan Caudill, and Matt DeLisi, *Lost Causes: Blended Sentencing, Second Chances, and the Texas Youth Commission* (Austin, TX: University of Texas Press, 2016); Chad Trulson, Matt DeLisi, Jonathan Caudill, Scott Belshaw, and James Marquart, "Delinquent Careers Behind Bars," *Criminal Justice Review* 35:200–219 (2010); Chad Trulson, Jonathan Caudill, Scott Belshaw, and Matt DeLisi, "A Problem of Fit: Extreme Delinquents, Blended Sentencing, and the Determinants of Continued Adult Sanctions," *Criminal Justice Policy Review* 22:263–284 (2011); Chad Trulson, Matt DeLisi, and James Marquart, "Institutional Misconduct, Delinquent Background, and Rearrest Frequency among Serious and Violent Delinquent Offenders," *Crime Delinquency* 57:709–731 (2011); Chad Trulson, Darin Haerle, Matt DeLisi, and James Marquart, "Blended Sentencing, Early Release, and Recidivism of Violent Institutionalized Delinquents," *The Prison Journal* 91:255–278 (2011).

offenders who are institutionalized, or state delinquents.) Significantly, the general profile of the chronic delinquent is remarkably similar regardless of whether the study group is from the United States or some other county. For all intents and purposes, the most delinquent and violent youthful offenders are the same type of persons across different societies and social contexts. For instance, Michael Rocque and his colleagues studied delinquent careers among nearly 11,000 participants from 30 nations as diverse as Armenia, Aruba, Belgium, Cyprus, Iceland, Russia, and the United States and found consistent risk factors for chronic, serious, and violent delinquent careers.[90] The remainder of the chapter explores some of the most important studies of delinquent careers and serious, violent, and chronic juvenile offenders.

Sheldon Glueck and Eleanor Glueck

The first criminologists to study chronic offenders were Sheldon Glueck and Eleanor Glueck, who conducted their research during the 1930s. Their study included 500 delinquent white males between the ages of 10 and 17 who had been committed to two Massachusetts correctional facilities, the Lyman School for Boys and the Industrial School for Boys. The Gluecks collected an array of data and created offender dossiers for each boy, including deviant and criminal history, psychosocial profile, family background, school and occupational history, and other life events such as martial and military history. The delinquent sample was matched on a case-by-case basis to 500 nondelinquent boys from the same area. Members of both samples were followed until age 32. The study design permitted the researchers to examine the long-term effects of early life experiences on subsequent social and antisocial behavior. In fact, the Gluecks' data set is so impressive that it was resurrected by Robert Sampson and John Laub in 1988 and used for more sophisticated data analysis.

The Gluecks' research produced some important findings. For example, an early onset of problem or antisocial behavior strongly predicted a lengthy criminal career characterized by high rates of offending and involvement in serious criminal violence. The Gluecks used the phrase "The past is prologue" to capture the idea of the stability in these males' behavior. However, the Gluecks also found that even high-rate offenders usually reduced their propensity for offending after they passed through adolescence into early adulthood. Similarly, even serious offenders could desist from crime, and seemingly ignore their own criminal propensity, by participating in conventional adult social institutions such as marriage, work, and the military.[91]

The Gluecks were also among the first criminologists to focus on psychopathy among serious delinquents. **Psychopathy** is a personality disorder that results in severe affective, interpersonal, and behavioral problems, such that psychopaths can victimize and manipulate others seemingly without conscience. The Gluecks found that psychopathy was a useful variable in differentiating delinquents from nondelinquents. They described psychopathic offenders as openly destructive, antisocial, asocial, and less amenable to therapeutic or educative efforts. Other characteristics included insensitivity to social demands or to others, shallow emotionality, self-centeredness coupled with a complete lack of empathy, impulsive behavior, lack of stress or anxiety over social maladjustment, gross irresponsibility, and emotional poverty. Psychopathic youth did not appear to respond to treatment or rehabilitative efforts, but instead seemed unconcerned about their consistent criminal behavior. The Gluecks also found that psychopathy was almost *20 times* more common among their delinquent sample than among the matched, nondelinquent control group.[92]

The relationship between psychopathy and serious, chronic, and violent delinquency that the Gluecks noted is still being studied today. Randall Salekin recently studied a cohort of 130 children and adolescents to examine the effect of psychopathic personality on legal problems and opportunities in life. Salekin found that psychopathy was stable across a 4-year follow-up period, meaning that children who had high scores on psychopathic traits early in life tended to remain that way later in adolescence. Additionally, psychopathy was a significant predictor of both general delinquency and violent forms of delinquency. Even more impressive, the effects of psychopathy on serious delinquency withstood the competing effects of 14 other correlates of delinquency, including demographic characteristics, intelligence, prior delinquency, school problems, parental factors, drug use, and delinquent peers, among others.[93]

Marvin Wolfgang and the Philadelphia Birth Cohorts

The landmark study that established the contemporary understanding of career criminals was *Delinquency in a Birth Cohort*, published by Marvin Wolfgang, Robert Figlio, and Thorsten Sellin in 1972. This study followed 9945 males who were born in Philadelphia in 1945 and who lived in the city at least from ages 10 to 18. The significance of this longitudinal birth cohort design was that it was not susceptible to sampling error because every male subject was followed. The researchers found that nearly two-thirds of the youths never experienced a police contact, whereas 35% of the population of boys did have such contact. For the minority of persons who were actually contacted by police, the police contacts were rare occurrences, occurring just once, twice, or three times.

By contrast, some youths experienced more frequent interactions with police. In the work of Wolfgang and his associates, persons with five or more police contacts were classified as chronic or habitual offenders. Only 627 members, or just 6% of the sample, qualified as chronic offenders. However, these 6% accounted for 52% of the delinquency demonstrated by the entire cohort. Moreover, chronic offenders committed 63% of all Crime Index offenses, 71% of the murders, 73% of the rapes, 82% of the robberies, and 69% of the aggravated assaults.[94]

A second study examined a cohort of persons born in Philadelphia in 1958. Conducted by Paul Tracy, Marvin Wolfgang, and Robert Figlio, the second Philadelphia cohort contained 13,160 males and 14,000 females. Overall, members of the 1958 cohort committed crime at higher rates than members of the 1945 cohort and demonstrated greater involvement in the most serious forms of crime, such as murder, rape, robbery, and aggravated assault. Roughly the same proportion of persons (33%) of the later cohort was arrested before adulthood. Approximately 7% of the population members were habitual offenders, and they accounted for 61% of all delinquency, 60% of the murders, 75% of the rapes, 73% of the robberies,

KEY TERMS

psychopathy
A personality disorder that results in affective, interpersonal, and behavioral problems, including violent criminal behavior that is committed without conscience.

BOX 2.9

A Window on Delinquency

Childhood Predictors of Serious, Violent, and Chronic Delinquency

Behavioral Characteristics

Troublesome
Dishonest
Antisocial
Poor self-regulation
Negative emotionality
Self-centered/narcissistic
Impulsive

Individual Characteristics

High daring/low fear
Lack concentration
Nervous
Few friends
Unpopular
Low nonverbal IQ
Low verbal IQ
Low educational attainment

Family Characteristics

Convicted parent
Delinquent sibling
Harsh discipline
Poor supervision
Broken family
Parental conflict
Large family size
Young mother
Frequent housing changes

Socioeconomic Characteristics

Low socioeconomic status (SES)
Low family income
Poor housing

Maria Ttofi, David Farrington, Alex Piquero, and Matt DeLisi, eds., "Protective Factors against Offending and Violence: Results from Prospective Longitudinal Studies." *Journal of Criminal Justice* 44, in press (2016); David Farrington, Maria Ttofi, Rebecca Crago, and Jeremy Coid, "Intergenerational Similarities in Risk Factors for Offending," *Journal of Developmental and Life-Course Criminology* 1:48–62 (2015); Rolf Loeber and David Farrington, *From Juvenile Delinquency to Adult Crime: Criminal Careers, Justice Policy, and Prevention* (New York: Oxford University Press, 2012).

and 65% of the aggravated assaults committed by the group as a whole.[95] A few years later, Paul Tracy and Kimberly Kempf-Leonard collected criminal records for the 1958 sample up to age 26. Their analysis showed that juveniles who were actively involved in crime as children were more likely to be adult criminals, whereas nondelinquents generally remained noncriminals in adulthood.[96]

When Marvin Wolfgang and his colleagues tracked 974 persons from their Philadelphia cohort through adulthood to age 30, they discovered that more than 50% of the chronic offenders were arrested at least four times between ages 18 and 30. In comparison, only 18% of persons with no juvenile arrests were ever arrested as adults.[97] This continuation of antisocial behavior across stages of the life span is known as the **continuity of crime**.[98]

Cambridge Study in Delinquent Development

The most important European contribution to the study of delinquent careers is the Cambridge Study

in Delinquent Development, a prospective longitudinal panel study of 411 males born in London in the years 1952–1953. Originally conceptualized by Donald West in 1961, the study continues today under the guidance of David Farrington. Now more than 50 years old, the study subjects have been interviewed nine times between the ages of 8 and 46, with their parents participating in eight interviews. Although the Cambridge study uses convictions rather than police contacts or arrests as its unit of analysis, its results relating to serious, violent, and chronic offenders are familiar. For example, 37% of the sample has been convicted of some criminal offense, most commonly theft or burglary. Six percent of the sample (25 youths) are chronic offenders who have accounted for 47% of all acts of criminal violence in the sample, including approximately 60% of the armed robberies. In addition to their versatile mix of delinquent acts, serious, violent, and chronic offenders in the Cambridge data are also much more likely to die earlier than their more well-behaved peers. In fact, Katherine Auty and her colleagues reported that serious, violent, and chronic offenders had seven times greater mortality risk than normal delinquents.[99]

As shown in **Box 2.9**, the "A Window on Delinquency" feature, thanks to the richness of the Cambridge panel data, Farrington has been able to publish widely on a variety of topics pertaining to chronic offenders, the criminal behavior of their siblings and parents, and the processes by which criminal behavior are transmitted from one generation to the next. Youthful chronic offenders in this study presented with a number of risk factors that served as predictors for a life in crime—for example, having a parent who had been incarcerated and having delinquent siblings. Young chronic offenders also tended to be daring, prone to trouble, impulsive, and defiant; had low intelligence and low school attainment; and were raised in poverty. The most antisocial boys in childhood were similarly the most antisocial adolescents and adults. Crime also tended to "run in families," as chronic offenders often had children whose life trajectories reflected a similar syndrome of antisocial behavior.[100] These findings not only lend support to the Gluecks' idea that the "The past is prologue," but also show the dangers of not intervening in the lives of serious delinquents—life-course persistent criminality and lives of despair are the usual outcome.

Dunedin Multidisciplinary Health and Human Development Study

The Dunedin Multidisciplinary Health and Human Development Study is a longitudinal investigation of the health, development, and behavior of a complete cohort of births between April 1, 1972, and March 31, 1973, in Dunedin—a medium-sized city with a population of approximately 120,000, located on New Zealand's South Island. Perinatal data were obtained at delivery, and the children were later traced for follow-up beginning at age 3. More than 90% of these births—more than 1000 people—are part of the longitudinal study. The study group members are now 36–37 years old, and the study also interviews their friends, spouses, children, and peers.[101]

Terrie Moffitt, Avshalom Caspi, and their colleagues have produced an impressive array of publications from the Dunedin data. These reports highlight the ways in which serious, violent, and chronic juvenile offenders develop; in Moffitt's theory, they are known as LCP offenders. For instance:[102]

- As early as age 3, several characteristics have been identified that predict LCP status, including an undercontrolled temperament, neurological abnormalities, low intellectual ability, hyperactivity, and low resting heart rate.
- LCP offenders are more likely to have teenage single mothers, mothers with poor mental health, mothers who are harsh or neglectful, parents who inconsistently punish them, and families characterized by a great deal of conflict.
- LCP offenders are youths who are usually the most aggressive and problematic across all life stages, ranging from childhood to adolescence and into adulthood.

National Youth Survey Family Study

The National Youth Survey Family Study (NYSFS) was launched in 1976 by Delbert Elliott and his collaborators (it was known as the National Youth Survey for nearly 30 years). This prospective longitudinal study focuses on the delinquency and drug use patterns among American youth. The sample contains 1725 persons from seven birth cohorts between 1959 and 1965, and multiple waves of data have been collected since the study's inception. The National Youth Survey Family Study has yielded plentiful information about the prevalence, incidence, correlates, and processes related to delinquency and other forms of antisocial behavior. In 2003, it was renamed the National Youth Survey Family Study to reflect additional data collection that included genetic information.

Chronic offender information based on NYSFS data is generally similar to information derived from studies employing official records. For most persons, involvement in crime generally and violence specifically proved short lived and limited in scope, although individual offending rates varied greatly. Delinquents tended to dabble in a mixed pattern of offenses, rather than focusing on one type of crime.

A small proportion of the NYSFS sample was habitual in its delinquency. For example, approximately 7% of youths in the survey were serious career offenders, defined as persons who committed at least three Crime Index offenses annually. These youth accounted for the vast majority of antisocial and violent behaviors in the sample and often committed many times the number of assaults, robberies, and sexual assaults than noncareer offenders. By comparison, only 2% of those identified as self-reported career criminals were identified as such using official records. This discrepancy suggests that serious and violent chronic offenders commit significantly more crime than their official records would indicate.

Additionally, information from offender self-reports suggests that there might be more career offenders at large than previously thought. For example, later research using additional waves of data found that 36% of African American males and 25% of white males aged 17 reported some involvement in serious violent offending.[103]

Program of Research on the Causes and Correlates of Delinquency

In 1986, the Office of Juvenile Justice and Delinquency Prevention created the Program of Research on the Causes and Correlates of Delinquency. The result was three prospective longitudinally designed studies: the Denver Youth Survey, the Pittsburgh Youth Study, and the Rochester Youth Development Study.[104]

- The Denver Youth Survey was a probability sample of 1527 youth living in high-risk neighborhoods

in Denver. Survey respondents included five age groups (7, 9, 11, 13, and 15 years old), and both they and their parents were interviewed between 1988 and 1992. This study was designed to obtain longitudinal data covering the 7- to 26-year-old age span to examine the effects of childhood experiences and neighborhood disadvantage on problem behaviors.

- The Pittsburgh Youth Study focused on 1517 boys in grades 1, 4, and 7 in public schools in Pittsburgh during the 1987–1988 school year. Data on delinquency, substance abuse, and mental health difficulties were obtained every 6 months for 3 years via interviews with the subjects and their parents and teachers.
- The Rochester Youth Development Study includes 1000 youths (75% male, 25% female) sampled disproportionately from high-crime neighborhoods. Interviews with multiple sources are ongoing to gather data on criminal offending and related behaviors.

Each study has included a "core measurement package" that encompasses official and self-reports of delinquent behavior and drug use; neighborhood characteristics; demographic characteristics; parental attitudes and child-rearing practices; attitudinal measures of school performance; information about peer and social networks; and views about committing crime.

The Denver, Pittsburgh, and Rochester studies have provided a substantive glimpse into the lives of youth who face multiple risk factors in these three cities. Not surprisingly, they have produced nearly identical findings about the disproportionate violent behavior of chronic offenders. Between 14 and 17% of the youth are habitual offenders who have accounted for 75 to 82% of the incidence of criminal violence. Just as Delbert Elliott and his colleagues found with respondents in the National Youth Survey, these researchers have found that 20 to 25% of adolescents in Denver, Pittsburgh, and Rochester are "multiple problem youth" who have experienced an assortment of antisocial risk factors, such as mental health problems, alcoholism and substance abuse histories, and sustained criminal involvement.

A small minority of youth in the Denver, Pittsburgh, and Rochester samples have been identified as the most frequent, severe, aggressive, and temporally stable delinquent offenders. These youths—all of whom are males—were reared in broken homes by parents who themselves had numerous mental health and parenting problems. These boys are also characterized by their impulsivity, emotional and moral indifference, and total lack of guilt with which they committed crimes. Indeed, as children they showed many of the characteristics of psychopathy.[105]

Pathways to Desistance Study

The Pathways to Desistance Study is the largest longitudinal study of serious adolescent offenders that has ever been conducted. It is a multisite study of 1354 adjudicated offenders from the juvenile and adult court systems in Maricopa County (Phoenix), Arizona and Philadelphia County, Pennsylvania. All of the participants were between the ages of 14 and 17 and had been adjudicated of a serious delinquent offense and were followed over a 7-year period. The study allows a unique look at the developmental pathways as delinquents mature into emerging adulthood and either desist from delinquency or graduate to adult criminal careers. The principal investigator of the Pathways to Desistance Study is Edward Mulvey and the study director is Carol Schubert.

Hundreds of studies have been published using Pathways data and scores of research findings have been produced. Generally, the study has demonstrated there is a considerable diversity of delinquent careers even among those who are generally severe offenders in the first place. Many formerly serious delinquents are able to disengage from a life of delinquency, especially if they have multiple protective factors such as positive personality features, higher cognitive functioning, prosocial family and peer relations, and other indicators of conventional society. Youth who have more risk factors along these domains tend to have greater difficulty disengaging from delinquency and continue to accumulate arrests into adulthood. The study has also shown additional evidence of a small, hard-core subgroup of offenders who engage in very high levels of delinquency and violence across adolescence and into adulthood.[106] Given the rich number of measures in the Pathways data, it is likely to continue to produce findings about various pathways of delinquent careers.

Other Studies of Serious, Violent, and Chronic Juvenile Offenders

Two other important studies of delinquent careers and serious, violent, and chronic juvenile offenders are the Dangerous Offender Project and the Racine, Wisconsin, birth cohorts.

Under the guidance of Donna Hamparian, Simon Dinitz, John Conrad, and their colleagues, the Dangerous Offender Project examined the delinquent careers of 1238 adjudicated youth born in Columbus, Ohio, between 1956 and 1960. Overall, these youths committed a total of 4499 offenses, 1504 crimes of violence, and 904 violent Crime Index crimes. Even among violent juvenile offenders, a small minority whom the researchers dubbed the "violent few" accounted for the majority of crimes. For instance, 84% of the youths were arrested only once for a violent crime as adolescents; 13% were arrested twice. The remaining 3%—*the violent few*—accumulated significantly more police contacts for violent crimes. In fact, they were arrested between 3 and 23 times.[107]

Lyle Shannon selected 1942, 1949, and 1955 birth cohorts from Racine, Wisconsin, that yielded 1352, 2099, and 2676 respondents, respectively, in an effort to examine the relationships between poverty, family structure, and delinquent criminal careers over time. Shannon followed the birth cohorts well into adulthood to further explore continuity in criminal behavior. This study included follow-up of the 1942 cohort to age 30, the 1949 cohort to age 25, and the 1955 cohort to age 22. As in prior studies, Shannon found that a small cohort of chronic offenders committed the preponderance of offenses.[108]

Because of the importance of serious, violent, and chronic delinquents to society, the juvenile justice system has taken special steps both to prevent serious delinquents from developing and to strengthen the juvenile justice system's response to them. These steps include primary prevention programs aimed at stopping serious delinquency before it starts.

WRAP UP

THINKING ABOUT JUVENILE DELINQUENCY: CONCLUSIONS

No one can say how much delinquency is committed or how many children commit delinquent acts. The uncertainty about delinquency rates arises because most crime never comes to the attention of police, but rather is hidden from them. As a consequence, criminologists are forced to estimate the nature and extent of delinquency by using a variety of measures, such as the Uniform Crime Reports (UCR), National Crime Victimization Survey (NCVS), and self-report studies, such as the National Youth Survey Family Study (NYSFS).

Clearly, some groups of children are arrested more often than others. All types of data show that boys commit more delinquency than girls, racial and ethnic minorities commit more serious delinquency than whites, and more serious offending is concentrated among youths from lower socioeconomic classes. Although nearly all children commit fewer crimes as they grow older, not all juvenile offenders completely stop committing crimes. Indeed, some children become chronic offenders.

CHAPTER SPOTLIGHT

- Delinquency is a difficult concept to measure. Over the years, several official, victimization, and self-report methodologies have been developed to quantify this issue.
- The *Uniform Crime Reports* Program is the most well-established way to measure delinquent and criminal behavior in the United States.
- The National Crime Victimization Survey is a nationally representative survey of persons ages 12 and older in U.S. households that measures annual delinquency victimization.
- The National Youth Survey is the longest-running self-report survey of delinquent behavior in the United States.

- From the 1960s until about 1993, there were dramatic increases in crime, delinquency, and youth violence in the United States. Today, delinquency levels are at their lowest level in several decades.
- All forms of crime data indicate that youths, males, nonwhites, and persons in lower socioeconomic groups have greater involvement in serious delinquency than do older adolescents, females, whites, and persons in higher socioeconomic status groups.
- Several studies have documented the existence of a small group of youths—less than 10% of the overall population—who are serious, chronic, and violent offenders.

CRITICAL THINKING

1. The police have a great deal of discretion in deciding which acts of delinquency to respond to. Is there any way to limit police discretion in crime reporting? Does the use of discretion taint official measures of delinquency, such as the *Uniform Crime Report* data?

2. All measures of delinquency are susceptible to measurement error, but especially self-reports. Would you tell strangers the truth about crimes you committed? If so, would you exaggerate or minimize your involvement? Why might people lie?

3. Criminologists have offered a variety of reasons for the decline in delinquency since the mid 1990s, including better and more policing, greater use of imprisonment, demographic changes, the economy, and even abortion. Which of these likely has had the greater impact and why?

4. There is evidence of a closing gender gap in delinquency and evidence that today's police are responding more harshly to female offenders than they have in the past. Based on behavioral differences between boys and girls, should they be treated differently by the juvenile justice system?

5. What are some of the reasons that have been advanced for racial and ethnic differences in delinquency? Why is the link between race and delinquency controversial? Does controversy similarly characterize the links between age, gender, and social class and delinquency? Why?

SECTION 2

Delinquency Theories

I n Section 2, we discuss theories of delinquency that have guided scholarship and policy development during the 20th and 21st centuries. Some of the theories are specific to juveniles; others apply to both children and adults.

In Chapters 3 and 4, we review *individual* theories of delinquency. These theories reject the idea that the environment is entirely responsible for behavior and instead blame delinquency on free will—that is, the choices people make—or on individual traits—for example, personality, temperament, genetics, brain chemistry, and so on. Chapter 3 examines choice and biological theories. Choice theories are based on the classical school of criminology and emphasize an individual's ability to make choices; by contrast, biological theories attribute delinquency and other types of antisocial behavior to biological traits and processes, such as brain dysfunction. Chapter 4 focuses on psychological theories, which also point to causes of delinquency within the individual, such as intelligence, temperament, and personality.

Chapter 5 reviews sociological theories, including cultural deviance, strain, and social control. Rather than blaming behavior on individual characteristics, these theories look at how the child's environment influences his or her behavior. Cultural deviance theories examine a child's interactions with social, cultural, and ecological factors that lead to delinquency; strain theories evaluate the role of a variety of stressors, including blocked opportunities that may push children into delinquency; and social control theories study how closely bonded or connected children are to family, peers, and the school.

Chapter 6 discusses critical theories. Two perspectives are presented: labeling theories and conflict theories. Labeling theories see delinquency as a product of the interactions between individuals and other persons or groups of people. The unequal distribution of the power to define behaviors as delinquent, the inability of some youths to resist the application of stigmatizing labels, and the process by which juveniles move from unwitting or spontaneous acts to behavior associated with more organized social roles and delinquent identities are among the concerns explored by these theories. By comparison, conflict theories examine the relationships among economic, social, and political factors, including how they interact to produce delinquency.

Chapter 7 reports on developmental theories of delinquency, which also are called life-course theories. These theories draw on earlier schools of criminological thought by integrating the strongest elements of those theories, such as social control and social learning. Additionally, developmental theories focus on protective

57

factors and risk factors associated with changes in behavior as people mature, conceptualizing delinquency as a pattern of behavior, rather than as a discrete event.

Theories of female delinquency are discussed in Chapter 8. A significant criminological reality is that nearly all theories of delinquency have been built around patterns of male delinquency; thus, they do not apply well when the goal is to explain why girls commit crime. After a brief examination of the development of female gender roles and identities, Chapter 8 discusses delinquency theories in terms of their relevance and applicability to female delinquency.

SECTION OUTLINE

Chapter 3: Choice and Biological Theories

Chapter 4: Psychological Theories

Chapter 5: Sociological Theories: Cultural Deviance, Strain, and Social Control

Chapter 6: Sociological Theories: Labeling and Conflict

Chapter 7: Developmental Theories

Chapter 8: Female Delinquency Theories

Choice and Biological Theories

The study of juvenile delinquency spans more than 200 years. During that time, criminologists have constructed a variety of **theories**, which are integrated sets of ideas that explain and predict *when* and *why* children commit crime. Many of those theories are discussed in this chapter and the following five chapters because *ideas have consequences*. You will notice when reading about them that *different* theories lead to *different* social policies (**Table 3.1**). This is because theories originate from different academic disciplines, such as biology, psychology, sociology, and many others, all of which make different assumptions about behavior. But how any theory explains delinquency will determine the social policies that will be recommended for preventing crime. For instance, criminologists who think delinquency is rooted in faulty brain chemistry may suggest a child take medication that targets the brain region responsible for the behavior in question. On the other hand, criminologists who believe delinquency is caused by social injustice may call for policies requiring the redistribution of societal resources.

OBJECTIVES

- Understand the different types of choice theories of delinquency that have evolved, from classical to neoclassical to rational choice theory.

- Explore early biological approaches to explaining delinquency, including atavism and body type theories, and understand the dark policies that grew out of these early approaches.

- Examine the ways that behavioral disorders, such as attention-deficit/hyperactivity disorder (ADHD), stem from neurological functioning.

- Identify the ways that "nature" and "nurture" forces interact to produce delinquency, including the role of intelligence, hormones, and genetics.

- Understand how environmental pathogens, such as maternal cigarette smoking, chemical poisoning, and nutrition, affect adolescent behavior.

KEY TERMS

Table 3.1 Overview of Criminology Theories and Their Policy Applications

Theory (Chapter)	Major Premise	Policy Application
Choice theory (3)	Children commit crimes because they anticipate more benefits from violating the law than from conformity.	Fixed-time sentences; shock probation; boot camps
Biological theory (3)	Crime is caused by a biological deficiency *inside* the offender.	Segregation; sterilization
Psychodynamic theory (4)	Crime is caused by an overdeveloped/underdeveloped superego.	Psychotherapy or aversion therapy
Behavioral theory (4)	Criminal behavior is learned.	Token economies
Cultural deviance theory (5)	Crime is caused by disorganized neighborhoods.	Chicago Area Project
Strain theory (5)	Crime is caused by society telling children what to seek without providing them with the means to do so.	Project Head Start
Social control theory (5)	Juveniles who are not bonded to society become delinquent.	Police Athletic League
Labeling theory (6)	Crime is caused by societal reactions to behavior.	Diversion programs; decriminalization of offenses
Conflict theory (6)	Crime is caused by imbalances in power.	Programs that equalize power, such as Project Head Start
Developmental theory (7)	Crime is caused by many cumulative factors that vary from childhood to early adulthood.	Age-appropriate interventions that interrupt the cycle of crime
Female delinquency theory (8)	Gender socialization creates different roles of males and females.	Interventions target gender-specific pathways

© Jones & Bartlett Learning.

What Theories Are

Theories are the ideas used to explain facts. They represent the viewpoints of criminologists who live in a particular place during a particular period in history. This is important to remember because theories are tied to real-life experiences. So as societies change, so do the experiences of its members. New experiences generate new ideas, which in turn lead to new theories. Although there are many theories to choose from, some theories clearly seem better than others.

Theories are evaluated on the basis of three criteria:

- Simplicity
- Testability
- Empirical validity

Each criterion forms its own continuum. As a consequence, a theory may be very strong on one or more of the criteria and weak on the remaining one(s). For instance, theories may be quite simple or

highly complex. A good theory effectively summarizes many separate observations into an easily understood statement. Simplicity is a virtue because the purpose of theory is to reduce a large body of information into a few simple laws.

A good theory is also testable. Why? Because other criminologists must be able to refute or verify it. A good theory makes clear and concise predictions that (1) confirm or modify the theory, (2) expand the parameters of the theory, and (3) have practical application. Some theories are not testable because their main concepts are unclear, not measurable, or both. For example, in Edwin Sutherland's *theory of differential association*, the concept of "differential association" cannot be completely verified because no one can monitor all of the interactions of a juvenile over an extended period of time.

If a theory is simple and testable, then a third feature to look for is whether it is supported by scientific evidence. Do research findings support the theory and its predictions? Some theories give rise to many predictions, and research tests could be carried out in many different settings and with many different samples and research methods.

Because there is *no* perfect theory, we discuss a variety of theories in order to provide a thoughtful, carefully crafted, and objective analysis of the most current literature, free of discipline jargon, so you

KEY TERMS

theory
An integrated set of ideas that explain and predict *when* and *why* children commit crime.

may make informed decisions about the theories that make the most sense to you. Our discussion begins with what are called **choice theories**.

Choice Theory

What does delinquency suggest about the rationality of people who commit crime? Do rational people commit crime? Do they exercise free will? Are they intelligent? Do they aim to maximize pleasure and minimize pain?

If you answered yes to these questions, you likely will agree with the causes of crime expressed in choice theories from the **classical school** of criminology. These theories tell us that juveniles are rational, intelligent people who have **free will**—that is, the ability to make choices. Young people calculate the costs and benefits of their behavior *before* they act. Crime is the result of them imagining that greater gains will come from breaking the law than from obeying it. In the same way, children who skip school weigh the likelihood of getting caught against the potential fun they will have. Juveniles who commit serious crime weigh the pleasure they imagine they will receive against the possibility of being caught, arrested, prosecuted, convicted, and sent to a correctional facility. Because behavior is a conscious decision children make, choice theories say that children should be held responsible for their choices and their consequences (see **Box 3.1**, the "Delinquency Around the Globe" feature).

Cesare Beccaria

A leading figure of the classical school was Cesare Beccaria, who formulated his ideas about crime control during the 18th century. At that time, the criminal justice systems throughout Europe were cruel and

Most delinquent acts are minor offenses. When young people commit these crimes, do they weigh the costs and benefits of their action before they act? Cold crimes such as shoplifting be prevented by increasing punishment?

© Fotosenmeer/Shutterstock.

ruthless and demonstrated a callous indifference to human rights. People were punished for crimes against religion, such as blasphemy or witchcraft, and for crimes against the state, such as criticizing political leaders. Worse yet, "offenders" were rarely told why they were being punished. No one was exempt. Any person could be hauled off to jail at any time for any reason. Wealthy persons were generally spared the most torturous and degrading punishments, which were reserved for ordinary citizens who sometimes were burned alive, whipped, mutilated, or branded.[1]

These conditions inspired Beccaria to write *On Crimes and Punishments*, where he laid out the framework for a new system of justice that emphasized humanity, consistency, and rationality (see **Box 3.2**, the "Theory in a Nutshell" feature). According to Beccaria:[2]

1. Social action should be based on the utilitarian principle of the *greatest happiness for the greatest number*.
2. Crime is an injury to society, and the only rational measure of crime is the extent of the injury.
3. Crime prevention is more important than punishment. Laws must be published so that the citizenry can understand and support them.
4. In a criminal procedure, secret accusations and torture must be abolished. *There should be speedy trials, and accused persons should have every right to present evidence in their defense.*
5. The purpose of punishment is to prevent crime. Punishment must be *swift*, *certain*, and *severe*. Penalties must be based on the social damage caused by the crime. *There should be no capital punishment;* life imprisonment is a better deterrent. Capital punishment is irreparable and makes no provision for mistakes.
6. Imprisonment should be widely used, but prison conditions should be improved through better physical quarters and by separating and classifying inmates as to age, sex, and criminal histories.

On Crimes and Punishments is one of the most influential papers ever written. It was the centerpiece for the 1791 criminal code of France and for some

KEY TERMS

choice theories
Theories that claim delinquency is an outcome of rational thought.

classical school
A school of thought that blames delinquency on the choices people make.

free will
The idea that people can and do choose one course of action over another.

BOX 3.1

Delinquency Around the Globe

Choice, Free Will, Brain, and Legal Responsibility

Different theories make different assumptions about human nature and the most basic aspects of our behavior. Classical theorists assume that people exercise free will, which is the power to make decisions. But what if free will itself is a myth? Neuroscientists at the Max Planck Society for the Advancement of Science in Germany performed magnetic resonance imaging (MRI) scans on 14 people after instructing the study participants to decide spontaneously whether to press a button on their left or their right. MRI scans indicated a flurry of activity in the unconscious brain long before the subject made his or her "spontaneous" decision. This finding suggests that the outcome of a decision is shaped very strongly by brain activity much earlier than the point in time when a person feels that he or she is actually making a decision. Thus, whether free will is, indeed, entirely free is an open scientific question.

In the United States and several nations around the world, scientists are daily making discoveries about the role of genetic and neurological factors in producing our personality, our temperament, and our behavior. For instance, Todd Armstrong and Brian Boutwell found that individuals with low resting heart rates (a physiological risk factor for delinquency) are more likely to perceive a low likelihood of getting caught for delinquency and are less likely to report shame or guilt following a confrontation. This shows that rational choice perspectives on crime commission are in part based on physiology. But does this reduce the legal responsibility for delinquency if a delinquent was in part driven to commit crime by biological deficits? The emerging field of neuroethics

grapples with the potentially destructive implications of fully understanding the role of biology in free will, behavior, and responsibility. Although some might suggest that biological deficits render delinquents innocent, that idea is neither likely to take hold in society nor become law.

The exciting scientific discoveries in this chapter simply provide more precise explanations to relationships that have long been known. Even if there are candidate genes for impulsivity, and impulsive decision making is involved in the commission of many delinquent acts, the offender is still legally and morally responsible. The late eminent social scientist James Q. Wilson brilliantly captured this idea:

> For all the advances in neurobiology and genetics— and for all the many sure to come—we are nowhere near a refutation of the basic fairness of a system of laws that takes free will seriously, and treats human beings as responsible agents. Those who believe such a change is at hand are not better informed about the science involved; they are just not informed enough about the practical and philosophical foundations of our morality and justice.

Wilson is correct that the justice system continues to process delinquents with the same basic notion of free will and criminal responsibility. But neuroscientific research will continue to improve the quality of psychiatric evaluations of youth, not only in terms of their legal responsibility, but also in developing interventions that can treat and reduce delinquency and, hopefully, to predict it.

Todd Armstrong and Brian Boutwell, "Low Resting Heart Rate and Rational Choice," *Journal of Criminal Justice* 40:31–39 (2012); James Q. Wilson, "The Future of Blame," *National Affairs*, Winter 2010, p. 114; Chun Soon, Marcel Brass, Hans-Jochen Heinze, and John-Dylan Haynes, "Unconscious Determinants of Free Decisions in the Human Brain," *Nature Neuroscience* 11:543–545 (2008); Gerben Meynen, "Neuroethics of Criminal Responsibility: Mental Disorders Influencing Behavior," pages 544–557 in Matt DeLisi and Michael Vaughn (eds.), *The Routledge International Handbook of Biosocial Criminology* (New York: Routledge, 2015).

BOX 3.2

Theory in a Nutshell

Cesare Beccaria

Beccaria believed that people are rational, intelligent, and exercise free will. They commit crime because they imagine they will receive greater gains from crime than from conformity. According to Beccaria, social action should be based on the utilitarian principle of the *greatest happiness for the greatest number*; because crime is an injury to society, the only rational measure of crime is the extent of the injury. Crime prevention is more important than punishment. Laws must be published so that the citizenry can understand and support them. For punishment to be effective, it must be certain, severe, and administered swiftly.

of the most important ideas in the United States Constitution:

- People are innocent until proven guilty.
- People cannot be forced to testify against themselves.
- People have the right to counsel and to confront their accusers.
- People have the right to a speedy trial by a jury of their peers.

Jeremy Bentham

The English economist Jeremy Bentham was impressed by Beccaria's essay.[3] Bentham also wanted to achieve "the greatest happiness of the greatest number." His work is grounded in **utilitarian principles**, a set of ideas that assume behavior is calculated and that people gather and make sense of information *before* they act. People determine whether the behavior they are contemplating will bring them more pleasure than pain; they are "human calculators." Behavior is, therefore, a consequence of a thoughtful plan.

Offenders must be punished because of the harm they have caused others. Punishment serves four purposes:

1. It prevents crime.
2. It reduces the seriousness of any crime committed.
3. It ensures that an offender will use only the minimum amount of force necessary to commit a crime, and no more.
4. It keeps the cost of crime to the lowest possible level.

The cruelty exercised by the criminal justice system during the 18th century prompted Bentham to suggest guidelines to regulate the relationship between crime and punishment:

1. The punishment must outweigh the profit derived from committing a crime.
2. The punishment must be increased in proportion to the degree that it falls short of certainty.
3. Repeat offenders (recidivists) must be punished more severely.
4. More serious offenses must receive harsher punishments.
5. When a person is considering committing one of two offenses, the punishment for the more serious offense must be sufficient to induce him or her to commit the less serious offense.
6. The punishment must fit the crime.
7. The punishment must not exceed what is necessary to prevent crime.
8. People who commit similar offenses should receive similar punishments.

Bentham's work had an immediate effect on English criminal law. Indeed, his ideas radically transformed the 19th-century English penal code, which was called "The Bloody Code" because people were executed for harmless and minor offenses, like stealing turnips, hanging out with gypsies, and damaging fish ponds. Between 1820 and 1861, the number of capital crimes in the code was reduced from 222 to just 3—murder, treason, and piracy—largely because of Bentham's work.[4] More important, however, the work of Bentham and his contemporary, Beccaria, fostered a new understanding about the relationship of people to society—one that affirmed the principle that *all* people should be treated equally under the law (see **Box 3.3**, the "Theory in a Nutshell" feature).

BOX 3.3
Theory in a Nutshell
Jeremy Bentham

Bentham, a leader in the utilitarian movement, was mostly concerned with the irrationality of existing laws and punishments and their failure to deter criminality. He advanced Beccaria's idea of the "greatest happiness principle," which holds that the purpose of criminal law is to provide for the "greatest happiness for the greatest number" of people. Crime must be prevented because it harms the "collective happiness." Bentham also believed that people exercise free will and are rational beings who choose to act on the basis of a pursuit of their own happiness. Bentham's most significant contribution was a series of guidelines to regulate the relationship between crime and punishment. His ideas profoundly affected criminal justice policy in England. Before Bentham's work, English law called for the death penalty for 222 crimes. After the publication of his theory, the death penalty was reserved for only three crimes—murder, treason, and piracy.

The Neoclassical School

Despite its good intentions, the classical school ultimately failed because of its own rigidity. Its major weakness was not taking into account *why* people committed crime, only that they did. The theories from this school held *all* people equally responsible for their behavior. Those who committed similar crimes received comparable punishments, regardless of why the crime was committed. Put differently, the classical school focused on the criminal *act* and not the criminal *actor*. Yet, in reality, people are different. Children and individuals who are insane or incompetent are not as responsible for their behavior as adults and individuals who are sane or competent. The idea that there are real differences among people led to the emergence of the neoclassical school.

Social reformers of the **neoclassical school** were sympathetic to what the classical school wanted to achieve. They agreed that people were rational,

KEY TERMS

utilitarian principles
A set of ideas that assume behavior is calculated and that people gather and make sense of information before they act.

neoclassical school
A school of thought that considers mitigating circumstances when determining culpability for delinquency.

intelligent beings who exercised free will, but they also thought some crimes were caused by factors beyond the offender's control. According to members of the neoclassical school, **mitigating circumstances**, or factors such as age or mental illness, sometimes influence the choices people make and affect a person's ability to form criminal intent or *mens rea* (guilty mind). This is why today most states establish minimum ages (typically age 7) for holding a child *legally* responsible for a criminal act.

The introduction of mitigating circumstances at criminal trials gave rise to the principle of **individual justice**, the idea that criminal law *should* reflect differences among people and their circumstances. Individual justice produced a series of important developments in criminal justice, including the insanity defense and inclusion of expert witnesses. Perhaps most important, it served as the cornerstone for a new explanation of crime that blamed delinquency on individual traits or characteristics that were in place *before* the act was committed. The foundation of this new way of thinking about crime was *scientific determinism*, which depended on the scientific method to explain crime and was the focus of the positive school of criminology.

Modern Classical School Theory

As delinquency and violence skyrocketed in the latter part of the 20th century, criminologists began to question the effectiveness of rehabilitation. A flurry of evaluation studies of rehabilitation programs concluded that *some* treatment works *some* of the time for *some* offenders in *some* settings.[5] This unconvincing endorsement of the rehabilitation model led to the proposal that criminals must be punished and not rehabilitated. One advocate of this change was James Q. Wilson, who said:

> Wicked people exist. Nothing avails except to set them apart from innocent people. And many people—neither wicked nor innocent, but watchful, dissembling, and calculating of their chances—ponder our reaction to wickedness as a clue to what they might profitably do.[6]

In Wilson's view, the reason to punish crime is that if crime is not punished, people "on the fence" will think crime pays and possibly commit it.

About the same time, other criminologists were busy constructing alternative theories to the neoclassical school's position. Ronald Clarke and Derek Cornish introduced **rational choice theory**. They argued that delinquents are rational people who make calculated choices about what they are going to do *before* they act. Clarke and Cornish think that offenders collect, process, and evaluate information about the crime and make a decision whether to commit it after they have weighed the costs and benefits of doing so (**Figure 3.1**). Thus, crime represents a well-thought-out decision: Offenders decide where to commit it, who or what to target, and how to execute it.[7]

Research has shown that many offenders *do* select a specific location to commit crime. Bruce Jacobs has reported that crack cocaine street dealers like to operate in the middle of a long block because they can see everything in both directions from this location.[8] It also has been found that offenders pick their crime targets only *after* they study the behavior of potential victims.[9] Criminals also learn how to avoid arrest. Successful crack cocaine dealers know where to hide drugs on their person, on the street, and at home.[10] Even robberies of drug dealers have been found to operate on rational principles (see **Box 3.4**, the "A Window on Delinquency" feature). Bruce Jacobs and Richard Wright described three general types of robberies among drug dealers:[11]

- *Market-related* robberies occur as a result of disputes among rival drug dealing offenders.
- *Status-based* robberies occur when one drug dealer's character or reputation is damaged or threatened by another drug dealer.
- *Personalistic* robberies occur when a drug dealer's autonomy is threatened by another drug dealer.

In other words, even the seemingly random violence of the drug underworld has been shown to unfold consistently with classical theory.

KEY TERMS

mitigating circumstances
Factors that may be responsible for an individual's behavior, such as age, insanity, and incompetence.

individual justice
The idea that criminal law must reflect differences among people and their circumstances.

rational choice theory
Theory stating that delinquents are rational people who make calculated choices regarding what they are going to do before they act.

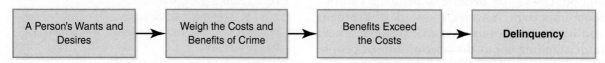

Figure 3.1 Mapping Delinquency Theory: Classical and Rational Choice Theories

BOX 3.4

A Window on Delinquency

Rational Predation?

Many acts of delinquency seem rational when they pertain to everyday types of crime. For instance, a young person might decide to steal from a store because he or she believes that stores have great resources and will not miss the stolen items. Other people might drive vehicles while intoxicated because they feel in control and figure that because they are only 20 minutes from home, little could go wrong. But is rational choice or classical theory also relevant for extreme forms of crime?

Eric Beauregard and his colleagues studied rational choice theory based on interviews with incarcerated serial sex offenders in Canada. All of the men had committed at least two prior sexual assaults or other sexually related crimes against stranger victims. The researchers found that serial sex offenders did not use a consistent method in selecting or "hunting" their victims. Instead, sexual predators studied the routine activities of potential victims to calculate the best way to carry out the crime. The offenders planned how to meet their victims, which attack strategy would be used to commit the crime, and how or if they would release the victim after the sexual assault. The offenders were keenly attuned to situational factors surrounding each attack and adjusted their approach and behavior as the situation warranted.

Beauregard and his associates have even found that some rapists have begun cleaning up their crime scenes to destroy forensic evidence that might assist in their apprehension. Offenders who engaged in more target selection, who burglarized their victims' homes to commit rape, and who displayed sexual signatures were most likely to be forensically aware. From this perspective, the most calculating, predatory, and violent rapists were the least likely to be caught by forensic methods. At times, rational predatory behavior backfires on the offender. Beauregard and Martineau found that sexual homicide offenders who moved the victim's body to another location were more likely to avoid detection; however, the victim's body was also likely to be recovered faster. Ultimately, this could lead to arrest with more certainty than if the offender had simply left the body at the crime scene in the first place.

In other words, serial sexual predators are guided by the same principle that a child uses when stealing candy from a candy store: rationality.

Eric Beauregard and Melissa Martineau, "Does the Organized Sexual Murderer Better Delay and Avoid Detection?," *Journal of Interpersonal Violence* 31:4–25 (2016); Eric Beauregard and Martin Bouchard, "Cleaning Up Your Act: Forensic Awareness as a Detection Avoidance Strategy," *Journal of Criminal Justice* 38:1160–1166 (2010); Patrick Lussier, Martin Bouchard, and Eric Beauregard, "Patterns of Criminal Achievement in Sexual Offending," *Journal of Criminal Justice* 39:433–444 (2011); Eric Beauregard, Kim Rossmo, and Jean Proulx, "A Descriptive Model of the Hunting Process of Serial Sex Offenders: A Rational Choice Perspective," *Journal of Family Violence* 22:449–463 (2007); Eric Beauregard and Benoit Leclerc, "Application of the Rational Choice Approach to the Offending Process of Sex Offenders: A Closer Look at the Decision-Making," *Sexual Abuse: A Journal of Research and Treatment* 19:115–133 (2007).

A similar theoretical explanation is advanced by Lawrence Cohen and Marcus Felson. Their **routine activities theory** examines the crime target or whatever it is the offender wants to take control of, whether it is a house to break into, a bottle of beer, merchandise from a department store, or illegal downloads of music off the Internet. Cohen and Felson argue that before a crime will be committed, three elements must converge:

- Motivated offenders
- Suitable targets
- An absence of people to deter the would-be offender

Thus crime increases when there are motivated offenders, vulnerable targets (e.g., keys left in the ignition), and only a few people to protect those targets (e.g., police).[12] (See **Figure 3.2**.)

There are two problems with the rational choice and routine activity theories. First, they do not identify which factors motivate offenders to commit crime. Second, they overlook factors that cause the criminalization of some behavior (e.g., smoking marijuana) and not other behavior (e.g., drinking alcohol). Nonetheless, both theories force criminologists to recognize that *every crime is a unique event*. Crime may have as much to do with situational factors and free will as it does with the offender's psychology.

Are Offenders Rational?

Are offenders rational? Do rational people murder their friends? Do they stab to death a 10-year-old child walking home from school? Do they drop a playmate from a 14th-floor window because he would not steal candy? In fact, juveniles have committed crimes such as these.

Research on whether offenders are rational has produced mixed results. Some studies have shown that street criminals, prostitutes, thieves, drug dealers and users, burglars, robbers, serial killers, and

KEY TERMS

routine activities theory
Theory arguing that motivated offenders, suitable targets, and absence of capable guardians produce delinquency.

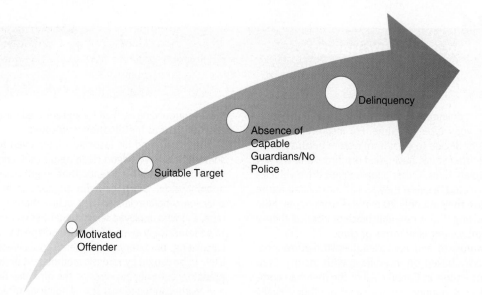

Figure 3.2 Mapping Delinquency Theory: Routine Activities Theory

© Jones & Bartlett Learning.

Until a person reaches age 7, the law does not recognize a child's ability to form criminal intent. Age is often used as a mitigating circumstance in sentencing, particularly when defendants are either very old or very young.

© Photodisc/Getty.

rapists do calculate the risks of getting caught. Gang leaders have been reported to be rational decision makers when they determine who their enemies are, which business deals to make, what the likelihood of being caught is, and how to recruit new members. However, others who commit the same offenses have been found to exercise less rationality than might have been expected.[13] Kenneth Tunnell studied the motivations of chronic property offenders and concluded:[14]

1. They do not consider the legal consequences of their behavior.
2. They focus on rewards and not risks, believing they will not get caught.
3. They do not consider the law, arrest, or imprisonment.

Ronald Akers suggests that the concept of rationality is itself problematic. If being rational means having full and accurate access to *all* potential outcomes of behavior, then classical theories are unrealistic because such predictable situations do not exist. If being rational means making a decision based on the available information, then offenders have "limited rationality." With limited rationality, the emphasis on free will and autonomy, which is the cornerstone of the classical argument, is lost.[15] The information that is available may be faulty or the individual's assessment of the situation may be incorrect. As a consequence, people may not be as free to choose between alternative courses of action as these theories suggest.

Under some circumstances, predatory crimes such as robbery are rational. What about bizarre crimes such as personal crimes of violence? Are these crimes rational? It is tempting to blame them on biological impulses and psychological delusions. Violence, however, may be rational in circumstances where offenders believe it will produce the desired rewards. When rival gangs fight, for example, the perceived reward is reputation. Boyfriends assault girlfriends to win arguments. Children murder classmates to stop being bullied. In other words, *some* juveniles *some* of the time in *some* situations may see violence as an effective means to get what they want.[16]

Another reason why some juveniles make some bad choices is their lack of morality. James Q. Wilson thinks juveniles who behave badly do so because they have not had a sense of morality instilled into them:

> The moral relativism of the modern age has probably contributed to the increase in crime rates . . . It has done so by replacing the belief in personal responsibility with the notion of social causation and by supplying to those marginal persons at risk for crime a justification for doing what they might have done anyway.[17]

Psychologist Hans Eysenck, who blames juvenile violence on parental and societal permissiveness, agrees. According to Eysenck, how young people are reared today has produced a serious problem: They have not developed a conscience because they have not been taught to connect their misbehavior with a negative outcome. Delinquency is the price we pay for society and parents who are not doing their job.[18]

Choice Theory and Delinquency Prevention

In choice theory, delinquency can be prevented in one of two ways: through the *justice model* or through the *utilitarian punishment model.* Both models hold children responsible for their behavior; that is, both assume children are sufficiently rational, intelligent beings who exercise free will. These models assume that children calculate whether to commit crime based on the rewards and punishments they imagine they will receive *before* they act. The models differ on the reasons cited for doling out punishment, however: The *justice model* punishes offenders because of the social harm they have caused, whereas the *utilitarian punishment model* punishes offenders to protect society.

The Justice Model

In *We Are the Living Proof,* David Fogel introduced the **justice model**, which promotes the notion of fixed-time sentences, seeks to abolish parole, and would use prisons to punish offenders. Fogel argues that **indeterminate sentences**—that is, sentences of varying time lengths, such as 5 to 10 years— should be abolished and replaced with **determinate sentences**—that is, sentences of a fixed amount of time—because the courts cannot discriminate

between offenders who can be reformed and those who cannot. A fairer system would be one in which people who committed similar crimes received equivalent punishments.

Fogel's thinking is grounded in the idea of **retribution**, which states that criminals must be punished because of the social harm they have caused: *Punishment is criminals' just desserts.* Underlying retributive philosophy is the notion that punishment should reflect the seriousness of the crime and the culpability of the offender. In addition, when sentencing offenders, it is wrong to consider their needs. Instead, sentences should reflect only the penalties criminals deserve for breaking the law.[19]

Critics complain that Fogel's remedies pander to a correctional policy of despair rather than one of hope. There also is not much empirical evidence to support the idea that the justice model leads to a more humane and impartial criminal justice system. To the contrary, some state legislatures have established determinant or fixed-time sentences as a way to create more punitive sentences.[20]

The Utilitarian Punishment Model

At the core of the **utilitarian punishment model** is the idea that offenders must be punished to protect society. According to Ernest van den Haag:

> If a given offender's offenses are rational in the situation in which he lives—if what he can gain exceeds the likely cost to him by more than the gain from legitimate activities he does—there is little that can be "corrected" in the offender. Reform will fail. It often fails for this reason. What has to be changed is not the personality of the offender, but the cost–benefit ratio which makes his offense rational. The ratio can be changed by improving and multiplying his opportunities for legitimate activity and the benefits they yield, or

KEY TERMS

justice model
A corrections philosophy that promotes flat or fixed-time sentences, abolishment of parole, and use of prison to punish offenders.

indeterminate sentence
A prison sentence of varying time length, such as 5 to 10 years.

determinate sentence
A prison sentence of a fixed amount of time, such as 5 years.

retribution
A punishment philosophy based on society's moral outrage or disapproval of a crime.

utilitarian punishment model
The idea that offenders must be punished to protect society.

by decreasing this opportunity for illegitimate activities, or by increasing their cost to him, including punishment.[21]

In Van den Haag's opinion, punishment *deters crime*. If he is right, then it should be possible to prevent crime by punishing offenders more severely. This idea has steadily increased in popularity, based on research findings published by criminologists who calculated the risk of *actual* time served for each Crime Index offense. The likelihood of a person who commits a serious crime serving prison time is very, very low. As time served has increased, however, the crime rate has dropped.

Several delinquency prevention programs are based on the utilitarian punishment model. In *shock probation*, offenders experience fear through a short period of incarceration preceding probation. In *boot camps*, offenders are drilled and tormented for 60 to 90 days. In *Scared Straight*, juveniles attend presentations at adult prisons where hardened convicts and inmates serving life sentences yell and scream threats of assault and rape at them, letting them know what will happen if they come to prison.

Research evaluating the effectiveness of these programs has generally been critical of their ability to deter juvenile offenders.[22] In fact, instead of controlling crime, such programs tend to increase it. When Anthony Petrosino and his colleagues conducted a systematic review of Scared Straight programs, they found that youths who went through the program had higher rates of offending than youths who did not. According to these researchers, "on average these programs result in an increase in criminality in the experimental group when compared to a no-treatment control group. According to these experiments, doing nothing would have been better than exposing juveniles to the program."[23]

Public Adoption of Choice Theory

The general public also protects itself from criminal victimization by following the principles of choice theory. Matthew Giblin examined the ways that Americans protect themselves from criminal harm using a sample selected from 12 large cities. Giblin found that people take a variety of rational

steps to increase their personal security, including avoiding areas characterized by disorder and crime, altering their lifestyles to avoid risky situations, and becoming aware of the services that community police officers provide in terms of crime safety.[24] In this sense, choice theory has an important application to the everyday lives of citizens. Indeed, research has revealed that simple, everyday situational prevention strategies are the best way to guard against becoming a crime victim.[25]

Choice theories locate the cause of crime in the brain in the sense that people are rational and choose to commit delinquency just as they choose not to and to lead a conventional, crime-free life. The theories explored thus far, however, view choice as a social cognitive process but do not explore the actual role of the brain, and specific neural pathways within the brain. Others do. The rest of the chapter explores theory and research that uses biological constructs, such as the brain, genes, and hormones to explain why some individuals are more at risk for delinquent behavior, and others less so.

Biological Theories

The idea that criminals are biologically abnormal is very old. It can be traced to the *positive* school of criminology, which marked a shift in thinking about crime from the *act* to the *actor*. Charles Darwin was largely responsible for this change. In *On the Origin of Species*, he argued that God had not created *all* the species of animals, but rather that people had evolved from lower forms of life over the course of millions of years. Then, in *Descent of Man*, Darwin proposed that God had not made people in his own image and suggested that there are actually very few differences between people and animals.

Darwin's ideas captured the attention of a group of 19th-century criminologists, who called themselves *Positivists* because they believed using the scientific method was the best way to study crime. These scholars, who formed the **positive school** of criminology, attributed crime to factors that were in place *before* the crime was committed.

Atavism

The Italian criminologist Cesare Lombroso constructed the first biological theory of crime. He argued that you could tell how highly evolved someone was from his or her physical appearance. Applying Darwin's teachings, Lombroso theorized that criminals were **atavistic beings**—that is, throwbacks to an earlier, more primitive stage of human development. Criminals more closely resembled their ape-like ancestors in terms of their traits, abilities, and dispositions. Because criminals were not so highly evolved as their noncriminal counterparts, they possessed **stigmata**—distinctive

---

KEY TERMS

positive school
A school of thought that blames delinquency on factors that are in place before a crime is committed.

atavistic beings
The idea that criminals are a throwback to a more primitive stage of development.

stigmata
Distinctive physical features of born criminals.

In *On the Origin of Species*, Charles Darwin suggested that God had not created all the species of animals and that human beings have evolved from lower forms of life over millions of years. In a second book, *The Decent of Man*, Darwin challenged the belief that God had created people in his image. He argued that there were few differences between humans and animals, and therefore that the behavior of both was regulated by the same set of laws.

Courtesy of National Library of Medicine.

physical features, such as an asymmetrical face, an enormous jaw, large or protruding ears, and a receding chin—that distinguished them from ordinary people. Through no fault of their own, criminals were incapable of obeying the complex rules and regulations of modern society; for this reason, Lombroso stated, they should be placed in restrictive institutions, such as prisons.[26]

Years later, the English economist Charles Goring challenged the validity of Lombroso's findings. Goring compared the physical measurements of 3000 English convicts on 43 traits with similar measurements from a sample of university students. He found *no* evidence of a physical type of criminal.[27] Goring's conclusion remained unchallenged until 1939, when Harvard anthropologist Earnest Hooton discovered that Goring had ignored his own data that refuted his argument (and supported Lombroso). Upon reexamining Goring's data, Hooton found relative differences between criminals and nonoffenders.[28] What is interesting is that more than 125 years after

Lombroso made his claims, Zeynep Benderlioglu and his colleagues found that men and women with asymmetrical extremities—ears, fingers, or feet of different sizes or shapes—were more likely to react aggressively when annoyed or provoked. The researchers argued that factors such as smoking or drinking during a pregnancy might stress a fetus in various ways, causing slight physical imperfections and also poorer impulse control.[29]

Today, the notion that delinquents are atavistic, evolutionary throwbacks is no longer believed; however, this does not mean that evolutionary processes are unrelated to delinquent behavior. For example, the field of **evolutionary psychology** examines how evolutionary forces shape patterns of human cognition and behavior. Specific antisocial forms of behavior may be refined, enhanced, or curtailed over evolutionary time as people adapt to their environment for survival. In some cases, antisocial behaviors can be helpful for survival, such as the use of violence to resolve conflicts. Over time, however, antisocial behaviors are modified so that human groups can evolve into functional societies.[30] The overarching thesis of evolutionary psychology is that humans and their environment interact to produce adaptations that influence human behavior.

Body Type

In 1949, William Sheldon theorized there was a relationship between body type and delinquency, an idea known as **somatotype** theory. Sheldon identified three ideal body types (see **Figure 3.3**):

- *Ectomorphs,* who are introverted and overly sensitive, and who love privacy
- *Mesomorphs,* who are active and assertive, and who lust for power
- *Endomorphs,* who are relaxed, comfortable, extroverted "softies"

Sheldon tested his thesis by "typing" the bodies of 200 incarcerated juvenile offenders and 4000 male college students. He found that delinquents were more likely to be mesomorphs and much less likely to be ectomorphs. He detected no significant differences between the groups on endomorphy.[31]

Sheldon's research has since been replicated as other criminologists continue to search for a link between

KEY TERMS

evolutionary psychology
A branch of psychology that examines the ways that evolutionary forces shape patterns of human cognition and behavior.

somatotype
The idea that criminals can be identified by physical appearance.

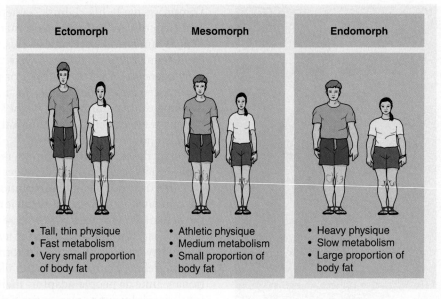

Figure 3.3 Sheldon's Types of Human Physiques

© Jones & Bartlett Learning.

mesomorphy and delinquency. For instance, when Sheldon Glueck and Eleanor Glueck compared the body types of 500 delinquents and 500 nondelinquents, they also found that delinquents were more likely to be mesomorphs.[32] Juan Cortes and Florence Gatti typed 100 delinquents and 100 high school students and reported similar findings—that 57% of the delinquents and only 20% of the nondelinquents were mesomorphs.[33]

More contemporary research has provided further support for Sheldon's hypothesis that mesomorphic people are more antisocial. Based on data from a sample of prisoners in the Arkansas Department of Corrections, Sean Maddan and his colleagues assessed the body type–delinquency relationship using the *body mass index* (BMI), which is calculated as a person's weight divided by his or her height squared. People who have a BMI over 26 are considered overweight (endomorphs). Those with a BMI between 19 and 25 are considered athletically fit and consistent with the mesomorphic body type. People who are frail and underweight have a BMI below 19, which is consistent with the ectomorphic body type. Maddan and his colleagues found that offenders with a mesomorph body type were significantly more likely than either ectomorphs or endomorphs to be incarcerated for a violent offense. Thus body type appears to have a minor, yet statistically significant effect on violent forms of delinquency.[34]

If there is a relationship between body type and delinquency, it could be linked to temperament. Adrian Raine, David Farrington, and their colleagues studied the effects of body size on delinquency in a sample of 1130 children. They found that large body size at age 3 was predictive of increased aggression at age 11. Large children tended to be more fearless

and stimulation seeking, but the effects of body size on delinquency remained even after controlling for temperament.[35] Using data from a national sample of American adolescents, J. C. Barnes and his colleagues found that height in adolescence predicts drug use in adolescence and young adulthood even when other important biological and social correlates of drug use are considered. Taller youths were more likely to use drugs, and the height–drug use link was found among boys and girls.[36]

Of course, there may be other explanations for this relationship. Perhaps mesomorphs are more effective at acting out their frustrations and desires than more delicately built children. Perhaps being muscular enables mesomorphs to be more readily admitted into delinquent gangs. Because masculinity allows someone to more easily dominate others, it might also encourage the use of violence and threats. Muscularity might also be perceived as a sign of masculinity and physical toughness, so that boys with muscles feel they need to play the role of "tough guy." In fact, ethnographic research suggests that male street offenders view criminal offending and substance abuse as ways to show their "manhood" and view others' inability to commit crime as a sign of weakness. Joshua Isen and his colleagues used data from two cohorts of children and found that childhood antisocial behaviors were associated with increased physical strength in boys between the ages of 11 and 17. In other words, more aggressive and delinquent boys were more likely to develop into physically strong—or mesomorphic—young men.[37] Finally, perhaps the relationship researchers have found between mesomorphy and delinquency results from juvenile justice officials—particularly law enforcement officers—regarding mesomorphy as a sign of danger and then reacting differently toward mesomorphs than they do toward juveniles with other body types.

Autonomic Hypoactivity and ADHD

In hindsight, early trait theories of delinquency seem almost laughable in their crudeness. However, scholarly investigations of the biological or physiological differences between serious delinquents and nondelinquents continued. Today, this line of research examines internal factors, such as heart rate, brain activity, and brain structure, rather than external differences, such as physical appearance.

The most consistently documented biological correlate of delinquency is *autonomic hypoactivity*—that is, an underaroused autonomic nervous system marked by a low resting heart rate. Low resting heart rate is more commonly found among males than females, among chronic offenders than normative delinquents, among violent offenders than nonviolent offenders, and among prisoners than those in the community. The relationship between low resting heart rate and problem behavior has been replicated in samples from Canada, England, Germany, Mauritius, New Zealand, and the United States.[38] When David Farrington examined the predictors of violence using 48 sociological, psychological, and biological independent variables, he found that low resting heart rate was *the* strongest and most consistent predictor of crime. More recent research by Todd Armstrong and his colleagues confirms that low resting heart rate is a robust predictor of delinquency and that individuals with the most hypoactive autonomic nervous systems are the most severe and aggressive offenders. In fact, low resting heart rate is also responsible for some of the association between social adversity and delinquency. Olivia Choy and her colleagues found that more than 20% of the relationship between exposure to social adversity and delinquency was explained by low resting heart rate. Autonomic indicators also explained more than 15% of the association between social adversity and overall antisocial conduct.[39]

Several explanations have been proposed for why resting heart rate is so strongly predictive of criminal behavior. For a variety of reasons—some known and others waiting to be discovered—there are important differences among people in terms of how their brains are structured and how their brains process information. A growing body of literature confirms that criminality is tied to differences in brain structure, which affects people's ability to exercise self-control (frontal lobe) and respond to environmental changes (temporal lobe). For some people, their brains produce either more or fewer neurotransmitters than they need. For example, those with brains that produce too little *serotonin* may have a behavioral condition that has been coupled with impulsivity, aggression,

and violent offending.[40] Recent evidence from brain scanning research suggests that persons with behavioral inhibition dysfunction have reduced activation or brain activity in the left dorsolateral prefrontal cortex, posterior cingulated gyrus, and bilateral temporal–parietal regions compared to children who are able to adequately modulate their behavior.[41] Another major area of research in neuropsychiatry focuses on scanning the brains of persons who appear to have physiological predispositions for behavioral problems (see **Box 3.5**, the "Delinquency Controversy" feature).

A possible consequence for children who have brains that produce too little serotonin or too much dopamine, which are important neurotransmitters that send communications between synapses in the brain, is **attention-deficit/hyperactivity disorder (ADHD)**. The most common neurobehavioral disorder of childhood, it affects between 4 and 12% of children ages 6 to 15. A physician in Providence, Rhode Island, while studying the causes of delinquency, discovered a medication-treatment for ADHD in the 1930s when he stumbled across a way to calm rowdy boys by giving them stimulants. Because low arousal is an unpleasant physiological state, youths seek stimulation to increase their arousal levels to normal levels. The stimulant helps persons with ADHD to achieve normal arousal levels. The discovery led to the creation of the first generation of drugs to treat ADHD.[42]

ADHD is generally recognizable by its symptoms, which include inattention and hyperactivity that cause difficulty in school, poor relationships with family and peers, and low self-esteem. Children with ADHD demonstrate the following behaviors:

- Are more than just fidgety—their "motor" is running all of the time
- Run, jump, and climb everywhere
- Constantly lose and misplace things
- Have difficulty following simple instructions
- Have trouble finishing work
- Need constant reminders to remain on task
- Do things without thinking about the consequences
- Are driven by the pursuit of immediate gratification

ADHD symptoms usually appear before age four. Often, children are not diagnosed with the disorder until they enter school, where they talk excessively, interrupt teachers, and commit physically dangerous acts. It is not easy, however, to determine whether a child has ADHD or some other disorder. In one

KEY TERMS

attention-deficit/hyperactivity disorder (ADHD)
The most common neurobehavioral childhood disorder, which is characterized by the following symptoms: inattention and hyperactivity that cause difficulty in school, poor relationships with family and peers, and low self-esteem.

BOX 3.5

Delinquency Controversy

Coming to Grips with ADHD

ADHD is one of the most common neuropsychiatric disorders worldwide and the label ADHD is a part of the public discourse in the United States. Unfortunately, that discourse often loosely uses the label ADHD to apply to children and adolescents with a wide range of symptoms, deficits, and conduct problems. ADHD is actually an umbrella term that includes three prototypes; one that refers mainly to inattention, one that refers mainly to hyperactivity and impulsivity, and a third combined type that encompasses both. It is ADHD Combined Type that is most intimately associated with conduct problems and delinquency.

Over a span of hundreds of years, scientists have struggled with how to describe and respond to what is today known as ADHD. Some of these labels throughout history include:

- defect of moral conduct
- defect of moral control
- postencephalitic behavior disorder
- hyperkinetic disease of infancy
- minimal brain damage
- minimal brain dysfunction
- sluggish cognitive temps
- hyperkinetic reaction in childhood

Because ADHD Combined Type includes broad deficits relating to social cognitive skills and self-regulation, it causes disruptions to children's development at school.

Unfortunately, because many of the same genes that are implicated in ADHD Combined Type are also involved with other conduct problems (this is known as the genetic concept of *pleiotropy*), children with ADHD Combined Type also commonly have other disorders. For example, about 50% of children with ADHD Combined Type also have Oppositional Defiant Disorder, and nearly 40% also have Conduct Disorder. Recent longitudinal research found that children with ADHD exhibit four to five times more symptoms of Conduct Disorder than their peers with an ADHD diagnosis.

ADHD is a disorder that is familiar to the general public, and its negative consequences are well known. Less well known are the characteristics of youth who display extremely low ADHD traits. A study of more than 2000 twin pairs from the Twins Early Development Study found that children and adolescents with very low ADHD traits have less depression, fewer emotional problems, and significantly better conduct. They also perform much better in English, math, and overall cognitive ability, are more prosocial, and report higher life satisfaction and greater happiness. Youth with extremely low ADHD traits also experience better parenting, less abuse, and are raised in more healthy home environments.

Thus, ADHD exists as a manageable disorder that is overcome with treatment and medication *and* a potent risk factor for severe conduct problems that lead to delinquency and adult crime.

Russell Barkley, "A Brief Note on the History of Executive Functioning," *The ADHD Report* 24:14 (2016); Dorothy Stubbe, "ADHD: An Overview," *Psychiatric Annals* 46:33–38 (2016); Klaus Lange, Susanne Reichl, Katharina Lange, Lara Tucha, and Oliver Tucha, "The History of ADHD," *ADHD* 2:241–255 (2010); Kate Langley, Jon Heron, Michael O'Donovan, Michael Owen, and Anita Thapar, "Genotype Link with Extreme Antisocial Behavior: The Contribution of Cognitive Pathways," *Archives of General Psychiatry* 67:1317–1323 (2010); Alison Pritchard, Carly Nigro, Lisa Jacobson, and Mark Mahone, "The Role of Neuropsychological Assessment in the Functional Outcomes of Children with ADHD," *Neuropsychology Review* 22:54–68 (2012); Corina Greven, Andrew Merwood, Jolanda van der Meer, Claire Haworth, Nanda Rommelse, and Jan Buitelaar, "The Opposite End of the ADHD Continuum: Genetic and Environmental Aetiologies of Extremely Low ADHD Traits," *Journal of Child Psychology and Psychiatry* 57:523–531 (2016).

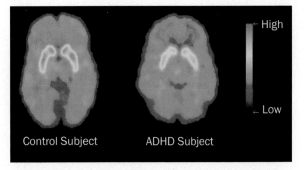

Research on ADHD has shown the essential role of the brain in self-regulation and overall behavior control.

© Science Source.

study, more than half of the children who received medication for ADHD did not have this condition.[43]

Estimates of the prevalence of ADHD vary. As noted earlier, it has been estimated that between 4 and 12% of the school-age population (children ages 6 to 12) are diagnosed with ADHD, and the disorder is approximately five times more common in boys than in girls.[44] The adult prevalence of ADHD in the United States has been estimated at 4% based on the National Comorbidity Survey Replication.[45] Because ADHD is a relatively stable disorder, the adult prevalence should be consistent with the ADHD prevalence in children and adolescents. ADHD in girls, however, may be as common as it is among boys and might be underdiagnosed because girls with ADHD have developed more passive and acceptable coping strategies than boys. Rather than being rebellious, ADHD girls often are inattentive and misdiagnosed as being lazy or spacey when they are not.[46] For instance, Teresa Nadder and her colleagues found that the symptoms of ADHD are similar for boys and girls.[47] Compared to girls who do not have ADHD, girls with the disorder are more likely to have conduct disorder, depression, anxiety, alcoholism, substance abuse problems, anorexia, and bulimia; they are also more likely to smoke.[48]

The causes of ADHD are not entirely known. In reports by the mainstream media, this condition has been tied to heredity, prenatal stress, neurological damage, food allergies, family turmoil, and more. In fact, *ADHD is almost entirely caused by genetic factors.* Soo Rhee and her colleagues assessed the genetic and environmental influences of ADHD using data from 2391 twin and sibling pairs from Australia. They found that between *85 and 90% of ADHD symptoms were* directly attributable to genes.[49] For instance, studies by behavioral geneticists found that persons with the 7-repeat allele of the dopamine D4 receptor gene (DRD4) develop ADHD.[50] Stephen Faraone and his colleagues confirmed that abnormalities in DRD4 are likely the genetic cause of ADHD. In addition, meta-analytic research has indicated that DRD4 is also broadly associated with attention and behavioral problems among youth with or without ADHD.[51]

What does this molecular genetics language mean? Basically, crucial parts of the brains of children with ADHD develop more slowly than other children's brains. These slower-developing regions are related to the parts of the brain that control the ability to focus attention, suppress inappropriate actions and thoughts, use short-term memory, work for reward, and control movement. When children have inefficient forms of genes—variants of genes are called *polymorphisms*—their brains do not perform at an optimal level.

There are many negative consequences of having ADHD. For instance, children with ADHD are more likely to be depressed, to have speech and language impediments, and to have learning disabilities. They also engage in more problematic behaviors throughout their lives. In turn, they are arrested, adjudicated delinquent, and become adult criminals much more often than non-ADHD children. Nondelinquents with ADHD have been found to have better cognitive functioning and verbal skills than ADHD delinquents, who, in turn, have more cognitive defects than non-ADHD delinquents. When James Satterfield and his colleagues compared 110 children with ADHD and 88 non-ADHD children, they found that the children with ADHD were more likely to be arrested for a serious crime and were 21 times more likely to be institutionalized for antisocial behavior.[52] Children with ADHD display a range of cognitive and behavioral problems that

often rub teachers and other students the wrong way, as a result, children with ADHD are more likely to be rejected by their peers. Peer rejection creates doubly negative consequences, the peer rejection worsens the ADHD traits and makes conduct problems and delinquency more likely. Although there is a consistent association between ADHD and delinquency, the fortunate news is that behavioral interventions are effective at improving the conduct and other problems of youth with ADHD. David Daley and his associates conducted a meta-analysis of behavioral interventions and found significant improvements in positive parenting, conduct problems, social skills, and academic performance among ADHD youth who participated in behavioral treatment regimes.[53]

In the United States, many medical centers treat ADHD. The most common treatment is drug therapy—specifically, methylphenidate (Ritalin) or an amphetamine (Adderall or Dexedrine). The ADHD drug treatment industry is a multibillion-dollar business. With children as young as age 5 being prescribed methylphenidate or an amphetamine, there is concern about the long-term side effects these drugs may have, such as psychosis, mania, loss of appetite, depression,

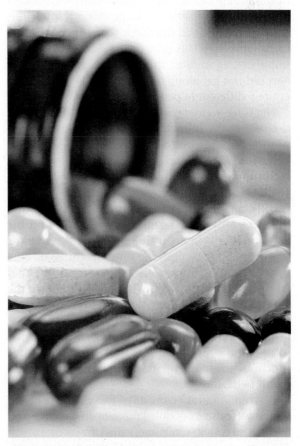

As researchers learn ever more about brain function and dysfunction, it is likely that additional drugs will be developed to treat behavioral disorders. The benefits of overcoming ADHD are many, but what are the costs?

© monticello/Shutterstock.

sleep problems, moodiness, and stunting of growth. Matthew Hutson reports that as many as 5% of children who are prescribed Ritalin complain of psychotic, delusional episodes where they believe that bugs are infesting their bodies.[54] Research indicates that children metabolize medications differently than adults; the brain also develops much more rapidly in children than in adults. Some studies have demonstrated that the maturing neurotransmitter system in children's brains is so sensitive to drugs that the drugs may cause permanent changes in the child's adult life.[55] This concern is the source of the current controversy over use of stimulants such as Ritalin in young children.

Frontal Lobes and Executive Functioning

On September 13, 1848, a freakish accident affecting railroad worker Phineas Gage occurred that would lead to an important scientific discovery about the human brain and its control over various aspects of behavior. While workers were setting railroad track, an explosives accident sent a tamping iron, 3 feet long and weighing about 13 pounds, through Gage's cheekbone and out the anterior frontal cortex of his head. Amazingly, not only did Gage survive the accident, but he appeared to be generally okay, suffering only minimal blood loss. His personality was another story. Before the accident, Gage was a responsible, hard-working, disciplined, congenial man who got along well with others. After the accident, he was highly impulsive, egocentric, irresponsible, and irreverent, and did not get along well with others. He seemed entirely different in personality and temperament.[56]

The Gage accident is commonly cited to illustrate the role of the human brain, and various sections of the brain, in controlling different aspects of our behavior. With the advancement of neuroimaging techniques, such as magnetic resonance imaging (MRI), functional magnetic resonance imaging (fMRI), and positron emission tomography (PET), neuroscientists have learned a great deal about the workings of the brain, including how different parts of the brain are responsible for different tasks. One of the more significant discoveries—and one that has direct application to delinquency—relates to the functions and operations of the prefrontal cortex.[57]

The radical change in the personality of Phineas Gage highlighted its biological origins. The frontal lobes are the anatomical location of the executive functions and have important implications for delinquent behavior.

The human brain consists of two main areas: the *subcortex* (sometimes called the subcortical area) and the *cerebral* cortex (sometimes called the cortical area). The subcortex is located beneath the cerebral cortex and contains the brain stem, the midbrain, and the forebrain. It performs many duties, but is primarily responsible for many of the lower order functions of humans, such as the regulation of breathing and the

activation of reflexes (see **Box 3.6**, the "A Window on Delinquency" feature for a look at the many deficits of the teenage brain).

Most research examining the neurological basis of antisocial behaviors has focused on the cerebral cortex.[58] The human brain has two hemispheres (i.e., the left hemisphere and the right hemisphere), and the cerebral cortex is found on the outer edges of both. Each hemisphere can be artificially divided into four lobes: the frontal lobe, the temporal lobe, the parietal lobe, and the occipital lobe. Although each lobe performs specialized functions for the human brain, the lobes most likely to be related to antisocial behaviors and traits are the two frontal lobes (one corresponding to each hemisphere).

The coordinated activities of the frontal lobes are referred to as *executive functions*; this cluster of higher order cognitive processes, involving initiation, planning, cognitive flexibility, abstraction, and decision making, collectively allows the execution of contextually appropriate behavior.[59] Terrie Moffitt describes the day-to-day operations of the frontal lobes in this way:

> [T]he normal functions of the frontal lobes of the brain include sustaining attention and concentration, abstract reasoning and concept formation, goal formulation, anticipation and planning, programming and initiation of purposive sequences of motor behavior, effective self-monitoring of behavior and self-awareness, and inhibition of unsuccessful, inappropriate, or impulsive behaviors, with adaptive shifting to alternative behaviors. These functions are commonly referred to as "executive functions," and they hold consequent implications for social judgment, self-control, responsiveness to punishment, and ethical behavior.[60]

Executive functioning has clear implications for involvement in delinquency because it deals with regulating impulsive tendencies, controlling emotions, sustaining attention, appreciating behavioral

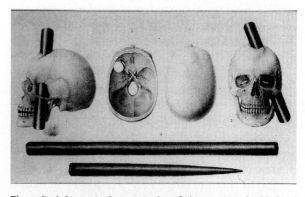

The radical change in the personality of Phineas Gage highlighted its biological origins. The frontal lobes are the anatomical location of the executive functions and have important implications for delinquent behavior.

Courtesy of National Library of Medicine.

BOX 3.6

A Window on Delinquency

The Criminology of the Teenage Brain

The impulsive behaviors that occur during adolescence have long been recognized and have been documented in scores of songs, television programs, and films throughout American history.

Increasingly, brain functioning is seen as a major reason why delinquency peaks during adolescence—the young brain is simply not as mature as it is in adults. In fact, in 2005, the U.S. Supreme Court used information about adolescent brain development to inform their decision to prohibit capital punishment for juveniles in the landmark case *Roper v. Simmons*. Laurence Steinberg—one of the foremost scholars in the study of adolescence—is also a major advocate for spreading neuroscientific findings about the brain bases of adolescent decision making and behavior. Recently, he suggested:

As a scientist who has been working in the field of adolescent development long enough to remember when such a field did not exist, I can say with great certainty that there has never been a more exciting time to be studying this phase of life. Much of this excitement comes from discoveries made within the laboratories of brain scientists, but the real excitement will come when this work is more fully integrated with psychological and contextual studies of this period of the life cycle.

In 2013, a special issue of *Current Directions in Psychological Science* was devoted to the teenage brain and the issue included brief summary reports from leading behavioral scientists from around the world. It is clear that adolescent delinquency and problem behaviors are far more widespread than simple impulsivity. On a variety of domains, including self-control, sensitivity to rewards, cognitive control, cognitive motivation, functional connectivity, sensitivity to social evaluation, fear processing, the effects of drug and alcohol, and others, the teenage brain is much weaker than the adult brain in terms of behavioral control. Thus, as adolescents become adults, so too do their brains and the numerous and extraordinary functions therein. The result is more adult behaviors, one of which is, fortunately, a sharp decline in antisocial conduct.

B. J. Casey and Kristina Caudle, "The Teenage Brain: Self-Control," *Current Directions in Psychological Science* 22:8287 (2013); Adriana Galvan, "The Teenage Brain: Sensitivity to Rewards," *Current Directions in Psychological Science* 22:88–93 (2013); Leah Somerville, "The Teenage Brain: Sensitivity to Social Evaluation," *Current Directions in Psychological Science* 22:121–127 (2013); Jiska Peper and Ronald Dahl, "The Teenage Brain: Surging Hormones—Brain-Behavior Interactions during Puberty," *Current Directions in Psychological Science* 22:134–139 (2013); Linda Spear, "The Teenage Brain: Adolescents and Alcohol," *Current Directions in Psychological Science* 22:152–157 (2013); Richard Bonnie and Elizabeth Scott, "The Teenage Brain: Adolescent Brain Research and the Law," *Current Directions in Psychological Science* 22:158–161 (2013); Laurence Steinberg, "A Behavioral Scientist Looks at the Science of Adolescent Brain Development," *Brain and Cognition* 72:160–164 (2010), p. 163.

consequences, and inhibiting inappropriate conduct. Research has clearly linked frontal lobe damage and impairments in executive functioning to delinquency, especially among the most severe types of offenders, such as life-course persistent offenders and psychopaths.[61]

In addition to injuries like those sustained by Phineas Gage, brain damage that results from many other causes may affect human behavior. Researchers have shown that genetic risks relating to one polymorphism, known as monoamine oxidase A (MAOA), predispose persons to impulsive behavior and affect the frontal lobes.[62]

Kathleen Heide and Eldra Solomon have documented how prolonged abuse and neglect of children can lead to biological changes in the ways their brains process and respond to social stimuli. These environmentally induced changes in brain chemistry place individuals at greater risk for delinquency, especially the most serious forms of violence.[63] Heide and Solomon's work points to the essence of biologically based theories of delinquency—namely, the interconnections between genes, biological functioning, and the social environment. The interplay between nature and nurture is complex and reciprocal, and the following sections highlight how these forces combine to produce delinquency.

How Does Biology Work? The Nature–Nurture Interplay

Early biological theories of crime pointed to features on the human body as evidence of criminality. Today, it is understood that biology affects behavior both through its heritability (for instance, through characteristics people inherit from their biological parents) and through its direct effects on human behavior (such as brain functioning). This section highlights how biological factors translate into social behavior, including delinquency.

An individual's genetic composition, or **genotype**, is largely responsible for shaping, structuring, and

KEY TERMS

genotype
A person's genetic composition.

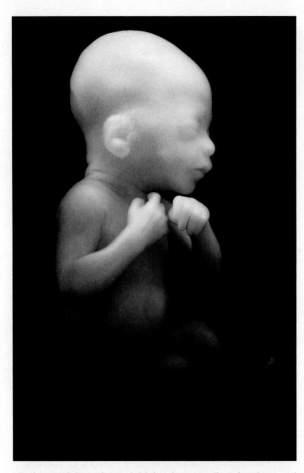

The brain of the unborn child develops rapidly. Fifty-thousand neurons per second are generated during the gestation of a fetus; 200 billion nerve cells throughout the body begin firing signals to an infant's brain with its first breath, while three billion learning connections per second are made in a child's brain.

© ninjaMonkeyStudio/E+/Getty.

selecting those environments that allow for optimal gene expression.[64] The ways that genes connect with environmental conditions is referred to as a gene x environment correlation. Gene x environment correlations (rGE) are important explanations for why researchers often find a correlation between an individual's personality or temperament and the environment in which the person finds himself or herself.

Most personalities and temperaments are partially heritable. People with certain personality traits, such as a penchant for thrill seeking, are apt to find themselves in dangerous or risky situations, such as bungee-jumping or skydiving classes. In contrast, an individual with a cautious or docile disposition would probably pass up the opportunity to jump out of an airplane in favor of a less hazardous and more mundane activity. In this case, the genes responsible for the creation of personality characteristics are also the genes responsible for the creation of the environment. Three main types of rGEs are distinguished—passive, evocative, and active—each of which accounts for a unique process by which genetic factors influence or otherwise mold the environment.[65]

Passive rGEs build on the fact that parents pass along two different elements to their children: genes and an environment. Because children receive half of their genes from each parent and are born into environments that are largely created from, or reflect, their parents' genetic makeup, it is not surprising that children's genetic propensities are correlated with the environment into which they are born. This type of rGE is referred to as a passive rGE because the child does not have an active voice in choosing his or her genotype or familial environment; instead, these elements are passively passed on from parent to offspring.

Evocative rGEs, the second type of rGEs, reflect the fact that people elicit certain responses from the environment based, in part, on their genes. A person with one genotype may evoke one type of response from the environment, whereas another person, owing to his or her own unique genotype, may evoke a completely different response. For example, family researchers have long recognized that parents treat their children very differently depending on how their children behave. A difficult and taxing child will likely be reprimanded, punished, and disciplined regularly by his or her parents. A sibling who has an easygoing personality and who is relatively obedient, in contrast, will be much more enjoyable for parents to raise, so punishment will be less frequent. In this case, children, depending on their unique genotypes, evoke differential responses from their parents.[66] These different familial environments are correlated with the child's genetically influenced temperaments. Evocative rGEs can be best summarized by stating that certain genetic polymorphisms elicit particular responses from the environment, and these responses are correlated with the person's genotype.

Active rGEs have the most relevance for criminologists because they help explain why some adolescents associate with delinquent peers.[67] Youths actively seek out and select environments or *niches* that are compatible with their personalities and other genetic predispositions. For some adolescents, especially those with a genetic proclivity to engage in mischief, antisocial friendship groups may be alluring and seductive. Other youths—particularly those who are not genetically predisposed to become involved in delinquency—may veer away from deviant peers and select more prosocial youths to befriend.[68] According to the logic of active rGEs, the individual person plays an important role in identifying and selecting environments that reinforce his or her genetic makeup (see **Box 3.7**, the "Delinquency Controversy" feature).[69]

Intelligence

The relationship between intelligence and delinquency has had a long and colorful history. In 1575,

BOX 3.7

Delinquency Controversy

Do Parents Matter?

Judith Rich Harris answers the question, "Do parents have any important long-term effects on the development of their child's personality?" with a resounding "No!" She contends that the peer relationships that children form with other children are primarily responsible for inculcating culture and modifying innate personality features. It is within these friendship groups that the psychological traits that a child is born with become permanently modified by the environment.

According to Harris, two processes—not our parents—make us who we are: assimilation and differentiation. *Assimilation* transmits cultural norms, smoothes off rough edges of the personality, and makes children more like their peers. In contrast, *differentiation* exaggerates individual differences and increases variability. Whether assimilation or differentiation occurs at a given point depends on the context of the interaction (e.g., participating in a sporting event, sitting in the classroom, playing at recess). In behavioral genetic parlance, this means that the effects of the nonshared environment are significantly more powerful than the effects of the shared environment.

Harris's work has had great public impact and is highly controversial mainly because *it contradicts the notion that parents are most directly responsible for people's personalities and behaviors because of the ways that they socialize their children*. Instead, according to Harris, parents are important simply because they pass on their genetic information to their children. Otherwise, personality and behavior are molded by peer relationships occurring outside the home.

Behavioral genetics research shows that genes and environmental influences are crucial to our development, but not all environmental influences have equal weight. Approximately 40 to 50% of the variance in delinquency is attributable to nonshared environment factors, whereas 0 to 10% is the result of shared (family) environment. According to Robert Plomin and Denise Daniels, "behavioral genetic studies consistently point to nonshared environment as the most important source of environmental variance for personality, psychology, and IQ after childhood. . . . children in the same family experience practically no shared environmental influence that makes them similar for behavior traits." Of course, behavioral genetic studies do not show that parents are irrelevant in the behavioral outcomes of their children. But, they show that most of the parental influence is genetic, and that environmental contributions mostly come from other sources, such as peers.

Judith Rich Harris, "Where Is the Child's Environment? A Group Socialization Theory of Development," *Psychological Review* 102:458–489 (1995); Judith Rich Harris, *The Nurture Assumption: Why Children Turn Out the Way They Do* (New York: Free Press, 1998); Judith Rich Harris, *No Two Alike: Human Nature and Human Individuality* (New York: W. W. Norton, 2007); David Rowe, *The Limits of Family Influence: Genes, Experience, and Behavior* (New York: Guilford Press, 1994); Robert Plomin and Denise Daniels, "Why Are Children in the Same Family So Different from One Another?" *Behavioral and Brain Sciences* 10:1–60 (1987); Kim Veroude, Yanli Zhang-James, Noèlia Fernàndez-Castillo, Mireille Bakker, Bru Cormand, and Stephen Faraone, "Genetics of Aggressive Behavior: An Overview," *American Journal of Medical Genetics Part B: Neuropsychiatric Genetics* 171:3–43 (2016).

the Spanish physician Juan Huarte formally defined **intelligence** as the ability to learn, exercise judgment, and be imaginative. Since the 16th century, scientists have designed different ways to measure intelligence. In 1905, Alfred Binet and Theophile Simon developed the first standardized IQ test. In 1912, the German psychologist William Stern introduced the idea of an "intelligence quotient" (IQ), claiming that every person has a mental age that can be represented by an **IQ score**, defined as the ratio of the person's mental age divided by the person's chronological age and multiplied by 100. The "average" ability for any age is 100, which is the point at which mental age and chronological age are equal.

Most of the early researchers who studied intelligence said very little about the heritability of intelligence. The idea that intelligence might be inherited was popularized in 1916 by Stanford University psychology professor Lewis Terman, who revised the Binet-Simon test and renamed it the Stanford-Binet Intelligence Test; the revised test remains widely used today. Criminologists at the beginning of the

20th century who were trained in medicine or in psychology made some inflated and inflammatory claims about the relationship between intelligence and crime. Specifically, they suggested that people of low intelligence were easily led into law-breaking activities by more clever people and did not realize that committing an offense in a certain way often led to getting caught and being punished.

One psychologist, Henry Goddard, who coined the term "moron," administered intelligence tests to prison and jail inmates and reported that 70% were "feebleminded." This very high percentage

KEY TERMS

intelligence
The ability to learn, exercise judgment, and be imaginative.

IQ score
Ratio of the person's mental age divided by the person's chronological age and multiplied by 100.

of low-intelligence inmates led the public, social reformers, and state legislators to conclude that low intelligence predisposed people to commit crime. Goddard's conclusion stood unchallenged for more than a decade.[70] In 1926, however, in a study comparing more than 1500 delinquent males with a group of male nondelinquents, John Slawson found no relationship between IQ and criminality.[71] Later replications and extensions of Slawson's pioneering work seemed to confirm his findings. In 1928, Barbara Burks, who studied the intelligence of children of mentally deficient parents, reported that when the children were placed in foster homes with a nurturing environment, their IQ scores reached normal levels.[72] In 1931, Edwin Sutherland evaluated IQ studies of delinquents and believed that he refuted the idea that any significant relationship might exist between IQ and delinquency.[73]

Intelligence and Delinquency

The early research on the relationship between IQ and delinquency relied on relatively simple methodologies and statistical techniques. In contrast, contemporary research, which is more methodologically sophisticated, consistently reports a connection between IQ and delinquency. In a groundbreaking study, Travis Hirschi and Michael Hindelang found that *IQ is a better predictor of involvement in delinquency than either race or social class* and that the IQ of the average delinquent is about eight points lower than the IQ of the average nondelinquent.[74] Other researchers have confirmed these conclusions. Donald Lynam and his colleagues reported that IQ predicted delinquency even when controlling for important correlates of delinquency, such as social class, race, and academic motivation.[75] Leslie Leve and Patricia Chamberlain reported that girls with low intelligence were significantly more likely to have an early onset of antisocial behavior, which often sets the stage for a sustained delinquent career.[76]

Intelligence also has been linked to the most serious forms of criminal behavior. For instance, Jean-Pierre Guay and his colleagues evaluated the intelligence–crime link among 261 sex offenders and 150 nonsexual violent offenders in Canada. They found that sex offenders have significantly impaired cognitive abilities compared to other criminals in areas such as vocabulary, comprehension, arithmetic, mental math computations, object assembly, letter–number sequencing, and perception.[77]

Exactly how intelligence affects delinquency is puzzling. There are no less than five possibilities.

First, intelligence might have no effect. Perhaps both intelligence and delinquency are affected by some third variable (a spurious relationship), such as social class. This hypothesis is commonly held, but it has no empirical support. Within the same social class, students with lower IQs have been reported as having higher rates of delinquency.

Second, Adrian Raine and his colleagues found that criminal offenders are more likely to suffer from brain dysfunction as a result of birth complications, environmental toxins, and head injuries, which lead to problem behaviors and having a low IQ. Raine thinks that early brain damage causes cognitive deficiencies that produce an array of endless problems for children, such as doing poorly in school and low self-esteem, which in turn lead to delinquency.[78]

Third, the relationship between intelligence and delinquency may be confounded by moral reasoning and *cognitive empathy* (which is the ability to understand and share in another person's emotional state or context). Darrick Jolliffe and David Farrington analyzed 35 studies of cognitive empathy, intelligence, and delinquency. They found that persons who have weak cognitive empathy are more likely than others to be criminal offenders, an effect that was particularly pronounced among violent offenders. Interestingly, the linkages between cognitive empathy and crime disappeared once intelligence was considered. From this perspective, both delinquency and ability to empathize with others are controlled by intelligence.[79]

Fourth, some criminologists believe that intelligence influences delinquency *indirectly*—that is, the effect is transmitted through school-experience variables. One purpose of IQ tests is to predict how well a person will do in school. Although they are not perfect, IQ tests do have a reasonably good prediction record in this regard: Students who perform well on IQ tests tend to get good grades. School performance (grades) affects various aspects of a student's life, but especially the student's attitude toward school. Students who receive good grades find school more enjoyable than students who receive poor grades, and they seem to be more accepting of a school's authority. Students who believe in the school's authority are not as likely to break the rules and are less likely to become delinquent. Looking at the issue from this perspective, we can say that low IQ leads to lower grades in school, lower grades lead to disliking school, disliking school leads to rejecting its authority, and this rejection of authority leads some students into delinquency.[80] Jean McGloin and her colleagues found that intelligence did not directly predict delinquency, but did predict poor school performance, association with deviant peers, and low self-control. In turn, all of these variables were directly related to delinquency.[81] Similarly, Chris Gibson and his colleagues have reported that the independent effect of low intelligence *interacts* with family adversity to explain delinquency.[82]

Fifth, Thomas Bouchard and his colleagues suggest that the abilities measured by IQ tests are partly genetic. For example, verbal abilities may be as inheritable as nonverbal abilities. Their theory is based on data from the Minnesota Twin Family Study, an ongoing 20-year longitudinal study of identical twins (also known as monozygotic [MZ] twins) and fraternal twins (also known as dizygotic [DZ] twins) who were reared apart. These researchers have found evidence of a strong genetic component in many psychological traits, including IQ. With respect to intelligence, the researchers concluded that 70% of the influence on IQ scores is genetic and 30% comes from the environment. According to Bouchard and his colleagues, "Although parents may be able to affect their children's rate of cognitive skill acquisition, they may have relatively little influence on the ultimate level attained."[83]

Hormones and Puberty

It is easy to recognize the effects of "raging hormones" and puberty on behavior during adolescence. For many parents, the years when their children are teenagers are the most challenging. Over the years, criminologists have explored the effects of hormones and puberty on delinquency. In particular, they have focused on the potential effects of testosterone, which is a hormone largely responsible for the maintenance of secondary sex characteristics in males.[84] Testosterone is also a correlate of aggression.

For instance, James Dabbs and Robin Morris assessed the relationship between testosterone, social class, and antisocial behavior using a sample of 4462 American military veterans. The majority of the sample, 4000 veterans, had normal testosterone levels. By comparison, 446 veterans had high testosterone levels. The latter group was characterized by significantly higher levels of childhood and adult delinquency; narcotic, marijuana, and alcohol use; sexual promiscuity; and military AWOL (absent without leave) behavior. Further, socioeconomic status (SES) moderated the independent effects of testosterone, as risk ratios were twice as high in the low-SES group compared to the high-SES group.[85] Alan Booth and Wayne Osgood similarly found a significant relationship between testosterone and deviance, and noted that this relationship was mediated by the influence of testosterone on social integration and prior delinquency.[86] Both studies demonstrate that hormonal factors interact with social and environmental conditions to produce various behavioral effects.

Hormonal effects on delinquency also have been found among correctional samples and among persons who demonstrate more extreme forms of antisocial conduct. James Dabbs and his colleagues reported a relationship between testosterone level and criminal violence among a sample of 89 male prisoners. Among the 11 offenders with the lowest testosterone levels, 9 had committed nonviolent offenses. Among the 11 offenders with the highest testosterone levels, 9 had committed violent crimes.[87]

It also has been reported that inmates who have been convicted of murder, rape, and child molestation have significantly higher testosterone levels than offenders convicted of other felonies. Moreover, testosterone level significantly predicts inmate infractions: Inmates with high hormonal levels tend to commit the most serious types of misconduct, such as assaulting inmates and committing other acts of overt confrontation.[88] Higher testosterone levels also have been reported among homicide offenders who were convicted of premeditated, more "ruthless" types of murder.[89]

The relationship between puberty and delinquency is multifaceted and important for both teenage boys and girls. Richard Felson and Dana Haynie have found that adolescent boys who are more physically developed than their peers are more likely to engage in violent and property crimes, drug use, and sexual activity. Interestingly, these effects of puberty on delinquency were direct and not explained by other individual factors. In fact, Felson and Haynie concluded that the effects of puberty on delinquency are stronger than the effects of social class, race, and family structure.[90]

Among adolescent girls, early pubertal development leads to more strained relationships with parents and "party"-related deviance, such as excessive drinking and drug use.[91] Research based on a nationally representative sample of American youths reported that adolescents who go through puberty early are also more likely to be the victims of crime—an effect that is notably stronger among physically developed girls who are dating.[92] When Kevin Beaver and John Wright assessed how puberty related to adolescent development and delinquency among a national sample of 6504 youths, they found that among both boys and girls, early puberty contributed to greater association with delinquent peers and, in turn, to greater delinquency. These effects of puberty on delinquency were more pronounced among males than females, however. During puberty, the early-developing boys tended to have poorer impulse control, have more negative interaction styles with parents and peers, and associate more frequently with other delinquent boys.[93]

Family, Twin, and Adoption Studies

Criminologists have commonly used family studies to examine the heritability of antisocial behavior. In family studies, index subjects, known as *probands*, who present the trait or behavior under investigation, such as criminality, are compared to a control group of persons who do not present the trait or behavior. From these study groups, the prevalence of the trait is examined among first-degree relatives (children, siblings, or parents) of the proband and control subjects. Genetic effects are inferred or estimated when the trait or behavior is more prevalent among relatives of the probands than among relatives of the control group.

Sheldon Glueck and Eleanor Glueck used family study designs to examine the heritability of crime among their classic samples of delinquent youth. In their sample of male delinquents, the Gluecks found that the prevalence of family member arrest was nearly

200% greater among probands than among controls.[94] For females, the prevalence of family member arrest was about 160% higher among probands than among controls. In short, the Gluecks provided speculative but empirically compelling evidence that crime "runs in the family."[95]

Robert Cloninger and Samuel Guze produced even stronger evidence for the heritability of crime in their studies of the transmission of sociopathy among families. In a study of 519 first-degree relatives of sociopathic males, the prevalence of sociopathy among proband subjects was more than 330% higher than among controls. The researchers found even stronger effects among female index subjects using arrests and sociopathy diagnosis as outcomes: The prevalence of arrest and sociopathy diagnoses were nearly 700% greater among probands than among control subjects. Their work provides compelling evidence that the most serious forms of delinquency are largely inherited.[96]

David Rowe and David Farrington examined the familial transmission of criminal convictions using data from 344 families with two or more children selected from a British sample. These researchers assessed whether the effect of parent convictions on children convictions was direct or was mediated through the quality of the family environment, as evidenced by parental supervision, child rearing, and family size. Rowe and Farrington found a direct effect without mediation from family environment and concluded that "unmeasured genetic or environment influences may determine convictions to a greater degree than measured aspects of the family environment."[97] It also has been reported that paternal criminality is the strongest familial predictor of delinquency in children.[98] To illustrate this point, children of murderers are a staggering *2400%* more likely to commit violent crimes than children whose parents were not murderers.[99]

Another way to evaluate the impact of heredity on behavior is to study twins. **Monozygotic twins (MZ)**, also known as identical twins, have identical DNA and come from one fertilized egg; **dizygotic twins (DZ)**, also known as fraternal twins, come from two separate eggs fertilized at the same time. Fraternal twins are no more alike genetically than nontwin siblings. If a genetic factor truly plays a role in determining delinquency, MZ twins should be more alike than DZ twins. This similarity, which is

called *concordance*, occurs when both twins share a characteristic. For example, if one twin is delinquent and the other twin is also delinquent, there exists concordance with respect to delinquency. Conversely, if one twin is delinquent and the other is not, the discrepancy is called *discordance*.

In 1929, Johannes Lange published the first study of twins and criminality. He examined 37 twin pairs including 13 MZ twins, 17 DZ twins, and 7 pairs who could not be classified. In each pair, at least one twin had been in prison. In 10 of the 13 MZ pairs, the other twin had also been in prison, whereas in only 2 of the 17 DZ pairs had both twins served prison sentences.[100]

Karl Christiansen completed the earliest comprehensive twin study in Denmark. He identified 3586 twin pairs born between 1870 and 1920 who were listed in the Danish Twin Register. Christiansen then reviewed police records and court documents for each twin set. A total of 926 twins belonging to 799 of the pairs had committed at least one criminal offense. When Christiansen computed the criminal concordance rates for the sample, he found much greater concordance among crime and criminal careers for MZ twins than for DZ twins.[101]

David Rowe and Wayne Osgood examined the genetic and environmental causes of antisocial behavior using a sample of 168 MZ twin pairs and 97 same-sex DZ twin pairs. They explored the frequency with which the youth committed assorted interpersonal (violent), property, and nuisance offenses during the prior year. These researchers found that more than 60% of the variation in antisocial acts and delinquent peer associations was accounted for by genetic factors. Among male twins, genes explained 61% of the variation and environmental factors explained 39% of the variation. Among female twins, genes accounted for 64% of the variation, with environmental factors explaining the remaining 36%.[102]

In a subsequent study, Rowe examined environmental and hereditary components of antisocial behavior. In his investigation, common-family environment—which includes social class, childrearing styles, parental attitudes, parental religion, and other factors—*did not* influence antisocial behavior, but heredity did. The primary genetic antecedents of antisocial behavior were deceitfulness and temperamental traits, such as lack of empathy, anger, and impulsivity.[103]

The most impressive behavioral genetic study in terms of size examined the heritability of violent crime in a population of more than 1.8 million people in Sweden. Nearly 60% of the variance in violent crime was attributable to genetic factors, which is comparable to heritable estimates for aggression, delinquency, and less severe forms of conduct. Genetic factors are not only important as a cause of behavior, but also for contributing to stability in behavior. Based on data from a national sample of adolescents and young

KEY TERMS

monozygotic twins (MZ)
Identical twins who develop from one fertilized egg. MZ twins have identical DNA.

dizygotic twins (DZ)
Fraternal twins who develop from two eggs fertilized at the same time.

adults in the United States, J. C. Barnes and Brian Boutwell found that 97% of the stability of criminal behavior across four waves of data collection was explained by genetic factors![104]

Another way to evaluate the relationship between heredity and behavior is by studying adoptees. Adopted children usually have little or no contact with their biological parents. Therefore, to the extent that their behavior resembles the behavior of their biological parents, an argument can be made that genes influence behavior. In a landmark study, Barry Hutchings and Sarnoff Mednick compared the criminal records of 662 adopted sons with the criminal records of their biological and adoptive fathers. When both the biological and adoptive fathers had a criminal record, 36% of the sons were criminal; when only the biological father had a criminal record, 22% of the sons were criminal; when only the adoptive father was criminal, 12% of the sons were criminal; and when neither of the fathers were criminal, only 10% of the sons had a record. In another study, Mednick and his associates matched the court convictions of 14,427 male and female adoptees with the court convictions of their biological mothers and fathers and their adoptive mothers and fathers. They found that the criminality of the child was more closely related to the criminality of the biological parents.[105]

Follow-up research has produced similar findings. For example, in a Swedish study of nearly 900 male adoptees, it was reported that the criminal histories of children were more similar to those of their biological parents than to those of their adoptive parents. In follow-up research, Raymond Crowe analyzed arrest records of 52 adoptees who had been separated from their incarcerated biological mothers. When he compared them to a group of adoptees whose biological mothers had no criminal record, he discovered that the adoptees of the "criminal mothers" were approximately 500% more likely than the adoptees of "noncriminal mothers" to have an arrest record.[106]

In a study of male adoptees from the National Longitudinal Study of Adolescent Health, Kevin Beaver and his colleagues examined the association between having criminal biological parents and subsequent psychopathic personality traits in their children who were placed into adoption. They found that having a criminal biological father (irrespective of the criminality of the adoptive parents) increased the odds of scoring in the extreme of the psychopathic personality scale by a factor between 4 and nearly 9 times. There was no effect for having a criminal biological mother and psychopathy.[107]

The most direct way to measure the effects of genetic factors on delinquency is to use *actual measured genes*—a feat made possible by the mapping of the human genome, which was completed in 2003. In recent years, behavioral scientists have explored the effects of genes on delinquent behavior using data from the National Longitudinal Study of Adolescent Health (Add Health), a data set in which a subsample of study participants were genotyped for five monoamine genes: 5HTT, DAT1, DRD2, DRD4, and MAOA. These genes are known to regulate the amounts of dopamine and serotonin in the brain; both dopamine and serotonin have important effects on mood, personality, and behavior. Thus far, variants of these genes (polymorphisms) have been linked to an array of outcomes. For instance:

- A study investigated the linkages between self-reported serious and violent delinquency and two dopamine genes (DRD2 and DAT1). Both polymorphisms were associated with greater involvement in serious and violent crime among both adolescents and adults.[108]
- In a related study, polymorphisms in three genes (MAOA, DAT1, and DRD2) were associated with serious and violent delinquency among young males.[109]
- Guang Guo and his colleagues found that all five genes included in the Add Health project predicted frequency of alcohol use and accounted for 7 to 20% of the variance in alcohol consumption.[110]
- Kevin Beaver and his colleagues found that DRD2 was associated with increased delinquency victimization, even when the researchers controlled for a variety of other correlates of victimization, including demographics, neighborhood disadvantage, maternal attachment, maternal involvement, maternal disengagement, and parental permissiveness.[111]
- In a related study, Beaver and his colleagues found that the genes included in the Add Health data are associated with desistance from delinquency and that some genes interact with marital status to predict desistance from delinquency.[112]
- Evidence suggests that males who have a certain variant of the dopamine transporter gene DAT1 are more likely to associate with delinquent peers, but only when they also live in a high-risk family environment.[113] In addition to these findings, a variety of other genes have been found to be associated with delinquency and other forms of maladaptive behaviors.

How Does Environment Work? The Nurture–Nature Interplay

Behavior is under the control of the brain. The brain is constructed of complex neural circuits that begin to form shortly after conception and grow and change throughout life as genes and cells *interact* with the environment. Researchers have found that those teens who play violent video games and then perform simple tasks use different parts of their brain than children who play other, nonviolent video games. Apparently, playing violent video games makes children's brains fire differently, especially affecting their ability to concentrate and modulate emotion. This effect, in which video games influence brain physiology, could potentially make a child more aggressive.[114]

Although the brain directs people's activities in everyday life, the activities themselves shape how the brain processes information throughout life. The environment, in other words, contributes to both the brain's contents and its wiring. Neuroscientists recently discovered that social deprivation and neglect like that experienced by children who are placed in institutions and orphanages has lifelong consequences not only for their behavior, but also for their genes. Early adversity prematurely shortened the tips of the children's chromosomes—called telomeres—which results in an earlier-developing aging process (see **Box 3.8**, the "A Window on Delinquency" feature).[115]

However, the brain of an unborn child is not a miniature of an adult's brain. Rather, it is a dynamically changing structure that is adversely affected by outside contaminants in social environments.

BOX 3.8

A Window on Delinquency

Genetic Underpinnings of Delinquent Conduct

There are approximately 23,000 genes in the human genome. Today scientists are seeking to identify genes that code for proteins that perform specific functions, with the resulting outcomes being known as phenotypes. A gene is simply a segment of DNA that codes for the amino acid sequences of a protein. The resulting protein products may take the form of enzymes, hormones, or cell-structured proteins and facilitate the ways that we experience the environment and behave. Genes that are hypothesized to be associated with antisocial behavior are known as candidate genes; in other words, because of their function, they are believed to be associated with traits or behaviors that are related to delinquency.

Two of the most important sources of candidate genes for delinquency are the serotonergic system and the dopaminergic system. Serotonin and dopamine are neurotransmitters. Serotonin is an inhibitory neurotransmitter which means that it functions to regulate emotions and behaviors that inhibit aggression by facilitating behavioral constraint. The more serotonin in the brain, the more inhibited and controlled the behavior. Conversely, people with deficient serotonin functioning show greater aggression and impulsivity—two important drivers of delinquent behavior. Dopamine is an excitatory neurotransmitter that is involved in behavioral activation, motivated behavior, and reward processing. A higher level of dopamine in the brain results in more excitable, impulsive, and aggressive behavior.

Numerous genes within these systems have been linked to antisocial behavior. For example, the dopamine genes DRD1, DRD2, DRD3, DRD4, DRD5, and DAT1 have been associated with delinquency, impulsivity, aggression, and ADHD diagnosis. Candidate genes in the serotonergic system, including 5HTT, HTR1A, HTR1B, HTR1DA, HTR2A, TDO2, and TRH, also have been linked to these phenotypes. Most molecular genetics research has found that complex phenotypes such as delinquency are partially caused by many genes. A phenomenon that has its roots in the actions of many genes is known as a *polygenic* effect. Another important finding is that individual genes are often associated with multiple but similar behavioral outcomes. For example, many of the genes discussed here and in the remainder of this chapter are associated not only with delinquency, but also with aggression, impulsivity, depression, alcoholism, substance abuse, and other maladaptive behaviors. In such a *pleiotropic effect*, a single gene influences multiple behavioral outcomes.

Although research into the molecular bases of delinquency is still new and much remains to be learned, more study has been conducted, and greater advances made, in other behavioral disorders. For example, at least four candidate genes for ADHD have been located: ADHD1 at 16p13, ADHD2 at 17p11, ADHD3 at 6q12, and ADHD4 at 5p13. In these examples, the combination of numbers and letters gives the address (cytogenic location) of the gene. The number indicates the chromosome on which the gene is located. The letter is the arm of the chromosome, with "p" used to indicate the short arm and "q" used to indicate the long arm of the chromosome. The final number is the region or band on the arm of the chromosome where the gene is located.

In the next few years, much more will be known about the genetic underpinnings of delinquency. Perhaps in time medications and other treatments will be created to address those genetic risks that contribute to antisocial conduct.

J. C. Barnes, Brian Boutwell, and Kevin Beaver, "Contemporary Biosocial Criminology: A Systematic Review of the Literature, 2000–2012," pages 75–99 in Alex Piquero (ed.), *The Handbook of Criminological Theory* (Malden, MA: Wiley Blackwell, 2016); Cody Jorgensen, Nathaniel Anderson, and J. C. Barnes, "Bad Brains: Crime and Drug Abuse from a Neurocriminological Perspective," *American Journal of Criminal Justice* 41:47–69 (2016); Joyce Weeland, Geertjan Overbeek, Bram Orobio de Castro, and Walter Matthys, "Underlying Mechanisms of Gene-Environment Interactions in Externalizing Behavior: A Systematic Review and Search for Theoretical Mechanisms," *Clinical Child and Family Psychology Review* 18:413–442 (2015); Jamie Vaske, Jamie Newsome, and John Paul Wright, "Interaction of Serotonin Transporter Linked Polymorphic Region and Childhood Neglect on Criminal Behavior and Substance Use for Males and Females," *Development and Psychopathology* 24:181–193 (2012); Matthew Ogdie, Simon Fisher, May Yang, Janeen Ishii, Clyde Francks, Sandra Loo, Rita Cantor, et al., "ADHD: Fine Mapping Supports Linkage to 5p13, 6q12, 16p13, and 17p11," *American Journal of Human Genetics* 75:661–668 (2004).

This section reviews some of the environmental conditions that are known to cause serious biological damage to developing children, create risk factors for delinquency, and preclude healthy human development.

Maternal Cigarette Smoking

The public health costs of cigarette smoking are great. More than 125 million nonsmoking Americans are exposed to secondhand smoke, including more than 20 million children between the ages 3 and 11. Each year, secondhand smoke kills nearly 50,000 adult nonsmokers via heart disease and lung cancer. Nearly 500 newborns die from sudden infant death syndrome induced by secondhand smoke. Also each year, children experience nearly 1 million ear infections and 200,000 episodes of asthma related to smoking.

In addition to secondhand smoke, nonsmokers can be exposed to *thirdhand smoke*, which is composed of the particles and gases given off by cigarettes that cling to walls, clothes, furniture, skin, and hair. Third-hand smoke can linger for months depending on the ventilation and level of contamination.

Because crawling babies explore the world by touching and putting everything in their mouths, the environmental effects of cigarette smoke and its by-products can be extensive. At a basic level, mothers who smoke while pregnant and parents who smoke around their children may be reflecting a tendency to place their personal desires ahead of a concern for the potential long-term detrimental consequences for their children.

Many criminologists have explored maternal smoking as a risk factor for delinquency and other problem behaviors. Nancy Day and her colleagues have studied the effects of prenatal nicotine exposure on preschoolers' behavior. They report that children whose mothers smoked while pregnant were significantly more likely to have the following characteristics:

- Emotionally unstable
- Physically aggressive
- Socially immature
- Affected by an oppositional defiant disorder

Tobacco exposure was the strongest predictor of oppositional and defiant behavior among children at age 3. At age 10, these children had severe deficits in learning and memory.[116]

Another important consequence of prenatal tobacco exposure is extremely premature birth, defined as children born at less than 26 weeks of gestation. Children who are born very prematurely are at risk for a variety of developmental and behavioral problems:

- Hyperactivity
- Conduct problems
- Cognitive problems
- Attention problems
- Problems bonding with parents

Research has found that, based on parent and teacher ratings, children who were born extremely prematurely are greater than four times more likely to have emotional problems at age 6 independent of other important predictors of child development.[117]

Patricia Brennan and her colleagues have studied the long-term effects of maternal smoking during pregnancy among a birth cohort of males from Denmark. Controlling for a host of predictors of crime, they found that children whose mothers smoked while pregnant were significantly more likely to engage in persistent criminal behavior into adulthood. In fact, smoking contributed to violent and property offending even when the males had reached age 34. Maternal smoking during pregnancy also caused psychiatric problems among the males well into adulthood.[118]

Chris Gibson and Stephen Tibbetts similarly found that prenatal and perinatal exposure to maternal smoking contributes to an early onset of delinquency and police contacts.[119] Reviews of research studies conclude that maternal smoking during pregnancy is a formidable risk factor for delinquency and related problem behaviors.[120] Moreover, this important public health threat is totally preventable.

Chemical Poisoning

Few people would blame delinquency on environmental toxins and chemicals. However, an abundance of evidence suggests that chemical pollutants such as mercury, a dangerous neurological toxin, are especially harmful when ingested by children. Much of this mercury is emitted into the air from coal-burning power plants. Mercury pollution from power plants is ultimately deposited into waterways and accumulates as it moves up the food chain until it ends up on our dinner plates. Exposure to mercury causes damage to the brain, kidneys, and cardiovascular system. Those most vulnerable to this threat are very young children, whose brains are still rapidly developing. Pregnant women, new mothers, and women who may become pregnant are especially at risk of passing this risk on to their children. In a study by the Centers for Disease Control and Prevention, researchers reported that one in six women of childbearing age has enough mercury in her body to put the health of her children at risk.[121]

Although chemicals do not cause children to commit crime, they indirectly affect behavior by interfering with the ability of the brain to perceive and react to the environment. Neurotoxins affect many of the executive functions described earlier in this chapter. Besides mercury, another toxin that adversely affects brain functioning and may cause changes in behavior in children is *lead*. In the 1970s and 1980s, the United States phased out leaded gasoline, which had poisoned more than 65 million children over the more than 50 years it was used. Public health advocates had warned politicians for many years that using lead in

The Flint water crisis began in April of 2014 when a new source of public drinking water exposed high levels of lead contamination to the community.

© Barbara Kalbfleisch/Shutterstock.

gasoline was dangerous. During these decades, lead pollution caused learning disabilities, hearing loss, reduced attention spans, and lower IQs—just as it has for centuries. For instance, composer Ludwig van Beethoven died in 1827 as the result of lead poisoning. Yet, more than 7 million tons of lead were burned in the United States before it was banned. The good news is that now that lead is illegal, the percentage of children with elevated levels of lead in their blood has decreased dramatically in recent decades. Unfortunately, there is always a threat of lead contamination. In 2016, Flint, Michigan, faced widespread lead contamination in the city's water supply. Given the number of children and adolescents who ingested lead-contaminated water, it is likely the city will see a spike in delinquency and violent conduct in future years, given the detrimental effects of the substance on behavior.[122]

Lead gets into the bodies of children in several different ways. For example, lead in the body of a pregnant woman may be transferred to her unborn child. In addition, children may ingest lead by inhaling dust particles traveling in the air or by eating sweet-tasting lead-based paints peeled or chipped from walls. Lead-based paint was banned in the United States in 1978 but is still found in 24 million housing units. In recent years, several cases of lead poisoning have made national headlines. For instance, an Illinois toddler was tested in 2006 and found to have blood lead levels of 136 micrograms per deciliter (mg/dL), which is an astounding 13 times the maximum safe level. The girl's mother has reported that her child can be very aggressive and attributes this behavior to lead exposure. It was discovered recently that several popular children's toys that were manufactured in

China contained high levels of lead; in fact, one study found that 35% of toys were unsafe.[123]

Once lead enters a child's body, it makes its way into the bloodstream, then into soft body tissues (which includes the brain and kidneys), and finally into hard tissues (bones and teeth).[124] Children are more susceptible to low levels of lead poisoning than adults because their nervous systems are developing rapidly, they are exposed to more lead, and their lead absorption rate is higher. Unfortunately, a high percentage of the lead that children absorb is not eliminated from their bodies for 20 or more years.

Lead damages internal organs, causes brain and nerve damage, and results in intelligence and behavioral problems, particularly in children (**Figure 3.4**). Lead poisoning has also been connected to delinquency. Herbert Needleman and his colleagues published a report that showed levels of lead in bone are much higher in adjudicated delinquents than in nondelinquents. Children with high levels of bone lead were more aggressive, self-reported more delinquency, and exhibited more attention difficulties. Lead poisoning also interfered with school performance.[125]

In a related study of 900 boys, Deborah Denno concluded that lead poisoning was a principal predictor of delinquency and chronic criminality in adulthood.[126] Rick Nevin has documented significant relationships between preschoolers' blood lead concentrations and aggression, juvenile delinquency, adult property and violent crime, and even murder.

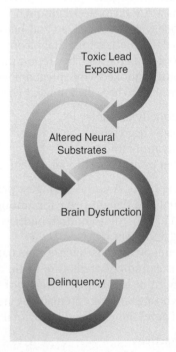

Figure 3.4 Mapping Delinquency Theory: Lead Poisoning and Delinquency

© Jones & Bartlett Learning.

These relationships were found in Australia, Canada, France, Germany, Great Britain, Italy, New Zealand, and the United States.[127] Scientists are also producing prospective evidence of the long-term effects of prenatal and childhood blood lead concentrations on criminal behavior throughout adolescence and into adulthood. Although the negative effects of lead exposure have been well documented, most studies relied on indirect measures of exposure and did not follow participants into adulthood to assess the long-term effects of excessive lead exposure. John Wright and his colleagues revealed the effects of prenatal lead exposure by taking multiple measures of child lead concentrations among 250 persons recruited at birth between 1979 and 1984. The participants lived in Cincinnati in impoverished neighborhoods characterized by a high concentration of older, lead-contaminated buildings. Those individuals with higher levels of lead in their blood were significantly more likely to be arrested and to be arrested for violent crimes later in life. Similarly, Jianghong Liu and her colleagues also found that early life lead exposure was associated with a broad range of behavioral problems and developmental deficits among youth.[128]

Children vary in terms of their exposure to lead and, therefore, in terms of their propensity to develop lead poisoning. The children most susceptible to lead poisoning are poor children. Their environments, including their homes and schools, are much more likely to be heavily contaminated with lead and other toxins than are the environments where wealthier children live. In fact, children living in poverty are eight times more likely than affluent children to have high and dangerous levels of lead in their blood.

The tendency to develop lead poisoning also differs by age. Children between the ages of 2 and 4 years old are most likely to suffer from elevated blood lead levels. By comparison, children younger than 1 year of age are the least likely to have been poisoned by lead.

Nutrition

Are children what they eat? Does the food children ingest affect their behavior? Is a partial remedy for delinquency to change the diets of children? These questions have baffled criminologists ever since 1942, when Hugh Sinclair suggested that poor diets—particularly diets deficient in vitamin B_3, vitamin B_6, and omega-3 essential fatty acids—were a cause of antisocial behavior and persuaded the British government to supplement the diet of all children with cod liver oil and orange juice.[129] Nutrition remains as important as ever as a health factor among children and adolescents.

Today, one in four U.S. children lives in a household that is *food insecure*, which means that the family has limited or uncertain availability of nutritionally adequate and safe foods. In poor households with infants, nearly 45% of households are food insecure. In addition, mothers in food-insecure homes report greater levels of depression and experience less positive interactions with their infant children. Moreover, children with risk alleles of the MAOA gene who are reared in food-insecure homes are not only more likely to display verbal deficits that compromise their school development, but also exhibit psychopathic personality traits that are linked to serious delinquency.[130]

Researchers have repeatedly confirmed the existence of a link between nutrition and behavior. Stephen Schoenthaler and his colleagues, for example, have conducted a variety of studies examining the association between diet and aggressive behavior. One of their experiments involved 80 working-class children who had been formally disciplined for violating school rules during the school year. Half of these children were administered a daily vitamin–mineral supplement for 4 months, whereas the others received placebos. Children who took the vitamin–mineral supplement exhibited a 47% lower average rate of antisocial behavior than the children receiving the placebos. This finding affirmed other research findings, which have consistently revealed reductions in disciplinary actions in incarcerated children who received a vitamin–mineral supplement. Moreover, the greatest decrease in rule-violating behavior typically occurs among children who previously have been identified as chronic offenders.

Schoenthaler and his colleagues also examined the relationship between diet and intelligence in more than 200 elementary school children, half of whom received vitamin–mineral supplements and half of whom received placebos. Again, significant differences between the groups emerged. After only 3 months, children receiving the vitamin–mineral supplement exhibited an average 16-point higher net gain in IQ scores than the matched placebo sample. Finally, in a series of three randomized controlled experiments in which half of 66 elementary school children, 62 confined teenage delinquents, and 404 confined adult felons received dietary supplements (the other half received placebos), Schoenthaler and colleagues found that for all three groups of subjects, those who received dietary supplements showed less aggressive behavior.[131]

Bernard Gesch and his colleagues have replicated and extend some of Schoenthaler's work in their study of 230 young adult prisoners. Like Schoenthaler's team, the Gesch team administered dietary supplements to half of their sample; the other half of the sample received placebos. The two inmate groups were matched on their number of disciplinary incidents as well as on their IQ scores, verbal ability, and levels of anger, anxiety, or depression. After 142 days, the subjects were compared. The researchers found that inmates who received the dietary supplements had 26% fewer offenses, with the greatest reduction in offenses (37%) being noted for serious violent incidents. In 2010, the United Kingdom's Wellcome Trust provided $2.3 million to conduct a nutritional supplement trial in British prisons to replicate Gesch's work.[132]

Poor nutrition and malnutrition have severe long-term consequences for deprived children. Jianghong Liu and his colleagues found that children who were malnourished at age 3 were more likely than other children to be aggressive and hyperactive at age 8; to exhibit aggressive, externalizing behaviors at age 11; and to exhibit conduct disorder and hyperactivity at age 17.[133]

Of course, no one suggests that nutrition is the sole cause of delinquency. Yet the evidence from the United States and Great Britain indicates that violent behavior might be reduced significantly with dietary supplementation in schools and correctional institutions. It is becoming clearer that a healthy diet improves brain function, intelligence, and performance in school—and all of these variables have been strongly linked to delinquency.

One of the most visible and destructive signs of social inequality is the concentration of lead in housing projects in the United States.

© Ronald Sumners/Shutterstock.

Biological Theory and Delinquency Prevention

In the past, social policy based on biological theories recommended that offenders receive drug therapy and/or be isolated from the general population. Because offenders cannot control their debilitating condition on their own, public safety concerns mandate that when the cause of the behavior is known, it must be neutralized. Practically speaking, offenders will likely submit to drug therapy to control their impulses, be institutionalized, or both.

Previous attempts to prevent delinquency in accordance with biological theory were benighted, cruel, and unsuccessful. Fortunately, contemporary biological criminology points to the critical importance of both biology and sociology/environment in producing delinquency. Many environmental risk factors, such as maternal smoking, alcohol consumption, and exposure to environmental toxins, can be reduced through education, public policy, and enforcement. Early-life home environments are the conditions that facilitate the transition of biological dispositions into antisocial behavior. As shown in **Box 3.9** (A "Window on Delinquency" feature), even sleep is a biosocial process related to delinquency. In other words, biological risk factors can be readily modified or reduced by straightforward environmental

changes. If the environment is "good," then the biological basis of delinquency is less likely to become manifest.[134]

Prevention is another way to reduce delinquency, particularly among the youngest potential offenders who present biological risk factors for crime. In her review of the promise of prevention as it relates to neurobiological research, Diana Fishbein concluded:

> As a result of the ineffective, unidimensional approaches of the past, we are now defaulting to the mental health and criminal justice systems with troubled individuals. Rather than ignoring the warning signs in childhood and waiting until adulthood to put these systems into motion, spending billions of dollars for legal remedies that do not produce favorable outcomes, the provision of sorely needed services and interventions to high risk individuals can yield far greater benefits.[135]

In other words, early intervention in the lives of at-risk children can help to promote factors that insulate children from delinquency, minimize or erase the risk factors that contribute to delinquency, and overall try to equalize the life chances for all children and adolescents to develop into healthy, prosocial adults.

BOX 3.9

A Window on Delinquency

Sleep and Delinquency

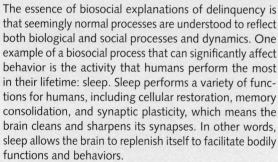

The essence of biosocial explanations of delinquency is that seemingly normal processes are understood to reflect both biological and social processes and dynamics. One example of a biosocial process that can significantly affect behavior is the activity that humans perform the most in their lifetime: sleep. Sleep performs a variety of functions for humans, including cellular restoration, memory consolidation, and synaptic plasticity, which means the brain cleans and sharpens its synapses. In other words, sleep allows the brain to replenish itself to facilitate bodily functions and behaviors.

The notion of sleep functioning to clean and sharpen the brain is understood best when we do not sleep at all or sleep very poorly. The day after lost or poor sleep is usually difficult, one does not think clearly or perform well, and it is difficult to regulate emotions. Those with low sleep are often irritable, crabby, short-tempered, and have lower self-control. Sleep disturbance makes individuals more likely to behave negatively or aggressively, in large part because the normal inhibition of emotions and aggressive impulses are weakened during periods of fatigue. Several studies have found that sleep deprivation, dysregulated sleep, and sleep problems are associated with a range of internalizing and externalizing symptoms in young children and adolescents.

Sleep deprivation has also been linked to delinquency. Drawing on data from the National Institute of Child Health and Human Development's Study of Early Child Care and Youth Development, Ryan Meldrum and his colleagues examined the linkages between sleep deprivation, low self-control, and delinquency. They found that youth who were more sleep deprived had lower self-control and greater delinquency. In addition, sleep deprivation was indirectly linked to delinquency via its effects on low self-control. Meldrum and his colleagues also controlled for a variety of other factors, including neighborhood context, depressive symptoms, parenting practices, peer effects, and prior involvement in delinquency.

While sleep performs a variety of biological functions, it is important to understand that sleep problems are largely controlled by environmental factors. Having a consistent and appropriate bedtime routine that allows for 8 to 12 hours of sleep (depending on the age of the child) is best to allow children to gain enough rest to perform well in school, control their emotions, and regulate their behavior. Thus, sleep is another example of a seemingly biological function that has important environmental or social connections and important implications for conduct problems and delinquency.

Ryan Meldrum, J. C. Barnes, and Carter Hay, "Sleep Deprivation, Low Self-Control, and Delinquency: A Test of the Strength Model of Self-Control," *Journal of Youth and Adolescence* 44:465–477 (2015); Marcos Frank and Rafael Cantera, "Sleep, Clocks, and Synaptic Plasticity," *Trends in Neurosciences* 37:491–501 (2014); Guillaume Bronsard and Fabrice Bartolomei, "Rhythms, Rhythmicity, and Aggression," *Journal of Physiology-Paris* 107:327–334 (2013); Jeanine Kamphuis, Peter Meerlo, Jaap Koolhaas, and Marike Lancel, "Poor Sleep as a Potential Causal Factor in Aggression and Violence," *Sleep Medicine* 13:327–334 (2012); Graham Reid, Ryan Hong, and Terrance Wade, "The Relation between Common Sleep Problems and Emotional and Behavioral Problems among 2- and 3-Year Olds in the Context of Known Risk Factors for Psychopathology," *Journal of Sleep Research* 18:49–59 (2009).

WRAP UP

THINKING ABOUT JUVENILE DELINQUENCY: CONCLUSIONS

Theories answer the questions of *why* and *when* something will happen. Theories are important because *ideas have consequences*. Two broad types of theories were discussed in this chapter: choice and biological theories. Choice theories assume children are rational and intelligent people who make informed decisions to commit crime based on whether they will benefit from doing so. Biological theories blame delinquency on factors over which the individual has very little, if any, control, such as body type, defective brain chemistry, hyperactivity, and low intelligence.

The classical school of criminology encompasses choice theories. Besides theorizing that people are

rational, intelligent beings who exercise free will, these theories state that people commit crime because they imagine it to be in their best interests. Classical theorists also think that punishment deters crime and that the best punishment is one that is certain, swift, and severe. The classical school ultimately failed because of its rigidity. In so doing, it gave rise to the neoclassical school, which introduced the ideas of mitigating circumstances and individual justice and laid the groundwork for the positive school of criminology.

Biological theories go hand-in-hand with the positive school of criminology. The theories discussed in this

chapter represent more than 200 years of thinking about crime. Theories that emphasize the biology of the offender blame delinquency on heredity or some other trait located *inside* of children. Biological theories that take environmental factors into account suggest that delinquency may be caused by an interaction of social factors (such as the environment, poverty, or racism) with biology, chemistry, nutrition, and other environmental issues.

CHAPTER SPOTLIGHT

- Classical theorists, including Cesare Beccaria and Jeremy Bentham, developed choice theories, which assumed that delinquency is the outcome of weighing the costs and benefits of antisocial conduct.
- Neoclassical approaches, including routine activities theory and rational choice theory, take an econometric perspective that suggests the causes and prevention of delinquency should follow rational principles.
- Early biological theories of crime were crude and framed delinquents as evolutionary throwbacks. Modern-day biological criminology is more scientifically rigorous and focuses on the brain as the driver of behavior.
- Nature and nurture interact and mutually reinforce each other to produce all forms of behavior, including juvenile delinquency.
- Several genes within the dopaminergic and serotonergic systems are associated with delinquency and other forms of antisocial behavior, including substance use.
- Early-life environmental factors, including exposure to maternal cigarette smoking, lead poisoning, and nutrition, have long-term effects on delinquency.

CRITICAL THINKING

1. Classical theorists such as Bentham suggested that the punishment should fit the crime. Does the U.S. juvenile justice system serve this purpose for serious felonies? Should legal condemnation and punishment match the barbarity of the most severe types of delinquency?
2. Children with ADHD are often difficult to parent and educate because of their consistently disruptive behavior. Should ADHD children be medicated to control their behavior? What are the benefits and costs of medicating children?
3. Chemical toxins, such as leaded paint, are a significant health risk to children. What are the implications for the social development of children who are exposed to such paint? Do you think exposure to leaded paint and delinquency are related?
4. The evidence is clear that maternal cigarette smoking produces antisocial behaviors, including delinquency. Should maternal cigarette smoking be viewed as a crime? Could such a law be enforced? Would it be enforced?
5. Since the mapping of the human genome was completed in 2003, scientists have been better able to identify the ways that nature and nurture interact to produce delinquency. Why might some people be concerned about genetic-based research on the causes of delinquency? Is it a better form of science than traditional delinquency research?

Psychological Theories

For more than a century, the study of crime in the United States has been dominated by sociologists. For this reason, most conceptualizations of delinquency and most theories that are covered in this section of the text derive from a sociological perspective. However, it is likely that many students do not "naturally" see things from a sociological perspective. Instead, many people view things from an individual-level perspective, and their conceptualization of what makes an individual delinquent often drifts toward psychological and psychiatric perspectives. In terms of delinquency, delinquents may be seen as persons who have a host of individual flaws, which in some way explain why they engage in deviant, antisocial, or delinquent conduct.

OBJECTIVES

- Understand broad psychological theories of behavior, including psychodynamic, behavioral, moral development, and personality theories.

- Learn about aggression as the raw material of delinquent behavior and about the specific childhood psychiatric diagnoses of oppositional defiant disorder and conduct disorder.

- Grasp psychopathy as an important theory of antisocial behavior.

- Explore the characteristics and behaviors of psychopathic youths, the causes of psychopathy, and the ways that psychopathic youths are treated.

- Assess ways that psychological theories inform delinquency prevention.

KEY TERMS

Psychological Theories

Proponents of this view—that individual deficits lie at the heart of delinquency—are not alone. Some criminologists also believe the cause of delinquency is psychological. After all, many delinquents live in dysfunctional homes and often find themselves in conflict with family members, neighbors, peers, classmates, and teachers. The existence of such an environment is a "red flag" that these youth may have disturbed personalities or a mental disturbance that causes them to commit crime. Support for this view comes from the fact that many delinquents *do* display antisocial characteristics. Nevertheless, psychologists disagree on *why* many delinquent youth are mentally disturbed and why these disturbances result in negative behaviors.

This chapter showcases broad psychological approaches to understanding delinquency. The first approach focuses on the formation of the **personality**, which is a set of characteristics that describe a person's beliefs, ways of thinking, motivations, and behaviors. Although some consistencies in personality may be noted across the population, each individual's personality is truly unique. Two of these theories of delinquency—psychodynamic theory and behavioral theory—are influential not just within criminology; the central ideas are also familiar to those outside of academia. Also included in this realm is the predominant conceptualization of the personality, known as the Five Factor Model of Personality.

The second approach is more psychiatric in nature and focuses on **psychopathology**, which is a set of behaviors and attitudes that show clinical evidence of a psychological impairment. A general rule of thumb is that youth who are good students, good sons and daughters, and who do not engage in delinquency have low psychopathology. Conversely, youth who have repeated problems at school, with peers, with parents, and with the police generally have high psychopathology.

KEY TERMS

personality
The set of characteristics that describe a person's beliefs, ways of thinking, motivations, and behaviors.

psychopathology
The set of behaviors and attitudes that show clinical evidence of a psychological impairment.

antisocial personality
The set of characteristics that describe a person's deviant beliefs, deviant ways of thinking, deviant motivations, and antisocial behaviors.

psychodynamic theory
Theory stating that unconscious mental processes that develop in early childhood control an individual's personality.

Interestingly, psychologists have shifted the focus on personality as it relates to behavior to a focus on **antisocial personality**, which is the set of characteristics that describe a person's deviant beliefs, deviant ways of thinking, deviant motivations, and antisocial behaviors. Four broad areas of psychopathology—aggression, oppositional defiant disorder (ODD), conduct disorder, and psychopathy—are reviewed here because of their close relationship with juvenile delinquency.

Psychodynamic Theory

According to **psychodynamic theory**, unconscious mental processes that develop in early childhood control our personality. The author of this theory was Austrian physician Sigmund Freud, who theorized that the personality consists of three parts: the *id*, the *ego*, and the *superego* (see **Box 4.1**, the "Theory in a Nutshell" feature).[1]

The id, which is present at birth, consists of blind, unreasoning, instinctual desires, and motives. It represents basic biological and psychological drives—the id does not differentiate between fantasy and reality. The id also is antisocial and knows no rules, boundaries, or limitations. If left unchecked, it will destroy the person.

The ego grows from the id and represents the problem-solving dimension of the personality; it deals with reality, differentiating it from fantasy. It teaches children to delay gratification because acting on impulse will get them into trouble.

The superego develops from the ego and comprises the moral code, norms, and values the child has acquired. It is responsible for feelings of guilt and shame and is more closely aligned with the conscience.

In mentally healthy children, the three parts of the personality work together. When the parts are in conflict, however, children may become maladjusted and primed to engage in delinquency (**Figure 4.1**). Although Freud did not write much specifically about delinquency, his work did influence criminologists, who took his ideas and applied them to the study of crime. Franz Alexander and William Healy conducted

BOX 4.1

Theory in a Nutshell

Sigmund Freud

Freud believed that unconscious mental processes developed in early childhood control the personality. The personality consists of three parts: the *id*, the *ego*, and the *superego*. In mentally healthy children, the three parts of the personality work together. When these parts are in conflict, children may become maladjusted and primed to engage in delinquency.

Sigmund Freud pioneered the study of the human personality as well as the importance of early childhood experiences in framing later life experiences.

Courtesy of the Library of Congress, Prints and Photographs Division, [reproduction number LC-USZ62-1234].

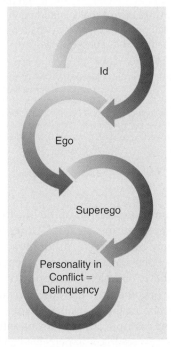

Figure 4.1 Mapping Delinquency Theory: Sigmund Freud

© Jones & Bartlett Learning.

criminological research during the 1930s and were peers of the then emerging and subsequently influential sociological perspectives on crime, such as social disorganization where crime is explained in ecological terms by neighborhood factors such as poverty, residential turnover, ethnic heterogeneity and other factors, and anomie where crime is explained by differential access to the means to achieve culturally defined goals. Alexander and Healy observed that criminals disproportionately come from lower-class areas despite the fact that most residents living in lower socioeconomic areas are not criminals. Many people reared in poor environments use their adversity as motivation to increase their class position or simply live their life without tremendous contemplation of their social position (in psychodynamic theory, this channeling of energy from the negative to the positive is a defense mechanism known as *sublimation*). On the other hand, others "suffering from ill-digested infantile hostilities and resentments against the members of the family has reason, because of his social handicaps, to replace his original hostilities with an aggressive antisocial behavior, he will be more likely to develop into a criminal."[2]

For example, one important theoretical disciple of Freud was John Bowlby, who developed attachment theory (see **Box 4.2**, the "A Window on Delinquency" feature). **Attachment theory** suggests that the enduring affective bond between child and caregiver (usually parents) is significantly related to child development because it provides a variety of benefits that serve as buffers or protective factors against the development of antisocial behavior. First, attachment helps to morally socialize children to understand the standards of behavior in society (in Freudian language, attachment helps the superego to develop). Second, attachment helps children to regulate their emotions and conduct so that they can function at home, in school, and in society. Third, attachment instills self-esteem, self-efficacy, and self-concept in children because of the confidence and support that the parent relationship provides. These skills help children to survive in society and also to be resilient when faced with adversity.[3]

Other criminologists' theories have generally blamed delinquency on children having either an underdeveloped or overdeveloped superego. In the case of an *underdeveloped superego*, the socialization process

KEY TERMS

attachment theory
Theory stating that the enduring affective bond between child and caregiver (usually parents) is importantly related to child development because it provides a variety of benefits that serve as buffers or protective factors against the development of antisocial behavior.

BOX 4.2

A Window on Delinquency

Attachment and Delinquency

Second only to Freud in popularity but equally important scientifically, John Bowlby produced a report, *Maternal Care and Mental Health,* on the welfare of homeless children that was commissioned by the World Health Organization. In it, Bowlby found widespread developmental problems among children living in institutions with no maternal care. Compared to a control group of children who were not raised in an institution, those who spent their first 3 years of life in an institution without a nurturing mother present, had significantly lower intelligence, poorer cognitive skills, speech problems, less social maturity, greater conduct problems, reduced capacity for guilt upon breaking rules, and reduced capacity for relationships. Children who did not attach to their mother were significantly unpopular with other children, were prone to restlessness and hyperactivity, had self-regulation problems, and had poor school achievement. In his concluding remarks, Bowlby noted that the early-life deprivation and the lack of a caregiver bond create an affectionless or psychopathic character in children.

In John Bowlby's work, the attachment process occurs in four stages of infant development. In the first phase, during the first 2 to 3 months of life, infants do not generally differentiate between people and attend to the environment in a generally unspecific way. However, infants do make eye contact with parents/caregivers and will cry, grasp fingers, and even smile. In the second phase, infants are able to distinguish their primary caregivers and can recognize them by smell and sight (the adage that an infant can smell his or her mother when she walks into a room is relevant here). It is during this stage that attachment behaviors such as crying are better resolved by caregivers than strangers. In the third stage, occurring around 6 to 8 months, infants direct attachment behaviors exclusively toward their mothers/caregivers and use their

mothers as a "secure base" to explore their environment. If separated from their mothers, infants express anger and sadness and then display characteristic responses when their mothers return depending on the security of their attachment (these responses are explored in the next section). In the fourth phase, children have a mental understanding of their caregiver relationship and how their caregiver responds to their attachment signals.

About 70% of children develop a *secure attachment,* which is the healthy, normative type. About 20% develop an *insecure/avoidant attachment* characterized by negative emotions, maternal inconsistency, and susceptibility to internalizing problems, such as anxiety and depression. About 10% of children develop an *insecure/ambivalent attachment* that is also characterized by negative emotions and maternal inconsistency as well as susceptibility for internalizing and externalizing symptoms.

Insecure attachments are largely responsible for the range of emotional and behavioral problems that many delinquent youth develop across childhood and adolescence. A fourth type of attachment occurs when abuse, neglect, and maltreatment disrupt the normal development of infant–parent attachment. This is known as *disorganized attachment* and is most centrally related to conduct problems and delinquency. Marinus van IJzendoorn and his colleagues have documented that youth who display disorganized attachment suffer from an array of psychological and behavioral problems, including disrupted ability to cope with stress, dissociation, aggression, externalizing problems, conduct problems, delinquency, and crime. Although Freud has the name recognition, Bowlby's work has been equally important in specifying how early childhood experiences lay the foundation for behavioral health and its consequences.

Marinus van IJzendoorn, Carlo Schuengel, and Marian Bakermans-Kranenburg, "Disorganized Attachment in Early Childhood: Meta-Analysis of Precursors, Concomitants, and Sequelae," *Development and Psychopathology* 11:225–249 (1999); Chantal Cyr, Eveline Euser, Marian Bakermans-Kranenburg, and Marinus van IJzendoorn, "Attachment Security and Disorganization in Maltreating and High-Risk Families: A Series of Meta-Analyses," *Development and Psychopathology* 22:87–108 (2010); John Bowlby, "Maternal Care and Mental Health," *Bulletin of the World Health Organization* 3:355–534 (1951); John Bowlby, *Attachment and Loss: Volume 1 Attachment* (New York: Basic Books, 1969); Irene Wilkinson, "Why Some Children Come to School with 'Baggage': The Effects of Trauma Due to Poverty, Attachment Disruption and Disconnection on Social Skills and Relationships," *Canadian Journal of Family and Youth* 8:173–203 (2016).

is viewed as having been inadequate or incomplete. As a consequence, the superego is too weak to curb the impulses and drives of the id. The child's behavior

KEY TERMS

Oedipus complex
A condition in which a child has an unconscious desire for the exclusive love of the parent of the opposite sex, which includes jealousy toward the parent of the same sex and the unconscious wish for that parent's death.

becomes a direct expression of the id—for example, "If you want something, steal it." Other delinquent behavior may be indirect. Although socialization inhibits the open expression of unacceptable urges, those urges never completely disappear; instead, they may merely become unconscious. Thus delinquent behavior may be a symbolic expression of unconscious impulses. For example, an adolescent with an unresolved **Oedipus complex** is perceived as having an unconscious desire for the exclusive love of the parent of the opposite sex, which includes jealousy toward the parent of the same sex and the unconscious wish for that parent's death. A son with Oedipus complex may "murder" his father in a figurative way, such as forging checks drawn on his bank account or killing a person who represents the authority of his father, such as a police officer.

Sometimes delinquent behavior is the result of too much socialization, which produces an *overdeveloped superego*. Impulses and urges of the id may elicit strong disapproval from the superego. This ongoing conflict causes the ego to experience guilt and anxiety. Because the ego knows that punishment must follow crime, it naturally leads the child to crime so as to minimize guilt. To ensure punishment, the ego will unconsciously leave behind clues, thereby ensuring the perpetrator is caught.

Psychodynamic theory is widely subscribed to by practicing psychologists who apply the theory in the treatment of adolescent offenders. Critics worry that this theory rests on some questionable assumptions. For instance, there is *no* evidence of a causal link between a child's "state of mind" and his or her behavior. It also is debatable whether personality consists of an id, ego, and superego. These traits were conceptualized by Freud, and there is no scientific evidence that any or all of the elements are present.

Behavioral Theory

In contrast to psychodynamic theory, **behavioral theory** proposes that behavior reflects our interactions with others throughout our lifetime (**Figure 4.2**). One leading behaviorist was psychologist B. F. Skinner,

BOX 4.3

Theory in a Nutshell

B. F. Skinner

Skinner argued that behavior is a consequence of the reinforcements and punishments it produces. Delinquents have their delinquency reinforced (and not punished) by others, either intentionally or unintentionally.

who applied the scientific method to his studies, rather than relying on unobservable mental processes as did Freud. Skinner theorized that children learn conformity and deviance from the *punishments* and *reinforcements* they receive in response to their behavior. He believed the environment shapes behavior. Children identify which aspects of their environment they find pleasing and which ones are painful, and their behavior responds to the consequences that the environment produces (see **Box 4.3**, the "Theory in a Nutshell" feature). Skinner concluded that children repeat rewarded behavior and terminate punished behavior.[4]

Some behaviorists have used Skinner's theory as a springboard to expand these ideas. Albert Bandura argues that learning and experiences couple with values and expectations to determine behavior. In his *social learning theory*, Bandura suggests that children learn by modeling and imitating others. They learn to be aggressive from their life experiences and learn aggression in different ways—for instance, by seeing parents argue, watching their friends fight, viewing violence on television and motion pictures, playing violent video games, and listening to "gangsta" rap music. In particular, children learn that aggression is sometimes acceptable and can produce a desired outcome (see **Box 4.4**, the "Theory in a Nutshell" feature).[5]

Bandura also pioneered the concept of *self-efficacy*, which is the belief in one's capabilities to carry out the necessary courses of action in everyday situations. Presumably if a person has weak self-efficacy, then he or she is less confident in his or her own abilities to handle interactions with others and, therefore, might be more susceptible to the influences of others.

Bandura's work and the general spirit of social learning theory have informed psychological approaches that

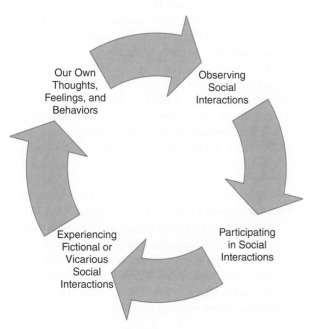

Figure 4.2 Mapping Delinquency Theory: Behavioral Theory
© Jones & Bartlett Learning.

KEY TERMS

behavioral theory
Theory suggesting that behavior reflects our interactions with others throughout our lifetime.

BOX 4.4

Theory in a Nutshell

Albert Bandura

Bandura thinks children learn how to behave from others whose behaviors they model and imitate. Delinquent behavior is learned from direct, face-to-face interaction or by observing others in person or symbolically in literature, films, television, music, and video games.

focus on social cognition. Generally, **social cognition** focuses on how people perceive, think, learn, and come to behave in particular ways as a result of the interactions with their social world. The social world includes observations of and participation in real social interactions, such as with parents and peers, and fictional social interactions, such as with the media. Theoretically, social cognition shows how a person's predispositions interact with situational and environmental factors to produce behavior.[6]

If Bandura is correct, then might children learn to be aggressive and commit violent crimes from what they see in the media? Is there a relationship between media violence and crime? Criminologists have studied these questions for about 80 years. In 1933, Herbert Blumer concluded from conversations with young people that movies did influence their behavior.[7]

On July 20, 2012, a movie theater became the scene of a horrific crime when James Holmes murdered 12 victims and injured 70 others at a theater in Aurora, Colorado, that was showing the Batman film, *The Dark Knight Rises*. Holmes had been homicidal for years and was obsessed with superheroes and violent media, including film. Decades after Blumer's conclusions, evidence continues to suggest that films still have this potential. For instance:[8]

- In 1979, shortly after release of *The Warriors*, three murders were committed that bore striking resemblances to acts in the film.
- Roughly 20 deaths have been blamed on *The Deer Hunter*. One incident involved a teenager who died after shooting himself with a .38-caliber handgun while playing Russian roulette, just as in the movie.

KEY TERMS

social cognition

A discipline that focuses on how people perceive, think, learn, and come to behave in particular ways as a result of the interactions with their social world. The social world includes observations of and participation in real social interactions, such as with parents and peers, and fictional social interactions, such as with the media.

- The would-be assassin of President Reagan, John Hinckley, Jr., identified with Travis Bickle, the character played by Robert De Niro in *Taxi Driver*. After seeing the film 15 times, Hinckley became obsessed with actress Jodie Foster, who played the teenage prostitute. In *Taxi Driver*, Bickle entertained the thought of assassinating a political candidate and stopped only after the plan had failed.
- Four days after watching *Born Innocent*, three teenage girls attacked a 9-year-old girl on a California beach and raped her with a bottle, just as had happened in the movie. The victim's mother filed an $11 million negligence suit against NBC, accusing the company of being responsible for the rape. The Supreme Court ruled that networks are not liable for damages unless they willfully seek to induce violence.
- When *Boyz N' the Hood* was released in July 1990, two people were killed and more than 30 injured near or outside movie theaters.
- Research has linked the film *Natural Born Killers* to at least 100 murders.
- Former Senator Robert Dole suggested that Columbia Pictures should share the blame for the torching of New York City subway clerk Harry Kaufman, the victim of a copycat crime based on a scene in *Money Train*.
- Following the premier of *Juice*, a movie about four African American juveniles who get involved in a robbery that ends in murder, violence broke out at theaters across the country. In Chicago, a 16-year-old was shot and killed by a stray bullet from a fight between two boys waiting for tickets to the last show. In Philadelphia, an 18-year-old was paralyzed from the chest down after he was shot coming out of the movie. In New York City, a 16-year-old was stabbed in a theater during a quarrel with another teenager.
- Two teens obsessed with *Scream* and *Scream II* were convicted of murder. They stabbed their victim 45 times with four knives and a screwdriver. In the movies, victims were knifed by killers obsessed with horror movies.
- A 9-year-old girl hanged herself with a shoelace while reenacting a scene from *The Man in the Iron Mask*.
- Newscasters have blamed at least one school shooting on Comedy Central's television show *South Park*, and MTV's *Jackass* was blamed when a 13-year-old Connecticut boy laid himself across a barbecue grill and suffered severe burns. Experts have also blamed *Tomb Raider*, a video game, for the precipitous increase in violent crime committed by adolescent females.

A persistent stream of data suggests a strong connection between children seeing violent entertainment

If children learn behaviors by watching and imitating others, what consequences, if any, should there be for adults who behave badly in the presence of children? Jail? Prison? Treatment?

© CarlaMc/E+/Getty.

and then behaving aggressively. Viewing violent entertainment affects children in at least one of three ways:

1. Children see violence as an effective way to settle conflicts.
2. Children become emotionally desensitized toward violence in real life.
3. Entertainment violence feeds the perception that the world is a violent and mean place and increases the fear of victimization.

In spite of the strong evidence supporting a relationship between media depictions of violence and real-world behavior, some criminologists believe that other factors are equally or more likely to cause juvenile violence. They think juvenile violence stems more from family breakdown, peer influence, youths' individual level of aggression, and the proliferation of guns in society, rather than from media violence. For example, Christopher Ferguson reports that the effects of playing video games on violent delinquency have been exaggerated. In his own research, Ferguson finds no statistical link between video game playing and delinquency once other variables, such as gender, exposure to family violence, and aggressive personality traits, are considered.[9]

Although some studies suggest that media-depicted violence has only a short-lived influence on children's behavior, other research consistently reports the opposite.[10] Rowell Huesmann and his colleagues have linked violent television viewing at ages 6 to 9 to adult aggression in members of both sexes. They surveyed 329 adults in the late 1970s, interviewing both the individuals and their spouses or friends about their television viewing habits; they then checked the study participants' crime records 20 years later. As children, the participants were rated for exposure to televised violence after they chose 8 favorite shows from 80 popular shows for their age group and indicated how much they watched them. The researchers also assessed these programs for amount of physical

violence. As young adults, the men who scored in the top 20% on childhood exposure to violence were approximately twice as likely as other men to have pushed, grabbed, or shoved their wives during an argument in the year preceding the interview. Women in the top 20% were roughly twice as likely as other women to have thrown something at their husbands.[11]

A related study by Gina Wingood and her colleagues found that teens that spend more time watching the sex and violence depicted in "gangsta" rap music videos were more likely to practice those behaviors in real life. After studying 522 African American girls between the ages of 14 and 18 from nonurban, lower socioeconomic neighborhoods, the researchers found that compared to those who never or rarely watched these videos, the girls who viewed these "gangsta" videos for at least 14 hours per week were far more likely to practice numerous problematic behaviors. Compared to their peers, these girls were[12]

- Three times more likely to hit a teacher
- Nearly three times more likely to get arrested
- Twice as likely to have multiple sexual partners
- Almost twice as likely to get a sexually transmitted disease, use drugs, or drink alcohol

These and the many hundreds of other studies on the topic of media violence, aggression, and crime have led the American Psychological Association to conclude that viewing violence on TV and other mass media *does promote aggressive behavior*, particularly in children.

In addition to showing the powerful effects of the media on adolescent behavior, youth violence and juvenile justice studies suggest that young people are underdeveloped in terms of the cognitive and moral appreciation of their behavior. Instances in which adolescents exhibit impulsive and violent behavior

Research suggests that chronic exposure to "gangsta" rap videos increases the likelihood of hitting a teacher, getting arrested, being sexually promiscuous, and using drugs. Do the lives and personas of "gangsta" rappers, such as 50 Cent, Tupac, Biggie Smalls, Dr. Dre, Snoop Dogg, TheGame, and Nas contribute to delinquency? What lifestyle and behaviors do "gangsta" rap videos portray?

© Joe Seer/Shutterstock.

during or after the course of using violent media demonstrate that youths may display a temporary or sustained lack of appreciation for the moral issues related to their behavior. The broader role of morality as it applies to delinquency is explored next.

Moral Development Theory

Recall from Bandura's work that social cognition is the way that people perceive, think, learn, and come to behave in particular ways as a result of the interactions with their social world. The social world includes observations of and participation in real social interactions, such as with parents and peers, and fictional social interactions (e.g., the media). Bandura also theorized about the importance of **moral disengagement**, which refers to an individual's tendency to use mechanisms conducive to a selective disengagement of moral censure. By doing things such as blaming their victims, moral disengagement allows people to engage in self-serving behaviors that are in contrast with moral principles while not experiencing negative self-evaluative emotions such as guilt.[13]

Despite Bandura's work on moral disengagement, behavioral theory has been more broadly criticized for not sufficiently taking into account other basic psychological differences between people that might help explain why individual-level differences in delinquency occur. Two of the most important psychological features that can affect how people respond to their environment are cognitive development (particularly as illuminated by the research by Jean Piaget) and moral development (particularly as discussed in the research by Lawrence Kohlberg).

Jean Piaget is best known for his work examining the development of thinking processes among children. One of his most significant contributions to the field of psychology was his recognition that the cognitive and moral development of children and adults is different. Through thousands of hours of observing children in clinical and community settings, Piaget developed a theory that outlined how children's cognitive abilities develop.

KEY TERMS

moral disengagement
An individual's tendency to use mechanisms conducive to a selective disengagement from moral censure.

morality of constraint
In Piaget's theory, the stage of development where children think rigidly about moral concepts and believe that people who break rules must be punished.

morality of cooperation
In Piaget's theory, the stage of development where children employ greater moral flexibility and learn that there are no absolute moral standards about behavior.

1. The *sensorimotor stage* occurs from birth to approximately age 24 months. It encompasses the development of object permanence (that is, the understanding that objects remain in certain places even if they are not being observed), reflexive behavior, and goal-oriented behavior.
2. The *preoperational stage* occurs from approximately ages 2 to 7 years. In this stage, children learn how to use symbols or words to represent objects such as people. In other words, language ability and the appreciation of language occur during this time. Also, children's thinking is egocentric and self-centered.
3. The *concrete operational* stage spans ages 8 to 11 and is characterized by the development of logical thought. During this time, thinking becomes broader and problem solving is less egocentric. In short, there is a realization that the world does not center on one's own thoughts and wants.
4. The *formal operational* stage occurs from age 12 onward. During this developmental stage, people can think abstractly and make sense of hypothetical situations.

Piaget also constructed a theory of moral development to illustrate how children symbolize and organize social rules and make judgments on the basis of that organization. In other words, as children develop cognitively, they also develop morally. Piaget believed that moral reasoning developed in two stages: (1) morality of constraint and (2) morality of cooperation. In the **morality of constraint** stage, children think rigidly about moral concepts and believe that people who break rules must be punished.

In the **morality of cooperation** stage, children employ greater moral flexibility and learn that there are no absolute moral standards for behavior. Around age 7, children's view of morality shifts from one of constraint to cooperation as they realize that good and bad are relative terms that depend on people's intentions and other factors.[14]

Although Piaget's work has been hugely influential in psychology, his theory of moral development has not received unanimous support. Some critics suggest that morality does not develop at all, but instead is an innate feature of humanity.[15] The idea of an innate moral sense was even noted by the 19th-century English naturalist Charles Darwin:

> Of all the differences between man and the lower animals, the moral sense or conscience is by far the most important . . . It is summed up in that short but imperious word *ought*, so full of high significance. It is the most noble of all the attributes of man, leading him without a moment's hesitation to risk his life for that of a fellow-creature; or after due deliberation, impelled simply by the deep feeling of right or duty, to sacrifice it in some great cause.[16]

Current research from evolutionary psychology and neuroscience reports that the human moral sense is housed anatomically in the limbic system of the brain. In particular, the amygdala, which controls emotions, fear, and empathy, plays a key role in the development of morality.

Other critics of Piaget's two-stage process insisted that his model was too simplistic and did not accurately capture the ways that young people develop. One of the most influential theories of moral development put forth since Piaget's work has been the moral reasoning model advanced by Lawrence Kohlberg. According to Kohlberg, moral development proceeds along three levels:[17]

- In the *preconventional level*, children's entire lives are governed by the rules established by others—usually the child's parents. At this level, children are almost entirely self-interested and generally obey rules simply to avoid punishment.
- In the *conventional level*, children adopt and abide by the rules of others and will at times subordinate their own interests to conform to others. At this level, there is increased appreciation of social norms and the recognition of social order.
- In the *postconventional level*, people learn how to create their own rules in terms of the values and ethical principles they have chosen to follow. At this stage, people also recognize their involvement in the tacit social contract that binds people in a society.

In keeping with this model, Kohlberg believed that youths who were morally immature were more likely to engage in antisocial behaviors than morally mature youths who recognized that delinquency was wrong. In his view, "Maturity of moral thought should predict maturity of moral action. This means that specific forms of moral action require specific forms of moral thought as prerequisites, that judgment–action relationship is best thought of as the correspondence between the general 'maturity' of the individual's moral judgment and the maturity of his moral action."[18] According to Kohlberg, an important part of moral development centers on the capacity with which individuals can minimize their own wishes and desires so as to better fit in with others.

Over the years, researchers have consistently documented a relationship between moral development, or morality generally, and delinquency. Compared to adolescents who are not delinquent, delinquent youths are delayed or immature in their moral development and have an almost childlike self-centeredness. With this kind of **egocentric bias**, the primary motivation for thought and behavior is to satisfy one's self-interest. Because delinquent youths are perceived as having lower moral development, treatment programs attempt to improve their social skills and social decision-making

processes to increase their awareness that others exist and that life is more than "me, me, me."[19]

How do these theories match up with real-life behavior? In a study of 152 male delinquents selected from a detention center in Scotland, Stavros Kiriakidis found that delinquents scored significantly higher on a moral disengagement scale compared to a community sample of adolescents. Youths with higher moral disengagement (and thus lower morality) were more likely to come from homes served by a social worker, had more unstable living situations, and had higher levels of drug use. More important, studies have shown that morality has predictive effects on delinquency even when researchers control for other known correlates of adolescent antisocial behavior. A study of 252 institutionalized juvenile offenders in Pennsylvania found that moral disengagement was significantly related to the emergence of delinquent behavior during childhood and adolescence. Children who displayed greater moral disengagement began to experiment with delinquency sooner, were contacted by police earlier, and appeared in juvenile court before their peers who had greater morality or moral engagement. Sam Hardy and his colleagues examined moral disengagement among a sample of 384 adolescents and found that youth who were morally disengaged were more aggressive and delinquent and also tended to have lower self-regulation.[20]

Greater immorality is also found among more violent and psychiatrically disturbed offenders. Aisling O'Kane and her colleagues found that persons who have more psychopathic personalities have less developed moral reasoning skills. Overall, the relationship between morality and delinquency is clear. Geert Jan Stams and colleagues conducted a meta-analysis of 50 studies to investigate whether delinquents had different moral development than their nondelinquent peers. The overall effect size—the average statistical effect across studies—was moderate to strong: Delinquents are less moral than their prosocial peers. In addition, the moral disparities are greatest when the delinquents are more severe, violent, and psychopathic.[21]

Although theorists such as Piaget and Kohlberg suggested that morality develops over time, more recent research has shown that morality is relatively stable. Marinella Paciello and her colleagues conducted an important study of stability and change of morality (or moral disengagement) as it relates to delinquency. Among their most important findings:[22]

- Four developmental pathways of moral disengagement were identified: One group of youths

KEY TERMS

egocentric bias
A condition in which the primary motivation of thought and behavior is related to satisfying one's self-interest.

was always moral, one group had slight moral disengagement at age 14 that declined quickly thereafter, one group had moderately high moral disengagement until age 16 that declined quickly thereafter, and a small group had moderate to high levels of moral disengagement across adolescence and into adulthood.

- Youths with the greatest levels of moral disengagement were the most delinquent, were the most aggressive, and committed the most acts of violence compared to youths with lower levels of moral disengagement.
- Girls demonstrated greater morality (or less moral disengagement) than boys.
- Youths with lower moral disengagement were more likely to feel guilty about their delinquent behavior.
- The members of the most severe group in terms of moral disengagement were also rated by their peers as the most aggressive.

In sum, morality is an important part of a person's psychology because it speaks to the individual's ability to use aggression, or refrain from using aggression, when deciding whether to pursue self-interest or conform to the greater social good. Morality is also related to the broader concept of personality, the topic that is explored next.

Personality Theory

The basic point of personality theory is that the set of traits that typify an individual's personality have important implications for his or her behavior—both conventional and delinquent. In other words, personality theory attempts to study the "character" of a person, taking a perspective that has obvious implications for delinquency. Even as psychologists such as Freud and Skinner were developing their psychodynamic and behavioral approaches, other researchers were studying ways to scientifically understand the personality and the ways that it influences behavior. For instance, in 1934, psychologist L. L. Thurstone described his research along these lines:

Sixty (60) adjectives that are in common use for describing people were given to each of 1300 raters. Each rater was asked to think of a person whom he knew well and to underline every adjective that he might use in a conversational description of that person . . . The coefficients for the sixty personality

traits were then analyzed by means of multiple factor methods, and we found that five factors are sufficient to account for the coefficients. It is of considerable psychological interest to know that the whole list of sixty adjectives can be accounted for by postulating only five independent common factors. . . . We did not foresee that the list could be accounted for by as few factors. This fact leads us to surmise that the scientific description of personality may not be quite so hopelessly complex as it is sometimes thought to be.[23]

The five dimensions that Thurstone found decades ago are today known as the **Five Factor Model of Personality**, sometimes referred to as the Big Five.[24] The Five Factor Model of Personality is a structural model of personality as measured by an instrument called the NEO Personality Inventory, which was developed by Paul Costa and Robert McCrae. The following five factors and six facets within each factor capture the essence of the human personality (see **Figure 4.3**):[25]

1. *Neuroticism* is assessed by the following facets: anxiety, hostility, depression, self-consciousness, impulsiveness, and vulnerability to stress.
2. *Extraversion* is assessed by the following facets: warmth, gregariousness, assertiveness, activity, excitement seeking, and positive emotion.
3. *Openness to experiences* is assessed by the following facets: fantasy, aesthetic, feelings, actions, ideas, and values.
4. *Agreeableness* is assessed by the following facets: trust, straightforwardness, altruism, compliance, modesty, and tender-mindedness.
5. *Conscientiousness* is assessed by the following facets: competence, order, dutifulness, achievement striving, self-discipline, and deliberation.

Although everyone's personality is a little bit different, certain traits or groupings of traits consistently tend to appear together in the same person. Take conscientiousness, for example. If a person scores very highly on all facets of conscientiousness, then

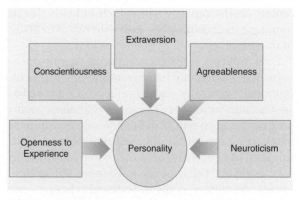

Figure 4.3 The Five Factor Model of Personality
© Jones & Bartlett Learning.

the person is a competent, orderly, duty-driven, ambitious, self-disciplined deliberator. This psychological profile describes a person who is probably successful, because these are the raw characteristics of a high-achieving person.

The same logic works when applying personality traits to young people involved in delinquency. Imagine a person who scores highly on hostility and impulsiveness, is very cold, and lacks concern for others. This psychological profile depicts someone who could easily victimize others, in part because of the collection of antisocial personality traits that

he or she possesses. In fact, Donald Lynam and Thomas Widiger recently used the Five Factor Model to illustrate how only a few personality traits, such as angry hostility, low affect or weak conscience, and interpersonal assertiveness, can form the basis for serious personality disorders such as psychopathy (which is explored in depth later in this chapter). See **Box 4.5**, for a closer look at the enduring effects of personality and personality disorder.[26]

Personality researchers have also identified the "Dark Triad," which includes narcissism or self-obsession, Machiavellianism (the ability to manipulate and exploit

BOX 4.5

A Window on Delinquency

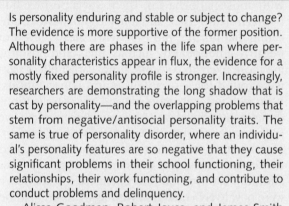

The Long Shadow of Personality and Personality Disorder

Is personality enduring and stable or subject to change? The evidence is more supportive of the former position. Although there are phases in the life span where personality characteristics appear in flux, the evidence for a mostly fixed personality profile is stronger. Increasingly, researchers are demonstrating the long shadow that is cast by personality—and the overlapping problems that stem from negative/antisocial personality traits. The same is true of personality disorder, where an individual's personality features are so negative that they cause significant problems in their school functioning, their relationships, their work functioning, and contribute to conduct problems and delinquency.

Alissa Goodman, Robert Joyce, and James Smith examined the longitudinal consequences of early life psychological functioning drawing on data from the National Child Development Study, which is a continuing study of nearly 18,000 children born in England during March 1958. Children with more negative personality features are those who are especially low in conscientiousness, which includes competence, order, dutifulness, achievement striving, self-discipline, and deliberation, and low in agreeableness, which includes trust, straightforwardness, altruism, compliance, modesty, and tender-mindedness, and greater hostility. Other symptoms of personality disorder occur for neuroticism (high angry-hostility scores and high impulsiveness) and extraversion (low warmth and high excitement seeking) and generally lower psychological functioning suffered from these conditions throughout their lives.

The wide-ranging implications included greater employment problems, less wealth, and reduced social

mobility. Childhood personality/psychological deficits resulted in nearly 30% reduced earnings by age 50 and a host of other problems including marital instability, lower agreeableness, lower conscientiousness, more emotional instability, and reduced self-efficacy.

Criminological epidemiologists recently examined the social welfare burden of personality disorders in the United States drawing on data from the National Epidemiologic Survey on Alcohol and Related Conditions, a nationally representative sample of more than 43,000 adults. They found that diagnoses for any personality disorder significantly predicted receipt of Medicaid, Supplementary Security Income, and Food Stamps. Moreover, persons who were diagnosed with Antisocial Personality Disorder—the personality disorder that most directly corresponds to a criminal personality—were significantly more likely to receive Medicaid, Food Stamps, and Women, Infant, and Children (WIC) assistance. These costs add to already large monetary costs that serious criminal offenders, particularly those with personality disorders, impose on society.

Meta-analytic research confirms that certain personality features are significantly associated with conduct problems during childhood, delinquency during adolescence, and substance abuse, crime, and violence during adulthood. In a nutshell, antisocial individuals have low agreeableness, low conscientiousness, low constraint, and high extraversion (especially impulsivity and sensation-seeking). In this sense, personality is not only central for understanding crime, but also central for understanding human development and its implications for society.

Alissa Goodman, Robert Joyce, and James Smith, "The Long Shadow Cast by Childhood Physical and Mental Problems on Adult Life," *Proceedings of the National Academy of Sciences of the United States of America* 108:6032–6037 (2011); Michael Vaughn, Qiang Fu, Kevin Beaver, Matt DeLisi, Brian Perron, and Matthew Howard, "Are Personality Disorders Associated with Social Welfare Burden in the United States?" *Journal of Personality Disorders* 24:709–720 (2010); Mieke Decuyper, Sarah De Pauw, Filip De Fruyt, Marleen De Bolle, and Barbara De Clercq, "A Meta-Analysis of Psychopathy, Antisocial PD, and FFM Associations," *European Journal of Personality* 23:531–565 (2009); Richard Howard and Conor Duggan, "Personality Disorders: Their Relation to Offending," pages 281–290 in David Crighton and Graham Towl (eds.), *Forensic Psychology* (New York: John Wiley & Sons, 2015); Julien Morizot, "The Contribution of Temperament and Personality Traits to Criminal and Antisocial Behavior Development and Desistance," pages 137–166 in Julien Morizot and Lila Kazemian (eds.), *The Development of Criminal and Antisocial Behavior: Theory, Research and Practical Applications* (New York: Springer, 2015).

others), and subclinical psychopathy. Although these people present with antisocial traits, they do not have them to such a degree that they meet the diagnostic criteria. For instance, personality researchers surveyed college students to examine the relationships between their personalities and behaviors. It was discovered that males who were narcissistic, somewhat psychopathic, and Machiavellian had more sexual partners and reported that they were frequently seeking brief sexual affairs. In others words, the study confirmed the popular notion that "bad boys get the girls." Moreover, these findings suggest that one facet of psychopathy that is often overlooked is that males with psychopathic traits tend to have prolific, albeit impersonal, sex lives. Research on the Dark Triad has shown that not all psychopathic traits are necessarily bad, particularly if they are present at subclinical levels. For instance, narcissism correlates with cognitive ability and can enhance work productivity and mastery of one's work. Subclinical psychopaths also score very low on neuroticism, which means that they rarely feel stressed. The impulsive lifestyle of the subclinical psychopath is also alluring to some because it is characterized by excitement seeking and little boredom—traits that also lend themselves to sexual adventurousness.[27]

Researchers have found important personality differences between delinquents and nondelinquents. In 1967, Gordon Waldo and Simon Dinitz reviewed 94 studies of the personality–delinquency link and found that 81% reported significant differences between the two groups.[28] In 1988, Robert Ross and Bambi Ross reviewed the personality and cognitive traits of delinquents:

> Many delinquents evidence developmental delays in the acquisition of a number of cognitive skills which are essential for social adaptation . . . many fail to stop and think before they act. . . . Many delinquents believe that what happens to them depends on fate, chance, or luck. Many offenders are almost totally egocentric. . . . Offenders encounter frequent interpersonal problems because they do not think about how others will feel.[29]

Recently, Avshalom Caspi and his colleagues examined the relationship between personality traits and delinquency among two samples of youth, one selected from a Dunedin, New Zealand, cohort and the other from the Pittsburgh Youth Study. The personality correlates of delinquency were strong and consistent across the different countries, in different age cohorts, across gender, and across race. Youths with greater delinquent participation tended to have personalities characterized by negative emotionality and weak constraint. The importance of this combination is that when negative emotionality or the tendency to experience aversive affective states is accompanied by weak constraint or poor impulse control, negative emotions may be translated more readily into antisocial acts.[30]

To further explore potential group differences in personality and to assess their relationship to delinquency, Estrella Romero and her associates studied more than 1000 male and female adolescents in school and a group of institutionalized male delinquents. They found that impulsivity and sensation seeking were strongly related to delinquency among groups of youth who were either "normal" or incarcerated.[31]

Joshua Miller and Donald Lynam reviewed 59 studies using the Five Factor Model or other structural personality models and found consistent links between antisocial personality traits and involvement in delinquency. Shayne Jones, Miller, and Lynam recently reviewed 53 studies to explore the association between the Five Factor Model and outcome measures for antisocial behavior and aggression. Overall, effect sizes for three of the five factors were significantly associated with antisocial behavior. There was a positive link between neuroticism and antisocial behavior, indicating that people who experience greater levels of negative emotionality, such as anger and hostility, are more likely to commit crime. Larger effect sizes were found for agreeableness and conscientiousness, with more antagonistic and less conscientious domains associated with antisocial behavior. All five factors were significantly associated with aggression. The direction for neuroticism, agreeableness, and conscientiousness was the same for aggression. In addition, extraversion and openness to experience were negatively correlated with aggression.[32] At the most extreme level, antisocial personality traits can come together in a person to such a degree that the person seems almost designed to engage in delinquency and other maladaptive behaviors. These types of psychopathology are examined next.

Aggression

Aggression is a troubling part of U.S. culture. Upwards of 75% of U.S. children between the ages of 8 and 11 have been targeted by bullies during school recess periods. This bullying is not always physical in nature. Instead, many times it involves children telling secrets to create fear and uncertainty in other children. Other forms of bullying include social ostracism, teasing, and rumor spreading.

Many types of behaviors can be categorized as aggressive. For instance, lying, stealing, and vandalism are often used as visible indicators of aggression. Although disruptive and socially annoying, these types of behaviors do not necessarily constitute acts of aggression and certainly are not signs of serious or chronic offending in adolescence and adulthood. As a result, scholars often divide aggression into different components, each reflecting a relatively distinct set of behaviors. The underlying assumption is that different types of aggression may have different causes and may differentially relate to the odds of engaging in delinquent behaviors later in life.

One of the most important distinctions made by psychologists is between reactive and instrumental aggression. **Reactive aggression** is impulsive, thoughtless, or unplanned; is driven by anger; and occurs as a reaction to some perceived provocation. It is also sometimes called hot-blooded, affective, angry, defensive, impulsive, or hostile aggression. **Proactive aggression**, by contrast, entails a premeditated means of obtaining some instrumental goal in addition to harming the victim.[33] The most extreme example of proactive aggression is found among serial sexual murderers, who stalk and kill their victims to satisfy deviant sexual interests. Proactive aggression is also sometimes called instrumental or (most commonly) cold-blooded aggression.[34]

Of these two types of aggression—proactive and reactive—proactive aggression is considered to be more severe because it describes a person who plans or calculates the use of aggressive force on another person. Youths who score highly on proactive aggression during childhood are significantly more likely to be diagnosed later with a behavioral disorder and to be involved in serious delinquency.[35] In other words, proactive aggression is predatory in nature. Reactive aggression is considered the "normal" type of aggression, because it illustrates the use of force in response to a real or perceived wrong; that is, it is defensive in nature.

An important caveat must be recognized when thinking about proactive and reactive aggression: If someone is extremely aggressive, he or she will be generally aggressive in all types of situations. Edward Barker and his colleagues recently found that if adolescent boys were identified as very aggressive on proactive forms, they were 100% likely to also be identified as very aggressive on reactive forms.[36]

Another distinction made by scholars who are trying to define aggression is between indirect aggression and direct aggression. **Indirect aggression** is usually verbal and covert and includes actions such as gossiping and ostracism. **Direct aggression**, in contrast, is typically physical and overt and includes behaviors such as hitting, kicking, punching, and biting. In general, females are more likely than males to use indirect aggression, whereas males are more likely than females to use direct aggression.

Although both forms of aggression have important ramifications, direct aggression is most applicable to the etiology of criminal behaviors. For instance, when Noel Card and colleagues conducted a meta-analysis of 148 studies of child and adolescent direct and indirect aggression, they found that direct aggression is more strongly associated with externalizing behaviors, poor peer relations, and low prosocial behavior.

The use of aggression is a universal and normal part of early childhood. Fortunately, most people develop the social skills needed to control aggressive thoughts. For those who do not adequately control themselves, aggression can contribute to serious behavioral disorders and delinquency.

© Cresta Johnson/Shutterstock.

By comparison, indirect aggression (more common among females) was more strongly associated with internalizing problems but higher prosocial behavior—or less delinquency. Across the 148 studies, the correlation between direct and indirect aggression was strong ($r = .76$). In other words, children and adolescents who are prone to using one form of aggression are also likely to use the other form, although there are important distinctions between them.[37]

Simply focusing on direct aggression leaves a lot of room for ambiguity and treats all forms of direct aggression as the same. As an example, consider two males, both of whom engaged in a serious physical fight in the past week. One of the males launched an unprovoked attack against an elderly woman. The other male, in contrast, was jumped by a group of teenagers and fought back in self-defense. Clearly, these two types of direct aggression are different and, therefore, it is essential that the definition of aggression be able to differentiate between the two. In the

KEY TERMS

reactive aggression
Aggression that is impulsive, thoughtless or unplanned, driven by anger, and occurring as a reaction to some perceived provocation.

proactive aggression
Aggression that includes a premeditated means of obtaining some instrumental goal in addition to harming the victim.

indirect aggression
Aggression that is usually verbal and covert; it includes actions such as gossiping and ostracism.

direct aggression
Aggression that is typically physical and overt; it includes behaviors such as hitting, kicking, punching, and biting.

preceding example, the behaviors were the same—both males were fighting—but their intentions were quite different. For one male, using aggression was a way of inflicting harm on someone; for the other male, using aggression was a defense mechanism.[38]

Aggression is evident during infancy. For this reason, many behavioral scientists focus on psychological constructs such as aggression when conducting research on delinquency. Their logic goes like this: If aggression is the raw material of what will one day become delinquent and criminal behavior, it must be important and better understood. In recent years, a group of researchers spearheaded by Richard Tremblay have examined aggressive behaviors in very young children and tracked them throughout childhood. The results of their studies have been quite striking:[39]

- Some children begin using aggression—including hitting and kicking—well before their first birthday and, in some cases, around 7 or 8 months of age.
- More than 80% of children in Tremblay's studies began using physical aggression by the age of 17 months.
- Within childhood, the peak age at which children use aggression and violence is around 2 to 3 years.
- After age 3, rates of aggression decline until mid-adolescence.
- Other types of antisocial behaviors that are not necessarily aggressive are also almost universal behaviors among children. For example, 90% of children in Tremblay's studies took things from others.
- With greater age, all of these types of behaviors become less prevalent.

Although important differences can be delineated between reactive and proactive aggression and indirect and direct aggression, there are also commonalities between these concepts. A wealth of studies has been conducted to examine the stability of antisocial behaviors, including violent aggression, over the life course and the results have been remarkably consistent. Across samples, generations, and countries, and regardless of the sample analyzed and the methodological techniques employed, extremely high levels of relative stability in aggressive behaviors have been observed. In a classic article, Dan Olweus reviewed studies that had examined the stability of aggressive behavior over time, discovering that aggression was extremely stable, even more so than IQ scores.[40]

Findings from more recent reviews have upheld the conclusions in Olweus's original article by showing that aggressive and violent behaviors are highly stable across long periods of the life course. Moreover, persons with the highest degrees of stability tend to score extremely high or extremely low on aggression. In other words, people who are the most aggressive (or the least aggressive) at one point in time are likely to be characterized as the most aggressive (or the least aggressive) at another point in time. Change, in other words, is highly unlikely. With this information in hand, it is probably not too surprising to learn that one of the best predictors of future delinquency is a history of aggressive behavior in childhood and adolescence.[41]

The reason that aggression remains relatively stable over time is because it is intertwined with other facets of the personality that deal with self-regulatory behaviors. Children and adolescents who experience actions as being guided by their own free will rather than external forces or who are *self-determined*, are *self-motivated* when faced with difficult or aversive situations, and can manage their moods and *self-soothe* during stress are also less likely to use aggression. Nevertheless, many aspects of self-regulatory behavior and cognition are positively related to aggression:[42]

- Tendency toward distraction
- Inability to visualize goals and intentions and keep them in mind
- Negative emotions, such as anxiety
- Lack of appropriate coping strategies when faced with failure
- Tendency toward doing what one likes as opposed to doing what is necessary
- Inability to "down-regulate" negative affect once it occurs
- Inability to restore positive affect after it has been dampened

In sum, aggression is a normal response to environmental annoyances. *Everyone* is aggressive from time to time. No one is exempt. The commonplace existence of aggression is most evident in infants and toddlers, who aggressively impose their will on others when things do not go their way. Fortunately, most people dramatically reduce their use of aggression over the life course—but some do not. For some people, aggression becomes a routine part of life. The clinical disorders discussed next illustrate how severe the use of aggression can become.

Oppositional Defiant Disorder

Oppositional defiant disorder (ODD) is a pattern of angry/irritable mood, argumentative/defiant behavior, or vindictiveness lasting for at least 6 months, as evidenced by at least four symptoms from any of the following categories, and exhibited during interaction with at least one individual who is not a sibling:

1. Often loses temper
2. Often touchy or easily annoyed

KEY TERMS

oppositional defiant disorder (ODD)
A clinical disorder characterized by a pattern of negativistic, hostile, and defiant behavior.

3. Often angry and resentful

4. Often argues with authority figures, or, for children and adolescents, with adults

5. Often actively defies or refuses to comply with requests from authority figures or with rules

6. Often deliberately annoys others

7. Often blames others for his or her mistakes or misbehavior

8. Has been spiteful or vindictive at least twice within the past 6 months

To differentiate oppositional defiant disorder from other childhood misbehavior, these criteria must occur more frequently than is typically observed in individuals of comparable age and developmental level.

The behaviors associated with oppositional defiant disorder cause clinically significant impairment in social, academic, or occupational functioning. Children with this disorder are not psychotic and do not suffer from mood disorders, however. Between 2 and 15% of all children meet the diagnostic criteria for oppositional defiant disorder. All children with oppositional defiant disorder are not the same; instead, there is variability within the diagnosis and classes or types of youth with the disorder. For instance, Robert Althoff and his colleagues studied three samples of adolescents in the United States and the Netherlands and found four classes of the disorder. One group of adolescents had no symptoms of the disorder, another group was mostly irritable, and another group was mostly defiant. The fourth, most severe group of adolescents, displayed all symptoms of the disorder and was most likely to also have conduct disorder, ADHD, and become violent offenders as adults. Other scholars have replicated findings about ADHD within the population, especially the existence of a large, unimpaired group that is 70% of the population and a small, severely impaired group that is 5 to 10% of the population.[43]

Oppositional defiant disorder can best be understood as the precursor to conduct disorder. Virtually all children who are diagnosed with conduct disorder also had oppositional defiant disorder. The relationship is not perfectly reciprocal, however: Of those who are diagnosed with oppositional defiant disorder, only 50% will later be diagnosed with conduct disorder. In a way, oppositional defiant disorder serves as a bridge between aggression and conduct disorder. The characteristics of oppositional defiant disorder read like a recipe for having disputes and confrontations with others.[44]

Joseph Biederman and his colleagues evaluated whether oppositional defiant disorder is a **prodrome**—that is, an early, nonspecific symptom (or set of symptoms) indicating the start of a disease before specific symptoms of conduct disorder appear. Among a sample of children who had behavioral disorders, 32% of those with oppositional defiant disorder also had conduct disorder. All but one child

Teens who are excessively argumentative, annoying, hostile, spiteful, and prone to conflict with others show clinical signs of oppositional defiant disorder. Left untreated, the condition can worsen into more troubling behavioral problems.

© Kamira/Shutterstock.

with conduct disorder also had oppositional defiant disorder that preceded the onset of conduct disorder by several years. Children with both oppositional defiant disorder and conduct disorder at the same time—a condition known as **comorbidity**—had more severe symptoms of the disorders, had more additional psychiatric disorders, exhibited lower functioning, and demonstrated more abnormal behaviors. In sum, Biederman and his colleagues found that children with more severe oppositional defiant disorder are very likely to develop conduct disorder during adolescence.[45]

Another disorder that is commonly comorbid with oppositional defiant disorder is ADHD. In a study of nearly 100 preschool boys, ages 4–5, with oppositional defiant disorder, nearly half also met the diagnostic criteria for ADHD. When the boys were assessed 2 years later, when they were in first grade, 76% of them had both oppositional defiant disorder and ADHD.[46]

What is troubling about these forms of psychopathology is that they do not simply go away, but rather require extensive treatment and behavioral interventions to alleviate their symptoms. Often, parents of children with oppositional defiant disorder are overwhelmed by the situation and have difficulty helping their child to deal appropriately with the disorder. When oppositional defiant disorder goes untreated, it usually culminates in conduct disorder—and it may also culminate in contacts with the juvenile justice system.

KEY TERMS

prodrome
A precursor of early symptoms; a warning sign of another disease or disorder.

comorbidity
The co-occurrence of two or more disorders.

For instance, Linda Teplin and her associates found that more than 40% of youths in detention centers in Chicago had diagnoses of oppositional defiant and/or conduct disorder.[47] Indeed, the prevalence of oppositional defiant disorder is so high among youths in juvenile facilities that staff members have sought to develop ways to better handle those who have oppositional defiant disorder. For example, staff members often refuse to argue with youth, allow youth time to vent and express their frustrations without penalty, redirect their attention and anger, and generally "pick their battles" so that each interpersonal exchange between youths with oppositional defiant disorder and treatment and educational staff is not characterized by conflict.[48]

Conduct Disorder

Conduct disorder is a repetitive and persistent pattern of behavior in which the basic rights of others or major age-appropriate societal norms or rules are violated. For children or adolescents to be diagnosed with conduct disorder, they must demonstrate three or more of the following 15 criteria in the previous 12 months, with at least one criterion being met in the past 6 months:[49]

1. Aggression toward people and animals
   a. Often bullies people, threatens, or intimidates others
   b. Often initiates physical fights
   c. Has used a weapon that can cause serious physical harm to others
   d. Has been physically cruel to people
   e. Has been physically cruel to animals
   f. Has stolen while confronting a victim, such as robbery
   g. Has forced someone into sexual activity
2. Destruction of property
   a. Has deliberately engaged in fire setting with the intention of causing serious damage
   b. Has deliberately destroyed other's property (other than by fire)
3. Deceitfulness or theft
   a. Has broken into someone else's house, building, or car
   b. Often lies to obtain goods or favors or to avoid obligations
   c. Has stolen items of nontrivial value without confronting a victim, such as by shoplifting

4. Serious violations of rules
   a. Often stays out at night despite parental prohibitions, beginning before age 13 years
   b. Has run away from home overnight at least twice while living in parental home
   c. Is often truant from school beginning before age 13 years
   d. Disturbances in behavior that cause significant impairment in social, academic, or occupational functioning

Conduct disorder affects between 3 and 5% of preadolescent boys and between 6 and 8% of adolescent boys. Its prevalence is much higher in boys than in girls, with the gender-based ratio being approximately 4:1 in childhood and 2:1 during adolescence. Conduct-disordered children create a host of problems for their parents, teachers, and others. Because of their aggressive and antisocial behavior, youths with conduct disorder frequently get into trouble and are likely to be suspended and expelled from school.[50]

One of the major interpersonal issues with conduct-disordered children is their difficulty in regulating or handling their emotions. They readily become aggressive not only in emotional situations, but also in the course of seemingly normal social interactions.[51] Carla Sharp and colleagues found that children with conduct problems respond negatively even to very neutral situations or stimuli. They have a relatively constant belief that others are against them—known as hostile attribution bias—and as such respond negatively to others.[52] In addition, children with conduct disorder are often shunned by their conventional peers, who may fear their erratic and volatile behavior. The social isolation and the recognition that their own antisocial behavior is causing them problems often contribute

Children and adolescents with conduct disorder face a lifetime of hardships, including a chronic and often serious delinquent career.

© ZouZou/Shutterstock.

KEY TERMS

conduct disorder
A repetitive and persistent pattern of behavior in which the basic rights of others or major age-appropriate societal norms or rules are violated.

to the development of substance abuse problems among conduct-disordered youth.[53]

The long-term outcomes in untreated conduct-disordered children are poor and include the following problems:

- Drug addiction
- Alcoholism
- Anxiety and depression
- School dropout
- Peer rejection
- Social isolation
- Victimization
- Financial problems
- Poor work history
- Unstable marital relationships
- Arrests and incarcerations

One of the more troubling aspects of conduct disorder centers on *callous–unemotional traits*, which are characteristics that suggest a deficiency in the ability to empathize with others. Children and adolescents who demonstrate callous–unemotional traits generally do not show their feelings or emotions, are not helpful if someone is hurt or upset, do not feel bad or guilty when they do something wrong, have few if any friends, are inconsiderate of others' feelings, are not kind to younger children, and are not concerned about how they perform in school. Put simply, they are callous and emotionally cold.

Callous–unemotional traits are strongly correlated with conduct disorder and other behavioral problems. When these traits and antisocial behaviors do occur together, the cause is generally genetic in origin. For instance, when Essi Viding and her colleagues recently studied callous–unemotional traits and antisocial behavior among 3687 twin pairs, they found that 67% of the variation in extreme callous–unemotional traits

Brilliant, successful, affluent, and psychopathic, the 1924 murder of Bobby Franks by Nathan Leopold and Richard Loeb horrified the nation and to this day is considered one of the most shocking crimes in American history.

© Stringer/Hulton Archive/Getty.

among 7-year-old children was attributable to genes. When the researchers examined extreme antisocial behavior in 7-year-olds with psychopathic tendencies, genes accounted for 81% of the variation. A subsequent study found that 71% of conduct problems in boys and 77% of such problems in girls were attributable to genetic influences.[54]

Some youths use aggression frequently and as a preferred means to handle interpersonal exchanges. These adolescents are at considerable risk for developing both oppositional defiant disorder and conduct disorder, and they usually commit delinquency at high levels. If left unchecked, these forms of psychopathology—especially when they include evidence of callous–unemotional traits—devolve into what is considered the most destructive personality disorder, psychopathy.

Psychopathy

The 1924 abduction and murder of 14-year-old Bobby Franks by Nathan Leopold and Richard Loeb shocked the country and remains one of the most disturbing crimes in U.S. history. Both of the young men came from prominent Chicago families and were brilliant students at the University of Chicago. On the surface, they seemed very unlikely to commit such an atrocious act of violence. As the case unfolded, however, the character of Leopold and Loeb became more startling. The crime had been perpetrated merely to see if they could get away with it, and the young victim had been selected at random. In part because of their superior intelligence, Leopold and Loeb viewed themselves as superior to others and had personalities characterized by a grandiose sense of self-worth, self-absorption, indifference to the victim and his family, and an apparent lack of conscience.[55] In short, they were psychopathic.

Psychopathy is a personality disorder that impairs interpersonal, affective, and behavioral functions and is closely linked to serious antisocial behavior. The disorder is significantly more likely to occur in boys as opposed to girls and does not discriminate by race, ethnicity, social class, or country of origin. In other words, psychopaths have been found in many racial groups and in many different countries.

Several core characteristics are associated with psychopathic individuals. They tend to be aggressive, self-centered or narcissistic, impulsive, and prone to risky activities. They often begin getting into trouble very early in life, even as early as age 3 (see **Box 4.6**),

KEY TERMS

psychopathy
A personality disorder that impairs interpersonal, affective, and behavioral functions and is closely linked to serious antisocial behavior.

BOX 4.6

Delinquency Controversy

Psychopathic at Age 3, Psychopathic at Birth?

One of the most heated controversies in psychological criminology centers on whether the theory of psychopathy should be applied to children and adolescents. This kind of application, which is known as the downward extension of psychopathy, takes information created from research on the antisocial personalities and behaviors of adults and superimposes it on youths. Labeling a child or adolescent as "psychopathic" can have serious implications for the youth's liberty and treatment options.

Andrea Glenn and her colleagues examined the temperament and psychophysiological responses among children at age 3 and conducted a follow-up when they were age 28. The findings from their research were intriguing:

- Those individuals with higher psychopathy scores in adulthood were significantly less fearful and inhibited at age 3 than those with lower psychopathy scores in adulthood.
- Psychopathic adults scored higher on stimulation-seeking measures at age 3 than did less psychopathic adults.

The work of Glenn and colleagues was the first study to demonstrate a prospective relationship between characteristics of preschool children and psychopathic-like personality in adulthood. It suggests that at least some biological and temperamental predispositions toward psychopathic personality may be in place even at a very young age. This makes perfect sense since all personality features are moderately heritable—which means that variance in them stems from genetic factors. Indeed, Essi Viding and Henrik Larsson reviewed genetic studies of psychopathy among children and adolescents and reached the following conclusion:

"[T]win studies that have examined the overlap between psychopathic personality traits and antisocial behaviors have all shown that common genetic influences account for much of the covariation between psychopathic personality traits and antisocial behavior. In addition, data on young twins suggest that early-onset antisocial behavior is more heritable for the group of children with concomitant callous-unemotional traits and antisocial behavior. These findings are consistent with the notion that a common set of genes influences psychopathic personality traits and antisocial behavior (as well as other disorders on the externalizing spectrum) and in line with the hypothesis that a shared set of genes affects various externalizing psychopathology."

As more researchers conduct longitudinal studies that track research subjects from the prenatal phase to death, it is likely that the long-term implications of our psychological makeup will become clearer.

Michael Rutter, "Psychopathy in Childhood: Is It a Meaningful Diagnosis?" *British Journal of Psychiatry* 200:175–176 (2012); Carla Sharp and Sarah Kine, "The Assessment of Juvenile Psychopathy: Strengths and Weaknesses of Currently Used Questionnaire Measures," *Child and Adolescent Mental Health* 13:85–95 (2008); Andrea Glenn, Adrian Raine, Peter Venables, and Sarnoff Mednick, "Early Temperamental and Psychophysiological Precursors of Adult Psychopathic Personality," *Journal of Abnormal Psychology* 116:508–518 (2007); Katherine Auty, David Farrington, and Jeremy Coid, "Intergenerational Transmission of Psychopathy and Mediation via Psychosocial Risk Factors," *The British Journal of Psychiatry* 206:26–31 (2015); Essi Viding and Henrik Larsson, "Genetics of Child and Adolescent Psychopathy," pages 113–134 in Randall Salekin and Donald Lynam (eds.), *Handbook of Child and Adolescent Psychopathy* (New York: The Guilford Press, 2010), p. 123.

engage in a wide variety of antisocial behaviors, and are prolific criminals.

The list of characteristics presented so far describes many serious, nonpsychopathic offenders as well as psychopaths. It is the other, more disturbing characteristics, however, that distinguish psychopaths from other individuals. Psychopathic delinquents are callous, lack guilt feelings, and have little to no fear or anxiety. They are exploitative, manipulative, deceptive, and seemingly unable to form warm relationships with other people. They are without conscience and appear to be impervious to efforts by the juvenile and criminal justice systems to intervene in their path toward serious criminal offending.[56]

Philippe Pinel was the first person to clinically study the construct of psychopathy with the publication of his *A Treatise on Insanity* in 1801 (his psychopathy concept was referred to as *manie sans délire*).

Pinel described a diagnosis for people who exhibited uncontrolled rage and outlandishly immoral behavior that was without psychotic features such as delusions. In other words, these people seemed to be extremely dangerous, yet simultaneously remained in control of their emotions and mental health.[57] In 1835, James Pritchard called the disorder "moral insanity," again noting that serious criminal conduct occurred without mental defect in these individuals.[58] Many other physicians, psychiatrists, and correctional clinicians also studied psychopathy throughout the 19th and 20th centuries.

The "modern" understanding of psychopathy was crystallized in 1941 with the publication of Hervey Cleckley's *The Mask of Sanity*. His work was the most systematic clinical study of psychopathy and laid the groundwork for contemporary research in this field. Among his many contributions, Cleckley described the sheer antisocial differences between psychopaths and even the most delinquent youths:

> In repetitive delinquent behavior, the subject often seems to be going a certain distance along the course that a full psychopath follows to the end. In the less severe disorder, antisocial or self-defeating activities are frequently more circumscribed and may stand out against a larger background of successful adaptation. The borderlines between chronic delinquency and what we have called the psychopath merge in this area.[59]

Cleckley identified 16 features of psychopathic individuals:[60]

1. Superficial charm and "good" intelligence
2. Absence of delusions and other signs of irrational thinking
3. Absence of "nervousness" or psychoneurotic manifestations
4. Unreliability
5. Untruthfulness and insincerity
6. Lack of remorse or shame
7. Inadequately motivated antisocial behavior
8. Poor judgment and failure to learn by experience
9. Pathologic egocentricity and incapacity for love
10. General poverty in major affective reactions
11. Specific loss of insight
12. Unresponsiveness in general interpersonal relationships
13. Fantastic behavior with drink and sometimes without
14. Suicide rarely carried out
15. Sex life impersonal, trivial, and poorly integrated
16. Failure to follow any life plan

Over the past 40 years, the major scholar in the area of psychopathy has been Robert Hare. He has developed an assessment tool called the Psychopathy Checklist Revised (PCL-R). As shown in **Figure 4.4**, current conceptualizations of psychopathy cover interpersonal, affective, lifestyle, and antisocial behavior dimensions.[61] Each area of psychopathy comprises various traits, behaviors, and characteristics; statistically, these traits are strongly correlated with one another. What this means is that the current study of psychopathy is very similar to the historical study of personality (and antisocial personality) in that relatively few traits are used to describe a person with the clinical disorder.

The majority of research on psychopaths has centered on adult criminals in prisons or psychiatric hospitals. Through this work, researchers have discovered that offenders demonstrate psychopathic characteristics

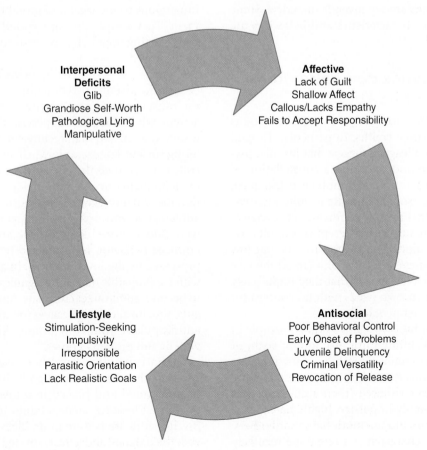

Figure 4.4 Psychopathy Dimensions

Data from Robert Hare and Craig Neumann, "Psychopathy as a Clinical and Empirical Construct," *Annual Review of Clinical Psychology* 4:217–245 (2008).

throughout their lives, even in early childhood and adolescence. Clearly, then, *juvenile psychopathy* is an important area of research for understanding the disorder and developing ways to prevent it or reduce its negative effects.

The application of the "psychopathy" label to children and adolescents has occurred for many decades. For example, in 1964 William McCord and Joan McCord expressed concerns that serious violent crime was the work of adolescent psychopaths.[62] In 1966, Lee Robins described children who appeared in local psychiatric clinics as follows: "Boys [who] had a history of truancy, theft, staying out late, and refusing to obey parents. They lied gratuitously, and showed little guilt over their behavior. They were generally irresponsible."[63] Technically, Robins referred to these children as "sociopathic," indicating that their antisocial behavior seemed to be produced largely by the abusive, impoverished home environments in which they were raised (the distinction between psychopathy and sociopathy is described later in this section).

In the 1980s, as crime rates increased and criminology focused more attention on the most serious types of offenders, serious juvenile offenders also began to receive more scrutiny from researchers. In recent years, criminologists in several countries have produced an impressive knowledge base on psychopathic traits among juvenile offenders. Some of their primary characteristics and behaviors are described next.

Characteristics and Behaviors of Psychopathic Youth

Criminologists have found that a certain set of traits typifies psychopathic youths. In particular, Donald Lynam and his colleagues suggest that juvenile psychopathy can be understood as a constellation of personality characteristics that contribute to delinquent behavior. This personality profile is quite negative, unfortunately. Psychopathic youths are very disagreeable and often are suspicious, deceptive, exploitative, arrogant, tough minded, and aggressive. They are low in conscientiousness and constraint (recall the Five Factor Model), which means that they impulsively seek to satisfy their own needs with no concern for the feelings of other people.[64]

Paul Frick and his colleagues studied a sample of more than 1100 children in third, fourth, sixth, or seventh grades to examine the stability of psychopathic traits. Like previous researchers, they found that the most psychopathic children (their average age was 10 years) were highly impulsive, highly narcissistic, and highly callous and unemotional toward others. Moreover, these characteristics remained relatively stable over a 4-year follow-up period. The research of Frick and colleagues suggests that psychopathic

traits develop early in life and, once established, are likely to persist throughout the life course.[65] In fact, recent research has found that scores on psychopathic tests among youths aged 13 are strongly correlated with psychopathy scores at age 24. Put simply, juvenile psychopathy often gives way to psychopathy in adulthood.[66]

If the personality profile of psychopathic youths is troubling, the behavioral profile is even more unsettling, particularly among institutionalized juvenile offenders. Mary Ann Campbell and her colleagues found that psychopathic youths are among the most aggressive, antisocial, and delinquent children within detention centers. Although they are the most prone to externalizing their problems (e.g., by hurting others), they are the *least* prone to internalizing their problems (e.g., by hurting themselves). In other words, psychopathic youths do not feel "stressed" about engaging in serious antisocial behavior. They also tend to have the most serious criminal records, have often been suspended or expelled from school, have multiple placements in foster homes and juvenile detention centers, and experience more abuse during early childhood.[67] In a similar vein, several other scholars have found that youths who present psychopathic traits have multifaceted involvement in delinquent behaviors.[68]

Unfortunately, psychopathic youths appear to be impervious to the legal and moral bases of punishment. They simply do not respond to punishment by correcting their behavior; instead, they appear to be unmoved.[69]

Compared to serious delinquents who are not psychopathic, juvenile psychopaths are noteworthy for their sustained criminal activity, continued criminal activity while under the supervision of the juvenile justice system, and high recidivism rates upon reentering society. For example, Michael Vaughn and his colleagues studied the effects of psychopathic traits on delinquent careers among a population of institutionalized delinquents in Missouri. They found that adolescents with psychopathic personality features were 300% more likely to have an early onset of criminal behavior, be contacted by police, and be processed by the juvenile court. In addition, youths with psychopathic traits were significantly more likely to become adult career criminals. Among delinquent girls, Vaughn and his colleagues found that narcissistic and impulsive youths were more likely to commit violent and property crimes.[70]

Diana Falkenbach and her associates studied psychopathic features among 69 children who had been arrested and placed in a juvenile diversion program. These researchers found that youths with psychopathic traits were more likely not to comply with the program and to be rearrested.[71] Based on data for Canadian youths between the ages of 12 and 18, Raymond Corrado and his colleagues determined that psychopathic youths are significantly more likely to commit general, violent, and nonviolent delinquent acts than youths who are not psychopathic. Moreover, psychopathic youths commit crimes faster and with greater frequency.[72]

Even while incarcerated, psychopathic youths tend to present more problems than their nonpsychopathic counterparts. When Daniel Murrie and his associates studied institutionalized youths in Virginia, they found that a prior record for crimes of violence, a record of violence that did not result in arrest, violence while incarcerated, assaulting other correctional residents with weapons, and inflicting great bodily harm were significantly correlated with psychopathy.[73] Similarly, among 85 adjudicated delinquents in Florida who were between the ages of 11 and 18, psychopathic youths accumulated more disciplinary infractions, committed more violent acts, and had worse treatment outcomes than nonpsychopathic children.[74]

What is remarkable about psychopathic personality traits is that their predictive validity is often more powerful than some biological and sociological correlates of crime. Michael Vaughn and his colleagues studied psychopathic traits among youths who were emancipated or leaving the foster care system, in a quest to determine those traits' effect on various delinquent outcomes. The psychopathic trait relating to coldness or being unemotional turned out to be the strongest predictor of number of arrests, exceeding the importance of male gender and being more than twice as powerful as having deviant peers and living in a disadvantaged neighborhood. Narcissism predicted arrests comparably to having deviant peers and living in a bad neighborhood. The psychopathic trait relating to fearlessness was *the* strongest predictor of drug sales and illegal money earning, ahead of correlates such as gender, deviant peers, and neighborhood factors.[75]

What Causes Psychopathy?

What causes some youngsters to be glib, deceitful, manipulative, callous, irresponsible, impulsive, mean, lacking in guilt, and so easily able to victimize others? Is their pathology innate? Did something happen to them that produced psychopathy? Does some combination of nature and nurture produce psychopathy? Based on the weight of the evidence, the best answer appears to be that psychopathy is produced by a combination of biopsychological and sociological factors—in other words, both *nature and nurture*.

Some behavioral scientists have distinguished between primary and secondary psychopaths as a way to explore **etiological** (causal) factors of antisocial behavior. *Primary psychopaths* are persons who have brain abnormalities that impair their ability to process and express emotion, such as empathy. Their antisocial behavior is largely innate.[76] Research by James Blair and his colleagues indicates that certain genetic factors produce neurotransmitter dysfunction, which in turn reduces the ability of the amygdala (the almond-shaped groups of neurons in the brain that control our emotional ability) to process emotional learning and, hence, impairs the individual's ability to socially relate to others.[77] Significantly, even the most biologically centered explanation (like the theory of Blair et al.) also points to the importance of the social environment in developing antisocial behavior. In other words, even primary psychopaths respond to the influence of others in determining their behavior.

Secondary psychopaths have the same characteristics as primary psychopaths; however, the pathology in the secondary psychopath is *developed*, often as an adaptation to some severe trauma in early life, and usually as the result of parental abuse or rejection. Because of the importance of early-life trauma in developing secondary psychopathy, many criminologists use the term **sociopath** to distinguish persons with psychopathic characteristics that are largely the result of early life abuse and neglect. As noted by Anthony Walsh and Huei-Hsia Wu, "Sociopathy appears to be a condition less strongly tied to genotype than psychopathy and more tied to development in extremely adverse environments rife with abuse, neglect, and violence."[78]

Donald Lynam has shown how these constitutional (biological) and environmental (sociological) factors interact to produce psychopathy in young people. Children who present with severe hyperactivity, impulsivity, and attention problems often suffer from conduct problems (e.g., conduct disorder and oppositional defiant disorder). These children are very difficult to parent and manage in school, and their behavior often alienates them from conventional peers, resulting in social isolation and labeling. Over time, the antisocial aspects of their behavior become reinforced or exacerbated, while the positive aspects of their behavior become more infrequent and difficult to reinforce. Unless a major treatment intervention occurs, these "fledgling psychopaths" may develop into the most serious, violent, and chronic delinquents.[79]

Treatment of Psychopathic Youth

Whether prevention and treatment programs that specifically address the needs of juvenile psychopaths might prove successful is unknown because almost all of the evaluation research has been conducted on adult offenders. By and large, criminal justice treatments attempt to increase the prosocial abilities of offenders.

KEY TERMS

etiological
Relating to the cause of a behavior.

sociopath
A person who shows psychopathic characteristics that are largely the result of early-life abuse and neglect.

In the case of psychopathic offenders, the emphasis is placed on increasing empathy through intensive cognitive therapy and behavioral modification.

Amazingly, prior research shows that in some circumstances, treatment actually makes psychopaths more dangerous. For example, Marnie Rice and her colleagues evaluated an intensive therapeutic community program that included up to 80 hours of intensive group therapy per week. Whereas the treatment reduced recidivism among 146 nonpsychopathic offenders, it *increased* recidivism among 146 psychopathic offenders. By learning to adopt others' perspective and behave in socially acceptable ways, psychopaths were able to enhance their ability to manipulate, exploit, and victimize others.[80] Robert Hare and his colleagues similarly found that recidivism rates for psychopathic offenders who had taken social skills and anger management classes were higher than those without treatment.[81] Indeed, in their comprehensive review of the literature on treatment of psychopaths, Grant Harris and Marnie Rice concluded that "there is no evidence that any treatment yet applied to psychopaths has been shown to be effective in reducing violence or crime."[82]

Despite this grim assessment, many of the people who have the most contact with psychopathic juvenile delinquents—probation and detention officers within the juvenile justice system—believe that the most violent and antisocial youths can be rehabilitated. Keith Cruise and his colleagues surveyed 424 juvenile detention and probation officers and found that many had hope that the most severe juvenile offenders could be reformed. Nearly 61% felt that psychopathic youths are candidates for rehabilitation, and nearly 63% of probation officers believed that psychopathy could be changed. This study suggests that some of those with the most frequent contact with juvenile offenders still detect admirable traits that suggest the youths are amenable to turning their lives around. Simon Wilkinson and his colleagues conducted a systematic review of the treatment literature for psychopathic youth. In seven studies that examined the effects of behavioral therapy, emotion recognition treatment, and multimodal interventions on psychopathic personality traits after release from custody, four showed improvements. Among 15 studies that examined the effects of treatment after juvenile justice interventions, seven studies indicated that psychopathic youth performed worse and the remaining studies showed no effects. In other words, there is evidence for treatment success with psychopathic youth, but it is modest because psychopathic delinquents are usually much more severe in their behavior before treatment, thus the programs face an uphill battle in trying to treat them.[83]

Recent experimental research is also promising for treating psychopathic children. Yoast van Baardewijk and colleagues conducted an experiment where participants played a computer-based competitive reaction-time game against a simulated opponent by blasting him or her with loud noise through a headphone. In one condition, the victim experienced considerable distress and in the other condition, the victim expressed no distress. They found that more psychopathic children were more aggressive and likely to blast their opponents with noise. However, when faced with the distress that their aggression was causing, psychopathic youths were less likely to be aggressive again.[84] This shows that the disorder is not immutable and that children with psychopathic tendencies can learn to respond appropriately to the suffering of others.

Moreover, in the end, it may simply be too expensive *not* to treat serious delinquents who present psychopathic traits. Individual criminal careers ultimately cost society substantially more than $1 million per offender in assorted victimization and criminal justice costs, with the costs of chronic offenders and homicide offenders in the range of $10–20 million per offender (see **Box 4.7**, the "A Window on Delinquency" feature).[85] Recent research by Michael Caldwell and his colleagues found that for every $1 spent to provide intensive treatment to violent, psychopathic delinquents, $7 in various costs was saved or effectively prevented.[86]

The treatment of youthful psychopathic offenders must borrow heavily from the treatment of juvenile homicide offenders. Both groups represent the extremes of delinquency and point to the need for intensive, multifaceted, and sustained treatment. Kathleen Heide and Eldra Solomon present the following treatment protocol for the most violent of juvenile offenders:[87]

- Comprehensive cognitive behavioral restructuring
- Prosocial skills training
- Positive peer communities
- Anger management and appropriate emotional release
- Empathy training
- Clear, firm, and consistent discipline
- Drug and alcohol counseling and education
- Transitional treatment, including family counseling when appropriate
- Aftercare
- Psychopharmacological management
- Educational and vocational programs and other activities that promote prosocial opportunities for success

Psychological Theory and Delinquency Prevention

Psychological theories recommend two strategies for preventing delinquency, both of which are widely practiced today.

BOX 4.7

A Window on Delinquency

Psychopaths and Violence

Psychopathic offenders are noteworthy for the extremity of their violence. In the community, they are the most active, versatile, and relentless offenders; in prison, they are among the most violent and noncompliant inmates.

Several criminologists have explored the nature of offending by psychopathic individuals. For example, Stephen Porter and his colleagues compared murders committed by psychopaths and nonpsychopaths among inmates in Canadian prisons. They found that murders committed by psychopaths were more often characterized by sadism and more gratuitous violence (e.g., stabbings with dozens or hundreds of entry wounds) than were killings by nonpsychopathic offenders. In fact, more than 82% of psychopathic offenders committed these types of murders compared to 52% of nonpsychopathic offenders.

Katherine Ramsland researched psychopathic violence among children and adolescents and unearthed several cases that confirm the more serious nature of the violent acts committed by psychopaths:

- In 1979, 16-year-old Brenda Spencer received a rifle for her birthday. She used it to shoot children at an elementary school near her San Diego home, wounding nine and killing two. A reporter asked her later why she had done it. Her answer: "I don't like Mondays. This livens up the day."
- In 1993, two bodies were found on a country road in Ellis County, Texas—one male, one female. The boy, 14, had been shot, but the 13-year-old girl had been stripped, raped, and dismembered. Her head and hands were missing. The killer turned out to be

Jason Massey, who had decided he was going to become the worst serial killer that Texas had ever seen. He tortured animals, stalked another young woman, and revered killers like Ted Bundy. Massey was 9 years old when he killed his first cat, and he added dozens more feline victims over the years, along with dogs and even six cows. He had a long list of potential victims, and his diaries were filled with fantasies of rape, torture, and cannibalism of female victims. Massey was a loner who believed he served a "master" who gave him knowledge and power. He was obsessed with bringing girls under his control and having their dead bodies in his possession.

- Nine-year-old Jeffrey Bailey, Jr., pushed a 3-year-old friend into the deep part of a motel pool in Florida in 1986. He wanted to see someone drown. As the boy sank to the bottom, Jeffrey pulled up a chair to watch. When it was finished, he went home. When he was questioned, he was more engaged in being the center of attention than in demonstrating any kind of remorse for what he had done. About the murder, he was nonchalant.

Many adult serial homicide offenders indicate that they experienced homicidal ideation throughout their childhood and these feelings are often what drove analogous acts, such as cruelty to animals and experimentation with violent attacks against other children. Given these disturbing images, it is clear why juvenile psychopathy is such an important area of research to enable the prevention of serious youth violence.

Stephen Porter, Michael Woodworth, Jeff Earle, Jeff Drugge, and Douglas Boer, "Characteristics of Sexual Homicides Committed by Psychopathic and Non-psychopathic Offenders," *Law and Human Behavior* 27:457–470 (2003); Norair Khachatryan, Kathleen Heide, Erich Hummel, and Heng Choon (Oliver) Chan, "Juvenile Sexual Homicide Offenders: Thirty-Year Follow-Up Investigation," *International Journal of Offender Therapy and Comparative Criminology* 60:247–264 (2016); Ewa Stefanska, Adam Carter, Tamsin Higgs, Daz Bishopp, and Anthony Beech, "Offense Pathways of Non-Serial Sexual Killers," *Journal of Criminal Justice* 43:99–107 (2015); Katherine Ramsland, "The Childhood Psychopath: Bad Seed or Bad Parents?," retrieved February 5, 2016 from http://newsgroups.derkeiler.com/Archive/Sci/sci.med.psychobiology/2011-03/msg00022.html.

According to psychodynamic theory, if children's instinctual drives are not controlled, they will experience internal conflicts that will manifest themselves in delinquent behavior. Delinquency is thus a symptom of deep-seated psychological problems, and offenders need counseling to acquire an understanding of the cause of their mental disturbance. The use of psychodynamic theory in juvenile justice peaked in the 1950s when influential groups championed counseling, group therapy, and other respectable and solid correctional techniques. In turn, these and other groups seized upon the idea embedded in psychodynamic theory that it was possible to identify "predelinquents" before they committed crime; today these children are labeled "at-risk" youths. Prevention

programs were developed for children in need. These antidelinquency programs marked the beginning of the child-guidance movement, the goal of which was to neutralize latent delinquency in the preadolescent.

In contrast, behavioral theories see delinquency resulting from the interaction between children and their environment. Social policies derived from this approach emphasize teaching children alternative ways of living. One very popular application of behavioral theory is *behavior modification therapy*, a method for changing behavior through conditioning. Behavior modification was widely practiced in the late 20th century to treat maladaptive behaviors such as overeating, drug use, alcoholism, and smoking. Two behavior modification therapies used then, and still

practiced today, are aversion therapy and operant conditioning.

In *aversion therapy*, children are taught to connect unwanted behavior with punishment. For example, juvenile alcohol offenders may receive treatment where they must ingest a drug that causes nausea or vomiting if they drink alcohol. The underlying idea of this aversion therapy is that children will connect drinking with unpleasantness and stop drinking to avoid the ill effect.

Operant conditioning uses rewards to reinforce desired behavior and punishment to abort behavior. One application of operant conditioning with juvenile delinquents is found inside the walls of many juvenile reformatories, where a *token economy*—a system of handing out points that can be exchanged for privileges such as watching television and punishing behavior by taking those same privileges away—is in place.

Stephen Scott and his colleagues conducted a study where adults who had conduct disorder as children were compared to adults who had milder conduct problems as children and adults with no childhood psychopathology. By age 28, the costs imposed by persons diagnosed with conduct disorder at age 10 were 10 times higher than the costs associated with persons without diagnoses and nearly four times higher than the cost associated with persons with milder behavior problems. These costs included delinquency, crime, and victimization costs; extra educational costs; foster and residential care; health care; and criminal justice interventions. In other words, childhood psychopathology is a major predictor of how much an individual will cost society in the long term.[88]

In recognition of the high costs imposed by delinquents with personality and behavioral disorders, many prevention programs in the United States have sprung up to assist youths with these forms of psychopathology. Many programs include parent training, which educates parents about the most effective ways to manage and reduce their children's problem behaviors. Often the parent training incorporates behavioral family therapy, where both parents and child work with clinicians to address the antisocial behaviors and seek ways to change them to healthy behaviors.[89]

Allen Grove and his colleagues conducted a meta-analysis of 45 studies that were designed to prevent problems associated with aggression, conduct disorder, and oppositional defiant disorder among 9366 children. They found that, overall, the prevention studies reflected a small, positive effect on the symptoms of oppositional defiant and conduct disorders up to 2 years after the completion of the intervention. Programs were best at reducing property damage, such as vandalism, followed by mitigation of oppositional behaviors directed toward parents and teachers, and aggression. However, Grove and his colleagues temper the promising findings stemming from prevention efforts with this assessment of the causes of oppositional defiant and conduct disorders:

> The knowledge that prevention programs as a whole are having a small effect over time on symptoms of ODD and CD is a sobering reminder of how difficult it is to prevent disorders with such a wide array of causes. A child born with a low resting heart rate to a father who regularly attacks his mother living in an area of town where it is just as likely to hear gunfire as it is to hear children playing has a lot of strikes against him. Even if he is motivated to learn positive ways to deal with his anger through a school-based prevention program, he will return home every day to an environment equipped to destroy the gains he made in school that day. Or, if his mother learns positive ways to handle his anger through behavioral parent training, as soon as she gets home she may have to defend herself and her son from his father's abuse.[90]

Other studies have found that prevention programs for conduct disorder can significantly reduce the amount of time serious delinquents spend in jail, their risk of being arrested, and the speed with which they are subsequently arrested. Interventions for psychological causes of delinquency are imperative because conduct problems and disorders are not only expensive for communities to deal with, but they significantly reduce the quality of life for both the affected delinquent and his or her immediate environment.[91]

WRAP UP

THINKING ABOUT JUVENILE DELINQUENCY: CONCLUSIONS

This chapter has showcased the broad psychological approaches taken to understanding how our innermost thoughts, attitudes, and individual characteristics translate into delinquency. Psychodynamic theory

and behavioral theory point to the elements of the personality (id, ego, and superego), mental processes, and the ways that we learn from the environment to define our own personality as an explanation for our conduct. Structural models of the personality, such as the Five Factor Model of Personality, identify core personality characteristics and facets within those characteristics as ways to describe a person's beliefs, ways of thinking, motivations, and behaviors. Over time, psychologists have moved from simply studying the personality to studying antisocial personalities in an attempt to show how the psychological profile of a person's traits reflects how and why he or she may engage in delinquent behavior.

Another psychological approach to studying delinquency stems from the field of psychiatry and focuses on psychopathology—that is, the set of behaviors and attitudes that show clinical evidence of psychological impairment. One of the most basic psychological constructs with implications for delinquency is aggression. Although aggression is a universal concept and a measure that everyone has used (especially during childhood), it becomes the primary way to respond to others for a small group of youths. If aggression becomes worse, it can spill over into conflictive behavior with parents, peers, and teachers, and ultimately may result in serious clinical diagnosis, such as oppositional defiant disorder and its successor, conduct disorder. If antisocial attitudes and behaviors persist, children and adolescents are at risk for psychopathy, the most serious personality disorder. Youths with these forms of psychopathology are at risk for serious and lifelong criminal behavior; as a consequence, the effective prevention and treatment of these disorders is important for both the individual and for society as a whole.

The quote from Allen Grove in the previous section about the multiple etiological bases of delinquency attests that there is more to our behavior than our own psychological makeup. Taking a different perspective, sociologists develop delinquency theories of their own that highlight the role of social forces that influence and mold the ways we think, feel, believe, and behave.

CHAPTER SPOTLIGHT

- Psychodynamic theory explores the ways that early life experiences influence the personality, which in turn affects behavior.
- Behavioral theory asserts that behavior is the outcome of social interactions that occur throughout the life course. People learn by observing and imitating what they see and experience.
- Important differences may be discerned between delinquents and nondelinquents in terms of their moral development, sociability, and personality features.
- Oppositional defiant disorder and conduct disorder are among the most severe psychiatric diagnoses of childhood; both are strongly related to antisocial behavior.
- Psychopathy is a severe personality disorder that is evident in childhood and adolescence and has clear connections with many forms of delinquency.
- There is strong overlap between psychopathy and serious, violent, and chronic juvenile delinquency.

CRITICAL THINKING

1. Even if violent media images contribute to delinquency, what can be done about them? Should video games and violent, R-rated movies be banned? Who decides which material is appropriate and which material should be censored? Could this practice lead to problems that are greater than juvenile delinquency itself?
2. Have you ever observed toddler behavior? In what ways are toddlers aggressive toward themselves, other toddlers, older children, and their parents? Are these examples of aggression upsetting or normal? Which types of aggressive behavior do you feel would be cause for alarm?
3. Males and females are differentially prone to use direct and indirect aggression. Are gender differences in delinquency reflective of powerful psychological differences between boys and girls? If so, what are some of the psychological differences between the sexes?
4. Cynics would say that all adolescents argue with their parents, fail to comply with their parents' rules, are often reluctant to follow school rules, and are full of negative emotions. Does this statement mean that all adolescents have oppositional defiant disorder? What are the essential differences between psychopathology and normal adolescent angst?
5. As scientific discoveries produce more knowledge about how genes influence personality, do you foresee a point where the precise genetic cause of psychopathy will be known? If so, what should be done with that information?

Sociological Theories: Cultural Deviance, Strain, and Social Control

OBJECTIVES

‹ Understand cultural deviance theories and the ways that sociologists theorize about how neighborhoods influence individual behavior.

‹ Describe the various economic, social, and psychological strains that come from social inequality and the ways that strain contributes to delinquency.

‹ Identify social control theories of delinquency and explain how this perspective uses distinct assumptions about human nature.

‹ Evaluate Gottfredson and Hirschi's self-control construct as advanced in their *general theory of crime*.

‹ Identify the ways that sociological theories influence juvenile justice policies.

KEY TERMS

Biological and psychological theories blame delinquency on conditions located within the child. In the early 20th century, sociologists challenged this idea when they attributed delinquency to factors outside the person. The first group of sociological theories to advance this new position was known as cultural deviance theories, which assumed that children are incapable of committing "deviant" acts. Although children may commit deviant acts by the standards of middle-class society, they are not committing deviant acts by the standards of their own immediate neighborhood or community. In other words, cultural deviance theories see deviance as conformity to a set of values that are, although not accepted by the larger society, nevertheless widely accepted by a particular subcultural segment of society.

A second group of explanations, strain theories, contend that people are moral beings and commit crime when they are under great pressure. This pressure comes from legitimate desires. Children, for example, desire success because everyone tells them they should. Some children are unable to succeed by following the legitimate rules of society, so, out of desperation, they turn to crime to acquire the unattainable, which they may consider rightfully belongs to them.

The final group of theories discussed in this chapter comprises social control theories. These theories state that if a

The rise and fall of manufacturing jobs in the United States not only affects economic conditions but also provides the background for delinquency to flourish.

© Anton Gyozidkov/Shutterstock.

BOX 5.1

Theory in a Nutshell

Clifford Shaw and Henry McKay

Shaw and McKay argue that (1) run-down areas of a city create social disorganization, (2) social disorganization fosters cultural conflicts, (3) cultural conflict allows delinquency to flourish, and (4) when allowed to flourish, delinquency becomes a full-time career. Within some neighborhoods, delinquency becomes a tradition through the process of *cultural transmission*, whereby criminal values are passed from one generation to the next.

child's bond or tie to society has been broken, that individual is "free" to commit delinquency. At the core of social control theories is the question: Why do children obey the rules of society? Social control theories take deviance for granted and conformity to rules is what must be explained.

Cultural Deviance Theory

In *cultural deviance theory*, delinquency is said to be the natural result of conditions that exist within certain neighborhoods in cities. The theory was popular in the early 20th century when the Northeast and Midwest regions of the United States were undergoing rapid population growth as a result of the migration of southern African Americans and Eastern European immigrants looking for industrial jobs to cities such as Boston, Chicago, New York, and Philadelphia.

Many of the new residents were poorly educated, had few marketable skills, and did not speak English. To adapt to this growth, large cities expanded outward. More affluent residents moved to the suburbs, leaving poor and uneducated people behind to fend for themselves in the old, rundown inner cities.

Clifford Shaw and Henry Mckay

Two criminologists who examined this transformation as it emerged in Chicago were Clifford Shaw and Henry McKay. They believed delinquency was caused by the neighborhood in which a child lived. Instead of focusing on individual traits, such as the

child's body type or psychological conflicts, Shaw and McKay studied how "kinds of places" (neighborhoods) created conditions favorable to delinquency. They discovered that delinquency rates declined the farther one moved from the center of the city (see **Box 5.1**, the "Theory in a Nutshell" feature).

Shaw and McKay reached this conclusion by dividing Chicago into five concentric circles, or zones. At the center was the Loop, or the downtown business district where property values were highest (Zone I). Beyond the Loop was the zone of transition (Zone II), containing an inner ring of factories and an outer ring of "first-settlement colonies, of rooming-house districts of homeless men and low-wage workers, of resorts of gambling, bootlegging, sexual vice, and of breeding places of crime."[1] Zones III and IV were suburban residential areas, and Zone V extended beyond the suburbs. Delinquency rates were highest in the first two zones and declined steadily as one moved farther away from the city center (see **Figure 5.1**).

Shaw and McKay had a ready explanation for their findings. Neighboring railroads, stockyards, and industries made Zone II the least desirable residential area, but also the cheapest. Therefore, people naturally gravitated to this area if they were poor, as many immigrants to the United States were.

What did these findings say about delinquency? Shaw and McKay interpreted the findings in cultural and environmental terms. Delinquency rates remained stable in some Chicago neighborhoods, regardless of the race or ethnicity of the people who lived there. Areas high in delinquency at the turn of the century were also high in delinquency 30 years later, even though many of the original residents had moved away

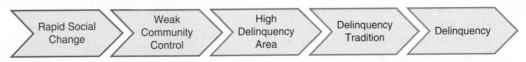

Figure 5.1 Mapping Delinquency Theory: Clifford Shaw and Henry McKay

© Jones & Bartlett Learning.

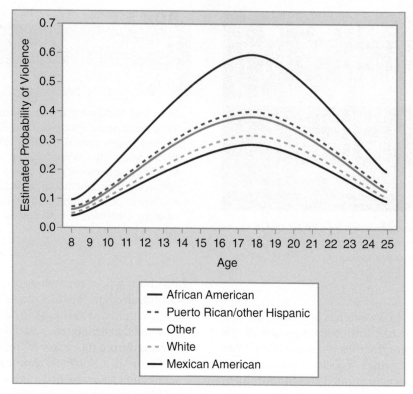

Figure 5.2 Racial and Ethnic Differences in Probabilities of Violent Delinquency

© Jones & Bartlett Learning.

or died. Shaw and McKay explained their findings in the following way:

- *Run-down areas create social disorganization.* At the time of Shaw and McKay's study, cities such as Chicago were expanding industrially, their populations were increasing, and segregation was forcing new immigrants into the slums. These immigrants were not familiar with the city's geography or culture; they arrived with different languages and work experiences; and they immediately faced new and overwhelming problems, including poverty, disease, and confusion.

- *Social disorganization fosters cultural conflicts.* In low-delinquency areas of the city, there typically was agreement among parents on which values and attitudes were the "right" ones, with general consensus regarding the importance of education, constructive leisure, and other child-rearing issues. Local institutions, such as the PTA, churches, and neighborhood centers, reinforced these conventional values. In contrast, no such consistency prevailed in high-delinquency areas. The norms of a variety of cultures existed side by side, creating a state of normative ambiguity, known as anomie. This condition was aggravated by the presence of people who promoted an unconventional lifestyle and defined behaviors such as theft as an acceptable way to obtain wealth. This value

system could count on the support of criminal gangs, rackets, and semilegitimate businesses.

- *Cultural conflict allows delinquency to flourish.* Children raised in low-socioeconomic, high-delinquency-rate areas were exposed to both conventional and criminal value systems. They saw criminal activities and organizations in operation daily. Successful criminals passed on their knowledge to younger residents, who in turn taught the knowledge to even younger children. Delinquency became a tradition in certain neighborhoods through the process of **cultural transmission**, whereby criminal values are passed from one generation to the next.

- *Allowed to flourish, delinquency becomes a full-time career.* Children in these Chicago neighborhoods dabbled in delinquency early in life, perhaps by age 5 or 6. Initial offenses were trivial, but their acts became increasingly serious, and delinquencies often became group efforts (see **Figure 5.2**).

For many years, few sociologists tested the ideas of Shaw and McKay. That changed beginning in 1989, when Robert Sampson and W. Byron Groves published research findings supporting Shaw and

KEY TERM

cultural transmission
The process through which criminal values are transmitted from one generation to the next.

McKay's general ideas.[2] Follow-up assessments of Shaw and McKay's theory have also found support for their propositions. Robert Sampson and Lydia Bean, for instance, used Shaw and McKay's propositions in their research on rural America and discovered the rate of juvenile violence was strongly correlated with rates of poverty concentration, single-parent families, and racial isolation.[3]

More recent research has shown that social disorganization theory is relevant not just in major cities, but also in the "hinterland." For instance, Matthew Lee found that rural communities characterized by a stable population base that is locally invested, a vibrant participatory civic culture, and an active middle-class experience lower rates of violent delinquency.[4] In other words, rural communities with ample social capital and a culture of investing in their community and its institutions have less delinquency. They are simply organized for prosperity. Today it is widely accepted that social ties or friendship networks lead to informal social controls, such as informal surveillance of the streets that ease the effects of social disorganization (e.g., poverty, residential instability, racial and ethnic heterogeneity).[5]

Collective efficacy provides an explanation for why some neighborhoods are unable to develop trust among residents and stop social problems from worsening.

It is also clear that different types of social ties vary in their ability to produce mechanisms of neighborhood control. The influence of friendship ties, for instance, may be weaker than the social control exerted by more formally organized networks. As has been reported by Mary Pattillo, whether social ties strengthen or weaken social controls depends on the particular neighborhood residents involved as well as on their specific interests. In her study of an African American neighborhood in Chicago, Pattillo found that some neighborhood networks (with law-abiding citizens) stimulated informal supervision of neighborhoods, whereas other networks (which included law-abiding citizens as well as gang members and drug dealers) undermined the neighborhood's efforts to fight delinquency. Similarly, Brian Stults examined the effects of social disorganization measures on homicide across 30 years of homicide data from Chicago. He found neighborhoods with greater family disruption and greater social disorganization were associated with homicide, but only in communities that had generally low levels of homicide. Otherwise, concentrated disadvantage and the associated concentration of serious violent felony delinquents was the strongest predictor of homicide.[6]

When Min Xie and David McDowall reviewed data from the National Crime Survey (now called the National Crime Victimization Survey), they found that housing turnover independently increases the risk that a dwelling will experience a crime, even when controlling for other relevant correlates of victimization. Consistent with social disorganization theory, neighborhoods characterized by high levels of residential turnover are prone to greater levels of delinquency and victimization. Irene Ng studied the relationship between neighborhood characteristics and serious juvenile delinquency in Wayne County (Detroit), Michigan. She found that poverty and inequality were associated with delinquency; however, there was no relationship between immigration and crime. In addition, residential stability was associated with more, not less serious delinquency. Drawing on data from the National Neighborhoods Study, which contains data on 7956 neighborhoods in 79 cities in the United States, Alyssa Chamberlain and John Hipp also found supporting evidence for social disorganization theory in terms of poverty and delinquency. However, they also found that relative deprivation—the difference in disadvantage between adjoining neighborhoods—was one of the strongest predictors of violent delinquency and property delinquency.[7]

For social ties to be effective at reducing delinquency, residents must be willing to take action—and whether they ultimately do depends on the level of mutual trust and solidarity among them. Robert Sampson and his colleagues have captured the core

of this idea in their notion of **collective efficacy**—the "mutual trust among neighbors combined with willingness to intervene on behalf of the common good, specifically to supervise children and maintain public order."[8] They found the degree of collective efficacy in a neighborhood is a better predictor of the violent crime rate in the neighborhood than either poverty or racial composition. Their findings have been supported by other researchers. In particular, Barbara Warner and Pam Wilcox have observed that concentrated disadvantage and the level of social ties both affect cultural strength, which in turn significantly affects informal social control. The importance of this work is that it illustrates the importance of weakened cultural strength in explaining informal social control in neighborhoods. Indeed, a recent study found that collective efficacy measures had weaker effects on reporting crime to the police in student neighborhoods near a large university because students lack the traditional community ties that other residents often have. Craig Uchida and his colleagues conducted one of the most nuanced and comprehensive studies of social disorganization and collective efficacy among eight diverse neighborhoods. These criminologists used refined measures of collective efficacy and of geographic neighborhoods to best capture the "essence" of each neighborhood, rather than relying on census tracts and other measures that are unable to capture the characteristics of people who live in each community. Their main finding was the linkages between social disorganization, collective efficacy, and crime depend on the socioeconomic, racial, and ethnic composition of the neighborhood. For example, within the entire sample there were significant relationships between collective efficacy and social cohesion and fear of crime, satisfaction with police, and perceived incivilities in the neighborhood. However, the satisfaction with the police was mostly associated with collective efficacy and social cohesion in nonwhite neighborhoods.[9]

Beyond crime, collective efficacy also affects other important facets of life. For instance, Catherine Ross suggests that the neighborhood disorder which reduces collective efficacy also poses a collective threat to the residents living there. This collective threat leads to alienation, powerlessness, and feelings of mistrust. The negative features that contribute to disorder, crime, and incivility also serve to undermine the confidence that residents can overcome the environment. To illustrate, Candice Odgers and her colleagues found that collective efficacy buffered children living in disadvantaged neighborhoods from antisocial behavior. But, that buffering effect is not possible if the levels of collective threat in a neighborhood are high.

Another important concept is street efficacy. **Street efficacy** is the perceived ability to avoid violent confrontations and be safe even in negative, violent environments. In other words, it describes a person who behaves in prosocial ways even in the face of street environments. In a study using data from the Project on Human Development in Chicago Neighborhoods, Patrick Sharkey examined the association between street efficacy and violent criminal behavior, including very serious delinquency, such as shooting someone or shooting at someone but missing. Sharkey found street efficacy was negatively associated with violence even while controlling for verbal ability, impulsivity, parental supervision, domestic violence, family criminality, marijuana use, alcohol use, school violence, and prior violence. He also controlled for neighborhood factors, including concentrated disadvantage, collective efficacy, and neighborhood violence. Youth with greater street efficacy were also less likely to use violence and less likely to associate with delinquent peers. Yue Yuan and his colleagues also found that youth with greater street efficacy are less fearful of crime.[10]

The **Project on Human Development in Chicago Neighborhoods** was designed to investigate the development of delinquency and violence in children and adolescents and has yielded a wealth of primary data with which to examine collective efficacy. The collective efficacy concept is useful for understanding how and why racial and economic differences between neighborhoods are related to the neighborhood's crime rate and general prosperity. Unfortunately, research shows the chilling levels of social inequality that exist in the United States for children of different racial, ethnic, and socioeconomic groups:[11]

- Children and adolescents raised in neighborhoods where most parents are unmarried and in neighborhoods largely populated with new immigrants have higher rates of violence.
- Witnessing or experiencing gun violence increases the likelihood of committing violence.
- The probability of violence varies greatly by race and ethnicity.
- Whites, African Americans, and Hispanics tend to flee neighborhoods that are low in collective

KEY TERMS

collective efficacy
Mutual trust among neighbors, combined with willingness to intervene on behalf of the common good—specifically, to supervise children and maintain public order.

street efficacy
The perceived ability to avoid violent confrontations and be safe even in negative, violent environments.

Project on Human Development in Chicago Neighborhoods
A study designed to investigate the development of delinquency and violence in children and adolescents; it has yielded primary data for examinations of collective efficacy.

efficacy, which in turn makes the problems of disorganized neighborhoods seem more intractable.

- Owing to their greater exposure to disorganized neighborhoods with low collective efficacy, African American children have deficits in verbal ability that are comparable to missing more than 1 year of school in comparison to white and Hispanic children.
- Among African American youth, exposure to a homicide in their neighborhood in the week prior to taking a standardized test at school was associated with a 0.5 to 1 standard deviation lower score on vocabulary and reading assessments. This amounts to about 15 fewer points on the exam because of the noxious environmental effects of homicide.

Even though Shaw and McKay's theory stands on solid footing, several questions remain to be answered in conjunction with their work. For example, do people living in high-crime-rate neighborhoods have different values than people living elsewhere? Edwin Sutherland has suggested that a **differential social organization** prevails among neighborhoods. Just because children in high-delinquency-rate neighborhoods might have regular contact with values that support criminality does not necessarily mean that they share the values or that their neighborhoods are disorganized. Perhaps their neighborhoods are just organized differently than other neighborhoods.

Ross Matsueda explored the idea of differential social organization by showing even in "bad" neighborhoods, people may band together to improve their community and work to reduce crime. Just by engaging in collective actions, such as attending city councils, participating in events at community centers, and using church services, people develop informal relationships that serve to deter others from committing crime. For instance, more than 10,000 African American males in Philadelphia recently launched a volunteer campaign to address the youth homicide problem in their city, a problem that has become so bad that the city has been nicknamed "Killadelphia." Similar efforts exist in cities across the United States, including Brooklyn, which suffers from a similar crime-inspired nickname of "Crooklyn." More recent support for differential social organization is seen in research by Markus Jokela. Using data on more than 20,000 people studied for more than a decade, Jokela found that in addition to delinquency, negative neighborhood characteristics were also associated with poorer health, reduced mental health, reduced healthy behaviors, more unhealthy behaviors, and other negative health features. However, these associations were due almost entirely to individual-level differences found between people. In other words, the negative traits of specific people is what makes certain neighborhoods bad.[12]

Simple exposure to violence in the most socially disorganized of neighborhoods creates multiple negative consequences. Dante Cicchetti and Michael Lynch developed an **ecological–transactional model of community violence**, which suggests that broad exposure to violence in the community stresses the ability of parents to protect their children from the pernicious effects of violence. Because of the toxic influences of gang activity and community violence, it becomes increasingly difficult for such parents to effectively monitor the activities of their children and adolescents. Over time, exposure to violence sets youth on a trajectory of increasingly declining parental monitoring. Cicchetti and Lynch's theory partially accounts for the entrenched nature of family dysfunction, gangs, and youth violence that characterize disorganized neighborhoods.

Richard Spano and his colleagues tested the ecological–transactional model of community violence using data from the Mobile Youth Survey—a sample of 360 youths living in 12 high-poverty neighborhoods in Mobile, Alabama. They found evidence of mutually reinforcing effects between exposure to community violence and parenting. Put simply, more violence exposure led to decreased parental monitoring; when dramatic exposure to violence occurred, this negative impact on parenting accelerated. Thus, community violence not only fuels the likelihood that youths will become juvenile delinquents and victims, but also undermines the ability of parents to protect their children from these effects.[13]

Sutherland does support the notion that some neighborhoods provide greater opportunities for children to learn criminal values. Some inner-city neighborhoods, for instance, are characterized by a predominance of delinquent gangs that *pull* adolescents into crime. Gangs influence the norms and behaviors of residents, thereby causing neighborhoods to appear as though they support criminal activity, even when they might not. As a consequence, crime rates in these neighborhoods will likely be higher than crime rates elsewhere in the city. Children living in high-crime-rate neighborhoods are at high risk for committing crime. Having ready access to firearms, for example, increases the risk

KEY TERMS

differential social organization
Neighborhoods are differentially organized based on a combination of prosocial and antisocial characteristics.

ecological–transactional model of community violence
Cicchetti and Lynch's theory, which suggests that broad exposure to violence in the community stresses the ability of parents to protect their children from the pernicious effects of violence.

If immersion in gang life is a central component of childhood socialization, is there any social policy that can prevent gang involvement? Who is most to blame if this child becomes a gang-affiliated juvenile delinquent?

© AlexandreNunes/Shutterstock.

of violence, and youths who carry guns are more likely to offend.[14]

Ruth Kornhauser thinks that all people share conventional values, including the desire to live in a crime-free neighborhood. According to Kornhauser, crime rates are high in some neighborhoods because the people living there have fewer opportunities to pursue conventional goals. These neighborhoods struggle to prevent crime because they lack the resources, willingness, or capacity to prevent it—not because they believe in oppositional values anchored in the community. In neighborhoods with weak conventional values, residents have little cultural support for exercising social control over others. It is also possible that high-crime-rate neighborhoods lack a consensus of moral values and residents are exposed to both law-abiding and deviant lifestyles. To put this idea differently, a segment of the neighborhood is attached to conventional values whereas another segment is not.[15]

That these differences exist speaks to the need for additional research. Of particular interest to criminologists is discovering how oppositional values arise in high-crime-rate neighborhoods. To what extent do residents of different neighborhoods reject conventional values and norms? Are conventional values attenuated or suspended because residents have learned to expect deviant behavior on the street? Are there neighborhoods in which the majority of residents believe it is acceptable to take the law into their own hands—for example, to retaliate against people who have offended or attacked them?

An important caveat must be heeded regarding Shaw and McKay's theory: Sometimes their theory leads to a misinterpretation of the crime problem. Recall that findings about a neighborhood *do not* necessarily apply to all of its residents. If you use neighborhood-level data to draw conclusions about individual residents, you are committing the **ecological fallacy**: Knowledge about a neighborhood says nothing about the behavior of specific individuals. It is not necessarily true that when a high crime rate is discovered in a crowded neighborhood where the residents are poor and uneducated that those uneducated and poor individuals are criminals. Indeed, many protective factors have been found to predict successful life outcomes among youths living in neighborhoods characterized by delinquency, poverty, and social disorganization. Using data from cohorts in Chicago and Denver, Delbert Elliott, William Julius Wilson, and their colleagues found many correlates to being a "good kid from a bad neighborhood."[16]

- **Personal competence**, which is characterized by generally high individual levels of self-esteem, self-efficacy, perceived popularity with peers, school attachment, future educational expectations, and perceived future opportunities in life.
- **Prosocial competence**, which is characterized by generally high individual levels of personal efficacy, educational expectations, grades, commitment to conventionality, and involvement in conventional activity.
- **Prosocial behavior**, which is characterized by good grades and involvement in sports, religious, and family activities.

Edwin Sutherland

Among Edwin Sutherland's most important contributions to delinquency is his *theory of differential association*, in which he described the process of becoming delinquent. Sutherland's work dominated U.S. criminology for nearly four decades, from the 1930s to the 1970s.

Sutherland first published the theory of differential association in 1939, revising it in 1947. Sutherland

KEY TERMS

ecological fallacy
An error that occurs when neighborhood-level data are used to draw conclusions about individual residents.

personal competence
The combination of generally high individual levels of self-esteem, self-efficacy, perceived popularity with peers, school attachment, future educational expectations, and perceived future opportunities in life.

prosocial competence
The combination of generally high individual levels of personal efficacy, educational expectations, grades, commitment to conventionality, and involvement in conventional activity.

prosocial behavior
The combination of behaviors such as good grades and involvement in sports, religious, and family activities.

BOX 5.2
Theory in a Nutshell
Edwin Sutherland

Sutherland told us that delinquent behavior is learned from intimate others, parents and peers, for instance. Children who become delinquents have learned an excess of definitions favorable to the violation of law over definitions unfavorable to the violation of law.

argues that behavior is learned through interaction with significant others, typically parents and peers (see **Box 5.2**, the "Theory in a Nutshell" feature). The likelihood of a youth becoming delinquent is determined by his or her interactions with both conventional and criminal associations. If a child has more contacts supporting criminal conduct than opposing it, then he or she will be more likely to commit crime than someone who has more positive than negative associations.

The theory of differential association consists of nine principles:[17]

1. Delinquent behavior is learned; it is not inherited. Biological and hereditary factors are rejected as explanations for the cause of delinquency. Only sociological factors explain why youth commit crime.
2. Delinquent behavior is learned through interaction with others by way of communication. This communication can be either verbal or nonverbal.
3. Learning occurs in intimate groups. It is in small, face-to-face gatherings that children learn to commit crime.
4. In intimate groups, children learn techniques for committing crime as well as the appropriate motives, attitudes, and rationalizations for doing so. The learning process involves exposure not only to the techniques of committing offenses, but also to the attitudes or rationalizations that justify those acts.
5. The specific direction of motives and drives is learned from definitions of the legal code as being favorable or unfavorable. The term "definitions" refers to attitudes. Attitudes favoring law breaking are common, for instance, among youths who engage in vandalism against schools or companies that adolescents feel "deserve" to have graffiti sprayed on their buildings.
6. A juvenile becomes delinquent because of his or her exposure to an excess of definitions favorable to the violation of law over definitions unfavorable to the violation of law. This sixth principle is the core of the theory of differential association. A parent who even hints through words or actions that it is acceptable to fight, treat women as potential conquests, cheat on income tax returns, or lie may promote delinquency in children unless these statements are outnumbered by definitions (attitudes) that favor obeying the law—for example, driving within the speed limit. Definitions favorable to the violation of law can be learned from both criminal and noncriminal people.
7. The tendency toward delinquency will be affected by the frequency, duration, priority, and intensity of learning experiences. The longer, earlier, more intensely, and more frequently youths are exposed to attitudes about delinquency (both pro and con), the more likely they will be influenced. Sutherland used the term *intensity* to refer to the degree of respect a person gives to a role model or associate. Thus correctional officers are not likely to become criminals, despite the positive things inmates say about living a life of crime. The reason is that officers do not respect the inmates and, therefore, do not adopt their beliefs, values, and attitudes.
8. Learning delinquent behavior involves the same mechanisms involved in any other learning. While the content of what is learned is different, the process for learning any behavior is the same.
9. Criminal behavior and noncriminal behavior are expressions of the same needs and values. In other words, the goals of delinquents and nondelinquents are similar. What is different are the means they use to pursue their goals.

Differential association theory shaped criminology for nearly a half-century. A clear signal of its widespread acceptance was the many research studies testing and critiquing it. These investigations generally revealed that children are more likely to commit delinquency and engage in other negative behaviors when they associate with delinquent peers.[18] Many studies have found that children with prosocial peers are not only less likely to commit delinquency, but also less likely to experience a range of problems in life. Pablo Vidal-Ribas and his colleagues studied a sample of nearly 8000 youth from the British Child and Adolescent Mental Health Survey and found that positive attributes of youth, such as hanging out with prosocial peers, led to significantly less psychopathology and other problems across life. Positive youth who hang out with other positive youth are less likely to have school problems, less likely to be truant, less likely to commit delinquency, less likely to ever be contacted by police, less likely to have emotional problems, and less likely to develop a psychiatric disorder.[19] Mark Warr even goes so far as to say that the nature of peer associations is the *best* predictor of delinquency:

No characteristic of individuals known to criminologists is a better predictor of criminal behavior than

the number of delinquent friends an individual has. The strong correlation between delinquent behavior and delinquent friends has been documented in scores of studies from the 1950s up to the present day . . . using alternative kinds of criminological data (self-reports, official records, perceptual data) on subjects and friends, alternative research designs, and data on a wide variety of criminal offenses. Few, if any, empirical irregularities in criminology have been documented as often or over as long a period as the association between delinquency and delinquent friends.[20]

Warr documented these statements through a comprehensive review of the large body of research on the group nature of delinquency and the role of peers in delinquency in the United States and throughout the world.

Nicole Piquero and her colleagues, who studied the impact of delinquent peers on the delinquency of boys and girls, extended Warr's study. These researchers found that delinquent peer association is a good predictor of delinquency generally, although it is a better predictor of delinquency for boys than girls.[21] By contrast, Dana Haynie and her colleagues found peer relationships—especially those involving romantic peers—have greater effects on girls' than boys' delinquency.[22]

Research has also found that peer associations have a greater impact on a child's behavior than do long-standing relationships.[23] Delinquent friends, in other words, do not have much of an effect on a child's attitudes, but rather have a temporary and short-term influence on the child's behavior. Delinquent behavior may not be the result of lifelong learning, but a result of immediate and current relationships with delinquent peers. Barbara Costello and Paul Vowell discovered that friends' attitudes and behaviors have direct effects on offending that are not mediated by the child's own attitudes. Associating with delinquent friends influences a child's behavior in ways that have nothing to do with the child's attitudes about crime.[24]

More recent research has shed light on the ways that differential association works depending on the strength, density, and relative nature of peer networks (see **Box 5.3**, the "A Window on Delinquency" feature).

Several investigations of the peers–delinquency relationship using the National Longitudinal Study of Adolescent Health have been conducted in recent years. Dana Haynie examined the effects of delinquent peers among a nationally representative sample of youths. She found that delinquent peers influence an individual's own conduct, but that the influence depends on how many friends a person has, how popular he or she is, and how close the friendship is. When adolescents are embedded in very deep, cohesive social networks, then peer effects are powerful. By comparison, the effects are less powerful when

friendships are peripheral or loose. Put differently, the effects of peer delinquency are relative to the strength or weakness of the friendship network. Adolescents also commit more delinquency if they have *highly* delinquent friends and if they spend a great deal of time in unstructured activities that lend themselves to getting into trouble. Interestingly, the effects of peers are more limited than the theory suggests, and peer effects do not necessarily increase even if a teen spends more time with peers.[25] This finding suggests that although differential association is an important theory of delinquency, peer effects do not work the same way for everyone.[26] For instance, Ilhong Yun and his colleagues observed that genetic factors are partially responsible for why people are differently affected by delinquent peers.[27]

A related shortcoming of Sutherland's theory is that he focused only on face-to-face interactions. In the late 1930s, when Sutherland was writing, the influence of film, the Internet, music, television, and video games on behavior was either nonexistent or was considered to have little impact. Notice that the nine principles of his theory listed earlier make no mention of how the mass media might influence behavior. This omission prompted criminologists to reexamine Sutherland's theory. To overcome this gap in the differential association theory, Daniel Glaser introduced the *differential identification theory*, in which he suggested that face-to-face interactions were only one way children might learn conventional and deviant values. According to Glaser, children might also learn values and social roles from characters in films.[28]

C. Ray Jeffery offered another modification to Sutherland's theory. In his *differential reinforcement theory*, Jeffery suggested that (1) children learn from the outcomes of their actions and (2) both social and nonsocial factors influence their behavior. A child who steals food, for instance, may receive reinforcement from the fact that the stolen goods provide the child with nourishment (nonsocial) and from the approval he or she receives from family and friends for being able to "get away with it" (social).[29]

Building on Jeffery's theory and his earlier work with Robert Burgess, Ronald Akers has restated differential association theory to incorporate their new ideas.[30] The result was a theory composed of seven propositions:[31]

1. Deviant behavior is learned according to the principles of operant conditioning.
2. Deviant behavior is learned in nonsocial situations that are either reinforcing or discriminating and through social interactions in which the behavior of other persons is either reinforcing or discriminating for such behavior.
3. The principal part of learning deviant behavior occurs in those groups that comprise or control the individual's major source of reinforcements.

BOX 5.3

A Window on Delinquency

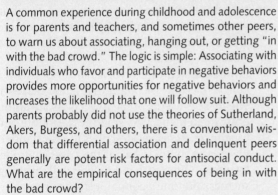

In with the Bad Crowd

A common experience during childhood and adolescence is for parents and teachers, and sometimes other peers, to warn us about associating, hanging out, or getting "in with the bad crowd." The logic is simple: Associating with individuals who favor and participate in negative behaviors provides more opportunities for negative behaviors and increases the likelihood that one will follow suit. Although parents probably did not use the theories of Sutherland, Akers, Burgess, and others, there is a conventional wisdom that differential association and delinquent peers generally are potent risk factors for antisocial conduct. What are the empirical consequences of being in with the bad crowd?

A survey of over 600 children and adolescents examined the validity of a range of predictors on seven forms of antisocial behavior, including child-reported and parent-reported aggression, child-reported and parent-reported rule-breaking, nonviolent crimes, violent crimes, and bullying behavior. Having delinquent peers was significantly associated with all seven of these antisocial outcomes, and in several cases was the strongest predictor despite controls for gender, depression, neighborhood factors, negative adult relationships, antisocial personality, family attachment, family conflict, psychological aggression, exposure to television violence, and exposure to video game violence.

In a study based on a natural experiment where juvenile delinquents were placed either in residential settings with intensive exposure to delinquent youth or in community-based settings with variable amounts of delinquent youth, Cheri Shapiro and her colleagues found that youths with residential placements had higher recidivism rates. This finding suggests that those with greater delinquent peer exposure were worse off than their less exposed peers. In follow-up analyses using propensity score matching, a statistical technique that controls for unobserved selection effects, the link between greater delinquent peer exposure and greater delinquency was confirmed.

Beidi Dong and Marvin Krohn examined 14 waves of data from the Rochester Youth Development Study to investigate the development of delinquent peer associations and gang affiliation across adolescence. They found that as delinquent peer associations increased so did involvement in delinquency, and the general effects of peer associations overlapped with gang affiliation. They also found that youth who were more involved in gangs were also the most violent and had more arrests. A large-scale meta-analysis of 133 studies published over a nearly 30-year span found that social learning based theories of crime—all of which point to the risks of being in the bad crowd—are significantly associated with conduct problems, delinquency, and violence. Differential association and holding definitions favorable to crime are most strongly related to crime. Reinforcement and imitation are also significantly related to crime, but their effects are smaller and less consistent.

In the biosocial age, criminologists have shown that delinquent peer association is partially caused by genetic factors, whereby youth with antisocial traits select peers who are similar to them in terms of their proneness for delinquency. Thus, the notion that certain people gravitate toward troubled others for friendship is supported by molecular genetic studies. All told, the conventional wisdom about antisocial peers and their negative effects on one's own conduct is true, and supported by criminological research.

Christopher Ferguson, Claudia San Miguel, and Richard Hartley, "A Multivariate Analysis of Youth Violence and Aggression: The Influence of Family, Peers, Depression, and Media Violence," *The Journal of Pediatrics* 155:904–908 (2009); Cheri Shapiro, Bradley Smith, Patrick Malone, and Alyssa Collaro, "Natural Experiment in Deviant Peer Exposure and Youth Recidivism," *Journal of Clinical Child and Adolescent Psychology* 39:242–251 (2010); Beidi Dong and Marvin Krohn, "Dual Trajectories of Gang Affiliation and Delinquent Peer Association During Adolescence: An Examination of Long-Term Offending Outcomes," *Journal of Youth and Adolescence* 45:746–762 (2016); Travis Pratt, Francis Cullen, Christine Sellers, Thomas Winfree, Jr., Tamara Madensen, Leah Daigle, Noelle Fearn, and Jacinta Gau, "The Empirical Status of Social Learning Theory: A Meta-Analysis," *Justice Quarterly* 27:765–802 (2010); Frank Vitaro, Mara Brendgen, and Eric Lacourse, "Peers and Delinquency: A Genetically Informed, Developmentally Sensitive Perspective," pages 221–236 in Julian Morizot and Lila Kazemian (eds.), *The Development of Criminal and Antisocial Behavior: Theory, Research and Practical Applications* (New York: Springer, 2015).

4. Learning deviant behavior includes specific techniques, attitudes, and avoidance procedures and is a function of the effective and available reinforcers and the existing reinforcement contingencies.

5. The specific class of behavior learned and its frequency of occurrence are a function of the effective and available reinforcers and the deviant or nondeviant direction of the norms, rules, and definitions that in the past have accompanied the reinforcements.

6. The probability that a person will commit deviant behavior is increased in the presence of normative statements, which, in the process of differential reinforcement of such behavior over conforming behavior, have acquired discriminative value.

7. The strength of deviant behavior is a direct function of the amount, frequency, and probability of its reinforcement.

Central to Akers' reformulation are propositions 2, 3, 5, and 6. Propositions 2 and 3 state that learning takes place in nonsocial situations; however, most learning occurs in social interactions with significant others. Propositions 5 and 6 speak to the importance of social definitions: Children who receive an excess of definitions favorable to the violation of law over definitions unfavorable to the violation of law are more likely to commit crime.

Walter Miller

Walter Miller worked for a number of years with delinquent gangs in Roxbury, Massachusetts, which is a poor neighborhood within the city of Boston. His experiences led him to see delinquency as an expression of a particular culture present in slum neighborhoods. (See **Box 5.4**, the "Theory in a Nutshell" feature.)

Miller's contribution to delinquency theory is explaining gang delinquency. His research methods have often included innovative approaches, using unobtrusive observation techniques. For example, Miller would go to a pizza parlor and pretend to be completely absorbed in his meal and newspaper. Actually, he was listening carefully to what the youths around him were talking about. He took extensive notes, which were later mined for theoretical nuggets. Miller's theory of juvenile delinquency is summarized here:[32]

- The lower class has a distinctive family structure. Female-based households and serial monogamy characterize lower-class families. Women run the household, and they go through a series of husbands or lovers. Because there are inevitably periods when no men are in their lives, women have to fend for themselves and their children.
- This family structure alienates boys, pushing them to join all-male peer groups. Miller believes that boys grow up with the traditional belief that a boy should not be told what to do by his mother,

aunt, or older sister. With no fathers or father figures present, however, lower-class boys are subject to the control and authority of women. Resenting this pattern, they seek the company of males who congregate on the street corner or in other gathering places, such as the pool hall.
- In these all-male peer groups, lower-class culture is created and transmitted. Boys develop values and standards that mirror those of lower-class culture in general.
- Lower-class culture revolves around six **focal concerns**—that is, values that guide behavior. The focal concerns of the lower class are autonomy, excitement, fate, smartness, trouble, and toughness. *Autonomy* describes the resistance of lower-class youths to having their lives controlled by others. Often such individuals will say things such as "No one's gonna push me around" or "He can shove this job up his ass." Curiously, the *actual* behavior of lower-class people contradicts the cultural value of autonomy. Typically, they seek out jobs in restrictive settings where they are told what to do and when to do it because they identify strong controls with being cared for. *Excitement* is the search for thrills, danger, or risk that often occurs through excessive drinking, fighting and gambling, and promiscuous sexual relationships. *Fate* is the belief that forces beyond their control determine lower-class individuals' lives. These forces are not religious, but rather refer to whether someone is naturally lucky or unlucky. *Smartness* is the ability to avoid being outfoxed; it refers to "street smarts," or the skill to take advantage of the weaknesses of others. *Toughness* is a physical prowess that is often displayed through machismo (lack of sensitivity and treating women as sex objects and conquests). *Trouble* is the most important concern. Getting into and staying out of trouble are major preoccupations of lower-class people. Children are judged (assigned status) based on their affinity for trouble. Focal concerns are not unique to the lower class; however, they are more significant to this group than they are to the middle and upper classes.
- Strong identification with the focal concerns of lower-class culture leads to violations of the law. Lower-class adolescent boys in gangs get into trouble because they live up to the standards presented to them in lower-class culture; according to the middle class, these standards or values are delinquent.

BOX 5.4

Theory in a Nutshell

Walter Miller

Miller blames delinquency on two structural features associated with the lower class: focal concerns and female-based households. Together, they produce sex-role problems for boys. Boys, who need to learn to become men, must learn from women. This learning is inadequate, so they join together and form a gang. Status is achieved in the gang by living up to focal concerns, some of which lead to delinquency.

KEY TERM

focal concerns
The primary values that monopolize lower-class consciousness.

Strong identification with these values explains why boys commit crime. Children participate in delinquency because they must live up to the standards of their neighborhood, regardless of what outsiders think about what they are doing. The focal concern of toughness, for instance, may mean the juvenile must fight when disrespected; possessing street smarts (smartness) may lead to drug dealing; and excitement may result in excessive drinking, gambling, or using of illegal drugs. The linkages among Miller's statements are illustrated in **Figure 5.3**.

Miller's theory focuses on the "culture of poverty" and America's underclass—concerns that are becoming more popular. The notion of a culture of poverty can be traced to Oscar Lewis, who, in his studies of Latin America, described a situation where people resigned themselves to being poor as a matter of fate. Children growing up in this environment eventually believed the same thing about their future: No matter what they did, fate had determined that they, too, would be poor.[33]

William Julius Wilson has also reported on the U.S. underclass. In the 1980s, Wilson explained why Chicago's inner-city neighborhoods deteriorated. This deterioration has been gradual and has often been blamed on structural changes occurring in society at large. As society became more integrated, opportunities for the professional and entrepreneurial class of African Americans increased. The members of this class, in turn, moved from the inner city to the suburbs to pursue the "good life." They took with them not only their money and their businesses, but also their values, which emphasized upward mobility. In their wake, they left behind a hard-core group of chronically unemployed, unskilled, and poorly educated people who lacked the social, economic, or political base from which to prosper. Ultimately, this migration resulted in the urban plight of the

1980s. In inner-city neighborhoods, an underclass of "truly disadvantaged" people emerged who lived in areas riddled with social ills: homicide, violence, fetal alcohol syndrome, illegal drug use, teen pregnancy, unemployment, and so on.[34]

Over the years, the United States has changed from a manufacturing to a service economy. In the past several decades, industrial production has declined and an increasing number of jobs have been outsourced to other countries, triggering a decrease in the demand for unskilled labor. Much of the production that remains has followed a trend of relocation—namely, shifting manufacturing jobs to foreign countries or to the suburbs. As opportunity declines, crime flourishes.[35] More recently, Wilson and his colleague, Richard Taub, documented some positive changes related to the emergence of the service economy. In Chicago and other major cities—many of which were recently urban wastelands to be avoided—disadvantaged neighborhoods have experienced reinvestment, developed increased cultural amenities, and even been the sites of professional sports stadiums. Although these businesses reflect the sway of a new type of economy, they have often resulted in renewal of the city.[36] Interestingly, although Wilson's thesis is widely supported, it has not fared well during the Great Recession, from 2008 to the present. Despite an economic downturn of a magnitude that has not been seen since the Great Depression, delinquency and violence actually have continued to decline.

The central issue, however, is not whether there is a culture of poverty or an underclass; experts agree that they exist. What experts disagree about is *why* they exist. Two competing lines of thought seek to explain this phenomenon. Edward Banfield believes that "birds of a feather flock together."[37] Poor people are attracted by, and relocate to, the inner city because of the presence of distinctive subcultural values that discourage personal achievement. In other words, they are looking for support for their low aspirations and lack of accomplishment. One aspect of inner-city living that Banfield finds particularly disturbing is its emphasis on immediate satisfaction rather than deferred gratification. Inner-city residents live for the moment rather than for tomorrow. As a result, they achieve very little. In effect, they perpetuate their own poverty and that of their children. According to this line of thought, many of our nation's poor people are irresponsible and reap what they deserve; they are responsible for their own circumstances.

Others disagree. For them, the poor are victims of unfair policies that regulate the distribution of wealth. According to these critics, Banfield is "blaming the victim."[38] This alternative view claims that

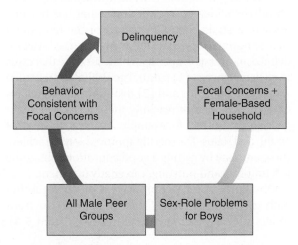

Figure 5.3 Mapping Delinquency Theory: Walter Miller
© Jones & Bartlett Learning.

the government purposely creates poverty because poverty is functional:[39]

- Poverty ensures that society's "dirty work" will be done. Society can fill these jobs by paying higher wages than for "clean work," or it can force people who have no other choice to do the dirty work.
- Because poor people must work at low wages, they subsidize many services that benefit the affluent. For example, domestic workers subsidize the upper middle and upper classes, making life easier for their employers.
- Poverty creates jobs for a number of occupations and professions that serve or "service" the poor or that protect the rest of society from them—for example, welfare agencies and the criminal and juvenile justice systems.
- Poor people can be identified and punished as alleged or real deviants to uphold the legitimacy of conventional norms.

According to this theory, poor people serve as a living example of the fate that befalls those who violate norms regarding work, family, and moral turpitude.

Strain Theory

One of the building blocks of strain theory is the idea of *anomie*, which was originally developed by the French sociologist Emile Durkheim, one of the founders of modern sociology.[40] Writing in the late 19th century, Durkheim wanted to understand the social change brought about by the Industrial Revolution and the ways in which it had influenced society. He believed unlimited aspirations and desires are a natural part of human nature. To temper the natural impulses people have and provide stability in society to ensure the greatest happiness for the greatest number, social controls are necessary. Preindustrial societies had a high degree of social cohesion and strong traditional

The shock of Hurricane Katrina created a sense of confusion and normlessness known as *anomie*. Without guidance, people often turn to delinquency.

Courtesy of Jocelyn Augustino/FEMA.

restraints, as reflected in the church and other institutions, which were later eroded in industrial societies.

In the aftermath of the Industrial Revolution, with the increased complexity of society, growth in individualization, and continued diversification of the division of labor, social bonds weakened, leading to the disruption of the normative structure. Social controls take the form of both norms and sanctions that regulate the day-to-day lives of people. Durkheim noticed that when a society goes through abrupt, rapid social change, such as a depression or war, the normative structure is disrupted. The resulting chaos can produce a period of **anomie**, or normlessness. Without norms, some people do not have the self-control to avoid deviance; they do not understand the rules well enough and will do anything to satiate their unlimited desires.

A state of anomie may affect an entire nation, such as the uncertainty and fear that gripped citizens in the United States during the Great Recession. Anomie can also affect certain groups of citizens, such as the victims of Hurricane Katrina, who experienced mass migrations from one area into culturally and normatively different regions. It can also affect smaller groups of people or individuals. For instance, a family moving from one area of the country to another might encounter a different sense of normative restraints and find themselves going through as radical a change from one value system to another as they would have experienced had they been caught up in a nationwide depression. Sometimes students going away to college for the first time experience anomie as they adapt to life outside their family structure. People bring their own norms with them, only to find another set of values and behaviors in the new locale. The process of meshing the old and new together can cause a radical change within people and society at large.

Robert Merton

In 1938, Robert Merton wrote an article that expanded Durkheim's idea of anomie into what has become known as strain theory.[41] Instead of the temporary state of normlessness that Durkheim described, Merton defined anomie as the permanent disjuncture that exists in society between (1) cultural goals that are regarded as worth striving for and (2) institutionalized means or approved ways of reaching these goals. The main goals in U.S. society, for example, are the acquisition of wealth and status. The socially approved ways to achieve these ends are by getting a good education, obtaining job training, and pursuing career advancement.

Obviously, some people have a much smoother path to follow to success than those who are born to less advantageous circumstances (see **Figure 5.4**).

KEY TERM

anomie
Normlessness leading to social disorganization.

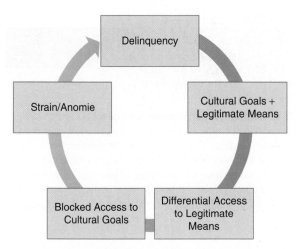

Figure 5.4 Mapping Delinquency Theory: Robert Merton

© Jones & Bartlett Learning.

The playing field is not equal, in that some people have ascribed qualities (male and white, for example), resources (wealthy parents and the "right" connections), and environmental advantages (growing up on the "right side of the tracks" or in a family that believes in the value of education and the work ethic) that are supportive of the pursuit of the goal. For many children, however, access to legitimate means of achieving socially acceptable goals is blocked. Doors to a good education or to a good job may be closed, which creates a problem, because those individuals desire wealth and status just as much as their more privileged counterparts.

Merton believed that this kind of strain between means and goals is always present in society and identified five ways people adapt to the frustration. Most people are *conformists*, meaning that they buy into the system and accept both the goals defined by the culture and the socially defined means to get there. Merton uses the term *innovators* to describe those individuals who strive for society's goals but do so through means that deviate from the norms of society. For example, criminals aspire to wealth, yet use unacceptable means to reach it. *Ritualists* are persons who do not subscribe to the goals of society, although they still participate in socially accepted means to support themselves. The assembly-line worker who shows up to work, day after day, minding the norms of society, satisfied with his or her safe routine with no hope or desire in reaching the goal of success, is such a ritualist. Individuals who have dropped out of society altogether, such as drug addicts, alcoholics, and many homeless people, believe in neither the means nor the goals of society; Merton labels them as *retreatists*. These people have withdrawn into what society considers a nonproductive world of their own. Finally, Merton discusses a method of adaptation he calls *rebellion*. Rebels are individuals who do not subscribe to either the means society feels are legitimate or the goals that society defines. These people are revolutionaries who define their own goals and find unique ways to achieve them.

Merton assumed that children are inherently good and commit delinquencies only when their backs are against the wall. According to Merton, if society could erase the conditions that produce strain, such as poverty and inequality, it might also be able to prevent delinquency.

Some criminologists believe Merton overstated the impact of strain on children. Others criticize him for failing to identify which juveniles, when denied access to legitimate means to obtain socially acceptable goals, will commit crime. Of course, other adaptations to strain might exist, including combinations of ideas that Merton developed. For example, Daniel Murphy and Matthew Robinson describe another adaptation type—the *maximizer*—who is a blend of a conformist and an innovator. The maximizer is usually involved in legitimate activities but will occasionally engage in illegitimate means, if the opportunity arises, to achieve his or her goals.[42]

Merton also did not say much about the relationship between frustration and delinquency. Why do some children who are frustrated refrain from committing crime, whereas others who appear to have less reason to become frustrated commit crime? Merton also did not answer an important question about the distribution of goals and means: In American society, what is the process for the assimilation of goals and how is accessibility to means to achieve those goals determined? It is also difficult to generalize, as Merton did, from the highly successful innovators to juvenile delinquents. Many juvenile offenses—for example, drinking alcohol, smoking marijuana, truancy, and fighting—net very little or no money. Often delinquency is not the lucrative career that Merton posits.

Margaret Farnworth and Michael Leiber believe that these criticisms of Merton's work are unfair. They think that critics have never really tested Merton's theory but instead tested their own misguided reinterpretations of it.[43] Nonetheless, its flaws aside, Merton's theory did inspire other criminologists to develop strain theories of their own. One who did was Albert Cohen.

Albert Cohen

In his 1955 book *Delinquent Boys*, Albert Cohen built upon Merton's ideas and explained why urban, lower-class boys commit crime.[44] The response to Cohen's book was very favorable, and the few critics who disagreed with him felt compelled to build rival theories.

Cohen's theory is a parable—a simple story with an obvious moral. Cohen described delinquents in terms of what he believed to be their main characteristics: They are *malicious, negativistic,* and *nonutilitarian.* Malicious behaviors are committed out of spite. Delinquent boys get their kicks from bullying nondelinquents, and they show the same kind of spite toward their

schools and teachers. Delinquents are also negativistic, believing their behavior is right precisely because it is wrong according to the norms and rules of the larger society. Their behavior is nonutilitarian because their activities do not produce a direct economic benefit. According to Cohen, delinquents "steal for the hell of it." His position is that delinquents are out to have fun—a point of view that stands in direct opposition to Merton's opinion that delinquents commit instrumental theft.

According to Cohen, the activities of delinquents show they have other traits as well, which he identifies as *versatility*, short-run *hedonism*, and *group autonomy*. Delinquents' versatility is shown in their tendency to dabble in many delinquent activities—stealing, vandalism, trespassing, truancy, and so on. Evidence of short-run hedonism is the fact that delinquents are often impatient and impulsive. These individuals are out for fun.

They do not take kindly to rules, schedules, or organization, nor do they plan ahead, study, or practice. Future gains and goals are of no importance to them. Delinquents also exhibit group autonomy: They are close to other members of their gang but hostile to outsiders.

Cohen also explains how these traits are acquired. Americans, he says, judge children in different ways. Middle-class parents, teachers, and social workers, for instance, judge the behavior of children in terms of a set of values or standards, which Cohen calls the **middle-class measuring rod**. All children—not just middle-class children—are expected to subscribe to these values:

- Ambition is a virtue; its absence is a defect and a sign of maladjustment. Ambition emphasizes an orientation toward long-range goals and deferred gratification, including an early determination to get ahead.
- Individual responsibility plays a key role in middle-class ethics. It applauds resourcefulness and self-reliance.
- Middle-class norms place a high premium on skills and tangible achievements.
- Hard work and frugality are admired.
- Rationality—as evidenced by exercise of forethought, conscious planning, and the budgeting of time—is highly valued.
- The middle-class value system rewards the cultivation of manners and courtesy.
- Control of physical aggression and violence, which damage personal relations, are important middle-class values.
- People should not waste time; rather, they should spend their time constructively.
- Middle-class values emphasize respect for property.

All children are expected to conform to these values. However, doing so is not so easy for some.

BOX 5.5
Theory in a Nutshell
Albert Cohen

Cohen believes that lower-class parents do not adequately socialize children in terms of widely accepted values and norms. In school, children compete for status from teachers who use a "middle-class measuring rod" to evaluate them. Lower-class children usually end up at the bottom of the status ladder, causing strain that encourages them to join together and form gangs, which in turn leads to delinquency.

Whereas most middle-class children may live up to these dictates effortlessly, lower-class children may not be taught these standards, or not taught them well. Consequently, they have difficulty adopting these values.

In school, regardless of their social class, children are judged by their ability to follow middle-class values. Children who do not or cannot lose status or prestige and are looked down upon by teachers and fellow students. Boys who are frustrated by their low status come together and form a delinquent subculture, which establishes its own set of values and standards for behavior that reject middle-class norms. By making a complete change—from accepting middle-class values to rejecting them, in a process called *reaction formation*—the youths achieve status in the eyes of their peers. However, once they adopt their new code, they lose any respect they had enjoyed in the larger society; once delinquent, they cannot turn back. (See **Box 5.5**, the "Theory in a Nutshell" feature.)

Based on this theory, Cohen sees delinquency as a male, lower-class phenomenon that is caused by status frustration and the inability to live up to middle-class standards. Frustrations are expressed as hostility toward middle-class norms and institutions (see **Figure 5.5**). Cohen's theory is simple and logically consistent. However, research testing it has produced mixed results. Certainly, academic performance and delinquency are related: The better a child's school performance, the lower the chances he or she will commit crime.[45] A substantial body of evidence also confirms that children commit their crimes in groups. By contrast, empirical support is lacking for the idea that delinquent boys reject middle-class values and adopt oppositional values. Lee Rainwater found that

KEY TERM

middle-class measuring rod
The standards used by teachers to assign status to students.

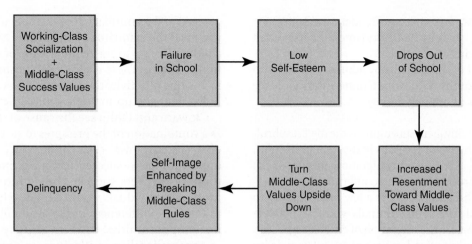

Figure 5.5 Mapping Delinquency Theory: Albert Cohen

© Jones & Bartlett Learning.

lower-class boys generally hold middle-class values but stretch them to fit their circumstances. However, they will conform to middle-class norms if they possibly can. David Downes reports that the typical response of delinquents to frustration is not rejection of middle-class values, but rather disassociation from those values. The delinquents in his study did not turn the values of their school upside down; instead, they psychologically withdrew. Steve Box observed that many lower-class boys never internalize the values of the school and teachers in the first place and are always distant from them.[46]

Richard Cloward and Lloyd Ohlin

In *Delinquency and Opportunity*, Richard Cloward and Lloyd Ohlin agreed with Cohen that delinquency is a male, lower-class, urban phenomenon.[47] Like Merton, they suggested that delinquency comes from the disjunction between what children are taught to want and what is available. Adolescents who join delinquent gangs want to achieve success, but because their legitimate path is blocked, they turn to illegitimate means in the form of delinquency. (See **Box 5.6**, the "Theory in a Nutshell" feature.)

According to Cloward and Ohlin, lower-class children who want to make a lot of money but stay with their lower-class friends are the most likely candidates to join a gang. They want, in the terminology of the 1940s and 1950s, "big cars, flashy clothes, and swell dames." Even so, they do not have a compelling urge to acquire middle-class status or a middle-class way of life.

When a lower-class boy senses he is not headed toward financial success later in life, he may blame his failure on society or on himself. If he blames society, the child will likely become alienated from it and consider its rule illegitimate, especially if he believes he is capable and deserving of success.

BOX 5.6

Theory in a Nutshell

Richard Cloward and Lloyd Ohlin

Cloward and Ohlin identified the existence of legitimate *and* illegitimate opportunity structures. In both systems, opportunity is limited and differentially available depending on where the child lives. Lower-class juveniles have greater opportunities for acquisition of delinquent roles through their access to deviant subcultures. They also have greater opportunities for carrying these roles out once they are acquired.

His failing will be attributed to a closed, unfair, and discriminatory social system. Boys who feel this way may join a delinquent gang whose rules are regarded by its members as the only legitimate rules. As the members of the gang come to realize how isolated they are from the rest of society, they become closer, more cohesive, and more dependent on one another.

Cloward and Ohlin identified three delinquent subcultures, where the particular type of subculture that develops in a neighborhood depends on how the neighborhood is organized (Sutherland) and which opportunities are available (Merton). A *criminal* subculture emerges in stable neighborhoods that provide children with illegitimate opportunities to become successful criminals. These opportunities to become wealthy arise because the neighborhood has the following characteristics:

- Adult role models who are successful criminals
- Integration of age levels, which makes it possible for children to learn from their elders how to commit crime and how to handle themselves when they are caught

- Cooperation between offenders and legitimate people, such as bail bondsmen, lawyers, and politicians
- Control of delinquents by adult criminals, who make youths cut down on unnecessary violence in favor of making money

A second delinquent subculture is the *conflict* subculture. This subculture develops in disorganized slums, where waves of in- and out-migration produce social and cultural rootlessness and conflict. In these neighborhoods, children have only a few opportunities to be successful. The adult criminals who live there are failures, so there is no integration of different age levels because the adult offenders have no useful knowledge to pass on. There is also little cooperation between offenders and legitimate members of the community because local lawyers and politicians have nothing to gain by associating with and assisting "losers." In addition, the adult criminals have neither the ability nor the inclination to help neighborhood delinquents reduce their violent activity. The absence of legitimate and illegitimate opportunities frustrates children, and they vent their frustrations by turning to violence.

The third delinquent subculture is the *retreatist* subculture. In this milieu, some children are eager to succeed in the criminal or conflict subculture but do not meet the standards of either one. Nor do these children live up to the requirements of the conventional culture. These *double failures* cannot succeed in any line of activity they attempt, so eventually the individuals give up and retreat into drugs or alcohol.

Cloward and Ohlin see the cause of delinquency as a combination of the pressures to succeed and the obstacles that lower-class children face. If they had opportunities to succeed using legitimate means, these researchers suggest, the delinquency rates for these individuals would decline. However, just as there are differences in the availability of legitimate opportunities, so there also are differences in the availability of illegitimate opportunities. Not everyone who wants to be a college professor, professional athlete, or rap musician can be one, nor can everyone who wants to be a drug dealer, pimp, or prostitute be successful at those endeavors (see **Figure 5.6**).

Cloward and Ohlin crafted a theory that was widely accepted, and numerous research studies have tested their central propositions, generally finding support for them. For example, research has shown that delinquents are more likely than nondelinquents to believe opportunities to be successful are limited.

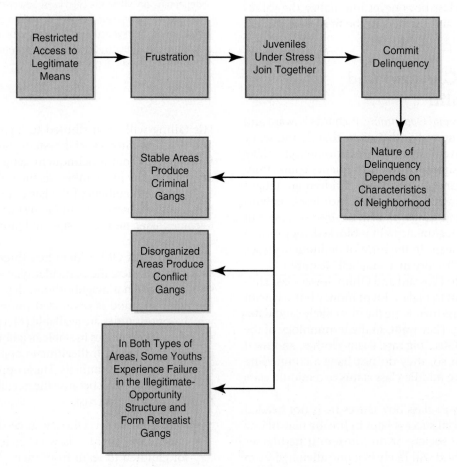

Figure 5.6 Mapping Delinquency Theory: Richard Cloward and Lloyd Ohlin

© Jones & Bartlett Learning.

SECTION 2 Delinquency Theories **131**

Strain theory contends that children are basically good. They commit crime as a last resort. The best strategy to prevent delinquency is to eliminate conditions that generate stress, such as poverty and inequality in schooling.

© 1000 Words/Shutterstock.

James Short and Fred Strodtbeck found that not only did delinquents perceive they had fewer legitimate opportunities, but they also perceived they had *more* illegitimate opportunities.[48]

Although Cloward and Ohlin's work is classic sociology theorizing, it also acknowledged that individual-level differences in delinquent propensity were important in determining who led a prosocial versus an antisocial lifestyle. Cloward and Ohlin suggest, "Because of the variations in personality characteristics, criminal propensity, and capacity to make the "right connections," or simply because of luck, some persons will find this avenue to higher status open, and some will find it closed." Christopher Salas-Wright and his colleagues recently examined those who subscribe to a retreatist subculture in their study of drifters, or persons who traveled about without any plan or resources for work or shelter for 1 month. They found that drifters engaged in a wide mix of delinquency, spanning property offenses, drug violations, and violent delinquency. They also had extensive substance abuse problems and an array of psychiatric problems.[49]

Robert Agnew

The theories of Merton, Cohen, and Cloward and Ohlin were developed many years ago. They were initially incorporated into a variety of delinquency prevention programs but eventually fell out of favor during the 1970s and 1980s when violent juvenile crime rates soared. Since 1985, these theories have experienced a revival, with Robert Agnew's introduction of *general strain theory*, in which he identified many more conditions that, if left unchecked, would cause frustration for children. (See **Box 5.7**, the "Theory in a Nutshell" feature.)[50]

Agnew claims that traditional strain theory is limited because it identifies only two possible sources of strain: economic failure or poor school performance. In reality, he suggested, strain might come from other sources. Teenagers may experience strain in response to doing poorly in an athletic event, being fired from a job, or being "dumped" by a boyfriend or girlfriend. Regardless of its origin, strain triggers a negative emotion that sometimes leads to delinquency. The relationship between strain and delinquency, in other words, is indirect. These events may lead to delinquency if the child responds by running away from home, assaulting an abusive parent or classmate, or drinking alcohol or using illegal drugs. Yet only some children who experience strain commit crime.

How children react to strain depends on specific conditioning factors, such as the youth's self-esteem, intelligence, social support, coping strategies, problem-solving skills, and associations with conventional and delinquent peers. Conditioning factors provide children with the necessary tools to imagine alternative reactions and solutions to strain. Some children, for example, respond to strain by ignoring or minimizing the event responsible for it, whereas others blame themselves or others for what happened. The type of strain, the assignment of blame for the strain, the intensity of the strain, and the emotion evoked by the strain all influence how a child might react (see **Figure 5.7**).

Agnew's reformulation has received considerable empirical support. Inga Sigfusdottir and her colleagues conducted one of the most impressive and comprehensive studies of general strain theory. Based on data

Theory in a Nutshell

Robert Agnew

Agnew tells us that many different sources of stress may trigger a negative emotion. Whether strain leads to delinquency depends on conditioning factors that the children possess, such as coping skills and intelligence. Children who have fewer coping skills are more likely to commit crime.

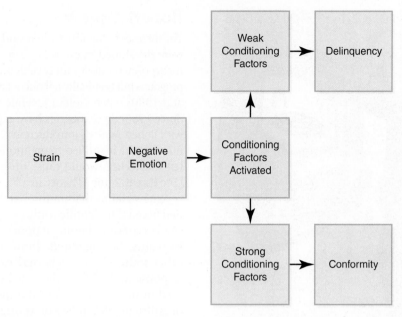

Figure 5.7 Mapping Delinquency Theory: Robert Agnew

© Jones & Bartlett Learning.

from nearly 13,000 individuals selected from cities in Bulgaria, Iceland, Latvia, Lithuania, and Romania, they examined the linkages between various sources of strain and violent and property crime while controlling for other important correlates of crime, such as age, sex, family factors, education, peer delinquency, and other social indicators. They found that several sources of strain, such as physical victimization, school failure, family conflict, and peer rejection were predictive of violent and property delinquency in five cities across Europe.[51]

An assortment of scholars detected a link between delinquency and interpersonal strain, including the finding that the effects of strain on delinquency partially depend on negative emotions, such as anger.[52] Ronald Simons and his colleagues examined the impact of strain on African American male and female children; they discovered the relationship between anger and strain is different for boys than for girls, suggesting that different theoretical models are needed to explain the behavior of the sexes.[53]

Of particular importance in Agnew's theory is the notion that criminal victimization might be among the most consequential strains experienced by a child, thereby representing an important cause of delinquency. Putting it differently, is criminal victimization a potential cause of a child's future involvement in crime? Carter Hay and Michelle Evans have examined this question. They found that violent victimization is a strong predictor of future participation in criminality, even when controlling for prior involvement in crime. Thus, when a child is the victim of a violent crime, it increases the likelihood that he or she will commit crime somewhere down the road.[54]

At the same time, findings from other studies have raised questions about general strain theory. Most forms of strain have been found to have only small to moderate effects on delinquency. Actually, only some adolescents respond to strain with delinquency. Based on data from 777 Korean youths, Byongook Moon and his colleagues explored the relationship between seven types of strain [family conflict, parental punishment, teachers' punishment, financial strain, school exam strain, being bullied, and delinquent victimization] and delinquency.

They found that delinquency victimization and punishment from teachers were related to general delinquency. Conversely, parental punishment and being the victim of bullying were unexpectedly found to be unrelated to delinquency.[55]

Charles Tittle, Lisa Broidy, and Marc Gertz produced similarly mixed support for general strain theory. They concluded:

Strain, especially with a general subjective measure, usually helps predict measures of projected criminal behavior. This is consistent with past research and is as GST [general strain theory] would have it. However, as some others have found, the theorized mediator of negative emotion, measured here as an item including several kinds of negative emotion, does not seem to work as theorized. Though strain is associated with negative emotions, these emotions do not, then, predict criminal outcomes; nor do they reduce the effect of strain on criminal outcomes . . . Strain does appear to be implicated in the production of criminal behavior, but GST notions about how and when it does so are called into question.[56]

The challenge facing general strain theory is to identify those factors that affect whether a youth will respond to strain with delinquency or in some other way.

In response to these and other concerns about general strain theory, Agnew more recently conducted an exhaustive review of evaluations of his theory and identified seven reasons why some individuals respond to general strains with violent forms of delinquency:[57]

1. These individuals have limited skills and resources for legal coping. Among other things, they have low intelligence, low constraint, low self-efficacy (i.e., the belief that they have the ability to cope with strain), and poor social and problem-solving skills.
2. They have abundant skills and resources for violent coping with strain, such as personality traits that are conducive to handling strain by means of force.
3. They have low levels of conventional social support, such as parents, teachers, and others who can provide assistance.
4. They demonstrate little social control and are not closely monitored or supervised by others.
5. They associate with other people who are violent.
6. They have beliefs that are favorable to using violence.
7. They are in situations where the costs of violence are low and the benefits are high.

Unlike other theorists who failed to innovate and modify their ideas, Agnew has steadfastly refined general strain theory and been open to ways that might improve it. For example, general strain theory was recently questioned for its relationship to criminal justice outcomes as well as its relevance to more extreme, violent offenders. A special issue of *The Journal of Criminal Justice* in 2012 was devoted to this topic. Agnew strives to develop a unified theory of crime of which general strain is one part of the larger theoretical puzzle.[58]

Steven Messner and Richard Rosenfeld

Steven Messner and Richard Rosenfeld have also presented a modified version of Merton's work, called *institutional anomie theory*. (See **Box 5.8**, the "Theory in a Nutshell" feature.) Messner and Rosenfeld think that American culture and social structure interact to produce conditions that lead to delinquency (see **Figure 5.8**). American culture is characterized by a culture of individualism, an orientation toward achievement, and pecuniary materialism—the notion that the amount of money one has determines his or her worth and self-worth. These cultural factors influence important social institutions, such as the family, schools, the economy, and political system. This culture permeates the entire society, such that even the most economically impoverished Americans generally subscribe to the ideals of the culture. Both poor and rich want to be independently successful. Because the poor lack adequate opportunities and access to resources, however, they are effectively barred from achieving success legitimately. This thwarting of their ambition creates frustration of anomie and is an incentive to use illegal means to achieve cultural goals.[59]

Evaluations of institutional anomie theory have produced mixed support. Factors including poverty, welfare spending, social support, economic inequality, and social altruism are related to a variety of crimes, ranging from murder to property crime. Thus, although anomie is one of the oldest theoretical perspectives in criminology, it still is relevant today.

BOX 5.8

Theory in a Nutshell

Steven Messner and Richard Rosenfeld

According to Messner and Rosenfeld, economic and materialistic interests dominate American society, with goals other than material success (e.g., being a good parent) being perceived as unimportant to many people today. Some children who are blocked from acquiring money legitimately will turn to crime, believing criminality is the most effective and efficient way for them to acquire wealth.

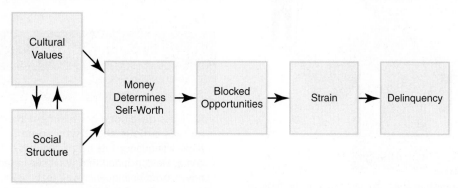

Figure 5.8 Mapping Delinquency Theory: Steven Messner and Richard Rosenfeld

However, not every study is supportive. Using data from the United Nations, World Bank, World Values Survey, and the Heritage Foundation, Lorine Hughes, Lonnie Schaible, and Benjamin Gibbs examined the theoretical relevance of institutional anomie theory and homicide in 50 nations. They found generally limited support for the theory. Homicides were not more common in market economies where other social institutions were weakened. Instead, region and geographic factors were better predictors of homicide.[60]

Social Control Theory

Social control theory can be traced to 17th-century philosopher Thomas Hobbes. In his book *Leviathan*, he argued that man is an aggressive, argumentative, shy creature in search of glory who would naturally use violence to master other men, their wives, and their children.[61] This profile was a quality of all men, not simply criminals. In Hobbes's view, men were basically bad, and to create order the state must strike fear into their hearts and punish them severely when they broke the law.

Twentieth-century criminologists expanded upon Hobbes' ideas to create social control theory. These theorists assumed that without controls children would break the law. Delinquency was expected behavior; conformity was unnatural. Rather than look for factors that push children into crime, social control theory seeks to identify those factors that stop or prevent children from participating in delinquency. In social control theory, what must be explained is why most children conform to society's rules most of the time. It is taken for granted that children will break rules. The real question to ask is: Why do children *not* commit crime? To make this very practical for you, ask yourself why are you reading this chapter when other students are not? Why do you go to class when others

skip? Are grades more important to you than to some others? What is it about you that makes you different from some of your classmates?

In the 1950s, social control theory was introduced to U.S. criminology. One of the first criminologists to explore this field was Walter Reckless, who developed containment theory. Reckless's theory was superseded by other social control theory explanations developed by David Matza, Travis Hirschi, and Michael Gottfredson and Travis Hirschi.

Walter Reckless

In 1956, Walter Reckless introduced *containment theory*, in which he focused on the child's self-concept. Reckless paid attention to the role of internal and external controls on the child's behavior. (See **Box 5.9**, the "Theory in a Nutshell" feature.) He had known for some time that only certain children were chronic offenders. As a student at the University of Chicago, where Clifford Shaw and Henry McKay were his mentors, Reckless became curious about the differential response of juveniles who lived in disorganized areas. In particular, he wanted to know why some boys in high-crime neighborhoods do *not* get into trouble with the law.

Studying this question in various ways for more than a decade, Reckless reasoned that "good boys" had a positive self-concept. He identified four pressures and pulls that influence whether a child will become delinquent:

- *Outer pulls*—environmental factors
- *Inner pushes*—psychological and biological factors
- *External containments*—attachments to persons and institutions representing the existing social order
- *Internal containments*—the element of a good self-concept

Outer pulls are living conditions such as poverty and unemployment that make delinquency look like an attractive solution to a difficult problem. Inner pushes are psychological factors such as drives and motives, as well as frustration, hostility, and feelings of inferiority, and biological factors such as brain damage.

The Hobbesian question about human nature is the basis of social control theory: Are idle hands the devil's workshop?

© Trinacria Photo/Shutterstock.

BOX 5.9

Theory in a Nutshell

Walter Reckless

Reckless developed containment theory because he was curious about why some boys living in high-delinquency-rate neighborhoods did not commit crime. He concluded that what separated the "good boys" from delinquents was that "good boys" had strong self-concepts that insulated them from the environmental pulls into delinquency.

Juveniles are equipped with two lines of defense to ward off pushes and pulls—namely, external containments (outer controls) and internal containments (inner controls) that insulate them from delinquency. External containments include family and community ties, which buffer children from the immediate pressures, pulls, and pushes they face, helping the juveniles to keep their behavior in check. Internal containments are strengths that stem from having a good, strong self-concept. A positive self-concept insulates children from the pressures, pulls, and pushes with which they are bombarded; it is the best defense against delinquent impulses. In support of this theory, research by Frank Scarpitti and his colleagues and Simon Dinitz and his associates has reported that boys with strong self-concepts were less likely to be delinquent.[62]

David Matza

David Matza studied delinquency in the mid-20th century, a period of civil unrest that was highlighted by protests over civil rights and the Vietnam War. The social and political struggles Matza observed as a professor at the University of California in Berkeley had a profound impact on his work in terms of the state defining what is appropriate or delinquent conduct. Matza came to believe that delinquency theorists had exaggerated the differences between delinquents and nondelinquents.[63] Strain theorists, such as Cohen and Cloward and Ohlin, see delinquents as part of a subculture completely committed to misdeeds, engaging in delinquency because they believe in ideas that require such behavior. These children are normal in all respects except for their belonging to this subculture, which teaches them it is all right to be delinquent.

Matza finds this notion hard to believe, and he criticizes strain theorists for not accounting for **maturational reform**: the idea that nearly all children who participate in delinquency reduce or stop such activity as they grow older. Strain theory persistently maintains that children are committed to stealing, vandalizing, and assaulting. If so, why do many delinquents change their behavior when they reach age 18, 21, or 25? Strain theory cannot answer this question.

Matza also suggests that if delinquents were really as committed to their misdeeds as strain theory claims, they would engage in delinquency for nearly all of their waking hours. They do not. Even the most delinquent youths spend most of their time in conventional, nondelinquent activities; they devote very little time to delinquency. Many delinquents who are caught also know they have done something wrong and feel sorry for their actions. If Matza is correct in thinking that youths know delinquency is wrong, why do these individuals participate in it? According to Matza, a youth may pick up cues in conversations with other youths that imply delinquency is acceptable and that those other youths think the individual is the only person who does not want to be delinquent. Faced with this implication, the youth may be reluctant to be the "chicken," the one who backs out of a delinquent escapade.

Because delinquents feel bad for what they have done, they develop **techniques of neutralization**, or rationalizations for their behavior to absolve themselves of guilt. There are five techniques of neutralization:[64]

1. *Denial of responsibility* is a technique to blame the delinquent act on an outside force. According to this perspective, youths are drawn into situations and are helpless to act any other way. They may blame their delinquency on growing up in an abusive family, on their residence in a bad neighborhood, or on delinquent peers. These juveniles might say, "I couldn't help it" or "It was not my fault."

2. *Denial of injury* occurs when the criminal act does not seem to hurt anyone; no one was seriously injured. A gang fight might be said to be only a private argument between consenting and willing participants. Thefts from Wal-Mart might be rationalized by suggesting that with all its wealth the company will never notice the losses from small thefts. Juveniles who use this technique might say, "A criminal act hurts someone and I did not hurt anyone."

3. *Denial of victim* is a technique used when a juvenile believes what he or she did was right because of the circumstances: The victim had it coming. Some adolescents will use this justification to explain their attacks on homosexuals or minorities. They might further legitimize their behavior by saying something like, "Robin Hood stole from the rich and gave to the poor because the rich deserved to be robbed."

4. *Condemnations of condemners* take place when children want to shift blame from their own illegal behavior to the behavior of others. They will try to create a negative image about those who are being critical of them. For example, they might label those who condemn them as "hypocrites." Juveniles might rationalize the legitimacy of their illegal drug use, for instance, by saying, "Police and

KEY TERMS

maturational reform
The idea that nearly all children who participate in delinquency reduce or stop such activity as they grow older.

techniques of neutralization
Rationalizations used to justify delinquent activities.

judges are corrupt hypocrites who are involved in the drug trade themselves."

5. *Appeal to higher loyalty* is used when juveniles feel they must break the law to benefit their friends, family, or another group they are closely tied to. Illegal acts might be justified by claiming they were committed in deference to a higher authority, such as a moral or religious belief, the gang, or a racial or ethnic group. Adolescents who steal necessities of life for their family might justify their behavior on this basis.

Although techniques of neutralization might be used as postevent explanations of delinquent behavior, Matza believes that the same justifications are used *prior* to delinquent acts to rationalize the delinquent's involvement. In other words, techniques of neutralization prepare a child for delinquency. They lessen the effectiveness of internal and external controls, thereby freeing the adolescent to commit crime. (See **Box 5.10**, the "Theory in a Nutshell" feature.)

If Matza is correct, juveniles can be delinquent without being committed to delinquency. They need simply believe that the circumstances surrounding their particular involvement are exceptional. Normally, most adolescents accept conventional rules and laws, but occasionally their acceptance of the law is overridden by some other factor, such as an attack or a provocation. In such circumstances, the youth may drift in and out of an acceptance of conventional values. When this happens, delinquency is possible but not inevitable. Whether delinquency occurs depends on many factors, including the juvenile's mood and his or her ability to neutralize the illegal act being contemplated.

The appeal of Matza's theory is that juveniles live in a state of flux and uncertainty. Some criminologists have criticized Matza because the central concepts of his theory, such as drift, are difficult to test. Matza is also vague about how children use techniques of neutralization. Nonetheless, Matza's theory has inspired others to conduct research, although studies examining his propositions have produced mixed results. It is true that delinquents accept conventional

values. It is also true that most children "age out" of delinquency, albeit possibly not without consequences. Travis Hirschi found evidence for three of the five techniques of neutralization (denial of responsibility, denial of injury, and condemnation of condemners), but he could not determine whether the rationalizations were in place before delinquent acts were committed or whether they followed only as postevent justifications.[65]

In addition, James Coleman discovered that white-collar criminals used techniques of neutralization to justify their criminal acts. The most common justification cited by the white-collar criminals in his study was "denial of injury," believing their actions did not hurt anyone.[66] Shadd Maruna and Heith Copes reported that auto thieves who were socially attached were more likely to use neutralization techniques than less-attached offenders. In addition, less-attached and more-attached thieves used different neutralization techniques. The most frequently used rationalizations for more-attached thieves were appeal to higher loyalty and denial of victim; low-attached thieves rationalized their behavior by turning to denial of the victim and denial of responsibility.[67]

Other criminologists, however, have not been able to generate much support for Matza's theory. Michael Hindelang found no support for the idea that juveniles use techniques of neutralization. In his studies, adolescents who committed crime were more likely to accept delinquent behavior than juveniles who were not involved in delinquency. Hindelang was also unable to provide support for Matza's contention that delinquents disapprove of delinquency but go along with it only because their friends expect them to do so. He concluded that a juvenile's perceptions of the feelings of his or her friends have almost nothing to do with the individual's decision to commit crime.[68] Likewise, Peggy Giordano found little support for Matza's claim that delinquents feel they are treated unjustly. In a study comparing delinquents and nondelinquents, she concluded that the two groups held similar attitudes.[69]

Travis Hirschi

In 1969, Travis Hirschi published *Causes of Delinquency,* in which he presented a detailed critique of cultural deviance, strain, and social control theories. He argued that no one should be surprised by delinquency because it is something *all* adolescents will do unless obstacles are thrown in their path. These obstacles chiefly consist of attitudes that are implanted effectively in most children but less so in others. The latter individuals have relatively weak bonds to society; their minds are not set firmly against delinquent activities. (See **Box 5.11**, the "Theory in a Nutshell" feature.)

BOX 5.10

Theory in a Nutshell

David Matza

Matza thinks that children are neither committed nor compelled to delinquency, and delinquents do feel guilty about their misdeeds. So that juveniles can feel better about themselves, they turn to techniques of neutralization to reduce guilt and justify their delinquencies.

BOX 5.11

Theory in a Nutshell

Travis Hirschi

"Why do juveniles conform?" This is the question asked by Hirschi, who suggests that children conform because of their bond to society. This bond consists of four elements: attachment, belief, commitment, and involvement. The stronger a child's bond to society, the less likely he or she is to commit crime, because the child has something to lose.

Warm, healthy family relationships build strong bonds, which prevent delinquency. What are some ways fatherhood equips children, particularly boys, to engage in successful endeavors?

© Volt Collection/Shutterstock.

Hirschi's version of social control theory is called *social bond theory*. A **bond** describes a person's connection to society. It consists of four elements: attachment, commitment, involvement, and belief. For every child, each component of the social bond forms its own continuum. When the continua are merged, they provide a gauge of how strongly a child is tied to society. The stronger the bond, the less likely the youth will commit crime.[70]

Hirschi thinks the best predictor of delinquent behavior is a child's attachments to parents, schools, and peers—the primary agents of socialization. For more than 40 years, criminologists have examined the relationship between attachment and delinquency. Studies have rather consistently reported that children who are strongly tied to parents are less likely to become delinquent; their positive feelings promote acceptance of the parents' values and beliefs. These children avoid delinquency because such behavior would jeopardize their parents' affection.[71] Interestingly, Trina Hope and her colleagues have reported that adolescent girls who become pregnant and keep their babies are much less likely to commit delinquency than adolescent females who end their pregnancies through abortion.[72] A parallel argument applies to peers. The closer juveniles are tied to their peers, the less delinquent they will be—even if their friends sometimes commit delinquency. This statement directly contradicts the more reasonable position taken by cultural deviance theory—namely, that closeness to delinquents will increase the likelihood of delinquency.[73]

With respect to school attachments, Hirschi argues that attitudes toward schooling and teachers are an important middle ground in the relationship between IQ and delinquency. Juveniles with high IQs usually earn better grades than do other students. Getting better grades makes school a more enjoyable experience, so

youths with better grades tend to like school more than their less-successful peers. Children who like school more easily accept—or at least endure—school rules and authority and are less likely to commit crime.

Belief in the moral validity of law also has been found to reduce the likelihood that a juvenile will commit crime. Hirschi maintains that in the United States, there is one belief system, which centers on conventional values. That is, there are no subcultures that regard theft and assault as proper and permissible, contrary to the claims of cultural deviance and strain theories. Belief in the moral validity of law does seem to reduce the likelihood of committing crime.[74]

Commitment, unlike attachment, is about success, achievement, and ambition, rather than respect, admiration, and identification. Recall that in strain theory, thwarted ambition causes frustration, which might lead to delinquent behavior—theft, in particular. Social bond theory proposes that ambition or motivation to achieve keeps juveniles on the "straight and narrow" path because they know getting into trouble will hurt their chances of success. In other words, children have a "stake in conformity." The more time and energy they have invested in building an education, a career, or a reputation, the less likely they are to risk their accomplishments by committing crime. Research examining the importance of commitment has reported that children who are more heavily invested in conventional activities are, indeed, less likely to be delinquent.[75]

Involvement in conventional activities has been seen as a way of preventing delinquency since 1386 when Chaucer suggested, "Idleness is the root of mischief." Today such thinking has inspired politicians and city planners to call for more and better playgrounds and after-school sports programs to keep children off the streets. If these facilities are available, children will have less time for delinquent pursuits. Unfortunately, involvement does not have as much impact

KEY TERM

bond
The glue that connects a child to society.

on preventing delinquency as other components of the bond to society. Delinquency is not a full-time job; it requires so little time that anyone—no matter how involved they are in conventional activities—can find time for delinquency if they want to.

Hirschi's theory became the most talked-about and tested theory of delinquency, as evidenced by the more than 9000 criminology articles that have referenced the importance of the social bond to behavior. Research is overwhelmingly more supportive of Hirschi's ideas than it is critical. Elaine Doherty found that persons with strong bonds to society are more likely to stop committing crime regardless of some of their individual characteristics, such as their level of self-control. In other words, attaching, committing, being involved with, and believing in the value of conventional behavior can override personal deficits that contribute to delinquency.[76] Similarly, Douglas Longshore and his colleagues found that persons with low self-control are less likely to attach to society and also have immoral beliefs that lend themselves to delinquency.[77] Jeb Booth, Amy Farrell, and Sean Varano recently reported that adolescents with greater involvement in prosocial activities, belief in traditional norms, and commitment to constructive school activities tend to engage in less delinquency than their peers who are not as bonded to school culture. The application of social control theory to delinquency is not limited to an American context. For instance, Sebahattin Ziyanak studied Kurdish adolescents in Turkey and found that those who expressed lower belief in conventional moral order, who reported lower involvement in conventional activities, who reported less commitment to conventional activities, and who were less attached to parents, peers, school, religion, and conventional others were more likely to commit minor and major forms of delinquency. Similarly, Heng Choon (Oliver) Chan and Wing Hong Chui found that youth in Hong Kong and Macau (China) who were less attached, committed, and involved and who believed less in conventional moral order were more likely to commit nonviolent and violent forms of delinquency.[78]

Other studies, however, have found the strength of empirical support for social bonding to be only weak to moderate. For instance, Marvin Krohn and James Massey found that commitment is a better predictor of delinquency than either attachment or belief. Hirschi's theory also predicts female delinquency better than male delinquency, and predicts minor delinquencies better than serious offenses.[79] Curiously, Özden Özbay found that social control theory was a better predictor of delinquency among males than females.[80] Although the behavior of adolescents is socially controlled by adults, the quality of that adult control has different kinds of effects on youthful delinquency. For instance, Deanna Wilkinson found that adults will intervene to prevent adolescents from fighting or committing vandalism, but not necessarily to prevent drug sales. In this way, the positive effects of the social bond depend on how committed adults are to enforcing the conventional behavior of neighborhoods youths.[81]

Some researchers suggest that social control theory is related to delinquency, but at very low levels. Randy LaGrange and Helen White discovered that the influence of the social bond on delinquency changes over time, such that social bonding explains only 1 or 2% of future delinquency. David Greenberg has reported that social control theory explains only 1 to 2% of delinquency outcomes and that much of control theory's appeal pertains to its ideological conservatism.[82] Conversely, Lisa Hutchinson Wallace found that more than 40% of the variation in delinquency was explained by an adolescent's social bond.[83]

Other concerns raised about Hirschi's theory have focused on how the various elements of the bond interact. How, for instance, do relationships between youths and their parents affect children's attitudes about school? How do attitudes toward teachers influence a child's future work history or involvement in criminality? How are attachments to the family influenced by relationships with peers? It is important for social control theory to do a better job of explaining these relationships.

Yet, its shortcomings aside, Hirschi's work has inspired criminologists to construct theories of their own. For example, Charles Tittle has developed the *control balance theory.* He explains criminality in terms of the ratio between the control imposed on a person by others and the control the individual can exercise over others.[84] What Tittle adds to Hirschi's theory is the idea that people have varying degrees of autonomy or command over their lives. Tittle predicts that persons with either a control deficit or a control surplus are most likely to commit crime.

Research by Nicole Piquero and Alex Piquero has produced mixed support for Titttle's control balance theory.[85] Similarly, Matt DeLisi and Andy Hochstetler have found that although control imbalances often can predict delinquency, they do not always do so as specified in the theory.[86] Using a sample of college students, George Higgins and Christopher Lauterbach found that control ratios were related to exploitative forms of delinquency.[87] More recent work by Stephen Baron and David Forde evaluated control balance theory by studying a sample of 400 homeless street youths; the researchers found that both control deficits and control surpluses were related to certain forms of delinquency, such as assault and serious theft.[88]

In part in response to such criticism of his theory, Tittle has recently revised the control balance theory to explain three general types of behavior. *Conformity* is achieved when people have a balance of control in their lives—they have things that they personally control, and they have situations where they are controlled by others. *Deviance* occurs when a control imbalance occurs or when people exert too much control over others or have too much control exerted on them. Finally, *submission* occurs when people have no control and are completely governed by others.[89]

Michael Gottfredson and Travis Hirschi

In 1990, Michael Gottfredson and Travis Hirschi published a theory of crime that deviated significantly from Hirschi's earlier work. In *A General Theory of Crime*, the child's self-control, or lack of self-control, took center stage. The theory is based on the Hobbesian view that people are pleasure seeking and self-gratifying. As such, they make choices based solely on the pleasure they imagine it will bring. Delinquency is committed because offenders imagine it will be gratifying. (See **Box 5.12**, the "Theory in a Nutshell" feature.)[90]

Consider the essence of self-control theory in the following anecdote:

Imagine that a female loved-one (e.g., daughter, sister, or mother) has brought home her fiancé. While the fiancé is in the other room, your loved-one briefly describes his personality and lifestyle. He is sporadically employed and generally stays at a job for only one to three months. While he has no official vocational training, he prefers work in the areas of construction and landscaping. He frequently quits or is fired because of disagreements with coworkers and supervisors . . . He recurrently collects unemployment benefits because he chooses to avoid underemployment. For the record, the fiancé, who described school as "not his thing," did manage to graduate from high school, but found his two months in college unrewarding and quit.

Socially, the fiancé enjoys going to bars and is an enthusiastic drinker. He also smokes cigarettes, dabbles recreationally with illicit drugs . . ., prefers to eat at fast-food restaurants rather than cook at home, and does not exercise. He is frequently bored and annoyed by others' expectations of him. The fiancé is friendly and only abusive, sullen, or

irritable when intoxicated or when "things are not going his way." He has been "common-law married" twice and briefly engaged once before, but your loved-one is confident that their impending relationship is "the one."[91]

Many readers will recognize someone they know as having a profile similar to the fiancé. Self-control theory is curious about why this profile is found in some people and not in others. Alternatively, it asks: Why do only some juveniles commit crime? Gottfredson and Hirschi say that delinquent youths cannot resist the easy, immediate gratification that goes with crime because they have low self-control. Children with low self-control are more impulsive, insensitive, physical (as opposed to mental), and shortsighted. They are also risk takers with low frustration tolerance and, therefore, are more likely to commit crime.

In contrast, children with high self-control are less likely throughout all periods of their lives to commit crime. Indeed, Gottfredson and Hirschi claim that differences in self-control account for most of the differences among children in criminal behavior. The relationship between self-control and crime is affected only slightly by concepts that sociologists have typically blamed as encouraging crime, such as strain, peer influences, social bonds, cultural influences, and others. These forces are overshadowed by self-control or are products of self-control.

In addition, Gottfredson and Hirschi propose that the effects of self-control are similar in every situation because post-childhood experiences do not influence self-control much, if at all. Instead, low self-control is essentially a function of child rearing. Parents help children to develop self-control when they engage in the following actions:

- Love a child enough to monitor and react to bad behavior
- Supervise the child
- Recognize naughtiness when it occurs
- Punish bad behavior

These children become adolescents with the self-control necessary to resist easy gratification and develop the will to succeed in school and later in the job market (see **Figure 5.9**).

Gottfredson and Hirschi's theory is one of the most widely tested explanations of delinquency (see **Box 5.13**, the "A Window on Delinquency" feature). Research has extensively examined the relationship between delinquency and self-control, and the theory has received very strong support. These studies have shown that measures of self-control are predictive of criminal behavior among criminals and noncriminals, college students, juveniles, males and females, and research subjects living within and outside the United States.[92]

For example, Alexander Vazsonyi and Rudi Klanjsek surveyed nearly 4000 students in Switzerland, some

BOX 5.12

Theory in a Nutshell

Michael Gottfredson and Travis Hirschi

Gottfredson and Hirschi theorize that delinquents have low self-control that can be traced to early childhood experiences. When parents do not supervise their children, do not recognize when their children are behaving badly, and do not punish poor behavior, they promote low self-control in their children. Children with low self-control are more likely to commit crimes.

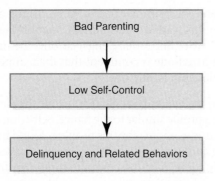

Figure 5.9 Mapping Delinquency Theory: Michael Gottfredson and Travis Hirschi

© Jones & Bartlett Learning.

of whom attended apprenticeship school (a type of school geared toward members of lower socioeconomic groups) and some of whom were affluent university students. Regardless of the very different social and economic backgrounds of these students, those with low self-control were more involved in delinquency.[93]

In another large-scale study, Vazsonyi and his colleagues surveyed more than 8400 youths from Hungary, the Netherlands, Sweden, and the United States to examine how self-control theory applied in different cultural contexts. The researchers found low self-control was correlated with deviant behavior for males, females, and five different age groups of

BOX 5.13

A Window on Delinquency

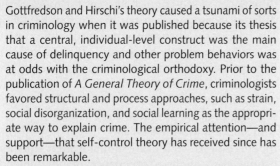

The T-Rex of Delinquency Theory

Gottfredson and Hirschi's theory caused a tsunami of sorts in criminology when it was published because its thesis that a central, individual-level construct was the main cause of delinquency and other problem behaviors was at odds with the criminological orthodoxy. Prior to the publication of *A General Theory of Crime*, criminologists favored structural and process approaches, such as strain, social disorganization, and social learning as the appropriate way to explain crime. The empirical attention—and support—that self-control theory has received since has been remarkable.

The reputation of self-control theory is so larger than life, that it has been referred to as the *Tyrannosaurus rex* of criminology. Various measures of self-control have been linked to the gamut of antisocial behavior, including violent, property, drug, and white-collar offending, noncompliance with the criminal justice system, victimization, smoking, drinking, cheating, and other imprudent behaviors. Scholars are busily examining the sources of self-control, including its genetic and environmental bases.

Of course, self-control is not only an issue in criminology and criminal justice, but in all facets of life. Terrie Moffitt and her colleagues recently advised, "The need to delay gratification, control impulses, and modulate emotional expression is the earliest and most ubiquitous demand that societies place on their children, and success at many life tasks depends critically on children's mastery of such self-control." There is ample evidence of this. For example, June Tangney and her colleagues examined an undergraduate sample and found that high self-control

was associated with earning higher grades, experiencing higher self-esteem, having fewer psychiatric symptoms, drinking less alcohol, having better eating habits, having better interpersonal skills, enjoying better relationships, and being more emotionally healthy. In fact, there were no negative effects from having high self-control, such as feeling overly controlled. Other scholars in diverse fields of study have similarly shown that self-control is an extraordinarily powerful construct that when it is high, generally explains overlapping positive outcomes in terms of behavior, health, and wealth, and when it is low, generally explains a multitude of negative outcomes in terms of delinquency, substance use, and unemployment.

Gottfredson and Hirschi were clearly onto something. Self-control is a powerful construct that influences life in positive and negative ways depending on whether one's self-control is mostly high or low. Where does self-control come from? When does it start? At conception? Is the womb the origin of self-control? Possibly, "self-control" begins to form when the child is outside the womb and living a full-time relationship with his or her environment, whether it is a nurturing one or not, or, most likely, it is some place in-between. This leads to asking how the child's particular gene-environment combination ties to the evolution of self-control. It may not be possible to answer all of these questions. Yet, it is possible to study them. As it stands today, self-control theory still is in its infancy and is maturing daily. Gottfredson and Hirschi have provided the criminology community with a solid beginning: A most formidable and inspiring start.

Michael Gottfredson and Travis Hirschi, *A General Theory of Crime* (Stanford, CA: Stanford University Press, 1990); Carter Hay and Ryan Meldrum, *Self-Control and Crime Over the Life Course* (Thousand Oaks, CA: Sage, 2015); Matt DeLisi, "Self-Control Theory: The Tyrannosaurus Rex of Criminology Is Poised to Devour Criminal Justice," *Journal of Criminal Justice* 39:103–105 (2011); June Tangney, Roy Baumeister, and Angie Boone, "High Self-Control Predicts Good Adjustment, Less Pathology, Better Grades, and Interpersonal Success," *Journal of Personality* 72:271–324 (2004); Patrick Converse, Katrina Piccone, and Michael Tocci, "Childhood Self-Control, Adolescent Behavior, and Career Success," *Personality and Individual Differences* 59:65–70 (2014); Gregory Miller, Tianyi Yu, Edith Chen, and Gene Brody, "Self-Control Forecasts Better Psychosocial Outcomes but Faster Epigenetic Aging in Low-SES Youth," *Proceedings of the National Academy of Science of the United States of America* 112:10325–10330 (2015); Terrie Moffitt, Louise Arseneault, Daniel Belsky, Nigel Dickson, Robert Hancox, HonaLee Harrington, Renate Houts, Richie Poulton, Brent Roberts, Stephen Ross, Malcolm Sears, Murray Thomson, and Avshalom Caspi, "A Gradient of Self-Control Predicts Health, Wealth, and Public Safety," *Proceedings of the National Academy of Sciences of the United States of America* 108:2693–2698 (2011).

adolescents from the four nations, suggesting that the effects of self-control are "invariant"—that is, that they apply universally across national and cultural contexts.[94]

David Evans and his colleagues found that self-control was related to "quality of family relationships, attachment to church, having criminal associates and values, educational attainment and occupational status, and residing in a neighborhood perceived to be disorderly." Self-control also predicts delinquent conduct among criminal populations. For instance, a recent study of prisoners reported linkages between offenders' low self-control and an array of outcomes, including social interactions with prison staff, correctional substance abuse, physical assaults against correctional staff, weapon carrying, placement in a disciplinary unit, infraction history, and retaliation against another inmate.[95]

In support of their theory, Gottfredson and Hirschi report that "throughout the twentieth century, evidence has accumulated that people who often lie, cheat, and steal also hit other people; these same people often drink, smoke, use drugs, wreck cars, desert their spouses, quit their jobs, and come to class late."[96] When James Unnever and his colleagues studied more than 2400 adolescents, they found that several aspects of "bad" parenting identified by self-control theory result in more aggression and delinquency. The effects of self-control are not limited to delinquency occurring among adolescents. Scott Wolfe and his associates studied more than 2000 elderly adults in Arizona and Florida and found those with lower self-control were more likely to engage in diverse forms of crime, such as drunk driving, domestic violence, traffic violations, theft, forgery, and taking nonprescribed medications.[97]

However, not all criminologists enthusiastically embrace self-control theory. For instance, Michael Cretacci argues that the importance of self-control theory has been exaggerated largely because of measurement problems in studies of the theory. Using data from the National Longitudinal Study of Adolescent Health, Cretacci found that persons with low self-control were more likely to commit property and drug delinquency, but that self-control was unrelated to violent delinquency. Cretacci also suggests that the importance of self-control wanes over time, meaning that it is not a truly general explanatory construct.[98] Strong associations between self-control and delinquency have not been found for all groups of people, particularly for serious young offenders and the homeless.[99]

Olena Antonaccio and Charles Tittle acknowledge that self-control is an important predictor of delinquency, but seriously question whether it is the quintessential predictor of delinquency, as Gottfredson and Hirschi suggest. Based on data from a survey in Ukraine, Antonaccio and Tittle found that the strongest predictor of delinquency was immorality, not low self-control.[100]

Some critics contend that a theory that blames crime on ineffective child rearing and dismisses the possibility that delinquency is a product of stress and strain (Merton), culture (Shaw and McKay), learning (Sutherland), or biology, is inherently flawed. In their study of twins, John Wright and Kevin Beaver demonstrated that self-control is not caused by parenting at all, once measures for genetics are included.[101] A follow-up study by John Wright and his colleagues reported that only 1% of self-control is caused by parenting practices. Approximately 25% of self-control is genetic in origin, and the rest is caused by nonshared environmental factors—that is, influences occurring outside the family, such as peer groups. In addition, Wright and his collaborators found that parenting did not account for any of the variance in delinquency committed during the second wave of data collection and that it accounted for only 2% of the variance in crime occurring during the third wave of data collection. In contrast, genetics accounted for 44% of the variance in delinquency and 29% of the variance in crime.[102]

Overall, this relatively new line of research shows that self-control is closely related to delinquency; however, its causes are more genetic than social. Similarly, Stacey Nofziger found that a child's self-control is predicted by his or her mother's level of self-control and not necessarily by parenting techniques. In fact, how a person parents his or her children is itself a product of that individual's own level of self-control. Jamie Gajos and Kevin Beaver also reported that neuropsychological deficits were involved in the development of self-control, suggesting that it is primarily a brain disorder and not an outcome of ineffective parental socialization.[103]

Studies by some researchers have failed to find any evidence to support Gottfredson and Hirschi's claim that peer groups have little or no influence on behavior. To the contrary, Constance Chapple discovered that children with low self-control were not only more likely to participate in delinquency, but also were more likely to be rejected by law-abiding peers and, out of necessity, more likely to associate with delinquent peers. For these children, it was better to have delinquent friends than no friends at all.[104] Other critics claim that Gottfredson and Hirschi pay too little attention to individual differences among children and ignore differences in power in relationships between adults and children and between children and other children that would affect the likelihood of a child participating in crime.[105]

These criticisms aside, if we assume just for the moment that Gottfredson and Hirschi are correct, delinquency may be inevitable. If self-control is internalized early in life, even before a child starts school, there may be little that the juvenile and criminal justice systems can do to overcome what has already been done.[106]

Policies based on these theories aim to change the relationship between the child and his or her environment. Most public policies for preventing delinquency include components from multiple theoretical perspectives. Few, if any, programs are based solely on one point of view.

Cultural Deviance Theory

Shaw and McKay and Miller believe neighborhoods are largely responsible for crime. The most comprehensive policy application of their theories is the Chicago Area Project (CAP), which began in 1931. The CAP was envisioned as a means to mobilize residents of high-crime neighborhoods to attack delinquency in three ways: direct service, advocacy, and community involvement. Community residents work with CAP officials to keep children out of trouble, assist them when they get into trouble, and keep the neighborhood clean. Research assessing the CAP has reported it is effective for reducing the incidence and prevalence of delinquency. Other programs have spawned from the CAP, including Neighborhood Watch, Operation Weed and Seed (a federal program to combat violent crime, drug use, and gang activity in high-crime neighborhoods), and community-oriented policing.[107]

Sutherland's theory also has had a major impact on delinquency prevention. The most notable programs based on his theory are "detached worker programs," which place law-abiding workers into gang settings to counsel gang members about their behavior before they commit crime. Other popular applications include mentoring programs, where at-risk children are paired with law-abiding citizens who serve as positive role models for the children, and the rating systems for films, music, television, and video games. All policies based on cultural deviance theory share the common goal of changing a child's social environment in ways that make it easier for the youth to be mainstreamed into society.

Strain Theory

According to strain theory, programs that reduce stress and frustration should be able to prevent delinquency. Proponents of this view suggest that children must be provided with legitimate opportunities to achieve success. In the 1960s, many delinquency prevention programs were based on these assumptions. Indeed, they provided the impetus for a reform package spearheaded by Presidents John F. Kennedy and Lyndon B. Johnson. Among the Great Society reforms were a wide range of social programs, which included Project Head Start for preschool children, job training programs for adults, and financial assistance for students in postsecondary education. Of these programs, Head Start is the most widely known.

Put into operation in 1965, Head Start may be the only antipoverty program embraced by both conservatives and liberals. It is a comprehensive child-development program that serves children from birth to age 5, as well as pregnant women and their families. A child-focused program, it has the overall goal of increasing the school readiness of young children in low-income families. Head Start teachers provide children with a variety of learning experiences that are appropriate to their age and development. Children are encouraged to read books, appreciate cultural diversity, express their feelings in appropriate ways, and learn how to play and interact with their classmates. Today, Head Start has an annual budget in excess of $6 billion, and nearly 1 million children are enrolled in its programs throughout the United States.

For years, critics debated whether Head Start was truly effective. Results from a 7-year national evaluation of the Early Head Start program provided evidence that 3-year-old children who completed the program performed better in cognitive and language development than those children who did not participate in the program. The participant children also developed behavior patterns that prepared them for success in school, such as engaging in tasks, paying attention, and showing less aggression. Parents in Early Head Start demonstrated more positive parenting behavior, reported less physical punishment, and did more to help their children learn at home through activities such as reading to them.[108] In short, the Head Start program prepares children for school and has a positive impact on their social development.

Social Control Theory

Social control theory serves as the foundation for a variety of delinquency prevention programs. The programs

What is the purpose of programs like Head Start? Does the very existence of such a program validate the ideas of cultural deviance, strain, and social control theorists?

© Jupiterimages/Stockbyte/Getty.

aim to reattach children to their parents, schools, and community by involving them in conventional and prosocial activities; they also require parents to become active participants in children's lives.

Several popular programs are based on this model. The Police Athletic League (PAL), for instance, offers children positive experiences with police and other youths, such as providing educational workshops and showing youths the positive aspects of police work. This program is intended to help to build a bridge between police and youth and reduce some of the animosity that can occur when people have misconceptions about what the police do.

An offshoot of the PAL is the Midnight Basketball League (MBL), a program that provides young males in lower-class neighborhoods an opportunity to play the game of basketball to stay out of trouble. The only difference between the MBL and normal basketball is the MBL is played between 10 PM and 2 AM, when young inner-city males are most vulnerable to drug-related activities, crime, and other negative activities. There is scant evidence, however, that the midnight basketball program is generally an effective delinquency prevention program. Although some evidence suggests it may have helped to reduce crime in certain neighborhoods, overall research studies of the program indicate that it is largely ineffective.[109]

A third important program based on social control theory is the Boys and Girls Clubs of America, a network of more than 2600 clubs serving more than 3.2 million school-age children. The clubs provide at-risk youths with guidance, discipline, and values from caring adults who serve as mentors, along with educational support, increased awareness of career options, and assistance for setting goals. A 3-year assessment of the Boys and Girls Club programs has confirmed that the clubs have had a significant impact on reducing juvenile crime (13% decline), drug activity (22% decline), and use of crack cocaine (25% decline).[110]

The self-control theory of Gottfredson and Hirschi does not lend itself as readily to the development of public policy. Most delinquency prevention policies have cultural deviance and strain theories as their underlying foundation. These theories rely on the deterrent and incapacitation functions of the juvenile justice system. In contrast, self-control theory calls for the implementation of early childhood interventions.

What *is* needed are programs that strive to improve the self-control of children, such as programs that assist single mothers to provide capable care for their children. One program whose goals complement the ideas inherent in self-control theory is "The Incredible Years: Parents, Teachers, and Children Training Series." The parent-training curriculum of this series, which is designed for parents of children ages 3 to 12, focuses on strengthening parents' monitoring and disciplinary skills and building their confidence. The curriculum includes an 11-week basic program that uses videotapes depicting real-life situations. Parents meet in groups and cover topics such as "Helping Children Learn," "The Value of Praise and Encouragement," "Effective Limit Setting," and "Handling Misbehavior."[111] Some evidence suggests that these kinds of early childhood prevention programs improve children's self-control and make delinquency less likely. For instance, the Stop Now and Plan Under 12 Outreach Project (SNAP ORP) is a cognitive-behavioral intervention designed to instruct youth to engage in strategies that improve their self-control, such as identifying, regulating, and appropriately responding to emotions; engaging in internal dialogue to prevent impulsive action and think through the implications of one's behavior; and using cognitive and verbal strategies to resolve interpersonal disputes and conflicts rather than aggression. An evaluation of SNAP ORP found that for every dollar invested in the program, between $17 and $32 were saved, depending on the severity of the delinquent's behavior (the benefit to cost ratio was greatest for low-risk boys).[112]

Even if self-control theory does not lend itself as well to delinquent prevention as other sociological theories of crime, this does not mean that ideas related to self-control have no implications for the serious, violent, and chronic juvenile offenders that populate the juvenile justice system. Matt DeLisi and Michael Vaughn, for example, have explored the overlap between low self-control and career criminality using a sample of institutionalized delinquents selected from detention centers in Missouri. They found that even when controlling for age, gender, race, ethnicity, receipt of welfare, head injury, psychiatric symptoms, prior psychiatric diagnoses, and ADHD, low self-control among youths predicted career criminality. In fact, low self-control was far and away the strongest predictor of a youth becoming a serious, violent, and chronic delinquent.[113]

Simply by keeping adolescents busy in constructive activities at night may produce reductions in delinquency and violence.

WRAP UP

THINKING ABOUT JUVENILE DELINQUENCY: CONCLUSIONS

This chapter reviewed theories from three schools of sociological thought. Cultural deviance theory was the first school of thought to reject biological and psychological theories. It shifted attention to considering the role of the environment in delinquency, particularly the child's neighborhood.

Strain theory distinguished itself by claiming that there is no unique lower-class culture. In the United States, the dominant culture emphasizes wealth and status—but not every person can achieve success because the legitimate means to do so are more broadly available to the middle and upper classes.

Thus lower-class children are more likely to give up chasing these goals or go about achieving them in illegal ways.

According to social control theory, children are amoral; without controls on their behavior, they will commit crime. The theories put forth by proponents of this school of thought ask, "Why do some children conform?" They answer the question in a variety of ways. For example, delinquency might be explained in terms of a child's self-concept; bond to his or her parents, school, or peers; or the quality of parenting that the child has received.

CHAPTER SPOTLIGHT

- Social disorganization theory suggests that neighborhoods characterized by poverty, residential turnover, renters, and ethnicity heterogeneity create social disorganization, which fosters cultural conflicts that then allow delinquency to flourish.
- Cultural deviance theories suggest that socially disorganized neighborhoods engender an oppositional subculture that lends itself to failure at conventional social institutions and delinquency.
- Social inequality contributes to anomie or strain, which—according to the theories of Merton,

Cloward and Ohlin, Agnew, and Messner and Rosenfeld—leads to financial and emotional stresses that result in delinquency.
- Differential association theory showcases how delinquency is learned from social relationships with family and friends in primary groups.
- Social control theory assumes that people are naturally self-interested and prone to delinquency.
- Two of the most important control theories are social bond theory (advanced by Hirschi) and self-control theory (advanced by Gottfredson and Hirschi).

CRITICAL THINKING

1. Even in the worst neighborhoods in the United States, the majority of residents are law abiding, suggesting that individual flaws explain delinquency. How might sociologists, psychologists, and biologists differ in the ways they address this issue?
2. Many crimes are not committed for financial reasons—that is, to alleviate strain. For example, some armed robbers commit crimes to obtain drugs, but rarely do they commit crimes to pay their rent. Are most juveniles who commit property crimes *really* economically motivated?
3. Is it wasteful to channel resources to retreatists, such as transients, drug addicts, and alcoholics?

Is it inevitable that some people will not succeed in life?
4. Some criminologists believe that children with low self-control are more likely to commit crime. What does this perspective suggest about the chances of rehabilitation or positive change for delinquents?
5. In West Palm Beach, Florida, police installed stereo systems that play classical music 24 hours per day in high-crime neighborhoods. Since the policy was implemented, crime has decreased in the area. Does this example demonstrate that neighborhoods and their delinquency rates can be altered by ecological change?

Sociological Theories: Labeling and Conflict

Because children are relatively powerless, they are subject to being labeled by adults who wield greater power. It has been argued that society produces delinquents and their delinquency through "a process of tagging, defining, identifying, segregating, describing, emphasizing, and evoking the very traits that are complained of. The person becomes the thing he [or she] is described as being."[1] The theories discussed in this chapter examine the nature of the labeling process; the role of conflict, differential power, and influence in creating and enforcing criminal law; and the consequences of how adults exert power to oppress children.

OBJECTIVES

◆ Understand labeling as a way to describe why adolescent behavior is partially driven by societal responses to the youth's identity and behavior.

◆ Distinguish different types of labeling theories, their empirical strengths, and their relationships to juvenile justice practice.

◆ Identify the history of conflict explanations of behavior dating to the work of Karl Marx and Friedrich Engels.

◆ Understand the theory of differential oppression, which states that delinquency is a consequence of the oppressive ways that adults think about and treat children.

◆ Identify the overall place of labeling and conflict explanations of delinquency compared to other theories of crime.

KEY TERMS

Labeling Theory

The labeling perspective has a rich tradition in sociology, and its conceptual and theoretical foundation can be traced to the writings of symbolic interaction theorists. The perspective borrows heavily from the works of Charles Horton Cooley, George Herbert Mead, and W. I. Thomas. At the heart of labeling theory is the idea that in their everyday lives children are bombarded with different cues and clues regarding how others perceive them (Mead). Through role-playing (Cooley) and defining situations (Thomas), adolescents become keenly aware of the meanings of symbols and gestures that other children and adults use to project labels onto them.[2] **Labeling theory** assumes that social control creates deviance when adolescents are negatively labeled.

Although labeling theory is sometimes criticized for being a dated, liberal defense of delinquency, its central ideas remain relevant today. For instance, Paul Hirschfield suggests that the social control policies used in U.S. schools are largely based on controlling behavioral problems among boys and are disproportionately applied to boys attending public schools in large cities. These policies promote punishment and exclusionary approaches (e.g., out-of-school suspension and expulsion) that effectively put some children on a "criminal justice system track." In this way, according to Hirschfield, the labeling effects that occur in U.S. schools prepare disadvantaged youths for prison.[3]

Research has also shown that criminal records—even when they are significantly dated—exert negative effects on people later in life. Megan Kurlychek and her colleagues, for example, found that people with old criminal records are behaviorally very similar to those without a criminal record, but that persons with records face negative consequences in terms of access to public housing, student financial aid, welfare benefits, and even voting rights.[4] Even an old criminal record can serve as a "scarlet letter" that must be worn throughout life.

Labeling theory is not so concerned with individual traits or environmental influences that might instigate initial deviant acts. Instead, it focuses on the stigmatizing effects of the juvenile justice system upon those who are labeled delinquent. The focal point of labeling theory is the power of the social response, especially in the form of formal social control, to produce delinquent behavior. Its aim is to understand how publicly or officially labeling someone as a delinquent may cause the person to become the very thing he or she is described as being.[5] As an illustration of the power of labeling, **Box 6.1**, the "A Window on Delinquency" feature, discusses how labeling might have contributed to Willie Bosket becoming one of New York's most dangerous prisoners.

Frank Tannenbaum

One early expression of the labeling perspective is found in Frank Tannenbaum's 1938 book, *Crime and the Community.* Tannenbaum professed that thinking of delinquents and nondelinquents as two fundamentally different types of people is a misleading notion, which he termed the **dualistic fallacy**. Earlier criminologists had believed undesirable qualities, such as atavistic physical features (Lombroso) and intellectual inferiority (Goddard), led to antisocial behavior. Tannenbaum rejected these notions, instead arguing that delinquents are rather well adjusted to their social groups.

Tannenbaum contended that delinquent activity begins as random play or adventure. Children do not think of their play as constituting delinquency, but a *play group* may later evolve into a delinquent gang as a result of conflict between the group and the community. Adults in the community might be annoyed with the group—which may, for example, be perceived as playing music too loud—and then try to subdue or crush it. This effort usually fails, however, and the children become more defiant, turning to fellow gang members for support. When conflict between a gang and community occurs, both sides resort to name calling. Adults call the youths' activity "delinquent" or "evil" and insist that the activity should no longer be tolerated. (See **Box 6.2**, the "Theory in a Nutshell" feature). According to Tannenbaum:

> There is a gradual shift from the definition of the specific act as evil to a definition of the individual as evil. . . . He [the child] has gone slowly from a sense of grievance and injustice to a recognition that the definition of him as a human being is different from that of other boys. . . . .The young delinquent becomes bad because he is not believed if he is good.[6]

Through this process, calling a child "delinquent" makes it more likely that the individual will accept the description and live up to it. Labeling and stereotyping lead children to isolate themselves from the rest of the community and to associate with others similarly identified. Tannenbaum believes that the

KEY TERMS

labeling theory
Theory assuming that social control leads to deviance; how behavior is reacted to determines whether it is defined as deviant.

dualistic fallacy
The mistaken notion that delinquents and nondelinquents are two fundamentally different types of people.

BOX 6.1

A Window on Delinquency

The Case of Willie Bosket

At the age of 26, Willie Bosket stabbed prison guard Earl Porter in the visiting room at Shawangunk Correctional Facility in New York. At his trial for the attempted murder of the guard, Willie explained his violent behavior as a direct product of having been labeled a delinquent at an early age and being institutionalized in the state's juvenile and adult correctional systems for most of his life. Acting as his own defense counsel, he told the jury, "Willie Bosket has been incarcerated since he was 9 years old and was raised by his surrogate mother, the criminal justice system . . . This being the case, Bosket is only a monster created by the system he now haunts." It is a strong claim for the effects of labeling. In Willie's case, however, it is difficult to disentangle the causes and effects of the labels.

At age 6, Willie was already a troublemaker in school, throwing temper tantrums, hitting teachers, fighting with other students, and playing hooky. When he was 8 years old and in second grade, he threw a typewriter out of a school window, nearly hitting a pregnant teacher. By 9 years of age, Willie was experimenting with sex with neighbor girls. Police reports on Willie at the time included offenses such as robbery, auto theft, threatening other children with a knife, and setting a number of fires; most of his crimes were never reported to the police. His first appearance in Family Court came as the result of his mother filing a PINS (Person in Need of Supervision) petition, which at that time was a status offense. The judge ordered Willie placed at the Wiltwyck School for Boys.

Over the next few years, Willie's disruptive and violent behavior led him to be moved from institution to institution, including both psychiatric and correctional facilities. At age 11, he was sent to the Highland School for Children, where he was soon punished for throwing a chair at another boy and attacking a supervisor with a broom.

At age 14, Willie's placement expired and he was sent home. Over the next few months he was arrested five times, mostly for robberies and burglaries, but received no serious sanctions for any of the crimes. According to

© Jim McKnight/AP Photo.

author Fox Butterfield, "[B]y age 15, Willie claimed that he had committed two thousand crimes, including two hundred armed robberies and twenty-five stabbings."

Three months after Willie turned 15, he went on a robbing and killing spree in the New York subways, resulting in the murder of two subway passengers and the serious wounding of a motorman. Although Willie was only 15 years old, the judge sentenced him to the maximum penalty allowed under the current state law: commitment to an initial period of 5 years with the Division of Youth Services and then a transfer to the adult system until he turned 21. Willie was eventually convicted of assault as an adult and sentenced to prison, where additional assaults on guards resulted in his being convicted of being a habitual offender, which carried a sentence of 25 years to life.

Labeling theory argues that labeling individuals causes problematic behavior. As Tannenbaum suggests, the person becomes the thing he or she has been described as being; according to Lemert, labeling, processing, and institutionalizing individuals merely promote recidivism. Is Willie Bosket a monster created by the juvenile justice system? Or was the labeling and official processing of Willie simply a response to his violent behavior?

Fox Butterfield, *All God's Children: The Bosket Family and the American Tradition of Violence* (New York: Vintage, 2008).

---

community expects the labeled youth to act in the manner prescribed by the label, and community members are unlikely to believe that the child has "turned over a new leaf" regardless of the individual's efforts at change. This process is illustrated in **Figure 6.1**.

Edwin Lemert

Edwin Lemert developed the ideas of primary and secondary deviation. **Primary deviation** is deviance that everyone engages in occasionally; it is

"rationalized, or otherwise dealt with as [part of] a socially acceptable role. Under such circumstances, normal and [deviant] behaviors remain strange and somewhat tensional bedfellows in the same person."[7] This situation can change, however, and the person may step into a deviant or delinquent role. This role

KEY TERMS

primary deviation
Deviant behavior that everyone engages in occasionally.

BOX 6.2

Theory in a Nutshell

Frank Tannenbaum

Tannenbaum argued that delinquents are well-adjusted people. "Delinquent behavior" is only that behavior so labeled by adults in a community. Adults though have more power than children and are able to have children labeled "delinquent." Once this label is attached to children, they become delinquent.

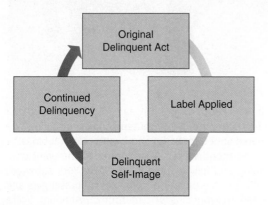

Figure 6.1 Mapping Delinquency Theory: Labeling Theory

© Jones & Bartlett Learning.

and the person's definition of himself or herself as a delinquent are affected by several factors:

- How much delinquency the person commits
- How visible such acts are to the community
- How serious others' reactions are
- How aware the delinquent is of their reactions

If the delinquency is highly visible and societal reaction is very obvious and negative, the youth will see him or herself differently, and it will be difficult for the person to hold onto past self-images and roles. The youth must choose new roles, which may be more or less deviant than the old ones. If the roles are more deviant, the adolescent has reached the stage Lemert calls **secondary deviation**:

> When a person begins to employ his deviant behavior . . . as a means of defense, attack, or adjustment to the overt and covert problems created by . . . societal reaction to him, his deviation is secondary. Objective evidence of the new role, . . . serve as symbolic cues to professionalization.[8]

KEY TERMS

secondary deviation
Deviant behavior based on the youth's taking on and accepting the deviant role as part of his or her identity.

Secondary deviation involves a long process—that is, it entails a dynamic relationship between the person's deviation and society's reaction to it. If the adolescent is eventually stigmatized, efforts to control him or her will shift from informal to formal legal ones, and the youth will be redefined as "delinquent." The sequence of interaction leading to secondary deviation typically involves the following steps:[9]

1. Primary deviation
2. Social penalties
3. Further primary deviation
4. Stronger penalties and rejections
5. Further deviations
6. Crisis reached in the tolerance quotient, which is expressed in formal action by the community stigmatizing of the deviant
7. Strengthening of the deviant conduct as a reaction to the stigmatizing and penalties
8. Acceptance of the deviant social status and the associated role

Lemert says that not all youths labeled "delinquent" accept this role; how receptive they are to such a label depends on their social class. If a youth comes from a family in which the parents are powerless and poor, he or she is more likely to accept the assigned delinquent role, especially if either parent is, for instance, an alcoholic. This tendency occurs because the status and self-conceptions of family members are transferred to children.[10] Also, lower-class parents may be frustrated by their situation and disturbed by inner conflicts. They may be quick to label their children "bad" or "worthless," overreacting to those qualities in their children that remind them of traits they despise in themselves. As a consequence, such parents may reject their children and, when trouble occurs, turn them over to community agencies such as the juvenile court. Once the child arrives in juvenile court, the individual's character and deviant behavior are redefined by the court and related agencies:

> . . . formal dispositions of deviants under the aegis of public welfare or public protection in many instances are cause for dramatic redefinitions of the self and role of deviants.[11]

Lemert believes that having a juvenile court record formally establishes a child's status as a deviant and segregates the youth from the community. Jail experience and contacts advance this process, further ensuring that the juvenile will develop a self-concept of "truly delinquent." Lemert takes it for granted that institutions fail to rehabilitate youths. He believes, rather, that they promote the opposite outcome: recidivism (see **Box 6.3**, the "Theory in a Nutshell" feature).

Howard Becker

In the 1960s, a new intellectual ferment began to brew. In sociology, labeling theory assumed new

Labeling theory suggests that official contact with the justice system sets into motion a range of identity changes and stigmatization processes that result in a delinquent self-image.

© Hill Street Studios/Matthew Palmer/Blend Images/Getty.

BOX 6.3

Theory in a Nutshell

Edwin Lemert

Lemert studied the process through which juveniles come to define themselves as delinquents. This process involves initial minor acts of delinquency (primary deviance), which are followed by negative social responses, further primary deviance, stronger penalties, more serious deviance, formal action by authorities, and eventual acceptance of the "delinquent" label (secondary deviance).

prominence and popularity; it was antiestablishment, liberal, unconventional, and "hip." Its guru was Howard Becker, who achieved fame with two books, *Outsiders* and *The Other Side*.[12]

Becker began by attacking criminologists, claiming that their research was flawed because it centered on the question, "Why do they do it?" Criminologists assume such a question is answerable because rule breaking is inherently deviant and some characteristic of rule breakers makes them do it; in other words, they assume that criminals are a particular kind of person. Becker disagreed, contending that criminologists often adopt the values of those in control—in other words, those who make the decisions about who is deviant and who should be institutionalized. According to Becker, in this way criminologists play a part in the oppression of children.

Deviants are not a homogeneous group. As a result, criminologists study a wide variety of people who have little in common with one another. Becker was curious to know how people acquire their labels, suggesting that

BOX 6.4

Theory in a Nutshell

Howard Becker

Becker told us that acquiring a label depends on how other people react to the behavior, not on the behavior itself. The process of *becoming* deviant progresses through a series of stages that lead to the person's deviance becoming a master status—that feature of the person that is most important to him or her as well as to others.

whether an activity is "deviant" depends *on how people react to it,* not on the activity itself. That is, *behavior is neither moral nor immoral in and of itself.* Rules are not always enforced regularly or consistently; some rules are even allowed to lapse completely.

Becker then considered the process of *becoming* deviant. The first step is to commit a deviant act (even if it is unintentional). The juvenile may have no idea that others consider what he or she did to be "deviant." The next step is getting caught, which puts the spotlight on the person and his or her behavior. Now the youth acquires a new status or label—"slut," "mental," or "juvenile delinquent." The labeled person is presumed to be likely to engage in the deviant behaviors on a repeated basis. Police will round up suspects (including this person) if a similar act occurs in the community at some later time. People also expect the delinquent to commit other offenses. In this way, the *stigma* (i.e., a negative label) becomes generalized so that juveniles accused of one kind of deviance—say, vandalism—are expected to lie, cheat, and steal as well (see **Box 6.4**, the "Theory in a Nutshell" feature).

This process can lead to delinquency becoming a **master status**—that is, "a status that takes precedence over all other statuses or characteristics of the individual."[13] The status of "delinquent" will carry the greatest weight in the minds of others. This labeling may also prove to be a self-fulfilling prophecy: The juvenile labeled "delinquent" may not be heavily involved or interested in delinquency but may feel pressured to engage in such behavior when labeling severs his or her ties with conventional people; thus the individual may turn to illegal activities as a means to survive. In addition, the "delinquent" label may cause conventional people to sever ties with the youth. In this way, deviance becomes a consequence of other

KEY TERMS

master status
The primary perceived status of an individual; it determines how other people initially react when they see or meet the person for the first time.

BOX 6.5

Theory in a Nutshell

Edwin Schur

Schur thinks the best we can do for children is to leave them alone. He emphasized three elements of the labeling process: stereotyping, retrospective interpretation, and negotiation. As these three elements work together to get the adolescent caught up in the deviant role, that role becomes increasingly difficult to disavow.

people's reactions, rather than a simple continuation of the original deviant act.

The final step in the process is for the delinquent to join an organized group or gang. Gang members know how to rationalize delinquency; for example, they may regard their victims as unworthy people (con artists call their victims "suckers"). Within the gang, delinquents learn reasons to continue their participation in delinquency, and tips on how to commit acts and avoid capture are passed along to others.

Edwin Schur

Edwin Schur has made a number of significant contributions to labeling theory, most notably through his analysis of the labeling process and his recommendations for reducing juvenile delinquency through radical nonintervention.[14] According to Schur, the labeling process involves stereotyping, retrospective interpretation, and negotiation. (see **Box 6.5**, the "Theory in a Nutshell" feature)

Stereotyping of youths is rampant in juvenile courts, with officials grouping the youths taken into custody in ways that best fit the minimal information available. For instance, a youth from a single-parent family may be viewed as unlikely to be given adequate supervision and control at home and being best served by institutionalization.

Retrospective interpretation is the process of reinterpreting the child's past behavior in an entirely new light on the basis of new information. Erving Goffman contends that retrospective interpretation frequently occurs when psychologists or psychiatrists evaluate children they believe have a mental illness. According to Goffman, "Almost anyone's life course could yield up enough denigrating facts to provide grounds for

KEY TERMS

radical nonintervention
An approach to juvenile justice whereby police and the courts would, whenever possible, "leave kids alone."

the record's justification of commitment."[15] Schur suggests that the juvenile justice system is particularly susceptible to inappropriate reinterpretation of youths because of the "vagueness with which delinquency and alleged predispositions to delinquency are defined." When examined with a cynical eye, almost every child's background has something that may suggest future trouble and delinquency.

The juvenile justice system generally avoids the kind of plea bargaining or *negotiation* that occurs in the adult criminal court, perhaps because juveniles have little power or influence. The paternalistic philosophy of the juvenile court assumes that the judge and the probation officer have the child's best interest in mind when making decisions. Because they have so much discretionary power, however, court officials can be quite arbitrary in their decisions, basing judgments on irrelevant and biased considerations. Schur contends that the inability of youths to negotiate effectively makes it more likely that they will be easily cast into a delinquent status—a status that becomes a crucial part of their identities and that they find increasingly difficult to disavow. Many people believe that "once a delinquent, always a delinquent."

Schur takes a rather tolerant view of delinquency, arguing that most of it is insignificant and benign—not violent, aggressive, or harmful to other people. Viewed from this perspective, punishment is unnecessary, as are most delinquency laws. In fact, these laws are actually seen as counterproductive, producing more delinquency than they deter. According to Schur, society should accommodate the widest possible diversity of behavior and not require persons to adapt to certain standards. Only very serious violations should be brought to the attention of the courts. If juveniles are adjudicated delinquent, they should *not* be committed to correctional facilities, but rather diverted to a less coercive and stigmatizing program. Schur's call for a **radical nonintervention** policy is very simple: Leave kids alone whenever possible.

John Braithwaite

Although most labeling theorists believe that societal reaction to deviance contributes to further and often more serious involvement in delinquency, some critics argue that reacting to deviance will prevent or deter it. Ronald Akers has noted:

Societal reaction to some deviance may actually prevent an individual from engaging in further deviant behavior. Applying a stigmatizing label and sanctions may have as much the intended consequence of deterring norm or law violation as the unintended consequence of fostering further violations.[16]

In his extension of labeling theory, John Braithwaite explores the nature and impact of *shaming*. He distinguishes two types of shaming: disintegrative shaming and reintegrative shaming.

Disintegrative shaming is a form of negative labeling by the juvenile justice system that is consistent with traditional labeling notions and that tends to stigmatize and exclude targeted youths, thereby tossing them into a "class of outcasts." For a juvenile who is marked as either delinquent or *pre*delinquent, legitimate avenues to membership in conventional society become severely restricted. As a result, the juvenile will likely turn to others who are similarly situated, and collectively those youths will develop a delinquent subculture or gang.

Reintegrative shaming, by contrast, involves expressions of community disapproval, ranging from mild chastisement to formal sanctions by the court, followed by indications of forgiveness and reacceptance into the community of responsible law abiders. In this type of shaming, the emphasis is upon a condemnation of the act rather than the actor:

> There is a stick followed by a carrot, condemnation followed by community responses aimed at binding the offender to the social order. In this case, shaming has two faces: It makes certain that the inappropriateness of the misconduct is known to the offender and to all observers, and it presents an opportunity to restore the offender to membership in the group.[17]

Braithwaite offers a thoughtful reformulation of the labeling perspective. His central proposition is that reintegrative shaming will reduce future offending, whereas disintegrative shaming will increase the possibility of future delinquency. A testament to the appeal of Braithwaite's theory is the fact that it is among the most empirically tested of the various labeling theories, although researchers have found mixed support for its ideas. In an initial test, Toni Makkai and John Braithwaite examined changes in compliance with regulations by nursing homes in Australia and found that reintegrative shaming increased compliance—evidence that argues on behalf of the theory. Similarly, Joongyeup Lee and Philip Kavanaugh studied perceptions of school discipline policies among youth in Philadelphia and found that students who perceived that their school punishment was reintegrative had more positive attitudes about the policy and were less likely to adopt antisocial attitudes.[18] In contrast, when Carter Hay examined the effects of perceived reintegrative shaming used in parental disciplining of self-reported delinquency among U.S. high school students, he found that reintegrative shaming in parental disciplining had only a negligible impact on future delinquency.[19]

When Jon Vagg surveyed 2280 youths from Hong Kong, however, he found that disintegrative shaming in which delinquents were swiftly punished and stigmatized was very effective as a method of social control. In practice, Hong Kong society preferred disintegrative rather than reintegrative shaming.[20] Similar findings on the effects of shaming on recidivism were produced from respondents in Iceland.[21] Using data from respondents in Russia, Ekaterina Botchkovar and Charles Tittle found that shaming of any sort—either reintegrative or disintegrative—had negative consequences.[22]

Lening Zhang and Sheldon Zhang explored the relationship between reintegrative shaming and predatory forms of delinquency using a national sample of youths. Consistent with the theory, they hypothesized that parent and peer disapproval of delinquent behavior and forgiveness of the transgressor would contribute to lower delinquency. Their findings were mixed, however. Parental forgiveness and peer shaming reduced the likelihood of predatory delinquency, whereas peer forgiveness significantly increased the likelihood of predatory delinquency. Another important concept is "anticipated guilt." Cesar Rebellon and his associates found that female adolescents experience much more guilt and anticipated guilt from even contemplating delinquency compared to male students. Self-sanctioning emotions like guilt were the best explanation for gender differences in delinquency, which suggests that shaming policies would be especially effective with girls.[23]

Kristina Murphy and Nathan Harris studied 652 tax violators in Australia and found that tax offenders who perceived the handling of their case as more reintegrative than stigmatizing were less likely to report that they had evaded their taxes in the years following their enforcement experience. These researchers also found that reintegration predicted slightly less shame acknowledgment—not more—and a desire to "put things right" was more influential in reducing reoffending than having a feeling of shame regarding the offense.[24]

Braithwaite's theory has also found its way into juvenile justice practice. For instance, many jurisdictions have developed drug courts to process offenders who have substance abuse problems but minimal other criminal history. By avoiding traditional court processing, drug offenders can focus on treatment and rehabilitation and avoid potentially stigmatizing labels that arise from adjudication. When Terance

KEY TERMS

disintegrative shaming
A form of negative labeling by the juvenile justice system that stigmatizes and excludes targeted youths, tossing them into a class of outcasts.

reintegrative shaming
The expression of community disapproval of delinquency, followed by indications of forgiveness and reacceptance into the community.

Miethe and his colleagues evaluated the effectiveness of drug courts in Las Vegas as it relates to reintegrative shaming, however, their findings contradicted the theory: Persons processed in drug courts had significantly *higher* recidivism rates than comparable defendants who were prosecuted in traditional criminal courts.[25]

Lawrence Sherman and his colleagues conducted experiments among Australian offenders that applied reintegrative shaming principles to 1300 violent offenders, drunk drivers, adolescent property offenders, and shoplifters. The offenders were randomly assigned to traditional court or to reintegrative conferences as a formal response to their crime. The reintegrative conferences significantly reduced recidivism among violent offenders and drunk drivers, but not among the other two groups.[26] Finally, Kenneth Jensen and Stephen Gibbons reported that shame is a powerful emotion that can help serious delinquents (even career criminals) to repudiate their criminal lifestyle, stop committing crime, and rejoin conventional society.[27]

Evaluation of Labeling Theory

Research testing the core assumptions of the labeling perspective has produced mixed results (see **Box 6.6**, the "A Window on Delinquency" feature). In support of labeling theory are studies that have reported on the impact of *formal* sanctions on delinquency. Many of these studies have concluded that juveniles who are formally processed through the juvenile justice system and who have formal contact with other social control agents are more likely to report greater delinquency than those who have not.[28]

For instance, Jon Bernburg and his colleagues studied the effects of juvenile justice intervention on subsequent delinquency among youths in the Rochester Youth Development Study. Controlling for relevant factors (e.g., gender, race, poverty, substance use, delinquency, and gang membership), youths who had been processed and labeled by the juvenile justice system were more likely than other youths to continue to commit crime. Further, youths who were labeled as "delinquents" had increased gang involvement and association with delinquent peers. In other words, the tarnishing effects of the juvenile justice system worsened the antisocial behavior of adolescents who were so labeled.[29] Identical results were produced in other studies. Emily Restivo and Mark Lanier examined 677 juveniles as part of the Children at Risk Study and found that official interventions with the juvenile justice system resulted in greater delinquent self-identity, increased associations with delinquent peers, and decreased expectations of prosocial activities and involvement—all of which contributed to subsequent delinquency. Jillian Turanovic and her

colleagues found that an arrest was associated with an assortment of life failures across adolescence and into adulthood. Even while controlling for self-control, IQ, drug use, delinquency, criminal behavior, concentrated disadvantage, age, sex, and race, being arrested increased the likelihood of getting fired, unemployment, repeating a grade in school, dropping out of school, marital dysfunction, and alcoholism. Recent research has also shown that official police contact results in labeling effects even when differences between research participants are controlled using advanced statistical techniques.[30]

Gary Sweeten found that high school students who were arrested and formally processed in juvenile court were more likely to drop out of school than their peers who were arrested but not processed in court. Again, these data suggest that a negative self-concept or other negative process is associated with going to court, which in turn negatively affects school performance.[31] In a study of juvenile delinquents in Australia, for example, Ieva Cechaviciute and Dianna Kenny found that approximately one-third of delinquent youths perceived that others labeled them as "delinquent" and felt that they were bad people. These youths were generally more hostile and angry, engaged in more defiant behaviors directed at a public they felt unfairly labeled them, and committed more serious forms of delinquency. In this way, even the perception that the "delinquent" label was being applied to offenders contributed to their poorer mental health and increased antisocial behaviors.[32]

It has been suggested that the higher recidivism rates noted among juveniles processed by the juvenile or criminal justice system make sense because these types of delinquents are, in fact, the most violent, dangerous, and recidivistic individuals. In other words, the labeling effects shown by system intervention could actually reflect selection bias in the types of adolescent offenders who are studied. One study suggests, however, that the negative labeling effects of criminal justice intervention are real. David Myers compared 494 violent youths, some of whom were prosecuted as adults and some of whom were prosecuted as juveniles. As part of his study, he controlled for several factors pertaining to the criminality or dangerousness of the juveniles. Even with these controls, youths processed as adults had higher recidivism rates than youths processed as adolescents.[33]

Lonn Lanza-Kaduce and his colleagues studied 475 pairs of Florida juveniles who were matched on seven factors, with one youth in each pair receiving adult punishment and the other paired youth receiving juvenile punishment. Controlling for delinquent career variables and demographic characteristics, these researchers found that youths waived to criminal court were not only more likely to recidivate but also more likely to commit a violent offense.[34]

BOX 6.6

A Window on Delinquency

Defiance Theory and a General Theory of African American Offending

Labeling theory is interesting in that it is a theory of delinquency that explicitly involves sanctioning agents, such as the juvenile justice system, in its conceptual framework. From this view, some youths engage in delinquency and continue to do so in part because of the perceived negative treatment that they receive from the police and juvenile court. A relatively recent theory within this broader perspective that shows how the juvenile and criminal justice systems play a part in perpetuating antisocial behavior is *defiance theory*.

Lawrence Sherman created defiance theory in 1993 and defined defiance as the increase in future offending against the community caused by a proud, shameless reaction to a criminal sanction. Four conditions make defiance possible:

1. The delinquent must define the sanction or legal penalty as unfair.
2. The delinquent must be poorly bonded to society.
3. The delinquent must consider the sanction to be stigmatizing.
4. The delinquent must deny the shame that normally accompanies sanctions or punishment.

In an empirical test, Nicole Piquero and Leana Bouffard analyzed more than 10,000 interactions between law enforcement and the public to see if situational or interactional dynamics were associated with citizens becoming defiant toward police. Consistent with the theory, they found that respectful, verbal interactions between police and public, even if the police lectured citizens, were not likely to produce defiant reactions. Moreover, physical coercion from police, such as handcuffing a suspect particularly when the suspect interpreted the police action as stigmatizing, was likely to produce defiant responses, such as resisting arrest.

Bouffard and Piquero examined defiance theory using data from the famous 1945 Philadelphia birth cohort. Their findings were generally supportive of defiance theory. Those who perceived sanctions to be fair were less likely to be contacted by police again and had less criminal history. On the other hand, those who perceived sanctions to be

unfair, were poorly bonded, or who denied shame, had more extensive criminal histories and were more likely to continue to commit delinquency. In fact, persons who had characteristics predicted by defiance theory, such as lack of shame, perceived unfairness, and poor social bonding had arrest histories that were more than 100% higher than those who perceived sanctions as fair.

Defiance theory is a useful approach for understanding why some delinquents appear to thwart the power of the police and criminal courts and engage in conduct that will only bring further punishment. From one perspective, it could be that delinquents simply do not learn from punishment. From another, their delinquent actions serve as a rejection of the perceived injustices and labeling that they receive from police.

A relatively new application of this idea is James Unnever and Shaun Gabbidon's theory of African American offending. According to the theory, the unique history of African American development in the United States means that they experience racism and racial stereotypes that are more pernicious and specialized than any other group. As a result, these real and perceived experiences produce increased feelings of alienation from social institutions, including the juvenile and criminal justice systems, that serve to drive feelings of hostility, resentment, and defiance against the rule of law. Unnever and Gabbidon believe that perceptions of racial injustice foster a global mood of anger, defiance, and depression, and that one result of these experiences is greater involvement in delinquency and crime, and thus, greater representation in the juvenile and criminal justice systems.

Thus far, studies have shown that perceived discrimination, perceived microaggressions, and experiences of racism and perceived criminal injustice are associated with greater delinquency, crime, violence, and externalizing symptoms among African Americans. Although the theory does not adequately address the veracity of their perceptions about injustice and racism—that is, whether they actually occurred—the theory is the latest innovation in labeling and defiance theory.

Lawrence Sherman, "Defiance, Deterrence, and Irrelevance: A Theory of the Criminal Sanction," *Journal of Research in Crime and Delinquency* 30:445–473 (1993); Nicole Piquero and Leana Bouffard, "A Preliminary and Partial Test of Specific Defiance," *Journal of Crime and Justice* 26:1–21 (2003); Leana Bouffard and Nicole Piquero, "Defiance Theory and Life Course Explanations of Persistent Offending," *Crime & Delinquency* 56:227–252 (2010); James Unnever and Shaun Gabbidon, *A Theory of African American Offending: Race, Racism, and Crime* (New York: Routledge, 2011); James Unnever, J. C. Barnes, and Francis Cullen, "The Racial Invariance Thesis Revisited: Testing an African American Theory of Offending," *Journal of Contemporary Criminal Justice* 32:726 (2016); Deena Isom, "Microaggressions, Injustices, and Racial Identity: An Empirical Assessment of the Theory of African American Offending," *Journal of Contemporary Criminal Justice* 32:27–59 (2016); Chenelle Jones and Helen Greene, "Race Discrimination, Racial Socialization, and Offending Trends among African American College Students: A Test of the Theory of African American Offending," *Journal of Contemporary Criminal Justice* 32:60–77 (2016).

Conversely, other research suggests that adult punishment presents certain advantages over the juvenile system approach. For instance, Aaron Kupchik interviewed 95 offenders who had served time in five adult or juvenile correctional facilities. Contrary to

expectations, juveniles reported that adult facilities did a better job than juvenile facilities at providing various treatment and counseling services.[35]

There is also evidence that labeling effects persist into adulthood. Ted Chiricos and his colleagues

studied nearly 100,000 offenders in Florida who had been convicted of felony offenses. Some were formally convicted and labeled as felons; others had the felon label withheld as long as the defendant completed a specified deferred sentence. In other words, the groups differed in the type of legal label they received but not necessarily in the underlying seriousness of their behavior. Consistent with labeling theory, the researchers found that those offenders who were formally tagged as "felons" were more likely to be rearrested within 2 years. Furthermore, the labeling effects were particularly strong among persons without any prior criminal history.[36]

In research examining the impact of *informal* sanctions on a juvenile's identity, David Ward and Charles Tittle concluded that the application of informal sanctions "significantly affects the likelihood that an offender will develop a deviant identity and that such identities significantly affect the likelihood of recidivism."[37] Evidence in support for this position has been reported by Karen Heimer and Ross Matsueda, who discovered that delinquency is produced by interactions between the youth and a referenced delinquent group or conventional others, such as parents, in which such factors as motives, norms, attitudes, and gestures coalesce into self-reflected delinquent identity.[38] These labeling effects are not limited to American youths: When Nicole Cheung and Yuet Cheung studied more than 1000 secondary school Chinese students in Hong Kong, they found that adolescents with low levels of self-control were negatively labeled by parents and teachers and perceived to be likely to commit delinquency *even though they actually were not involved in delinquent behavior.*[39]

A half century after Becker introduced his theory, criminologists continue to explore his ideas about labeling and delinquency. For instance, John Hagan and Holly Foster examined "secret deviants" among a national sample of American youth to see if race affected whether youths who committed moderate drug offenses are contacted by juvenile authorities. They found strong evidence of a "partying" drug subculture among affluent white youths, who are rarely contacted or punished by the justice system. In contrast, there is a smaller group of African American youths who dabble in substance use but whose racial and class position does not protect them from police scrutiny. Hagan and Foster suggest that these differences in the attention paid to their offenses allow privileged whites to be secret deviants, but not members of other racial and social groups.[40]

It has also been argued that structural gender inequality affects the meaning that people attach to themselves, situations, and behaviors such as delinquency. A youth's definition of a situation as favorable or unfavorable to delinquency, for example, is affected by the significant others and reference groups that the youth considers in the process of role taking. The selection of these influential others and groups is, in turn, shaped by the youth's gender. According to Karen Heimer, the delinquency gender gap "emerges in part because inequality teaches girls to express their motivations through behavior that differs from that of boys."[41] In short, the meaning of behavior varies across gender. These observations regarding role-taking behavior may also apply to boys. Dawn Bartusch and Ross Matsueda reported that the negative effects of informal labels are greater for boys than for girls, especially for boys with strong self-identities as males.[42]

Mike Adams and his colleagues discovered that informal labeling by teachers and peers had a more significant impact on the child's self-conception than formal labeling by police or the juvenile court. Being sent to the principal's office or shunned by peers also has a greater impact on the child's self-concept than do the actions of his or her parents.[43] Indeed, informal social control and the various "labels" that parents, friends, neighbors, and other relatives affix to youths can affect their conduct.[44]

Other studies have *not* found support for the claims of labeling theory. Major criticisms of the labeling perspective tend to fall into one of two categories:[45]

- The theory disregards the actual behavior of the deviant, instead focusing on the *image* of the deviant being coerced by the labeling process.
- The key concepts of the theory are vague and imprecise, making it difficult to empirically validate its core propositions.

Charles Thomas and Donna Bishop, for instance, reported *no* evidence for the idea that sanctioning offenders pushes them toward acceptance of a deviant label.[46] Steven Burkett and Carol Hickman found that official processing of youths charged with marijuana offenses affected changes in girls' identities but not boys, although the identity changes in the girls did not lead to future delinquency.[47] Jack Foster and his colleagues concluded that youths who had been officially labeled as delinquents *did not* feel the label made much of a difference. Labeling, in other words, *did not* have much impact on their self-concept or what they believed was possible to achieve.[48]

When John Hepburn compared "official delinquents" with nondelinquents, he found that arrest record had *no* direct influence on self-concept.[49] Lisa Thrane and her colleagues' study of homeless adolescents found that youths with criminal friends were significantly more likely to be harassed by police officers; however, being labeled as having criminal friends had no effect on being arrested.[50]

Finally, some research has produced findings that are just the opposite of what labeling theory predicts. Specifically, it has been reported that youths who are sent to juvenile court have lower rates of future delinquency than those handled less severely.[51] Put differently, formal intervention appeared to *decrease* the likelihood of future offending.

Juvenile Justice Policy Applications

One fairly consistent finding from research on labeling is that official labels produce a negative effect when applied to *not-so-serious* offenders. Official or formal labeling *does not* have much of an impact on more serious delinquents. In the minds of these youths, the official label may be just one facet of their life to which they have become acclimated. Labeling theory also suggests that formal intervention by the juvenile justice system simply instills a deviant self-identification, thereby increasing delinquency. As a consequence of these understandings, the logical policy implications of labeling theory are to either (1) ignore delinquent acts; (2) react informally, diverting the child away from the juvenile justice system; or (3) bring the offender, victim, and community together to "right the wrong" and to restore justice. Whatever the juvenile justice system might do, it should do less—that is, it should decline to formally intervene in the lives of children unless absolutely necessary and divert youths at every possible stage in the juvenile justice process.

Such an approach may require, in the terms used by Schur, policies of *radical nonintervention*. He argues that we overcriminalize youths by bringing too many into the juvenile justice system and enforcing unnecessary laws. Therefore, we should consider fully removing status offenses (and related violations of court orders produced by such offenses) from the system. In addition, we should remove all but the most serious juvenile offenders from the nation's

Inspired by Braithwaite's reintegration theory, many juvenile justice systems use restorative justice techniques to avoid the stigmatizing effects of formal juvenile justice processing. Are restorative justice programs likely to empower adolescent offenders and victims?

© clearstockconcepts/E+/Getty.

juvenile corrections system. To do otherwise would be, in the words of Randall Shelden, to perpetuate a "war on kids."[52]

Diversion programs at both the police and court levels should be used whenever possible. Fortunately, diversion has long been practiced by police officers when responding to delinquent conduct. A variety of informal means, such as giving a youth a stern glare, lecturing a child about their delinquency and the consequences of it, and driving a juvenile offender home in a police car are ways that the police can get the message across in terms of deterrence, without actually having to formally involve the youth in the juvenile justice system. A variety of police diversion programs, such as Big Brothers Big Sisters and Police Athletic League (PAL) Clubs have been extensively developed around the United States. Similarly, court diversion provides alternatives ranging from informal adjustment and mediation to referral of adolescents to youth service bureaus and community youth boards. A number of diversion programs also exist at the correctional stage. For instance, wilderness programs, such as Vision Quest, Outward Bound, the Stephen French Youth Wilderness Program, and the Florida Associated Marine Institute, combine fitness, survival skills, and personal challenges as alternatives to secure institutional placements.[53]

Although numerous diversion programs exist, they are not nearly as popular today as they were in the mid-1970s. In the past, the lack of empirical evidence in support of the labeling theory and concerns over diversion actually "widening the net" and bringing more youths into the system have raised serious questions as to its usefulness. In fact, labeling theory and diversion policies were clearly on the decline by the late 1970s.

The one variation in labeling theory that appears to be most appealing to policymakers today might be that of John Braithwaite and his advocacy of reintegrative shaming. Three practical policy implications may be derived from Braithwaite's work:

1. The community's disapproval of the delinquent act may be expressed through the use of informal agencies or institutions of social control.
2. The repentant role may be reintegrated with rehabilitation programs.
3. Media coverage may be increased for not only the delinquent acts of juveniles, but also individual juvenile offenders, who may then be held up as examples of successful reform following their delinquencies.

Restorative justice programs also have extensively drawn upon Braithwaite's ideas. These programs bring the offender, victim, and community together to respond to less serious forms of delinquency and attempt to collectively assist in the rehabilitation process.

Restorative justice programs have been attempted in juvenile courts, juvenile corrections, victims' organizations, school-based treatment programs, and community-based social service programs.[54] Overall, some programs rooted in reintegration/restorative justice have been found to be mostly positive. For instance, when Jeff Latimer and his colleagues analyzed 35 studies of restorative justice, they found that the approach was more effective at reducing recidivism than were traditional correctional methods.[55]

Conflict Theory

Cultural deviance, strain, and social control theories share similar assumptions about the organization of society. Specifically, they see society as being organized around functionally interdependent institutions. Each institution has a function, or reason, for existing as it does. In a healthy society—one in which all the institutions are functioning smoothly together—there is social order. Social values are shared throughout society and serve as the basis for the creation of laws. These theories assume that society has reached a consensus regarding appropriate norms; they do not question why institutions are organized as they are, nor do they question why law has developed as it has. According to these perspectives, juvenile delinquency is behavior identified and prohibited by law because it violates consensual norms and values of society.

Conflict theory challenges these assumptions. It rejects the idea that society is organized around a consensus of values. Instead, **conflict theory** contends that in its normal state, society is held together by force, coercion, and intimidation. The values of different groups are often the basis of conflicting interests between those groups. Law represents the interests of those groups that have attained the power or influence to decide legislation. The first theorists to articulate a conflict view of social relations were Karl Marx and Friedrich Engels.

Karl Marx and Friedrich Engels

Karl Marx and Friedrich Engels saw delinquency as stemming from competition between social classes over scarce resources as well as from the historical inequality of the distribution of resources. Writing in the latter half of the 19th century, these two philosophers argued that the character of every society is determined by its particular mode of economic production. The primary conflict in society arises between the material forces of production and the

social relations of production. By "material forces of production," Marx and Engels meant the ability of a society to produce material goods. The term "social relations of production" refers to relationships among people, especially those relationships that are based on property, and the way material goods produced are distributed. In industrialized societies, then, the primary relationship reflects conflicts between the incompatible economic interests of the owners of the means of production (the *bourgeoisie*) and people who sell their labor (the *proletariat*). The class conflict between these two groups produces (both directly and indirectly) the conditions for delinquency.[56]

Because the *bourgeoisie* controls the means of production, it can also control all aspects of social life—*even the production of ideas*. Those ideas include those that create the criminal law as well as the ideological or philosophical beliefs that become the basis for policies of law enforcement. According to Marx and Engels, law and its enforcement are tools of the powerful, designed to protect their own economic interests. In short, the police, courts, and correctional system of society operate to control the working class. Behaviors prohibited by criminal law or selectively enforced by the police and courts reflect acts or values that threaten the interests of the dominant class. (This process is illustrated in **Figure 6.2**.)

Marx and Engels also produced a modest explanation of crime and delinquency (see **Box 6.7**, the "Theory in a Nutshell" feature). They believed that crime is the product of a demoralized working class. It is part of human nature to work and be productive, yet capitalist societies create large surplus populations of unemployed and underemployed workers. Over time, their unproductiveness leaves these individuals demoralized and vulnerable to committing crime and vice. Marx and Engels called criminals and their juvenile counterparts the *lumpenproletariat* (the "dangerous class") and described them as a "parasite class living off productive labor by theft, extortion and beggary, or by providing 'services' such as prostitution and gambling. Their class interests are diametrically opposed to those of the workers. They make their living by picking up the crumbs of capitalist relations of exchange."[57]

Marx and Engels are often criticized for being outdated. One of the better translations of their ideas is Thomas Bernard's basic principles of conflict criminology. His 12 propositions summarized the logic of Marx and Engels, while making it seem more applicable and relevant to delinquency and crime control:[58]

1. One's "web of life"—that is, the conditions of one's life—affects one's values and interests.
2. Complex societies are composed of groups with widely differing life conditions.
3. Complex societies are composed of groups with disparate and conflicting values and interests.

KEY TERMS

conflict theory
Theory arguing that society is held together by force, coercion, and intimidation and that the law represents the interests of those in power.

Figure 6.2 Mapping Delinquency Theory: Conflict Theory

© Jones & Bartlett Learning.

BOX 6.7

Theory in a Nutshell

Karl Marx and Friedrich Engels

Marx and Engels proposed that the ruling class in capitalist societies is responsible for the creation and application of criminal law. Acts threatening interests of the bourgeoisie will be handled by criminal law. In addition, crime reflects the demoralization of the surplus population, which consists of both unemployed and underemployed workers.

4. The behavior of individuals is generally consistent with their values and interests.

5. Because values and interests tend to remain stable over time, groups develop relatively stable behavior patterns that differ in varying degrees from the behavior patterns of other groups.

6. The enactment of laws is the result of a conflict and compromise process in which different groups attempt to promote their own values and interests.

7. Laws usually represent a combination of the values and interests of many groups, rather than the specific values and interests of any one particular group. Nevertheless, the higher a group's political and economic position, the more the law in general tends to represent the values and interests of that group.

8. The higher a group's political and economic position, the less likely it is that the behavioral patterns characteristic of that group (behaviors consistent with their values and interests) will violate the law.

9. The higher the political and economic position of an individual, the more difficult it is for official law enforcement agencies to process that person when his or her behavior violates the law. This difficulty may arise because the types of violations are more subtle and complex, or because the individual has greater resources to conceal the violation, to legally defend against official action, or to exert extralegal influence on the law enforcement process.

10. Because they function as bureaucrats, law enforcement agencies will generally process easier cases rather than more difficult ones.

11. Law enforcement agencies will preferentially process individuals from lower political and economic groups rather than individuals from higher groups.

12. Because of the processes of law enactment and enforcement described previously, the official crime rates for groups will be inversely proportional to their political and economic position, independent of any factors that might also influence the distribution of crimes rates.

Willem Bonger

Willem Bonger was an early-20th-century Marxist criminologist and the author of *Criminality and Economic Conditions* (1916). Bonger saw modern capitalist society as being divided into two classes: a ruling class and a ruled class. Furthermore, he viewed capitalism as being based on competition and profit making. Indeed, Bonger believed that economic production is carried on exclusively for profit. More important, he argued that because capitalism brings about *egoistic impulses* (selfishness and personal ambition), it makes people less sensitive to the misery or happiness of others. In more "primitive" societies, he said, people lived in a state of communism, and modes of production were designed for personal consumption, not exchange: "They had neither rich nor poor; their economic interests were either parallel or equal . . . the interest of one was the same as that of his comrade." Indeed, in such societies, *altruistic impulses* (a concern for the well-being of others) were developed and encouraged.[59]

By contrast, the modern class structure found in capitalism inhibits tendencies toward mutual helpfulness and instead fosters social irresponsibility. The egoistic tendencies of capitalism have "weakened the moral force in man which combats the inclination toward egoistic acts, and hence toward the crimes which are one form of these acts."[60] According to Bonger, crime and delinquency reflect the egoistic behavior fostered by the desire to get ahead and to think only of one's personal needs and desires (see **Box 6.8**, the "Theory in a Nutshell" feature).

Capitalism also creates conditions that encourage delinquency. In Bonger's time, child labor was still extensively practiced in industrialized countries. He saw the exploitation of child labor as a singularly capitalist phenomenon—one that contributed to delinquency in many ways. On the one hand, labor forced the child to think only of his or her own interests, thereby instilling egoistic feelings. Paid labor also made children more independent at an

BOX 6.8

Theory in a Nutshell

Willem Bonger

Bonger thought that capitalism engenders egoistic impulses in all people, which inhibit their tendencies toward developing a sense of responsibility to the larger group. For Bonger, the solution to delinquency was clear: A socialist society, built upon socialist modes of production, will produce altruistic impulses in all people. When adolescents are motivated by altruism, they are unlikely to commit crimes against others.

age when they most needed the guidance of others. Finally, according to Bonger, involvement in paid labor brought children "into contact with persons who are rough and indifferent to their well-being."[61] All these factors increased the child's vulnerability to the enticements and pressures of delinquency.

For Bonger, the solution to crime and delinquency was to be found in the construction of a socialist society. In a society based on a socialist mode of production, altruistic influences would dominate, both in the behaviors of persons and in the legal system. Altruistic adolescents would be more likely to help others instead of taking advantage of vulnerable people. "Such a society will not only remove the causes which now make men egoistic, but will awaken, on the contrary, a strong feeling of altruism."[62]

Not all conflict theorists cite the economic competition between classes or the unequal distribution of economic resources as the sources of delinquency. Thorsten Sellin and George Vold (discussed next) explored the nature of group conflict in socially heterogeneous societies. They contend that groups in society reflect associations based on common interests, such as the pursuit of goals or the protection of vested interests (power, wealth, and status).

Thorsten Sellin

Thorsten Sellin's *Culture and Conflict in Crime* (1938) was one of the first textbooks to put forth the idea that delinquency was the product of conflicting norms. Sellin distinguished between *crime norms* (norms found in the criminal law) and *conduct*, or *group*, norms

KEY TERMS

crime norms
Criminal laws that prohibit specific conduct and provide punishments for violations.

conduct norms
Rules that reflect the values, expectations, and actual behaviors of groups in everyday life. They are not necessarily the norms found in the criminal law.

(norms that are specific to localized groups and that may or may not be consistent with crime norms).

Crime norms reflect rules that prohibit specific conduct and provide punishments for violations. The particular character of the laws, the specific conduct prohibited, and the punishments meted out reflect the character and vested interests of those groups able to influence legislation. According to Sellin, "In some states these groups may comprise the majority, in others a minority, but the social values which receive the protection of the criminal law are ultimately those which are treasured by dominant interest groups."[63]

Conduct norms, by contrast, reflect the values, expectations, and actual behaviors of groups in everyday life. These norms can be very specific to particular groups, may be shared by many diverse groups, and may conflict with one another. Conduct norms are not necessarily the norms found in criminal law, and sometimes may directly conflict with crime norms. Sellin answered the question of which conduct norms are likely to be incorporated into the criminal law this way:

> The conduct which the state denotes as criminal is, of course, that deemed injurious to society, or in the last analysis, to those who wield the political power within that society and therefore control the legislative, judicial, and executive functions which are the external manifestations of authority.[64]

As societies become more heterogeneous and complex, the likelihood that group norms will collide with crime norms increases. In turn, delinquency rates will be higher in neighborhoods with the greatest diversity of group norms. Sellin believed, for instance, that urban neighborhoods with a variety of recently arrived immigrant groups living in close proximity would have a higher level of delinquency than suburban neighborhoods where residents had little contact with "outsiders." Culture and conflict is not limited to the American context. A study in Israel compared youth versus adult assessments of the seriousness of crimes and found that youths were more likely to rate crimes as generally unserious and punishment as less appropriate whereas adults held opposite views. Based on these data, juvenile delinquency and the generally liberal attitudes among adolescents about delinquent behavior represent a "cultural conflict" of sorts against adult order.[65]

Sellin's emphasis on the normative conflict that arises in neighborhoods complements the principles underlying cultural deviance theory, particularly the work done by Shaw and McKay. (see **Box 6.9**, the "Theory in a Nutshell" feature)

George Vold

In 1958, George Vold published *Theoretical Criminology*, in which he argued that human nature leads people into groups. According to Vold, groups form

BOX 6.9

Theory in a Nutshell

Thorsten Sellin

Sellin argued that conflict naturally arises between the conduct norms of groups and the crime norms reflected in criminal law. The specific behaviors prohibited by law, as well as the punishments specified by the law, will reflect the character and vested interests of those groups with sufficient power to influence the legislative process.

because common interests draw people together. As new interests arise, new groups are created. However, "groups come into conflict with one another as the interests and purposes they serve tend to overlap, encroach on one another, and become competitive."[66] This competitiveness generates a continuous struggle to maintain or even enlarge the position of one's own group relative to others. This conflict may eventually lead to the creation of new laws. "Whichever group interest can marshal the greatest number of votes will determine whether there will be a new law to hamper and curb the interests of the opposing group."

Not surprisingly, group members who support the new law will be more likely to obey it and call for its strict enforcement. People who oppose the law will be less sympathetic to it and, consequently, more likely to violate it. People with little power or influence hold little sway over the legislative process. As a consequence, behaviors reflecting their interests are more likely to be legislated as criminal by groups that have the necessary influence.

Richard Quinney

Richard Quinney believes that criminal laws are consciously created mechanisms that enable the ruling class to maintain political and economic control over the rest of society. This basic Marxian framework is found in Quinney's book, *Critique of Legal Order*, in which he outlines the following principles:[67]

1. American society is organized around advanced capitalism.
2. The state exists to serve the interests of the dominant capitalist class.
3. Social and economic order are maintained and perpetuated by the ruling class through the application of criminal law.
4. Crime control is accomplished through the criminal justice system, which is administered by governing elites. This system of law and control represents ruling-class interests and is designed to establish domestic order.

5. The inherent contradictions of advanced capitalism require the oppression of the lower classes through the coercion and violence of the legal system.
6. The crime problem can be solved only by the collapse of capitalism and the creation of a new society built upon socialist economic principles.

By the time he prepared the second edition of his book *Class, State, and Crime*, however, Quinney's views had shifted substantially. In this work, rather than relying entirely on a Marxist critique of capitalist society, Quinney considered the problem of crime and delinquency within a *religious* context: "The contemporary capitalist world is caught in what Tillich, going beyond Marx's materialistic analysis of capitalism, calls a *sacred void*, the human predicament on both a spiritual and sociopolitical level."[68] Citing Old Testament prophets, Quinney suggests that a "prophetic understanding" of reality is necessary for a proper analysis of crime and justice and states that Marx was wrong about religion being an "opium of the people." Quinney does maintain an essentially Marxian orientation: "The socialist struggle in our age is a search for God at the same time that it is a struggle for justice in human society."[69]

John Hagan

John Hagan, who focused on the role of the mother as a worker, suggests a different approach to explaining delinquency. In his *power-control theory*, Hagan suggests that children's participation in delinquency is affected by the relative position of fathers and mothers in the workplace:

> Positions of power in the workplace are translated into power relations in the household and . . . . the latter, in turn, influence the gender-determined control of adolescents, their preferences for risk taking, and the patterning of gender and delinquency.[70]

According to Hagan, delinquency is a male-dominated phenomenon because of the class structure of modern patriarchal families. The *patriarchal family* consists of a husband whose employment outside the home carries some degree of authority and a wife who is not employed outside the home. This type of family is more likely to socially reproduce daughters who are like their mothers—females who focus on domestic labor and consumption, activities preparing them for a cult of domesticity. The sons in patriarchal families are more likely to be prepared to participate in the external labor force in direct production.

The opposite of the patriarchal family is the *egalitarian family*, in which both parents are employed in positions of authority outside the home. In such families, both males and females engage in consumption and production activities equally. Parents

then attempt to socially reproduce both sons and daughters for entry into the production sphere of the labor force.

In the patriarchal family, females are both instruments and objects of informal social control. Although both fathers and mothers exert much more control over their daughters than over their sons, daughters are even more controlled by their mothers than by their fathers. In egalitarian families, parents redistribute their informal controls in a manner that treats sons and daughters more equally.

The relationship between parents and daughters in patriarchal families is also responsible for daughters' significantly lower interest in risk taking (an activity viewed as more acceptable for sons). Patriarchal families teach daughters to avoid risk taking, whereas egalitarian families are more likely to encourage both sons and daughters to take risks. Consequently, patriarchal families are characterized by large sex-ratio differences in common forms of delinquency. In egalitarian families, where girls are treated more like their brothers, minimal differences in common delinquency are detected.

Tests conducted by Simon Singer and Murray Levine have lent support to power-control theory. These researchers reported that gender differences in delinquent behavior were largely tied to variations in parental authority.[71] Brenda Sims Blackwell and her colleagues found partial support for Hagan's theory when they found that it explained gender differences in delinquency in their study of middle school and high school students in a small Florida city. Tamela Eitle and David Eitle tested power-control theory using a sample of American Indian youth and found that patriarchal family structure and father-daughter bonds were associated with drug-related delinquency.[72]

Conversely, other tests of power-control theory have found little or no support. Gary Jensen and Kevin Thompson examined data from three surveys conducted between 1964 and 1979 that were based on samples 3 to 30 times larger than the Toronto sample used by Hagan and his associates. Whereas Hagan had predicted significant relationships between social class and delinquency and between gender and class, data produced by Jensen and Thompson did not support these hypotheses. To explain this discrepancy, the researchers suggested the lack of supportive findings may be the result of differences between American and Canadian youths or methodological differences between the studies.[73]

Merry Morash and Meda Chesney-Lind have reported mixed support for power-control theory. They found that girls were less delinquent than boys in each type of family. Furthermore, the key explanatory variable was not the mother's relative workplace power, but rather the absence of a father and presence of a step-father, as well as the quality of the child's relationship with his or her parents. Their data also yielded several other important findings:

> In some types of families, boys were controlled more than girls. Specifically, if the mother was alone and unemployed, she controlled more of the decisions about boys than about girls, and was more punitive toward boys. The family with an unemployed mother alone also differs from other types in that the children identify less with their mother.[74]

Daniel Curran and Claire Renzetti argue that Hagan's theory defines patriarchal control in the home as simply "parental supervision" and, therefore, is too narrowly conceived.[75] James Messerschmidt suggests that it may be incorrect to assume that the authority a person has at work translates in exactly the same way as authority in the home and family.[76]

Ronald Akers takes the power-control theory to task, claiming that although Hagan's own Canadian study supported the theory, the findings from other studies are much less supportive:

> The class and gender differences, the low involvement of fathers in exercising parental control, and other internal family variables have no or very weak effects on delinquency. The gender differences in delinquency are about the same for patriarchal and egalitarian families. . . . Furthermore, the effects of family control variables on delinquent behavior are equally weak for both males and females.[77]

Over the years, Hagan has responded to his critics and modified his power-control theory to compensate for its shortcomings. In its most recent form, this theory assumes that the links between patriarchal structures in employment and in parenting styles with girls and boys, as well as differences in risk affinity and delinquency, are mediated by the ideologies of gender role preferences and hierarchic self-interest. A study of families in Canada and Germany found that the gendered structure of the work environment contributed to the emergence of gender differences in aggressive behavior by increasing either gender differences in socialization within the family or parental ideological commitments to socialization according to gender.[78]

Finally, a basic and powerful critique of power-control theory is that gender differences in delinquency have little to do with patriarchy or gender socialization—or any environmental feature, for that matter. Biological criminologists and psychological criminologists would explain gender differences by citing the profound evidence of immutable biological differences between males and females in terms of their use of aggression and coercion as it relates to delinquent behavior and profound gender differences in the psychological expression of antisocial behaviors.[79]

Mark Colvin and John Pauly

Mark Colvin and John Pauly's **integrated structural-Marxist theory** argues that serious delinquency results from the reproduction of coercive control patterns tied to the relationship between production and class structure in capitalist societies. Their approach assumes that the "objective structure of social relations [is] grounded in the process of material production under capitalism."[80] The struggle between the three major classes (capitalist, working, and petite bourgeoisie) produces distinctive "fractions" within each major class. The different control structures, operating within the various fractions of the working class, "solicit and compel certain types of behavior from individuals and shape ideological orientation for the individual in relation to the agents and apparatuses of social control." Within the working class, there are three important fractions:

1. Fraction 1 is primarily composed of workers located in very competitive, secondary labor market industries. Given the minimal job security and dead-end nature of the work, control tends to be simple and coercive.
2. Fraction 2 provides greater job security than Fraction 1, largely as a result of the unionization and protective contracts that these workers typically have. The control structure relies more on the workers consciously bonding to work and authority on the basis of the possibilities of promotions and wage increases.
3. Fraction 3 comprises mainly workers located in jobs that provide greater amounts of independence and require or expect individual initiative (this includes both blue- and white-collar occupations). Controls in Fraction 3 take a more bureaucratic, normative form in which the worker is manipulated through valued symbols and statuses.

According to integrated structural-Marxist theory, the coercive control patterns that exist for lower-class parents in the workplace are reproduced in the home, thereby shaping the parents' behavior as they interact with each other and with their children. Fraction 1 parents—who hold jobs that are inferior, tightly controlled, lacking in personal authority, and regulated by superiors through coercive means—then reproduce these control patterns in the home. The result: the increased alienation of the child from authority in general. In addition, the use of coercive controls in the home, including physical punishment, tends to weaken the bond between parent and child.

Social bonds of lower-class adolescents may also be weakened by aspects of the school setting. Colvin and Pauly argue that the control structures of schools are designed to support the labor requirements of capitalism. Consequently, these structures use coercive controls similar to those in the workplace.

When entering school, the child, whose initial bonds were produced in a family control structure, confronts a new structure of control. The school, like parents' workplaces, contains gradations of control (within "tracks") that are exercised over students. A child with negative initial bonds is likely to be placed in a control structure at school that parallels the coercive family council structure that produced the child's negative bond.[81] According to Colvin and Pauly, the reproduction of coercive controls in school is accomplished in four ways:

1. IQ and aptitude testing are likely to identify more negatively bonded children and dictate their placement in lower level tracks.
2. Negatively bonded children may give behavioral cues to school authority figures that identify them as potential "problem students." Such cues may be self-fulfilling prophecies, with the child becoming what he or she is expected to become.
3. The differential placement of lower-class students into lower-level tracks will lead to a greater strain on, and alienation of, those students.
4. Differential financial resources of schools in lower-, working-, and middle-class neighborhoods will produce differences in the availability of rewards and punishments in the school setting. Schools with fewer resources will rely on more coercive controls.

The various school control structures lead to differential patterns of rewards and punishments, resulting in differential reinforcement or weakening of social bonds. Lower-class adolescents who have become alienated at home and school are more likely to join peer groups composed of similarly alienated individuals. Criminal, violent, or delinquent patterns of behavior will emerge from these relationships.

Colvin and Pauly's approach may be summarized as follows:

1. Parents' *class position* is negatively associated with their experience of coercion in *workplace control structures*, a situation that leads to more alienated bonds in lower-class parents.
2. Alienated parental bonds contribute to the development of more coercive family control structures, which in turn result in more alienated initial bonds in juveniles.
3. Juveniles with alienated initial bonds are more likely be placed in more coercive school control

KEY TERMS

integrated structural-Marxist theory
Theory suggesting that serious delinquency is the result of the reproduction of coercive control patterns tied to the relationship between production and class structure in capitalist societies.

structures, reinforcing the juveniles' alienated bonds.

4. Juveniles' reinforced alienated bonds lead to greater association with alienated peers who form their peer-group control structures, which interact with class-related, community and neighborhood distributions of opportunities to create qualitatively different paths of delinquent development.

Tests of Colvin and Pauly's theory have found only modest support for their claims. Studies by Steven Messer and Marvin Krohn and by Sally Simpson and Lori Elis, for example, have reported the basic relationship between social class and delinquency is largely structured by gender.[82] These researchers suggest that traditional gender controls in the home interact with workplace controls to produce more rigid discipline and control for girls.

Mark Colvin

Nearly two decades after Colvin and Pauly developed their integrated structural-Marxist theory, Colvin alone developed a second integrated theory using a conflict framework he called **differential coercion theory**. (See **Box 6.10**, the "Theory in a Nutshell" feature.) Colvin defines *coercion* as a force that causes a child to behave in a certain way out of the fear and anxiety it creates. According to Colvin, children who are exposed to coercive environments are more likely to develop social–psychological deficits that increase the possibility of their committing crimes.[83] Differential coercion theory borrows heavily from previously published works showing, among other things, that aversive family interchanges and coercive disciplining patterns are strongly correlated with juvenile delinquency in adolescents. Indeed, research supports the idea that children who are physically abused and who receive erratic discipline are more likely to commit crime.[84] Some examples of the types of coercive interchanges Colvin identifies include physical attacks, teasing, humiliation, yelling, and threats. Through aversive family interchanges, children growing up in these environments learn to use the coercion mechanism when they find themselves in undesirable situations, both in family and nonfamily settings. In short, children bring what they learn from coercive family interactions into other social settings. These children are more likely to become "early starters" in delinquency and life-course persistent or career offenders.[85]

BOX 6.10
Theory in a Nutshell
Mark Colvin

In differential coercion theory, Colvin argues that children who are exposed to coercive environments are more likely to develop social–psychological deficits that increase their likelihood of committing crimes. He defines coercion as a force that causes a child to behave in a certain way out of the fear and anxiety it creates. Children who grow up in coercive environments are more likely to behave inappropriately in settings they find to be unpleasant.

Colvin identifies two dimensions of coercion: the *strength* of the coercive force, which ranges from no coercion to total coercion, and the *consistency* with which coercion is applied or experienced. Children usually experience coercion on either a more or less consistent basis or an erratic basis. Juveniles who experience coercion erratically will develop a different set of social–psychological deficits than juveniles who experience coercion consistently. The most notable difference between these two groups is the direction of their anger and the degree of self-control induced in the child.

Erratic coercion leads to anger directed at *others* because the child's perception of unjust and arbitrary treatment is heightened because of an unpredictable schedule of coercion. Erratic coercion also induces low self-control. Coercion that is applied inconsistently teaches children that they cannot control the effects of being punished because the punishment occurs randomly, rather than as a predictable outcome of their behavior. Thus, when children believe their punishment is random, there is no pattern or incentive for them to learn self-control.

By contrast, coercion that is applied more or less consistently produces *self*-directed anger and engenders a rigid type of self-control that is based on a steady fear of reprisal from external sources. Colvin argues that erratic coercion creates children who are prone to committing predatory crime, whereas consistent coercion produces children who are submissive. Although children who experience consistent coercion are less likely to commit crime, they are more likely to experience mental illness.[86]

Whereas consistent coercion might prevent crime in theory, it is very difficult for adults to maintain such consistency in their interpersonal relations with children in practice. Doing so requires constant monitoring to detect noncompliance. Except for extreme situations of monitoring (such as that exercised over females in highly repressive, patriarchal households), consistent coercion typically becomes erratic because of the demands it imposes on adults who are trying to maintain close surveillance. Consequently, the crime-controlling effect of consistent coercion is short lived. Given these difficulties in applying the coercive mechanism, coercion may be best at controlling delinquency when it is coupled with an array of social supports in which coercion remains subtle and in the background and used only as a last resort when social supports fail to create compliance.

Finally, Colvin distinguishes between *interpersonal* and *impersonal* forms of coercion. The first type of coercion occurs within direct interpersonal relations of control (e.g., adults and children). The second type of coercion grounded in Merton's strain theory is linked to pressures from larger structural arrangements that create an indirect experience of coercion. On the one hand, interpersonal coercion uses the threat of force and intimidation to create compliance in interpersonal relations. These *micro*levels of coercive processes of control might involve the actual or threatened use of physical force or the actual or threatened removal of social supports. On the other hand, impersonal coercion results from pressure arising from structural arrangements and circumstances beyond the individual's control that produce stress, frustration, anxiety, desperation, and anger. These *macro*level sources of coercion may include economic and social pressures that stem from unemployment, poverty, or competition among groups. Coercion can involve the removal of social supports at both the microlevel, such as love, food, and clothing, and the macrolevel, such as unemployment benefits, health care, and housing.

Francis Cullen

In 1994, Francis Cullen introduced *social support theory* as a general framework for understanding criminology and criminal justice. **Social support** is defined as the perceived and actual amount of instrumental and expressive or emotional supports that a person receives from primary relationships, social networks, and communities. Having a neighbor, friend, or family member to help with babysitting, job searching, bill paying, and providing other advice and counsel are examples of social support. Across multiple levels of social life, social support may be provided informally and formally through churches, schools, government assistance programs, and even the criminal justice system.

According to Cullen, social support is theoretically important to criminology because it serves as a protective factor that both insulates persons from delinquency and assists them in the process of correctional rehabilitation. In this sense, social support is applicable to crime prevention and offender treatment. In particular, Cullen's "general" proposition is that, all things being equal, individuals—ranging

BOX 6.11
Theory in a Nutshell
Francis Cullen

Cullen's social support theory argues that the perceived and actual amount of instrumental and expressive or emotional support that one receives from primary relationships, social networks, and communities can insulate youths from delinquency. In addition, social support is an important way to help former offenders desist from crime and reconnect or reintegrate into conventional society.

from would-be offenders to those who have already broken the law—who receive higher levels of social support will be at a lower risk for engaging in wayward behavior in the future (see **Box 6.11**, the "Theory in a Nutshell" feature).[87]

In the correctional setting, social support may serve as a resource and safety net to help steer former delinquents and prisoners along conventional pathways. Indeed, in subsequent work, Cullen and his colleagues articulated that the social support approach was particularly well suited to rehabilitate prisoners because research shows that recidivism can be reduced via programs that develop interpersonal skills, provide supportive counseling from caring providers, and furnish multiple social services. Thus social support theory predicts that many of the potentially harmful effects of prison conditions on an inmate's behavior can be mediated by the provision of social support.[88] Actually, Cullen and Colvin have linked their theories by showing that social support is an important way to reduce the noxious effects of social coercion in people's lives.[89]

Criminologists have produced impressive empirical support for social support theory using an array of data sources and analytic methods. By analyzing data from the National Youth Survey, for example, John Wright and his colleagues found that familial social support (also known as family capital) was positively related to moral beliefs, time spent studying, and grades and negatively related to having delinquent friends. Youths who had a strong family support system were also more likely to exercise, maintain a healthy lifestyle, and be committed to their jobs. In addition, youths who had family support had relatively few criminal

KEY TERMS

social support
The perceived and actual amount of instrumental and expressive or emotional supports that one receives from primary relationships, social networks, and communities.

friends and were less likely to use drugs. Overall, Wright and his associates reported, family social support produced other beneficial forms of social support/capital, reduced delinquency over a 6-year period, and exerted effects that led to a range of outcomes associated with prosocial adult development.[90]

James Unnever and his colleagues tested the theory using a sample of nearly 2500 middle school students selected from Virginia and found considerable support for differential coercion theory. Specifically, parental coercion, school coercion, neighborhood coercion, and coercive ideation were significantly predictive of involvement in delinquency despite controls for several sociodemographic and social bond measures. In fact, peer coercion was the only type of coercion that was not significantly associated with delinquency. Similarly, Stephen Baron found that coercion, coercive modeling, and coercive ideation were associated with violent delinquency among a sample of 400 homeless youths.[91]

Benjamin Cornwell examined the effects of social support on mental health outcomes using data from the National Longitudinal Study of Adolescent Health and found that adolescents with reduced parental and friendship support experienced higher levels of depression than youths who had greater connectedness with their peers and families. Elise Peplin and Victoria Banyard found that social support mediated the effects of child maltreatment on developmental outcomes in young adults. In other words, people who were mistreated as children could overcome the harmful effects of maltreatment with emotional and other forms of support from friends and family. In a study of youth selected from the Project on Human Development in Chicago Neighborhoods, Sara Anderson and her colleagues found that adolescents who experienced more social support from their peers engaged in significantly fewer delinquent acts than youth with lower social support. These effects were pronounced in the worst neighborhoods, which suggests that social support can be an important buffering effect to delinquency in dangerous environments.[92]

Social support theory has also been supported using offender samples. In a study of male offenders who were recently released from prison, Andy Hochstetler and his colleagues found that ex-prisoners with strong social supports—such as family, friends, and community activities—had lower feelings of hostility and bitterness about their incarceration experience.

This, in turn, led to more productive reintegration to society. Similar effects have been shown among prisoner inmates in South Korea.[93]

Researchers have shown that although the general public holds many punitive attitudes with regard to delinquents, they also espouse social support. For instance, Melissa Moon and her colleagues reported that citizens believe in the importance of rehabilitation to change delinquents and support establishment of prevention programs. In fact, many people are even willing to volunteer their time to provide social support to juvenile delinquents.[94]

Social support is also linked to crime at the aggregate level. By analyzing data from 46 countries, Travis Pratt and Timothy Godsey examined the relationship between a society's degree of social support and its murder rate. They found that nations with greater levels of social support have lower violent crime rates; in comparison, nations that do not invest in social support have more homicides.[95]

Robert Regoli and John Hewitt

In their **differential oppression theory**, Robert Regoli and John Hewitt focus on the fact that children have little power to influence their social world. They have almost no choice regarding with whom they associate, and they have limited resources available to influence others or to support themselves independently of adults. Therefore, they have the least access to resources that could allow them to negotiate changes in their environment.[96] In comparison to parents, teachers, and other adult authority figures, children are relatively powerless and are expected—often required—to submit to the power and authority of adults. When this power is used to deny children self-determination and impede them from developing a sense of competence and self-efficacy, it becomes oppression (see **Box 6.12**, the "Theory in a Nutshell" feature).[97]

Regoli and Hewitt think *all* children are oppressed. The amount of oppression children experience falls along a continuum, ranging from simple demands

KEY TERMS

differential oppression theory
Theory stating that delinquency is the culmination of a process that begins at conception and evolves through adolescence; the more a child is oppressed, the greater the likelihood he or she will become delinquent.

BOX 6.12

Theory in a Nutshell

Robert Regoli and John Hewitt

According to Regoli and Hewitt, children develop in an arena of oppression that affects who and what they become. Children are differentially oppressed—some more frequently and more severely than others. Children who experience more frequent and severe oppression are more likely to turn to delinquency and engage in other problem behaviors.

for obedience to rules designed for the convenience of adults to physical, sexual, and emotional abuse. These researchers contend that the problem behaviors of children—including crime and delinquency, drug and alcohol abuse, and mental disorders—can be understood as adaptive reactions to oppressive social situations created by adults. Although many children grow up under oppressive conditions that fail to support their developmental needs, the actual psychological, emotional, or physical consequences that a child suffers depend on the duration, frequency, intensity, and priority of the oppression and on the child's stage of development.

The theory of differential oppression is organized around four principles:

1. Because children lack power because of their age, size, and lack of resources, they are easy targets for adult oppression.
2. Adult oppression of children occurs in multiple social contexts and falls along a continuum ranging from benign neglect to malignant abuse.
3. Oppression leads to adaptive reactions by children. The oppression of children produces at least four adaptations: passive acceptance, exercise of illegitimate coercive power, manipulation of one's peers, and retaliation (**Figure 6.3**).
4. Children's adaptations to oppression create and reinforce adults' views of children as inferior, subordinate, and being troublemakers. This view enables adults to justify their role as oppressors and further reinforces children's powerlessness.

Forms of Oppression

Oppression is a summary term used to describe the abusive, neglectful, and disrespectful relations that children often confront. Oppression of children by adults occurs in multiple social contexts and falls along a continuum ranging from benign neglect to malignant abuse; it occurs whenever adults act in ways that belittle or trivialize children as being something less than authentic and feeling human beings. Children are exposed to different levels and types of oppression that vary depending on their age, level of development, and beliefs and perceptions of their parents.

Although adults sometimes exercise power over children out of sincere concern for the child's welfare, Regoli and Hewitt focus on the times when an adult's use of power over children is about the needs and interests of the adult, rather than those of the child. In fact, much of the oppression children suffer stems from their parents' inability to meet their needs, either because adults are uninformed about what the needs of children are at various stages of development or because they are not capable of responding to those needs. Oppressive structural forces—such as poverty, social isolation, and residing in a disadvantaged neighborhood—also negatively influence parenting practices. Nevertheless, the underlying source of adult oppression may be found in the mistreatment parents received when they were children and continue to experience as adults. In essence, the oppression adults inflict on children is likely a part of a chain of coercion and abuse that is transmitted from one generation to the next.[98]

Healthy development requires that social contexts provide opportunities for children to fulfill their physical, intellectual, psychological, and social developmental needs. Unfortunately, for many children, rather than being supportive and nurturing, their surrounding social contexts are oppressive and damaging. Using a developmental–ecological perspective can provide a means for understanding how the oppression of children is likely to occur within multiple social contexts that may interact to produce harmful outcomes for children. These contexts include both micro-level relationships with family and friends and macrolevel structural elements such as race, class, neighborhood, and age, which expose people to more or less oppression of different types.

Microlevel Oppression

The most severe and damaging oppression adults inflict upon children is officially defined as maltreatment. The major forms of child maltreatment include physical abuse, sexual abuse, neglect, and emotional abuse. According to data from the U.S. Centers for Disease Control and Prevention, more than 3.4 million cases of child abuse or neglect involving more than 6 million children are reported to the various state protective services each year. Thirty percent of these cases are referred for investigation, with slightly less than 30% of the investigated cases resulting in a disposition of either substantiated or indicated child maltreatment. Approximately 78% of the victims

The adult oppression of children results in delinquency and other maladaptive behaviors, according to Regoli and Hewitt's theory of differential oppression. Should hitting or whipping a child be a criminal offense, based on the negative outcomes it helps to produce?

© VMJones/E+/Getty.

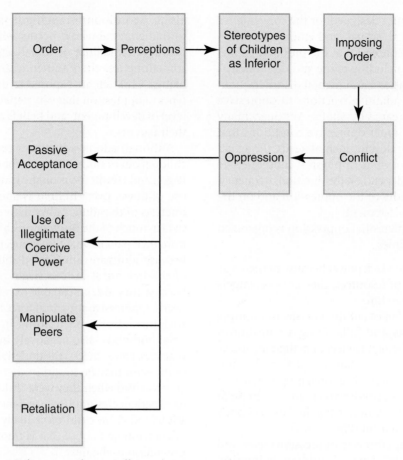

Figure 6.3 Mapping Delinquency Theory: Differential Oppression Theory

© Jones & Bartlett Learning.

have suffered neglect, 18% have experienced physical abuse, 9% have been sexually abused, and 11% have suffered emotional maltreatment.[99] Official data are reinforced by the findings from a self-report study based on a national sample of 3346 adults, in which 63% of parents reported they had used at least one form of psychological aggression on their children in the previous year.[100]

Certain parenting styles are more likely to oppress children. Some parents oppress children as they attempt to impose and maintain adult conceptions of social order. Such parents may view their children as extensions of themselves rather than as individuals and, therefore, feel free to impose their will on their children.[101] In any case, the children are required to obey rules designed to reinforce adult notions of right and wrong behavior. In an attempt to exert greater control over their children, some parents and other adults use coercion or force. According to Richard Gelles and Murray Straus, American cultural norms regarding violence in families dictate that it is acceptable to hit a child if he or she is doing something wrong and "won't listen to reason." Such coercion may become excessive, however, leading to physical harm and long-term psychological damage; it is also a mechanism for transmitting an ageist ideology that

diminishes the value of children in relation to adults across society.[102]

Other parents oppress their children through neglectful parenting that fails to meet their children's physical, emotional, and educational needs. Examples of physical neglect include the refusal of or delay in seeking health care, abandonment, expulsion from the home or refusal to allow a runaway to return home, and inadequate supervision. Emotional neglect includes inattention to the child's needs for affection, refusal of or failure to provide needed psychological care, and spousal abuse committed in the child's presence. The allowance of chronic truancy, failure to enroll a child of mandatory school age in school, and failure to attend to special educational needs are all examples of educational neglect. Generally, neglect occurs whenever a caretaker permits a child to experience suffering or fails to provide one of the basic ingredients essential for developing a child into a physically, intellectually, emotionally, and psychologically healthy person.

Although single incidents of neglect may have no noticeable harmful effects, in some cases they can result in death. Chronic patterns of neglect also may result in developmental delays or emotional disabilities. According to Munkel, "Neglected children suffer hurts in their bodies, their minds, their emotions, and their spirits."[103]

Macrolevel Oppression

Macrolevel social forces such as poverty also oppress children. Put simply, children living in poverty are more likely to experience oppression than children living in more affluent conditions. This oppression can be viewed developmentally and is likely to be cumulative in nature as children continue to grow and develop in destitute conditions. During their early years of life, socioeconomic disadvantage oppresses children by impairing their physical health status at birth and providing less access to resources that may moderate the negative consequences of those problems. Socioeconomic disadvantage has the added burden of conferring greater exposure to violent delinquency and various forms of victimization. Data from the National Crime Victimization Survey, for instance, indicate that poor households have more than double the rate of violent victimization than persons in high-income homes. For healthy development, young children need exposure to stimulating materials or experiences. Unfortunately, children living in poverty are less likely than their wealthier counterparts to have access to these materials or experiences. Often their homes are unsafe, lacking heat and adequate plumbing. In addition, they have increased exposure to chemical toxins such as lead (which is associated with cognitive deficits), lower school achievement, and long-term impairment of neurological function. Indeed, early-life poverty contributes to reduced brain volume in the orbitofrontal cortex, and the subsequent neurological deficits have been linked to delinquency and problem behaviors occurring 25 years later.[104]

Rather than receiving cognitively stimulating experiences, young children living in disadvantaged neighborhoods may rarely leave their homes. Environmental and work-related conditions often limit their access to the outdoors. Poor children are more likely than nonpoor children to live in housing located in commercial and industrial areas, which often lack safe outdoor places for children to play and limit opportunities for social interaction and cognitive development. Poor children's environments are also characterized by greater risk exposures, such as access to gangs and active criminal offenders, proximity to sexual predators, exposure to prostitution, substance use, and other social incivilities. These experiences have long-term negative effects on their well-being and health.[105]

Poverty and economic disadvantage also have oppressive influences on school-age and adolescent children. During middle childhood and adolescence, children increasingly come into direct contact with their neighborhoods through involvement in school, youth-serving organizations, and informal neighborhood groups. For young people, the physical features of their neighborhood establish the boundaries of their social universe. Some neighborhoods offer youth a variety of supervised instruction and structured activities, whereas others send the majority of the children out on the street.[106] As a result of the restricted tax base in poor distressed neighborhoods, limited public resources are available to support the education, recreation, and health needs of youth and their families. In contrast, youth in wealthy neighborhoods have opportunities that poor children are not offered, such as summer camp, music lessons, sports training, home computers, and special tutoring. In stark contrast, adolescents in dilapidated inner-city neighborhoods have higher exposure to physical danger, criminal activity, and drug use.[107]

Because successful adaptation at each stage of youth development is influenced by earlier developmental histories, long-term exposure to oppressive living conditions typically results in worse developmental outcomes for some children. African American and Hispanic children, for example, are more likely than white children to experience persistent poverty and to live in areas of concentrated poverty.[108] Thomas McNulty and Paul Bellair found that concentrated poverty is so segregated by race that virtually no white children live in the worst neighborhoods in which many African American and Hispanic children do.[109]

High-risk contexts such as poverty, chronic stress, and child maltreatment may have lasting effects when they damage or impair crucial adaptive systems such as adult–child attachment, intelligence, and self-regulation of emotions and behavior. Persistent poverty is consistently found to have more adverse effects than transitory poverty on children's cognitive development and school achievement. Children living for long periods in impoverished conditions experience more negative life events and adverse conditions that may place demands on their coping resources well beyond what they can handle.[110] Consequently, exposure to chronic adversity exacts a toll on a child's mental, physical, and emotional health. This may trigger a cycle of lifelong deficiencies encompassing many contexts of their lives:

> Children who enter school with few resources, cognitive difficulties, and self-regulatory problems often have academic problems, get into trouble with teachers, are more likely to be rejected by peers and are at risk for disengaging from normative school and peer contexts, which sets them up for considerable difficulties.[111]

Because many social problems are significantly clustered and correlated with concentrated poverty, cumulative oppression and its ensuing pathways to long-term developmental problems are much more frequently encountered among children who endure lifelong exposure to impoverished social environments.

Adaptations to Oppression

Most children adapt to oppression through *passive acceptance* and subsequent obedience—an obedience built upon fear, which derives from implied threats and intimidation. This adaptation is characterized by the child's passive acceptance of his or her subordinate and inferior status. Passive acceptance is more common among females, owing to the higher status generally accorded to males.[112]

Because children are subjected to adult domination in all facets of their lives, they quickly learn that obedience is expected. Such adaptations among children are similar to the passive acceptance of the slave role, adaptations of prison inmates, and immersion in the cycle of violence for battered women. These children outwardly accept their inferior positions but develop a repressed hatred for their oppressors, even while adapting to the structures of domination in which they are immersed. Once a situation of violence and oppression has been established, it engenders an entire way of life and behavior for those caught up in it—oppressors and oppressed alike. Both are submerged in this situation and both bear the marks of oppression. For their part, the oppressed are likely to believe they have no purpose in life except what the oppressor prescribes for them.

Passive children do not fully explore personal autonomy; they never become the "authors of their own lives." This repression results in negative self-perceptions that may manifest themselves in a wide range of problematic behaviors, including alcoholism, drug addiction, eating disorders, low self-esteem, and psychiatric disorders.[113]

A second adaptation to oppression is the *exercise of illegitimate coercive power*. Many adolescents are attracted to delinquency because it helps them to establish a sense of autonomy and control. This anticipatory delinquency reflects a yearning for adult status.[114] Delinquent acts can immediately and demonstratively make things happen, thereby providing the child with a sense of restored potency despite the power denied him or her by adults and parents. Sexual misbehavior, illicit use of drugs or alcohol, and violations of the criminal law possess greater symbolic importance for the child to the extent they demonstrate resistance to adult attempts to exert control over his or her behavior.

A third adaptation is the *manipulation of one's peers*, in which the child attempts to become empowered. Through the manipulation of others within the peer group, a child who has experienced oppression at the hands of adults may acquire a sense of strength and control or a degree of empowerment not otherwise felt. Gerald Marwell suggests that "at any given point of time this potential [for social power] lies primarily in the opinions of the actor held by those with whom one interacts. If one is thought strong, one, by and large, is strong, or at least, may use

'strength' to manipulate others."[115] The school bully is an example, as is the child who spreads gossip in hopes of gaining status and prestige in the eyes of others. Unfortunately, the mere involvement of a child with his or her peers leads many adults to view the involvement as problematic in itself. Adults may then react by exercising even greater control over the child's interaction with others.

The fourth adaptation is *retaliation*, which may include delinquent acts ranging from property crimes to violent offenses. Retaliation is the most severe and least common of the adaptations to oppression. It is more common among males than females. Children may engage in retaliation to get back at the people or the institutions they believe are the source of their oppression. School vandalism sometimes occurs because a student is angry with a teacher or principal, for example. Some children may strike directly at their parents or peers by assaulting or killing them. Others may try to hurt their parents by turning inward, becoming chronically depressed and contemplating or committing suicide. A study of income gradients in antisocial behavior found that greater poverty and childhood disadvantage was associated with six general forms of delinquency and maladaptive behaviors, including aggression, nonaggressive delinquency, oppositional behavior, defiance, psychopathic traits, and negative affect.[116] In other words, when confronted by oppressive forces, children will find a way to adapt.

Also, although children *as a group* are oppressed, the effects of oppression are most significantly experienced at the individual level. Oppression is differentially experienced, both in its application and its impact. Likewise, children adapt differentially, though the individual reasons for how particular children adapt are generally unknown. Even children growing up in the same family, in the same neighborhood, and experiencing similar oppressive situations will often exhibit different adaptations.

Current research has firmly established the connection between oppression and problem behaviors of children. For instance, Carolyn Smith and David Farrington explored the extent to which antisocial behavior in parents predicted antisocial behavior in children in two successive generations. They also examined the degree to which a man's childhood antisocial behavior predicted antisocial behavior in his own children, the ways that parenting problems were related to delinquency in two successive generations, and the extent to which intergenerational continuities in antisocial behavior were mediated by parenting. The findings were interesting. Between generations, antisocial parents in the first generation predicted conduct problems among children in the next two generations. Within generations, second-generation child conduct problems predicted adult antisocial behavior and antisocial partnerships, which in turn predicted conduct problems among their own children (the third generation). Parental conflict and authoritarian parenting resulted in early childhood conduct problems in two successive generations. Second-generation boys who were poorly supervised by their parents were themselves poor supervisors as fathers. Both first- and second-generation individuals displayed assortative mating—that is, antisocial males tended to marry antisocial females. In this way, parents specifically, and adults generally, cultivated delinquency, violence, and other maladaptive behaviors directly as a consequence of the way they treated children.[117]

Future research is needed to explore why one child adapts to abuse by passively accepting the situation and developing low self-esteem, whereas another child experiencing similar abuse adapts by manipulating or bullying others, perhaps even abusing age peers, and still another child retaliates by murdering the offending adult. For information about the various adverse childhood experiences children in the United States endure, see **Box 6.13**, the "A Window on Delinquency" feature.

Evaluation of Conflict Theory

Conflict theories have been criticized for a number of reasons. Jackson Toby, for instance, contends that conflict theory is nothing more than a rehashing of the traditional liberal approach of helping the underdog. He claims that most crime is committed for profit and luxury, not for survival.[118]

Conflict theory has also been accused of relying too heavily on historical and theoretical approaches that fail to produce testable hypotheses. Statements or postulates offered under the aegis of this theory tend to be untestable; they are not subject to scientific verification and instead must be accepted as a matter of faith.

In addition, Francis Allen[119] and David Shichor[120] suggest that conflict theory oversimplifies and

overemphasizes the political and economic nature of juvenile delinquency. Their concern has received some support from J. A. Sharpe, who analyzed patterns of law violations in England between the 15th and 19th centuries and found little evidence to support the claims of conflict theorists that crime and delinquency increased with the development of capitalism.[121]

Ronald Akers has taken conflict theory to task for portraying modern society as too heterogeneous in terms of the general population to arrive at any significant value consensus. Instead of viewing society as a precarious balancing of crisscrossing, conflicting, and competing interest groups, Akers contends "society is also held together by the larger or smaller number of widely supported values, common assumptions, and images of the world. This is a chief factor in providing some continuity and unity in a diversified society."[122] Akers also notes that most delinquency cannot be explained by group conflict inasmuch as most delinquency is *intra*group in nature—that is, it is committed by members *within* the group against other members *within* the group rather than by outsiders.

Donald Shoemaker is critical of the suggested direct link between capitalism and delinquency. He questions the existence of such a link for four reasons:[123]

- Delinquency is widespread in the middle and upper middle classes.
- Juveniles appear to have little concern for their status in the economic system.
- Racial and ethnic factors have as much or more influence on crime and delinquency as social class factors do.
- There is a failure to demonstrate "a necessary connection between capitalism per se and industrial or demographic conditions within a society."

Despite these critiques, criminologists in the 21st century continue to show the relevance of conflict theory in explaining delinquency and helping offenders become rehabilitated and reintegrated into society. Propositions derived from conflict theory have been linked to overcoming abuse,[124] homicide rates,[125] racial profiling by the police,[126] and coercive encounters between the police and the public.[127] Social support theory, in particular, holds promise in terms of its applicability to criminal justice practice. Research has indicated that social support is linked to inmate misconduct at both the individual and facility levels. When Shanhe Jiang and his colleagues analyzed data from the National Survey of Inmates in State and Federal Correctional Facilities, which encompassed more than 9000 inmates and 275 correctional institutions, they found that inmates who received telephone calls from their children were significantly less likely to accumulate rule violations than those without contacts from their children. At the structural

Adverse childhood experiences not only negatively affect children during their youth, but are associated with delinquency and continued problem behaviors into adulthood.

BOX 6.13

A Window on Delinquency

Adverse Childhood Experiences

Conflict theories of delinquency address the various forms of abuse, neglect, and oppression that occur in the lives of children and adolescents. Often these forms of abuse result in delinquency, along with a range of other negative behaviors and health problems. In 1998, Vincent Felitti and his colleagues conducted a survey of 9508 adults in the Adverse Childhood Experiences (ACE) Study, where respondents provided information about various adverse childhood experiences from their youth. They found many health and behavioral consequences of various forms of childhood abuse and exposure to household dysfunction. Among its many findings, the original ACE study reported a gradient of adverse childhood experiences was associated with significant health impairments in adulthood. Those who had experienced four or more adverse childhood experiences including psychological abuse, sexual abuse, physical abuse, exposure to substance abuse, exposure to mental illness in household, mother treated violently, and criminal behavior in household were 4 to 12 times more at risk for alcoholism, drug abuse, depression, suicide attempt, and also were significantly more likely to smoke, suffer poor health, engage in promiscuous sexual behavior and develop sexually transmitted disease, and other health problems.

Adverse childhood experiences are the specific negative experiences that occur in impoverished and dysfunctional homes. David Finkelhor and his colleagues found that many adverse childhood experiences, including poverty,

having a parent go to prison, peer victimization, peer social isolation, and exposure to community violence, are associated with health problems and psychiatric problems.

Adverse childhood experiences are also importantly related to delinquency and to more serious pathways of delinquency. Studies of more than 60,000 youth who have been referred to the Florida Department of Juvenile Justice found that each additional adverse childhood experience increases the likelihood of a youth becoming a serious, chronic, and violent offender by 35%. Thus, an adolescent with 10 adverse childhood experiences is 350% more likely to become a severe delinquent offender. In addition, youth with more extensive adverse childhood experiences become delinquent sooner, are contacted by police sooner, and are more likely to continue their delinquent career into adulthood.

Although the precise ways by which adverse childhood experiences translate into delinquency are unclear, Kevin Wolff and Michael Baglivio suggest that negative emotionality is the key. Adverse childhood experiences create huge increases in anxiety, frustration, hostility, and coping problems, and these emotions have been shown to predict not only delinquency, but also continued delinquent acts after release from a juvenile justice facility. Adverse childhood experiences are more likely to occur in dysfunctional, oppressive, and impoverished homes, and are a pressing research need for conflict theorists to consider when conceptualizing the causes of delinquency.

Vincent Felitti, Robert Anda, Dale Nordenberg, David Williamson, Alison Spitz, Valerie Edwards, Mary Koss, and Makes Marks, "Relationship of Childhood Abuse and Household Dysfunction to Many of the Leading Causes of Death in Adults: The Adverse Childhood Experiences (ACE) Study," *American Journal of Preventive Medicine* 14:245–258 (1998); David Finkelhor, Anne Shattuck, Heather Turner, and Sherry Hamby, "A Revised Inventory of Adverse Childhood Experiences," *Child Abuse & Neglect*, 48:13–21 (2016); Bryanna Hahn Fox, Nicholas Perez, Elizabeth Cass, Michael Baglivio, and Nathan Epps, "Trauma Changes Everything: Examining the Relationship between Adverse Childhood Experiences and Serious, Violent and Chronic Juvenile Offenders," *Child Abuse & Neglect* 46:163–173 (2015); Michael Baglivio, Kevin Wolff, Alex Piquero, and Nathan Epps, "The Relationship between Adverse Childhood Experiences (ACE) and Juvenile Offending Trajectories in a Juvenile Offender Sample," *Journal of Criminal Justice* 43:229–241 (2015); Kevin Wolff and Michael Baglivio, "Adverse Childhood Experiences, Negative Emotionality, and Pathways to Juvenile Recidivism," *Crime & Delinquency*, in press (2016).

level, facility participation in religious programs was negatively related to facility rule violations.[128] Similarly, Jiang and Thomas Winfree reported that (1) female inmates have greater social support than male inmates based on calls, mail, and visits from their children; (2) male inmates experience greater social support from their spouses compared to female inmates; and (3) inmates with more social support commit fewer prison infractions per month.[129] It has also been reported that ex-convicts who have greater social support are better able to successfully transition from the status of inmate to the status of citizen.[130]

Conflict theory also has been linked to extreme forms of delinquency and violence perpetrated at

the national level. For instance, John Hagan and his colleagues used conflict theory to show how campaigns of murder and rape in the Darfur region of Sudan are examples of the Arab-dominated government's attempts to impose its will on non-Arabic African groups. During the campaigns of violence, Sudanese government officials spared villagers who were Arabic, instead focusing their violence on groups whose members were seen as different and, therefore, expendable.[131] To date, nearly 500,000 people have been killed in the genocide in Sudan, and these acts of violence are entirely consistent with the basic ideas of conflict theory.

Nonetheless, critics of conflict theory must reconcile the fact that research connecting the more extreme forms of oppression of children (including beatings, sexual abuse, hitting, slapping, screaming, ridicule, verbal insults, and serious neglect and deficiencies in child care) to subsequent delinquency is substantial.[132] Several studies have illuminated this relationship, including Cathy Spatz Widom and Michael Maxfield's research on more than 1500 children, James Unnever and his colleagues' study of coercion and delinquency among nearly 2500 students from six middle schools, Stephen Baron's research on Canadian skinheads, and a series of studies conducted by Lisa Hutchinson Wallace and her colleagues.

The research by Widom and Maxfield is interesting because it updates data initially collected in 1988 on the link between child abuse and offending. Their study followed 1575 cases from childhood through young adulthood. The research design included a study group of 908 substantiated cases of childhood abuse or neglect and a comparison group of 667 children, not officially recorded as abused or neglected—all matched on sex, age, race, and family socioeconomic status. According to Widom and Maxfield:

> Those who had been abused or neglected as children were more likely to be arrested as juveniles (27 percent versus 17 percent), adults (42 percent versus 33 percent), and for a violent crime (18 percent versus 14 percent). . . . The abused and neglected cases were younger at first arrest, committed nearly twice as many offenses, and were arrested more frequently.[133]

Unnever and his associates tested core propositions from differential coercion theory. They evaluated whether involvement in delinquency was related to four coercive environments: parental coercion, peer coercion, school coercion, and neighborhood coercion. They found consistent support for the theory: Students exposed to coercive environments were more likely to develop social–psychological deficits and to be involved in relatively more serious delinquency.[134]

Stephen Baron wanted to explain the violent behavior and political consciousness of Canadian male street skinheads. Using the framework of Regoli and Hewitt's theory of differential oppression, he discovered—as the theory would predict—that skinheads came from homes characterized by extreme violence and oppression. Their family and school experiences destroyed any trust these young people might have for authority, and they modeled the violent behavior of their oppressors. As such, they were themselves vulnerable to violent behavior. According to Baron:

> Their serial abuse negates their ability to empathize with others and leaves them vulnerable to

frustration, while their familial oppression exposes them to violent cultural influences and leads them to seek opportunities for deviance.[135]

Their violence also was exacerbated by their oppressive school experiences, which increased their proneness to violence by stifling their creativity and individuality through an environment that the skinheads characterized as being dictatorial and authoritarian. They reacted to these conditions through detachment and attack. By withdrawing, the skinheads found themselves in a situation where the only doors open to them were ones that fueled their violence. Baron concluded that the political consciousness of the skinheads he interviewed was tied to their long histories of experiencing oppression.

In a series of empirical tests, Lisa Hutchinson and her associates provided a comprehensive evaluation of how differential oppression theory might be used to explain school delinquency. They assessed three of the four adaptive reactions set forth in the theory. They reported that students who perceived themselves to be oppressed by teachers frequently adapted to oppression through passive acceptance and the use of marijuana, beer, wine, and other types of alcohol. In addition, Hutchinson and Seydlitz found oppression by teachers and having low self-esteem to be predictive of more serious forms of drug abuse, such as ecstasy, heroin, and cocaine use.

Oppression resulting in the use of passive acceptance is not limited to substance abuse. Hutchinson reported on the effects of oppression in student experiences with delinquency in the schools. She found that students who were oppressed by teachers were more likely to be the victims of school delinquency than those who had not experienced such oppression. In an effort to examine the relationship of oppression in the home to other forms of victimization, Hutchinson and Mueller studied the linkage between parental oppression and peer victimization. They noted that children who had experienced parental oppression were more likely to be *both* verbally and physically abused by their peers. Further, self-esteem played a significant role in future victimization, as children who were oppressed by their parents, but exhibited high levels of self-esteem, were less likely to be victimized by their peers.

In looking at the relationship between differential oppression and the use of the exercise of illegitimate coercive power, it was discovered that students who experienced oppression by parents and teachers were more likely to commit acts of low-level delinquency within the school. Low levels of self-esteem increased students' use of this particular adaptive reaction.

Finally, Hutchinson tested the role of oppression in the use of retaliation. Although the measures she

BOX 6.14

A Window on Delinquency

Reducing Social Inequality by Mentoring

A central idea of conflict theories is that American society is plagued by social inequality and that families with fewer social and material resources have greater difficulty helping their children compared to families with more social and material resources. A simple policy to reduce this gap between the haves and the have-nots is mentoring. Mentoring is the pairing of a successful adult caregiver who devotes his or her time to an at-risk child. Although mentoring programs vary, the basic idea is that the mentor works with the mentee to organize and plan the student's school work, complete assignments in a timely manner, and follow through with the student's responsibilities. In addition, the mentor participates with the child in fun community activities, such as bowling, fishing, going to the library, attending museums, or playing sports. The mentor is a successful person who is employed, often has a college degree, and is active in the community. The mentor and mentee are often paired in terms of sociodemographic characteristics, and it is hoped that the mentor serves as a role model for the youth.

There are more than 5000 mentoring programs in the United States and over 3 million children and adolescents participate. David DuBois and his colleagues recently conducted a systematic review of mentoring programs and found evidence for program effects in an array of outcome areas. For example, mentoring has been shown to:

- reduce conduct problems
- improve school engagement
- improve school performance
- improve emotional health
- improve psychological functioning
- increase school motivation

Mentoring programs are not necessarily going to prevent delinquency. Adam Matz reviewed the empirical literature of evaluation studies of mentoring programs and found that although they are effective overall, the effects are rather small in size. Sema Taheri and Brandon Welsh's meta-analysis of after-school programs, including mentoring, similarly found significant, albeit quite small, effects. However, the larger importance of mentoring is that children and adolescents are shown that healthy, prosocial adults care about them, care about their development, and care about their future. Because many delinquents are exposed to considerable deprivation and various forms of negativity, that positivity of mentoring can make all the difference.

David DuBois, Nancy Portillo, Jean Rhodes, Naida Silverthorn, and J. C. Valentine, "How Effective Are Mentoring Programs for Youth? A Systematic Assessment of the Evidence," *Psychological Science in the Public Interest* 12:57–91 (2011); Adam Matz, "Commentary: Do Youth Mentoring Programs Work? A Review of the Empirical Literature," *Journal of Juvenile Justice* 4:83–101 (2015); Sema Taheri and Brandon Welsh, "After School Programs for v: A Systematic Review and Meta-Analysis," *Youth Violence and Juvenile Justice*, 14:272–290 (2016).

---

used were merely indicative of students' thoughts of retaliation, she found that oppression by parents and teachers significantly increased the frequency of retaliatory thoughts by students. As with exercise of illegitimate coercive power, low levels of self-esteem increased the likelihood of this reaction.[136]

Juvenile Justice Policy Applications

Conflict theories have traditionally had little direct impact on either juvenile jvustice policy or broader social policy (for an exception, see **Box 6.14**, the "A Window on Delinquency" feature). Federal and state legislative bodies have been understandably hesitant to consider policy changes that would require a restructuring of the larger society along socialist lines. Similarly, they have generally balked at dramatically redefining crime to either include broadly accepted business and economic practices associated with capitalism or to exclude "revolutionary" crimes of the economically or socially deprived or marginalized underdog.[137]

Nevertheless, conflict theory has contributed in many ways to the discourse within criminology and the larger society regarding the need to reduce structural inequalities based on economic, social, racial, and gender differences, and to eliminate discriminatory practices within the juvenile and adult justice systems. Today, tremendous amounts of resources, interventions, and research attention are devoted to children and adolescents deemed to be at greatest risk for antisocial behaviors. Significantly, at-risk youths are not identified simply for the sake of labeling efforts but rather with the goal of providing the services needed to help them develop along prosocial, conventional pathways as opposed to delinquent pathways.[138] Differential oppression theory has led to recent calls for adults to refuse to define children as objects, but instead to empower children with the essential fundamental constitutional rights that adults enjoy. At a minimum, seriously abused and neglected children should be quickly removed from dangerous and threatening home environments and placed in foster care or group homes designed to provide loving and supportive adult care and supervision.

WRAP UP

THINKING ABOUT JUVENILE DELINQUENCY: CONCLUSIONS

The theories discussed in this chapter represent ideas about delinquency that have been popularized during the last third of the 20th century. Unlike strain and social control theories, labeling and conflict theories show little interest in the immediate causes of individual delinquency; instead, they are more concerned with reactions to behavior and imbalances in power that stem from social arrangements. These theories, therefore, tend to side with the adolescent and view the juvenile justice system in a critical light.

Labeling theory assumes that social control efforts produce more serious problem behaviors, especially juvenile delinquency. The social response to acts socially defined as delinquent results in the labeling of individuals who engage in such acts as delinquents. It is this interactional process, including the impact of the response and the label, that is of greatest interest to labeling theorists. According to proponents of this theory, if solutions to the problem of delinquency exist, they will be found in the juvenile justice system doing less, not more.

Conflict explanations of delinquency assume that social order in contemporary, heterogeneous societies is maintained through coercion, force, and confrontation. These theories stress the effects of economic and political power, influence, and group or vested interests on the development and enforcement of law. Solutions to delinquency from the conflict perspective largely focus on major social and economic structural changes designed to eliminate discriminatory laws and legal processes and to equalize wealth and power. For example, differential oppression theory assumes that children develop in an arena of oppression. This oppressive environment has consequences for what children become and who they are in relation to adults. Adults impose their sense of order on children, whom they see being inferior, which in turn leads to maladaptive responses from those children, including delinquency. Differential oppression theory, then, argues that the solution to delinquency lies not so much in reforming the juvenile or changing the juvenile justice system, but rather in changing adult perceptions of children.

Labeling and conflict theories of delinquency emphasize the interrelationships between societal factors, group characteristics, and people as they relate to defining and responding to delinquency. In contrast, developmental and life-course explanations of delinquency suggest that human development molds behavior along both positive (prosocial) and negative (antisocial) pathways.

CHAPTER SPOTLIGHT

- Labeling theories of delinquency reject the idea that delinquents and nondelinquents are fundamentally different types of people, but instead suggest that the societal response or labeling of behavior sets into motion a self-fulfilling prophecy, wherein adolescents internalize their delinquent reputation and adjust their behavior accordingly.
- John Braithwaite's theory suggests that reintegrative shaming punishes the act while affirming the actor, whereas disintegrative shaming punishes both the act and the actor.

- Conflict theories suggest that struggle and exploitation characterize society, and that delinquency and its control represent the interests of powerful elements of society.
- Social inequality contributes to delinquency and other social problems, according to conflict theorists.
- The theory of differential oppression blames delinquency on the oppressive ways in which adults define and control the behavior of children and adolescents.

CRITICAL THINKING

1. From the labeling theory perspective, what might happen if a child thinks that he or she is a trouble-maker? Why should elementary school teachers be especially delicate in disciplining young children?

2. Whose interests are best served by radical nonintervention policies? Is it more important to protect delinquents from having a deviant label affixed to them or to protect society from delinquency?

3. Do some delinquents deserve to be shamed and ostracized because of their illegal behavior? Isn't it helpful for society to have a "class of outcasts" as a stern reminder of what is appropriate and lawful behavior?

4. If labels have such formidable power, why don't more parents label their children as "gifted," "intelligent," or "athletic"? In turn, why don't youths affix a positive label to themselves and then allow the self-fulfilling prophecy to occur?

5. Part of the undeniable allure of conflict theory is that subordinated groups are disproportionately involved in delinquency. The glaring exception to this idea is gender: Males are much more delinquent than females. Does this discrepancy suggest that biology is more important than sociology in explaining delinquency?

Developmental Theories

Most theories of delinquency could be called "snapshot" theories because they explain fairly specific conduct, such as delinquency occuring during a fairly specific period, such as middle to late adolescence. For example, various sources of strain or anomie can motivate a person to shoplift, prompt a group of friends who regularly engage in sexting to coerce another teen to do the same, or lead an adolescent to commit delinquent acts because he or she is not closely bonded to society. In all of these scenarios, specific events come together to *push* an adolescent into delinquent conduct.

However, "snapshot" theories of delinquency leave many unanswered important questions. If individuals are susceptible to engaging in delinquency during adolescence, are they necessarily prone to committing crime as adults? Are these adolescents also prone to exhibiting other forms of antisocial behavior when they are children? Do people stay the same, change slightly, or change greatly in terms of their propensity toward antisocial behavior? Do certain types of people exist in terms of when they first commit delinquency?

Unlike theories of delinquency that take a narrow snapshot approach to human behavior, *developmental theories* constitute a diverse group of explanations that share several important

OBJECTIVES

- Understand the development of antisocial behavior from early childhood through adolescence.

- Assess ways that delinquency and other problem behaviors change over time.

- Identify the ways that social institutions, such as the family, education, and employment, buffer individuals from delinquency.

- Grasp the empirical standing of developmental theories of crime and delinquency.

- Know the ways that juvenile justice system policies can be informed by ideas from developmental theories.

KEY TERMS

features. Developmental theories have the following characteristics:

- They pull together or integrate the strongest elements of earlier theories.
- They suggest that the key risk factors associated with delinquency change as individuals grow older.
- They suggest that the key protective factors associated with delinquency also change as people age.
- They view delinquency as a pattern of behavior rather than an isolated event.
- They recognize the heterogeneity in the delinquent population, meaning that most youths who commit delinquent acts will be modestly antisocial and a small group will be severely or even pathologically antisocial.

Developmental theories are not as interested in accounting for why a child commits a particular delinquent act; rather, they seek to identify those factors that drive an individual's entire criminal career. Today there is little doubt that the science of developmental theories is becoming more popular within criminology. Some of the most frequently cited works in criminology that have advanced our understanding of antisocial behavior are described in this chapter. Over time, the developmental theory perspective has broadened the study of delinquency into the past (childhood) as well as into the future (adulthood) and made criminology more compatible with ideas from the psychological and biological sciences.

One reason that developmental theory is so popular is that research has shown the troubling costs of allowing delinquent careers to develop. For example, Mark Cohen calculated the lifetime costs imposed by a high-risk youth whose antisocial tendencies were left unchecked and developed into an adult criminal career. He found that the average cost of a single serious, violent, and chronic juvenile offender totaled approximately $1.5 million in criminal justice system costs, victimization costs, and lost productivity.[1] Subsequent research similarly found that a single chronic delinquent can impose costs on society exceeding $1 million and that the most violent and habitual criminals impose costs in excess of $10 million, notwithstanding the human toll of their violent acts.[2]

These early studies of the developmental costs of a delinquent career omitted many types of offending.

More recent studies revealed even higher costs associated with chronic delinquents:

- A high-risk youth who is a chronic offender imposes between $4.2 million and $7.2 million in costs on society.
- If these juveniles can be prevented from becoming career criminals, the savings would be enormous. For instance, the typical career criminal imposes about $65,000 in costs on society through age 12 and about $230,000 in costs through age 14. However, throughout a lifetime these costs aggregate to nearly $6 million.
- The worst offenders—defined as persons with 15 or more police contacts—impose costs estimated to range between $3.6 million and $5.8 million by age 26.[3] Based on data from a sample of convicted homicide offenders, investigators recently found that the average cost per murder exceeded $17 million and the assorted costs imposed by the average murderer (when other offenses are also considered) is a staggering $24 million. Serious and violent offenders who happen to murder multiple victims can singly produce societal costs in excess of $100 million.[4]

Given these tremendous costs, criminologists are eager to identify risk factors for sustained involvement in delinquency, with the goal of forestalling such costly careers from unfolding.

What Is Developmental Theory?

Over the past decade, **developmental theories** (sometimes called life-course theories because they trace human development across most stages of the life span) have become among the most popular theories in criminology. Developmental theories assume that delinquency *has to develop* and is not simply the manifestation of an underlying condition. Rather than attributing delinquency to the pathologies of the individual, such as damaged frontal lobes, low self-control, bad temper, or psychopathy, the developmental perspective points to life experiences that mold individuals and send them along trajectories or pathways. These life trajectories can be positive, such as going to school or playing on a sports team, or negative, such as joining a criminal gang. Thus, developmental theories assert that everyday problems with family, school, and work can snowball into larger problems such as alcohol and drug use, gambling, and criminality.

Studies from diverse parts of the globe illustrate the stepping-stone nature of developmental theories and the various pathways to delinquency. Jukka Savolainen and his colleagues conducted a large-scale study of nearly 5000 men from the 1986 Northern Finland Birth Cohort Study to show the developmental paths from childhood into adulthood. They found that childhood deficits in self-regulation, such as ADHD and general

KEY TERMS

developmental theories
Theories that focus on an individual's entire life course, rather than one discrete point in time.

disruptive behaviors, were associated with poorer academic performance, peer marginalization, and alcohol use. Children with these behavioral problems often felt lonely and isolated from their better-behaved peers, often felt inferior to their classmates who could perform better in class and better control their conduct, and were often teased and ostracized by conventional peers. Over time, disruptive youth gravitated toward alcohol and drug use and their academic performance deteriorated. Upon reaching adulthood, the children who had self-regulation and conduct problems were more likely to be convicted of felony offenses, but these effects were indirect and operated through the adolescent peer marginalization, substance use, and school failures.

Joseph Murray and his associates examined developmental steps from birth to adulthood using data from a birth cohort of 3600 children in Pelotas, Brazil, and another birth cohort of 4100 children in Avon, Britain. They found that pre/perinatal risk factors, such as exposure to alcohol, tobacco, and infection during gestation; low birth weight; and premature birth were the strongest predictors of conduct problems and delinquency at age 11 years. Similar to the findings from the Northern Finland Birth Cohort Study, childhood and adolescent conduct problems and hyperactivity set into motion a cascade of problems at school, at home, with peers, and with the juvenile justice system. Conduct problems were associated with continued violence and crime into adulthood.[5]

Developmental theories are popular among criminologists for two main reasons. First, as mentioned earlier, theories of delinquency were usually designed to explain whether juveniles were likely to become delinquent during a certain period or how much trouble they were likely to get into. Accordingly, they devoted little attention to the time ordering of potential causes of misbehavior and the acts of misbehavior themselves. Many theorists simply assumed that key risk factors, such as exposure to violent behavior, weak bonding, or status frustration, caused delinquency soon after they were experienced. Alternatively, some criminologists, such as Gottfredson and Hirschi, proposed that a *static* characteristic, such as a lack of self-control, was responsible for causing both delinquency and other problem behaviors.

They assumed that the effect of low self-control persisted throughout one's life and that the characteristic itself remained relatively stable across life. In addition, traditional criminologists did not usually devote much attention to *how* events that occurred during one part of a person's life (e.g., childhood) might influence behavior during later stages (e.g., adolescence). Indeed, the criminologists who considered this problem failed to allow for the possibility that key risk factors might change as people mature.

For instance, a research study on a major historical event is helpful for understanding how delinquency development changes over time. Conventional wisdom

Some scholars explain a life of crime as the result of criminal propensity, whereas others point to life circumstances. Evidence supports both perspectives.

© edfuentesg/E+/Getty.

holds that going to war is a traumatic event and that engaging in active combat is even more traumatic. It is also commonly speculated that combat military service can contribute to antisocial behavior, particularly substance abuse. John Wright and his colleagues studied a sample of men over a 15-year period from the time when they were high school sophomores in 1964, through their military service, and continuing until 1979. Upon completion of high school, men who ultimately served in Vietnam had lower self-control, had worse grades, were poorer, and had lengthier juvenile arrest records than their peers who did not go to Vietnam. Nevertheless, regardless of a young man's criminal propensity, fighting in the Vietnam War led to increased drug use and ultimately enhanced his risk of getting arrested later in life. As demonstrated by this study, a historical event can change or modify a person's own criminal propensity and result in more delinquent conduct.[6]

Second, traditional theorists have often treated delinquency exclusively as an outcome measure. That is, they have been interested in examining only why risk factors, such as bad parenting, poor school performance, or association with deviant peers, cause

delinquent behavior. What they have not done is to allow for the possibility that delinquency itself may have important causal effects on its own presumed risk factors.[7] For instance, Robert Agnew, in formulating his general strain theory, suggests that delinquency is the product of different types of strain, all of which can lead to delinquent behavior, depending on several conditioning factors. Nevertheless, Agnew's theory *does not* explicitly state that delinquency itself can produce strain. For instance, Agnew would contend that being expelled from school should produce strain, which under the right circumstances might drive a youth to delinquent behavior. Yet it is also possible that committing delinquency—for example, going to school under the influence of drugs or stealing from another student's locker—can be an important factor in why a youth is suspended or expelled. In such a situation, the delinquent act *precedes* the student's experience of strain. Accordingly, it would be less likely for the strain of being expelled to *cause* the delinquent behavior.

Developmental theories differ from other criminological theories in terms of how they approach these issues. First, rather than being interested in predicting the **prevalence** (a measure of *whether* an individual has committed any delinquency during a given period of time) or the **incidence** (a measure of *how much* delinquency someone has committed over a given period of time) of delinquency, developmental theories explain changes in the progression of delinquent behavior over time—a progression that criminologists call the **delinquent career**. (For an example of the development of an extreme delinquent career, see **Box 7.1**, the "A Window on Delinquency" feature.)

Second, instead of being interested only in understanding why a juvenile has committed a crime or how many crimes that person is likely to commit in the following year, a developmental theorist is more interested in explaining why the youth who seemed to be a "good kid" throughout his or her childhood suddenly started getting into trouble as a teenager. For instance, a social control theorist might try to figure out whether a troubled teenage girl's attachment to her parents is currently weak or strong, whereas a developmental theorist is likely to be interested in the teen's entire history with her parents. The developmental theorist would contend that the parenting a child received at various ages is as important to understanding her present behavior as is the parenting that she is currently receiving.

In formulating their explanations, developmental theorists look beyond what happened in the lives of children immediately before they got into trouble. Instead of focusing on this short period of time, they try to determine what has taken place in an individual's life for many years before the criminal or delinquent incident. These life situations are classified into two broad categories: risk factors and protective factors. **Risk factors** are situations, settings, events, or characteristics that *increase* the likelihood that a person will become delinquent. **Protective factors** are situations, settings, events, or characteristics that *decrease* the likelihood that a person will become delinquent. Protective factors shield youths from contexts that contribute to delinquency or provide the resilience to avoid crime. A list of protective factors for delinquency appears in **Box 7.2**, the "A Window on Delinquency" feature.

Some developmental theorists explicitly recognize that delinquency itself influences the factors that are typically assumed to cause it. Thus, while strain theorists such as Merton, Cohen, Cloward, Ohlin, and Agnew would likely argue that juveniles who become frustrated by their lack of access to legitimate means of achieving success often band together to commit crimes, developmental theorists would assert that the very act of committing crime is likely to push children further into delinquent subcultures. After all, juveniles who routinely break the law will probably become ostracized by their nondelinquent peers and have little choice except to associate with other youths more like themselves.

A study conducted in 2008 illustrates the ways that the causes of delinquency can also be related to the effects of delinquency and identifies how these relationships overlap. Sonya Siennick and Jeremy Staff studied educational deficits among delinquent youths among more than 7500 persons selected from the National Education Longitudinal Study. Compared to nondelinquents, delinquents completed less education; even if they attended college, they were less likely to obtain a degree than their nondelinquent peers. In addition, delinquents made less effort in school (based on teacher assessments) and were less aware of their performance in school.[8] Taken together, a variety of issues—including delinquency, school commitment,

KEY TERMS

prevalence
A measure of whether an individual has committed any delinquency during a given period of time.

incidence
A measure of how much delinquency someone has committed over a given period of time.

delinquent career
The pattern of delinquent behavior that an individual exhibits over the course of his or her life.

risk factors
Situations, settings, events, or characteristics that increase the likelihood that one will be delinquent.

protective factors
Situations, settings, events, or characteristics that decrease the likelihood that one will be delinquent.

BOX 7.1

A Window on Delinquency

Development of an Extreme Delinquent Career

Although delinquency does not develop in a strict linear fashion, criminologists have found that delinquent careers are marked by escalation from more trivial forms of delinquency during childhood to more serious types of property and violent offending. The following delinquent history comes from a young man who by age 19 had committed five murders and multiple rapes (he admitted to at least six more rapes after his confinement). Noted profilers Robert Ressler, Ann Burgess, and John Douglas interviewed the offender after his confinement and found a fairly predictable background: broken home with multiple divorces and father figures, high school dropout, frequent drug and alcohol use, and multiple diagnoses for psychiatric disorders.

This delinquent history also shows a seeming unpredictable mix of offenses—which is one of the reasons why it is so difficult to accurately predict what offenders will do next. Even so, the big picture of this case study shows that when left untreated (many crimes were either never formally charged or received a light sentence of probation) minor forms of juvenile delinquency can lead to extreme forms of violence.

Age	Offense	Disposition
9	Vandalism	Community service
12	Petty larceny	Probation
12	Assault	Probation
12	Breaking and entering	Probation
12	Disrupting school	Probation
13	Driving without a license	Case continued
14	Burglary and rape	Sentenced to state psychiatric center
14	Petty larceny	Sentenced to state psychiatric center
14	Breaking and entering	Sentenced to state psychiatric center
16	Rape	Never charged
16	Rape	Never charged
16	Burglary and rape	Never charged
16	Rape	Never charged
17	Attempted armed robbery	Probation and outpatient therapy
18	Rape	Never charged
18	Rape and murder	Life imprisonment
19	Rape and murder	Life imprisonment
19	Rape and murder	Life imprisonment
19	Rape	Never charged
19	Rape and murder	Life imprisonment
19	Rape and murder	Life imprisonment

Robert Ressler, Ann Burgess, and John Douglas, "Rape and Rape–Murder: One Offender and Twelve Victims," pages 123–132 in John Campbell and Don DeNevi (eds.), *Profilers: Leading Investigators Take You Inside the Criminal Mind* (New York: Prometheus Books, 2004).

school performance, and educational attainment—appear to be interrelated. Likewise, the problems that cause educational deficits among delinquents can also be related to these individuals' propensity to continue committing crimes after unsuccessfully leaving school. In short, the causes and consequences of delinquency can and often do overlap in confusing ways. Fortunately, developmental theories can help in clarifying how these relationships unfold over time.

Finally, developmental theories of delinquency are interdisciplinary; they borrow constructs or ideas from diverse academic disciplines including sociology, psychology, psychiatry, and genetics, among others. This interweaving of disciplines brings an excitement and scientific freshness to developmental theories that are sometimes lacking in older theories, and there is little doubt that they are among the most popular approaches currently used by criminological

BOX 7.2

A Window on Delinquency

Developmental Protective Factors Against Delinquency and Youth Violence

Although nearly everyone engages in *some* form of delinquency during childhood or adolescence, most people are able to avoid becoming serious, violent, and chronic delinquents, and frankly, are able to avoid this behavioral outcome with ease. The main reason is that most people have a host of protective factors that insulate them from environmental risks and run counter to risk factors for delinquency.

There are varieties of protective factors. A *direct protective factor* is one that predicts a low probability of delinquency. Direct protective factors are also known as *promotive factors*. A *risk-based protective factor* is one that predicts a low probability of delinquency among a risk category. An *interactive protective factor* is one that predicts a low probability of delinquency among a risk category but not among a non-risk category. An interactive protective factor is also known as a *buffering factor.*

Longitudinal studies are those that prospectively follow research subjects over time so that developmental patterns can be observed and understood. These studies have produced several important findings on protective factors against delinquency. For instance:

- Intelligence and cognitive ability is a protective factor against delinquency. The protective effects of intelligence are especially important for youth raised in high-risk environments where their smarts are able to navigate potentially dangerous settings and interpersonal situations. Intelligence is less

of a protective factor for youth raised in low-risk environments.
- High academic achievement is an important interactive protective factor against violent delinquency among African American youth, but is less important among white youth.
- A greater number of cumulative protective factors can significantly offset the emergence of delinquency and violent conduct, even among youth with assorted risk factors for delinquency.
- David Farrington and his colleagues found that school attainment and high parental interest in education could overcome poor child rearing to prevent delinquency. In addition, high family income can overcome the effects of having an incarcerated parent.
- Anna-Karin Andershed and her colleagues' study of delinquent careers in Sweden found that, compared to youth with no protective factors, youth with 10 protective factors are 10 times less likely to be adjudicated of an offense.

In other words, developmental theories assert that the likelihood of delinquency is effectively the outcome of a mixture of risk and protective factors. Youth with a multitude of risk factors, in the absence of protective factors, are nearly guaranteed to have conduct problems, whereas youth with the opposite mixture (many protective and few, if any, risk factors) usually lead conventional, productive, prosocial lives.

Maria Ttofi, David Farrington, Alex Piquero, Friedrich Lösel, Matt DeLisi, and Joseph Murray, "Intelligence as a Protective Factor against Offending: A Meta-Analytic Review of Prospective Longitudinal Studies," *Journal of Criminal Justice*, 45:4–18 (2016); Darrick Jolliffe, David Farrington, Rolf Loeber, and Dustin Pardini, "Protective Factors for Violence: Results from the Pittsburgh Youth Study," *Journal of Criminal Justice*, 45:32–40 (2016); David Farrington, Maria Ttofi, and Alex Piquero, "Risk, Promotive, and Protective Factors in Delinquent Development: Results from the Cambridge Study in Delinquent Development," *Journal of Criminal Justice*, 45:63–70 (2016); Anna-Karin Andershed, Chris Gibson, and Henrik Andershed, "The Role of Cumulative Risk and Protection for Violent Offending," *Journal of Criminal Justice*, 45:78–84 (2016); Miguel Basto-Pereira, Rita Comecanha, Sofia Ribiero, and Angela Maia, "Long-Term Predictors of Crime Desistance in Juvenile Delinquents: A Systematic Review of Longitudinal Studies," *Aggression and Violent Behavior* 25:332–342 (2015).

researchers. As noted by Stephen Tibbetts and his colleagues:

> Criminology is once again exciting. After years of unproductive theorizing and bitter academic debates concerning the appropriateness of including evidence from other disciplines—namely biology— the life course paradigm has ignited a firestorm of research. This research has the potential to usher in a new era in criminology—an era where advances

occur at a startling rate; the strength of evidence is measurable; and better, deeper questions are asked about the causes of criminal conduct.[9]

Developmental Theory and the Age–Crime Curve

Much of the early impetus for the creation of developmental theory came from a growing understanding of the **age–crime curve**, which is a line illustrating how crime rates increase during preadolescence, peak in middle adolescence, and steadily decline thereafter (see **Figure 7.1**).[10]

Remarkably, the curve does not depend on which type of crime is being studied; where the investigation

KEY TERMS

age–crime curve
The notion that crime rates increase during preadolescence, peak in middle adolescence, and steadily decline thereafter.

criminologists would agree that in the United States, *proportionally*, inner-city, African American males engage in more delinquent acts than middle-class, white females, the delinquent behavior of both groups tends to peak during adolescence. Young children and mature adults from both groups commit relatively few crimes in comparison to their teenage counterparts. The age–crime curve is also seen in societies that are very different from the United States, that have an entirely different cultural and ethnic history, and that have very different levels of delinquency, crime, and violence, such as Bosnia-Herzegovina, Cyprus, Lithuania, Japan, and Venezuela.[11]

The universality of this finding led criminologists to ask a number of important questions. First, is the age–crime curve universal? Does it accurately represent the behavior of all adolescents, or is it a composite of many different patterns of delinquent development? (To better understand these distinctions, see **Figure 7.2**.) Second, what causes the near-universal spike in delinquent behavior during adolescence? Criminologists began wondering whether this phenomenon occurs simply because teenagers are exposed to higher levels of risk factors than people of other ages. For instance, some began wondering whether teenagers might experience higher levels of strain than younger children or adults. Perhaps lower-class youths were simply more likely to become frustrated with the inequities of the school system, much like Cohen originally suggested.

Other criminologists theorized that there could be something unique about young people going through this developmental period that might explain their behavior. Put differently, perhaps it is not the fact that the external factors affecting teenagers are unique, but rather that young people themselves perceive the factors differently. Perhaps teenagers place greater or lesser importance on certain risk factors than do

There are many protective factors, such as the love and parental care, which insulate youths from antisocial influences. How does something as small as reading to a child provide positive outcomes throughout his or her life?

© Rob Marmion/Shutterstock.

occurred; which ethnic, racial, or socioeconomic group subjects belong to; or whether they are male or female. In all cases, the shape of the age–crime curve tends to be very similar. For instance, although most

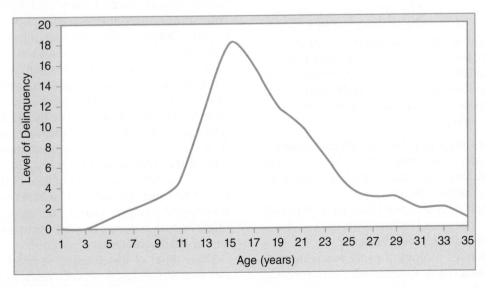

Figure 7.1 Representative Age–Crime Curve

© Jones & Bartlett Learning.

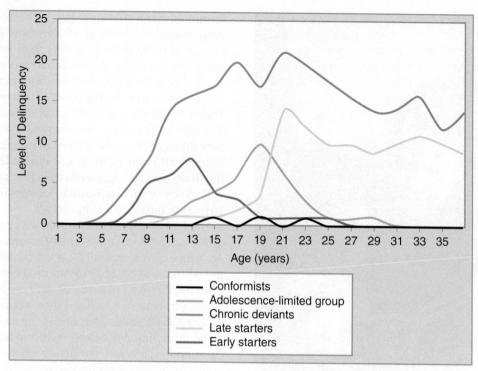

Figure 7.2 Various Delinquent Trajectories

© Jones & Bartlett Learning.

people of other ages, For example, Sung Jang and Marvin Krohn have shown that parental attachment may be more important to younger children than to teens.[12] Thus, although a strongly bonded child finds it almost impossible to engage in delinquency, an older adolescent—even one with a strong bond to his or her parents—may still feel free to engage in illegal activity. Similarly, Persephanie Silverthorn and Paul Frick contend that young children look up to their teachers and place a great deal of importance on their schoolwork. These prosocial influences help keep young children out of trouble. As they grow older, however, the importance of these factors to youths fades, and the world of delinquency opens up.[13]

Others suggest that the age–crime curve is readily understandable from a biosocial criminological perspective. Criminologist Anthony Walsh thinks much of the behavior characterizing adolescence is rooted in the following sources:[14]

- The intermingling of biology with environmental influences causes teens to come in conflict with their parents, take more risks, and experience wide swings in emotion.
- The lack of synchrony between a physically mature body and a still maturing nervous system explains adolescent delinquency.
- A variety of biological processes relating to hormonal changes, neurological development, changing neural pathways, and developments in neurotransmitter systems occur during this

period and explain changes in self-regulation and behavior.
- Adolescents' sensitivities to rewards appear to be different than those of adults, with young people being more prone to seek higher levels of novelty and stimulation to achieve the same feeling of pleasure.

Another explanation of the age–crime curve is that it represents millions of years of human evolution. Drawing on research from evolutionary psychology, Satoshi Kanazawa and Mary Still argue that the crime-prone years during adolescence comprise a period of intense competition among young males, who use violence and other antisocial methods to gain reproductive access to women. According to Kanazawa and Still, nature and sexual selection have calibrated the "teenage male" psychological profile to take into account both the benefits and the costs of competition as a function of the men's age and life stage. As a result, males become rapidly more criminal immediately following puberty and become equally rapidly less deviant around the time of the birth of their first child. Viewed from this perspective, the sociological interpretations of the age–crime curve might be true; however, they represent extensions of a more basic evolutionary process.[15]

These types of observations sparked interest in developmental theory. In fact, research into these matters continues today. For example, criminologists still do not completely agree if the age–crime curve applies universally to all adolescents, especially chronic offenders, or if it represents a composite of many possible developmental pathways. Although most criminologists embrace the latter idea, those who believe that some individual-level construct accounts for criminal behavior do not. These theorists reject the argument that delinquent behavior and the factors that influence it fluctuate over time. Instead, they suggest, a child's delinquent propensity—that is, an inner or constitutional indicator of criminality that influences the likelihood of becoming delinquent—becomes established during childhood and remains almost unaltered thereafter.[16]

For example, Marcus Jokela, Chris Power, and Mika Kivimäki conducted a longitudinal study of 11,537 participants from a 1958 British birth cohort to see how sturdy propensities, such as childhood externalizing symptoms and internalizing symptoms, affected behavior and health over the life span. Their study examined developmental patterns by including teacher assessments of the child's behaviors and symptoms at ages 7 and 11, parent reports at ages 7, 11, and 16, and self-reports at ages 23, 33, 42, and 46. They found that individuals who scored one standard deviation above the mean on externalizing symptoms in childhood were 10 to 20% more likely to incur an injury at home, at work, from traffic, or from violent assault. In other words, the "acting out" behaviors that children display—especially when the behaviors are pronounced—represent a syndrome or propensity that similarly manifests in injuries across life.

Drawing on birth cohort data from the Dunedin Multidisciplinary Health and Development Study, Terrie Moffitt and her colleagues evaluated the predictive validity of childhood self-control on a range of life outcomes during adulthood. The findings were startling. Persons who displayed low self-control during childhood displayed a range of difficulties at age 32. These included worse physical health, greater depression, higher likelihood of drug dependence, lower socioeconomic status, lower income, greater likelihood of single-parenthood, worse financial planning, more financial struggles, and most importantly for a criminological audience, more criminal convictions. Indeed, 45% of participants with low self-control during childhood had criminal convictions at age 32, a level that is nearly fourfold higher than the prevalence of criminal convictions for persons who had high childhood self-control. Moffitt and her co-researchers reported that childhood self-control predicted life outcomes as well as intelligence and low social class origin, both of which they noted are difficult to improve through intervention. Interestingly, Moffitt and her colleagues also found that an individual's self-control is essentially mirrored by their credit score. Credit scores are predicted by factors such as educational attainment, cognitive ability, and self-control and have wide-ranging predictive validity for many behavioral and health outcomes. For example, a 100-point increase in credit score was associated with a 13-month difference in heart age, or cardiovascular fitness. Although the participants in the Dunedin birth cohort were the same age (38 years), their heart age ranged from 22 to 85 years! Those with much younger heart age were fit, followed strict diet and exercise regimens, and had high self-control. Those with older heart age had poor health habits and lower self-control.[17]

Richard Herrnstein described this rationale in the following way: "It would be an overstatement to say 'once a criminal, always a criminal,' but it would be closer to the truth than to deny the evidence of a unifying and long-enduring pattern of encounters with the law for most serious offenders."[18] Put differently, life events and circumstances may have subtle influences on a person's behavior at any given point in time; for instance, getting a good job or starting a family may keep a person with low self-control out of trouble temporarily, but not indefinitely. Along these lines, some criminologists assert that people with a high delinquent propensity will relapse into antisocial lifestyles and eventually engage in behavior that jeopardizes their jobs and families, thereby falling back into antisocial, self-destructive, and ultimately delinquent behavior.

The next section reviews the major developmental theories in criminology and explores how these theoretical ideas attempt to explain the development of both conventional and delinquent (i.e., good and bad) behavior over the life course.

Developmental Theories of Delinquency

At first glance, some of the theories discussed in this section may appear to have little in common with one another. However, two things will become clear as you read about them. First, all of the theories borrow heavily from earlier, nondevelopmental perspectives that emerged from an array of academic disciplines, including developmental psychology, child psychology, human development and family studies, behavioral genetics, criminology, and criminal justice. The ideas on which they are based (e.g., poor parenting, problems in school, and association with delinquent peers) are not new, but rather are factors that criminologists have long considered to be related to delinquency. However, this *new* set of developmental theories casts many of the traditional risk factors into a different

KEY TERMS

delinquent propensity
The likelihood of committing delinquency and other antisocial acts; it is a trait that is largely set in early childhood.

light. Developmental perspectives focus on *how* the importance of these individual components varies over the life course. Second, many of the theories describe how experiencing a given risk factor at one stage of life might influence behavior at subsequent stages of life—something that traditional theories of delinquency usually did not do.

One of the first sociologists to propose the idea that events that occur during one stage of life can have strong influences on later behavior was Glen Elder, who believed that historical events, such as economic depressions and wars, can affect a variety of developmental outcomes, including delinquency. Precisely *when* such events occur in an individual's life is important in regard to *how* they are experienced. For example, the effects of an economic depression would not be the same for people who experience that event as young children and for people who experience it as teenagers.

Moreover, **precocious transitions** (key life events that occur much earlier than usual) are likely to have adverse effects on development.[19] This kind of event, in turn, can set a cycle of undesirable outcomes into motion. For instance, adolescents who become parents early in life may find it difficult to finish school and achieve a stable position in the job market, which can push them into lifestyles characterized by poverty, substance abuse, and crime. According to this theory, the more precocious transitions an individual experiences, the more likely he or she is to engage in problem behaviors. For example, a boy who becomes sexually active at age 11, fathers a child at age 14, drops out of school at age 15, and marries at age 16 is more likely to participate in crime than a boy who experiences only one of these precocious transitions.[20]

One of the most serious precocious transitions is early exposure to drugs and alcohol, which has been found to predict delinquency and other problem behaviors from the point of exposure onward. A study of youths from the Dunedin Multidisciplinary Health and Development Study who were followed over a 30-year period illustrates how powerfully destructive a substance abuse precocious transition can be. Candice Odgers and her colleagues used a statistical technique called propensity-score matching, which essentially controls for a person's innate propensity, while examining the effect of an event occurring at one time period (e.g., exposure to drugs and alcohol) on an event occurring at a later period (e.g., committing delinquency because of exposure to drugs and alcohol). These researchers found that even among persons with no history of conduct problems, those who were exposed to drugs and alcohol at ages 13 and 15 were more likely than persons without early exposure to develop substance abuse problems, test positive for sexually transmitted diseases, have an early pregnancy, and be convicted of criminal offenses. In fact, early exposure more than doubled the odds of these later events occurring.[21]

Gerald Patterson

Gerald Patterson's *coercive exchange theory* explores how early parenting influences delinquent behavior. He focuses on the exchanges that take place between parents and children immediately after the children have misbehaved. If the parents consistently react to antisocial behavior with fair, effective discipline, then children quickly learn that misbehavior carries unpleasant consequences. In turn, the children learn to behave and abide by societal rules. In contrast, if parents fail to monitor their children and if parental discipline is lax or inconsistent, then children fail to internalize this important lesson. Even worse, some children actually learn to use extreme misbehavior, such as temper tantrums, to discourage parental discipline. When this situation—which is called a **coercive exchange**—occurs, the usual roles become reversed and the child ends up controlling the behavior of the adult.[22]

Imagine, for example, a situation in which a child sees a toy in a store and asks her parents to buy it. The parents decide that the toy is too expensive and refuse. The child reacts by becoming angry, stomping her feet and using a loud, assertive voice to demand that the parents reconsider. This situation is both embarrassing and uncomfortable for the parents. At this point, they can react in at least one of two ways. First, they can give in and buy the child the toy to avoid making a scene in the store. Second, they can reassert their authority and, if necessary, discipline the child for throwing a temper tantrum.

Although the first alternative will likely be easier on the parents, Patterson argues that choosing it sets a dangerous precedent. First, it teaches children that they can force their parents to reconsider a negative answer by increasing their level of misbehavior. As a consequence, misbehavior can be used as a method of getting exactly what a child wants. Second, if the parents give in, the child's temper tantrum ceases; that event serves as a negative reinforcement that teaches parents to "give in" in future confrontations. Patterson believes that such early exchanges can have profound effects on children's development. Children who are inconsistently disciplined—and especially those who master coercive exchanges—grow up to be teenagers

---

KEY TERMS

precocious transitions
An important life event (e.g., pregnancy) that is experienced unusually early in life.

coercive exchange
A test of wills, in which a child uses misbehavior to extort a desired outcome from his or her parents.

and adults who commit crimes. Such individuals are taught to defy authority figures, reject rules, and use violence and other forms of misbehavior to solve their problems.

Patterson was one of the first scholars to differentiate the two general classes of offenders: those for whom the onset of delinquent behavior occurred early in life and those for whom the onset occurred later in life. Subsequent criminologists, such as Terrie Moffitt, have used this conceptualization in their theories. *Early starters* are exposed to inept, coercive, or authoritarian parenting. These experiences instill an overall negativity that leads to their rejection by conventional peers, dislike of school, anger, low self-esteem, and mental health problems such as depression. As early as fourth grade, these children are identifiable for their school failure and are especially prone to associate with similarly situated peers. Early starters are often arrested by age 14 and are most likely to engage in chronic criminality.[23]

By comparison, such problems are not expected from *late starters*, individuals whose onset of delinquency occurs after age 14. Late starters are normative delinquents who are particularly prone to the influences of delinquent peers if their parents failed to monitor their behavior closely. For late-starting, "normal" delinquents, the significant relationship between delinquent peer association and delinquency is so robust that it has been found to mediate other known correlates of crime such as socioeconomic status.

Patterson's theory has enjoyed much empirical support. His approach has proven crucial in demonstrating the contributions that families and peers have in producing delinquent behavior.[24] (See **Box 7.3**, the "Theory in a Nutshell" feature.)

Terrie Moffitt

Like Patterson's work, Terrie Moffitt's developmental taxonomy suggests that there are two types of delinquents: **adolescence-limited** and **life-course persistent offenders**.

BOX 7.3

Theory in a Nutshell

Gerald Patterson

Patterson focuses on the exchanges that take place between parents and children immediately after the child misbehaves. If parents consistently react to antisocial behavior with fair, effective discipline, children learn that misbehavior carries unpleasant consequences. Conversely, if parental discipline is lax or inconsistent, children are likely to become teens who engage in delinquency.

Adolescence-limited offenders account for the bulk of the delinquent population; more than 90% of delinquents are of this type. These individuals are generally able to resist any antisocial impulses that they may have and are generally law-abiding citizens. As the label implies, however, adolescence-limited offenders engage in delinquency for a brief period during their teen years. Driving their deviance is the ambiguity of puberty and the internal confusion associated with adolescent development. During this phase, youths often have difficulty grappling with quickly changing expectations and responsibilities that are a function of age, such as obtaining a driver's license, dating, having a job, the demands of peer relationships, and the overall angst of being a teenager. By observing the delinquent behavior of serious delinquents, a process Moffitt calls "social mimicry," adolescence-limited offenders come to believe that a certain level of autonomy and adult reinforcement actually comes from "bad" behavior.[25]

Moffitt also described a small group of youths who abstain almost entirely from delinquent conduct during adolescence (see **Box 7.4**, the "Delinquency Prevention" feature, to know more about abstainers). What does this group look like? Brian Boutwell and Kevin Beaver examined youths who abstain from delinquency and found that they are youths who have very high levels of self-control, have less exposure to delinquent peers (e.g., they are more likely to be loners), and have variants of specific dopamine genes that protect them from delinquency.[26]

A desire for adult status is the primary motivation for delinquent behavior in adolescence-limited offenders, in that their delinquency consists of generally low-level offenses, such as underage drinking, marijuana use, shoplifting, and vandalism. Alex Piquero and Timothy Brezina studied offending patterns of approximately 2000 males and found that adolescence-limited offenders, as theorized by Moffitt, engaged in rebellious but not violent forms of delinquency during the difficult stages of puberty.[27] Seth Schwartz and his colleagues similarly found that young people are more likely to conform to societal rules as they move into adulthood.[28] Because adolescence-limited offenders are portrayed as non-serious delinquents, criminologists have paid less attention to them. Nevertheless, studies of criminal careers have generally demonstrated that a substantial group

KEY TERMS

adolescence-limited offenders
Juveniles whose delinquent behavior is confined to their teenage years.

life-course persistent offenders
Individuals who suffer from a number of neuropsychological deficits that likely cause them to engage in delinquency throughout their lives.

BOX 7.4

Delinquency Prevention

The Wonderful People: Moffitt's Abstainer Subgroup

Moffitt's developmental taxonomy offers three general types of individuals: a large group of normative adolescents who flirt with delinquency during their teen years, a small pathological group whose conduct problems are essentially lifelong, and another small group who abstain from antisociality altogether. The latter group has not received much research attention because they do not commit delinquency, and for this reason criminologists have viewed them as somewhat unimportant. In addition, there is also the idea that abstainers are isolated teenagers who lack the peer networks and opportunities to commit delinquency. In this way, their abstention is viewed as more the result of social ineptitude than prosocial characteristics they might have.

Research indicates such a cynical view is incorrect. Individuals who never commit delinquency have characteristics that suggest that they are simply better than the majority of people who do. Two studies based on nationally representative data sets from the United States indicate that delinquency abstainers have many characteristics that suggest they "have their act together" at an early age. In the National Longitudinal Survey of Youth, investigators found that abstainers have high levels of attachment to their teachers, high interaction and monitoring with parents, high involvement with prosocial peers, and low levels of internalizing symptoms, such as depression. In addition, there was no evidence that abstainers were socially alienated from their peers who happened to commit some delinquency. In the National Epidemiologic Survey on Alcohol and Related Conditions, which is a massive

sample of more than 43,000 Americans, Michael Vaughn and his colleagues found that abstainers are significantly less likely than nonabstainers to experience mood, anxiety, or personality disorders over their lifetime.

The beneficial features of abstainers are also found elsewhere. Researchers in Sweden found that abstainers have the most prosocial family backgrounds and are psychologically healthier than youths who follow the adolescence-limited and life-course persistent pathways. A major explanation for the positive profile of abstainers is personality, especially the facet conscientiousness. People who are high scoring on conscientiousness, which is a central component of structural models of personality, are less likely to use drugs, less likely to drink alcohol, less likely to have unhealthy eating habits, less likely to have psychiatric disturbance, less likely to smoke, and less likely to engage in any form of deviant behavior. Using data from the Cambridge Study in Delinquent Development, Wesley Jennings and his colleagues found that abstainers were the most well-adjusted across various life domains and had the best functioning through age 56 compared to those who had been adolescence-limited or life-course persistent offenders. Using the same data, Natalie Mercer and her associates reported that abstainers were honest and conforming in their behavior.

Given this profile, it is likely that delinquency abstainers will receive increased research attention from criminologists who are looking for protective factors that guard against delinquency. In this way, abstainers are a naturally occurring experiment of delinquency prevention.

Alex Piquero, Timothy Brezina, and Michael Turner, "Testing Moffitt's of Delinquency Abstention," *Journal of Research in Crime and Delinquency* 42:27–54 (2005); Michael Vaughn, Qiang Fu, Stephen Wernet, Matt DeLisi, Kevin Beaver, Brian Perron, and Matthew Howard, "Characteristics of Abstainers from Substance Use and Antisocial Behavior in the United States," *Journal of Criminal Justice* 39:212–217 (2011); Håkan Stattin, Margaret Kerr, and Lars Bergman, "On the Utility of Moffitt's Typology Trajectories in Long-Term Perspective," *European Journal of Criminology* 7:1–25 (2010); Tom Bogg and Brent Roberts, "Conscientiousness and Health-Related Behaviors: A Meta-Analysis of the Leading Behavioral Contributors to Morality," *Psychological Bulletin* 130:887–919 (2004); Wesley Jennings, Michael Rocque, Bryanna Hahn Fox, Alex Piquero, and David Farrington, "Can They Recover? An Assessment of Adult Adjustment Problems among Males in the Abstainer, Recovery, Life-Course Persistent, and Adolescence-Limited Pathways Followed up to Age 56 in the Cambridge Study in Delinquent Development," *Development and Psychopathology*, 28:537–549 (2016); Natalie Mercer, David Farrington, Maria Ttofi, Loes Keijsers, Susan Branje, and Wim Meeus, "Childhood Predictors and Adult Life Success of Adolescent Delinquency Abstainers," *Journal of Abnormal Child Psychology*, 44:613–624 (2016).

of delinquents limit their antisocial conduct to the teen years.[29]

Life-course persistent offenders have received much more empirical attention from criminologists because such offenders are considered to be the most threatening to society. According to Moffitt, two types of neuropsychological defects, affecting verbal and executive functions, give rise to an assortment of antisocial behaviors. Verbal functions include reading ability, receptive listening, problem-solving skill, memory, speech articulation, and writing. In short, these relate to verbal intelligence. Executive functions relate to behavioral and personality characteristics,

such as inattention, hyperactivity, and impulsivity. Children with these neuropsychological deficits are restless, fidgety, destructive, and noncompliant, and they can be violent. They are also noteworthy for the intensity of their aggression, the intensity of their defiance and argumentativeness, and the range of problem behaviors they commit.[30]

As these children grow, their tendencies toward antisocial behavior create friction in most of their social interactions with family, school, and peer groups. This ongoing conflict causes life-course persistent children to be shunned and ostracized by both other adolescents and adults, such as parents and teachers.

This social rejection pushes them to begin associating with other problem children and encourages further misbehavior. Eventually, life-course persistent offenders become locked in cycles of increasingly serious misbehavior and negative reactions that culminate in adult criminal careers, a process known as **cumulative disadvantage**.[31]

Two other circumstances cause disadvantages for children with life-course persistent offender characteristics. First, such children often resemble their parents in terms of temperament, personality, and cognitive ability. To put it differently, the parents of life-course persistent offenders often are themselves poorly tempered, impulsive, and prone to use violence to resolve disputes. This cycle of disadvantage further worsens their children's social development.[32]

Second, such children are disproportionately raised in impoverished home environments that are appalling by material, social, and health standards. One of the more damaging environmental factors is early exposure to lead, which is more commonly found in environments characterized by poverty. Douglas Ris and his colleagues supervise the Cincinnati Lead Study, which is a longitudinal examination of the effects of lead exposure on adolescent development. They report that children who have been exposed to lead have increased educational and cognitive risks and that the effects are more pronounced in boys than girls.[33] Bruce Lanphear and his colleagues similarly report that children who are exposed to lead and mercury suffer from an array of behavioral problems, intellectual deficits, and health problems that limit their development. Moffitt and her colleagues have also shown that children on the life-course persistent pathway of problem behaviors suffer from additional environmental exposures specifically exposure to violence that damages them medically and behaviorally. Severe exposure to violence during childhood, for instance, has been linked to erosion of telomeres, which are the endcaps of chromosomes and are an indicator of aging. Thus, abusive environments also ages children with severe behavior problems at a much faster rate than children reared in healthy environments.[34]

Researchers surveyed 4704 children from the National Health and Nutrition Examination Study to examine the long-term consequences of exposure to environmental lead. They discovered that children with the highest lead concentrations in their blood were more than 400% more likely to develop attention-deficit/hyperactivity disorder (ADHD) than children with lower lead exposures. Indeed, lead exposure accounts for more than nearly 290,000 excess cases of ADHD in U.S. children.[35]

Although children with ADHD are different from Moffitt's life-course persistent offenders, they share many of the same characteristics.

Once thrust into impoverished circumstances, youths described as life-course persistent offenders

BOX 7.5

Theory in a Nutshell

Terrie Moffitt

Moffitt believes delinquents are either life-course persistent or adolescence-limited offenders. Life-course persistent offenders suffer from a variety of psychosocial deficits, and the process of cumulative disadvantage frequently turns them from troubled adolescents into career criminals. Conversely, adolescence-limited offenders become involved in delinquency during a brief period of teenage rebellion.

continually behave poorly and face consequences that narrow their options for future success. As Moffitt stated in her original conceptualization of the taxonomy, the behavioral repertoire of the life-course persistent offender is limited to negativity, rejection, and delinquency. It is well documented that such youths often suffered through adverse childhoods, demonstrated an array of problematic and antisocial behaviors, and generally led lives of crime and involvement with the criminal justice system.[36] Many of the environmental causes that wrought harm on this group could have been prevented (see **Box 7.5**, the "Theory in a Nutshell" feature).

Robert Sampson and John Laub

Robert Sampson and John Laub think that the development of delinquency is influenced by factors ranging from structural conditions (such as socioeconomic status and family structure) to individual traits (such as temperament) to traditional social control concepts (such as bonding, attachment, and supervision). Unlike many earlier theorists, however, they argue that the importance of these factors varies over the life course. Specifically, Sampson and Laub's *age-graded theory* of informal social control argues that informal social controls—such as involvement in family, work, and school—*mediate* structural context and explain criminal involvement even in the face of the underlying level of criminal propensity.

Like theorists who favor "kinds of people" explanations for delinquency, Sampson and Laub acknowledge that people differ both in their underlying criminal propensity and the likelihood that they will place themselves in troublesome situations. Unlike other theorists, they suggest that people acquire different

KEY TERMS

cumulative disadvantage
The process by which successive misbehavior leads to a serious detriment for an individual's life chances.

amounts of social capital from informal social control networks, and that this social capital explains the continuity in antisocial behaviors across various life stages. Persons with low social capital (and past criminal involvement) mortgage their future life chances—a process referred to as the *cumulative continuity of disadvantage*. Conversely, the development of conventional adult social bonds or experiencing of particular *turning points* (discussed later in this section) can "right" previously deviant pathways such as juvenile delinquency, unemployment, and substance abuse, and place an individual onto a trajectory toward more successful outcomes. Rather than viewing the causes of delinquency as overly simplistic and deterministic, Sampson and Laub stress that *change* or *dynamism* characterizes criminal careers, because even the most active offender stops committing crime over the life course. For instance, 60-year-old criminals are not as active and violent as they were at age 17, and Sampson and Laub's theory helps to account for such changes.[37]

Sampson and Laub's theory has been very influential. Their own research has applied modern statistical methods to data for 500 officially defined delinquents and a matched sample of 500 nondelinquents originally collected by Sheldon and Eleanor Glueck. Overall, Sampson and Laub have found that family-related issues—such as the amount of maternal supervision, parental discipline style, and attachment to parents—are among the most robust predictors of serious delinquency. These family variables largely mediate background social class factors and predict

Even youths with prior involvement in delinquency can turn their lives around by participating in conventional "turning points."

© Paul Matthew Photograph/Shutterstock.

delinquency even when considering the antisocial dispositions of both children and their parents.[38] By the term "mediate" Sampson and Laub mean that if adults are currently involved in the "right" types of behavior, such as having a job or marriage, they can stop committing crime, even if they had an extensive criminal background. In contrast, even previously nondelinquent people may begin engaging in crime during adulthood if they are not effectively bonded to society through marriage, work, military, or some other positive social institution.

Even though Sampson and Laub's theory stresses the importance of local life circumstances, these criminologists do not entirely ignore the negative consequences of antisocial behavior that occurs during childhood. For instance, they have found that childhood delinquency is predictive of an array of deviant characteristics in adulthood. However, such relationships often disappear once adult social bonds are considered. In their words, "adult social bonds not only have important effects on adult crime in and of themselves, but help to explain the probabilistic links in the chain connecting early childhood differences and later adult crime."[39]

Sampson and Laub's theory helps us to understand the entire life course or human development aspects of delinquency. Although poverty and family circumstances set the *initial conditions* for delinquency, in that children born in disadvantaged areas are more frequently exposed to criminogenic conditions, these factors do not directly explain why these children tend to grow up delinquent. Instead, they influence what is *likely* to happen to the children as they grow up. Young people born into impoverished, disorganized neighborhoods are more likely to experience scholastic difficulties and are less likely to have good relationships with their parents. As adolescents, they are less likely to build strong ties within their families and experience frequent and effective parental supervision. For their part, impoverished parents will be more likely to work long hours and to have less time to devote to their children. Taken together, these factors increase the risk that disadvantaged children will begin spending time in the company of other disadvantaged children, in settings where delinquency is likely to take place. For instance, middle- and upper-class children are likely to spend much of their time at home, in organized extracurricular activities, or in places where there is at least some adult supervision, whereas many lower-class children will spend much of their time hanging out on street corners—a setting where gang recruitment is a very real possibility.

In general, Sampson and Laub tell us that problems experienced during the early stages of life have adverse effects on later stages of development. If a child experiences structural disadvantage, this factor makes it more likely that he or she will experience

BOX 7.6

Theory in a Nutshell

Robert Sampson and John Laub

Sampson and Laub argue that the development of delinquency is influenced by many factors, ranging from structural conditions to individual traits to traditional social control concepts. The importance of these factors varies over the life course. Problems experienced during the early stages of life have adverse effects at later stages. Sampson and Laub also suggest that key life events can "derail" delinquent careers and move individuals back to prosocial developmental pathways.

poor parenting in early adolescence, which in turn will lead to increased associations with delinquent peers later in adolescence. These steps represent the "building blocks" of a typical *delinquent career*. Nevertheless, Sampson and Laub do allow for the possibility that **turning points**—key life events that can either drive someone toward delinquent behavior or initiate the process of desisting from it—can "derail" delinquent careers and push people back onto prosocial developmental pathways. Two of the most important turning points in this regard are marriage and steady employment.

Imagine, for example, a situation in which a delinquent boy who spends much of his time on the street in the company of gang members can land a steady job and then meets a prosocial girlfriend. Sampson and Laub think that this young man will then spend much less time associating with his delinquent peers and will less often find himself in situations where delinquency is both possible and encouraged. He may also come to realize that he now has much to lose by being delinquent. He may, for instance, begin to think that committing crimes with his friends is not worth the risk of getting arrested, fired, or rejected by his new girlfriend. Over time, Sampson and Laub suggest, this boy will become more deeply involved in a conventional, prosocial lifestyle and eventually his delinquent career will end (see **Box 7.6**, the "Theory in a Nutshell" feature). In this way, their theory (see **Figure 7.3**) offers not only an explanation for how children become delinquent, but also an argument for how delinquent youth and adults are able to "go straight."[40]

Terence Thornberry

Terence Thornberry's *interactional theory* is another important developmental approach, which stresses that all human behavior occurs in the context of social interaction. Social interaction affects everyone and is often complex, overlapping, multidirectional, and reciprocal. Children who are attached to their parents

are likely to harbor conventional values and beliefs (provided, of course, that their parents harbor and teach such values and beliefs) and, therefore, are likely to be committed to school. Over time, this serious commitment to school will bolster these children's support of conventional beliefs and solidify their relationships with their parents, who will be pleased their child is performing well in school. Conversely, children who are not committed to school are more likely to weaken their relationships with their parents and to initiate or strengthen their relationships with peers who are not committed to school. Social interactions that lead to both prosocial and antisocial values and behaviors are constantly in flux, overlapping, and in the process of development.[41] In other words, the causes and consequences of delinquency are difficult to separate.

These ideas have been supported with data from the Rochester Youth Development Study, a panel study of middle school children from Rochester, New York. As conceptualized by Thornberry, these data reveal that school and family bonding variables predict delinquency, which in turn weakens school and family bonding.[42] Once involvement in delinquency has begun, its interactional effects are often difficult for youths to overcome. Delinquent behavior and association with delinquent peers have a synergistic effect, whereby antisocial or delinquent beliefs become increasingly important to the youth. In other words, their delinquent beliefs and personas become hardened, further influencing the types of people with whom delinquent youth associate. For this reason, stopping committing crime is a process (not a discrete event), whereby offenders gradually transition from a social network centered on delinquency to one centered on conventional behavior. Most important for developmental theory, Thornberry's theory asserts that an individual's involvement in social institutions such as family, school, and work are directly, indirectly, and variably related to delinquency. In addition, considerable behavioral change and responsiveness to parents, peers, and social institutions occur *within individuals* as they pass through adolescence.[43]

Like many theories of delinquency, interactional theory suggests that the roots of delinquent behavior can be traced to structural disadvantage, particularly low socioeconomic status. This situation results in low initial levels of parental attachment, belief in conventional values, and commitment to school. These factors, in turn, lead to increased associations with delinquent peers and the promotion of delinquent

KEY TERMS

turning points
Key life events that can either drive someone toward delinquent behavior or initiate the process of desisting from it.

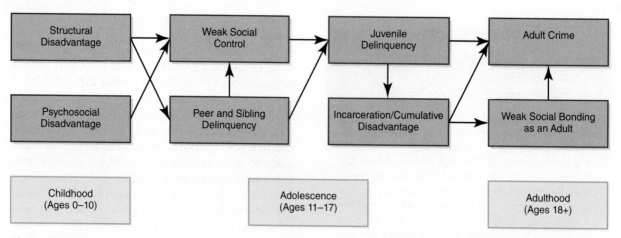

Figure 7.3 Mapping Delinquency Theory: Sampson and Laub's Life Course Theory
© Jones & Bartlett Learning.

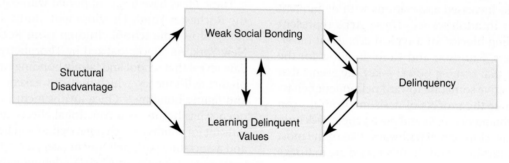

Figure 7.4 Mapping Delinquency Theory: Thornberry's Interactional Theory
© Jones & Bartlett Learning.

values, both of which are subsequently related to delinquency (see **Figure 7.4**). Like Sampson and Laub, Thornberry believes that the importance of these key factors changes as people age (see **Box 7.7**, the "Theory in a Nutshell" feature). For instance, he argues that the importance of parental attachment declines as people move from early to late adolescence.

According to interactional theory, the more delinquent a child becomes, the more likely he or she is to experience all of the other identified criminogenic factors. Terence Thornberry and Marvin Krohn extended

BOX 7.7
Theory in a Nutshell
Terence Thornberry

Thornberry believes that delinquency begins with structural disadvantage, which leads to initially low levels of parental attachment, belief in conventional values, and commitment to school. Such factors promote increased associations with delinquent peers and elevated delinquent values, which subsequently lead to delinquency. Thornberry further suggests that delinquency itself can initiate an amplifying cycle that leads to more serious delinquency.

this theory to explain continuity and changes in the criminal careers of serious offenders. For instance, suppose that an adolescent boy has a very poor relationship with his parents. This factor makes it less likely that he will spend much time at home and more likely that he will associate with delinquent peers. Taken together, these factors increase the probability that this boy will engage in delinquent behavior. The more delinquency he commits, however, the more likely he is to continue associating with his delinquent peer group rather than with his parents or other prosocial friends. If the parents become aware of his delinquent behavior, it may also create family strife, which will further damage the boy's relationship with his parents, causing him to spend even less time at home. These developments, in turn, will further increase the probability of deeper involvement with the delinquent peer group and more serious delinquent behavior. Eventually, the boy may become hopelessly locked into an amplifying cycle of delinquent behavior.[44]

Joseph Weis, Richard Catalano, and J. David Hawkins

Since 1981, Joseph Weis, Richard Catalano, J. David Hawkins, and other researchers at the University of

Washington have conducted the Seattle Social Development Project, which is a longitudinal study of more than 800 children who were enrolled in fifth grade in 1985 in 18 Seattle public elementary schools. The study is based on the researchers' *social development model*, which claims that the causes of delinquency are complex, multifaceted, and ultimately the outcome of an individual's journey along overlapping prosocial and antisocial paths.

The social development model is rooted in the theoretical traditions of differential association, social control, and social learning, and focuses on four specific periods of development: (1) preschool, (2) elementary school, (3) middle school, and (4) high school. According to the theory, socializing agents such as family, school, peers, and others teach and inculcate both "good" and "bad" behaviors to children. At each stage of development, children are faced with risk factors that push them toward delinquency and protective factors that pull them away from delinquency. Four factors influence the socialization processes occurring during the four periods of development: (1) opportunities for involvement in activities and interactions with others, (2) the degree of involvement and interaction, (3) skills to participate in these involvements and interactions, and (4) the reinforcement forthcoming from performance in activities and interactions.[45]

An interesting component of the social development model is its explicit focus on developmental processes across various stages of childhood development for all types of individuals. In other words, this theory views antisocial behavior and the risks for antisocial behavior generally—not prescriptively for high-risk groups. Perhaps for this reason, the results of some of the empirical tests of the social development model are slightly at odds with the claims made by other developmental theories. For example, researchers have found that the theory applies equally well to males and females and to children from divergent social class backgrounds.[46] Although it is well known that these groups have varying involvement in delinquency and victimization, the processes by which they are exposed or protected from delinquency reflect commonality, not differences in development. Similarly, children for whom the onset of delinquent behavior occurred at different ages nevertheless followed similar developmental patterns toward violent behavior when assessed at adulthood.

Overall, the social development model speaks to the delinquencies and conventional behaviors of many social groups.[47] It claims that social structure sets the initial conditions that determine how strongly an individual is bonded to conventional society. For poor children, this bond is typically weak. Disadvantaged adolescents usually see little opportunity or hope for prosocial involvement, and they typically lack the skills necessary to succeed in the conventional

BOX 7.8

Theory in a Nutshell

Joseph Weis, Richard Catalano, and J. David Hawkins

Weis and his colleagues contend that disadvantaged youths have few opportunities for prosocial involvement and lack the skills necessary to succeed in the conventional world. At the same time, these youths have ready access to delinquent opportunity structures and possess the skills necessary to excel at delinquency. For these reasons, they frequently associate with delinquent peers and participate in crime. However, early interventions may interrupt this process.

world. At the same time, such children frequently have access to delinquent opportunity structures and possess the skills necessary to excel at delinquency. As a consequence, they may begin associating with delinquent peers and end up on antisocial developmental pathways. Just the opposite is true for more affluent children: Not only are such youth socialized with the skills necessary to succeed in conventional society, but they often lack access to illegitimate opportunities. In addition, they frequently have much to lose by engaging in delinquent behavior and often form strong bonds with parents, teachers, and prosocial friends who push them toward conventional developmental pathways.

Social development theory is heavily geared toward delinquency prevention. To this end, its authors have painstakingly identified the mechanisms by which social institutions and socialization agents promote healthy development (e.g., protective factors) and maladaptive development (e.g., exposure to risk factors). (See **Box 7.8**, the "Theory in a Nutshell" feature.)

Ronald Simons

Ronald Simons and his colleagues have empirically tested many of the developmental theories described in this chapter. Using data from an ongoing longitudinal study of more than 450 Iowa families, they were able to examine how antisocial behavior that occurs during childhood and adolescence affects various outcomes in adulthood. Like Sampson, Laub, Patterson, and others, Simons and his colleagues show that both delinquency and prosocial behavior are long-term processes that are strongly affected by participation in social institutions. In addition, these researchers are among a relatively small number of criminologists who have studied individuals living in rural areas. As such, they can consider the multiple routes that adolescents may take in becoming delinquent and see if traditional pathways are limited to youths living in urban settings.

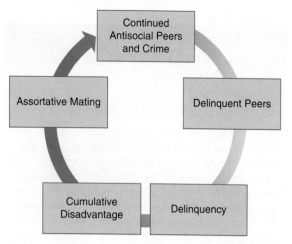

Figure 7.5 Mapping Delinquency Theory: Simons and Assortative Mating

© Jones & Bartlett Learning.

Does the theory of assortative mating explain why delinquent youths often select other delinquent youths to become romantically involved with? In what ways can a romantic partner increase or decrease one's own delinquent beliefs and behaviors?

© BananaStock/age fotostock.

For instance, Simons and his colleagues have reported that association with deviant peers, socioeconomic status, and parenting techniques can steer youths into positive or negative pathways. "Late starters"—defined as persons who initially engaged in delinquency after age 14 and who were in strong marriages—have been found to be significantly less involved in crime than their peers who were single or in problematic marriages. Simons and his colleagues argue for "consideration of the manner in which peer friendships, as well as other social relationships, may operate to amplify or moderate the antisocial tendencies fostered by ineffectual parental behavior."[48] In other words, criminal propensity, as measured by childhood and adolescent misconduct, often disappears once the effects of family, school, and peers are considered. The importance of this point should not be missed: It means that informal social control networks and mundane experiences, such as getting married, having a job, or being in school, are more powerful explanations of delinquency than latent, kinds-of-people trait explanations.[49]

A unique contribution from Simons and colleagues' research relates to how a romantic relationship with a prosocial partner can help "derail" a delinquent career. Simons and his associates suggest that individuals who have been delinquent throughout their adolescent years and those who have become strongly committed to a deviant peer group are unlikely to form stable unions with nondelinquent partners. This trend arises because these delinquent persons are unlikely to associate with the same groups as prosocial individuals and will not appear to be attractive partners to potential prosocial mates. Many serious delinquents and their prospective romantic partners will have poor social skills, substance abuse problems, lengthy criminal records, little education, and a poor work history. For these reasons, chronically antisocial individuals are more likely to become romantically involved

BOX 7.9
Theory in a Nutshell
Ronald Simons

Simons thinks adolescents with a long history of delinquency, who have become committed to a deviant peer group, are unlikely to form stable unions with prosocial partners. Instead, these individuals often become romantically involved with other antisocial individuals, which promotes their continued involvement in delinquency.

with other antisocial individuals, because they often come into contact with them. This process, known as **assortative mating**, leads to continued involvement with deviant peer networks, dysfunctional domestic relationships, and a lack of success in the job market (see **Figure 7.5**). All of these factors predict a continuation of delinquent careers into adulthood.[50] (See **Box 7.9**, the "Theory in a Nutshell" feature.)

Interestingly, the effects of romantic relationships on delinquency appear to work differently for males and females. Although delinquency and affiliation with delinquent peers tend to lead to having an antisocial romantic partner as a young adult, romantic relationships exerted more influence on girls than on boys. Research by Dana Haynie and her colleagues has also reported that during adolescence, delinquency by girls is more dependent on romantic partners than

KEY TERMS

assortative mating
The concept that people tend to choose mates who are similar to themselves.

is delinquency by boys. Why would this discrepancy occur? For a variety of reasons, males and females draw potential romantic partners from very different groups. Especially during adolescence, it is not uncommon for girls—even prosocial girls—to date delinquent boys. Conversely, it is highly unlikely that conventional boys will date delinquent girls. Andrea Leverentz found that formerly delinquent girls almost exclusively date former drug users or exoffenders.[51] As a consequence, girls are more susceptible to the delinquent influences of their significant others.

Simons and his colleagues also utilize the Family and Community Health Survey, an African American sample that examines developmental trajectories of delinquency and other problem behaviors among minority youth. Most of their studies reinforce research findings that were based on white or European youth, while others provide novel findings. For instance, African American youth who experience more racial discrimination, and who perceive that they experience more racial discrimination, are more likely to have an early onset of delinquency and to have their delinquent career worsen over time.[52]

David Farrington

One of the most prolific researchers of developmental theories is David Farrington, who for more than 40 years has served as director of the Cambridge Study in Delinquent Development, a multigenerational study of a cohort of 411 London males. After years of studying the causes and correlates of serious delinquency and violence from many different theoretical perspectives, Farrington developed his own theory, called the *integrated cognitive antisocial potential theory*. This theory has the following characteristics:

- It integrates ideas from many other theories, including strain, control, learning, labeling, and rational choice approaches.
- It uses as its key construct *antisocial potential*, which refers to the potential to commit antisocial acts including violence.
- It assumes the translation from antisocial potential to antisocial and violent behavior depends on cognitive thinking and decision-making processes that take account of opportunities and victims.

Farrington suggests that in terms of antisocial potential, people are ordered on a continuum from low to high, but that the distribution of antisocial potential is highly skewed. In other words, most people have very little antisocial potential but a small subgroup of persons has very high (i.e., pathological) antisocial potential. In terms of their behavior, the latter group is similar to Moffitt's idea of the life-course persistent offender. The ordering of people on the antisocial potential continuum is relatively but not absolutely stable. Those with very low and very high antisocial

Theory in a Nutshell

David Farrington

Farrington's integrated cognitive antisocial potential theory uses concepts from many other theories, including strain, control, learning, labeling, and rational choice approaches. His main argument is that antisocial potential, which refers to the potential to commit antisocial acts, including violence, is the basis for delinquency. Farrington's integrated theory assumes the transition from antisocial potential to antisocial and violent behavior depends on cognitive thinking and decision-making processes that take account of opportunities and victims.

potential will remain so throughout their lives generally. By comparison, those in the middle have ups and downs of antisocial behavior that coincide with age and situational experiences, such as going to bars and getting into altercations.[53] (See **Box 7.10**, the "Theory in a Nutshell" feature.)

An important cognitive process that translates antisocial potential to antisocial behavior is empathy, which is an affective and cognitive trait that facilitates the experience of another person's emotions and the understanding of another's emotions (**Figure 7.6**). Individuals who lack empathy find it easier to victimize others because they do not relate to their victims on a personal level and feel their common humanity. Darrick Jolliffe and David Farrington have found significant evidence that youths with low levels of empathy have higher levels of delinquent behavior.[54]

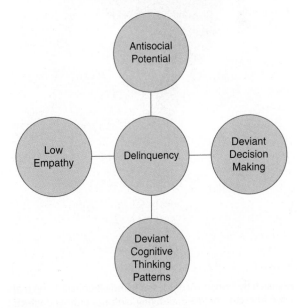

Figure 7.6 Farrington's Integrated Theory

The integrated cognitive antisocial potential theory might also explain why males and females have such different levels of delinquent involvement, especially for more serious violent crimes. People respond to stressful life events based both on their perception of the event and on their individual cognitive processes. These responses to stimuli are informed by how individuals encode information, interpret the information, and perceive risks and benefits of particular actions. Females generally have better prosocial skills and acquire social cognitive skills earlier in life compared to males. The superior social cognitive skills of females are attributed to many factors, including superior hemispheric communication in the brain, fewer frontal lobe deficits, and greater verbal ability. By comparison, males are more likely to use their temper and their fists as opposed to dialogue to handle disputes.[55]

The idea of antisocial potential in the integrated cognitive antisocial potential theory has at times been called delinquent propensity, criminality, criminal propensity, and population heterogeneity. Research has consistently supported the idea that those individuals with high antisocial potential are usually the worst delinquents and has shown that

Research by Sarnoff Mednick and Patricia Brennan shows that what transpires before and during birth has profound effects on delinquent conduct occurring decades later.

© wavebreakmedia ltd/Shutterstock.

their delinquent behavior is often present very early in life. For example, when Graham Ousey and Pamela Wilcox studied adolescents in Kentucky, they found that antisocial propensity or potential magnified the risk factors that youths faced during adolescence. In other words, traditional theoretical risks for delinquency, such as having delinquent friends or feeling general strain, are heightened in those persons who score high on antisocial potential. Similarly, Stacey Bosick and her colleagues found that clusters, or types, of delinquents during adolescence generally translated into similar clusters during adulthood. Thus, youth who are highest in antisocial potential at one time in their life are usually the most severe offenders later on in life. Moreover, these effects pass from one generation to the next. Several risk factors for high antisocial potential, such as having convicted parents, harsh discipline, large family size, poor housing, low school attainment, and a daring, risk taking personality style are linked to the most severe delinquents, and a generation later, to their children.[56]

Russell Dobash and his colleagues studied the developmental history of delinquency among 786 men convicted of murder in the United Kingdom. Although all of these men were convicted killers, they varied in terms of their antisocial potential based primarily on the onset of their delinquent career. Fewer than 20% of the murderers in the sample were early starters, but they rated significantly worse than late starters and individuals without criminal records on almost every measure associated with delinquency. Those with high antisocial potential were more likely to come from broken homes; have alcoholic and criminal parents; live in poverty; have multiple caretakers during childhood; suffer physical and sexual abuse; have school, psychiatric, and behavioral problems; and have extensive adolescent and adult criminal histories. Those with high antisocial potential are also more likely to be killed early in life. Katherine Auty and her colleagues reported that people who were high-rate, chronic offenders were seven times more likely to die by age 57 than those in the general population. In addition, people with high antisocial potential usually die from causes related to social pathologies, including drug overdoses, health problems associated with poor health habits, and from violent means, such as suicide and homicide.[57]

Sarnoff Mednick and Patricia Brennan

Sarnoff Mednick, Patricia Brennan, and their colleagues are the investigators behind the Danish Birth Cohort Studies, a massive effort that includes all 358,180 people born in Denmark between 1944 and 1947 and followed by police records through age 44. These researchers have also developed a sample of 4169 males born in Copenhagen, Denmark, between

1951 and 1959 and followed by criminal records to age 34. The latter sample has provided extensive information on prenatal and perinatal factors that contribute to the development of delinquent and related antisocial behaviors. In terms of their sheer magnitude, the Danish studies are arguably the most impressive data set in developmental criminology. Also, a major difference between the work by Mednick, Brennan, and their associates and other researchers into developmental theories is that the focus of the former group is on a broader range of the life span from birth to middle age, which truly allows for an assessment of the ways that delinquency develops, occurs, persists, and declines over time.

The Danish research program has produced many interesting and important findings about the ways that delinquent behaviors during adolescence and even adulthood unfold from causes occurring at birth. For instance:

- One of the most damaging prenatal risks is maternal cigarette smoking. In fact, prenatal cigarette smoking predicted persistent criminal behavior at age 34 in the Danish studies.[58]
- Children with both biological risk factors (e.g., neuromotor scores at age 1) and social risk factors (e.g., unstable family environment) have the highest risk for becoming delinquent later in life.
- Children with biosocial risk factors (biological and environmental) accounted for more than 70% of the delinquency in the entire cohort.[59]
- Children and adolescents with very early onsets of violent behavior are significantly more likely to have birth complications and be rejected by their mother (e.g., child placed in a public care institution) during the first year of life.[60]

Mednick and Brennan's work is less of a theory and more of a research program that shows the long-term effects of health and behavioral problems among mothers and their children occurring at birth. (See **Box 7.11**, the "Theory in a Nutshell" feature.) Events occurring immediately after birth can unfold into serious forms of antisocial behavior that persist decades into life (see **Figure 7.7**).

BOX 7.11

Theory in a Nutshell

Sarnoff Mednick and Patricia Brennan

Mednick, Brennan, and their colleagues have used extremely large samples of Danish citizens to show that prenatal and perinatal problems or dysfunctions occurring at birth set into motion a change of developmental problems that result in delinquency during adolescence and criminal behavior during adulthood.

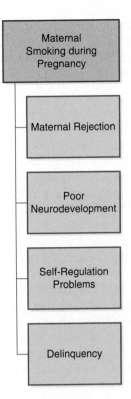

Figure 7.7 Mapping Delinquency Theory: Mednick and Brennan and Pre-/Perinatal Complications

© Jones & Bartlett Learning.

Evaluation of Developmental Theory

The individual building blocks of developmental theories—such as poverty, neuropsychological deficits, weak bonding, association with delinquent peers, coercive exchanges, and assortative mating—are all associated with criminality. Most criminologists agree that adolescents can follow more than one pathway to delinquency and that the key predictors of misbehavior likely change over time. Many also recognize that the risk and protective factors associated with delinquency are involved in reciprocal causal relationships. As a whole, the developmental perspective has enjoyed widespread support within the research community.[61] As noted by Terrie Moffitt, "[B]efore 1993, virtually no research compared delinquent subtypes defined on a developmental basis, but now this research strategy has become almost commonplace."[62]

Consider the following point about the developmental differences between individuals whose delinquency first appears during childhood as compared to those whose onset occurs during adolescence:

The taxonomy of childhood versus adolescent-onset antisocial behavior has been codified in the *DSM-IV* [produced by the American Psychiatric Association], presented in many abnormal psychology and criminology textbooks and invoked in the NIMH Factsheet *Child and Adolescent Violence Research*, the U.S. Surgeon General's report *Youth Violence*,

the World Health Organization's *World Report on Violence and Health*, and the National Institutes of Health's *State-of-the-Science Consensus Statement in Preventing Violence*.[63]

Thus, in part because of their real-world application, developmental theories of delinquency have been extremely successful.

Developmental theories have also opened the door to a dynamic and interesting area of research focusing on how person-specific and environmental factors interrelate to produce all types of behavior, including delinquency. For instance, Hozefa Divan and her colleagues used data from the Danish National Birth Cohort to study the effects of cell phone exposure to behavioral problems in children through age 7. In their study, which included more than 13,000 children, the researchers found that prenatal exposure to cell phones was associated with behavioral difficulties such as emotional regulation and hyperactivity. In fact, children whose mothers used cell phones while pregnant had behavioral problems that were nearly double those of children without cell phone exposure.[64]

Developmental perspectives are also shedding light on the ways that genetic factors and socialization factors interact. For instance, Elisabeth Binder and colleagues collected data from 900 patients visiting an inner-city hospital for nonpsychiatric care. These researchers asked the patients if they had experienced childhood abuse and other traumas experienced in childhood or adulthood. In addition, each patient contributed a saliva sample for DNA testing. Binder and her associates found that 80% of the patients reported experiencing one or more significant traumas, and one-fourth of them met the criteria for posttraumatic stress disorder (PTSD). Approximately 30% reported being physically or sexually abused as children. The researchers found that four variations in a specific gene called FKBP5 (which is responsible for regulating stress) interacted with the severity of child abuse to predict the level of adult PTSD symptoms. This association remained significant even when the researchers controlled for depression severity, age, sex, genetic ancestry, and levels of trauma exposure other than child abuse.[65]

Working in a similar area, Kevin Beaver used genetic data from the National Longitudinal Study of Adolescent Health to see how dopamine genes interacted with childhood sexual abuse victimization to predict delinquency. Beaver found that young males who had certain risk-related variants of three dopamine genes and who were sexually molested as children were significantly likely to develop into serious delinquents, as shown in **Figure 7.8**. No such effect was found for females.[66]

Of course, developmental theories are not without their weaknesses. Although the theories pay lip service to social structure, these theories are overwhelmingly individualistic. For instance, Per-Olof Wikstrom and Robert Sampson make the following arguments:[67]

- Studies of developmental pathways neglect the influence of a wider social context.
- Research on individual risk factors has largely failed to specify the causal mechanisms that link the risk factors to acts of crime or delinquent pathways.

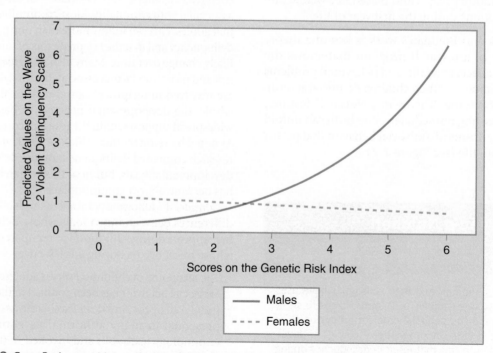

Figure 7.8 Gene-Environment Interactions Predict Violent Delinquency

© Jones & Bartlett Learning.

- Research on environmental influences has largely failed to specify the causal mechanisms that link social context to crime.
- Interactions between individual characteristics and community contexts are poorly understood.
- Existing approaches to crime prevention and policy are poorly integrated.
- If developmental theories claim to take a multilevel, comprehensive perspective on delinquency, they must do a better job of including sociological influences on behavior.

Developmental theories can also be criticized for not being theories at all but rather descriptive models of how conventional and delinquent behavior unfolds over time. Michael Gottfredson suggests that most development theories lack parsimony, have difficulty explaining the versatility or generality of delinquency, and minimize the evidence of criminal propensity, whereas general theories of crime account for these issues.[68]

Another problem with developmental theories is the fact that they assume antisocial traits and behavior have to develop over time; in contrast, general theories argue that some individual-level construct explains delinquency at all life stages. For example, Michael Vaughn and his colleagues evaluated parent and teacher reports of impulsivity and self-control among a national sample of kindergarteners. They found that kindergarteners with extremely poor self-control and impulsivity also demonstrated other serious risk factors relating to school performance and behavioral regulation. Moreover, parenting processes explained very little of the variance in self-control and impulsivity—a finding that suggests these constructs do not develop but rather are already present within individuals.[69]

Developmental theories are also amazingly similar in terms of their focus on social institutions as determinants of behavior and offer only slight variations in terminology. For instance, Janet Lauritsen argues that it is unclear how developmental theories differ from one another, in that they all strive to understand reciprocal relationships among families, peers, schools, and individuals. Lauritsen is also critical of these theories' failure to consider family composition and the ways in which different types of families can affect a youth's development.[70]

Furthermore, although developmental theories stress development, all of them (except for Moffitt's developmental taxonomy and research by Mednick, Brennan, and colleagues) ignore the earliest stages of individual development. In contrast, Robert Regoli and John Hewitt's theory of differential oppression is the *only* criminological theory to focus attention on the potential contextual effects of conception, pregnancy, infant care, and ways that adults create oppression in the lives of their children. The development that occurs at the earliest points in life can propel youths down conventional and delinquent pathways. To fully understand delinquency you must *begin at the beginning*; not at some point down the road. By starting later, too much water will have already moved under the bridge.

There is less than complete agreement regarding exactly how many delinquent pathways are open to adolescents, and precisely how the various risk factors are related to one another. For example, Moffitt's theory suggests that adolescents can follow one of three possible developmental pathways. She believes that most individuals will fall into the adolescence-limited group, whereas substantially fewer persons either will become life-course persistent offenders or will never engage in delinquency. However, as shown in **Figure 7.2**, adolescents may follow many distinct developmental pathways. For example, a study by Amy D'Unger and her colleagues explored how many distinct "types" of offender classifications exist in famous birth cohort studies from London, Philadelphia, and Racine (Wisconsin). D'Unger reported that four or five distinct classes emerged, which is certainly a more complex account than Moffitt's developmental taxonomy would suggest.[71]

For their part, Margit Wiesner and Deborah Capaldi have pointed to the existence of six distinct groups of offenders. Two of the groups in their study aged out of crime by early adulthood, whereas two clearly did not. Substantial differences between these groups were also noted in terms of the total amount of offending that occurs over the delinquent career: One group engaged in a generally low level of offending, one group engaged in a moderate level of offending, and two groups engaged in high levels of offending. In addition, a substantial number of individuals engaged in sporadic offending over the life course. In Wiesner and Capaldi's work, no clear developmental pattern was evident in the last group.[72]

Tim Brennan and his colleagues identified seven categories of offending groups, including two groups similar to those in Moffitt's developmental taxonomy:[73]

1. Internalizing youth A: withdrawn, abused, and rejected
2. Socially deprived: subcultural or socialized delinquents
3. Low control A: versatile offenders
4. Normal: "accidental/situational" delinquents
5. Internalizing youth B: with positive parenting
6. Low control B: early-onset, versatile offenders with multiple risk factors—essentially the life-course persistent offender group
7. Normative delinquency: drugs, sex, and delinquent peers—essentially the adolescence-limited offender group

Moffitt's own work has expanded the universe of offenders beyond the two prototypes identified in her original developmental taxonomy. For instance, a recent study found four groups: a life-course persistent group, adolescent-onset group, childhood-limited group, and low-offending group.[74] These finding are somewhat difficult to reconcile with Moffitt's taxonomy because many studies show that delinquents do not fit neatly into exclusively the life-course persistent or adolescence-limited category.

There is also dispute regarding exactly how the building blocks that constitute the different developmental models are related to one another. For example, interactional theory indicates that most of the effect of peer deviance on delinquency is *direct*. That is, when a child begins associating with deviant individuals, he or she is automatically placed at higher risk for delinquent involvement.

Conversely, the social development model shows that much of this effect is *indirect*: Associations with delinquent peers lead to delinquent behavior only after an individual has learned a deviant value system from the peer group and has had time to internalize it. Thus, it is the learning of deviant values that directly causes delinquency, not the association with delinquent peers.

In general, none of these issues represents a serious challenge to the developmental perspective.[75] Developmental theories will likely continue to provide a foundation for many future studies of juvenile delinquency. As more studies are conducted, however, modifications will likely be made to the existing developmental theories. Perhaps an integrated developmental perspective will emerge that will systematically consider the insights offered by the theorists discussed in this chapter.

Researchers are currently testing how well developmental theories apply to different groups of children under various conditions. For instance, it remains an open question whether particular developmental theories apply universally to both males and females and to adolescents from different cultures and social class backgrounds. To date, the findings of this research have generally been supportive of the universality of developmental theories. Delinquent development appears to take place in roughly the same way throughout North America, South America, Europe, Asia, and Australia.[76] Moreover, initial investigations suggest that both boys and girls follow similar pathways to delinquency, although boys more often traverse chronically deviant pathways.

Of course, more work remains to be done. Many of the best-known studies in this area have been based exclusively on samples of boys or have drawn their samples from relatively restricted geographical areas. Nevertheless, it is likely that developmental theory will continue to be very influential in guiding research in the area of juvenile delinquency for years to come (see **Box 7.12**, the "The Face of Delinquency" feature).[77]

Juvenile Justice Policy Applications

Developmental theories blame delinquency on many different causes, ranging from psychosocial deficits to weak social bonding. As a consequence,

these theories have a wide range of implications for juvenile justice policy, many of which are consistent with the implications suggested in earlier chapters.

Developmental theories that borrow heavily from the social control perspective would likely agree that reconnecting children with their parents should be an important goal of any intervention strategy. Similarly, because some of these theories incorporate aspects of the strain perspective, they suggest a focus on providing children with legitimate opportunities to succeed. For example, providing skills training and mentoring for disadvantaged elementary and junior high school students can act as a powerful shield against criminogenic influences.

Because Gerald Patterson's theory is more closely associated with Albert Bandura's behavioral perspective, it implies that consistent punishment of negative behavior is the key to preventing delinquency. If it is desirable to avoid the criminogenic consequences of coercive exchanges, then parents must be taught to avoid becoming trapped in such exchanges. This perspective clearly implies the need to provide parents with training. Young mothers and fathers must be taught to recognize coercive exchanges when they occur and given the necessary tools to prevent them from continuing. In his review of developmental theories, David Farrington argues that a variety of preventive measures can be taken to delay the onset of delinquency, especially parenting, life skills, and social skills training for parents, thereby ensuring that they can better recognize how to enhance protective factors and minimize risk factors.[78]

Developmental theories extend the policy implications of earlier explanations of crime by making policymakers aware of the fact that events experienced during one stage of life may have important consequences at subsequent stages. Because developmental theorists believe that the most important predictors of delinquency vary as people age, their models imply that interventions that may be highly effective during one stage of life may no longer work at the next stage.

Finally, because these theories integrate existing explanations of delinquency and because research using developmental perspectives has identified a variety of pathways that youth might follow into delinquency, this set of theories strongly cautions against adopting a "one size fits all" approach to delinquency intervention. To illustrate, according to these theories, a child's ties to his or her parents are the key to predicting delinquent behavior in early adolescence. Adolescents who are weakly bonded to their parents are at particularly high risk.[79] As adolescence progresses, however, the influence of parental attachment wanes and peer relationships become more important as key predictors of delinquent behavior. As adolescence gives way to early adulthood, assortative mating becomes a key process that predicts continued involvement in delinquency.

BOX 7.12

The Face of Delinquency

Temperament: The Raw Ingredients of Delinquency and Problems Across Life

Temperament is the stable, largely innate tendency with which an individual experiences the environment and regulates his or her responses to that environment. Temperament reflects core differences in central nervous system reactivity that manifest in differential activity level, emotionality and mood, approach and withdrawal behavior, and self-regulation among individuals. It is likely that one's parents mentioned positive and negative aspects about their temperament.

Temperament is a very old scientific concept. Hippocrates developed the four humors model of distinct temperaments. These comprise the *melancholic* person, who was described as moody and anxious, with a predominance of black bile; the *sanguine* person who was described as cheerful, spirited, and good natured, with a predominance of blood; the *choleric* person, who was angry and irritable, with a predominance of yellow bile; and the *phlegmatic* person, who is slow to arouse and possesses substantial phlegm. In terms of relationship to delinquency, the choleric person would be most likely to be delinquent.

Drawing on this rich heritage, Matt DeLisi and Michael Vaughn advanced a developmental theory that uses temperament as its explanatory focus. They suggest that two temperamental constructs—effortful control and negative emotionality—are significantly predictive of self-regulation deficits and behavioral problems in infancy, toddlerhood, childhood, adolescence, and across adulthood. In addition, their theory asserts that people with poor self-regulation and generally negative moods also tend to have problematic interactions with others, such as parents, peers, and juvenile and criminal justice practitioners. Thus, their theory not only explains delinquency, but also the often negative consequences that delinquents face in their interactions with the legal system.

Unlike most theories of delinquency, which are heavily and often exclusively rooted in criminology, DeLisi and Vaughn's work is multidisciplinary and draws on studies of research subjects as young as infants and as old as octogenarians. There is considerable evidence supporting their work. Michelle Horner and her colleagues, for instance, found that temperament disturbances in infancy, specifically low self-regulation and poor negative emotional regulation, predict substance use disorders 20 years later. Other researchers have found stable evidence of people with particularly difficult temperaments relating to effortful control (self-control) and negative emotions, and these features are consistently associated with behavioral problems across life.

Criminologists have provided supporting evidence as well. Kevin Wolff and his colleagues found that adolescents with low effortful control and high negative emotionality are more likely to engage in delinquency and recidivate after release from juvenile custody compared to youth without these temperamental features. Similarly, Glenn Walters reported that temperamental features consistent with this theory are associated with parenting problems and are the origin of the self-control problems that are so strongly associated with delinquency.

The theory is likely to inspire additional tests, in part because so many academic disciplines draw on temperament as a foundational method of understanding behavior.

Matt DeLisi and Michael Vaughn, "Foundation for a Temperament-Based Theory of Antisocial Behavior and Criminal Justice System Involvement," *Journal of Criminal Justice* 42:10–25 (2014); Michelle Horner, Maureen Reynolds, Betty Braxter, Levent Kirisci, and Ralph Tarter, "Temperament Disturbances Measured in Infancy Progress to Substance Use Disorder 20 Years Later," *Personality and Individual Differences* 82:96–101 (2015); Charles Beekman, Jenae Neiderhiser, Kristin Buss, Eric Loken, Ginger Moore, Leslie Leve, Jody Ganiban, Daniel Shaw, and David Reiss, "The Development of Early Profiles of Temperament: Characterization, Continuity, and Etiology," *Child Development* 86:1794–1811 (2015); Hannah Snyder, Lauren Gulley, Patricia Bijttebier, Catharina Hartman, Albertine Oldehinkel, Amy Mezulis, Jami Young, and Benjamin Hankin, "Adolescent Emotionality and Effortful Control: Core Latent Constructs and Links to Psychopathology and Functioning," *Journal of Personality and Social Psychology* 109:1132–1149 (2015); Soo Jin Lee, C. Robert Cloninger, Soo Hyun Park, and Han Chae, "The Association of Parental Temperament and Character on Their Children's Behavior Problems," *PeerJ* 3:e1464 (2015); Kevin Wolff, Michael Baglivio, Alex Piquero, Michael Vaughn, and Matt DeLisi, "The Triple Crown of Antisocial Behavior: Effortful Control, Negative Emotionality, and Community Disadvantage," *Youth Violence and Juvenile Justice*, in press (2016); Glenn Walters, "Early Childhood Temperament, Maternal Monitoring, Reactive Criminal Thinking, and the Origin(s) of Low Self-Control," *Journal of Criminal Justice* 43:369–376 (2015).

Young adults who form strong bonds with prosocial partners are more likely to mature out of crime than those who do not.[80]

If developmental theorists are correct, different types of delinquency prevention programs must be designed for adolescents of different ages. For middle and junior high school children, such programs might focus on family ties. Programs aimed at building good relationships and effective communication between parents and their children would probably be most effective, as would programs that give parents the opportunity to spend more time with their children. By high school, however, such programs might be discontinued. Instead, it would be more important to focus on peer pressure, gang involvement, and other issues related to the peer groups of at-risk children. By late high school, intervention strategies should probably begin focusing on making effective transitions to the job market and teaching older adolescents how to avoid dysfunctional personal relationships.

Developmental theories also imply that the same intervention strategy is not likely to work for all people,

BOX 7.13

Delinquency Prevention

The Seattle Social Development Project

The Seattle Social Development Project is one of the longest running studies in the field of developmental criminology. This study was initiated in 1981 at the University of Washington by Joseph Weis and J. David Hawkins. It is based on a prospective longitudinal panel design, which means that it follows a group of subjects over a period of many years to foster an understanding of the various developments that occur throughout the life course. At its inception, the project enrolled 808 fifth graders from 18 public elementary schools in Seattle, Washington. Follow-up research continues to this day, as the subjects are now in their late 20s and many are starting families.

What makes the Seattle project different from other long-running developmental studies of delinquency is its focus on intervention and change. From the very beginning of the study, Hawkins and his colleagues sought not only to understand *why* children got into trouble but also to discover *how* the process could be interrupted.

The Seattle approach is multifaceted. The researchers believe that delinquency prevention must focus on family, schools, peer groups, and the community. Parents must be taught how to communicate and interact with their children in ways that encourage good behavior. Teachers are encouraged to use inclusive learning strategies that promote scholastic commitment in *all* students—not just those who show an affinity for learning. Perhaps most important, the adolescents themselves must be made to believe that they can achieve success through prosocial behavior. To this end, they must be taught the skills necessary to succeed in the conventional world and the value system associated with a prosocial lifestyle. In practical terms, this process equates to showing children that they have much to gain by studying and working hard and much to lose by becoming involved in deviant peer groups, gangs, and delinquent activity.

Does the Seattle project prevent delinquency? The available research strongly suggests that it does.

Repeated studies have found that children who receive the program interventions are less likely to be involved in delinquency, substance abuse, and other antisocial behaviors as compared with subjects who do not receive any interventions. Importantly, the treatment effects are not limited to delinquency prevention. Follow-up studies of the youths into early adulthood continue to show that children who receive the interventions are healthier; lead more successful, conventional lives; and are significantly less likely to engage in crime, substance use, and other harmful acts. Indeed, the longer subjects participate in the program, the more effective it seems to be. For instance, Catalano and Hawkins have shown that children enrolled in a program called "Catch Them Being Good" from grades 1 through 6 did significantly better than those children who participated in the program only in grades 5 and 6.

Another important prevention program is Communities That Care, a five-phase project that identifies community problems and the individuals and agencies that can address them, organizes them according to prevention-science principles, develops a community action plan, and implements and monitors the effectiveness of the plan. Communities That Care seeks to improve the behavioral health of youth and targets substance use, delinquency, and violence. Evaluation studies have shown that Communities That Care cities were 25 to 33% less likely than control communities to have health- and delinquency-related problems among youth.

The Seattle research is also unique in that it has synthesized both theories and research findings into practical, step-by-step programs that can be implemented by delinquency prevention agencies or school administrators. As such programs are implemented in more areas, researchers will have expanded opportunities to see developmental theory in action and determine whether it is an effective delinquency prevention strategy.

J. David Hawkins, Richard Catalano, Rick Kosterman, Robert Abbott, and Karl Hill, "Preventing Adolescent Health Risk Behaviors by Strengthening Protection during Childhood," *Archives of Pediatrics and Adolescent Medicine* 153:226–234 (1999); J. David Hawkins, Jie Guo, Karl Hill, Sara Battin-Pearson, and Robert Abbott, "Long-Term Effects of the Seattle Social Development Intervention on School Bonding Trajectories," *Applied Developmental Science* 5:225–236 (2001); J. David Hawkins, Rick Kosterman, Richard Catalano, Karl Hill, and Robert Abbott, "Promoting Positive Adult Functioning through Social Development Intervention in Childhood," *Archives of Pediatrics and Adolescent Medicine* 159:25–31 (2005); Heather Lonczak, Robert Abbott, J. David Hawkins, Rick Kosterman, and Richard Catalano, "Effects of the Seattle Social Development Project on Sexual Behavior, Pregnancy, Birth, and Sexually Transmitted Disease Outcomes by Age 21 Years," *Archives of Pediatrics and Adolescent Medicine* 156:438–447 (2002); Sabrina Oesterle, J. David Hawkins, Margaret Kuklinski, Abigail Fagan, Christopher Fleming, Isaac Rhew, Eric Brown, Robert Abbott, and Richard Catalano, "Effects of Communities That Care on Males' and Females' Drug Use and Delinquency 9 Years After Baseline in a Community-Randomized Trial," *American Journal of Community Psychology* 56:217–228 (2015); Communities That Care, retrieved February 15, 2016, from http://www.communitiesthatcare.net/; Seattle Social Development Research Group, retrieved February 15, 2016, from http://www.sdrg.org/.

even those within the same age group. A major reason that multiple approaches are needed is that people have different underlying genetic dispositions for certain types of antisocial behaviors. For instance, Moffitt's theory clearly implicates genetic causes as leading to

delinquency; however, her theory cites neuropsychological deficits as the main producer of delinquency. Recent research suggests that neuropsychological deficits are only part of the equation; ultimately, they interact with genetic risks to produce delinquency.

For instance, Kevin Beaver and his colleagues found that adolescents with neuropsychological deficits and risk-specific alleles of the MAOA gene are significantly likely to be delinquent, to engage in violent delinquency, and to have low self-control.[81] Consequently, the most serious and violent delinquents will be more difficult to help than normal delinquents.

Different subpopulations require different interventions. For life-course persistent offenders, the roots of their misbehavior often can be traced to psychosocial deficits and the process of cumulative disadvantage. Moffitt's theory suggests trying to minimize the deficits themselves or interrupting the disadvantage process to prevent delinquency in these individuals. In keeping with this perspective, it would be important to identify problem children as early as possible and teach them effective anger management and impulse control skills. Furthermore, it would be important to minimize any stigmatization or secondary deviation caused by excessive reactions to initial misbehavior; in this regard, Moffitt would likely agree with proponents of labeling theory. Many school districts, which are now doing their best to keep problem students integrated with other students, appear to be following this approach. Although school administrators likely do not use the same terminology as Moffitt, such programs have the equivalent aim of trying to minimize the process of cumulative disadvantage by not separating difficult children from their peers and keeping them in the mainstream educational system.[82]

Victor Battistich and his colleagues have shown that this approach may be successful through their evaluation of the Child Development Project, a comprehensive, 3-year program involving more than 5500 elementary school children from 24 schools distributed throughout the United States. Battistich and his colleagues found that the program increased prosocial behavior, academic achievement, attachment, and commitment to school. In addition, the program reduced substance abuse among all students. In schools that were more effective at implementing the program, the treatment effects were even stronger, resulting in significant declines in marijuana use, weapons possession, car theft, truancy, and threatening behavior.[83]

Of course, not all well-intentioned early childhood interventions are effective at reducing problem behaviors.

An evaluation of an Australian universal parenting program for mothers of 8-month-old children found that at age 24 months, children who received the program services had externalizing negative behaviors comparable to those demonstrated by children who did not receive the program. This program was also not effective at reducing depression and anxiety symptoms among mothers.[84]

For adolescence-limited offenders, these types of measures may not be necessary. Moffitt argues that these children commit delinquency largely from a desire to appear "grown up." It is unlikely that such individuals need early childhood skills training; in fact, providing it would probably be wasteful and even counterproductive. It is also less important to worry about a labeling or cumulative disadvantage process developing for this group of juveniles. Although fewer and fewer criminologists are willing to accept a "boys will be boys" view of delinquent behavior, Moffitt's theory suggests that this perspective might be acceptable, at least for adolescence-limited offenders who mostly engage in minor delinquency. Such individuals will likely age out of crime on their own when they enter adulthood. Thus interventions for adolescence-limited offenders could conceivably be limited to situational responses to each delinquent act. These responses should probably be kept as informal as possible, given that involving the formal criminal or juvenile justice systems might do more harm than good. If these ideas sound familiar, it is because they are precisely what Edwin Schur advocated decades ago with his notion of radical nonintervention.

Because developmental theory is relatively new, little applied research as yet has explored how effectively it might guide criminal justice policy in comparison to older theories. Many of the theories remain in the nascent stage, and some have not been tested in the real world. One notable exception, the **Seattle Social Development Project**, is discussed in some depth in **Box 7.13**, the "Delinquency Prevention" feature.

KEY TERMS

Seattle Social Development project
A leading study in the creation and application of developmental theory.

WRAP UP

THINKING ABOUT JUVENILE DELINQUENCY: CONCLUSIONS

Interest in developmental theories of delinquency was sparked by the observation that delinquent behavior seems to trend almost predictably over time. Specifically, it has been repeatedly observed that most illegal acts are committed by adolescents and young adults in contrast to young children and mature adults. Some criminologists began to recognize that deviant behavior is governed not only

by what is currently happening in an individual's life, but also by what has happened in the past. As criminologists subjected the age–crime curve to more sophisticated testing, however, they discovered that it was not nearly as universal as once thought. Although most delinquency does occur in adolescence and early adulthood, children exhibit very different patterns of behavior. This finding led developmental theorists to consider what causes these different patterns and to develop theories that could account for them. Developmental theories borrow heavily from earlier work, but ultimately move beyond it by paying special attention to the roles of time, maturation, and social institutions on delinquent behavior.

Developmental theory has important applications to juvenile justice policy. It suggests that to reduce delinquency, policy analysts must develop age-appropriate interventions as well as interventions that are tailored to particular groups of troubled children. A "one size fits all philosophy" is not likely to be successful given that the available research clearly suggests multiple risk factors are associated with deviant development for diverse groups of children at different stages of the life course.

Criminology has historically been a male-dominated discipline and feminist criminologists have reacted to and addressed this problem by exploring how the development of delinquent behavior and the experience of being delinquent are conditioned by gender.

CHAPTER SPOTLIGHT

- Developmental theories integrate the strongest elements of earlier theories of delinquency and suggest that key risk factors for offending change as individuals grow older.
- Protective factors are characteristics that protect individuals from committing delinquency. They include such behaviors as school attendance, employment, and having relationships with others not engaged in delinquency.
- Social institutions are the structural framework that provides turning points for delinquents to desist from offending and become conventional citizens.
- A variety of developmental theories have been proposed that share a common element: the role

of early family life as setting youths on either an antisocial or prosocial pathway.
- Because of their interdisciplinary design, developmental theories of delinquency are among the most popular approaches in criminology and lend themselves to linking behaviors in childhood, adolescence, and adulthood.
- Various typologies of delinquents have been developed, among which the most influential are categories defined by Patterson and Moffitt that distinguish offenders based on the age at which they begin committing antisocial behavior.

CRITICAL THINKING

1. If the seeds of delinquent behavior are planted in early childhood, is it too late to do anything when teenagers begin misbehaving? Should society require parenting classes to make sure that everyone "gets it right" during childhood?
2. If most adolescents "age out" of delinquency, why spend time and money on delinquency prevention?
3. How practical is Patterson's advice? Are there situations where social norms *force* parents into

coercive exchanges? Should parents spank children to stop a temper tantrum?
4. If assortative mating leads to adult crime, should steps be taken to restrict it? Would you favor a measure to deny marriage licenses to couples when both parties have criminal records?
5. Is there a place for "get tough on crime" initiatives within developmental theory? Can a "Scared Straight" program or a boot camp program be considered a turning point?

Female Delinquency Theories

OBJECTIVES

- Examine the ways that female identities and gender roles are framed by socialization, which results in gendered pathways into delinquency.

- Understand similarities and differences between girls and boys in terms of their delinquency.

- Assess the relationship between gender and violence, and examine how it has changed over time.

- Identify theoretical explanations for female delinquency.

- Identify juvenile justice policies that specifically target female offenders.

KEY TERMS

According to criminologist Allison Morris, "[C]riminology, like most academic disciplines, has been concerned with the activities and interests of men."[1] She is correct. For more than a century, the study of delinquency has focused almost exclusively on the behavior of males. This emphasis reflects the simple reality that males' law-violating behavior exceeds that of females in both frequency and seriousness. However, it also illustrates that criminology, as a discipline, has been dominated by men, who have often tended to see the world through their own eyes. In addition, the vast majority of people who create laws, make arrests, prosecute offenders, defend clients, and administer the juvenile justice system have been—and still are—males.

The United States has traditionally been a patriarchal society. **Patriarchy** describes a social, legal, and political climate that values male dominance and hierarchy. The existence of a patriarchy affects not only social structures (including the family and the economy), relationships, and definitions of appropriate social roles but also the way in which people (both males and females) perceive the world around them. Gender stratification as a product of patriarchy has led to unconscious assumptions about female and male behavior and misbehavior. Research suggests that a patriarchal social structure produces inequality and other social problems, including delinquency. In

fact, recent research has revealed that patriarchy may have a significant, independent effect on crime rates among women.[2]

To the extent that patriarchy extends into the academic arena of criminological research and writing, the delinquent behaviors of girls and the causes of those behaviors remained largely invisible until only recently. Although sex is one of the most statistically significant factors in predicting delinquency, criminologists have rarely shown much interest in including girls in their samples. Criminologist Joanne Belknap states the case quite succinctly:

> When the researchers did include girls in their samples, it was typically to see how girls fit into boys' equations. That is, rather than include in the study a means of assessing how girls' lives might be different from boys' lives, girls' delinquency has typically been viewed as peripheral and unnecessary to understanding juvenile offending and processing.[3]

When females have been studied as delinquents, the focus has nearly always been on comparing them to males: *why* girls are less delinquent than boys, *why* girls commit less serious crimes, *why* girls are more likely to be arrested for status offenses, and *how* the causes of female delinquency differ from those of male delinquency.

Although both the amount and seriousness of female delinquency has increased over the past few decades, many of the stronger correlates predictive of male delinquency (such as associating with antisocial peers, having an antisocial personality, and holding antisocial attitudes) have also been found to be strong predictors of female delinquency.[4] This chapter examines specific theories and explanations of female delinquency. We begin by examining how patriarchy and gender stratification affect the lives of girls as they grow up. Such an examination is critical for understanding the nature of female delinquency and the appropriateness of explanations put forth to explain it.

Growing Up Female

In Charlotte Bronte's 19th-century novel *Jane Eyre*, the young protagonist paces the roof of Thornfield Hall, frustrated over the contrast between her confined existence and the possibilities that lie in the larger world:

> Women need exercise for their faculties and a field for their efforts as much as their brothers do; they

KEY TERMS

patriarchy
A social system that enforces masculine control of the sexuality and labor power of women.

suffer from too rigid a restraint, too absolute a stagnation, precisely as men would suffer; and it is narrow-minded in their more privileged fellow-creatures to say that they ought to confine themselves to making puddings and knitting stockings, to playing on the piano and embroidering bags.[5]

The frustration that came from realizing the unfair situation she and other women faced in life because of their sex was not unique to Jane Eyre. In generation after generation, young girls have experienced the same frustration after realizing the same unfairness. Somehow, their place in society has been defined as being different from that of boys. But Jane Eyre's sense of a self-identity as a female was perhaps more consciously formed than that of many other young girls, and such awareness may in part explain why some girls feel more frustration than others over their defined place in society.

Throughout most of human history, girls have grown up in societies that have viewed them as "inferior" to boys. Jean Stafford illustrates the pervasiveness of this belief in her novel *The Mountain Lion*. Ralph, at age 11, already senses his superiority to his 9-year-old sister, Molly:

> It was natural for her to want to be a boy . . . but he knew for a fact that she couldn't be. Last week, he had had to speak sharply to her about wearing one of his outgrown Boy Scout shirts . . . she had not taken the "Be Prepared" thing off the pocket and he had to come out and say brutally, "Having that on a girl is like dragging the American flag in the dirt."[6]

What accounts for Jane Eyre's confinement to an existence less fulfilling than that of the men of her community or for Ralph's assumption of his superiority over his sister? The differences between girls and boys suggested in these two passages reflect widely held perceptions of the superiority of boys over girls. The relegation of girls to more restricted lives also reflects the influence of a patriarchal society, in which males have managed to maintain control over females. For both girls and boys, one's sense of self, and of oneself in relation to others, is strongly influenced by society's perceptions of gender roles. In patriarchal societies, then, growing up female is quite different from growing up male—and this difference has significant implications for how girls confront their lives (see **Box 8.1**, the "A Window on Delinquency" feature).

The limits that patriarchal societies impose on girls extend to criminal behavior. In some circumstances, the ways that gender is defined mean that certain types of delinquency are viewed as typically male or typically female. In the case of crimes, such as prostitution, patriarchal society frames the crime almost entirely as a female problem. In other ways,

BOX 8.1
A Window on Delinquency
Gendered Legacies of Crime

A large research program on the development of female delinquents is the Ohio Life Course Study, which tracked serious juvenile offenders who were in Ohio institutions in 1982. Although the Ohio Life Course Study included both boys and girls, there was a particular focus on female offenders and their development. More recently, Peggy Giordano and her colleagues have examined what became of those delinquent children, particularly how their delinquent history affects the social and antisocial development of their own children. Using both quantitative and qualitative data, Giordano has shed new light on how the intergenerational transmission of positive and negative personal and social factors contributes to legacies of crime.

Two competing explanations for the intergenerational transmission of crime are biological explanations (e.g., the genetic risk factors that antisocial individuals pass on to their children) and family dysfunction explanations (e.g., family dissolution, early childbearing, family violence). However, Giordano demonstrates the complex ways in which the children of formerly antisocial individuals develop. An important factor is the strength of the parent–child relationship and how it continues to be an important source of support for adult children. Giordano has found that adults who have strong bonds to their parent(s) are more likely to desist from delinquency and drug use compared to their peers with fractured parental relationships.

Some of the findings from the Ohio Life Course Study challenge long-held views about antisocial development, especially among women. For example, although poverty is an important risk factor for continued crime, its effect depends on whether women are pregnant or have already started families. In addition, the "wantedness" of the pregnancy as well as the woman's relationship with the biological father condition the relationship between juvenile delinquency and adult crime. Finally, although parenthood generally leads to desistance from crime, that relationship does not hold for women who are highly antisocial and enmeshed in a criminal lifestyle. In other words, legacies of crime are complex and depend on an intricate blending of person, relationship, and social dynamics.

The gendered legacies of crime are not limited to Giordano's Ohio data. Studies from other regions and nations have produced similar findings on delinquent behavior among females and the gender-specific ways that delinquency harms them, jeopardizes their motherhood status, and contributes to behavioral problems among the delinquent's children. Christopher Salas-Wright and his colleagues studied a nationwide sample of pregnant adolescents and found evidence of a subgroup of girls with extensive substance abuse problems during their pregnancy. These girls experienced very little parental warmth, parental monitoring, or parental involvement in their life and were significantly disengaged from school. Because of their extreme drug use during pregnancy, their children were at great risk for similar behavioral problems and delinquency. Cohort studies in Stockholm, Sweden similarly show that female delinquents have significant victimization histories, face greater social exclusion because of their conduct problems, and have complicated family relationships with their children, many of whom have similar delinquent behaviors.

Peggy Giordano, *Legacies of Crime: A Follow-Up of the Children of Highly Delinquent Girls and Boys* (New York: Cambridge University Press, 2010); Ryan Schroeder, Peggy Giordano, and Stephen Cernkovich, "Adult Child–Parent Bonds and Life Course Criminality," *Journal of Criminal Justice* 38:562–571 (2010); Peggy Giordano, Patrick Seffrin, Wendy Manning, and Monica Longmore, "Parenthood and Crime: The Role of Wantedness, Relationships with Partners, and SES," *Journal of Criminal Justice* 39:405–416 (2011); Christopher Salas-Wright, Michael Vaughn, and Jenny Ugalde, "A Typology of Substance Use among Pregnant Teens in the United States," *Maternal and Child Health Journal* 20:646–654 (2016); Felipe Estrada and Anders Nilsson, "Does It Cost More to Be a Female Offender? A Life-Course Study of Childhood Circumstances, Crime, Drug Abuse, and Living Conditions," *Feminist Criminology* 7:196–219 (2012).

patriarchal society and its gender roles serve to insulate girls from delinquency. For instance, Jean Bottcher has shown that traditional gender roles insulate girls in very high-risk, crime-ridden communities from delinquency because the criminal population believes that girls should engage in certain behaviors (e.g., taking care of children) and not others (e.g., hanging out and getting into trouble). Megan Bears Augustyn and Jean McGloin studied a national sample of female and male delinquents and found that unstructured and unsupervised socializing with peers was strongly associated with predatory forms of delinquency among boys, but had no effect among girls, in part because this risk factor was not compatible with gender expectations for girls. In contrast, the peer effects were associated with substance use delinquency among girls, in part because their delinquency is largely defined by drug use.[7]

The long shadow of patriarchy even extends to behaviors where females are "worse" than males, such as relational aggression. **Relational aggression** refers

KEY TERMS

relational aggression
Behaviors that employ damage to relationships, or the threat of damage to relationships, as a means to harm another person.

to behaviors that focus on damage to relationships, or the threat of damage to relationships, as a means to harm another person. These behaviors can be either direct or indirect. For example, a direct relationally aggressive act might involve telling a friend that she cannot come to your birthday party unless she does what you want her to do. An indirect relationally aggressive act might involve starting a rumor about someone to damage that person's reputation or giving an acquaintance the "cold shoulder" to ostracize that individual. Unlike physical aggression, which is much more commonly used by males, relational aggression is more often used by females. A range of studies of preschool children, elementary school children, and adolescents, based on investigative techniques such as researcher observations, teacher reports, peer reports, and self-reports, supports the notion that relational aggression is *the* "female" form of aggression.[8]

One reason why relational aggression is more common among girls is that females are more inclined to not only invest more heavily in relationships than males but also derive more satisfaction from interpersonal relationships. In addition, relational aggression is consistent with stereotypes about females—that they are prone to gossip, manipulative, and emotional—and children pick up on these stereotypes and expectations of appropriate behavior as they age. The importance of gender roles is explored next.

The Development of Girls' Gender Roles

The creation of **gender-role identities** begins at conception (given ultrasound identification of the child's sex) with the announcement of "It's a girl!" or "It's a boy!" Almost immediately, in describing their infants, parents start using typical gender stereotypes. In one study, parents described boy babies as being firm, large featured, alert, and strong, while girl babies were characterized as delicate, fine featured, soft, and small. Parents also respond to toddlers differently on the basis of the child's sex. They discourage rough-and-tumble play by girls and doll play by boys. They listen to girls and respond to them more attentively when girls are gentle or talk softly, but they attend more to boys when boys demonstrate assertiveness. Parents encourage dependence in girls and independence in boys. By age 4 or 5, children have become aware of their gender and the behaviors appropriate to it.[9]

Although prescriptions and proscriptions regarding gender roles have shifted in many ways over the past few decades (i.e., women now account for the majority of college enrollments and law school admissions,

Relational aggression entails seemingly benign acts, such as keeping secrets and spreading rumors about other people. However, its effects can be serious.

© MBI_Images/iStock/Getty.

Should girls and boys be socialized in near-identical ways to try to eliminate gender differences? If so, should girls be raised like boys, or vice versa?

© BlueOrange Studio/Shutterstock.

participate extensively in professional sports, engage in street-level police patrol, and are killed in combat in the armed forces), a great amount of everyday socializing into gender roles has not evaporated entirely. For example, research has shown that early-adolescent daughters of mothers who are employed are more likely to hold nontraditional gender-role attitudes than daughters of unemployed mothers.[10]

Throughout much the 20th century, girls' gender roles were reinforced through toys and games in early adolescence. Boys frequently were given toys that encouraged creativity and manipulation, such as construction and chemistry sets, whereas girls were given toys that encouraged passivity and nurturance, such as stuffed animals and dolls. Today, girls are more likely to play in small, unstructured groups; their games have few rules and emphasize cooperation rather than competition. In contrast, boys typically play in larger groups, often teams; their games have

KEY TERMS

gender-role identities
Individual identities based on sexual stereotypes.

more complex rules and often emphasize cooperation to facilitate competing.

Going to school provides both girls and boys with ample opportunities to learn the *four Rs*: reading, 'riting, 'rithmetic, and (gender) roles. Conscious and unconscious patterns of interaction between teachers and students as well as the formal and informal activities of girls and boys in school encourage stereotyped gender roles. Girls receive reinforcement from teachers for being passive, verbal, and dependent, whereas boys are encouraged to explore, examine how things work, and be independent.

Schools also provide avenues for children to develop self-esteem. For boys, these avenues are being tough, developing a good physique, participating in sports (including competition and aggressiveness), being cool (not showing emotions), and being good at something (e.g., sports, school, cars, and sex). Although girls' involvement in sports has increased significantly, other avenues for building self-esteem in girls were traditionally more problematic: being pretty, being popular, being liked as sociable and pleasant, and being preoccupied with body weight, which may lead to eating disorders (e.g., anorexia or bulimia). In general, teachers encourage boys to be more assertive in the classroom, have higher expectations for male students, and believe that male students are better at math and science.[11]

The socialization into sex-appropriate gender roles for adolescents has also been reinforced in the home. In traditional family arrangements, girls are kept more dependent and cloistered through closer supervision and more restrictive rules. Parents encourage girls to stay at home or in close proximity to their mothers, to avoid risks, and to fear social disapproval. Girls generally join groups later than boys, are less likely than boys to have a regular meeting place outside the home, and are less likely to belong to single-sex groups at all. Conversely, parents typically encourage boys to be independent, aggressive, and group oriented, and they allow boys to date earlier than girls, to stay out later than girls with their friends, to be left alone at home, and to participate in organized activities.

All agents of socialization—including the family, schools, work, and the juvenile justice system—play a part in gender socialization and shaping girls' gender roles. Stephen Gavazzi and his colleagues studied the life histories of 305 youths who had been detained in juvenile facilities. Female delinquents were significantly more likely than boys to be detained for family violence and psychiatric problems. The family violence problems were especially noteworthy because girls were likely to be detained for exhibiting "out-of-control" types of behavior and not obeying their parents. Although male delinquents similarly caused their parents trouble, they were not detained for violating gender roles within the family. Instead, boys were detained for more serious violent and property delinquent acts. These effects often continue into adulthood. A study of chronic delinquents found that girls who experienced parental divorce were three times more likely to be arrested as an adult compared with girls from intact families. In addition, exposure to family violence increased the likelihood of adult arrest for girls nearly threefold; whereas for males, prior delinquency and prior juvenile justice system involvements were the best predictors of adult arrest.[12]

The importance of socialization to the development of girls has also been emphasized by a surprising line of research—that dealing with genetics. A recent study by Jason Boardman and his colleagues explored gender differences in **resilience**, which is the ability to withstand environmental stressors and general forms of adversity. They found that 52% of resilience in males is explained by genes, whereas just 38% of resilience in females has a genetic origin. Thus, in females, 62% of the ability to overcome environmental stress comes from environmental sources.[13] For this reason, negative components of gender socialization render girls more vulnerable to stresses that cause problem behaviors, such as delinquency (for a provocative counter argument, see **Box 8.2**, the "Delinquency Controversy" feature).

Girls' Identities

What are the effects of gender-role socialization and other constructs on girls' identities and self-esteem? The patterns lead many girls to identify with traditional female roles, anticipate economic dependence and a more restricted adult status, and accept lesser political, social, and sexual privileges than those accorded to boys. Such socialization creates narrower boundaries of opportunities for girls than for boys and instills in them a self-perception of powerlessness and dependence. Girls also learn that to be feminine means to nurture, prompting them to focus on relationships.

Carol Gilligan suggests that girls are raised to identify with the primary caretaker (the mother) and, therefore, experience a strong bonding relationship that becomes a model for the rest of their lives. This emphasis on relationships or "making connections" also encourages in adolescent girls the development of a "morality of response" or "ethic of care," which emphasizes the creation and maintenance of interdependence and responsiveness in relationships. Males, by contrast, develop values or ethics of justice, fairness, rationality, and individuality. Female moral reasoning, because it focuses on care, connection, and relationships, is

KEY TERMS

resilience
The ability to withstand environmental stressors and general forms of adversity.

BOX 8.2

Delinquency Controversy

Gendered Socialization: Perception or Reality?

Parents raise girls as girls and boys as boys from not long after conception to adulthood, correct? Scores of studies have demonstrated the multifaceted ways that gender socialization creates different realities for girls and boys, and these differences have important implications for social development and maladjustment. But not all research supports these conclusions.

In a landmark study, Hugh Lytton and David Romney conducted a meta-analysis of 172 studies to see if parents socialized their children according to gender norms. They produced a number of counterintuitive findings:

- Across studies, there were no significant differences in the ways that parents socialized their children by sex/gender.
- Where there were significant differences, the size of these differences were small.
- Among studies conducted in North America, 18 of 19 failed to produce evidence of gender social-ization. The only significant effect was parental encouragement of sex-typed activities, and both mothers and fathers were likely to push involvement in sex-typed activities.
- In Westernized nations, there is a significant differ-ence in the use of physical or corporal punishment, and it is more likely to be applied to boys. This can be interpreted as potentially reflecting a gender norm to not use physical force against females.

- Fathers are more likely than mothers to differentiate socialization of their children based on the gender of the child.

Lytton and Romney concluded that because there is little evidence for gender socialization, other factors must explain behavioral differences between girls and boys. One hypothesis is that socialization practices are experienced differently by girls and boys based on other constructs. For example, Danielle Boisvert and her colleagues found that self-control—a construct that is increasingly shown to be largely genetic in origin—is an important variable that explains gender differences in delinquency. Boisvert and her collaborators found that maternal attachment and maternal rejection were associated with higher levels of delinquency, but their effects operated through lower levels of self-control found among boys. Robert Eme reviewed sex differences in delinquency and other forms of externalizing behaviors and reported that there are many biosocial variables that favor girls, in the sense that greater behavioral risk is conferred by male gender. For instance, girls have advantages in terms of intelligence, temperamental features, self-regulation, attentional control, genetic protective factors, and reduced likelihood of neurobehavioral disorders relative to boys. In other words, future investigators will specify how parenting practices operate on mostly biopsychological constructs that in turn are predictive of delinquency.

Hugh Lytton and David Romney, "Parents' Differential Socialization of Boys and Girls: A Meta-Analysis," *Psychological Bulletin* 109:267–296 (1991); Danielle Boisvert, Jamie Vaske, Justine Taylor, and John P. Wright, "The Effects of Differential Parenting on Sibling Differences in Self-Control and Delinquency among Brother–Sister Pairs," *Criminal Justice Review* 37:5–23 (2012); Robert Eme, "Sex Differences in the Prevalence and Expression of Externalizing Behavior," pages 239–266 in Theodore Beauchaine and Stephen Hinshaw (eds.), *The Oxford Handbook of Externalizing Spectrum Disorders* (New York: Oxford University Press, 2016).

likely to discourage girls from framing attitudes and responses to situations in ways that would produce competition, conflict, or aggressiveness.[14]

Gender identity has been shown to influence delin-quency. An interesting study that speaks to this issue was conducted by Lisa Broidy and her colleagues, who compared gender differences in empathy and delinquency. Broidy and her colleagues used two very different samples, 425 high school students from Philadelphia and 232 youths who had served time in the California Youth Authority. Across all groups, empathy was negatively related to serious violence. In other words, adolescents who could empathize with other people and potential victims were unlikely to physically harm them. Conversely, youths who could not feel the common humanity of other people could fairly easily use physical force against them. Perhaps because of their gender socialization, girls were observed to be significantly more empathic than boys in terms of emotional and behavioral expression. They also

found that female delinquents were more empathic than male nondelinquents.[15]

As this line of research suggests, girls begin to operate very early within a network of intimate interpersonal ties that reinforce their acceptance of a more nur-turing and caring role. Also, because girls are more likely to define themselves relationally, they do not develop the same precise and rigid ego boundaries common to boys.[16] According to Erik Erikson, "Much of a young woman's identity is already defined in her kind of attractiveness and in the selective nature of her search for the man (or men) by whom she wishes to be sought."[17]

In a 3-year study of 100 teenage girls in London, Sue Lees explored some of the problems of identity for adolescent girls. Lees found that a girl's sexuality is central to the way she is judged in everyday life:

To speak of a woman's reputation is to invoke her sexual behavior, but to speak of a man's reputation is to refer to his personality, exploits, and his standing in the community. For men sexual reputation is, in the main, separated from the evaluation of moral behavior and regarded as private and incidental.[18]

Although a boy's social standing is typically enhanced by his sexual exploits, a girl's standing can be destroyed by simple insinuations; therefore, she is often required to defend her sexual reputation to *both* boys and girls. The use of slang terms and insults, such as "slut" or "whore," functions to control the activities and social reputations of girls. A girl need not actually have slept with a boy to have her reputation threatened. As one girl commented, "When there're boys talking and you've been out with more than two, you're known as the crisp they're passing around . . . . The boy's alright but the girl's a bit of scum."

The possibility of being labeled "bad" or a "slut" is a form of moral censure reflecting dominant perceptions of departure (or potential departure) from male conceptions of female sexuality. More important, such terms are applied to "any form of social behavior by girls that would define them as autonomous from the attachment to and domination by boys."[19] According to Meda Chesney-Lind and Randall Shelden, teenage girls are coerced into cultivating a hegemonic, heterosexualized "teen femininity" that "recreates and reinforces the sexual double standard by labeling girls who are too overtly sexual as 'sluts'" and that ties a girl's self-esteem and prestige far more to external factors (primarily male approval) than is typical for boys. Indeed, many problems relating to social media, such as sexting and sending sexually provocative photos via smart phone, are more problematic for girls than boys. In many ways, a girl's apparent sexual behavior is seen as a barometer, testing her capacity to learn appropriate codes of social conduct with boys.[20]

Gendered Pathways into Delinquency

Today, the understanding of the gender–delinquency relationship owes much to the developmental or life-course perspective that is currently popular in criminology. The developmental perspective is interested in the ways that life events occurring during childhood influence outcomes during adolescence and adulthood. Negative events or circumstances, often called *risk factors*, increase the likelihood that young people will be delinquent. Positive events or circumstances, often called *protective factors*, decrease the likelihood that young people will become delinquent (or help them desist from crime if they have already engaged in delinquency). In fact, Joanne Belknap has described developmental criminology as directly compatible with feminist perspectives on crime:

In many ways the life-course [developmental] perspective is seemingly pro-feminist in nature: It purports to address significant childhood and adult experiences and to view how these, particularly social bonds, are related to delinquent, criminal, and deviant behavior.[21]

Scholars have examined how pathways into delinquency unfold into delinquent careers among women. For example, Marguerite Warren and Jill Rosenbaum studied 159 women who had been incarcerated in California. They found that women had similar criminal careers as men in the sense that they displayed a generalized involvement in many types of crimes, such as violence, property, and drug offenses. However, women were disproportionately likely to have arrests for prostitution, theft, forgery, fraud, and drug violations. Other criminologists have also shown that women's offending careers feature mostly arrests relating to drug abuse. Another major concept in gendered pathways of crime is that girls are more likely to develop internalizing behaviors as a result of childhood abuse and adversity, whereas boys are more likely to develop externalizing behaviors as a result of childhood abuse and adversity. Using data from the Lehigh Longitudinal Study, Hyunzee Jung and her colleagues found that childhood abuse significantly increased internalizing symptoms, such as anxiety and depression, among girls, and these problems facilitated drug problems. Internalizing behaviors were significantly associated with adult crime for girls as well, but these effects were not found among boys.[22]

Stephen Cernkovich and his colleagues studied female offenders from 1982 to 1995. In 1982, they compared two groups of delinquent girls who were living in juvenile institutions; one group was less delinquent and one group was severely delinquent (these are the youths from the Ohio Life Course Study previously discussed in Box 8.1). On many measures, the severely delinquent group had more risk factors. For instance, these girls had less family caring and trust and less communication with parents, received less parental control and supervision, were subjected to more parental conflict, and received less disapproval of their delinquent behaviors from their parents. Both groups of girls, however, experienced comparable levels of physical abuse, sexual abuse, money worries, and changes in residence. At follow-up, the members of the two delinquent groups—who were now criminal women—closely resembled one another on virtually all variables.

Their study also highlighted the fact that early childhood abuse can result in a serious criminal career. For instance, those girls who had the worst sexual abuse histories were *334%* more likely than others to become chronic adult offenders. Girls who were physically abused as minors were *600%* more likely than other girls to be habitual criminals. Finally, those girls who experienced both forms of

victimization were an additional *260%* more likely to be serious offenders.[23]

Compared to male delinquents, female offenders typically have significantly more extensive victimization histories, including sexual, physical, and emotional abuses. Often, this abuse begins at home when girls are very young, especially if there is a nonbiological male parental or authority figure in the household. A typical response to this abuse—and one that is consistent with Regoli and Hewitt's theory of differential oppression—is for girls to run away from home; the resulting exposure to street life often leads them to engage in delinquency. When girls have these experiences at relatively young ages, the victimization, oppressive home life, and vulnerabilities of the street collectively lead them toward drug use. Bipasha Biswas and Michael Vaughn found that girls in juvenile confinement facilities engage in an array of serious and unhealthy delinquencies, including intravenous polydrug use, risky sexual behavior, and recurrent institutional involvement. They also have severe histories of childhood trauama.[24] Indeed, Ronald Mullis and his colleagues describe the typical female delinquent as one who is young, impoverished, likely to have experienced abuse or exploitation, an abuser of drugs and alcohol, and likely to have unmet medical and mental health needs; lacks hope for the future; and perceives that life is oppressive.[25]

The gendered part of this development equation centers on how female offenders live on the streets and sustain their drug and delinquent careers. In many ways, the abuses that female criminals experience reflect their sexualized and subordinated status in a patriarchal society. For example, Kimberly Kempf-Leonard and Pernilla Johansson's study of more than 6400 juvenile offenders in Texas found that serious delinquent careers often began with seemingly minor offenses, such as running away. However, many girls in their study ran away from home and were living on the streets to avoid physical and sexual abuses occurring in their home. Once on the street, as Kempf-Leonard and Johansson discovered, the runaway girls often had much worse drug problems than male runaways, were prone to join gangs, and were likely to commit diverse forms of delinquency.[26]

Other studies have also explored this line of research. Among a sample of women who had been arrested a minimum of 30 times, Matt DeLisi found that, in an ironic twist, their status as sexual objects helped many female offenders survive—namely, by engaging in prostitution. Along with theft, forgery, and fraud, prostitution is the primary way that women on the streets obtain money, with this money often quickly used to obtain drugs to help these women "numb themselves." Darrell Steffensmeier and his colleagues' analysis of *UCR* data similarly found that larceny, forgery, fraud, and embezzlement were among the most common offenses of female delinquents.[27]

When Kim English studied 200 women prisoners, she found that forgery was the primary criminal offense committed by the women, but they also dabbled in an assortment of offenses. More women reported committing assaults than men in her study, but women tended to commit just one assault in a year, which was usually domestic in nature. When men were involved in assaults, they committed several annually against both partners and strangers. Women also reported greater frequency of participation in drug sales than men, primarily because women's income from drug trafficking was lower than that for male offenders. This finding suggests that a "pay gap" may even exist among female and male drug dealers.[28]

Cathy Spatz Widom has chronicled the *cycle of violence* whereby physical abuse, sexual abuse, and neglect incurred during childhood dramatically increase an individual's risks for delinquency and a host of maladaptive behaviors during adolescence and adulthood, especially among girls who are sexually abused.[29] Along with various forms of victimization, the cycle of violence is also characterized by social isolation and marginality. Peggy Giordano and her colleagues found that delinquent girls are often those who have difficulty in school and are labeled as outcasts, which in turn fuels more antisocial behavior by these females. Over time, girls with these kinds of backgrounds associate with other troubled youth, which further increases their chances for additional victimization and withdrawal from conventional peers. As these women cycle in and out of jail and prison, they are left behind their nondelinquent peers in terms of their job skills and often become reliant on governmental assistance.[30]

Evidence suggests that abusive backgrounds and victimization experiences are manifested differently among females based on race. For instance, Kristi Holsinger and Alexander Holsinger compared African American and white female delinquents and found racial differences in their responses to abuse. Although both groups experienced significant trauma, African American girls had more violent crimes in their delinquent histories and generally better mental health. White girls internalized their violence and had more severe mental health problems and self-injurious behaviors, such as suicide attempts. The role of race and ethnicity is also seen in studies of gang-involved female delinquents. Eryn O'Neal and her colleagues found that African American and Hispanic gang-involved females experienced many problems even after leaving the gang. For instance, 40% were attacked by rival gangs even after they had left the gang, nearly 60% were still viewed as gang members by police even though they had left, and more than 14% had family members attacked because they left the gang.[31] In this way, the gendered pathway to delinquency illustrates a cycle where one type of abuse and victimization engenders many more, a process that Abigail Fagan calls the "gender cycle of violence."[32]

Girls and Violence

Female delinquency has been increasing in recent years at a faster rate than delinquency committed by males. Concern is also growing about the increase in violent delinquency among girls. To better understand how much violence is committed by girls, including whether rates are increasing, decreasing, or remaining steady, and to assess the types of violent delinquency girls commit, the Office of Juvenile Justice and Delinquency Prevention convened the Girls Study Group to guide the development, testing, and dissemination of strategies to reduce or prevent girls' involvement in delinquency and violence. Recently, this agency produced a report with several important findings:[33]

- Girls are arrested for simple assault more today than in previous years based on official, victimization, and self-report data.
- Nevertheless, the actual incidence of serious violence has not increased, thus there does not appear to be any looming national crisis of serious violence among adolescent girls.
- In terms of peer violence, girls fight with peers to gain status, to defend their sexual reputation, and to act in self-defense against sexual harassment.
- Girls fight at home with their parents more frequently than boys do.
- When girls fight at school, it is more likely the result of self-defense, feelings of hopelessness, and negative teacher labeling.
- Like boys, girls in disadvantaged neighborhoods are at increased risk to commit violence and be victimized by violence.

Increasingly, criminologists are studying female delinquents for some of the characteristics that seem to buffer them from delinquency relative to the characteristics of boys. Robert Eme suggested that the "substantial sex difference [in antisocial behavior and especially serious, violent delinquent behavior] is due in great part to the greater male vulnerability to a host of neurodevelopmental risk factors that in interaction with family and environmental adversity exponentially increase the probability of violent behavior."[34] To what extent are delinquencies among girls acts of rebellion against the constraints of the restricting and oppressive sex roles imposed on them during adolescence? If they are not revolts, what might account for girls' involvement in delinquency? When girls do violate the law, why are their delinquencies generally less serious, and how might we account for the increasing involvement of girls in delinquent behavior? Finally, how adequate are male-oriented criminological theories in explaining

female delinquency? The next section discusses theories of female delinquency in detail.

Theories of Female Delinquency

Criminology as a discipline has, by and large, been the domain of males. As a consequence, it should come as no surprise that early explanations of female delinquency reflected only male perceptions of females. For the most part, those perceptions evolved from beliefs about innate or biological differences between males and females. Even when sociological explanations of delinquency entered the mainstream, the theories were largely developed from studies of boys; girls were still viewed as "naturally" less delinquent. The relative inattention given to female delinquency was also due in part to the fact that most criminological theory has been policy driven; that is, because males made up most of the delinquent population in the courts and correctional institutions, policies designed to respond to delinquency sought out theories that dealt primarily with boys.

An example of this perspective is seen in research on attractiveness. Attractiveness is an important characteristic that influences how people are viewed and evaluated in a variety of ways. Researchers in Canada have found that parents often treat their own children differently, with attractive children benefiting from more attention. For example, attractive children—defined as those with good facial symmetry, cleanliness, nice attire, and other features—get more positive attention, get less negative attention or punishment, and are better protected than their less attractive siblings. Consistent with the arguments of feminists who believe that our patriarchal society defines people in sexual terms often based on attractiveness, these findings are intriguing.

Attractiveness has also been found to be a correlate of delinquency. When Naci Mocan and Edral Tekin studied the effects of attractiveness on delinquency and other life outcomes among a national sample of Americans between the ages of 18 and 26, they found that being very attractive reduced involvement in crime. Conversely, being unattractive increased criminal involvement in a variety of crimes, such as burglary and drug violations.

Attractiveness also has a significant and independent effect on relationships with teachers, grades, high school social history, adult vocabulary, and labor market performance. These effects are *especially pronounced* for females. In addition, very attractive women (but not very attractive men) receive more favorable treatment from the criminal justice system—that is, they are more likely to receive positive discretion, such as being let go with a warning instead of being issued a ticket. In some circumstances, it certainly pays to be considered attractive. If girls garner human capital

from their looks, it is likely that looks will continue to be a source of status in society.[35]

As more women have entered the field of criminology over the past 30 years, they have brought with them a greater interest in female delinquency, its nature and causes, and differences in its origins relative to the origins of male delinquency. In this section, we examine biological and psychological theories of female delinquency, consider how sociological theories may apply to girls, and look at the more recent feminist and critical theories.

Biological and Psychological Theories

Although the earliest explanations of delinquency located its causes in demons and later in free will, they did not make causal distinctions on the basis of the sex of the delinquent. It was not until the rise of the positive school of criminology in the 19th century, with its emphasis on biological and psychological causes of behavior, that female law violators were seen as uniquely "different" from male criminals.

In *The Female Offender*, published in 1895, Cesare Lombroso and William Ferrero applied to females the principles of Lombroso's earlier work on the male criminal. Inasmuch as criminals were viewed as "throwbacks," or atavistic by their nature, the female criminal was also seen as biologically distinct and inferior to noncriminal women. Lombroso and Ferrero believed that women ranked lower on the evolutionary scale than men and, therefore, were closer to their "primitive" origins. Consequently, they suggested, female criminals were not as visible as their male counterparts and showed fewer signs of degeneracy than males.

According to Lombroso and Ferrero, women are naturally more childlike, less intelligent, lacking in passion, more maternal, and weak—characteristics that make them less inclined to commit crimes (see **Box 8.3**, the "Theory in a Nutshell" feature). Women also share other traits with children: Their moral sense is deficient and they are "revengeful, jealous, [and] inclined to vengeances of a refined cruelty." However,

because "women are big children; their evil tendencies are . . . more varied than men's, but generally . . . latent. When . . . awakened and excited they produce results proportionately greater." Therefore, when a woman does turn to crime, she is "a monster," as "her wickedness must have been enormous before it could triumph over so many obstacles."

For Lombroso and Ferrero, women's criminality is a product of their biology—yet this biology also keeps most women from crime. To the extent that women's nature is antithetical to crime, and with criminality seen as a characteristic more common to men, the female criminal is not only an abnormal woman, but also biologically more like a man, albeit "often more ferocious." It should be noted that Lombroso and Ferrero believed most female delinquents were only "occasional criminals," as were most male delinquents. The physical features of these occasional female delinquents did not appear to reflect any atavistic degeneration, according to these theorists, and their basic moral character was essentially the same as that of their "normal sisters."[36]

In 1923, in *The Unadjusted Girl*, W. I. Thomas postulated that males and females are biologically different. Although both males and females are motivated by natural biological instincts leading to "wish fulfillment," how they approach the fulfillment of the wishes differs. Thomas identified four distinct categories of wishes:

- The desire for new experience
- The desire for security
- The desire for response
- The desire for recognition

Thomas believed that women naturally have stronger desires for response and love than men and that they are capable of more varied types of love as demonstrated by maternal love, a characteristic atypical of males. This intense need to give and receive love often leads girls into delinquency, especially sexual delinquency, as they use sex as a means to fulfill other wishes.

Nevertheless, Thomas did not believe girls are inherently delinquent. Rather, he saw their behaviors as resulting from choices circumscribed by social rules and moral codes designed to guide people's actions as they attempt to fulfill their wishes. Girls, more than boys, are limited by their gender roles in society and consequently are more likely to become demoralized and frustrated as they perceive their deprivations.[37]

The origins of female delinquency, according to Thomas, are found in the girl's impulsive desire to obtain "amusement, adventure, pretty clothes, favorable notice, distinction and freedom in the larger world. . . . Their sex is used as a condition of the realization of other wishes. It is their capital." Such impulsive behavior is also likely to drive girls into the arms of boys who will take advantage of them,

BOX 8.3

Theory in a Nutshell

Cesare Lombroso and William Ferrero

According to Lombroso and Ferrero, female criminals are biologically distinct from and inferior to noncriminal women. Because women rank lower on the evolutionary scale than men generally, criminal females are not as visible as male offenders and show fewer signs of degeneracy.

frequently leading to pregnancy, prostitution, and eventual ruin.

In *The Criminality of Women*, Otto Pollak argued that women are as criminal as men but that their criminality is hidden or "masked." The masking of their crimes and delinquencies is a result of "natural" physiological differences in the sexes, as well as the tendency of males to overlook or excuse offenses by women. Pollak believed that the physiological nature of women makes them more deceitful than men. Owing to their lesser physical strength as compared to men, women must resort to indirect or deceitful means to carry out crimes or to vent their aggression; women also are more likely to be "instigators" and men "perpetrators" of crime. Pollak further argued that social norms force women to conceal their menstruation each month and to misrepresent or conceal information regarding sex from their children, at least for some time. Pollak thought that social norms "thus make concealment . . . in the eyes of women socially required and commendable, . . . condition[ing] them to a different attitude toward veracity than men."[38]

In Pollak's view, the lower rates of crime found among females reflect men's deference and protective attitude toward women, whereby female offenses are generally overlooked or excused by males—a premise known as the **chivalry hypothesis**. Male victims of female delinquencies, police officers, prosecutors, judges, and juries, Pollak suggested, are hesitant to report, arrest, prosecute, and convict women. Thus the actual rate of female delinquencies is much higher than the official statistics reported in the *UCR*.

Recent Biological and Developmental Explanations

The idea that girls' behavior is largely controlled by their biology, physiology, or sexuality continued to be the subject of studies for some time, although today it is rare to find any expression of the "natural" inferiority of girls in criminological literature. Instead, many of the more recent studies from this perspective suggest that girls' biological nature interacts with social forces, usually those found in the family, to produce delinquency.

In *Delinquency in Girls*, John Cowie and his colleagues describe female delinquency as being dominated by sexual misbehaviors. They argue that female delinquents are unhappy and that "their unhappiness is commonly related to disturbed emotional relationships with the parents." These theorists think that delinquent girls often come from families characterized by low moral standards, poor discipline, conflict, and disturbed family relations. In addition, delinquent girls are more likely than delinquent boys to have pathological psychiatric problems and overall impaired physical health. For Cowie and his colleagues, the notion that girls are less likely than boys to be delinquent is accounted for, in part, the fact that girls are more timid and lacking in enterprise.[39]

The belief that girls are led to sexual delinquencies because of dysfunctional families and unsatisfactory peer relations is also presented in Clyde Vedder and Dora Somerville's *The Delinquent Girl*. Feeling unloved and facing the disapproval of family and peers make some girls more likely to engage in sexual delinquency to gain acceptance and love. Official female delinquency, according to Vedder and Somerville, is dominated by five offense categories (listed here in order of decreasing frequency): running away, incorrigibility, sexual offenses, probation violation, and truancy. These authors suggest that running away and incorrigibility are typically the less "serious" charges filed, even though such behavior is actually nearly always linked to sexual misbehaviors. To "protect" the girl, officials are more likely to charge her with the more innocuous offense, thereby masking the true extent of sexual delinquency among girls.[40]

A more recent and exciting area of research that investigates gender differences is the field of *evolutionary psychology*, which argues that male and female behaviors represent adaptations to the environment that have evolved over evolutionary time. As is the case in criminology, most researchers in evolutionary psychology have focused on male adaptations as a way to explain gender differences in offending. For instance, violent delinquency is viewed as a way for males to compete for sexual partners to guarantee their survival. Owing to this evolutionary development, males are psychologically more competitive, take more risks, and are prone to using violence to defend their honor or interpersonal threats.[41]

But does this mean that evolution sheds light only on male behavior? In *A Mind of Her Own*, Anne Campbell suggests that gender-based behavioral differences stem from reproductive investments that males and females make. For males, the reproductive investment is extraordinarily brief, even fleeting. For females, the reproductive investment is, of course, the entire process of pregnancy and the profound bonds that flow from it. Consequently, females have no incentive to engage in reckless, impulsive acts that could jeopardize their ability to reproduce.[42]

According to evolutionary psychology, significant psychological differences by gender have developed over time. Many of these variations relate to males'

KEY TERMS

chivalry hypothesis
The notion that the lower crime rates for females reflect men's deference and protective attitude toward women, whereby female offenses are generally overlooked or excused by males.

and females' tendency to commit delinquency and to refrain from delinquency. For example:[43]

- Although females and males experience anger at roughly equivalent levels, their expression of that anger is different. Males are more likely to directly confront or attack the person with whom they are angry, which naturally increases their opportunities for offending. Females are more likely to discuss their anger with a third party or cry as a result of their anger.
- Meta-analyses confirm that females experience much higher levels of fear than males do; fear has a strong inhibitory effect on aggression and delinquency.
- Research consistently shows that females exhibit greater levels of effortful control—that is, the ability to regulate one's behavior or inhibit one's desires—compared to than males.
- Research finds that females demonstrate greater self-control and lower impulsivity than males, who tend to demonstrate reduced self-control and thus greater impulsivity.

More recent attempts to link biological and physiological factors to female delinquency have stressed the effects of hormonal differences between girls and boys. Normally, males produce six times as much testosterone and twice as much androgen as females. Females, by contrast, produce estrogen in far larger amounts than do males. These hormonal differences, which are associated with many of the basic masculine and feminine characteristics of males and females, may also have some effect on gender-role behavior. A number of researchers have reported levels of testosterone are higher among violent female offenders than among female offenders considered nonviolent. Although hormonal changes in females linked to the premenstrual phase of the menstrual cycle (known as *premenstrual syndrome*) may increase irritability, no connection has been found between irritable mood and aggressive behavior. Indeed, many of the changes in mood may be caused by other factors, such as stressful external events.[44]

Researchers from various fields in the neurosciences have also produced compelling evidence that gender differences in all forms of behavior—conventional and delinquent—stem from basic differences in the brain chemistry of males and females. For instance, Simon Baron-Cohen argues that neurological functioning and behavioral expression between boys and girls are fundamentally different. The brains of males are organized for *systematizing*, which lends itself to organizational and analytical tasks. In contrast, the brains of females are organized for *empathizing*, which lends itself to emotional relatedness to others, sociality, and taking the perspective of others.[45] Viewed from this neurological perspective, females would be expected to have lower levels of antisocial behavior because they have greater and more fundamental connections to others, which in turn would make it more difficult to victimize them. Conversely, male brains are significantly less designed for empathy, which facilitates delinquency.

Other neuroscience research has also highlighted gender-specific brain differences, thereby refuting the idea that socialization explains all gender-based differences in behavior. According to Sarah Bennett and her colleagues:

> Males and females vary on a number of perceptual and cognitive information-processing domains that are difficult to ascribe to sex-role socialization. The human brain is either masculinized or feminized structurally and chemically before birth. Genetics and the biological environment in utero provide the foundation of gender differences in early brain morphology, physiology, chemistry, and nervous system development. *It would be surprising if these differences did not contribute to gender differences in cognitive abilities, temperament, and ultimately, normal or antisocial behavior* [italics added].[46]

Other studies from a biosocial criminology perspective have focused on early physical development and puberty's effects on girls and delinquency. For example, Dana Haynie examined whether parents treat daughters who are more physically developed differently than less developed girls and whether early physical development in girls is related to delinquency. Using data from the National Longitudinal Study of Adolescent Health, Haynie found that girls who are more physically developed than their peers and who are more developed overall are more likely to report smoking cigarettes, drinking alcohol, smoking marijuana, exhibiting disorderly conduct, selling drugs, joining a gang, participating in group fights, and having shot or stabbed someone compared to girls who report average or lower pubertal development. Haynie suggests that this relationship may reflect the more physically developed girl's increased social distance from parents, increased association with male adolescents, increased exposure to older friends, and greater likelihood of involvement in romantic relationships.[47]

Terrie Moffitt and her colleagues in continuing analysis of data from the Dunedin Study reported similar findings. They reported that most antisocial girls' behaviors appear to be related to an attempt to escape a *maturity gap*. That is, these girls' biological maturity has outpaced their social maturity, such that they begin to associate with older peers or peers who appear to be older. Moffitt and her colleagues also noted that "females are most antisocial soon after puberty, and when they are under the influence of relationships with males, who are more antisocial than females on average."[48] Sonya Negriff and her colleagues similarly found that early puberty among girls is a serious risk factor for depression and delinquency.[49]

In 2005, Lee Ellis presented the *evolutionary neuroandrogenic theory*, which makes two key assertions:

- Aggressive and acquisitive criminal behavior evolved as an aspect of human reproduction, especially among males.
- The probability of aggressive and acquisitive criminal behavior is linked to neurochemistry—most notably to gender-related hormones that promote "competitive/victimizing" behavior.

In theorizing that males are more biologically prone to criminal behavior than females, Ellis assumes that this gender difference in behavior must be related to the one chromosome that males and females do not share: the Y-chromosome. According to Ellis, the Y-chromosome is important because testosterone promotes competitive and victimizing behavior related to brain functioning. The resulting theory helps move criminology beyond strictly social environmental theories toward a new, more comprehensive paradigm that envisions behavior as stemming from the interaction of biological factors rooted in evolutionary history, learning, and social environmental factors.[50]

Overall, contemporary developmental explanations of female delinquency are less biological (with the exception of Lee Ellis' work) and more *biosocial* in their perspective. This line of research shows the ways that biological factors—such as reproductive capacity, for example—set into motion a range of consequences that positively and negatively affect women and influence their social development. According to Bruce Ellis and his associates:

> In modern Western societies, adolescent girls face a biosocial dilemma. On the one hand, the biological capacity to reproduce ordinarily develops in early adolescence; on the other hand, girls who realize this capacity before adulthood often experience a variety of negative life outcomes. Specifically, adolescent childbearing is associated with lower educational and occupational attainment, more mental and physical health problems, inadequate social support networks for parenting and increased risk of abuse and neglect for children born to teen mothers.[51]

In this way, much biological and psychological research focuses on the implications and outcomes of female traits.

Sociological Theories

Biological and developmental theories of female delinquency continued to dominate the literature long after theories of male delinquency had shifted to address the role of social forces. Their popularity reflected the lingering belief, even among many sociologists, that biological differences between females and males were deterministic of their social behaviors as

well. In this section we examine the ideas of several theorists whose work influenced the development of major bodies of criminological theory.

Emile Durkheim, a 19th-century French sociologist, provided the first sociological explanation for why gender differences in homicide exist and how gender murder rates may change across various stages of societal development. Durkheim's ideas were reexamined by Bruce DiCristina, who suggested that Durkheim rejected a biological reason for women's lower homicide rates and instead argued that because women were less active in collective life, they experienced less exposure to the causes of homicide. Durkheim also noted that opportunities to commit homicide differed between the genders and observed that the effects of gendered socialization caused "homicidal passions" to be ignited in men and not women. Thus his argument is that men have higher rates of homicide than women because their social structural location provides them with greater homicidal opportunities and their socialization has provided them with the "seeds of strong homicidal passions."[52]

Sociological theories of delinquency stressed male patterns of behavior almost exclusively. Misbehavior by girls was treated as extraneous, marginal, and irrelevant. In his 1927 study of 1313 gangs, for example, Frederic Thrasher devoted only slightly more than one page to the handful of female gangs he found. He attributed the relative absence of girl gangs to the fact that the traditions and customs underpinning socially approved patterns of girls' behaviors are contrary to the activities of gangs. Thrasher accounted for the few girls who did become involved in gangs in stereotypic and simplistic terms: "The girl *takes the role of a boy* and is accepted on equal terms with the others. Such a girl is probably a tomboy in the neighborhood."[53]

Clifford Shaw and Henry McKay's studies of the impact of social disorganization on delinquency included analyses of more than 60,000 male delinquents in Chicago. Although Shaw and McKay noted the persistence of high delinquency rates in particular zones of the city and argued that these rates were linked to characteristics of the community rather than to the groups of people living in them, they made only brief reference to female delinquency. Delinquency was implicitly defined as a part of the male domain. Whether female delinquency was also a product of social disorganization was not explored.[54] Barbara Warner suggests that social disorganization theory essentially ignores cultural influences, such as gender socialization, on crime.[55] In fact, criminologists have begun to investigate the role of gender in Shaw and McKay's theory. For example, Walter DeKeseredy and his colleagues have noted that women who live in socially disorganized neighborhoods report higher levels of domestic violence and fear of crime than women living in more affluent neighborhoods.[56]

Robert Merton's strain theory also fails to address the issue of female delinquency. Neither Merton nor his followers attempted to apply his typology of adaptations to women, even though interesting but contradictory implications for females could have been derived from his work.[57] For example, Ruth Morris suggests that the goals of women are fundamentally *relational* (for example, marriage, family, friends, love), whereas men typically pursue material goals. She argues that because most women have lower material aspirations and their goals are more accessible, they do not experience the same stressful conditions as men and, therefore, are less likely to turn to delinquency. At the same time, Morris argues that women do have aspirations similar to men (for example, jobs, education, and money) but are denied the same opportunities to achieve them. If this is so, then it would follow that female rates of delinquency should be higher than the corresponding male rates.[58]

Özden Özbay and Yusuf Ziya Ozcan tested Merton's strain theory among nearly 2000 high school students in Ankara, Turkey. Although they found gender differences in terms of educational aspirations and expectations, none of these differences were significantly related to delinquency. In fact, upper-class boys and girls were more likely than lower-class youths to commit delinquency, a direct refutation of the theory.[59]

There is support for the general idea that economic disadvantage among women does influence the types of delinquency they commit. For example, Amy Reckdenwald and Karen Parker found that women engaged in certain types of offenses that were related to specific structural factors that limited opportunities and marginalized them economically. Economic marginalization was particularly closely related to drug sales and robbery rates, suggesting that females commit these crimes out of economic necessity. By comparison, women committed intimate-partner homicide for very different reasons, possibly because of the strain and frustration that stems from females' lack of resources and power. Elaine Rodermond and her colleagues reviewed 44 studies on desistance from delinquency among girls and women and found that economic independence, in addition to supportive family relationships, were the main causes of desistance.[60]

General strain theory has been extended by Agnew and his associates in an attempt to account for differences in the nature and causes of female delinquency. These theorists argue that females experience different types of strain and respond differently to strain than males, thereby producing different behavioral outcomes. Females, for example, experience strain from abusive situations, excessive demands of family members, problems in maintaining relational networks, low prestige in work and family roles, and

restrictions of their behavior as females. The female response to strain also varies and is likely to be tied to gender-based differences in coping skills, a sense of mastery, and positive self-esteem. According to Broidy and Agnew, boys experience types of strain that are more likely to lead to serious property and violent crimes, whereas the types of strain experienced by girls lead them to domestic violence, running away, and self-directed delinquency, such as drug use. Many of the strains experienced by girls derive from the greater levels of social control to which they are subjected and the limitations on their opportunities to engage in delinquency. Whereas both boys and girls may respond to strain with anger, the anger of girls is usually tied to emotional problems, such as depression, anxiety, and shame—all of which also decrease the likelihood of their involvement in other-directed delinquent behavior.[61]

In a test of Broidy and Agnew's hypotheses, Nicole Piquero and Miriam Sealock examined data from 150 youths detained in juvenile detention facilities in a mid-Atlantic state. Although these researchers found that both males and females who reported more strain were also more likely to self-report higher levels of delinquency, they found no significant differences in the amount of strain experienced between females and males. Instead, what appeared to differ was that females reported higher levels of anger and depression and lower levels of physical and cognitive coping resources than did males. Moreover, and as Piquero and Sealock note:

> The effect of strain on delinquency was not diminished after [they] controlled for negative emotions, and this was especially the case among males. . . . On the other hand, the results indicated that among females, anger was positively related to interpersonal aggression even when strain was not significant in the model, an effect that was not observed for males.[62]

Walter Miller also seemed unconcerned with explaining female delinquency in his study of lower-class culture and gang delinquency, although he did devote some attention to females in an article on "The Molls" 15 years later. His analysis of the "focal concerns" of the lower class is limited to male adaptations and assumes that such aspirations are exclusive to the lower class. That is, his definitions of "masculinity" are exclusive to the lower class rather than common to all social classes.[63]

Eileen Leonard argues that Miller's focal concerns are not particularly relevant to females even in the lower class: "Given their different location in society, they [girls] are unlikely to be as concerned as males about trouble, toughness, smartness, excitement, fate, and autonomy."[64] Leonard further suggests that if lower-class males and females did have the same focal concerns and that if these concerns alone explained the development of delinquent subcultures, their delinquency rates would be similar.

Albert Cohen explicitly defined the problem of delinquency and the development of the delinquent subculture as a male phenomenon. Even so, he devoted 11 pages to a discussion of why his work did *not* apply to girls. According to Cohen, boys and girls have different adjustment problems requiring different solutions. The delinquent subculture develops largely as a response to the problems faced by boys; thus it is not an appropriate response for dealing with the problems of girls arising from the female role. Boys, Cohen says, are most interested in their own achievements compared with those of other boys; girls are more interested in their relationships with boys. According to Cohen, "It is within the area of these relationships . . . that a girl finds her fulfillments *as a girl*. It is no accident that 'boys collect stamps, girls collect boys.'" Cohen does recognize the existence of female delinquency, but he defines it primarily as sexual delinquency. According to Cohen, "sex delinquency is one kind of meaningful response to the most characteristic . . . problem of the female role: the establishment of satisfactory relationships with the opposite sex."[65]

In a feminist critique of Cohen's work, Ngaire Naffine states:

> The message from Cohen is manifest. Men are the rational doers and achievers. They represent all that is instrumental and productive in American culture. Women's world is on the margins. Women exist to be the companions of men and that is their entire lot. . . . While men proceed with their Olympian task of running all aspects of the nation, women perform their role of helpmate.[66]

Richard Cloward and Lloyd Ohlin's work on delinquency and opportunity focused exclusively on male delinquency produced by the frustrations associated with the unequal distribution of both legitimate and illegitimate opportunities. In their view, females are important only in terms of how they contribute to the difficulties boys have in developing a clear masculine image. Boys, in their attempts to establish themselves as males in female-dominated homes and schools, often experience strain:

> Engulfed by a feminine world and uncertain of their own identification, they tend to " protest against femininity." This protest may take the form of robust and aggressive behavior, and even of malicious, irresponsible, and destructive acts.[67]

Because girls are seen as having no difficulty in adapting to their own prescribed female roles within this feminine world, they do not experience this strain. The fact that girls also experience similar unequal distributions in opportunities and that some girls *do*

become delinquent was apparently of no interest to Cloward and Ohlin.

Edwin Sutherland offered his *theory of differential association* as a general theory of crime that explains all types of law-violating behaviors. Despite the broad claims made for his theory, he made *no* reference to females and did not attempt to explain how differential association may account for their lower rates of delinquency. The implication in his work is that, compared with boys, girls encounter more anticriminal patterns and are exposed to fewer criminal associations and definitions favorable to violation of law. Some years later, Sutherland noted that the differences in rates of male and female delinquency are explained by differential associations: "Parents and other intimate associates define one kind of propriety for girls and another for boys, and exercise one kind of supervision over girls and another over boys."[68] Sutherland presumably believed that girls who become delinquent have less parental supervision and, therefore, develop the same kind of delinquent associations as those developed by delinquent boys.

The social learning theory developed by Albert Bandura is also helpful for understanding expressions of delinquency among females. According to Bandura, girls learn to be aggressive in their behavior, encounter situations that trigger further aggression, and develop internal and external ways that reinforce or mute their expression of aggression. Gretchen Snethen and Marieke Van Puymbroeck showed how gendered expressions of aggression—and, by extension, antisocial behavior—are maintained by direct reinforcement, vicarious reinforcement via media images, and self-reinforcement. In this way, the gender socialization and gendered images that are relentlessly presented through the mass media provide "instructions" for females to behave in specific, gender-constrained ways.[69]

Although Sutherland did not specifically test how differential associations might affect gender differences in delinquency, other criminologists have conducted such investigations. Numerous studies have looked at how girls' association with delinquent friends affects their likelihood of engaging in delinquency.[70] Kristan Erickson and her colleagues, for example, conducted a longitudinal analysis of gender differences among students from six high schools in California and three high schools in Wisconsin. These researchers found a significantly greater positive effect of having delinquent friends on subsequent delinquency for males than for females.[71]

Shari Miller, Rolf Loeber, and Alison Hipwell found that girls' association with delinquent friends—whether the friends were boys or girls—was associated with conduct problems during early elementary school. They also found that girls associated with delinquent youths to a greater extent when they had been subjected to harsh parenting characterized by little

parental warmth.[72] When Xiaoru Liu and Howard Kaplan studied 2753 junior and senior high school students in Houston, Texas, they found that although females and males engaged in similar levels of minor delinquencies, exposure to delinquent peers was more positively associated with delinquency for males than for females.[73]

Lonn Lanza-Kaduce and his colleagues studied the links between gender, alcohol use, and sexual behavior among students selected from eight universities. Their findings showed that men and women who were members of fraternities and sororities were more likely to use alcohol before having sex compared to students who were not Greek-society members, whether male or female. Fraternity men were most likely to use alcohol before having sex, followed in frequency by sorority women. Both social learning and differential association theories help us to understand why sorority women frequently engaged in drinking before sex: These women associated with fraternity men who were engaging in the same behavior. Having less academic success (as measured by grades) had a greater impact in increasing females' alcohol use before sex as compared to men who had less academic success.[74]

Travis Hirschi's notion of the *social bond*, reflecting a social control perspective, provides a framework for explaining differences in rates of female and male delinquency, although Hirschi himself never explored this possibility. Hirschi's explanation of delinquency was developed from his analysis of a sample of approximately 4000 boys; girls were intentionally excluded from the analysis. Coramae Mann commented on this exclusion:

> Travis Hirschi stratified his samples of race, sex, school, and grade. He included 1076 black girls and 846 nonblack girls; but in the analysis of his

data Hirschi admits "the girls disappear," and he adds, "Since girls have been neglected for too long by students of delinquency, the exclusion of them is difficult to justify. I hope I return to them soon." He didn't.[75]

Because social control theory appears to be one of the most powerful explanations of juvenile delinquency generally, it is understandable that criminologists would soon test its ability to explain female delinquency. Rachelle Canter discovered that girls had stronger bonds to their parents than did boys, although this attachment had a greater inhibitory effect on delinquency for boys.[76] Other studies have observed that boys are more likely than girls to be negatively influenced by their attachments to delinquent friends and are subsequently more likely than girls to engage in delinquency and substance abuse.[77] A study of homeless and runaway youths by Constance Chapple and her colleagues similarly found that boys are more likely to get arrested than girls primarily because they have stronger attachments to delinquent peers.[78] Despite these results, some studies have reported no differences in boys' and girls' attachment to their parents; however, gender differences in attachment to parents and peers seem to provide more protection for girls than for boys and consequently reduce the severity of delinquency among girls.[79]

In an extension of social control theory, Michael Gottfredson and Travis Hirschi argued that delinquency is more likely to occur among youth who lack self-control—a phenomenon that applies equally to girls and boys. (See **Box 8.4**, the "Theory in a Nutshell" feature.) Gottfredson and Hirschi also suggested that gender differences in delinquency "appear to be invariant over time and space."[80] The explanation for this difference is found in the substantial gender differences in self-control resulting from early childhood socialization: Compared to boys, girls are socialized to be less impulsive, to engage in less risk-taking behavior, and to be more sensitive and verbal (rather than physical), more resistant to temptations, and more obedient. According to Gottfredson and Hirschi, it

According to Gottfredson and Hirschi's self-control theory, girls have higher levels of self-control because they are not only more closely monitored by their parents but also socialized to be more verbal, less impulsive, and more cautious—traits not related to delinquency.

© Rob Marmion/Shutterstock.

BOX 8.4

Theory in a Nutshell

Michael Gottfredson and Travis Hirschi

Gottfredson and Hirschi blame delinquency on low self-control. They think that girls are less delinquent than boys because girls are socialized to be less impulsive, to take fewer risks, and to be more sensitive and verbal (rather than physical), more resistant to temptations, and more obedient.

is this difference in socialization—rather than differences in levels of attachment or parental supervision (as suggested in social bond theory)—that accounts for gender differences in frequency and seriousness of delinquency.

Interestingly, several scholars, including George Higgins and Richard Tewksbury, report that the processes of instilling self-control in children work differently for boys and girls.[81] Teresa LaGrange and Robert Silverman found that the effects of self-control on delinquency operated differently among 2095 Canadian high school students.[82] Brenda Sims Blackwell and Alex Piquero discovered similar gender differences using a sample of U.S. adults.[83] Likewise, Özden Özbay's study of self-control among university students in Turkey found that self-control predicted deviance in the same ways for both females and males.[84] Although self-control is useful as a general theoretical concept, it seems to explain delinquency better among men than women.

Recent tests of the general theory provide support for the argument that differences in self-control largely account for the gender differences in delinquency. Boys exhibit lower self-control than do girls at all ages, which has direct effects on the prevalence of delinquent behavior by gender. Low self-control may also be predictive of female delinquency *and* victimization. When Eric Stewart and his colleagues studied a group of 466 drug-using offenders in Atlanta, they found that young women with low self-control were more likely both to engage in risky behaviors and to have higher levels of violent victimization than were women with higher self-control. A final point to observe about gender differences in self-control and their relation to delinquency is that female delinquency is more nuanced in his etiology than that of males. For example, Sarah Cusworth Walker and her colleagues performed a latent class analysis of nearly 2000 female adolescents who had been charged in juvenile court. This statistical technique allows criminologists to observe various "types" of delinquent within the data. They found four classes of female delinquents: (1) those with high family conflict and trauma, (2) those with few adverse childhood experiences but substance abuse needs, (3) those with complex treatment needs with antisocial peers, and (4) those with mental health needs but strong social and family assets. Notice that self-control was not an important part of their delinquency, but instead paled compared to psychiatric problems, substance use, family conflict, and trauma.[85]

Writing from the labeling perspective, Edwin Schur argues that women are negatively labeled with great regularity as "aggressive," "bitchy," "hysterical," "fat," "homely," and "promiscuous." According to Schur, these negative labels set into motion social reactions that can have a negative impact on an individual's life chances.

The process of labeling is used to maintain an informal form of social control over females. Earlier in this chapter, we discussed how the development of girls' identities works to keep women in their "place" and how girls are devalued through use of terms such as "slut" or "whore." (See **Box 8.5**, the "Delinquency Controversy" feature discusses the issue of sexual labeling and control of girls.) According to Schur, "When women are effectively stigmatized, it reinforces their overall subordination and makes it more difficult for them to achieve desired goals." Furthermore, the differential enforcement of status offenses for girls can be seen as punishment for "violating or threatening to violate gender-related norms."[86]

Current research shows that labels affect men and women differently. For example, Brenda Geiger and Michael Fischer conducted a study where offenders were given various labels, such as "criminal," "prostitute," "drug dealer," and "incompetent parent." Male offenders were able to ignore or justify each label and still form a positive self-image. Conversely, female offenders were negatively affected by the labels, especially the charge of being an incompetent parent—regardless of whether it was true.[87] Just as Schur theorized, females appear to feel devalued by pejorative or negative labels.

Marxist-Feminist Theories

Marxist-feminist theories combine the notions of patriarchal male dominance in the home and interpersonal relationships with male control of the means of production. In such an environment, the criminal justice system "defines as crimes those actions that threaten this capitalist-patriarchal system."[88] James Messerschmidt believes that in societies characterized by patriarchal capitalism, male owners or managers of capital control workers, and men control women. Thus, under patriarchal capitalism, women experience *double marginality*: They are subordinate to both capitalists and men.

Messerschmidt suggests that girls are less likely to be involved in serious delinquencies for three reasons:

1. Most serious crimes are "masculine" in nature; physical strength, aggressiveness, and external proofs of achievement are facets of the male personality.
2. Because women are subordinate and less powerful, they have fewer opportunities to engage in serious crimes.
3. Males control even illegitimate opportunities, and females are relegated to subordinate roles even in criminal activities.

When women do engage in crime, their criminal activity is usually a response to their subordinate and powerless position in patriarchal capitalist society (see **Box 8.6**, the "Theory in a Nutshell" feature and

BOX 8.5

Delinquency Controversy

Sexual Labeling and Control of Girls

Although adolescent girls and boys frequently engage in harmless bantering, kidding, and joking with each other, all too often the informal verbal interactions take on an insidious, demeaning, and manipulative flavor designed to facilitate boys' control of girls. Mark Fleisher suggests that the use of insulting terms in the verbal dueling of girls and boys in the Freemont area in Kansas City helps to establish social hierarchies, allows for the release of tensions without violence, and defines group membership and friendships: "Boys call girls by the standard list of insulting terms, including 'bitch,' 'rotten bitch,' 'stank bitch,' 'pussy,' 'cunt,' and 'slut,' among others. Girls retaliate with a vengeance, shouting, 'bastard,' 'prick,' 'pussy,' 'bitch,' 'little dick,' . . . among others. Girls call one another by the standard list of insults." The seeming equality of insults, however, masks the actual inequalities in the relationships. According to Fleisher:

> Girls think about relationships as moral contracts; boys don't. Beyond the street rhetoric of the gang, girls' implicit construction of relationships, especially with boys, includes fairness, reciprocity, and equality. . . . In what they perceive to be long-term relationships, girls feel an inherent responsibility toward the boys with whom they are involved, but the boys feel neither reciprocity nor fairness nor equality.

Elijah Anderson's study of the informal street code that guides interactions between boys and girls in the inner city of Philadelphia reflects a similar pattern of control in relationships. Whereas many girls "offer sex as a gift" in their attempt to gain a boy's attention, boys define the exchange as only a means to enhance their self-esteem. According to Anderson, "The girls have a dream, the boys a desire. The girls dream of being carried off by a Prince Charming who will love them. . . . The boys often desire either sex without commitment or babies without responsibility for them." The boys want to "score" with as many girls as possible—the more girls a boy has sex with, the higher his esteem in the eyes of his male peers. "But the young man not only must 'get some'; he also must prove he is getting it. This leads him to talk about girls and sex with any other young man who will listen." Labels may also be used to control boys. If his peers suspect him of becoming too committed to a girl, they are likely to sanction him with "demeaning labels such as 'pussy,' 'pussy whipped,' or 'house husband.'"

Many of the interviews Mark Totten conducted with 90 Canadian boys ages 13 to 17 in Ottawa, Ontario, reflected the boys' willingness to use demeaning labels to control girls. Steve, a 15-year-old, responded to Totten's question. "Do you like girls?:"

No, not really . . . I think most of them are stupid bitches. I'll call them bitch, slut, whore all the time. They're always trying to show me up—make me look stupid, like a goof. . . . It's all about knowing your place in society. Some girls do, but most girls don't know what they're supposed to do. . . . We all think that girls should do what we want them to. And it pisses us off when they don't. So I've seen some of them when they've hit girls. And all the time we are just joking around, calling them names—slut, cunt, whore, bitch, fat cow—we all do it.

When boys label girls in this manner as part of their oppression and control of girls, it should not be surprising that boys also express an attitude of negative fatalism with regard to future generations of girls. Philippe Bourgois spent 5 years studying the neighborhood culture of the crack trade in East Harlem. Getting girls pregnant seemingly produced some ambivalence. Many boys took pride in noting how many girls they had impregnated. Luis, for example, bragged about getting a number of girls pregnant in just a 9-month period, but then referred to them as "holes out there." The ambivalence came from thinking about the possibility of the pregnancy producing a daughter. According to one youth, "That's why I would never want to have a daughter, if I was to get my girl pregnant. I couldn't handle the fact of having a baby, and then I have to see her being a 'ho.'" And an 11-year-old commented about his mother's pregnancy: "He told us he hoped his mother would give birth to a boy 'because girls are too easy to rape.'"

Elijah Anderson, *Code of the Street: Decency, Violence, and the Moral Life of the Inner City* (New York: W. W. Norton, 1999); Philippe Bourgois, *In Search of Respect: Selling Crack in El Barrio* (New York: Cambridge University Press, 1995); Mark Fleisher, *Dead End Kids: Gang Girls and the Boys They Know* (Madison, WI: University of Wisconsin Press, 1998); Mark Totten, *Guys, Gangs, and Girlfriend Abuse* (Peterborough, Ontario: Broadview Press, 2000); Deborah Prothrow-Stith and Howard Spivak, *Sugar and Spice and No Longer Nice: How We Can Stop Girls' Violence* (San Francisco: Jossey-Bass, 2005); Kelly King, Dexter Voisin, and Ralph DiClemente, "The Relationship between Male Gang Involvement and Psychosocial Risks for their Female Juvenile Justice Partners with Non-Gang Involvement Histories," *Journal of Child and Family Studies* 24:2555–2559 (2015).

Figure 8.1). Such activity may take the form of *privatized resistance* (alcoholism, drug abuse, or suicide) or *accommodation* (generally less serious economic crimes, including shoplifting, embezzlement, and prostitution).[89]

Ronald Akers and Christine Sellers have raised important questions about Messerschmidt's general reliance on the patriarchal social structure as an explanation of all types of crimes committed by both females and males. They believe that for the theory to truly be testable, researchers must be able to measure the specific nature and impact of patriarchy in different parts of society, as well as to examine the relationship of gender inequalities and male and female crime

BOX 8.6
Theory in a Nutshell
James Messerschmidt

Messerschmidt argues that girls commit less serious delinquency than boys for three reasons: Girls lack physical strength, they have fewer opportunities to commit crime, and they occupy subordinate roles even in criminal activities.

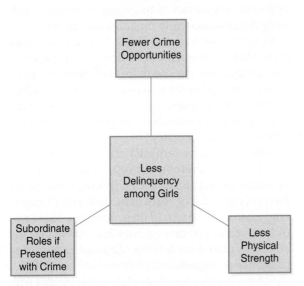

Figure 8.1 Mapping Delinquency Theory: James Messerschmidt

© Jones & Bartlett Learning.

patterns within a cross-cultural perspective.[90] One such test, conducted by Darrell Steffensmeier, Emilie Allan, and Cathy Streifel, involved the examination of arrest data for homicide and major and minor property crimes in a wide range of societies. Steffensmeier and his colleagues found that neither "gender inequality" nor "female economic marginality" was related to female–male arrest ratios in different societies. Instead, the arrest ratios were more significantly related to the degree to which women had access to consumer goods and to the general formalization of social control within the societies. These findings provide very little support for Messerschmidt's claim that patriarchal inequalities produce gender-specific differences in crime patterns.[91]

Conversely, some research does provide support for Marxist theories of delinquency. A study by Lynne Vieraitis and her colleagues examined whether women's structural position had any effect on their chances of being murdered. It did: Women in poverty were more likely to be murdered. According to the authors, this finding is consistent with Marxist-feminist theory, which suggests lower-class women often interact with men who are frustrated by their own economic conditions, and this frustration leads to violence against

women, including homicide. In addition, women's poverty often leads to dependence on men, even if the men are abusive.[92]

Power-control theory, which was developed by John Hagan and his associates, argues that girls engage in less delinquency because their behavior is more closely monitored and controlled by parents (especially the mother) in patriarchal families. In *patriarchal families*, the father works outside the home and has control over others, while the mother stays at home and raises the children. Because the father has a higher control position than the mother, he maintains control over both the wife and the children in the home.

Egalitarian families, by contrast, are characterized by a lack of gender differences in the consumption and production spheres. In such families, both parents work and have control positions outside the home, and both share child-rearing responsibilities within the home. Parental control is redistributed so that the control over daughters is more like that over sons, and daughters, like sons, are prepared to enter the production sphere and given greater opportunities for risk taking. This differential treatment leads boys in such families, more so than girls, to engage in greater risk taking and, consequently, in delinquency.[93]

Meda Chesney-Lind and Randall Shelden suggest that power-control theory is "essentially a not-too-subtle variation of the **liberation hypothesis** that women's liberation directly led to increases in female criminality. Now, mother's liberation or employment causes daughter's crime."[94] Chesney-Lind and Shelden argue there is no evidence to support Hagan's claim that as women's participation in the labor force increases, so, too, will female delinquency. Note, however, that Roy Austin's analysis of labor force participation, divorce rates, and female arrests for minor, major, and occupational offenses *does* lend support to the claim that female liberation is associated with an increase in female criminality. Despite different research findings, more recent surveys indicate that most Americans do not believe that maternal employment is a cause of delinquency. Justin Pickett's analysis of 10,144 voters found that just a fraction of them thought that working mothers contributed to delinquency among girls or boys.[95]

In recent years, Hagan and his associates have extended their work to more specifically consider gender differences. Their *gendered power-control theory*

KEY TERMS

power-control theory
Theory that emphasizes the consequences of the power relations of husbands and wives in the workplace on the lives of their children.

liberation hypothesis
The notion that changes brought about by the women's movement triggered a wave of female crime.

links delinquency to subsequent gendered patterns of feelings of anger, despair, and aggressiveness as youth move through adolescent life-course stages. These theorists argue that the lower levels of instrumental control possessed by males compared to females in more patriarchal families increases the likelihood of males moving from more direct aggressive delinquency to the use of alcohol and drugs. Alternatively, they suggest, "in more patriarchal families higher levels of relational control of females compared with males may yield sequences in which females more often move from indirect, relational involvements in delinquency to feelings of depression."[96]

Numerous tests of power-control theory have been conducted over the past two decades, which have yielded mixed results. For example, Simon Singer and Murray Levine analyzed data from 705 high school youths and 560 parents and found that, consistent with power-control theory, parents exerted less control over boys than girls and mothers exerted greater control over girls. However, these researchers also found that boys were more delinquent than girls in egalitarian households, which is contrary to the theory's predictions.[97] Merry Morash and Meda Chesney-Lind, found, in their analysis of data from the National Survey of Children that sex differences in delinquency were present regardless of patriarchal or egalitarian family structures.[98]

Whereas Hagan and his associates assumed that single-parent families were sufficiently similar to his classification of egalitarian families, other researchers have questioned this assumption. Michael Leiber and Mary Ellen Wacker examined data from two samples of juveniles living in single-mother households in Washington and Iowa. Although associations with delinquent peers were related to delinquency in these samples, the researchers failed to find any support for power-control theory.[99]

Christopher Uggen examined the relationship between parents' perceptions of their workplace power and control and the delinquencies of their children. According to his study, "Parental power and control in the workplace increases the rate of arrest among males and decreases it among females. Maternal authority position, in contrast, dramatically raises the risk of arrest among females and reduces this risk among males."[100]

Kristin Mack and Michael Leiber explored how race differences in delinquency between African Americans and whites could reflect differences in household structure. Their research produced surprising results, however: among both racial groups, boys simply committed more delinquency than girls, regardless of household structure. Although not a test of power control theory, Monique Morris contends that patriarchal structure and racial stereotypes and discrimination are likely the best explanations for delinquency among African American girls, particularly

in the school context. Many times, school officials ignore or fail to investigate severe risk factors that black girls experience and that contribute to adjustment and behavioral problems.[101]

Daniel Mears and his colleagues suggest that sex differences in delinquency are more appropriately explained by how girls and boys are differentially affected by the same criminogenic factors because of differences in their moral development. They argue that "the primary socialization of women instills moral values that strongly discourage behavior that hurts or harms others." As a consequence, moral evaluations by females counteract criminogenic conditions, such as dysfunctional family organization, poverty, and exposure to delinquent friends. Not only are boys more likely than girls to have delinquent friends, it appears that boys are also more likely than girls to be strongly affected by their delinquent peers. According to Mears and his associates, this "reflects the greater effect of moral evaluations in counteracting peer influence among females."[102]

Although many feminist criminologists have called for the development of a "feminist" theory of female delinquency, *no* clearly articulated theory has yet emerged. The work of Morash and Chesney-Lind may come closest. In their view, girls' lower rate of involvement in delinquency is explained by the emphasis placed on females' developing nurturing relationships. Morash and Chesney-Lind contend that children—whether female or male—who identify with a nurturing parent who cares for others are likely to develop identities built on an ethic of care and concern for others rather than identities conducive to harming others. They also note that men can take on nurturing roles and—because sons can identify just as easily with a nurturing father as with a nurturing mother—can likewise promote prosocial behavior in boys (see **Box 8.7**, the "Theory in a Nutshell" feature and **Figure 8.2**).[103]

Feminists acknowledge that girls do become delinquent and that any feminist theory of female delinquency must take into consideration the various influences of gender. From this perspective, female delinquency

BOX 8.7

Theory in a Nutshell

Merry Morash and Meda Chesney-Lind

Morash and Chesney-Lind believe that girls are less delinquent than boys because girls are more often socialized to be nurturing; as a consequence, they develop identities that emphasizing caring for others rather than causing harm to others.

Figure 8.2 Mapping Delinquency Theory: Merry Morash and Meda Chesney-Lind

© Jones & Bartlett Learning.

Differential oppression theory contends that girls turn to prostitution because it helps establish a sense of power and autonomy. Does it? What are other reasons girls turn to prostitution? Is sex a form of social capital?

© RapidEye/E+/Getty.

is accounted for by the gender and sexual scripts in patriarchal families, which lead girls, more so than boys, to be victims of family-related sexual abuse. In patriarchal societies, male–female relationships are unequal, and young women are defined as sexual objects and seen as sexually attractive by older men. Girls become more vulnerable to both physical and sexual abuse because of norms that give males control over females and that keep females at home where victimizers have greater access to them.

Furthermore, victimizers (usually males) can call upon official agencies of control to keep girls at home. Put simply, the juvenile court system has historically been willing to uncritically support parental control and authority over daughters. Girls who react to abuse by running away from home are often returned to their parents by juvenile authorities. If girls persist in running away, the court may then incarcerate them. Girls who successfully run away often find themselves unable to enroll in school or to obtain reasonable jobs. They may then be forced into the streets, where their survival may depend on their committing petty crimes such as theft, panhandling, or prostitution.

Differential Oppression Theory

Robert Regoli and John Hewitt's **differential oppression theory** provides another framework for understanding why girls become delinquent as well as why they are less inclined toward delinquency than males. This theory argues that adults oppress children as they attempt to impose and maintain adult conceptions of social order. Children are perceived as objects, devalued and defined as inferior to adults, and consequently experience a sense of powerlessness and marginality. Adults often impose their social order on children through oppressive means. The level of oppression falls along a continuum, ranging from simple demands for obedience to rules designed for the convenience of adults to the physical or sexual abuse of children. Adults' perceptions of children as inferior, subordinate, and troublemakers allow adults to rationalize their oppressive acts.

Generally, the more oppressed the child is, the more likely she or he will become delinquent.[104]

Girls in patriarchal societies are **doubly oppressed**: They are oppressed as children *and* as females. To counteract this oppression, girls have four modes of adaptation available to them:[105]

- Passive acceptance of their status
- Manipulation of their peers to gain power
- Exercise of illegitimate coercive power
- Retaliation

Most girls adapt to oppression through *passive acceptance* of their subordinate and inferior status (also known as conformity). Their obedience is built upon fear, which derives from implied threats and intimidation. In some cases, this passive acceptance may be only a facade, presenting to the oppressor the appearance of conformity. Girls outwardly appear to accept their inferior positions, but develop a repressed hatred for their oppressors, adapting to the structures of domination in which they are immersed. Once an atmosphere of violence and oppression has been established, it engenders an entire way of life and behaviors for those caught up in it.[106]

Some girls adapt to their oppression through the exercise of *illegitimate coercive power*. These individuals are attracted to delinquency because it helps them to establish a sense of autonomy and control; the anticipatory delinquency also represents a yearning

KEY TERMS

differential oppression theory
A framework for understanding why girls become delinquent as well as why they are less inclined to delinquency than males.

doubly oppressed
Description of adolescent girls as being oppressed both as children and as females.

for adult status. Delinquent acts can immediately and demonstratively make things happen. Sexual misbehavior, illicit use of drugs or alcohol, and violations of the criminal law possess greater symbolic importance for the girl to the extent they exert control over her behavior. The "sneaky thrill" that accompanies shoplifting, drug use, or illicit sexual encounters, for example, is not simply a product of the rush of the act, but also a consequence of the girl knowing that *she* is controlling the event. In addition, when a young girl perceives that she has little or no control over her own life and that her parents determine all important activities and goals, she may choose to exert absolute control over what food is taken into or kept in her body (at least until she is force fed); the result is an eating disorder.

Through *manipulation of their peers,* girls who have experienced oppression at the hands of adults may acquire a sense of strength and control or a degree of empowerment not otherwise felt. Bullying younger or smaller children at school may be a form of displacement of a girl's anger at a parent or teacher. Girls may also verbally bully or manipulate peers, especially female peers, in an attempt to establish social hierarchies, eliminate competition for attention, release tensions without violence, or define group membership and friendships.[107]

Some girls may engage in *retaliation*—that is, "getting back" at the people or the institutions they believe are the source of their oppression. Some adolescent girls who are severely physically or sexually abused by parents may retaliate by striking directly at their parents, assaulting or killing them. Not only larger, stronger girls strike back at an abusive parent, however: Some smaller, physically weaker children may fight back by compensating with speed and choice of weapon. For example, a young girl may wait until her parents are asleep and then torch the home. Alternatively, she may retaliate by striking at a substitute, such as a younger sibling who is viewed as representative of her parents. Finally, many girls retaliate against their parents by turning inward—by becoming chronically depressed or contemplating or committing suicide. In a study carried out by the Centers for Disease Control and Prevention (CDC), one in four female students reported seriously considering suicide at some time during the 12 months before the survey, 16% had made a specific plan to attempt suicide, 11% had actually attempted suicide, and 3% made a suicide attempt resulting in an injury, poisoning, or overdose requiring medical attention.[108]

Adult conceptions in patriarchal societies of the *girl as female* (relational, nurturing, and passive) contribute to their oppression. Adoption of this perspective reinforces traditional gender roles and, consequently, the girl's identity as "object." When treated as an "object," a girl may adapt by developing an identity through relationships with boys; she does not have

to "prove" her own worth as long as she is "related" to a proven person. Consequently, her delinquencies may be indirect and relational. Being defined as a female "object" may also reinforce the girl's identity as a "sexual object." In this case, adaptations may take the form of sexual delinquencies and prostitution.

Even as it contributes to the delinquency of some girls in the previously described ways, oppression of girls as females carries with it a reinforcement of more domestic, passive, relational, and nurturing roles that often exclude girls from the outside world of male street–peer groups. Girls are not only more closely monitored and kept closer to home, but are also encouraged to identify with their mothers and to concentrate on building and maintaining relations. In addition, girls learn to anticipate economic dependence and the need to develop intimate interpersonal ties through which a sense of value and self-esteem may be gained. At the same time, they are discouraged from pursuing independent acts and risk-taking activities. As girls develop identities that reinforce positive, prosocial, and nurturing relations with others stressing caring and fairness, they are less likely to engage in behaviors harmful to others (see **Box 8.8**, the "Theory in a Nutshell" feature and **Figure 8.3**).

Differential oppression theory, as applied to female delinquency, builds on earlier work stressing differences in socialization patterns of girls and boys and views the role of socialization of adolescent girls within the context of oppression. Whereas male adolescents experience the oppression of being a child, female adolescents experience the *double* oppression of being a female child. The socialization of girls leads to their being less likely to engage in delinquency in general; when they do commit delinquent acts, however, they typically engage in particular forms of delinquency.

So which theory works best at explaining delinquency among females? Leah Daigle and her colleagues compared several theories of delinquency, including strain theory, social bond theory, differential association theory, learning theory, developmental theories, and feminist perspectives. They found value in all of the theories yet also determined that general theoretical perspectives are too sweeping to capture the subtleties

BOX 8.8

Theory in a Nutshell

Robert Regoli and John Hewitt

Regoli and Hewitt think girls commit less delinquency because girls are doubly oppressed: They are oppressed as children and as females. Adult conceptions of the "girl as child" lead to oppressive acts by adults that alienate the girl and lead her into adaptive reactions as she seeks to become a "subject" instead of an "object."

| Double Oppression of Girls | → | Adult Conception of Girl as Child | → | Adult Oppression Creates Alienation | → | Adaptive Reaction to become Subject Instead of Object |

Figure 8.3 Mapping Delinquency Theory: Robert Regoli and John Hewitt

© Jones & Bartlett Learning.

that exist between boys and girls and the risk factors that propel them to commit delinquency.[109] In this sense, feminist and developmental theories are likely to more accurately predict delinquency among girls.

Juvenile Justice Policy Applications

At the beginning of this chapter, we noted that criminological theorizing about delinquency has typically focused on male rather than female delinquency. The same criminological gaze through male eyes has led to marginalization or minimization of policies and programs aimed at preventing or treating female delinquency. Recognizing this uneven treatment, Meda Chesney-Lind argues that "girls involved in the juvenile justice system are particularly invisible in terms of programming." According to Chesney-Lind, most programs offered for females are based on stereotypes of "girls' issues," such as teen pregnancy, sexual abuse, or gang violence, and focus on intervention in the lives of girls already in trouble rather than on prevention for girls who are at risk of becoming involved in delinquency. Moreover, most traditional delinquency programs for girls have been built around common-sense understandings about what adolescent *boys* need. These programs may sometimes work for girls or work for some girls, but sometimes they may not work at all.[110]

According to Chesney-Lind, certain approaches may be particularly effective for girls, including policies and programs designed to protect girls from physical and sexual violence, to reduce the risk of sexually transmitted diseases and pregnancy, to deal with unemployment and job training, to locate safe and affordable housing, to assist in managing family problems and stress, and to develop a sense of empowerment. Finally, Chesney-Lind suggests that programs for at-risk girls need to create separate time and space for girls, away from boys, so that issues related to sexism will not be overshadowed by boys' more disruptive behavior.

When juvenile justice officials do pay attention to girls, there continues to be evidence of double standards in the ways that female delinquents and male delinquents are treated and supervised—a dual nature referred to as the **gendered juvenile justice system**. The informal and biased application of gendered

The gendered juvenile justice system suggests that correctional personnel use double standards in the way they monitor and supervise females compared to male offenders. Are there any situations where different treatment by gender is warranted?

© Rob Chapple/Thinkstock/Alamy.

juvenile justice has a long history in the United States, dating back more than a century. Traditionally, juvenile justice systems were unduly harsh toward female delinquents, particularly when their deviance was sexual in nature.[111] Nicole Flynn and her colleagues evaluated 84 females and 167 males in aftercare

KEY TERMS

gendered juvenile justice system
The existence of double standards regarding how female delinquents and male delinquents are treated and supervised within the justice system.

BOX 8.9

Delinquency Prevention

Improving Programming for Girls

A model for developing gender-appropriate delinquency prevention programs through the identification of special needs of female adolescents may be discerned in a series of studies undertaken by Barbara Bloom and her colleagues. Their needs assessment, which was funded by the California Office of Criminal Justice Planning, gathered information on the needs of girls and young women in California through extensive interviews and focus groups with juvenile justice personnel, including judges, probation officers, and program staff, as well as with girls and young women around the state. Data were collected on the following issues:

- Factors contributing to delinquency and other risky behavior
- Types of problems experienced by girls and young women
- Types of help and services needed
- Obstacles in seeking help
- Program gaps and barriers
- Effective program elements

The researchers noted a number of key findings. First, family issues—including parent–child conflicts, parental absence, parental drug use and criminality, and lack of parent–child communication—were believed to make significant contributions to female offending. Second, emotional, physical, and sexual abuses were significantly related to delinquency, yet few programs addressed the girls' specific needs. Third, although running away from home was likely to lead to delinquency, there were very few safe options for girls who believed they could no longer live at home. Fourth, although drug abuse typically leads to other delinquent behaviors, few substance abuse programs (including prevention and residential care) specifically focused on the needs of girls. Fifth, adolescent females' attitudes of independence and ambivalence toward parental discipline and guidance appeared problematic, often leading to resistance to seeking help from adults. Sixth, because school difficulties and negative attitudes toward school often lead to excessive truancy and dropping out, schools were identified as key locations and opportunities for early intervention in at-risk girls. Finally, early sexual activity by girls was found to be related to other risky behaviors, predictive of delinquency, and suggestive of the need for special female-focused sex education.

Bloom and her associates also found significant barriers to effective programming for female delinquents. In particular, these barriers included such problems as deficiencies in funding and resources, especially for female-focused programs; family resistance, especially lack of parental involvement or support; long waiting lists for services; and girls' distrust and fear of people in positions of authority.

Many suggestions for program change were offered. Most respondents said that greater and improved information about what works for girls was needed and that existing programs should be redesigned to address the wide range of specific problems, issues, and needs of girls. Ideally, programs should use gender-specific models to address issues of care and services for girls; a gendered focus should be applied to aftercare and follow-up services as well. In addition, training and education of those working with girls in the juvenile justice system must provide insight into the unique dynamics of female crime and lead these personnel toward understanding that the needs of girls are very different than those of boys. Finally, programs should be designed to address the particular situations of girls in society and tailored to the real-world problems faced by girls. All of these efforts should be gender specific and gender appropriate.

Fortunately, juvenile justice practitioners and policymakers have listened, and there are promising gender-specific programs. The Movimiento Ascendencia (Upward Movement) program is an intervention that targets Mexican-American females in gangs and provides services relating to conflict resolution, social support, and cultural awareness. The program also provides a safe, structured environment and was effective at reducing girls' delinquency and improving their school functioning and performance.

Recently, a meta-analysis of 37 studies involving nearly 22,000 female offenders found that girls and women who participated in correctional interventions were 22 to 35% more likely to succeed upon release from custody than females who did not participate in programming. Moreover, gender-specific programs and interventions were significantly more likely to produce reductions in crime and delinquency compared to programs that were not gender-specific. Hopefully, these evaluation data will lead to more programs that target the unique delinquency needs of female offenders.

Barbara Bloom, Barbara Owen, Elizabeth Deschenes, and Jill Rosenbaum, "Moving Toward Justice for Female Juvenile Offenders in the New Millennium: Modeling Gender-Specific Policies and Programs," *Journal of Contemporary Criminal Justice* 18:37–57 (2002); Barbara Bloom, Barbara Owen, Elizabeth Deschenes, and Jill Rosenbaum, "Improving Juvenile Justice for Females: A Statewide Assessment in California," *Crime & Delinquency* 48:526–552 (2002); Barbara Bloom, Barbara Owen, Jill Rosenbaum, and Elizabeth Deschenes, "Focusing on Girls and Young Women: A Gendered Perspective on Female Delinquency," *Women & Criminal Justice* 14:117–136 (2003); Joanne Belknap and Kristi Holsinger, "The Gendered Nature of Risk Factors for Delinquency," *Feminist Criminology* 1:48–71 (2006); Rebecca Peterson and James Howell, "Program Approaches for Girls in Gangs: Female Specific or Gender Neutral?" *Criminal Justice Review* 38:491–509 (2013); Vera Lopez and Lidia Nuño, "Latina and African American Girls in the Juvenile Justice System: Needs, Problems, and Solutions," *Sociology Compass* 10:24–37 (2016); Renée Gobeil, Kelley Blanchette, and Lynn Stewart, "A Meta-Analytic Review of Correctional Interventions for Women Offenders Gender-Neutral Versus Gender-Informed Approaches," *Criminal Justice and Behavior* 43:301–322 (2016).

programs and found that officials sanctioned girls for less serious behaviors than boys. Girls were also monitored more closely as part of these programs. Both of these findings are evidence of differences in the ways that the justice system controls girls and boys and are consistent with gendered norms that regulate and restrict girls' behavior. Interestingly, Flynn and her colleagues found *no* gender differences in risk assessment, rule violations, and the odds of receiving high-level sanctions.[112]

Today, there is greater emphasis on addressing the gender-specific needs of female delinquents so that the juvenile justice system can be more effective at reducing recidivism. (See **Box 8.9**, the "Delinquency Prevention" feature.) In addition, the days of overtly differential treatment of delinquents as a function of their gender are gone, although there is still lingering evidence of gendered treatment, to the detriment of females. For instance, Charlotte Lyn Bright and her colleagues studied 700 girls referred to juvenile justice services and found that many of the girls who had the greatest number of risk factors and the most extensive victimization and trauma histories nevertheless received the fewest services. In this way, the justice system is not only missing opportunities to address girls' unique risk profiles, but is also likely contributing to recidivism by not effectively intervening in their delinquent career.[113]

WRAP UP

THINKING ABOUT JUVENILE DELINQUENCY: CONCLUSIONS

The study of delinquency over the past century has focused almost exclusively on male behavior. The marginal treatment of females reflects the predominance of a patriarchal structure in which males control the sexuality and labor of women. In such a society, girls are presumed to be "inferior" to boys and are socialized into sexually stereotypic gender roles beginning at birth.

Early explanations of female delinquency stressed the biological and developmental differences between the constitutional makeup of females and that of males: Female delinquents were seen as atavistic, inferior, unadjusted, and inherently deceitful. More recent biological and developmental theories have explored girls' emotional problems and differences in their hormonal levels and early physical development as factors leading to delinquency.

Early sociological theories shifted attention from individual characteristics or flaws to the role of social forces in delinquency. Although the men who constructed these theories often ignored female delinquency or saw it as irrelevant in explaining the real problems of crime, more recent studies appear to provide partial explanations for gender differences in patterns of delinquency. Marxist and feminist theories, which stress how a social order based on patriarchy and capitalism affects females, have focused attention on the role of control and supervision of girls in limiting their activities, including delinquency. Finally, differential oppression theory emphasizes the implications of the double oppression that girls face as children and as females. These modes of oppression account for both the lower rates of female delinquency and the particular adaptive reactions of girls to oppression, which often include delinquencies.

CHAPTER SPOTLIGHT

- Studies of female delinquency have historically been lacking for two reasons: the focus on male behaviors and the empirical reality that women commit less crime than men.
- Female delinquents typically follow gendered pathways of offending that are characterized by high levels of physical, emotional, and sexual abuse early in life, running away, and delinquent acts such as prostitution, forgery, and fraud that center on drug abuse.
- Clear gender differences exist for a variety of psychological traits that are related to aggression and antisocial behavior, such as anger expression, effortful control, self-control, and impulsivity.
- Biological, biosocial, and evolutionary psychology theories point to profound differences between males and females in terms of the way that they behave, think, and act.
- Sociological and psychological theories emphasize socialization and learning processes that steer females toward certain ways of behaving and conforming to normative gender roles.

CRITICAL THINKING

1. How might our understanding and conceptualization of delinquency differ if females had historically dominated criminology instead of males? Do male and female criminologists study delinquency differently?

2. Data from international studies indicate that boys are more frequently involved in delinquency than girls in all countries. What are the implications of this finding for those who argue that gender-role identities and gender socialization explain delinquency? In your opinion, what percentage of delinquency is explained by socialization and what percentage is explained by biological factors?

3. Are males and females fundamentally different because of their reproductive capacity and investment (the idea advanced by evolutionary psychologists)? How might feminists debate this question?

4. Inadequate parental socialization may produce children with low self-control. Based on the disproportionate role of women in parenting and nurturing, are they to blame for children having low self-control? Or are "deadbeat" or absent dads the main culprits in producing children with low self-control?

5. Edwin Schur argues that females are regularly labeled as "aggressive," "bitchy," "hysterical," or "promiscuous." Given that they face an assortment of negative labels whenever they step "out of line," shouldn't women be more involved in delinquency? Is the female ability to nullify negative labels a testament to women's resilience or another piece of evidence contradicting labeling theory?

The Social Context of Delinquency

SECTION **3**

Previous sections of this text examined the nature of juvenile delinquency as it has been defined, measured, and explained. How delinquency is defined and measured largely determines how criminologists explain it. The theories and explanations that have evolved, however, must also be connected to the social reality of delinquency. Section 3 examines juvenile delinquency within its societal context.

Juvenile delinquency is closely tied to those social groupings or institutions where children spend most of their time: the family, school, and friends. It is here, in these contexts, that the groundwork for delinquency, drug use, and violence are laid. Chapter 9 examines conditions in the family that contribute to a child's delinquency. The traditional functions of the family—socializing of children, inculcating moral values, regulating sexual activity, and providing material, physical, and emotional security—as well as the traditional structure of the family have undergone substantial change during the past 40 years. Many of these changes have increased the levels of tension, anxiety, and conflict within the family. Single-parent families, working mothers, and inadequate parenting skills have been identified as contributing in one way or another to delinquency. So, too, have the problems associated with divorce, including custody battles, forced visitation, and failure to pay court-ordered support for noncustodial children. To whatever extent basic parenting skills and structural change within families affect the likelihood of delinquency for their children, current research rather consistently suggests there are even greater effects produced by familial maltreatment of children.

Children spend close to half their waking hours in school. Chapter 10 explores how schools not only are locations of adolescent crime, but also may directly or indirectly contribute to the problem of youth crime. Although violent crime has declined in schools in recent years, students and teachers continue to be victimized in this setting. Bullying has recently gained national attention as a possible correlate—if not a cause—of school violence. Schools continue to grapple with the problems associated with both high dropout rates and troublesome students who stay in school. To what extent do the built-in stresses and conflicts of the schooling process, the temptations and pressures of peers, and the enforcement of school rules with sanctions ranging from suspensions to corporal punishment contribute to disruptive behaviors and more serious delinquencies?

Chapter 11 addresses two of the most troubling aspects of delinquent behavior: drug use and violence. Both types of delinquency can be found on a wide continuum ranging from less serious forms of drug use and violence, such as experimenting with alcohol or marijuana and getting into a fistfight, to severe forms, such as

229

Opener image: © Banana Republic images/Shutterstock; Spray icon: © sabri deniz kikil/ShutterStock, Inc.

narcotics use, addiction, drug selling, and crimes such as murder, rape, and armed robbery. Chapter 11 explores the ways that adolescents commit drug and violent crimes and examines the linkages between these behaviors and more general forms of delinquency.

Chapter 12 considers juvenile delinquency within the context of peer groups and gangs. Are children more likely to violate norms and laws when they are with their friends? Are juvenile gangs simply more formal and violent expressions of normal school and neighborhood peer groups? Why do juveniles form gangs? How do the cultural experiences of various racial and ethnic groups affect the development of juvenile gangs? Although criminologists may ponder the difficulties in defining what constitutes a "gang," local law enforcement and politicians often draw upon statutory definitions to support get-tough approaches to gang suppression. Might intervention and prevention policies provide a more effective long-term solution to the gang problem?

SECTION OUTLINE

The Family and Delinquency

OBJECTIVES

- Learn the traditional functions of the family and the ways that family dynamics govern adolescent behavior.

- Explore structural changes in family composition in American society and their effects on delinquency and other youth behaviors.

- Understand the effects of parenting on prosocial and delinquent behaviors.

- Grasp the nature and extent of the maltreatment of children.

- Explore how public policies attempt to reduce delinquency by targeting family factors.

KEY TERMS

socialization 233
single-parent
  families 238
latchkey children 244
authoritative
  parents 246
authoritarian
  parents 246
indulgent parents 246
indifferent
  parents 247

maltreatment 248
physical abuse 248
sexual abuse 248
emotional abuse 248
physical neglect 248
educational
  neglect 249
emotional neglect 249
Family Dependency
  Treatment
  Courts 253

The family is the most important social institution. The earliest and most critical stages of a child's socialization occur within the family. The family is largely responsible for instilling in children important moral and religious values and understanding about right and wrong. However, as a Chinese proverb says, "No family is perfect." In other words, in all families there are problems. Family problems, however, vary greatly in both type and magnitude. In addition, there is substantial variation in the degree to which delinquency is part of a family's history (see **Box 9.1**, the "A Window on Delinquency" feature). The problems of some families may be minor and produce only small consequences for family members. Other families may experience greater problems, and their impact on family members may be significant. One problem families often face is juvenile delinquency.

The family has long been considered to play an important role in producing or reducing delinquency. For example, in 1915 Douglas Morrison wrote that "among social circumstances which have a hand in determining the future of the individual it is enough for our present purpose to recognize that the family is chief."[1] Now, a century later, we are bombarded in the news with

BOX 9.1

A Window on Delinquency

Delinquency, Abuse, and Violence Runs in Families

It has long been understood that crime runs in families. Virtually every criminological theory uses some family characteristic or process to explain how delinquency is proportionately more likely to occur in families where members are already engaged in antisocial behavior. Researchers in Sweden demonstrated how strongly delinquency and violence tends to cluster within families. Using data from 12.5 million individuals in the nationwide Multi-Generation Register, Thomas Frisell, Paul Lichtenstein, and Niklas Långström compared the violent convictions among relatives of violent individuals with relatives of matched nonviolent controls using a nested case-control design. They produced several interesting findings:

- The odds of violence are 4.3 times higher among first-degree relatives of violent offenders.
- The odds of violence are nearly two times higher among distant relatives of violent offenders.
- Among siblings, there is dramatically higher likelihood of violence if one's sibling is involved in violent delinquency. The odds ratio by offense are:
  12.8 for homicide
  22.4 for arson
  35.7 for kidnapping
  13.5 for robbery
  4.7 for assault
  6.8 for threats and violence against a police officer
  15.2 for unlawful coercion
  6.1 for unlawful threat
  4.8 for intimidation

The effects are not limited to blood relatives. The odds of violence are 5.2 times higher among unrelated mating partners. Their findings demonstrate the salience of the family to delinquency and violence and the interactive effects of biological and social variables in the production of antisocial conduct.

Other studies examined the intergenerational continuity in delinquency and violent behaviors and the various forms of family abuse and dysfunction that produce them. One such study using the Swedish data found that males who had a brother who was convicted of a sexual offense were five times more likely to commit rape or sexual abuse. Boys with a father who was a sex offender were nearly four times more likely to commit sexual delinquency. Genetic factors explained about 40% of the variance of family aggregation in sexual offending. Cathy Spatz Widom and her colleagues also have shown intergenerational clustering and transmission of child abuse and neglect and its close association with delinquency, violence, and other problem behaviors.

The good news is that positive family behaviors are also clustered and transmitted across generations. A study of an epidemiology sample from the United States found that 20% of families are characterized by a history of problem behaviors, delinquency, alcoholism, and diverse criminal involvement. However, more than 70% of families have minimal family history of problem behaviors and are essentially delinquency-free. In addition, these families have higher socioeconomic functioning and less psychopathology. Whether good or bad, experiences, traits, and behaviors indeed run in families.

Thomas Frisell, Paul Lichtenstein, and Niklas Långström, "Violent Crime Runs in Families: A Total Population Study of 12.5 Million Individuals," *Psychological Medicine* 41:97–105 (2011); Niklas Långström, Kelly Babchishin, Seena Fazel, Paul Lichtenstein, and Thomas Frisell, "Sexual Offending Runs in Families: A 37-Year Nationwide Study," *International Journal of Epidemiology* 44:713–720 (2015); Cathy Spatz Widom, Sally Czaja, and Kimberly DuMont, "Intergenerational Transmission of Child Abuse and Neglect: Real or Detection Bias?" *Science* 347:1480–1485 (2015); Michael Vaughn, Christopher Salas-Wright, Matt DeLisi, and Zhengmin Qian, "The Antisocial Family Tree: Family Histories of Behavior Problems in Antisocial Personality in the United States," *Social Psychiatry and Psychiatric Epidemiology* 50:821–831 (2015).

appalling cases of delinquency and violence occurring by and within families:[2]

- In Texas, two young men were sentenced to up to 8 years in prison for coaxing two toddlers in their care to smoke marijuana. The toddlers were ages 2 and 4 at the time of the incident, an incident that was also videotaped and showed the adults laughing as the children smoked marijuana. Toxicology tests later found that the toddlers also had cocaine in their systems.
- In Arizona, a mother and a man who agreed to babysit her 3-year-old daughter were arrested for sexual trafficking, kidnapping, sexual conduct with a minor, and child abuse. The child was found bound with duct tape and placed in

a trash bag in a closet. The male defendant in the case had sexually abused the girl and also offered her sexually to other adults who visited the apartment. Authorities called it among the worst cases of child abuse they had ever witnessed.

- In California, a mother doused herself and her children, ages 4 years and 18 months, with gasoline and set her family on fire because she was stressed about her marriage. All parties died in the blaze.
- In Ohio, a mother was convicted of killing her 1-month-old daughter by incinerating her in a microwave oven.
- In Texas, a 25-year-old woman and her boyfriend were arrested by FBI agents for attempting to

sell her 5-year-old daughter on the Internet to a child molester.

- A mother in California was convicted of several crimes for driving her son and his friends to a rival gang member's house to take part in a drive-by shooting.
- In Florida, a 12-year-old boy who was left to babysit his 17-month-old cousin was charged with murder after killing the toddler with a baseball bat when he became enraged that she cried and interrupted his cartoon show.

Based on these reports, it is no wonder that the family is related in some way to antisocial behaviors.

Of course, we are also daily bombarded with the truly wonderful effects that come from parents loving and investing in their children. This is an important point to consider when assessing the role of the family in delinquency. Just as many negative parental behaviors create harm for their children and place them at risk for delinquency, many positive parental behaviors protect and insulate children from an assortment of risks, including delinquency and victimization.

For instance, Jacinta Bronte-Tinkew and her colleagues used data from the Early Childhood Longitudinal Study–Birth Cohort to examine how father involvement is positively associated with infant cognitive outcomes including language development, such as babbling and exploring objects with a purpose. They found that various types of father involvement, such as cognitively stimulating activities, physical care, paternal warmth, and caregiving activities, are associated with a reduced likelihood of infant cognitive delay. Interestingly, father involvement is related to greater reductions in infant cognitive delay for male infants than for female infants and for infants with disabilities than for infants without. These findings point to the importance of considering fathers' roles in early infant outcomes, which, of course, have implications for outcomes occurring later in life. Another mundane and perhaps overlooked feature of positive families is regular mealtime and bedtime routines. Children who are raised in homes where there is a clear schedule, characterized by organization, security, and routine, fare much better than children reared in more chaotic homes. A study of 3136 families participating in the Generation R Study, a large-scale population study in the Netherlands, found that children who were raised in families where there were clear routines for meals and bedtime were less aggressive and engaged in fewer disruptive and delinquent behaviors. In addition, boys who were already displaying anger and emotional regulation problems had significant reductions in their oppositional behaviors when in homes characterized by family regularity.[3]

How do families contribute to the delinquent behavior of their children? In this chapter, after discussing traditional functions of the family, we explore the effects of various types of family structures, family dynamics, and parenting styles on delinquency.

Traditional Functions of the Family

Traditionally, the family has performed four principal functions: socialization of children, inculcation of moral values, reproduction and regulation of sexual activity, and provision of material, physical, and emotional security.

The Socialization of Children

The family is the first and most important social unit to affect children; it is the first social world the child encounters. **Socialization** is the process through which children learn the ways of a particular society or social group so that they can function within it. Individuals learn the attitudes, behaviors, and social roles considered appropriate for them from already socialized individuals, typically parents and other family members. Through the socialization process in families, the personalities, values, and beliefs of children are initially shaped. Families aid in the development of stable and emotionally secure individuals and enhance the cognitive and language development of children by providing a variety of intellectually rich and stimulating experiences. Parents and older family members also serve as role models, transmit educational values, and provide environments in which children can safely develop a sense of autonomy.[4]

Of course, families are not isolated groups. Rather, they exist within a larger social and cultural context and will reflect the family's particular class, ethnic, racial, religious, political, and regional characteristics. As a consequence, a child's socialization is somewhat selective, depending on the background and contextual experiences of his or her particular family. The socialization of children also entails guidance about the proper ways to act and to avoid improper—that is, delinquent—behavior. It appears that the traditional or "nuclear" family is best at insulating children from delinquency, as evidenced by delinquency levels for children from such families that are 15% lower on average than delinquency levels for youths from nonintact families. When Robert Apel and Catherine Kaukinen analyzed data from the National Longitudinal Survey of Youth, they found youths in two-biological-parent or intact families committed the fewest kinds of antisocial behaviors. They also found that youths in *blended families* (in which the child lives with both

KEY TERMS

socialization
The process through which children learn the norms and values of a particular society or social group so that they can function within it.

biological parents, but has half- and stepsiblings who may or may not reside in the household) and *intact cohabiting families* (in which unmarried biological parents live together) were significantly more antisocial than their counterparts in *nuclear households* (defined as two married biological parents with no half- or stepsiblings). The difference between blended and nuclear households is accounted for by a variety of structural and experiential factors, the most important of which include disadvantage related to family income, government aid, teenage motherhood, grade repetition, scholastic performance, antisocial peers, and prior antisocial behavior.

Apel and Kaukinen also report that youths who live in one-biological-parent families have the highest risk of antisocial behavior when the biological father is the custodian. Their findings are not exclusive to American delinquency. A study of 508 adolescents who were seen for psychiatric services in Finland found that adolescents from single-parent families, from child welfare placements, and those not living with their biological parents were at greater risk for delinquency than adolescents from two-parent families.[5] Of course, a major reason for this finding is that two parents are better able to supervise and monitor children than one parent. This is particularly important for parental monitoring of peers. Keeping children away from delinquent peers goes a long way toward preventing a child from becoming delinquent. For instance, research by Frank Dillon and his colleagues has revealed that parental monitoring of peers can significantly reduce a host of adolescent delinquency behaviors, including drug use, externalizing behaviors, and risky sexual behaviors. Whether or not parents are around and *when* they are around also matters. Joshua Hendrix and Toby Parcel found that children reared in traditional homes where both parents work nonstandard hours, such as the night shift, have less family bonding and greater delinquency. However, homes where the mother works nontraditional hours,

but the father works traditional hours are associated with lower delinquency among children.[6]

At a theoretical level, families are also the primary locus for teaching children self-control, which is a major inhibitor of delinquency. Gottfredson and Hirschi argue that adolescents who have low self-control are more likely to participate in delinquency than are youth with greater self-control, and the primary "'cause' of low self-control is ineffective child rearing."[7] A key ingredient in the socialization of children is the development of an appropriate level of self-control.

Our own families and even the age order of our family structure can affect the likelihood of delinquency. Recently economists who study birth order discovered that merely having an older sibling increases the likelihood that younger brothers and sisters will misbehave. Younger siblings were 3 to 7% more likely to smoke cigarettes, drink alcohol, smoke marijuana, and be sexually active if they had an older brother or sister. While the purpose of the family is to socialize children for positive behaviors, such socialization also has negative consequences (see **Box 9.2**, the "A Window on Delinquency" feature).[8]

Inculcation of Moral Values

One of the most critical aspects of socialization is the development of moral values in children. Moral education, or the training of the individual to be inclined toward the good, involves a number of things, including learning the rules of society and developing good habits.[9] Youths who have developed higher levels of prosocial moral reasoning, such as operating according to empathetic motives and internalizing values that would lead them to act in ways to benefit others and society, are less likely to engage in aggressive behavior and delinquency.[10] Although the church and school complement the family in both teaching and setting examples of moral behavior, it is in the family where the development of moral virtue or good character is effectively formed or left unformed.[11] Psychologist Robert Coles puts it this way:

> Good children are boys and girls who in the first place have learned to take seriously the very notion, the desirability, of goodness—a living up to the Golden Rule, a respect for others, a commitment of mind, heart, soul to one's family, neighborhood, nation—and have also learned that the issue of goodness is not an abstract one, but rather a concrete, expressive one: how to turn the rhetoric of goodness into action.[12]

Similarly, the Children's Defense Fund advocates that every child deserves a *moral start* in life, meaning that he or she should be taught the enduring values of honesty, hard work, discipline, respect for self and others, responsibility, and the Golden Rule ("Do unto others as you would have done to yourself").[13]

Socialization occurs at all times throughout a child's development and the long-term effects of good parenting are many.

© iofoto/Shutterstock.

BOX 9.2

A Window on Delinquency

Parents Behind Bars

Children who grow up to be well-functioning adults experience security and stability as they develop and are effectively socialized to take on roles in society. In contrast, children who grow up in families where a parent is incarcerated may have experiences that do not promote their development into well-functioning adults. In other words, having a mother or father in prison is not normal and probably will result in many negative outcomes for children. What are these outcomes?

Anne Dannerbeck examined 1112 juvenile offenders in Missouri, 31% of whom had a parental history of incarceration. She found that parents who had previously been imprisoned:

- Exhibited lower levels of effective parenting.
- Exhibited higher levels of ineffective parenting.
- Exhibited more substance abuse problems.
- Exhibited more psychiatric problems.
- Were more likely to physically abuse their children.
- Were more likely to lose their children to out-of-home placement.
- Were significantly more likely to have children with serious delinquent histories.

A parental history of incarceration also strongly correlates with a host of other adverse childhood experiences, including physical, emotional, and sexual abuse; neglect; and exposure to family violence. Kevin Wolff and his colleagues studied a sample of nearly 28,000 youth who were referred to juvenile justice facilities and found that those with more adverse childhood experiences, including parental incarceration, were more likely to continue committing delinquent acts upon release to the community. Interestingly, epidemiological researchers have found that those whose parent or parents were incarcerated during their childhood are much more likely to suffer a heart attack during adulthood, even while controlling for many other factors.

The multifaceted negative effects of prisoner parents on children are not limited to the United States. For instance, when Joseph Murray and David Farrington evaluated the effects of parental imprisonment on a cohort of London boys during the first 10 years of life, they uncovered dramatic results. Boys whose mother or father had been imprisoned were significantly more delinquent than their peers who had more normal upbringings. In fact, the independent effect of parental imprisonment continued to predict antisocial behavior and crime when the boys were 32 years old. In short, prisoner parents inflict a variety of serious risks on their children, many of which continue to cause problems into adulthood.

Anne Dannerbeck, "Differences in Parenting Attributes, Experiences, and Behaviors of Delinquent Youth with and without a Parental History of Incarceration," *Youth Violence and Juvenile Justice* 3:199–213 (2005); Holly Foster, "The Strains of Maternal Imprisonment: Importation and Deprivation Stressors for Women and Children," *Journal of Criminal Justice* 40: 221–229 (2012); Kevin Wolff, Michael Baglivio, and Alex Piquero, "The Relationship between Adverse Childhood Experiences and Recidivism in a Sample of Juvenile Offenders in Community-Based Treatment," *International Journal of Offender Therapy and Comparative Criminology*, in press (2016); Bradley White, Lydia Cordie-Garcia, and Esme Fuller-Thomson, "Incarceration of a Family Member During Childhood is Associated with Later Heart Attack: Findings from Two Large, Population-Based Studies," *Journal of Criminal Justice* 44:89–98 (2016); Joseph Murray and David Farrington, "Parental Imprisonment: Effects on Boys' Antisocial Behavior and Delinquency through the Life Course," *Journal of Child Psychology and Psychiatry* 46:1269–1278 (2005).

Religion

Nineteenth-century French sociologist Emile Durkheim believed the integrative function of religion was crucial for maintaining social order. According to Durkheim, social cohesion is enhanced through shared values and norms generally originating from religious practice. When parents view religion as important, communicate religious values and practices to their children, and involve their children in religious activities, inclinations toward delinquency are reduced. Religious beliefs, according to Bruce Chadwick and Brent Top, have long been understood to be the foundation for moral behavior; thus "the more religious a person is, the less likely he or she will be to participate in delinquent or criminal behaviors."[14]

There is much evidence that an adolescent's religiosity—typically measured by religious participation, including church attendance, private prayer, bible study, discussing one's belief in God with others, belief in this-world or other-worldly sanctions, and attitudes and behaviors reflecting the individual's commitment to the religious teachings of his or her faith—is negatively related to delinquency. A recent analysis of 60 published studies conducted over the last 30 years examining the relationship between religion and delinquency concluded that "religious behavior and beliefs exert a significant, moderate deterrent effect on individuals' criminal behavior."[15] Byron Johnson and his colleagues examined the impact of religiosity on over 2300 at-risk African American juveniles living in poverty tracts in Boston, Chicago, and Philadelphia. They found that church attendance—even after controlling for background and other nonreligious variables, such as secular bonding and informal social controls through the family and school—had an independent effect on nondrug crime, drug use, and drug dealing among the disadvantaged youth.[16]

Other studies have also found religion to have a deterrent impact on delinquency. For example, Brent Benda and Robert Corwyn looked at random samples of youths from two public schools in an inner-city area of a large, East Coast city and from three rural public schools in the South. They concluded that religion is inversely related to crime among adolescents in both urban and rural public schools, although this factor did not appear to affect illicit drug use. Benda and Corwyn speculate that drug use may have reached a widely "normalized" level of acceptable behavior within teen culture. One way that religion might buffer against delinquency is by its habilitative effects on self-control. Kevin Rounding and his associates conducted experiments in which they found that exposure to religious themes increased the subject's self-control. Even when they were taxed in their self-control capacity, religious content was found to replenish it. Thus, religion could indirectly guard against delinquency by boosting youth's self-control.[17]

Interestingly, the most frequently cited work on the topic of religiosity and delinquency is an article titled "Hellfire and Delinquency" by Travis Hirschi and Rodney Stark. These authors reported that there was *no* link between belief in hell and religiosity (the latter measured by church and Sunday school attendance) and delinquent behavior. The popularity of the study's findings "that religion fails to guide teenagers along the straight and narrow was soon enshrined in undergraduate textbooks."[18] Subsequent research, however, consistently has found strong negative initial effects of religion on delinquency. Stark accounts for the relative uniqueness of the original findings as a product of their study being done on the West Coast, where there is very low religious involvement compared to other regions of the country. Studies conducted in the East, South, Midwest, and Rocky Mountain states have consistently found an adolescent's religiosity, especially when reinforced by family and peer religiousness, to have a preventive effect on delinquency.[19] Today, Stark is not hesitant to state the opposite conclusion to his original work: "Other things being equal, religious individuals will be less likely than those who are not religious to commit deviant acts."[20]

Sex

The family is the traditional social unit for sexual reproduction. The family teaches children society's norms related to sexual conduct, including both what is acceptable and what is unacceptable. In the family, children learn at what age, with whom, and under which circumstances they may engage in sexual relationships. Children also learn in the family about the consequences of sexual activity—that is, if pregnancy occurs, who is responsible for the care and maintenance of the infant and how such care should be provided.[21]

Jennifer Manlove and her colleagues assessed the link between religiosity and risky sexual behaviors among a large sample of more than 6000 youths from the National Longitudinal Survey of Youth. Following are some of their findings:[22]

- Family religiosity led to stronger parent–child relationships, higher parental monitoring and awareness of where the child is, and more routine family activities, such as eating dinner together regularly.
- These elements of family cohesion reduce risky teen sexual behavior regardless of family religiosity.
- Sexually active male teens from more religious families are less likely to use contraceptives consistently, which conveys the importance that such families place on abstaining from sex, but also highlights the need for contraception once youths become sexually active.
- For girls, being from a more religious family is indirectly linked with having fewer sexual partners and greater contraceptive consistency through a later age at first sex, more positive peer environments, and higher levels of parental monitoring and awareness.
- The benefits of delaying sex include reduced exposure to the risk of pregnancy and sexually transmitted diseases and greater contraceptive use.

Provision of Material, Physical, and Emotional Security

Families are the primary providers of the material well-being of their members. Specifically, the family clothes, feeds, and provides shelter for these individuals. Parents or older siblings provide supervision and monitoring of younger children to ensure their safety

Children with a strong moral fiber are significantly more likely to engage in conventional activities and significantly less likely to be delinquent. Is the role of morality in behavior respected or minimized by today's culture?

© sonya etchison/Shutterstock.

and obedience. In addition, the family provides for the physical security of its members, and the mere presence of family members in the home functions to protect the family from potential thieves, vandals, and burglars.[23] Finally, the family provides emotional security to its members through giving encouragement, support, and unconditional love.

The support that families—and especially parents—provide to their children is cumulative. In turn, one of the best predictors of a child's life outcomes is the background of his or her parents. Steven Levitt and Stephen Dubner suggest that "who" the parents are is more meaningful in explaining their children's success or failure than their parenting ability. Levitt and Dubner found that a child with at least 50 children's books in his or her room scores about five percentile points higher on standardized intelligence tests than a child with no books, and a child with 100 books scores another five percentile points higher than a child with 50 books. Highly educated, well-paid parents who waited until they reached age 30 to start their families tend to have children with the highest test scores. Other important parenting factors, such as how much TV watching was allowed, whether the mother worked outside the home, whether children went to museums, and whether they attended Head Start programs, did not affect test scores nearly as much.

Levitt and Dubner suggest that efforts to improve parenting techniques are highly overrated when it comes to assessing the material and human resources actually provided to children. By the time most parents pick up a book on parenting techniques, it's too late. Many of the things that matter most were decided long ago, such as how much education the parents have, how hard they worked to build careers, who they married, and how long they waited to have children.[24]

The world is not perfect, of course, and many families fail at achieving one or more of these goals. Families often transmit values that promote violence or criminality and undermine the development of positive self-concepts among their children. Too often, families fail to inculcate moral values or virtues in their young. Likewise, too many families fail to provide adequate material, physical, and emotional security to their members when parents divorce or fail to marry in the first place or when they engage in disreputable or criminal behavior, thereby ignoring the primary needs of the children.

The Changing Family

A number of changes in the American family during the past few decades have prompted both controversy and debate over the meaning and implications of the trends. In 1970, 85% of children younger than age 18 lived with both mother and father; 35 years later only 67% of children lived with both parents. By 2015, 69% of children lived with both parents. Approximately 23 million children live with one parent—nearly 18 million with their mother and nearly 3 million with their father. During the first decade of the 21st century, a majority of children were expected to spend a portion of their childhood in families with only one parent.[25] In 2006, for the first time in American history, the majority of U.S. households (50.2%) consisted of unmarried couples.

Also that year, nearly 40% of babies born in the United States were out-of-wedlock (referred to as "illegitimate births" in the past). Whereas out-of-wedlock births were once considered taboo, today they are so commonplace that they are statistically almost the norm. In fact, 17% of fathers aged 16 to 45 have had children with more than one woman. Approximately one-third of these fathers have children with multiple women across a series of nonmarital relationships. Overall, nearly 41% of all births in the United States are to unmarried women.[26]

The number of children's books in a child's room has been shown to influence his or her test scores in subsequent years. What other benefits may come from owning books and reading with a child?

These trends are troubling. James Q. Wilson observed that:

> . . . those [children] raised by mothers, black or white, who have never married are more likely to be poor, to acquire less schooling, to be expelled or suspended from school, to experience emotional or behavioral problems, to display antisocial behavior, to have trouble getting along with their peers, and to start their own single-parent families. These unhappy outcomes afflict both girls and boys, but they have a more adverse effect on boys.[27]

Changes in the American family have many unintended consequences, including those related to the most serious forms of delinquency. For example, Jennifer Schwartz examined whether family structure influences the murder rate. It does: Counties with greater levels of family disruption (defined as single-parent, female-headed households) have higher murder rates than counties with predominantly traditional family structures. Schwartz found that a 1% increase in a community's level of family disruption increased homicides by women by 11% and homicides by men by 25%. In places where at least 20% of the households are female headed, the male homicide rate is 125% higher and the female homicide rate is 55% higher.[28]

Many other changes are occurring in the American family during the 21st century—some good, some bad, and some just different. For example, the United States is becoming a more adult-focused society after being a child-centered society for decades. Longer life expectancy, delayed marriage and child rearing, and more childlessness equate to a longer life span without children. In a way, raising children—an activity that was once central to most adults' lives—has become a niche lifestyle, just a small part of the life course. At the same time, other research indicates that both married and single parents are spending more time with their children, almost as much as they did 40 years ago. Also, men perform more housework than ever before.[29]

How do these trends relate to satisfaction with family life? The Pew Research Center conducted a poll of 3000 Americans and found that family ties are as strong as ever. Approximately 42% of adults see or talk to a parent daily, an increase of 10% from 1989. Nearly 80% of adults have daily contact with distant relatives each day usually via e-mail or telephone. Overall, 72% of adults indicated that they were very satisfied with their family life.[30]

Perhaps because of these changing trends, people in other countries hold conflicting opinions of the American family. According to family researchers, people living in certain Asian, African, and South American countries consider the American nuclear family of husband, wife, and children (and not extended relatives and in-laws) to be the ideal family composition. American families are also lauded for marriages based on love and companionship (rather than arranged marriages), material comfort, and independence. Conversely American families are criticized for placing too much emphasis on work and not enough emphasis on children as well as for being selfish and overly individualistic.[31] The central point made by opinion surveys is that family structure directly affects quality of life and other social indicators.

Single-Parent Families

What might account for the increase in **single-parent families**? Linda Gordon and Sara McLanahan point out that in 1900 only 5% of all children in single-parent homes were living with a parent who was divorced or had never married; instead, most of the parents in these homes were widowed.[32] By the early 21st century, however, only 5% of all female-headed households with children had experienced the death of the father and 37% had experienced parental divorce; in 36% of these homes, the parents had never married. The remaining 22% of the households were classified as "married, spouse absent."[33]

Nearly 1 million American teenagers become pregnant each year; most teen pregnancies end in abortion, and approximately 275,000 teenagers give birth. The birth rate for teenagers ages 15 to 18 is 31 per 1000, though these rates vary by race. For example, the birth rate for white, non-Hispanic teenagers is 22 per 1000, for African American teenagers 47 per 1000, and for Hispanic teenagers 49 per 1000. Since 2007, teenage births among whites have dropped by 20%, teenage births among blacks have dropped by 30%, and teenage births among Hispanics have dropped by 40%. Most teenage births are to *unmarried teenagers*. Although the birth rate for unmarried teenagers has fallen since 1991, babies born to unmarried girls ages 15 to 17 account for 88% of all teenage-parent births, whereas 97% of births to girls younger than 15 years involve unmarried parents.[34]

Single-parent families are not evenly distributed across racial and ethnic groups. Today, approximately 26% of white children, 42% of Hispanic children, and 66% of African American children are being raised by a single parent. Single-parent families also are disproportionately at or near the poverty level: The poverty rate for single-parent families is approximately five times higher than that for two-parent families. Ten percent of children in two-parent families live in poverty, and 46% of children in female-headed families reside in households at or below the poverty level. And although race and ethnicity are related to poverty, such dramatic differences in family poverty rates are not a function of race or ethnicity. Only 18% of African American children living with their married parents live in poverty, whereas nearly 60% of African American children living in female-headed households live below the poverty level.[35]

Teenage mothers are three times more likely than other teenagers to drop out of school, and they earn less money than unmarried mothers who did not have their first child until they were in their 20s. They are also likely to spend longer periods of time living in poverty. For instance, Sara Jaffee and her colleagues studied the effects of teenage motherhood on these women's children 20 years later. Approximately 40% of the negative life outcomes that these youths experienced (e.g., delinquency, unemployment, school failure, adult crime) were directly and independently explained by their mother giving birth as a teenager.[36] Overall, teenage childbearing is costly to taxpayers, with the federal government spending nearly $40 billion each year to assist families that began with a teenage birth. More generally, the costs of family fragmentation costs U.S. taxpayers at least $112 billion each year.[37]

Travis Hirschi points out, however, that the teenage mother herself should not be targeted as the primary problem. According to Hirschi, "the teenage mother is not the problem. . . . The problem is the mother without a husband. Her children are likely to be delinquent, and she is likely to have more of them." He argues there should be two parents for every child and that delinquency can be reduced by improving the quality of child-rearing practices. This means strengthening the bonds not only between parents and children but also between husbands and wives.[38] Indeed, father absence creates a host of problems for girls. Compared to girls with both parents, those without fathers are more likely to be diagnosed with conduct disorder, to be diagnosed with mood and anxiety disorders, to attempt suicide, to drop out of school, and to commit violent forms of delinquency.[39]

What about teenage fathers? What are the consequences of fatherhood for adolescent boys? Between 2 and 7% of male teenagers are fathers. Teen fatherhood is associated with growing up in poverty and hanging out with friends who engage in delinquency and other problem behaviors. Like teenage mothers, teenage fathers experience many negative educational, financial, social, health, and other developmental consequences. They are more likely to drop out of school and to enter the workplace earlier than their peers and to earn less money than their peers when they reach their mid-20s. Interestingly, boys who become teenage fathers are also more likely to engage in a variety of other problem behaviors,

such as status offenses, disruptive school behavior, and illicit drug use. According to Terence Thornberry and his colleagues:

Young fathers tended to be troubled young men who were significantly more likely than their matched controls to have engaged in varied serious acts of delinquency in the year of fatherhood and in the year after. . . . They were more likely than non-fathers to have had a court petition alleging delinquency, to be drinking alcohol frequently, to be involved in drug dealing, or to have dropped out of school.[40]

Often times teen fathers are unlikely to be in a position to provide financial, emotional, or other parental support for their children; as a consequence, they are likely to serve as poor role models for those children. As Thornberry and his associates note, "Their legacy to their children is likely to be one of socioeconomic disadvantage, poorer health, and poorer education, among other hardships."[41]

There is also an interesting relationship between teenage fatherhood and serious delinquent behavior. That is, chronic delinquents are significantly more likely to father children than are less seriously delinquents and nondelinquents. Evelyn Wei and her colleagues' analysis of a sample from the Pittsburgh Youth Study found that by age 19, nearly half of the serious repeat offenders had caused at least one pregnancy (which could have terminated by miscarriage or abortion) and one-third had fathered at least one child. They also report that "repeat serious delinquents were not only more likely to father children during adolescence; many had fathered multiple children, accounting for 65% of the offspring produced by teenage fathers. And although these youth produced many children, they were less likely to be living with or to spend time with their children."[42]

Children in poor, single-parent families, especially those headed by teenage mothers, clearly face special difficulties. They are more likely to experience chronic psychological distress, to engage in health-compromising behaviors (including drug and alcohol use, cigarette smoking, and unprotected sex), to perform less well academically, to be expelled or suspended from school, to drop out of school, to suffer from mental illness, to commit suicide, to have trouble getting along with their peers, and to start their own single-parent families.[43] Jeffrey Grogger reports that the sons of adolescent mothers are nearly three times more likely to be incarcerated at some point in their 20s than the sons of mothers who delay childbearing until they are in their early 20s.[44]

Economic and emotional supports are critical for single-parent families—yet relatively few noncustodial fathers provide that kind of support. For example, one-third of families with children receive none of the financial support awarded by courts; when those

families do receive support, it usually amounts to only 60% of the award. Furthermore, noncustodial fathers are unlikely to have much—if any—contact with their children. Based on a National Survey of Children report, approximately 26% of noncustodial divorced fathers manage a visitation with their children on just a bimonthly basis, and 23% had no contact with their children ages 11 to 16 in the previous 5-year period. Fathers never married to the mothers of their children had much less contact with their children.[45]

Of course, not all children being raised in single-parent homes live in poverty, nor are all born to unmarried or teenage mothers. Many children are being raised by a divorced parent. The process and consequences of divorce on children may have negative effects independent of the mother's age or economic status. It is not unusual for intact families to be fraught with conflict between husbands and wives or for a pervasive silence to be cast over the members of the family as each attempts to avoid provoking outbursts in others. Frequently, relations improve after divorce or separation. Nevertheless, much current research suggests that both the structural reality of single parenting as a consequence of divorce and the very process of going through divorce produce adverse consequences for the children in the family.[46] The adverse consequences are often long lasting. Frances Rice and her colleagues report that family conflict increases the likelihood of children experiencing clinical depression during childhood and adolescence.[47]

Each year approximately 2%—nearly 2 million families—of all married couples in the United States get divorced, and more than half of these breakups involve children younger than age 18. According to the National Center for Health Statistics, 12% of couples divorce within 3 years of getting married, 20% within 5 years, and 33% within 10 years.[48] Those couples who divorce and then remarry other partners are even more likely to find the subsequent marriage falling apart, and multiple divorces are harder on the children. Children who have experienced multiple divorces are more likely to report higher levels of anxiety and depression, to fail in school, and eventually to have more troubled marriages of their own than are children who have experienced a single divorce or children whose families remain intact. Frank Furstenberg and Andrew Cherlin estimate that 15% of all children in divorced families will see the parent they live with remarry and redivorce before they reach age 18.[49] The Family Research Council has long suggested that marriage and keeping a family intact provides numerous benefits to family members (both adults and children) and to society as a whole (see **Box 9.3**, the "A Window on Delinquency" feature).

Single Parents, Divorce, and Delinquency

The relationship between single-parent families and delinquency has been widely studied. Much research reports that children from single-parent families are more likely to become delinquent than children from two-parent families.[50] For example, Ann Goetting found that only 30% of the children arrested for homicide in Detroit over an 8-year span lived with both parents.[51] Edward Wells and Joseph Rankin's analysis of 50 studies led them to conclude that the effect of the single-parent family on delinquency is real and consistent but of relatively low magnitude and that the effect is greater for minor offenses and weaker for serious offenses.[52] When Michelle Miller and her colleagues surveyed approximately 500 students in 11 public schools, they found that adolescents in single-parent families are more likely to engage in both serious and minor delinquencies than are youths in two-parent families.[53] William Comandor and Llad Philip analyzed the impact of family structure on a youth's involvement with the criminal justice system using data from the National Longitudinal Survey of Youth. They concluded that "the most critical factor affecting the prospect that a male youth will encounter the criminal justice system is the presence of his father in the home. All other factors, including family income, are much less important." In addition, the effects of divorce on delinquency are certainly not limited to boys. A study of youth who participated in Multidimensional Treatment Foster Care found that girls whose parents were divorced were three times more likely to be arrested in adulthood than girls from non-divorced families.[54]

Explanations offered to explain the greater likelihood of delinquency among children from single-parent families include the following suggestions:[55]

- Single parents can less effectively supervise their children because one parent can do less than two.
- Children in single-parent families grow up too fast.
- Single mothers give adolescents greater say in what they can do or give too early autonomy, thereby reducing their control over youths.
- Children from single-parent families are more susceptible to peer pressure.
- Children in single-parent families experience lower levels of parental attachment.

The Impact of Divorce on Children

How does the breakup of a family affect children? According to Ronald Simons and his colleagues, divorced parents make fewer demands on their children, provide less monitoring, are more likely to

BOX 9.3

A Window on Delinquency

Marriage Benefits

Several theoretical perspectives point to family processes as being crucial in understanding the causes of delinquency. Both sociological and biosocial perspectives assert that intact families, featuring married parents, promote many health and behavioral benefits for children. Indeed, studies of national data found that marriage explains a significant proportion of the race differences in health, wealth, and behavior in the United States, particularly in comparing whites to African Americans. Indeed, there are many ways that marriage benefits children:

How Marriage Benefits Children

- Children living with married parents are safer than children living with single parents, because they are less likely to be abused or neglected.
- Compared to children in single-parent families, children raised in married-parent homes have better emotional and physical health and engage in fewer risky behaviors, such as premarital sex, substance abuse, delinquency, and suicide.
- Children with married parents do better academically and fare better economically.
- Children raised in intact homes are less likely to cohabit and more likely to view marriage positively and maintain lifelong marriages.

How Marriage Benefits Adults

- Married people have better emotional and physical health and live longer than do unmarried people.
- Married couples have higher incomes than do single adults. The longer they stay married, the more wealth they accumulate.
- Married couples enjoy greater sexual satisfaction than do unmarried people.
- Married women are safer than unmarried women: Never-married, cohabiting, separated, and divorced women experience higher rates of domestic violence than do married women.

How Marriage Benefits Society

- Marriage helps ensure that human life is protected and cherished, because married women are less likely to abort their children than are unmarried women.
- Marriage makes homes safer places to live, because it curbs social problems such as domestic violence and child abuse.
- Communities with more married-parent families are safer and more attractive places to live, because they are less likely to be the sites of substance abuse and crime among young people.
- Married people are more likely to be healthy, productive, and engaged citizens, benefiting businesses and, ultimately, the economy.

Woojin Chung and Roeul Kim, "Are Married Men Healthier Than Single Women? A Gender Comparison of the Health Effects of Marriage and Marital Satisfaction in East Asia," *PLoS ONE* 10:e0134260 (2015); Yuriy Pylypchuk and James Kirby, "The Role of Marriage in Explaining Racial and Ethnic Disparities in Access to Health Care for Men in the US," *Review of Economics of the Household*, in press (2016); Bridget Maher, *The Benefits of Marriage* (Washington, DC: Family Research Council, 2004); James Q. Wilson, *The Marriage Problem: How Our Culture Has Weakened Families* (New York: HarperCollins, 2003); Shelly Lundberg and Robert Pollak, "The Evolving Role of Marriage: 1950–2010," *The Future of Children* 25:29–50 (2015).

display hostility, and tend to use less effective disciplinary techniques than do married parents. Each of these factors contributes to the greater likelihood of delinquency found among the children of a divorced family.[56] Mavis Hetherington reports that in the year following the breakup, children in single-parent families are more likely to suffer psychological distress, but in the long run they cope more successfully than children in intact families where parents do not get along. She sees three major effects of divorce on women that dramatically affect children: Divorced mothers are overloaded from both work and child rearing, face financial strains, and are likely to be socially isolated.[57]

Divorce also may produce "family wars," in which relatives and friends pick sides and attempt to "win" by attacking the former spouse. Children are caught in the middle, often being defined as victims or expected to accept new definitions of the former spouse. In

either case, the stress produced for the child may manifest itself in many ways. Some studies have found a relationship between father absence and a host of social and emotional ills, including decreased school performance and self-control and increased rates of psychological disturbance, drug use, gang affiliation, and involvement in violent crime.[58]

Judith Wallerstein and Joan Kelly studied families in the early stages of breaking up, after 18 months apart, and after 5 years. In the first period, both parents typically felt the pinch of a lower standard of living and were depressed and lonely. Mothers were also overburdened by having to juggle breadwinner and homemaker roles and had to stay up late to do so. Children were often upset and thoroughly opposed to the divorce. They became more angry, aggressive, and unruly during this initial stage of the breakup, partly because of their deteriorating relationships with their mothers. Eighteen months later, some mothers

were still depressed, but parent–child relations were healing and children themselves improved, with fewer feeling deprived or lonely. At the 5-year point, conditions were slightly worse than at 18 months. Among children, there was increased evidence of anger and depression.[59]

Judith Wallerstein and Sandra Blakeslee published results from a study in which 60 families and 131 youths were interviewed at 1-, 5-, 10-, and 15-year intervals after divorce in an attempt to discover both short- and long-term effects of divorce. After 5 years, one-third of the children were doing well, but another third were significantly worse off, suffering both academic and psychological difficulties. Some specific consequences of divorce on children resulted from the diminished capacity of parents to supervise almost all dimensions of child rearing. While in the process of divorce, parents spent less time with their children and were less responsive to their needs. Wallerstein and her colleagues published their findings from follow-up interviews with these same 131 subjects, now 25 years after divorce. Many still suffered from anxiety and had difficulty in establishing healthy relationships.[60]

Constance Ahrons argues that many divorces are actually "good," producing what she calls the binuclear family—a family that spans two households while continuing to meet the needs of the children. If the divorce is managed correctly, the divorcing parents and children will be able to emerge as emotionally healthy as they were before the divorce.[61] Divorce can also be portrayed as a positive factor if it reduces the incidence of family strife and arguing to which children are exposed. For instance, Patrick Davies and his colleagues found that children whose parents frequently argue and experience conflict have impaired ability to pay attention in school and are more likely to experience school problems than children whose parents have a good relationship.[62] Households characterized by stress and conflict affect both parents and children, and the results are reciprocally negative. For instance, Henrik Larsson and his colleagues found that childhood antisocial behavior increases parental negativity—that is, parents' feelings of stress, anger, and impatience toward their children. These negative feelings, in turn, contribute to increased antisocial behavior among children and adolescents.[63]

Taking the contrarian position is Elizabeth Marquardt, who believes that there are no "good" divorces when it comes to children. She contends the concept of a "good" divorce is an adult-centered vision. Children of divorce must go from a world that seemed safe to shuttling back and forth between two worlds, often perceived by the children as "polar opposites, left without clear guidance on right and wrong, and required to keep secrets about the different households."[64]

Remarrying after divorce does not necessarily eliminate the negative effects of the divorce. Children raised in stepfamilies do less well in school, experience higher levels of family conflict, have more adjustment problems, and are more likely to engage in delinquency than are children in two-parent, never-divorced families. Children in stepfamilies are two to three times more likely to engage in delinquency. Some evidence indicates that although the presence of a stepfather seems to increase the likelihood of delinquency, the presence of a stepmother may reduce it, although only a very small percentage of children from divorce live with stepmothers (see **Box 9.4**, the "Delinquency Controversy" feature).[65] Cesar Rebellon's analysis of data from the National Youth Survey suggests that youths who have been raised in the long-term presence of a stepparent are more likely to engage in violent delinquency than youths with minimal or no exposure to a stepparent.[66]

Finally, although divorce is related to or even causes multiple problems for children and adolescents, recent research suggests that delinquency may *not* be one of those problems. Jui-Chung Li analyzed data on more than 6300 children from the National Longitudinal Survey of Youth and found that children of divorce had higher levels of delinquency. Once other correlates of delinquency were considered, however, the effect of divorce disappeared. In other words, children may fare either well or poorly in terms of their behavioral adjustment whether their parents divorce or stay married because other factors explain delinquency.[67]

Working Mothers and Latchkey Children

Most women participate on either a full-time or part-time basis in the labor force today. Three-fourths of married women with children between the ages of 6 and 17 are employed; 78% of single mothers with children in this same age group are employed. But mothers with much younger children are also working outside the home: Today, more than 10 million women with children younger than age 6 are employed. This number includes 60% of married women and 68% of single women with children younger than age 6.[68] In view of this, some criminologists have asked whether there is a connection between women in the labor force and delinquency.

Research has found one definite effect of mothers being in the labor force: They have less time to spend with their children. As Russell Hill and Frank Stafford report, college-educated working mothers try hard to compensate for their absence: They cut down on time spent sleeping and relaxing more than they cut down on time spent with their children. The same authors also note that by the time children reach adolescence, parents in general spend only an hour or two per week in nurturing them; under these circumstances, there is little difference between working and nonworking mothers in terms of the time they give to their teenage children.[69] Therefore, having less time to spend

BOX 9.4

Delinquency Controversy

Are Delinquents Raised by Their Parents or Lowered by Them?

Despite the findings from hundreds of studies, the relationship between family structure and delinquency remains controversial. Anecdotally, there are millions of people who were raised in single-parent or divorced homes who did not commit delinquent acts. Moreover, millions of people who were reared in intact, nuclear families nevertheless display problem behaviors. These large exceptions cause some to question the scientific literature. In fact, a meta-analysis of 74 studies that included more than 55,000 participants reported that level of attachment to parents was significantly associated with delinquency; however, the effect was small in size.

Perhaps family structure is less important than the antisocial traits or delinquent potential of parents in producing antisocial outcomes in children. Recent research has shown how important parent antisociality is for children. Dylan Jackson and Kevin Beaver examined data from the Early Longitudinal Child Survey, Kindergarten (ECLS-K) and found that the antisocial traits and behaviors of children and parents are similar and mutually affect each other across the child's early years and into adolescence. Sara Jaffee and her colleagues studied a

sample of 1116, 5-year-old twin pairs and their parents and found children with less contact with their fathers (where the father lived in the same home as the child) had more conduct problems. That is expected. But they also found that this effect was true only if the father had low involvement in crime. Antisocial fathers contributed to delinquency in their children even when they lived at home with their children. In this way, having an antisocial father away would be beneficial to the child in terms of delinquency.

But it is not all dad's fault. Psychologists examined the biosocial predictors of aggressiveness among 12-month-old infants. They found that the mother's mood disorder during pregnancy and history of conduct problems predicted aggressiveness in her children. Drawing on data from the Fragile Families and Child Wellbeing Study, Brian Boutwell and Kevin Beaver found that maternal self-control and paternal self-control predicted their child's level of self-control. In sum, the antisocial traits and behaviors of parents are critically important for understanding whether youth will commit delinquency. Irrespective of family structure, a child's exposure to criminal parents wreaks havoc on their social development.

Machteld Hoeve, Geert Jan Stams, Claudia van der Put, Judith Semon Dubas, Peter van der Laan, and Jan Gerris, "A Meta-Analysis of Attachment to Parents and Delinquency," *Journal of Abnormal Child Psychology* 40:771–785 (2012); Dylan Jackson and Kevin Beaver, "A Shared Pathway of Antisocial Risk: A Path Model of Parent and Child Effects," *Journal of Criminal Justice* 43:154–163 (2015); Sara Jaffee, Terrie Moffitt, Avshalom Caspi, and Alan Taylor, "Life with (or without) Father: The benefits of Living with Two Biological Parents Depend on the Fathers Antisocial Behavior," *Child Development* 74:109–126 (2003); Dale Hay, Lisa Mundy, Siwan Roberts, Raffaella Carta, Cerith Waters, Oliver Perra, and Stephanie van Goozen, "Known Risk Factors for Violence Predict 12-Month-Old Infants' Aggressiveness with Peers," *Psychological Science* 22:1205–1211 (2011); Brian Boutwell and Kevin Beaver, "The Intergenerational Transmission of Low Self-Control," *Journal of Research in Crime and Delinquency* 47:174–209 (2010).

with her children does not necessarily mean that the mother is failing to perform her role adequately. As Keith Melville states, "[W]hen working mothers derive satisfaction from their employment and do not feel guilty about its effects, they are likely to perform the mother's role at least as well as nonworking women."[70]

Studies examining the effects of mothers' employment on children and their development have produced mixed results. For instance, Matthijs Kalmijn reports that having mothers who work in high-status jobs leads to positive school effects for their children: Sons and daughters do better academically and are more likely to complete high school, attend college, and eventually graduate.[71] Jay Belsky and David Eggebeen found that a variety of measures of adjustment, such as behavior problems, insecurity, and sociability, reflected no negative effects of employment of mothers.[72]

In one study, Travis Hirschi compared sons of homemakers, sons of women who worked part time, and sons of women who worked full time. He found

that 20% of sons of full-time working mothers, 17% of sons of part-time workers, and 16% of sons of homemakers were delinquent. Given the small magnitude of these differences, we can safely say that there is at most only a weak relationship between delinquency and mothers' employment status.[73]

What about working fathers? Between 80 and 90% of married and single fathers with children are employed. In the past, traditional gender roles guided fathers into breadwinning rather than into child-rearing and caregiving roles; the latter were considered the primary domains of mothers. David Popenoe notes that with the majority of mothers now in the labor force, "men are being asked to return to domestic roles. Fathers are badly needed as comprehensive childrearers on an equal basis with mothers."[74] Nevertheless, conflicts between fathers' and mothers' employment schedules tend to not only reduce the time fathers have available for caregiving but also contribute to increased stress and role conflict between husbands and wives. Only when fathers work different schedules

than their wives are they more likely to provide care for their children.[75]

When both mothers and fathers are employed outside the home with overlapping schedules, most children face the prospect of coming home to empty houses after school. The number of **latchkey children**—that is, children who regularly care for themselves without adult supervision after school or on weekends—has increased dramatically in the United States. More than 3 million children ages 6 to 12 now spend 5 or more hours per week unsupervised or in the care of a young sibling. More than 10% of these unsupervised children spend 10 or more hours per week alone while their parent or parents are at work.[76] Many experts believe that latchkey children, especially those in their teenage years, are more susceptible to opportunities for getting involved in delinquent situations.

Laurence Steinberg suggests that latchkey children face a variety of subtle fears and worries, such as exposure to dangers while alone and increased susceptibility to peer pressure. They have less adult supervision and, therefore, are more vulnerable to peer pressure to engage in delinquent acts.[77] Latchkey children are likely to "find other [children] who are coming home to empty houses. They create a peer-group culture, and it's likely to be an ugly culture—a culture of destroy, of break, of acting-out."[78]

In a study of the behavioral consequences of leaving children in self-care, students who spent 11 or more hours per week in self-care were twice as likely to use alcohol, tobacco, and marijuana as children of the same age whose after-school time was supervised by adults.[79] A recent national longitudinal study on adolescent health involving more than 12,000 middle and high school students, conducted by Michael Resnick and his associates, found the presence of parents at home at key times during the day (in the early morning, after school, at the evening meal, and at bedtime) provided moderate protection against emotional distress for children, reduced the frequency of use of alcohol and marijuana, and delayed adolescents' initiation of sexual intercourse.[80]

With the numerous problems posed by self-care, it is understandable that many parents turn to childcare providers. More than 60% of children younger than age 6 are cared for on a regular basis by caregivers other than their parents. Nearly 80% of children younger than age 5 are in some sort of childcare arrangement during a typical week, with 49% being cared for by nonrelatives. Preschoolers spend an average of 28 hours per week in child care.[81] Children who spend a large amount of time in day care may be more likely to develop behavioral problems than either children who spend less time in such programs or children who are cared for only by parents. In one study, approximately 17% of children who spent more than 30 hours per week in nonparental child care were found to be more demanding, more noncompliant, and more aggressive than their peers, compared to only 6% of children who spent less than 10 hours per week with nonparental caregivers. The former group of children was also more likely to engage in hitting, bullying, and explosive behavior and to demand a lot of attention. Jean-Baptiste Pingault and colleagues studied 1544 children in Canada and found that those who received nonparental child care were more oppositional, more aggressive, and less shy than their peers upon entry to school. However, they also found these group differences disappeared across the elementary school period as children who were not raised in child care "caught up" with their childcare peers in terms of aggressive and oppositional conduct.[82]

The solution may be problematic. Some critics argue that instead of reducing the amount of time spent in child care, high-quality child care should be expanded. Only 8% of daycare facilities qualify as "high-quality" operations. What distinguishes "high-quality" child care? Such programs provide intense, personal attention over an extended period of time—the same thing that real mothers do. Thus, instead of expanding child care, other critics argue that mothers should be urged to work less and spend more time with their children.

The difficulties in finding high-quality child care may be one of the factors contributing to the trend of more working married mothers with very young children choosing to leave the work force and stay home. Although approximately 74% of mothers with children younger than age 18 continue to participate in the work force, the proportion of working married mothers with children younger than age 3 has dropped over the past two decades.[83]

Parenting in Families

Although the relationships among broken homes, absent fathers, and working mothers have been extensively studied, research findings in these areas are inconsistent. Indeed, one body of research suggests that the most important determinant of whether a child will be involved in delinquency is the quality of the parent–child relationship rather than family structure alone (the nature and impact of parenting are discussed later in this chapter).[84] For example, a study of nearly 2500 middle and junior high school students in Dade County (Miami), Florida, reported that a strong attachment between parent and child significantly reduced the likelihood of delinquency, whereas family structure had only a weak indirect effect.[85] In addition, Marc Zimmerman and his colleagues studied the effects of family structure and parental attachment among 254 African American male adolescents from a large East Coast city. Regardless of family structure, the amount of time spent with their fathers and their perceptions of their fathers' emotional support were associated with lower levels of delinquency and marijuana use among the sons.[86]

Perhaps delinquency has more to do with family process than with family structure—an idea proposed by sociologists more than 50 years ago.[87] The link between family process variables and delinquency is examined next.

A standard assumption is that married adults automatically know how to be good parents—presumably there is some universal common sense transmitted from one generation to the next. In reality, effective parenting depends on many things. The quality of parenting (as well as interactions within the family) changes as a child's misbehavior or delinquency increases over time. Often parents become angry and short tempered with a child who consistently gets into trouble or become disillusioned when they find they cannot believe what the child tells them. Over time, parent–child conflicts may escalate, or the relationship between parent and child may become more distant and alienated. In circumstances where the child's antisocial behavior is directed against the parents, many parents are less able to exercise reasonable parental authority and may even abdicate their parental responsibilities altogether.

Gerald Patterson found the type of deviance children engage in most is the type parents tolerate most. In the case of children who steal, for example:

Many of the parents maintained that since they had never actually seen their child steal, they could not prove that their child had stolen, and therefore could not punish the child. In numerous instances, someone else had actually seen the child steal, but the child's "story" would be accepted by the parents, who would then rise to the child's defense and accuse others of picking on the child. As the parents used the word "steal," it could be used as a label only if it could be proven, which was usually impossible; ergo the child did not really steal, ergo no punishment could be applied.[88]

James Snyder and Gerald Patterson have identified two divergent disciplinary styles that characterize families with delinquent children: enmeshed and lax. Parents who practice the *enmeshed* style are overly inclusive in what they define as problematic behavior. Even trivial misbehaviors by the child result in sharp parental reactions ranging from cajoling to verbal threats. Nevertheless, enmeshed parents "fail to consistently and effectively back up these verbal reprimands with nonviolent, nonphysical punishment . . . [and]

inadvertently provide more positive consequences for deviant child behavior." At the other extreme, parents who engage in the *lax* style tend to be very liberal in what they define as excessive or antisocial behavior.

Problem solving and negotiating disagreements or conflict are ways to forestall violence. Snyder and Patterson believe that parental violence often erupts at the end of a chain of events that began with a trivial incident such as the child "sneaking" candy or food. To avoid such violence, parents must learn to break the chain and practice techniques of negotiating a settlement before minor matters get out of hand.[89]

But can Patterson's prescription be effective for all parents? Travis Hirschi has identified a few problems with this approach:

The parents may not care for the child (in which case none of the other conditions would be met); the parents, even if they care, may not have the time or energy to monitor the child's behavior; the parents, even if they care and monitor, may not see anything wrong with the child's behavior; finally, even if everything else is in place, the parents may not have the inclination or the means to punish the child.[90]

Hirschi also reminds us that families with more children face greater strain on parental resources such as time and energy. And single-parent families are strained even more:

The single parent . . . must devote a good deal to support and maintenance activities that are at least to some extent shared in the two-parent family. Further, she must do so in the absence of psychological or social support. As a result, she is less able to devote time to monitoring and punishment, and is more likely to be involved in negative, abusive contacts with her children.[91]

Parental Supervision

Patterson's rules of parenting also note the need for effective parental supervision, such as establishing a set of "house rules" and clearly communicating them. House rules should cover with whom the child associates, which places are considered off limits, when curfews are set, and when the child should be home from school. Parents must be aware of the child's performance in school as well as school attendance, the possibility of drug or alcohol use, and the activities the child is involved in with friends. "Good supervision . . . indirectly minimizes the adolescents' contact with delinquency—promoting circumstances, activities, and peers."[92]

Common sense suggests that unsupervised children are more likely to participate in delinquency, and substantial research has confirmed this relationship. For example, Grace Barnes and Michael Farrell studied

a sample of 699 adolescents and their families; they found that high levels of parental monitoring, when combined with high levels of parental support, were the key factor in preventing delinquency.[93] Jaana Haapasalo and Richard Tremblay examined aggressiveness in samples of more than 1000 boys in Montreal in an attempt to predict which boys would become "fighters" and which would be "nonfighters"; they concluded that nonfighters appeared to be the most closely supervised children and that low levels of supervision were associated with higher levels of fighting.[94]

Although the findings from a variety of studies indicate that poor parental supervision is a significant factor contributing to delinquency, Sung Jang and Carolyn Smith suggest that parental supervision and delinquency are reciprocally related. Their analysis of data collected from 838 urban adolescents led them to conclude that although parental supervision has a significant negative impact on delinquency, the effects of supervision vary over time, with the influence of parents declining as adolescents mature. These researchers also found that weak parental supervision not only promotes delinquency, but to the extent the child is delinquent, his or her participation in delinquency also leads to further erosion in the perception of effective parental supervision. Selma Salihovic and her colleagues' study of 875 adolescents in Sweden reported similar reciprocal effects between the youth's psychopathic personality traits and the parenting they received. More delinquent and psychopathic youth elicited more negative forms of parenting, including angry outbursts, coldness and rejection, limited understanding, and erratic supervision. Thus parenting should not be thought of as a single avenue process; instead, positive and antisocial forms of parenting affect children whose positive and delinquent conduct affects how their parents respond to them.[95]

John Wright and Francis Cullen argue that parents who are supportive of their children—for example, by encouraging hobbies, facilitating special lessons or activities, and becoming involved in a child's activities—are more likely to provide greater supervision and to exhibit a stronger attachment than less supportive parents. According to Wright and Cullen, "[P]arents who are nurturing, reliable, and closely attached to their youths and who provide guidance in the form of rules and supervision reduce the delinquency of their adolescents."[96] Positive parenting involves interactions between parent and child that have positive effects on interpersonal, academic, and work skills for the child and that reinforce conventional values and norms. Positive parenting requires taking a consistent approach to the child as well as providing positive feedback when the child behaves as desired.

Parenting Styles

Research has also shown that the style of parenting employed influences the behavior of children. Diana Baumrind theorizes that there are two critical aspects of parents' behavior toward children: parental responsiveness and parental demandingness. *Responsiveness* is the degree to which parents are supportive of the needs of their children. *Demandingness* is the extent to which parents demand age-appropriate behavior from children.[97] Parents will vary on each dimension. They can be supportive and demand much (*authoritative*) or rejective and demand much (*authoritarian*). Similarly, parents can be supportive and demand very little (*indulgent*) or rejective and demand little (*indifferent*). A description of these four parenting styles follows.

Authoritative parents are warm but firm. They set standards for the child's conduct but form expectations consistent with the child's developing needs and capabilities. They place a high value on development of autonomy and self-direction but assume the ultimate responsibility for their child's behavior. Authoritative parents deal with their child in a rational, issue-oriented manner, frequently engaging them in discussion and explanation about rules and discipline.

Authoritarian parents place a high value on obedience and conformity, tending to favor more punitive, absolute, and forceful disciplinary measures. These parents are not responsive to their child and project little warmth and support. Verbal give-and-take is uncommon in authoritarian households because authoritarian parents believe that the child should accept without question the rules and standards established by the parents. Such adults tend not to encourage independent behavior, but instead focus on restricting the child's autonomy.

Indulgent parents behave in responsive, accepting, benign, and more passive ways in matters of discipline. They place relatively few demands on the child's behavior, giving the child a high degree of latitude to act as he or she wishes. Indulgent parents are more likely to believe that control is an infringement on the child's freedom that may interfere with healthy

KEY TERMS

authoritative parents
Parents who are warm but firm; they set standards of behavior for their child and highly value the development of autonomy and self-direction.

authoritarian parents
Parents who place a high value on obedience and conformity, tending to favor more punitive, absolute, and forceful disciplinary measures.

indulgent parents
Parents who are relatively more responsive, accepting, benign, and passive in matters of discipline and place few demands on their child.

development. Instead of actively shaping their child's behavior, indulgent parents view themselves as resources the child may or may not use.

Indifferent parents are fairly unresponsive to their child and try to minimize the time and energy they must devote to interacting with the child or responding to the child's demands. In extreme cases, indifferent parents may be neglectful. They know little about their child's activities and whereabouts, show little interest in their child's experiences at school or in his or her friends, and rarely consider the child's opinion when making decisions. The child is typically ignored except when making demands on parents, which often results in hostile or explosive responses toward the child.

Parental Attachment

Another way parents influence the behavior of children is through emotional closeness. Presumably, children who like their parents will respect their wishes and stay out of trouble. Research supports the conclusion that the children who are least likely to turn to delinquency are those who feel loved, identify with their parents, and respect their parents' wishes. By contrast, delinquents often lack a supportive relationship with their fathers, have minimal supervision of their activities, are closer to their mothers, and come from broken homes. Strongly attached children are more likely to have more open communication with parents, whereas youths who have problems communicating with either parent or who communicate less frequently are more likely to engage in serious forms of delinquency.[98]

Likewise, parental love may reduce delinquency because it is something children do not want to lose. Randy LaGrange and Helen White found this relationship to hold true especially for juveniles in middle adolescence. They suggest that attachment to a positive role model is important because it functions as a "psychological anchor" to conformity.[99] For some adolescents, the attachment to parents is reflected in their family pride. That is, establishment of a positive family identity appears to significantly reduce levels of delinquency for white and African American youths.[100] Weak attachments may also have greater negative effects on female adolescents. For example, Angela Huebner and Sherry Betts report that attachment bond variables explain three times more delinquency among girls than boys.[101]

The positive effects of attachment vary somewhat in single-parent versus intact families. Michelle Miller and her colleagues found that attachment to mothers and fathers in intact families was negatively related to delinquency. By comparison, in single-mother households, parental attachment was negatively related to serious delinquency, but was inconsistently predictive of minor delinquency.[102]

The sins of the parent are often visited upon the child. Delinquents are more likely to have parents who abuse drugs and alcohol, commit crimes, or abuse them.

© EkaterinaBonda/iStock/Getty.

Of course, not everything in the family flows from parent to child: Some things flow back from child to parent and from child to sibling—so-called *child effects*. Thus, across all types of parenting, children mutually influence their parents and the dynamics that characterize their family. For instance, Kevin Beaver and John Wright recently found that among youths from the Cambridge Study in Delinquent Development, family risk did not have a major effect in determining whether boys became embedded in a delinquent career. Boys' involvement in delinquency, however, did significantly increase the overall risk level of the family.[103] Similarly, Ronald Simons and his associates found that children with low self-control, hostility, anger, and acceptance of deviant norms were involved in delinquency irrespective of parenting practices.[104] In this way, the behavior of children and adolescence feeds back into the family, which in turn makes family dynamics complex in the ways they produce behavior.

Parental Deviance

Studies show that children with criminal parents are more likely to participate in delinquency. Donald West and David Farrington's longitudinal study of British boys led them to conclude that delinquency is transmitted from one generation to the next: Criminal fathers are likely to produce delinquent sons.[105] John Laub and Robert Sampson similarly conclude: "Parental deviance of both the mother and father strongly disrupts family processes of social control, which in turn increases delinquency."[106] Helen Garnier and Judith Stein's analysis of data from the

KEY TERMS

indifferent parents
Parents who are unresponsive to their child and may, in extreme cases, be neglectful.

18-year longitudinal Family Lifestyles Project led them to conclude that early maternal drug use was linked with adolescent drug use, "signaling a more deviant lifestyle to which children were exposed and which could increase their exposure and attraction to deviant peers."[107]

One of the best studies of family deviance was conducted by David Farrington and his colleagues. These researchers were interested in the interrelationships among offending by three generations of relatives (fathers, mothers, sons, daughters, uncles, aunts, grandfathers, and grandmothers) and the concentration of offending in families. They also studied the extent to which criminal relatives predict a boy's delinquency based on data from 1395 Pittsburgh boys aged 8, 11, or 14. Farrington and colleagues found that offenders were highly concentrated in families: If one relative had been arrested, there was a high likelihood that another relative also had been arrested. Arrests of brothers, sisters, fathers, mothers, uncles, aunts, grandfathers, and grandmothers all predicted a boy's delinquency. The most important relative in this regard was the boy's father; arrests of the father predicted his son's delinquency independently of all other arrested relatives. In fact, boys whose fathers had been arrested were 500% *more likely* to be arrested themselves.[108] When parents are involved in deviant lifestyles (for example, crime or illicit drug use), they are less likely to be conscientious and responsible parents. It is this ineffective parenting—not necessarily the deviant activities modeled by the parents—that increases the child's risk of delinquency.

More recently Joseph Murray and his colleagues replicated Farrington and his associates' work by comparing delinquency levels in adult offspring of prisoners using data from England and Sweden. They found that parental criminality and parental incarceration contributed to offending among those individuals' offspring throughout the life course. In addition, a relationship was found between the number of times parents were incarcerated and the subsequent delinquent career of their children: Put simply, habitually incarcerated parents had children who habitually violated the law. However, among the sample in Sweden, the effect of parental incarceration on children's deviance went away once the parent's criminality was considered. In England, the effect of parental incarceration persisted. Despite this difference, there is no question that the offspring of parents who go in and out of prison face a variety of uphill battles, including a propensity for delinquency.[109]

The Maltreatment of Children

Parenting methods clearly affect a child's behavior. Some parents are too harsh, too irritable, and too inconsistent in discipline. Other parents are too neglectful and preoccupied with building their careers or maintaining the lifestyle they had before having children. As a consequence, many of the problem behaviors of children can be tied back to the behavior of parents and other adults who have regular contact with children.

Regoli and Hewitt's theory of differential oppression suggests that adults generally, and parents particularly, attempt to establish and maintain order and social control in the home in ways that are broadly oppressive of children. In more rigid and authoritarian families, when children violate the rules they are punished, often severely. Children are also exposed to a variety of forms of abuse and neglect more generally known as **maltreatment**.

Maltreatment consists of six general types of child abuse and neglect:[110]

1. **Physical abuse** comprises acts of commission that result in physical harm, including death.
2. **Sexual abuse** entails acts of commission of sexual acts against children that are used to provide sexual gratification to the perpetrator.
3. **Emotional abuse** consists of acts of commission that include confinement, verbal or emotional abuse, and other types of abuse, such as withholding sleep, food, or shelter.
4. **Physical neglect** comprises acts of omission that involve refusal to provide health care, delay in providing health care, abandonment, expulsion of a child from a home, inadequate supervision, failure to meet food and clothing needs, and conspicuous failure to protect a child from danger. The failure to provide medical care to children is also known as *medical neglect*.

KEY TERMS

maltreatment
Severe mistreatment of children, involving several types of abuse and neglect.

physical abuse
Acts that cause physical harm, including death.

sexual abuse
Acts of commission of sexual acts against children that are used to provide sexual gratification to the perpetrator.

emotional abuse
Acts of commission that include confinement, verbal or emotional abuse, and other types of abuse, such as withholding sleep, food, or shelter.

physical neglect
Acts of omission that involve refusal to provide health care, delay in providing health care, abandonment, expulsion of a child from a home, inadequate supervision, failure to meet food and clothing needs, and conspicuous failure to protect a child from danger.

5. **Educational neglect** encompasses acts of omission and commission that include permitting chronic truancy, failure to enroll a child in school, and inattention to the child's specific education needs.
6. **Emotional neglect** includes acts of omission that involve failing to meet the nurturing and affection needs of a child, exposing a child to chronic or severe spouse abuse, allowing or permitting a child to use drugs or alcohol, encouraging the child to engage in maladaptive behaviors, refusing to provide psychological care, and other inattention to the child's developmental needs.

In response to such maltreatment, a child is likely to develop a sense of powerlessness, leading to negative and often harmful adaptations, such as delinquency and adult criminality. A list of risk and protective factors for child maltreatment appears in **Box 9.5**, the "A Window on Delinquency" feature.

Nature and Extent of Maltreatment

How extensive is the maltreatment of children, and what are its consequences? Marije Stoltenborgh and her colleagues conducted a meta-analysis of 244 publications on child maltreatment and found that child maltreatment is a worldwide problem. Based on self-reported data, the prevalence of sexual abuse is 127 per 1000 children, but it is much more common among girls, with a prevalence of 180 per 1000, than boys, with a prevalence of 76 per 1000 children. The prevalence of other forms of maltreatment is also rather high, including 226 per 1000 children for physical abuse, 363 per 1000 children for emotional abuse, 163 per 1000 for physical neglect, and 184 per 1000 children for emotional neglect. Child maltreatment varies by continent. For instance, physical abuse is highest in South America, emotional abuse is highest in Africa, physical neglect is highest in North America, emotional neglect is highest in Australia, and sexual abuse is similarly high in Africa, Australia, and North America. A report by the Centers for Disease Control and Prevention found that about 2% of infants suffer from some form of maltreatment. Maltreatment comes in a variety of forms, such as when parents kick, bite, punch, and beat their children and threaten them with guns, knives, and baseball bats. Children are sometimes beaten unconscious and occasionally killed by parents or other guardians.

Such maltreatment has consequences for the child, the family, and the larger community. Children who experience maltreatment are more likely to become unhealthy adults—they have increased risks for smoking, alcoholism, substance abuse, eating disorders, obesity, depression, suicide, and other problems. Assaf Oshri and associates examined the effect of child maltreatment on 361 college students and found that sexual abuse and emotional abuse during childhood was associated with anxious and avoidant attachment style. In turn, these forms of attachment were significantly associated with alcohol use, drug use, risky sexual behaviors, and delinquency.[111] In addition, the negative effects of maltreatment are evident in differences between offenders and the general population. For instance, a study of childhood exposure to violence and maltreatment found that approximately 50% of delinquents were abused as children; this prevalence rate is two and five times higher than the rate for the general population, in which maltreatment estimates range from 10 to 30%.[112]

Some 3.1 million cases of child abuse or neglect are reported to state child protective services agencies each year. Children in the first year of life had the highest rate of victimization. Approximately 60% of reported cases are referred for investigation, and 30% of the investigated cases result in a disposition of either substantiated or indicated child maltreatment. Roughly 80% of the estimated 679,000 victims of maltreatment suffer neglect, 18% suffer physical abuse, slightly more than 9% are sexually abused, 5% are psychologically maltreated, and the remainder

Children who observe their parents fighting or physically punishing siblings are more likely than children who do not observe these events to regard them as normal ways of resolving conflicts.

© Chris Bernard Photography Inc./E+/Getty.

KEY TERMS

educational neglect
Acts of omission and commission that include permitting chronic truancy, failure to enroll a child in school, and inattention to the child's specific education needs.

emotional neglect
Acts of omission that involve failing to meet the nurturing and affection needs of a child, exposing a child to chronic or severe spouse abuse, allowing or permitting a child to use drugs or alcohol, encouraging the child to engage in maladaptive behaviors, refusing to provide psychological care, and other inattention to the child's developmental needs.

BOX 9.5

A Window on Delinquency

Child Maltreatment: Risk and Protective Factors

Child maltreatment produces $24 billion in direct costs related to the criminal justice and social service responses to child maltreatment cases each year. The indirect, long-term economic consequences are estimated to total $69 billion annually, and the total lifetime economic burden of child maltreatment in the United States is estimated at $124 billion. In other words, each year the United States experiences nearly $100 billion in costs to respond to child maltreatment. The pain and suffering to child victims, however, is in many ways incalculable.

A combination of individual, family, community, and societal factors contribute to the risk of child maltreatment. For example, children younger than 4 years are at greatest risk of severe injury or death. Children younger than 4 years account for nearly 80% of all maltreatment-related injuries to children, and infants younger than 12 months account for 44% of deaths from this cause.

A variety of risk and protective factors are linked to child maltreatment.

Risk Factors

- Disabilities or mental retardation in children
- Social isolation of family
- Parents' history of domestic violence
- Family disorganization, dissolution, and lack of cohesion
- Family violence
- Substance abuse in family
- Young, single, nonbiological parents as caregivers
- Parental stress and mental health problems

Protective Factors

- Supportive family environment
- Nurturing parenting skills
- Stable family relationships
- Household rules and monitoring of the child
- Parental employment
- Adequate housing
- Access to health care and social services
- Caring adult role models or mentors
- Communities that support parents and take responsibility for preventing abuse

Child maltreatment is a critical issue, with important implications for delinquency. Children who have been maltreated are significantly more likely to engage in delinquency and to have sustained and serious involvement in violence, substance use, and crime, relative to their peers who were not maltreated. Indeed, child maltreatment is a significant risk factor for virtually all forms of externalizing and problem behaviors.

Centers for Disease Control and Prevention, *Child Maltreatment: Fact Sheet 2014* (Atlanta: National Center for Injury Prevention and Control, 2015); Susan Snyder and Rachel Smith, "Do Youth with Substantiated Child Maltreatment Investigations Have Distinct Patterns of Delinquent Behaviors?" *Children and Youth Services Review* 58:82–89 (2015); Adrienne VanZomeren-Dohm, Xiaoyenan Xu, Eric Thibodeau, and Dante Cicchetti, "Child Maltreatment and Vulnerability to Externalizing Spectrum Disorders," pages 267–285 in Theodore Beauchaine and Stephen Hinshaw (eds.), *The Oxford Handbook of Externalizing Spectrum Disorders* (New York: Oxford University Press, 2016).

experience medical neglect or some other form of maltreatment.

The highest victimization rates by age are among children younger than 4 years (13 per 1000); rates decline as age increases. Victimization rates by race–ethnicity vary from a low of 2 per 1000 for Asian-Pacific Islander children to 16 per 1000 for African American children. Approximately 49% of child victims of maltreatment are male; 51% are female. The youngest children, those from birth to 3 years, account for 25% of all child maltreatment offenses. They are also most likely to experience recurrence of maltreatment during their childhood.

Eighty percent of child victims are maltreated by one or both parents. Maltreatment by both mother *and* father accounts for 19% of the cases, 18% of cases involve victimizations by the father only, and mother-only victimizations account for 41%.[113]

Although the corporal punishment of children is presently prohibited in nine countries (Austria, Cyprus, Denmark, Finland, Germany, Italy, Latvia,

Norway, and Sweden), more than 90% of American parents report having spanked their children by the time those children have reached age 3 or 4. Corporal punishment is more likely to be used in authoritarian-style parenting, where discipline is inconsistent or developmentally inappropriate, or where there is minimal parent–child communication. Even small amounts of physical punishment can have an adverse effect on the psychosocial development of children, however: Such behavior has been found to predict intelligence failure, emotional dysfunction, impaired ability to empathize, hostility, depression, conduct disorders in children, and criminality and violence in adulthood. A 2012 study based on a national sample of Americans found that physical punishment during childhood increased the likelihood of adult depression by 41%, increased the likelihood of alcohol abuse or dependence by 59%, increased the likelihood of drug abuse or dependence by 53%, and increased the likelihood of manic symptoms by 93%.[114]

Approximately 1530 children die of maltreatment each year. Thirty-six percent of children die from neglect, 28% die from physical abuse, and 29% die from multiple maltreatment types. Children younger than 12 months old account for 41% of the fatalities, 58% of maltreatment deaths occur in children younger than age 2, and 85% of such deaths occur in children younger than age 6. According to CDC data, in those cases in which children died as a result of abuse or neglect, 68% involved mothers as perpetrators and 49% involved fathers as victimizers.

Maltreatment, Corporal Punishment, and Delinquency

The nonlethal consequences of maltreatment frequently include delinquent, aggressive, and violent behavior by its victims. According to Gail Wasserman and Angela Seracini, compared to non-maltreated children, maltreated toddlers are significantly more likely to respond with fear, threats, or aggressive behavior to another child's distress. In addition, abused and neglected children are significantly more aggressive in their interactions with peers, and abused preschool and elementary school-age children are perceived by parents and teachers to have higher rates of externalizing behavior at home and at school.[115]

In John Lemmon's study of a cohort of 632 male juveniles from low-income families, maltreatment significantly influenced the initiation and continuation of delinquency among the study participants. The maltreated boys had significantly higher scores on all measures of delinquency, were more likely than their non-maltreated counterparts to be referred to the juvenile court, and were more likely to be adjudicated delinquent. The maltreated group represented the overwhelming majority of youths in the juvenile justice system, accounting for 84% of those youths receiving placement dispositions and 78% of those transferred to criminal court for prosecution. The maltreatment group also accounted for most of the serious delinquencies by juveniles: 78% of aggravated assaults, 83% of robberies, and 86% of weapons offenses. Male delinquents who had been maltreated were significantly more likely to be persistent and violent offenders, whereas non-maltreated delinquents tended to be routine, infrequent offenders.[116]

Timothy Ireland and his colleagues report that persistent maltreatment dramatically increases the risk of chronic delinquency in both early and late adolescence. In their study, persistent maltreatment throughout childhood and adolescence and maltreatment limited to adolescence were predictive of both delinquency and drug use. By comparison, children who were maltreated only during childhood, rather than in adolescence, were no more likely than controls to engage in violent delinquency in early adolescence.[117]

Jane Siegel and Linda Williams conducted a prospective study of 206 women treated in a hospital emergency room to examine the maltreatment–delinquency relationship in females. Women reporting childhood sexual abuse were twice as likely as members of the non-abused group to have been arrested as juveniles for violent offenses, nearly twice as likely to have been arrested as adults and to have engaged in violent offenses, and five times more likely to have been arrested for drug offenses.[118]

Cathy Spatz Widom has reported results from four maltreatment–delinquency studies conducted in different parts of the United States over a 25-year period. Her Midwest study determined that abused and neglected children were more likely to be first arrested about 1 year earlier than matched non-maltreated children and significantly more likely to become chronic offenders. Findings from a subset of data from the Rochester Youth Development Study confirmed that both self-reported and official delinquency was significantly related to child maltreatment. A study in North Carolina revealed that maltreated children had higher rates of reported delinquency and violence than controls, while research conducted in Washington concluded that abused and neglected children were *5 times* more likely to be arrested for nonviolent delinquencies and *11 times* more likely to be arrested for violent offenses than their matched controls. These studies, when taken together, provide support for the "cycle of violence" hypothesis, whereby children who experience maltreatment are predicted to grow up to become perpetrators of violence.[119]

Candice Odgers and her colleagues have examined the long-term development of behavior using the Dunedin Multidisciplinary Health and Development Study, which focused on a birth cohort in New Zealand. These researchers found that maltreatment was strongly correlated with a person's subsequent delinquent career. For instance, among those persons who demonstrated very low levels of delinquency, just 2% had ever been maltreated. By comparison, among those who became life-course persistent offenders, nearly 25% had been maltreated. This finding indicates that maltreatment increases the odds of being a lifelong criminal by nearly *15 times*! In addition to their delinquency, members of the high-maltreatment group suffered from a host of personal and social problems, including school failure, unemployment, mental health problems, substance use, and poorer health.[120] These effects are not unique to New Zealand: A study based on data from U.S. youths found that maltreatment negatively affected a range of outcomes occurring 12 years later.[121]

Although few people would ever condone child abuse and neglect, many parents both condone and advocate the use of corporal punishment as a form of discipline. However, corporal punishment also produces negative consequences for youths. Although

BOX 9.6

Delinquency Around the Globe

Has Sweden's Anti-spanking Law Reduced Child Abuse?

Nearly two-thirds of Americans approve of spanking, down from 74% in 1946. College-educated parents are twice as likely to disapprove of spanking as are parents who did not complete high school, and whites are roughly twice as likely to disapprove of spanking as are African Americans. Many anti-spanking advocates express concern that spanking children produces a variety of psychological and behavioral problems, including delinquency. Other anti-spankers are concerned that spanking a child is just the beginning of a slide down the slippery slope toward more serious forms of child abuse. For example, recent surveys report that nearly 20% of parents admit hitting their children on their bottoms with brushes, belts, or sticks, and another 10% report spanking their children with "hard objects." In addition, two-thirds of mothers with children younger than 6 years of age report spanking them at least three times per week.

In 1979, Sweden passed the first law in the world prohibiting parents from spanking their children in a major effort to reduce child abuse. Eight other countries have passed similar laws (Austria, Cyprus, Denmark, Finland, Germany, Italy, Latvia, and Norway). Did Sweden's anti-spanking law reduce child abuse? Much of the evidence suggests that it *did not*. Robert Larzelere, director of residential research at Boys Town in Nebraska, has examined all published studies evaluating the Swedish spanking ban and concluded "it has made little change in problematic forms of physical punishment." Although significantly fewer Swedish parents spanked their children or hit them with an object than did American parents, more serious forms of physical punishment occurred more frequently in Sweden during the year after the ban than in the United States. Furthermore, Swedish police records indicate that reported abuse of children younger than the age of 7 actually increased 489% from 1981 to 1994.

Larzelere also reports that "the rate of beating a child up was three times as high in Sweden as in the United States, the rate of using a weapon was twice as high, and the overall rate of very severe violence was 49% higher in Sweden than the United States average." Moreover, "the rate of pushing, grabbing, or shoving was 39% higher in Sweden than the average rate in the United States." Larzelere concludes that although parents in Sweden were significantly less likely than American parents to spank their children, they were also significantly more likely to use physical aggression and to engage in child abuse than their American counterparts.

Larzelere believes that parents need to be empowered with "milder, effective disciplinary tactics" incorporating limited spanking. He and other experts argue that it is not so much *whether* parents spank their children, but *how* they spank them. Most "limited spanking" advocates argue that children younger than 2 years of age should never be spanked because the risk of serious physical injury is too great and because spanking children under 2 may actually increase their misbehaviors. Spanking, they believe, is most effective with children between the ages of 2 and 6. According to these observers, spankings should be done in private to reduce humiliation, never done in anger, and applied only with an open hand on the child's bottom. Indeed, a meta-analysis found that conditional spanking was an effective means of disciplining children, whereas severe or predominant spanking led to negative outcomes.

The lessons from Sweden are also applied in the United States. One part of the Head Start program is to teach parents to respond to their children in more productive and positive ways than spanking them. A study found reduced spanking was associated with increased parental reading to their children, which was associated with cognitive gains and reductions in aggression.

Robert Larzelere, Marjorie Lindner Gunnoe, Mark Roberts, and Christopher Ferguson, "Children and Parents Deserve Better Parental Discipline Research: Critiquing the Evidence for Exclusively 'Positive' Parenting," *Marriage & Family Review*, in press (2016); J. E. Durrant, "Evaluating the Success of Sweden's Corporal Punishment Ban," *Child Abuse & Neglect* 5:435–448 (1999); Robert Larzelere, "Child Abuse in Sweden," retrieved March 1, 2016 from http://humansciences.okstate.edu/facultystaff/Larzelere/sweden2.html; Robert Larzelere and Brett Kuhn, "Comparing Child Outcomes of Physical Punishment and Alternative Disciplinary Tactics: A Meta-Analysis," *Clinical Child and Family Psychology Review* 8:1–37 (2005); Elizabeth Gershoff, Arya Ansari, Kelly Purtell, and Holly Sexton, "Changes in Parents' Spanking and Reading as Mechanisms for Head Start Impacts on Children," *Journal of Family Psychology*, 30:480–491 (2016).

low-impact spanking, when used with young children by warm and caring parents, *does not* appear to be predictive of later adolescent conduct problems, more severe forms of corporal punishment *are* associated with delinquency. Longitudinal studies have found a strong relationship between severe punishment (such as slapping, kicking, shoving, and hitting) and both self-reported and official delinquency.

A number of studies have reported physical punishment to be more widely accepted among African Americans than among whites. Whereas white parents may be more tolerant of moderate misbehavior, African American parents may perceive the consequences of disobedience as being more serious in their neighborhood context, in which respect for authority might reduce harassment by the police. Viewed from this perspective, firm discipline is believed to help protect the child from the variety of dangers in the child's social environment. For example, a study by Delores Smith and Gail Mosby found Jamaican child-rearing practices to be highly repressive and severe, with fogging being the most common form of corporal punishment. In this environment, children might be disciplined for a variety of misbehaviors, ranging from lying and stealing to being impolite and failing to complete their chores. Such punishment was found to be highly related to depression, posttraumatic stress disorders, prostitution, teen pregnancy, criminality, and violence.[122] **Box 9.6**, the "Delinquency Around the Globe," feature discusses how Sweden's anti-spanking law affected rates of child abuse in that country. Beyond corporal punishment, the juvenile justice system has developed special courts to deal with family violence and other family issues that relate to delinquency. One such set of courts comprises the **Family Dependency Treatment Courts**, which were established in Reno, Nevada, in 1994. These family courts Specifically adjudicate child welfare cases involving child abuse and neglect and parental substance abuse. Family Dependency Treatment Courts strive to ensure that children are safe and provided for, while simultaneously providing support, treatment, and access to social services to help parents get sober. Brief stints in jail for the substance-abusing parent are used as incentives to participate in the program.

Family Dependency Treatment Courts use a multidisciplinary team of child protective workers and drug counselors to address the needs of the family. The ultimate goal is to unify the family in a healthy environment. Although formal evaluation studies of these courts have not been conducted as yet, anecdotal information from child protective services workers and drug counselors suggest that both children and parents believe that the hands-on, specialized attention that Family Dependency Treatment Courts provide is helping reduce family-related problems.[123]

Finally, one of the most promising policy developments is the establishment of early family/parent training programs to provide parenting, educational, and other social service modalities to the parents of young children who are most at risk for delinquency and other maladaptive behaviors. According to a recent meta-analysis, early family interventions that target parenting practices can effectively reduce the emergence of delinquency in adolescence.[124] In other words, public policy is following the ideas presented in theories of delinquency, most of which point to the powerful importance of the family in either contributing to children's delinquency or insulating them from it.

KEY TERMS

Family Dependency Treatment Courts
Family courts that specifically adjudicate child welfare cases involving child abuse and neglect and parental substance abuse.

WRAP UP

THINKING ABOUT JUVENILE DELINQUENCY: CONCLUSIONS

Few people would contend the family has no effect whatsoever on whether a child becomes delinquent. But what is the nature of that effect? Which specific aspects of the family are most significant in this arena? Is it the inculcation of moral values? The structure of the family? The role played by working mothers? Or do delinquency outcomes have more to do with parenting styles and degree of supervision? This chapter explored these issues and presented what often appear to be conflicting findings from research.

Studies suggest that a relationship between divorced or single-parent families and delinquency exists, but that it is strongest for girls and for trivial offenses. However, this finding may be misleading. The relationship between broken or single-parent homes and delinquency might actually be a weak one because these variables are separated by a number of important intervening variables. In other words, the absence of one parent may affect delinquency by producing weak attachments between the parent and child.

Parenting skills have a considerable effect on delinquency. Patterson's techniques for making children more conforming to conventional norms include reinforcing conformity and providing sane punishment for transgressions. Nevertheless, reinforcement alone is not enough, particularly with very problematic children. Research shows that parents can be taught how to be more effective: When parenting skills improve, children's misbehavior tends to decline.

Child maltreatment, including corporal punishment, abuse, and neglect, is widespread in modern society. Nearly 3 million cases of abuse and neglect are reported each year, and approximately 1530 children die each year as a result of maltreatment. The maltreatment of children also creates an oppressive environment that leads to a variety of negative outcomes, including drug use, teen pregnancy, low academic achievement, emotional problems, and juvenile delinquency.

Although the family is the most critical social institution, children may actually spend more time

in direct interaction with other children and adults in another major social institution, the school. For at least 9 months every year, from about age 5 until approximately age 18, children spend nearly half their waking hours in school. Does this time in school deter or contribute to problem behaviors in children?

CHAPTER SPOTLIGHT

- The traditional functions of the family are to socialize children, inculcate moral values, produce children and regulate the sexual activity of those children, and provide material, physical, and emotional security.
- Family structure has changed dramatically in recent decades, as the two-parent, married family unit has given way to new units as a result of widespread divorce and bearing of children out of wedlock.

- A variety of parental skills and styles are related to both conventional and delinquent behaviors of children.
- The maltreatment and abuse of children is a pressing social problem in the United States and contributes to delinquency and a host of behavioral and social problems.
- Promising results have been produced by programs that target early family issues—specifically, parenting instruction to forestall delinquent careers.

CRITICAL THINKING

1. Abused children are likely to become delinquent in part because of their maltreatment. Should maltreatment be used to mitigate a youth's future delinquency?
2. Is sexual behavior during adolescence intrinsically delinquent? Do real differences exist between the sexual behavior of boys and girls?
3. What do the various data on the disintegration of the African American family suggest about the effects of this trend on delinquency? Which factor likely explains a greater portion of African American crime: biases in the criminal justice system or family-disintegration?

4. Given the implications of divorce for delinquency and the maladjustment of children, should divorce become a criminal offense? If there were criminal consequences of getting divorced, how would the American family change? Would delinquency increase or decrease?
5. Latchkey children are disproportionately from the working class. Are criminologists projecting their views of appropriate parenting in lamenting the existence of the latchkey child? In other words, is the latchkey child a problem only for middle-class parents who cannot afford to stay at home?

CHAPTER

10

Schools and Delinquency

OBJECTIVES

- Trace the origins of compulsory public education in the United States.
- Know the various types of activities that occur at or nearby schools that create an unsafe environment for students.
- Identify the U.S. Supreme Court decisions that control the behavior of students and school officials on school property.
- State the differences among the alternative explanations of school violence.
- Compare the strategies for preventing school violence.

KEY TERMS

The United States has a long history of providing free public education. Its success can be traced to the Massachusetts Act of 1642, which required parents to provide children with education and literacy. However, many parents did not comply with this law, which forced political leaders to pass the General School Law of 1647, requiring towns with 50 or more families to hire a schoolmaster to teach children, servants, and apprentices to read and write. The teacher's salary was to be paid by parents or the community's tax dollars. Towns with 100 or more families were also required to establish grammar schools. More than two centuries later, in 1851, Massachusetts passed the nation's first **compulsory school attendance law**, which required *all* children between the ages of 8 and 14 to attend school for a minimum of 3 months each year. **Truant officers**, whose job was to check for school absences, were hired to enforce the law. By 1929, compulsory education laws had been passed in all 48 states and the territories of Alaska and Hawaii (both of which became states in 1959).

How long a child is legally required to attend school varies by state. States including Arkansas, Maryland, and Oklahoma require school attendance upon reaching age 5. States including Arizona, Florida, and Georgia require school attendance upon age reaching 6. And states including Indiana, Missouri, and Wyoming mandate

school attendance upon reaching age 7. Some states, such as Colorado, Massachusetts, and New York, allow students to exit school at age 16 with parental consent. In other states, such as Illinois, Mississippi, and Nevada, students can exit school at age 17. Other states, such as California, Ohio, and Utah, require school attendance until age 18.[1]

In the United States, approximately 76 million children and adolescents are in school from pre-kindergarten to college. This represents 23% of the U.S. population. About 55 million children are enrolled in preschool through grade 12. Nearly 10 million additional children are enrolled in private schools, religious schools, or are home schooled. Approximately 20% of U.S. students will not graduate from high school. Graduation rates vary considerably by race and ethnicity. *Diplomas Count*, a report produced by the Editorial Projects in Education Research Center, reported that according to the most recent data, graduation rates for Asian American and white students were 89% and 86%, respectively. In contrast, graduation rates for American Indian, Hispanic, and African American students were 54%, 73%, and 69%, respectively. The overall high school graduation rate for *all* U.S. students was 81%, which represented the highest graduation rate in two decades.[2] As shown in **Box 10.1** in the "A Window on Delinquency" feature, education and the successful completion of school is an essential buffer against delinquency and many other problem behaviors.

In addition, graduate rates vary greatly between urban and suburban schools. In some cities, such as Baltimore, there is a 50% difference in the graduation rate between urban and suburban schools. In part, these differences in high school graduation rates correlate with the fact that the schools some children attend are blessed with an abundance of resources, dedicated teachers, a culture of learning, and an endless supply of educational enrichment opportunities. Other students toil in dysfunctional, racially divided, overcrowded schools with high rates of teacher absenteeism, few resources, outdated books, lack of opportunities, and an infestation of violent gangs, illegal drugs, and deadly weapons.[3]

These are only a few examples of the inequalities found in American schools. Researchers Wayne Welsh and his colleagues concluded that nonwhite children—especially African Americans and Hispanic Americans—are significantly more likely to attend schools that are unsafe and contain high levels of student misconduct and delinquency. According to Graham Ousey and Pamela Wilcox, nonwhite children are much more likely than whites to attend schools where the underlying culture emphasizes misbehavior and delinquency rather than learning.[4] Jonathan Kozol has described U.S. schools as representing "savage inequalities," "the shame of a nation," and "evidence of apartheid."[5]

Schools are a microcosm of the larger society, in which children are placed in a subordinate position to teachers. Albert Cohen's theory blamed delinquency on teachers who adopt the "middle-class measuring rod" and apply it to all students. This results in some students landing at the bottom of status hierarchy; in response, they turn to misbehavior as a way to reduce their status frustration. Students at the bottom will sometimes fight back by misbehaving and committing delinquencies.[6]

In a classroom setting, teachers wield power because students have little control over what they are taught. The educational interests of the nation, state, school district, administrators, teachers, and parents prevail over the interests of children. The teacher is a taskmaster whose job is to impose a curriculum upon students, regardless of whether children learn anything. It is no wonder that some students feel their school has a hostile and uninviting environment. Many schools are characterized by a structured-conflict environment, where teachers often unknowingly coerce and belittle students into obedience and force them to follow routines and submit to authority. Teachers use a variety of methods to achieve these goals. Some teachers reprimand students, for example, each time they leave their seats without permission. Other teachers punish children by removing them from the classroom for 15-minute periods of isolation. Some teachers take away a child's rewards, tokens, or privileges he or she has previously earned as a punitive measure. What teachers sometimes forget is that punishment affects children differently: Some students who are punished become powder kegs, waiting to explode and act out in ways that are dangerous to them as well as to their classmates, teachers, their school, and the neighborhood.[7]

Schools must be safe havens and free of crime and violence for teaching and learning to take place. Crime and violence have no place at school. When they are present, they not only affect the individuals involved, but also disrupt the educational process and affect bystanders, the school, and the surrounding community. For both students and teachers, victimization at school can have lifelong effects. Criminologists have found that in addition to experiencing loneliness, depression, and adjustment difficulties, victimized children are more prone to truancy, poor academic performance, dropping out of school, and violent behaviors. For teachers, becoming a crime victim may

KEY TERMS

compulsory school attendance law
A legislative act that requires students to attend school between specific ages (e.g., 6–16 years old).

truant officers
Individuals whose job is to check for student absences from school.

BOX 10.1

A Window on Delinquency

Schools, Behavioral Functioning, and Life Chances

Students spend an enormous amount of time in school—more than 15,000 hours—from kindergarten through high school, and these experiences have profound effects on their skill development, behavioral functioning, and life chances. Consistent with social control and social learning theories—two of the most prominent theories of delinquency—schools are a social institution that promotes positive social bonds, provides access to conventional role models, and encourages attachment to conventional role models and activities. In addition to the many educational activities, such as reading, writing, math, public speaking, critical thinking, debate, research, homework, exercise, and others, school trains individuals how to devote their time toward long-term goals that are not realized in the present but rather in the distant future. Students who invest or "buy in" to the educational process are often rewarded with greater educational attainment, greater income and wealth, better health, and better social functioning. A recent longitudinal study is revealing. Megan McClelland and her colleagues examined data from 430 individuals who were part of the Colorado Adoption Project and examined the association between their attention span persistence during preschool and subsequent outcomes. They found that attention span persistence, which is a measure of executive functioning associated with attentional control, cognitive flexibility, and more generally self-regulation, at age 4 years was significantly correlated with the person's math ability and reading ability at age 7, math ability and reading ability at age 21, and whether or not they completed college by age 25. They also found children whose attention span persistence was one standard deviation above the mean were nearly 50% more likely to complete college by age 25 than their peers with lower attention span persistence. In other words, just one skill that is cultivated and promoted at school has wide-reaching cognitive and behavioral effects that have important social and financial implications.

Those who do well in school have greater human and social capital than their peers who perform poorly in school, are often truant from school, or drop out. Indeed, the type of student you were during elementary school bears on your socioeconomic status and even when you will die. Mario Spengler and associates analyzed a sample of 2543 students who were assessed in 1968 in Luxembourg and followed to the present. They found that students who were more studious, focused, and disciplined during elementary school, as measured by both self-reports and teacher ratings, had significantly lower mortality than those who were less studious, even after controlling for IQ, parental socioeconomic status, and demographic characteristics. On the other hand, student characteristics such as inattentiveness, impatience, pessimism, and defiance of parental authority were linked to elevated mortality 40 years later. The latter traits were also associated with lower socioeconomic functioning.

School functioning is also importantly related to delinquency and violent offending even into adulthood. Antonis Katsiyannis and his colleagues examined data from the National Longitudinal Study of Adolescent to Adult Health to see how academic and behavioral functioning during elementary school was associated with subsequent violent delinquency. Several factors, including repeating a grade, homework problems, truancy, problems with other students, and suspensions were correlated with violent conduct into adulthood. Students who were frequently truant and often suspended were three times more likely to commit violent crime 15 years after high school.

In sum, school inculcates much more than reading, writing, and math skills. It sets into motion the behavioral functioning that is required for competence in society, and when it is impaired, is often a harbinger of delinquency, crime, and correlated social problems.

Allison Ann Payne and Kelly Welch, "How School and Education Impact the Development of Criminal and Antisocial Behavior," pages 237–251 in Julien Morizot and Lila Kazemian (eds.), *The Development of Criminal and Antisocial Behavior: Theory, Research and Practical Applications* (New York: Springer, 2015); Megan McClelland, Alan Acock, Andrea Piccinin, Sally Ann Rhea, and Michael Stallings, "Relations between Preschool Attention-Span Persistence and Age 25 Educational Outcomes," *Early Childhood Research Quarterly* 28:314–324 (2013); Marion Spengler, Brent Roberts, Oliver Lüdtke, Romain Martin, and Martin Brunner, "The Kind of Student You Were in Elementary School Predicts Mortality," *Journal of Personality*, in press (2016); Marion Spengler, Martin Brunner, Rodica Damian, Oliver Lüdtke, Romain Martin, and Brent Roberts, "Student Characteristics and Behaviors at Age 12 Predict Occupational Success 40 years Later Over and Above Childhood IQ and Parental Socioeconomic Status," *Developmental Psychology* 51:1329–1340 (2015); Antonis Katsiyannis, Martie Thompson, David Barrett, and J. B. Kingree, "School Predictors of Violent Criminality in Adulthood: Findings from a Nationally Representative Longitudinal Study," *Remedial and Special Education* 34:205–214 (2012).

lead to disenchantment with educating students and an early departure from the profession.[8]

School-Associated Violent Deaths

Violent deaths at schools, although rare, are tragic events with far-reaching consequences. A **school-associated violent death** is a homicide, suicide, legal

KEY TERMS

school-associated violent death
A homicide, suicide, legal intervention (involving a law enforcement officer), or unintentional firearm-related death where the fatal injury occurred on the campus of a functioning elementary or secondary school.

intervention (involving a law enforcement officer), or unintentional firearm-related death where a fatal injury occurs on the campus of a functioning elementary or secondary school. According to the most recent *Indicators of School Crime and Safety* report, which is jointly published by the U.S. Department of Justice and the U.S. Department of Education, in 2013–2014, there were 45 school-associated violent deaths.[9] Of these deaths, 26 were homicides, 14 were suicides, and 5 were legal interventions.

Over the past two decades, the United States experienced many other shocking violent episodes at or near schools. In May 2006, for instance, 12 boys between the ages of 6 and 8 at an elementary school in St. Louis were expelled for the school year after sexually assaulting a second-grade girl during recess.[10] In 1997, a principal and a student were killed in Bethel, Alaska; three students were killed and five more wounded in West Paducah, Kentucky; one teacher and five students were killed in Jonesboro, Arkansas; a teacher was killed and a student wounded in Edinboro, Pennsylvania; and a teacher and 13 students were killed at Columbine High School in Littleton, Colorado. In the wake of the Columbine mass murder, a few students tried to copy the rampage. One week after Columbine, a disgruntled teenager who had dropped out of school killed a student and wounded another at the W. R. Meyers High School in Taber, Canada. In Pennsylvania, 52 bomb scares were reported the week after the Columbine attack. Bomb scares or plots to copy the Columbine massacre were attempted in dozens of other states. In December 2012, a young man with multiple psychiatric problems, Adam Lanza, murdered 20 children ages 6 to 7 and six teachers and school personnel at Sandy Hook Elementary School in Connecticut. Lanza committed suicide as law enforcement descended upon his position.[11]

Even though shootings have been part of the school landscape for many years, they nevertheless remain relatively uncommon. As early as the 1950s, a number of movies, including *High School Confidential* and *Blackboard Jungle*, focused on violence in high schools. Before the late 1980s and early 1990s, when the rate of juvenile gun violence was rising dramatically, school shootings usually involved only single victims; students in lower grades rarely even witnessed the violence, much less took part. It was not until the shooting of Kayla Roland in 2000 that U.S. elementary schools were no longer seen as inviolate islands of safety for children.[12] Guns are now being brought into first-grade classrooms and 6-year-olds are being murdered, as in the case of Sandy Hook.

Perhaps caused by the large amount of media attention given to the series of incidents involving multiple-shooting victims in schools, polls report that school violence and bullying are among the greatest concerns related to the safety of children in the United States. Despite the fear engendered by the highly publicized incidents, however, school-associated violent deaths remain rare. According to the recent *Indicators of School Crime and Safety* report, children were approximately *76 times* more likely to be murdered away from school than at school.[13]

Nevertheless, school shootings have galvanized public concern about school safety. Two national studies of school homicides have been conducted by the Centers for Disease Control and Prevention (CDC) in collaboration with the U.S. Departments of Education and Justice. The first study covered a 2-year period and identified 68 students killed on or near school grounds or at school-sponsored events.[14] The victims generally were males and were killed with firearms. These homicides accounted for less than 1% of all youth homicides in the period studied, and the estimated incidence of school-associated violent death was 0.09 per 100,000 student-years. Students with the greatest risk of being killed were racial or ethnic minority males who attended public high schools in urban neighborhoods. The study found that the homicide rate in urban schools was nine times higher than the corresponding rate in rural schools. The most common motives cited for killing a classmate were interpersonal disputes or gang-related activities. The second study updated the original study. It identified 177 students between the ages of 5 and 19 who were killed over a 5-year period; the vast majority of the homicides (84%) involved firearms. Today, school-associated violent deaths continue to account for less than 1% of all juvenile homicides, but the frequency of homicides involving more than one victim has increased.[15]

Although school-associated violent deaths are rare, the events that contribute to them are mundane. Martha Smithey suggests that the first steps in the development of lethal violence at schools are often the social rejection of the school shooter in the form of persecution, teasing, and bullying. These experiences produce emotional responses including humiliation, loneliness, unwantedness, and despair. These feelings contribute to broken school bonds, and because the social interaction occurs at school, parents are less able to help repair them. Over time, youth become isolated and ostracized and limit their social interaction to similarly situated peers or vicarious friendships over the Internet. Once this point is reached, disaffected youth often gravitate toward violent and extreme media content and begin to develop plans for violence that are believed to "right the wrong" of their original persecution.[16]

Nonfatal Student Victimizations

Most school delinquencies and violence are nonfatal. Even so, nonfatal crimes such as theft and assault create a disruptive and threatening environment, which may in turn result in physical injury and emotional stress that impede student achievement. Data from the most recent Indicators of School Crime and Safety report reveal that students ages 12 to 18 were victims of about 1.4 million nonfatal crimes at school. This includes about 966,000 violent victimizations such as assaults and nearly 455,000 theft victimizations. The rate of victimization at school is about 55 victimizations per 1000 students compared to 30 victimizations per 1000 students away from school. The higher rate of victimization at school is driven primarily by simple assaults (e.g., fistfights) that are much more common at school compared to away from school.

The victimization rates for students ages 12 to 18 vary related to student characteristics. Younger students (ages 12 to 14) are more likely than older students (ages 15 to 18) to be victims of school crime, but the reverse is true away from school. Students who live in suburban areas have a lower rate of violent victimization both at and away from school than do students living in urban communities; there is no measurable difference between the rate of violent victimizations at or away from school in suburban and rural areas. Generally, student victimizations at school follow a similar pattern to delinquency and victimization in the general population. Male gender, racial minority status, family dysfunction, neighborhood disadvantage, and various indicators of emotional and behavioral disorders are associated with more victimizations occurring at school.[17] **Box 10.2**, the "A Window on Delinquency" feature, presents a snapshot of delinquency that occurs after school.

Nonfatal Teacher Victimizations

Teachers are also victims of threats and physical attacks. For instance, the American Psychological Association Classroom Violence Directed Against Teachers Task Force conducted a survey of 2998 kindergarten through 12th grade teachers to examine the prevalence of victimizations directed against teachers. They found

BOX 10.2

A Window on Delinquency

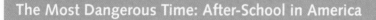

The Most Dangerous Time: After-School in America

In the United States, roughly 76 million students are enrolled in prekindergarten through grade 12 in schools. A major social issue and policy concern is the safety of students and teachers in American schools. A major preventive advantage of school, however, is the monitoring and social control that principals, teachers, and other school staff provide. Those safeguards are not present in the hours immediately after the end of the school day, and indeed, the after-school hours are among the most dangerous for youth. For instance:

- More than 20 million schoolchildren are on their own after school because their parents are at work.
- More than 2 million elementary school students in grades K through 5 are on their own after school.
- Roughly 50% of youth do not participate in after-school programs.
- After-school hours from 3 PM to 6 PM are a dangerous time as youth have unsupervised opportunities to commit delinquency and experiment with tobacco, alcohol, and drugs.
- Adolescents who do not participate in after-school programs are three times more likely than their peers who do participate in programs to skip classes and use marijuana.

Given these risks, after-school programs are important programs to keep children and adolescents engaged in structured, prosocial activities until their parents return from work. Engagement in after-school programs is associated with numerous positive outcomes, such as higher scores on standardized tests, more school engagement, less truancy, better grades, and better self-esteem among youth. In addition, the more that youth are involved in school and after-school programs, the less likely they will begin to experiment in delinquency and substance use.

Although after-school programs are a sensible policy idea, the effectiveness of the programs is surprisingly small. Two recent meta-analyses are revealing. Kristen Kremer and her colleagues examined the effectiveness of after-school programs with at-risk youth in terms of improving their school attendance and reducing their delinquency. Among 16 programs that address school attendance and 49 programs that address delinquency, the overall effect magnitudes were small and non-significant. That is, although the programs provide monitoring for at-risk youth, they do not improve their school attendance nor reduce their delinquency. Sema Taheri and Brandon Welsh similarly reviewed 17 after-school programs for delinquency prevention and found small, non-significant effects. That is, the programs did not reduce delinquency.

Simone Robers, Anlan Zhang, Rachel Morgan, and Lauren Musu-Gillette, *Indicators of School Crime and Safety: 2014* (Washington, DC: U.S. Department of Justice and U.S. Department of Education, 2015); Kristen Kremer, Brandy Maynard, Joshua Polanin, Michael Vaughn, and Christine Sarteschi, "Effects of After-School Programs with At-Risk Youth on Attendance and Externalizing Behaviors: A Systematic Review and Meta-Analysis," *Journal of Youth and Adolescence* 44:616–636 (2015); Sema Taheri and Brandon Welsh, "After-School Programs for Delinquency Prevention: A Systematic Review and Meta-Analysis," *Youth Violence and Juvenile Justice*, 14:272–290 (2016).

that 80% of teachers reported at least one form of victimization and among these, 94% were victimized by students. About 75% of teachers had been harassed, 50% were victims of theft, and 44% were physically attacked or assaulted. Three percent of teachers had been threatened with a weapon. Male teachers and those teaching in urban settings were more likely to be victimized, and African American teachers were less likely to be victimized.

To prevent violence against teachers and to put teachers in a position to deter school violence, the Harrold (Texas) School District board decided to permit teachers to carry concealed guns. The decision was made following 2 years of research examining the best school security options. Although the school superintendent, David Thweatt, did not say how many teachers were carrying concealed firearms, he did say that any teacher carrying a firearm must first be approved by the school board based on his or her personality and reaction to crisis. In addition to undergoing the training required to obtain a state concealed weapons license, teachers must be trained to handle crisis intervention and hostage situations. When approving the plan, the school board took extra safety steps, such as requiring teachers to use bullets that will minimize the risk of ricochet, similar to the bullets used by U.S. air marshals. The school's policy is being challenged by the Brady Center to Prevent Gun Violence, which argues if a school board authorizes an employee to carry a firearm, then that person should be a law enforcement officer.[18]

In the Schools and Staffing Survey, teachers were asked whether they were threatened with injury or physically attacked by a student from their school during the past year.[19] Ten percent of teachers in public schools and 3% of teachers in private schools reported being threatened with injury by a student from their school. Fewer teachers—approximately 6% of those in public schools and 3% in private schools—had been physically attacked. A greater percentage of teachers in city schools reported being threatened with injury or physically attacked in comparison to teachers in suburban, town, or rural schools.

Teachers' reports of being threatened or physically attacked varied based on the type of school in which they were teaching. Teachers in public schools are more likely to be threatened and attacked than teachers at private schools. A slightly lower percentage of secondary school teachers (9%) reported being threatened with injury by a student than did elementary school teachers (10%). However, a greater percentage of elementary school teachers reported having been physically attacked (8% for elementary school teachers and 3% for secondary school teachers). More elementary and secondary teachers in city schools reported being threatened with injury or physically attacked than did teachers in either suburban or rural schools.

School Environment

School discipline contributes to an environment that can either facilitate or deter violence and crime. In the *School Survey on Crime and Safety*, school principals were asked how often specific disciplinary problems took place at their schools.[20] In particular, they were asked about the daily or weekly occurrence of student racial tensions, sexual harassment of other students, verbal abuse of teachers, widespread classroom disorder, and acts of disrespect toward teachers. Nine percent of the respondents reported that student acts of disrespect toward teachers were a common occurrence. With regard to other frequently occurring discipline problems (those taking place at least once per week), 5% of principals reported students verbally abusing teachers, 3% reported students sexually harassing other students, 3% reported racial and ethnic tensions among students, and 2% reported chaos in classrooms.

Other disciplinary problems documented by the *School Survey on Crime and Safety* occurred far more frequently—and have a greater impact on students' ability to learn. Twenty-three percent of public schools reported that bullying of students occurred on a daily or weekly basis. Seventeen percent of principals and 16% of students acknowledged the presence of gang activities at their school. Almost 25% of students reported seeing hate-related graffiti at school. By further examining the statistics drawn from the *School Survey on Crime and Safety*, it becomes possible to pinpoint the most disruptive and corrupting influence on students—namely, bullying.

Bullying

Bullying is widespread. A national study found that 30% of U.S. students are involved in bullying: bullies (13%), bullied (11%), or both (6%). Both bullying and being bullied are correlated with violence-related behaviors such as carrying weapons, drug use, and fistfights. There is evidence that bullying has stabilized in terms of its prevalence. According to *Child Trends*, the prevalence of bullying has remained steady at between 28 and 30% among youth 12 to 18 from 2005 to 2011 based on the *School Crime Supplement* and has been about 20% based on the *Youth Risk Behavioral Surveillance Study* from 2009 to 2014.[21]

Bullying is formally defined as using one's strength or status to intimidate, injure, or humiliate another person of lesser strength or status. It happens whenever students are picked on or forced to do things

KEY TERMS

bullying
Negative acts by students carried out against other students repeatedly over time.

One of the most pervasive and serious problems at schools today is bullying. Bullying can take many forms. What would you recommend schools do to prevent bullying? What steps should be taken and how should they be implemented?

© manley099/E+/Getty.

they do not want to do. Five types of bullying have been distinguished:

- *Physical bullying,* which involves hitting, kicking, spitting, pushing, and taking personal belongings
- *Verbal bullying,* which includes taunting, teasing, name calling, and making threats
- *Emotional bullying,* which includes spreading rumors, manipulating social relationships, or engaging in social exclusion, extortion, or intimidation
- *Sexual bullying,* which involves sexual harassment and sexual abuse
- *Cyberbullying,* which is bullying through the use of electronic communications

Who Are the Bullied Students?

In the School Crime Supplement to the National Crime Victimization Survey, students were asked if they had been bullied at school during the past 6 months. Nearly 22% of students reported being bullied. Nearly 14% said the bullying consisted of being made fun of; 13% were the subject of rumors; 4% were threatened with harm; and 6% were pushed, shoved, tripped, or spit on. Among bullied students, 77% were bullied inside the school or on school grounds and 23% were bullied outside of school. More than 67% of the bullied students reported being bullied once or twice during the survey period, 19% had been bullied once or twice a month, nearly 8% were bullied once or twice a week, and almost 6% had been bullied daily.

White and African American students were bullied more often than Hispanics. White students were also more likely to report being bullied and to report being the subject of rumors. Grade level was found to be inversely related to being bullied. As students' grade level increased, they were less likely to be bullied. Approximately 28% of sixth graders, 23% of ninth graders, and 14% of 12th graders reported being bullied. Students in public schools were bullied more often than private school students. Of students who reported bullying that involved being pushed, shoved, tripped, or spit on, about one in five sustained an injury. Although no measurable differences were found by sex in students' likelihood of being bullied, males were more likely than females to be injured from bullying.

There is considerable variance in the types of children who are bullied. Gia Barboza performed a latent class analysis on data from the School Crime Supplement of the National Crime Victimization Survey and found that 77% of students were *not* victims of bullying. Nearly 12% of youth were victims of relational bullying, verbal bullying, and cyberbullying, 8% were victims of face-to-face bullying but not cyberbullying, and 3.1% of students were highly victimized by all forms of bullying. Girls and nonwhite students were more likely to be highly victimized. Youth who were bullied more extensively were also more likely to engage in school-related delinquency compared to youth who were not bullied.[22]

Who Are Bullies?

Bullies have many of the same risk factors as serious and chronic delinquents. They tend to be aggressive; have oppositional, defiant, and difficult interpersonal styles; and often come from dysfunctional home environments. Although bullies can be popular, their popularity is more a function of fear that students have for them. Instead, bullies are often socially inept children who perform poorly in class, have low attachment to school, and often dislike school. A study by the National Institute of Child Health and Human Development found that nearly 2 million children in grades 6 through 10 are bullies. Eleven percent of students reported bullying others "sometimes" (moderate bullying) and 9% bullied others "once a week" or more often (frequent bullying). Bullying most often occurs from the sixth to eighth grades, with little variation in this pattern between urban, suburban, and rural areas.[23]

Although both boys and girls may act as bullies, they do so differently. Girls are emotional and verbal bullies, whereas boys are physical bullies. Certain risk factors or warning signs have also been identified to suggest that a child may be a bully. At-risk children are impulsive, hot tempered, and lack empathy. Bullies have difficulty following rules, are often bored and frustrated, and are not so interested in school. They are often raised in homes where there is modest parental warmth and involvement, plus harsh and inconsistent parental discipline.[24]

Consequences of Bullying

Bullying has both long- and short-term consequences for bullies and the bullied (see **Box 10.3**, the "The Face of Delinquency" feature). Bullies and their targets are

BOX 10.3

The Face of Delinquency

Echoes of the Schoolyard: The Long-Term Consequences of Bullying

Bullying has negative consequences that endure long after children and adolescents have left school. There is increasing evidence about the detrimental effects of bullying on both its perpetrators and victims and the ways that antisocial traits contribute to bullying. Bullying does not randomly occur. Bullying victimization and perpetration are more likely among children who display family, emotional, and conduct risk factors. In addition, bullying is stable across time suggesting that bullies and their victims interact across school years. Bullying creates a wide range of negative consequences for victims, including psychiatric problems, self-harm, delinquency, and even psychotic symptoms.

Longitudinal and meta-analytic studies show how specifically damaging bullying is over time. Maria Ttofi and her colleagues found that being bullied imposes a twofold higher likelihood of depression 36 years later, and this effect withstood the explanatory effects of 20 other predictors of depression. The long-term effects are also damaging for the bullies themselves. A recent study found that boys who bully others at age 14 are significantly more likely to have violent convictions during adolescence and adulthood, more likely to be unemployed or have low job status during adulthood, more likely to abuse drugs during adulthood, and more likely to lead an unsuccessful life at age 48. Again, the relationship between bullying and these outcomes persisted despite the competing effects of other predictors.

Often, children who bully others display a range of risk factors for delinquency generally, suggesting that bullying is just one part of their delinquent career. Essi Viding and her colleagues found that callous-unemotional traits are a particularly pernicious predictor of bullying (these traits are the affective deficits in psychopathy). Children who are more callous and unemotional commit higher levels of direct and indirect bullying, and have more severe conduct problems. These children are also more difficult to help through anti-bullying programs. In their case, bullying is simply an early stop on what will likely be a lengthy criminal career.

Finally, bullying has noxious, long-term effects for bullied children who bully as well. Analysis of longitudinal data from the Great Smoky Mountains Study of youth found that those who were bullied and those who were bullied and bullied others suffered significant problems into adulthood. People who had exposure to bullying as perpetrator, victim, or both had more health problems, engaged in more risky and illegal behaviors, had poorer educational and work outcomes, and more strained social relationships.

Susan Carter, *The Hostile Environment: Students Who Bully in School* (Lanham, MD: University Press of America, 2015); Maria Ttofi, David Farrington, Friedrich Lösel, and Rolf Loeber, "Do the Victims of School Bullies Tend to become Depressed Later in Life? A Systematic Review and Meta-Analysis of Longitudinal Studies," *Journal of Aggression, Conflict and Peace Research* 3:63–73 (2011); David Farrington and Maria Ttofi, "Bullying as a Predictor of Offending, Violence and Later Life Outcomes," *Criminal Behaviour and Mental Health* 21:90–98 (2011); Essi Viding, Elizabeth Simmonds, K. V. Petrides, and Norah Frederickson, "The Contribution of Callous-Unemotional Traits and Conduct Problems to Bullying in Early Adolescence," *Journal of Child Psychology and Psychiatry* 50:471–481 (2009); Dieter Wolke, William Copeland, Adrian Angold, and Jane Costello, "Impact of Bullying in Childhood on Adult Health, Wealth, Crime, and Social Outcomes," *Psychological Science* 24:1958–1970 (2013); Frederick Rivara and Suzanne Le Menestrel (eds), *Preventing Bullying Through Science, Policy, and Practice* (Washington, DC: National Academies Press, 2016).

more likely than other youths to engage in violent behaviors such as fistfights. Victims of bullying often become adults with more acute depression and lower self-esteem. Children who are bullied are also more likely to feel lonely, have trouble making friends, and not get along well with classmates. Sometimes they are insecure, embarrass easily, and are fearful of going to school. The effects of chronic childhood bullying often follow them into adulthood, where they face a substantial risk of suffering from depression, developing schizophrenia, and committing suicide.

Children who bully are also affected by their behavior, and bullying is usually just one of several problems they have. These individuals also tend to abuse animals, vandalize buildings, shoplift, drop out of school, be involved in fistfights, and use illegal drugs and alcohol. Dan Olweus and Susan Limber found that bullies were more likely to be *chronic juvenile offenders* and adult criminals. They also discovered that 60% of boys who bullied others

in grades 6 through 9 were convicted of at least one crime as adults, compared with 23% of boys who did not bully their classmates. More striking is the fact that 40% of boys who bullied others had three or more criminal convictions by age 24, compared to only 10% of boys who did not bully. There is also evidence that the most serious career criminals began their careers in violence as school bullies.[25]

Prevention of Bullying

Education professors Peter Gill and Max Stenlund conducted a case study where three friends of a bully acted as "law enforcement officers" who intervened when their friend started to victimize other students. The three peers forcefully pinned the bully to the ground and commanded him or her to stop harassing and using violence toward others. Seeing the class bully being physically overpowered reduced the perception among other students that the bully was someone to fear. In addition, the case study caused the bully to change his or her behavior because he or she did not like being physically handled.[26]

According to Dan Olweus, who has developed a widely implemented bullying prevention program, bullying can be reduced by 30 to 70%. The Olweus Bullying Prevention Program is a multilevel, multicomponent, school-based program designed to prevent or reduce bullying in elementary, middle, and junior high schools (students ages 6 to 15). The program restructures the existing school environment to reduce opportunities and rewards for bullying.[27]

However, Christopher Ferguson and his colleagues recently analyzed findings from published research reports assessing the success of bullying programs implemented over the period 1995–2006 and concluded that "school-based anti-bullying programs are not practically effective in reducing bullying or violent behaviors in schools."[28] There are two reasons why school-based anti-bullying programs are ineffective.

First, bullies weigh the costs and benefits of their behavior *before* they act. At that point, they decide whether they will receive more benefits from bullying or from the meager rewards of the anti-bullying program.

Second, anti-bullying programs are based on the assumption that behavior is caused by environmental factors that can be manipulated—an approach that ignores the role of biology in some students' propensity to bully. It was recently reported, for instance, that bullies do not inflict pain on others solely to establish dominance; instead, they inflict pain because they receive emotional pleasure in witnessing the suffering of others. Researchers from the University of Chicago used magnetic resonance imaging (MRI) to monitor the emotional reactions of teenagers who watched video clips of strangers getting hurt as the result of accidents (such as having a bowl dropped on their hands) or deliberately inflicted cruelty (such as a bully stamping on their victim's feet). They found the brains of most people responded to these images with a reaction in their own brain pain center; they showed empathy with the victim's pain. However, teenagers with a history of bullying showed increased activity in the brain's pleasure and reward centers. Not only were bullies indifferent to the pain of others, they actually enjoyed it.[29] The behavior of bullies who have a genetic predisposition toward violence cannot be attenuated by anti-bullying programs; for these children, anti-bullying programs are ineffective.

Bullying, unlike other forms of peer aggression and conflict, always involves an imbalance of power between the bully and the bullied.[30] Whether it is power against authority or power over other students, when this element enters the picture, it creates an intimidating, threatening atmosphere that impairs students' ability to learn. Besides bullying, gangs, drugs, carrying weapons, fistfights, and use of hate-related words are other significant factors that contribute to an unstable school environment that can be very challenging for students to navigate.

Students' Perceptions of Personal Safety

School violence can make students fearful and affect their readiness and ability to learn. Overall, concerns about vulnerability to attacks detract from a positive school environment. In the *School Survey on Crime and Safety*, students were asked how often they had been afraid of attack "at school or on the way to and from school" and "away from school" during the previous 6 months. Three percent of students reported they were afraid of attack or harm *at* school, and 3% reported they were afraid of attack or harm *away* from school.

African American and Hispanic students were more likely than white students to fear for their safety regardless of location, either at school or away from school. As grade level increased, students' fear of an attack at school or on the way to and from school decreased. School location, however, was found to be related to students' fear of attack. Students who attended urban schools were more likely than students enrolled in suburban and rural schools to fear being attacked at school or on the way to and from school.

Avoiding School Activities and Places at School

School crime causes students to perceive school as unsafe. In trying to ensure their own safety, they may skip school activities or avoid certain places within the school. The percentage of students who avoid school activities and certain areas in school is, therefore, a measure of their perceptions of school safety. About 5% of students reported avoiding a school activity or an area in the school because they were fearful that someone might attack or harm them.[31] African Americans, Hispanics, and students in urban areas were the most likely to avoid one or more places at school for fear of being harmed.

Disciplinary Actions Taken by Schools

In the *School Survey on Crime and Safety*, public school officials were asked to report the number of disciplinary actions their schools took against students for specific offenses.[32] Thirty-nine percent of public schools (approximately 40,000 schools) took at least one serious disciplinary action against a student—including suspensions lasting 5 days or more, expulsions, and transfers to specialized schools—for specific offenses. The targeted offenses included physical attacks or fights; insubordination; distribution, possession, or use of alcohol; distribution,

possession, or use of illegal drugs; use or possession of a weapon other than a firearm or explosive device; and use or possession of a firearm or explosive device. Of the more than 433,000 disciplinary actions taken, 74% consisted of suspensions of 5 days or more, 6% comprised removals with no services, and 20% were transfers to specialized schools.

The largest percentage of schools that reported taking a disciplinary action did so in response to a fistfight (29%). Of the schools that reported taking a serious disciplinary action, 20% took action for insubordination and for distribution, possession, or use of illegal drugs; 14% took action as a result of use or possession of a weapon other than a firearm or explosive device; 9% did so for distribution, possession, or use of alcohol; and 3% did so for use or possession of a firearm or explosive device.

Safety and Security Measures Implemented by Schools

Public schools have implemented a variety of practices to promote the safety of their students and

As a precautionary measure, an increasing number of schools have students walk through metal detectors or similar detecting equipment in an attempt to reduce the number of firearms and other weapons or contraband brought onto school property. Do you believe metal detectors and similar devices increase school safety?

© Don Tremain/age fotostock.

staff. In the *School Survey on Crime and Safety*, public school officials were asked about their school's use of such measures and procedures.[33] Some practices, such as use of locked or monitored doors or gates, are intended to limit or control access to school campuses. Other measures, such as use of metal detectors, security cameras, and drug sweeps, are intended to monitor or restrict students' and visitors' behavior while on campus.

Approximately 88% of public schools control access to the school building by locking or monitoring doors during school hours, and 44% control access to school grounds with locked or monitored gates. Most public schools require faculty and staff to wear badges or picture identification, and 77% use one or more security cameras to monitor the school. Five percent of public schools perform drug testing on athletes, and 3% do so for students who participate in other extracurricular activities. Students are required to wear uniforms in 19% of public schools.

The percentage of schools using security measures has changed dramatically over the past few years. Between the 1999–2000 and 2013–2014 school years, the percentage of schools using one or more security cameras to monitor the school increased from 39% to 77%. The percentage of public schools having locked entrances or exit doors during the day was 38% during the 1999–2000 school year and 76% during the 2013–2014 school year. In other words, American schools have gotten much tighter in their security and accessibility to visitors, which likely has helped reduce delinquency and victimization occurring in the schools.

Schools, Children, and the Law

Schools constantly struggle to create an environment that fosters learning. As part of this effort to control the behavior of students, schools have put in place many rules and regulations. The student handbooks children receive when they enter secondary school are roughly the same across the nation. These manuals list behaviors that constitute violations of school policy and identify the consequences for engaging in such behaviors. In some schools, for instance, students cannot bring cell phones, pagers, cameras, electronic games, iPods, and any other electrical device that rings, buzzes, or otherwise causes a disruption or distraction. In addition, students often face restrictions on their attire: Students may not wear their hair in a distracting style, girls cannot wear spaghetti straps, and students may not wear baseball caps. Some specific professional sports jerseys and teams are banned because specific numbers and colors are associated with various delinquent gangs.

Students who violate these school rules may be disciplined. They may have their electronic devices confiscated, they may not be allowed to participate in an activity, or they may be placed in "time-out." For more serious violations, students may be required to have their parents sign and return a discipline form. If a student continues to misbehave, he or she may be suspended for a specific number of days or, on rarer occasions, may be expelled from school. In some schools, students may be physically punished for their transgressions.

Due Process Rights

The Fifth and Fourteenth Amendments of the U.S. Constitution guarantee due process of law; that is, they specify the procedural rights given to people charged with breaking the law and/or facing deprivation of life, liberty, or property by the government. In ***Goss v. Lopez*** (1975), the U.S. Supreme Court considered the due process rights of students who were suspended from school for violating school rules.[34]

In *Goss*, the Court ruled that students who face suspension have specific legal rights. The school must follow minimal due process procedures when suspending a student from school for 10 or fewer days. Students facing such a suspension must at least receive oral or written notice of the charges against them and an opportunity for a hearing to present their side regarding the charges. However, students facing a short-term suspension do not have the rights to obtain legal assistance, to question witnesses against them, or to call their own witnesses to refute the charges against them—all of which are due process rights set forth in the Sixth Amendment of the Constitution. In *Goss*, the Supreme Court also said that notice of charges and a hearing should be provided before suspension, unless a student's presence in school threatens the safety, property, or educational opportunities of others. See **Box 10.4**, the "From the Bench" feature. In *Goss*, the Court made it clear that it was responding only to suspensions of students for 10 or fewer days. The Court advised school officials that "longer suspensions or expulsion for the remainder of the school term, or permanently, may require more formal procedures." Since this ruling, each state has developed procedures for "long-term suspensions or expulsions." In Illinois, for example, a student may be expelled for "gross disobedience or misconduct." To determine the severity of the misconduct, the student's parents or guardian have the right to appear at a meeting of the school board or with a hearing officer selected by the board to discuss the student's alleged misconduct. The parent or guardian must be notified of this meeting by certified or registered mail or delivery of notice in person. At the hearing, the reasons for the expulsion must be discussed. The student may be represented by an attorney, who can present evidence and cross-examine witnesses on the student's behalf. The board then takes whatever action

BOX 10.4

From the Bench

Goss v. Lopez

The issue before the Supreme Court in *Goss v. Lopez* was whether the suspension of a student for a period of up to 10 days without a hearing constitutes a violation of the individual's due process rights. In this case, several public high school students (including D. Lopez) were suspended from school for misconduct but were not given a hearing immediately before or after their suspension. School authorities in Columbus, Ohio, claimed that a state law allowed them to suspend students for as long as 10 days without a hearing. The students brought legal action claiming that the statute was unconstitutional because it allowed school authorities to deprive students of their right to a hearing, violating the due process clause of the Fourteenth Amendment.

The Court said that education is protected by the Fourteenth Amendment and affirmed that any suspension requires prior notice and a hearing. Permitting a suspension without a hearing is, therefore, unconstitutional. The Court said that oral or written notice of the charges brought against a student must be given to the student who is being suspended for more than a trivial period. If he or she denies the charges, the student must be given a hearing. This hearing may be an informal one where the student is simply given an explanation of the evidence against him or her and an opportunity to tell the student's side of the story.

Goss v. Lopez, 419 U.S. 565 (1975).

it deems appropriate. The maximum length of time a student may be expelled is 24 months.

In 1988, the Supreme Court ruled on the due process rights of disabled students in ***Honig v. Doe***. In *Honig*, the Court decided that before school officials may expel a disabled student, the school must first determine whether the offending behavior was caused by the student's disability. If so, then the student cannot be expelled. Nevertheless, the disabled student may be suspended from school for 10 or fewer days even if the offending behavior was the result of his or her disability. If the offending behavior was not caused by the child's disability, the student may be expelled but

KEY TERMS

Goss v. Lopez
U.S. Supreme Court decision stating that students who are to be suspended for 10 or fewer days must receive a hearing.

Honig v. Doe
U.S. Supreme Court decision stating that before school officials may expel a disabled student, the school must first determine whether the offending behavior was caused by the student's disability.

has the same due process rights as all other students. Any disabled student who is expelled from school may not be totally deprived of educational services provided by the public school system.[35]

Corporal Punishment

Corporal punishment is the infliction of pain as a penalty for a student who violates a school rule. Historically, it has included a wide range of punishments designed to inflict pain and discomfort, such as pinching, pulling ears and hair, shaking, slapping, smacking, spanking, swatting, hitting, kicking, punching, paddling, using switches, hair brushes, belts, and ironing cords, and making the student kneel on gravel or a grate. In the United States, teachers and other school officials have administered these and other forms of punishment for many years to children who break school rules.[36] Much earlier, in 17th-century Jesuit schools, for example, it was *expected* that teachers would hit their students. Serious student offenders were often "stripped in front of the whole community and beaten until they bled." Whipping was considered a standard teaching aid. One student complained, "My master . . . beat me horribly; he used to seize me by the ears and lift me off the ground."[37]

In America during the Colonial era, corporal punishment was also widely practiced. Disobedient students were tied to whipping posts and beaten. Violence against students was justified on the basis of an Old Testament passage attributed to Solomon (in the book of Proverbs): "He that spareth his rod hateth his son; but he that loveth him chastiseth him betimes."[38] Thus the "right thing to do" was for teachers to physically punish unruly students.

From the end of the 19th century into the early 20th century, discipline problems in schools were a daily occurrence. Teachers resorted to threats, intimidation, coercion, and beatings in an attempt to control students. Today corporal punishment in schools is banned in every industrialized nation except the United States, Canada, and Queensland, Australia. In the United States, 29 states and the District of Columbia have banned corporal punishment in schools.

The U.S. Supreme Court has ruled twice on the use of corporal punishment in schools. In 1975, in ***Baker v. Owen***, the Court decided that teachers could administer reasonable corporal punishment for disciplinary purposes.[39] In 1977, in the case of ***Ingraham v. Wright***, the Court added that corporal punishment *does not* violate the cruel and unusual punishment clause of the Eighth Amendment (see **Box 10.5**, the "From the Bench" feature).[40]

While school officials in some states may hit children, in 1987, in ***Garcia v. Miera***, the Supreme Court ruled that punishment must not be excessive—that is, it may not leave welts and bruises.[41] In *Garcia*, a 9-year-old New Mexico girl was held upside down and struck five times with a broken wooden paddle, leading to bleeding and permanent scarring. She was paddled a second time 3 months later, causing severe bruising. The 10th Circuit Court of Appeals

KEY TERMS

corporal punishment
The infliction of physical pain as a penalty for violating a school rule.

Baker v. Owen
U.S. Supreme Court decision stating that teachers can administer reasonable corporal punishment for disciplinary purposes.

Ingraham v. Wright
U.S. Supreme Court decision stating that corporal punishment does not violate the cruel and unusual punishment clause of the Eighth Amendment.

Garcia v. Miera
U.S. Supreme Court decision stating that school authorities who use excessive or extreme punishment against a child may be sued for damages suffered by the student and must pay attorney fees if they lose the lawsuit.

BOX 10.5

From the Bench

Ingraham v. Wright

In *Ingraham v. Wright*, the Supreme Court was asked to decide whether school authorities have the right to use corporal punishment. This case involved James Ingraham, who was a junior high school student in Dade County (Miami), Florida. Ingraham was paddled 20 times by the school principal, Willie Wright, for not leaving the stage of the school auditorium promptly. Principal Wright hit Ingraham repeatedly on the buttocks with a 2-foot-long wooden paddle. When Ingraham went home, his mother examined him and then took him to a local hospital. At the hospital, doctors prescribed pain pills, ice packs, and a laxative and recommended Ingraham stay home from school for 1 week.

The Court ruled that the "cruel and unusual punishment clause" of the Eighth Amendment does not apply to corporal punishment in schools and the "due process clause" of the Fourteenth Amendment does not require schools to give students notice before punishing them. The Court declared that corporal punishment is not "cruel and unusual" punishment because it is the traditional method for maintaining discipline in public schools. The justices also stated that the punishment must be reasonable; if the punishment is extreme, criminal charges may be brought against the offender. In other words, school authorities may hit children, but the extent of the punishment cannot be excessive.

Ingraham v. Wright, 439 U.S. 651 (1977).

ruled that school officials had used excessive force in administering corporal punishment and, therefore, had violated the student's federal constitutional right of substantive due process. Both the school district and the administrators were held liable for damages suffered by the student. Thus the *Garcia* case makes it clear that school officials may be sued for excessive punishment—a time-consuming and expensive process.

But what happens if a school district within a state allows corporal punishment but the student's parent(s) object to the teacher or principal hitting their child? That question was answered in 1980 by the Fourth Circuit Court of Appeals in **Hall v. Tawney**, when it was decided that parents have *no* constitutional right to exempt their children from corporal punishment in public schools.[42]

In the 21 states that allow corporal punishment, in the 2006–2007 school year, teachers, principals, coaches, and bus drivers used corporal punishment on more than 220,000 students. Although this number may alarm some readers, it represents a steady decline in the use of corporal punishment since 1976, when more than 1.5 million students were corporally punished.

In spite of the trend toward the elimination of corporal punishment in public schools, each year some 5000 children are beaten badly enough by school officials that they require medical attention. Almost 40% of corporal punishment cases take place in two states, Texas and Mississippi. If statistics for Alabama, Arkansas, and Georgia are added to the mix, then these five states account for nearly 75% of all school paddlings. African Americans and males are hit the most often. Boys, who represent approximately 51% of the student population, receive 80% of the paddlings. Similarly, African American students, who constitute 17% of all public school students in the United States, account for 36% of children who receive corporal punishment—more than twice the rate of punishment found among white students.[43]

An array of reasons is cited for banning corporal punishment:[44]

- It perpetuates a cycle of child abuse. It teaches children to hit someone smaller and weaker when angry.
- Injuries occur. Bruises are common, and broken bones are not unusual. Children's deaths have occurred in the United States as a result of corporal punishment.
- Corporal punishment is used much more often on poor children, racial and ethnic minorities, children with disabilities, and boys.
- Schools are the only institutions in the United States in which striking another person is legally sanctioned. Corporal punishment is not allowed in prisons, the military, or mental hospitals.
- Educators and school boards are sometimes sued when corporal punishment is used in their schools.

- Schools that use corporal punishment often have poorer academic achievement, more vandalism, truancy, pupil violence, and higher dropout rates.
- Corporal punishment is often not used as a last resort, but rather is the first resort for minor misbehaviors.
- Many alternatives to corporal punishment—including time-out, losing recess, and calling parents—may be more productive. Alternatives teach children to be self-disciplined rather than cooperative out of fear.

Alternatives to corporal punishment emphasize positive behaviors of students, realistic rules that are consistently enforced, instruction that reaches all students, conferences with students for planning acceptable behavior, parent/teacher conferences about student behavior, use of staff such as school psychologists and counselors, detentions, in-school suspension, and Saturday school.

Research examining the impact of corporal punishment on children has found that it may lead to more serious problems for the child, the school, and other students through increased aggression and depression. For instance, Andrew Grogan-Kaylor has reported that children who are paddled have an earlier onset of antisocial behavior, which often leads to behavioral problems. In addition, the effects of corporal punishment on delinquency appear to be longer lasting among boys than among girls.[45]

Emily Douglas and Murray Straus explored the experience of corporal punishment on children as it related to adult dating behavior. Using a sample of 9549 students in 26 universities in 19 countries, they found that being spanked as a child exerted an independent effect on assault in adult dating behavior: Adults who were paddled as children were more likely to use violence in romantic relationships while in college.[46]

Today, in the United States, there is a nationwide movement to ban corporal punishment in public schools. (Private schools are exempt from state and federal laws on corporal punishment.) More than 40 professional organizations, including the American Academy of Pediatrics, American Bar Association, American Medical Association, American Psychiatric Association, and the National Education Association, oppose corporal punishment, but these and other organizations face stiff opposition and a somewhat unsympathetic public.[47] Many opponents of the ban believe in the disciplinary methods recommended by James Dobson, whose book *The New Dare to*

KEY TERMS

Hall v. Tawney
U.S. Supreme Court decision stating that parents do not have a constitutional right to exempt their children from corporal punishment in public schools.

Discipline instructs parents that to soften the child's rebellious spirit, it may be necessary to spank the child hard enough to cause tears.[48] Dobson has many supporters: In a national public opinion poll, 24% of the U.S. public answered "yes" when asked, "Do you think it is okay for a school teacher to spank a student?" Thus, although the drive to ban corporal punishment in schools is making steady, slow progress, it faces an unbending opposition from both a significant number of people and a number of significant people.[49]

Does corporal punishment prevent unwanted behavior in its victims? No widespread deterrent effects of corporal punishment have been found, regardless of whether the spanking or paddling was administered by parents or teachers. Instead, the effects of corporal punishment include a range of physical, psychological, emotional, and behavioral problems.[50] Ralph Welsh discovered that corporal punishment produces fear and anger in students. When the fear subsides, the anger remains. Angry students are more likely to strike out at whomever and whatever they blame for their pain and suffering.[51]

Searches and Seizures

School officials may search students and their lockers without consent. This practice may seem to violate the protections afforded by the Fourth Amendment to the U.S. Constitution, but it does not. The standard is lowered for searches in schools to protect and

KEY TERMS

Thompson v. Carthage School District
U.S. Supreme Court decision stating that school officials may legally search students and their lockers without consent.

sweep search
A search of all students' lockers.

New Jersey v. T.L.O.
U.S. Supreme Court decision stating that school officials can conduct warrantless searches of individuals at school on the basis of reasonable suspicion.

Vernonia School District 47J v. Acton
U.S. Supreme Court decision stating that students participating in school athletic activities must submit upon request, to a drug test (urinalysis).

Board of Education of Independent School District No. 92 of Pottawatomie County et al. v. Earls et al.
U.S. Supreme Court decision that expanded the *Acton* ruling; it stated that schools may require students to submit to a urinalysis for illegal drugs before participating in all competitive extracurricular activities.

maintain a proper educational environment for all students. This decision was reached in **Thompson v. Carthage School District**, after Ramone Lea was expelled from Carthage High School when school officials found crack cocaine in his coat pocket while looking for guns and knives reported to be on school grounds. The district court awarded $10,000 to Lea in damages for "wrongful expulsion" because the search violated his Fourth Amendment rights. The Carthage School District appealed the ruling to the U.S. Court of Appeals, which concluded that under the circumstances the search was constitutionally reasonable.[52]

School officials may also search student lockers because the school is the rightful owner of both the locks and the lockers. Students, in effect, "borrow" these items for the purpose of storing clothes, schoolbooks, supplies, and personal items necessary for school. Lockers cannot be used to store items that interfere with any school purpose. Therefore, lockers and their contents are subject to search to ensure they are being properly used.

A search of all lockers, called a **sweep search**, can be ordered whenever a principal believes an inspection of lockers is necessary. For example, such a search might be carried out for the following reasons:

- Interference with a school purpose or an educational function
- Physical injuries or illness
- Damage to property
- Violation of state law or school rules
- Disposal of confiscated contraband
- Involvement of law enforcement officials
- Locker cleaning

Unlike the probable cause requirement of the Fourth Amendment, the decision to search lockers is based on the less restrictive notion of reasonableness and school officials' interpretation of what "reasonableness" is. The "reasonable suspicion doctrine" was applied in 1985 in **New Jersey v. T.L.O.**, when the Supreme Court ruled that school officials can conduct warrantless searches of individuals at school on the basis of reasonable suspicion.[53] (See **Box 10.6**, the "From the Bench" feature.)

The decision in *T.L.O.* was affirmed in 1995 in **Vernonia School District 47J v. Acton**.[54] In *Acton*, the Court held that students participating in school athletic activities *must* submit to an involuntary drug test upon request. (See **Box 10.7**, the "From the Bench" feature.) The *Acton* ruling, in effect, allows schools to "seize" the urine of particular students to "search for" chemical traces of unlawful drugs, without any evidence of grounds for suspicion that drug testing is warranted. The Court's ruling in *Acton* was expanded in 2002 in **Board of Education of Independent School District No. 92 of Pottawatomie County et al. v. Earls et al.**, a case involving the

BOX 10.6

From the Bench

New Jersey v. T.L.O.

In *New Jersey v. T.L.O.*, the Supreme Court was asked to decide whether the state of New Jersey and its agent, a public school's assistant vice-principal, violated T.L.O.'s Fourth Amendment right of protection from "unreasonable search," her Fifth Amendment right of protection from self-incrimination, and her right to due process as provided in the Fourteenth Amendment. In 1980, a teacher at New Jersey's Piscataway High School discovered two girls smoking in the lavatory. Because smoking was a violation of a school rule, the two students (T.L.O. and a companion) were taken to the principal's office. There they met with the assistant vice-principal, who demanded to see T.L.O.'s purse. Upon opening the purse, he found cigarettes and cigarette rolling paper. The assistant vice-principal proceeded to look through the purse and found marijuana and drug paraphernalia, money, lists of names, and two letters that implicated her in drug dealing. T.L.O. argued that the search of her purse was unconstitutional.

The Supreme Court decided in favor of the school and its assistant vice-principal. It reasoned that to maintain discipline in school, school officials who have "reasonable suspicion" that a student has done something wrong can conduct a reasonable search of the suspicious student. A school's main objective is to educate students in a legal, safe learning environment. Police need "probable cause"—a higher standard—to search people, places, and things. School officials, unlike the police, need only reasonable suspicion to search students when they suspect unlawful conduct.

New Jersey v. T.L.O., 469 U.S. 325 (1985).

legitimacy of a school district's drug testing policy.[55] In *Earls*, the court decided that a school could require students to submit to a urinalysis for illegal drugs before participating in *any* competitive extracurricular activities such as an academic team, Future Farmers of America, Future Homemakers of America, band, choir, and cheerleading, as well as athletics. In spite of these efforts by the Supreme Court and school districts across the nation to thwart illegal drug use, however, research examining the relationship between schools' drug testing policies and self-reported student drug use has found *no* relationship between them.[56]

In April 2009, in *Safford Unified School District v. Redding*, the U.S. Supreme Court considered the latitude school administrators should have when deciding to search students. In *Redding*, the vice-principal directed the school nurse and an administrative assistant, both women, to strip search eighth-grader Savana Redding, based on a tip from another student that the 13-year-old possessed prescription-strength ibuprofen. The nurse and the assistant had Savana take off her shoes and socks, then her shirt and pants. Then they ordered Savana to pull out her bra and pull open her panties to see whether she was hiding pills. No pills were found. Savana challenged the search, arguing that it violated her Fourth Amendment rights when she was required to expose her breasts and pelvic area in an effort to find the pills. The Supreme Court held that the search violated her Fourth Amendment rights; however, they also held that school officials were shielded from liability by qualified immunity. Despite the constitutionality of school searches, they are nevertheless controversial. Some scholars view school searches as having essentially the same logic as stop-and-frisk policies of suspected criminals, and worry that treating students as suspected delinquents will contribute to greater delinquency and estranged relationships with police officers.[57]

BOX 10.7

From the Bench

Vernonia v. Acton

The issue before the Supreme Court in *Vernonia v. Acton* was whether drug testing of student athletes violates these individuals' protection against unreasonable search and seizure as provided in the Fourteenth Amendment to the Constitution. The Vernonia school district, concerned about the drug problem among athletes and students in its community, sought to reduce the problem by creating a student-athlete drug policy. School officials worried that drug use by athletes might increase the risk of sports-related injuries among these students. For this reason, the Vernonia school district student-athlete drug policy authorized urinalysis drug testing of student athletes. James Acton brought suit against the district after he refused to take the urinalysis test and was disallowed participation in the school's junior high football program.

In a 6–3 decision, the Court reasoned that drug testing of student athletes was constitutional. It accepted the argument that student rights could be lessened at school if such a practice was necessary to maintain safety and to fulfill the educational mission of the school.

Vernonia v. Acton, 515 U.S. 646 (1995).

Free Speech

No one in the United States has absolute free speech. The guarantee of free speech in the First Amendment is a relative one—that is, no one can say whatever they want, whenever they want, or wherever they want, without possible consequences. (See **Box 10.8**, the "Delinquency Controversy" feature.) Furthermore, the free speech of students in school is more restricted than is the free speech of adults, although students do have the right to some free speech. For instance, in 1943, the Supreme Court ruled in *West Virginia State Board of Education v. Barnette* that the free speech rights of students had been violated when they were required to salute the flag while reciting the Pledge of Allegiance.[58]

Twenty-six years later, in the 1969 case of *Tinker v. Des Moines Independent Community School District*, the Supreme Court revisited the issue of students' free expression. In *Tinker*, several students who wore black armbands to school in protest of the Vietnam War had been suspended. The school argued that the armbands violated the dress code policy. Once again, the Supreme Court ruled in favor of the students, stating that their dress "neither interrupted school activities nor sought to intrude in the school's affairs or the lives of others."[59]

The Supreme Court has, however, placed limits on students' right to free expression. In *Bethel School District No. 403 v. Fraser*, it ruled that schools may ban vulgar and offensive language.[60] On April 26, 1983, Matthew Fraser, a student at Bethel High School in Pierce County, Washington, delivered the following speech nominating a fellow student for student elective office:

> I know a man who is firm in his pants, he's firm in his shirt, his character is firm—but most of all, his

belief in you, the students of Bethel, is firm. Jeff Kuhlman is a man who takes his point and pounds it in. He doesn't attack things in spurts—he drives hard, pushing and pushing until finally he succeeds. Jeff is a man who will go to the very end—even the climax, for each and every one of you. So vote for Jeff for ASB vice-president; he'll never come between you and the best our high school can be.

Roughly 600 high school students, many of whom were 14-year-olds, attended the assembly. Students were required to attend the assembly or to report to the study hall. The assembly was part of a school-sponsored educational program in self-government. During the entire speech, Fraser referred to his candidate in terms of an elaborate, graphic, and explicit sexual metaphor.

Two of Fraser's teachers, with whom he discussed the contents of his speech in advance, informed him that the speech was "inappropriate and that he probably should not deliver it" and that his delivery of the speech might have "severe consequences." During Fraser's delivery of the speech, a school counselor observed students' reactions. Some students hooted and yelled; some used gestures to graphically simulate the sexual activities pointedly alluded to in Fraser's speech. Other students appeared to be bewildered and embarrassed by the speech. One teacher reported that, on the day following the speech, she found it necessary to forgo a portion of the scheduled class lesson to discuss the speech with the class.

The morning after the assembly, the assistant principal called Fraser into her office and notified him that she believed his speech violated a disciplinary rule of the school that stated, "Conduct which materially and substantially interferes with the educational process is prohibited, including the use of obscene, profane language or gestures." Fraser was also presented with copies of five letters submitted by teachers, describing his conduct at the assembly. He was given a chance to explain his conduct and admitted to having given the speech described and deliberately using sexual innuendos in the speech. Fraser was then informed that he would be suspended for 3 days; he was also told that his name would be removed from the list of graduation speaker candidates.

Fraser sought review of this disciplinary action through the school district's grievance procedures. The hearing officer determined that the speech given by Fraser was "indecent, lewd, and offensive to the modesty and decency of many of the students and faculty in attendance at the assembly." The examiner determined that the speech fell within the ordinary meaning of "obscene," as used in the disruptive-conduct rule and affirmed the discipline in its entirety. Fraser served 2 days of his suspension and was allowed to return to school on the third day.

Soon after the ruling in *Fraser*, in the 1988 case, *Hazelwood School District v. Kuhlmeier*, the Supreme

KEY TERMS

West Virginia State Board of Education v. Barnette

U.S. Supreme Court decision stating that students do not have to salute the flag while reciting the Pledge of Allegiance.

Tinker v. Des Moines Independent Community School District

U.S. Supreme Court decision stating that students have the right of free expression, as long as their behavior does not interrupt school activities or intrude in school affairs or the lives of others.

Bethel School District No. 403 v. Fraser

U.S. Supreme Court decision stating that schools may prohibit vulgar and offensive language.

Hazelwood School District v. Kuhlmeier

U.S. Supreme Court decision stating that school administrators can regulate the content of student publications in public schools for educational purposes.

BOX 10.8

Delinquency Controversy

Religion, Schools, and Students

The relationship between religion, schools, and students has evolved over the past 60 years. The Supreme Court has heard many cases where the First Amendment of the Constitution is at issue. With respect to religion, the First Amendment states: Congress shall make no law requiring an establishment of religion or prohibiting the free exercise of religion.

The Court has been asked to establish the boundaries that govern the relationship among religion, schools, and students. Some of the more notable Court decisions on this topic are the following:

1948: In *McCollum v. Board of Education*, the Court disallowed the practice of having religious education take place in public school classrooms during the school day.

1962: In *Engel v. Vitale*, the Court ruled it was unconstitutional for a school to require students to recite school prayers.

1963: In *Abington School District v. Schempp*, the Court overturned a Pennsylvania law that permitted the reading of 10 verses from the Bible at the opening of each school day.

1968: In *Epperson v. Arkansas*, the Court found the state law prohibiting the teaching of evolution to be unconstitutional.

1972: In *State of Wisconsin v. Jonas Yoder*, the Court ruled that compulsory schooling of Amish children beyond the eighth grade was a violation of the free exercise of religious rights.

1980: In *Stone v. Graham*, the Court ruled a Kentucky law requiring the posting of the Ten Commandments in each public school classroom in the state to be unconstitutional.

1985: In *Wallace v. Jaffree*, the Court found that an Alabama law requiring each school day begin with a 1-minute period of "silent meditation or voluntary prayer" was unconstitutional.

1992: The Court ruled in *Lee v. Weisman* that the graduation prayer during a high school graduation was unconstitutional.

2000: In *Santa Fe School District v. Doe*, the Court held that official student-led prayers before a high school football game were unconstitutional.

2002: In *Zelman v. Simmons-Harris*, the Supreme Court ruled 5–4 that a Cleveland program that spent large amounts of public money on subsidizing education at religious schools was constitutional.

2004: In *Elk Grove Unified School District v. Newdow*, the Court ruled that the words "under God" in the Pledge of Allegiance did not violate the First Amendment and, therefore, it is within the bounds of the Constitution to include the words.

These rulings are based on the Supreme Court's interpretation that the First Amendment guarantees that the government will not coerce any person to support or participate in religion or its exercise.

McCollum v. Board of Education, 333 U.S. 203 (1948); *Engel v. Vitale*, 370 U.S. 421 (1962); *Abington School District v. Schempp*, 374 U.S. 203 (1968); *Epperson v. Arkansas*, 393 U.S. 97 (1968); *Wisconsin v. Yoder*, 406 U.S. 208 (1972); *Stone v. Graham*, 449 U.S. 39 (1980); *Wallace v. Jaffree*, 472 U.S. 38 (1985); *Lee v. Weisman*, 505 U.S. 577 (1992); *Santa Fe School District v. Doe*, 168 F.3d 806 (2000); *Zelman v. Simmons-Harris*, 536 U.S. 639 (2002); *Elk Grove Unified School District v. Newdow*, 542 U.S. 1 (2004).

Court decided that school administrators can regulate the content of student publications, but only if doing so serves an educational purpose.[61] The *Hazelwood* case involved a disagreement between students and school officials over the administrative censorship of two pages in the school's student-run newspaper. (Students in private schools do not have First Amendment protection against censorship by their teachers and principals, who are not government employees.) The topics the students had written about were important to them: teenage pregnancy and divorce. The Court ruled that "censorship will only be prohibited in school-sponsored activities when school officials have no valid educational purpose for their action."

The Court's decision in *Hazelwood* was widely protested on the grounds that it constituted an unreasonable form of censorship. Critics complained that censorship does not enhance the education of young journalism students unless the purpose is

to teach them not to report on unpopular issues. Since the ruling, students across the United States have taken it on themselves to circumvent the censorship laws imposed by *Hazelwood* by establishing independent student Web publications that are not under school control.[62] (**Box 10.9**, the "From the Bench".)

In 2007, the Supreme Court once again revisited the free speech rights of students in ***Morse v. Frederick***.[63] The circumstances giving rise to *Frederick* occurred in 2002, when the Olympic torch passed through Juneau, Alaska. During the festivities, high school senior Joe

KEY TERMS

Morse v. Frederick
U.S. Supreme Court decision that further clarified juveniles' right to free speech at school and in public areas.

Morse v. Frederick made clear that juveniles' right to free speech is tempered at school.

© Bill Clark/CQ-Roll Call Group/Getty.

BOX 10.9

From the Bench

Hazelwood School District v. Kuhlmeier

In *Hazelwood v. Kuhlmeier*, the Supreme Court was asked to decide whether the school district violated students' freedom of expression right, protected by the First Amendment, by regulating the content of their school newspaper. In this case, Kathy Kuhlmeier and two other journalism students wrote articles on pregnancy and divorce for their school newspaper. Their teacher submitted page proofs to the principal for approval. The principal objected to the articles because he felt that the students described in the article on pregnancy, although not named, could be identified, and because the father discussed in the article on divorce was not allowed to respond to the derogatory article. The principal also said that the language used was not appropriate for younger students. When the newspaper was printed, the two pages containing the articles in question as well as four other articles approved by the principal were deleted.

In *Hazelwood*, the Court ruled that the school district did not violate the First Amendment right of the students. The justices stated that, although schools may not limit the personal expressions of students that happen to occur on school grounds (see the discussion of *Tinker*), they do not have to promote student speech with which they disagree. This decision permits schools to censor activities, such as school newspapers, as long as the school finances the activities and grounds for censorship exist. In *Tinker*, the Court said that to censor students' expression, the expression must either disrupt the school's educational process or impinge upon the rights of others. *Hazelwood* broadened this guideline to include censorship of unprofessional, ungrammatical, or obscene speech, or speech that goes against the fundamental purpose of a school.

Hazelwood School District v. Kuhlmeier, 484 U.S. 260 (1988).

Frederick thought of an unusual way of getting on television. As the torch relay passed his school, Joe, with a little help from his friends, unfurled a banner that read, "Bong Hits 4 Jesus." The school's principal, Deborah Morse did not find Frederick's antics funny. She tore down the banner and suspended him for 10 days on the grounds that because the word "bong" was a reference to marijuana, the sign violated the school's antidrug policy.

Following his suspension, Frederick filed a suit against Morse and other school officials, claiming they violated his First Amendment rights. The U.S. Supreme Court disagreed. In a 5–4 decision, Chief Justice Roberts stated that school officials did not violate Frederick's First Amendment rights because (1) Frederick's banner was displayed during a school-supervised event, making this a "school speech" case (see the discussion of *Fraser*) rather than a normal case of free speech on a public street, and (2) the school's officials reasonably concluded that the banner promoted the use of an illegal drug.

Since the *Tinker* ruling the free speech rights of students have become somewhat more narrowly defined.[64] Students do not entirely leave their free speech rights at the schoolyard gates, however. In the recent case of *Marineau v. Guiles*, the U.S. Supreme Court let stand a ruling by the U.S. Court of Appeals for the Second Circuit, concluding that a school district had violated a student's rights by censoring his T-shirt, which bore a controversial message. In *Guiles*, school officials suspended Zachary Guiles for wearing a T-shirt that derided President George W. Bush as the "Chicken-Hawk-in-Chief."[65] The shirt showed the president as a chicken with a martini in one wing and a cocaine straw in the other.

With assistance from the American Civil Liberties Union, Guiles filed a lawsuit against school officials. Although the district court agreed with school officials that the shirt was offensive and, therefore, school officials were within their right to suspend Guiles for wearing it, its decision was reversed on appeal. According to the appellate court, even though the shirt used harsh rhetoric and imagery to express disagreement with the president's policies and character, it did not cause any disruption at the school. Based on the ruling in *Tinker*, Guiles was permitted to wear the shirt. In other words, the ruling in *Guiles* states that school officials cannot restrict student speech that contains a political message simply because the message contains a reference to an illegal activity. Student speech may be restricted only when it is reasonably apparent that the message *promotes* illegal activity.

Explanations of School Violence

School violence has roots in many areas, and the existing rules and regulations generally have not controlled the chaos found in some schools. How do criminologists explain school violence and disruption? Why do some children behave badly in school? What are the reasons some children act violently toward their classmates and teachers? This section presents three theories that offer rather different answers to these questions.

Loss of Teacher Authority

In *The Literacy Hoax*, Paul Copperman introduced a theory of school violence that focused on the loss of teacher authority, which is primarily the result of "open" classrooms established in the late 1960s.[66] Open classrooms have the following characteristics:

- Children study the things that interest them, virtually whenever they want to do so.
- A wide variety of learning activities are made available to students within the classrooms.
- During their learning activities, children may move freely around the classroom and interact with other students as they desire.
- The teacher is to be democratic, nonmanipulative, warm, and respectful of students, providing them with a pleasant and enjoyable educational experience.

The open-education movement can be traced to A. S. Neill's book *Summerhill*, which was published in 1960.[67] It spawned an educational approach that advocates flexible scheduling, more electives, and lighter course loads, though in many instances such freedoms are detrimental to learning. Flexible scheduling gives students more free periods. As a result, teachers who see students in the hallways do not know whether the children are legitimately unscheduled or are just skipping class. Teachers tend to give students the benefit of the doubt, and students may take advantage of this confusion to cut more classes.

Copperman argued that teachers face another challenge today, in addition to the chaos wrought by the open-education movement: Many students choose not just their electives but also the teachers who will conduct their required classes. Teachers, accordingly, are put in a difficult position. Without wanting to sacrifice quality, teachers realize they must get a reasonably large number of students to take and like their courses if they are to remain employed. Many students (not all) tend to like courses that are entertaining and easy. This situation generates a popularity contest among teachers, where one of the ways to "win" is to inflate grades. If one teacher inflates grades, then others are almost forced to follow suit. As a result of such pressure, standards for students become increasingly more relaxed. With life so easy, students are more likely to become lazy and unmotivated. Poor study habits present no worry, because the students will receive good grades anyway. As their teachers' expectations decrease, students work less and learn less, and their skills erode.

This lack of control makes it easier for students to get away with deviant behaviors such as drug use, violence, and vandalism. If there is a great deal of free time and teachers are reluctant to intervene, then delinquent and disruptive behaviors are likely to increase. For instance, Michael Turner and his colleagues found that well-run, traditional schools instill self-control in children, inhibiting their delinquency and enhancing their school performance. In contrast, schools in the most disadvantaged neighborhoods, where there has been the greatest loss of teacher authority, fail to foster self-control in students; as a consequence, both the school and the students suffer.[68]

Gary Gottfredson and Denise Gottfredson and their colleagues developed the idea of a communal school organization, which in many ways reflects more traditional school discipline than the open classrooms described by Copperman. A **communal school organization** exists when teachers have shared values and expectations of learning and appropriate student behavior. Schools that follow this model emphasize activities designed to foster meaningful social and learning interactions among students. In short, communally run schools empower students, while teachers and administrators remain clearly in control. Studies of such schools have shown that they produce positive results. For example, in a national survey of 254 high schools, researchers found that communal school organization reduces school disorder, student delinquency, and victimization of both teachers and students.[69]

James Coleman conducted a nationwide survey of nearly 60,000 students from more than 1000 high schools in the early 1980s. Much of Coleman's work compared public and private school students. Coleman points out that students' scholastic achievement is much higher in private schools primarily because of the firm teacher control that exists in these institutions:

First, given the same type of student . . . private schools create higher rates of engagement in academic activities. School attendance is better, students do more homework, and students generally take more rigorous subjects. . . . The indication is that more extensive academic demands are made in the private schools, leading to more advanced courses and thus to greater achievement. This is a somewhat obvious conclusion, and the statistical evidence supports it. Second, student behavior in a school has strong and consistent effects on

KEY TERMS

communal school organization
A partnership of teachers who have shared values and expectations of student learning and appropriate student behavior.

student achievement. . . . [The] greatest differences in achievement between private and public schools are accounted for by school-level behavior variables (that is, the incidence of fights, students threatening teachers, and so forth).[70]

Private schools experience fewer behavioral problems in their students because they are selective in terms of who they admit and retain, whereas public schools must accept any student regardless of the behavioral problems he or she may bring to the facility. According to Coleman, "the *average* public high school is outside the whole range of Catholic schools in the direction of more behavior problems."[71] He believes that private schools have fewer behavioral problems because of their disciplinary climate. Three-fourths of the private school students he interviewed said discipline in their school was strict and effective; by comparison, only 40% of the public school students said the same about their schools. Because of the higher standards of discipline enforced in private schools, fewer behavioral problems such as absenteeism, cutting classes, threats to teachers, and fights among students occur in these schools.

Although private schools were clearly superior to public schools during Coleman's era, this situation may no longer hold true, at least in terms of academic achievement. The U.S. Department of Education reported that independently run, publicly financed charter schools perform no better than comparable public schools. Students in public schools, in fact, performed slightly better in math and reading at the fourth- and eighth-grade levels than their private school counterparts.[72] Overall, however, poorly controlled and supervised schools where teachers have lost control of the school environment have poorer school safety records and create opportunities for school violence to thrive.[73]

Tracking

Some criminologists have singled out tracking (ability grouping) as a factor contributing to school violence. **Tracking** is the grouping of students into curricular categories, such as the college-preparatory, general, vocational, business, agricultural, and remedial tracks. Students in the college-preparatory track usually take a foreign language, algebra or some other form of advanced mathematics, and a science course during their freshman year in high school. Students in other tracks take different courses. Segregation and differentiation, therefore, begin very early in students' high school careers.

KEY TERMS

tracking
The grouping of students into curricular categories, such as the college-preparatory, general, vocational, business, agricultural, and remedial tracks.

The theory behind the tracking movement is that students learn better in groups whose members are similar to themselves. Thus the goal of tracking is to make classes as academically homogenous as possible. Students who achieve at the same level can work at the same pace, proceeding rapidly and uniformly through the material under the supervision of the teacher. Students who are slower will not hold up higher ability students, according to tracking theory, and lower ability students can receive specialized instruction that might make it possible for them to catch up with their peers later on.

Teachers and guidance counselors decide which track a student will be placed in. Researchers have found that their decisions regarding placement of students in particular tracks do not rest entirely on the students' academic abilities. Instead, the higher the family income of students, the more likely they will be placed in higher ability groups or the college-preparatory track. Conversely, students from low-income families are more likely to be placed in the vocational track or in the low-ability group.

August Hollingshead published *Elmstown Youth*, the first major study of tracking. He divided the population of Elmstown High School into five social classes, with students being assigned to one of three tracks of study: college preparatory, general, and commercial. Hollingshead then examined the social class of students in each track. Nearly two-thirds of students from upper- and upper-middle-class families were in the college-preparatory track. More than half of the middle-class and lower-middle-class students were in the general track, with a large proportion in the commercial track and many fewer in the college-preparatory track. Lower-class students were overwhelmingly in the commercial and general tracks; only 4% were in the college-preparatory track.[74]

Sometimes teachers *expect less* from lower-class students. One of the best-known studies examining teacher expectations and student performance was conducted by psychologists Robert Rosenthal and Lenore Jacobson, who published their findings in the book *Pygmalion in the Classroom*.[75] These researchers gave students a standard intelligence test. Next, teachers were provided with the names of students the researchers called "late bloomers" and were told to expect a sudden burst of learning from them. What the teachers did not know was that the names of the "late bloomers" were selected randomly from the class.

One year later, the researchers administered the intelligence tests again. The scores of the "late bloomers" were compared with those of the other students who received scores on the original test similar to the group of supposed late bloomers. The researchers found that students who were identified to teachers as late bloomers made significant gains on their intelligence test scores as compared to the group of "ordinary" students. The principal inference of Rosenthal and

Jacobson's study is that teacher expectations make a strong difference in the educational achievement of children. To the extent teachers expect children from poor families to fail or to struggle in school, there exists a major barrier to what these students might be capable of achieving. Interestingly, these effects are nearly identical to the effects of labeling children as "delinquent," in that the label may become a self-fulfilling prophecy.

Obviously students have different academic abilities. Tracking of children based on those abilities, however, may have a negative side: It may be discriminatory. The labels affixed to students are important because they set in motion a course that may be irreversible. Once a student is assigned to a particular track, that individual has little chance of ever being reassigned. Going from a noncollege-preparatory track to a college-preparatory track, for instance, is difficult because schools establish prerequisites. For example, freshman algebra must be taken before a student can take sophomore geometry.[76] Walter Schafer and Carol Olexa found that only 7% of students switch from a college-preparatory track to a noncollege-preparatory track or vice versa.[77]

Furthermore, the tracks to which students are assigned influence their future careers and determine their associates in and out of school, their grades, their participation in extracurricular activities, and their self-esteem. Tracking also affects students' attitudes toward school, their chances of failing, their attendance, and their involvement in misbehavior inside and outside a school setting. Karen Randolph and her colleagues have reported on the experience of being held back to repeat first grade and found that retention produces an array of educational deficits throughout children's school career. A school track that includes "flunking" first grade is very difficult to overcome.[78]

The connection between track position and delinquency is also important. Delos Kelly correlated track position, sex, and social class with self-reported incidents of delinquency and—somewhat surprisingly—found delinquency was more closely associated with track position than with either sex or social class. Students in the lower ability tracks were more likely to be involved in gang fights, smoking, and school expulsion.[79] The results obtained by Adam Gamoran and Robert Mare in their study of high school sophomores further supported Kelly's findings. These researchers discovered that a student's track position was related to the probability of high school graduation and, conversely, to the likelihood of dropping out. They suggest that tracking assignments in school reinforce preexisting inequalities in achievement among students from different socioeconomic backgrounds.[80]

Tracking might also serve as a proxy for other variables that are related to delinquency. Eric Stewart used data from the National Educational Longitudinal Study, which surveyed nearly 11,000 students from 528 high schools, and found that students who have strong school bonds are less likely to be involved in delinquency. In this sense, different school tracks reflect real scholastic and behavioral differences between children.[81] Many juveniles take school seriously and do not have time to participate in delinquency; for others, engaging in misbehaviors is their priority. Richard Felson and Jeremy Staff suggest that tracking does not reflect social class, IQ, or academic skills, but does influence self-control. Tracking groups are organized in a way that reflects students' abilities to defer gratification and display diligence, tenacity, and persistence in performing schoolwork. Felson and Staff found that a child's self-control was the best predictor of his or her delinquency both inside and outside of school.[82]

Not all research has found tracking to be harmful or discriminatory. First, if students with equal academic ability are compared, the track they enter is not significantly affected by their social class background.[83] Second, students do not always know which track they are in. In fact, both students and staff are often unsure what the tracks are.[84] Students in the noncollege-preparatory track are most likely to misperceive their track and think they are in the college-preparatory track. Far from feeling stigmatized and frustrated, these students are unrealistically optimistic. Third, the college-preparatory track is becoming less popular as more students opt for general and vocational tracks; many of those individuals will still be able to enter college.[85] Together, these findings appear to contradict study results that are critical of the tracking theory, which claim that tracking is prejudiced against particular groups of students.

Michael Wiatrowski and his associates reached a similar conclusion after looking at a national sample of 500 white males in high school and then following them for several years. These researchers found *no* relationship between a student's track and (1) delinquency among 10th graders, (2) delinquency among 12th graders, (3) extent of delinquency 1 year after high school, or (4) seriousness of delinquency 1 year after high school.[86]

In a review of the study conducted by Wiatrowski and his colleagues, Kenneth Polk agreed that tracking is less important than tracking theorists claim. However, Polk found that other school factors were important in producing delinquency. He examined the relationship between school performance (measured by high school grades) and adult criminality. The four groups compared were (1) youths with a high grade-point average (GPA) and a record of delinquency, (2) youths with a high GPA and no record of delinquency, (3) youths with a low GPA and a delinquency record, and (4) youths with a low GPA and no delinquency record. When Polk looked at the adult lives of these people, he discovered that those

who had committed delinquent acts as youths were more likely to be criminals as adults. But grades also made a difference in adult life: Students with a low GPA but no record of delinquency were 40% as likely to become adult criminals as all students; students with a delinquency record and a high GPA were 50% as likely to become adult criminals as all students. Polk's findings suggest that high school grades have a long-term effect on social behavior.[87]

Social Reproduction and Resistance

According to social reproduction theory, schools reproduce the social class structure of the larger society for the benefit of the economic elite. In other words, schools perpetuate inequality. In turn, some students react to that inequality by engaging in delinquency. In recent years, the concept of the **school-to-prison pipeline**, defined as the cycle of disproportionate suspension and serious disciplining of African American children that is consistent with disparities seen in the juvenile and criminal justice systems, has been advanced to account for interrelated issues of school problems, school discipline, and juvenile justice system involvement of African American youth (see **Box 10.10**, the "Delinquency Controversy" box feature).

In *Schooling in Capitalist America*, Samuel Bowles and Herbert Gintis argued that the public school system is the vehicle used to transmit social class differences among children and to point them toward differential occupation and income opportunities. Schools achieve this feat by instructing children differently depending on their social class backgrounds. For instance, schools with a high proportion of children from low-income families tend to be more authoritarian and require more conformity to school rules compared with schools with a high percentage of youths from high-income families. Often lower-class children are educated to fill low-paying jobs that do not require much independent thinking and decision making. The reverse is true for upper-class children, so the schools they attend socialize them to be bosses and creative and critical thinkers.[88]

One problem with the social reproduction theory has been pointed out by Henry Giroux in *Theory of Resistance*. Giroux writes that this theory assumes children are passive recipients of outside forces who are easily manipulated by school authorities.[89] Teachers know this is not true: Students are not easily controlled

and manipulated. To the contrary, an ever-increasing complaint among teachers is the growing willingness of some students to challenge teachers' authority. Many students balk at the prospect of blindly following teacher instructions and go out of their way to make life difficult for teachers. Some students have an agenda regarding their own lives that may have very little to do with the goals of the school and, for this reason, may resist the plans teachers and school officials have made for them. In fact, some students join together to construct an *oppositional culture* that resists the goals of the teachers and the school. In the book *Ain't No Makin' It*, Jay MacLeod describes how entrenched the oppositional culture is in inner-city America and suggests that schools in these areas are viewed as a waste of time, rather than as opportunities for advancement.[90]

Paul Willis tested a similar idea with a group of students from working-class backgrounds who attended an all-male comprehensive high school in an industrial area of England. The students learned to manipulate the school environment to make sure they always "had a good time." They established a peer culture that was antisocial and that differed sharply from the culture of students they called the "ear-'oles," who in their opinion did nothing but sit and listen in school, conforming to school authority and expectations. The working-class students resented both the ear-'oles and the authority of the school. For them, the school was out of touch with the "real world" and had little to offer them in preparation for the life they would enter into as adults. These students reacted by taking every opportunity to play pranks on the school officials, teachers, and ear-'oles, as their culture rejected the notion of upward mobility coming through schooling and the value of learning. Willis portrays their "opposition culture" as preparation for the generalized labor force these students would enter. The pranks the students played in school were similar to the pranks their adult versions would play in the future on the shop floor. The peer culture they developed complemented both the culture of their fathers at work and the cultures they would experience in the everyday world of the work force. The students Willis studied created an antischool culture that played a determining role in ensuring the perpetuation of their working-class status. In his account, the culture of the school was in conflict with the culture of the students. Sometimes this conflict manifested itself in the form of school violence and crime.[91]

Over a generation later, Willis' theory remains relevant. Consider the work of Elizabeth Stearns and Elizabeth Glennie, who examined data from all public high schools in North Carolina to explore why dropouts leave school. For younger adolescents, dropping out usually occurred for disciplinary reasons. By contrast, among students age 16 and older, the decision to leave school was driven by work and family

KEY TERMS

school-to-prison pipeline
The cycle of disproportionate suspension and serious disciplining of African American children that is consistent with disparities seen in the juvenile and criminal justice systems.

BOX 10.10

Delinquency Controversy

School-to-Prison Pipeline

The school-to-prison pipeline is a relatively new concept characterizing the disproportionate involvement of African American youth in various forms of school discipline, restraint, and exclusion. Disproportionate social control of African American children occurs at all levels. In preschool, black youth account for 18% of the total enrollment but 48% of preschoolers who receive out-of-school suspensions. Although black students account for 16% of students in the United States, they account for 32% of in-school suspensions, 33% of out-of-school suspensions, 42% of multiple out-of-school suspensions, and 34% of expulsions. Black students represent 27% of students referred to law enforcement and 31% subjected to school-related arrest.

To many, these statistics reflect school systems that are too likely to criminalize the conduct of black children and subject them to more punitive school sanctions. In 2016, the U.S. Departments of Education and Justice issued advisements to school districts stating that disproportionate minority outcomes for school discipline could violate federal Title VI regulations. An implication is that quotas could be tacitly imposed to create more equal outcomes in terms of school sanctions.

A problem with out-of-school suspensions and expulsions is that they create more time and opportunity for youth to engage in delinquency, in part because they are not being monitored at school. Alison Cuellar and Sara Markowitz found that out-of-school suspensions doubled the likelihood of arrest and the effect is stronger among black than white youth.

Of course, disproportionate school sanctions should be expected for racial groups, given the underlying differences in delinquency. For instance, John Wright and his colleagues analyzed data from the Early Childhood Longitudinal Study, Kindergarten Class (ECLS-K) and found that racial differences in school suspensions are *entirely* accounted for by prior behavior problems. Their findings seriously challenge claims of racial bias or differential enforcement.

President Obama has attempted to slow the school-to-prison pipeline with the creation of My Brother's Keeper, an organization that seeks to improve the school and socioeconomic functioning of African American youth and adults in the United States. My Brother's Keeper has six primary goals:

- Entering school ready to learn
- Reading at grade level by third grade
- Graduating from high school ready for college and career
- Completing postsecondary education or training
- Successfully entering the workforce
- Reducing violence and providing a second chance

It is likely that policies intended to stem the school-to-prison pipeline, and studies about whether it even exists, will continue.

Christopher Mallett, "The School-to-Prison Pipeline: A Critical Review of the Punitive Paradigm Shift." *Child and Adolescent Social Work Journal* 33:15–24 (2016); U.S. Department of Education Office for Civil Rights, *Civil Rights Data Collection Data Snapshot: School Discipline* (Washington, DC: Author, 2014); Alison Cuellar and Sara Markowitz, "School Suspension and the School-to-Prison Pipeline," *International Review of Law and Economics* 43:98–106 (2015); John Paul Wright, Mark Morgan, Michelle Coyne, Kevin Beaver, and J. C. Barnes, "Prior Problem Behavior Accounts for the Racial Gap in School Suspensions," *Journal of Criminal Justice* 42:257–266 (2014); Broderick Johnson and Jim Shelton, *My Brother's Keeper Task Force Report to the President* (Washington, DC: Author, 2014).

responsibilities that conflicted with school demands. Lower-class youths felt "locked into" their social class position and believed that completing school would not appreciably improve that position.[92]

Similarly, Roslyn Caldwell and her colleagues found that some African American students who live in disadvantaged communities *perceive* that their future is uncertain because of violence in their neighborhoods. In their research, students with a sense of fatalism and uncertainty about the future were more likely to be delinquent and have behavioral problems in school. However, many younger students living in the same neighborhoods could picture themselves going to college, getting married, and successfully transitioning into adult roles; those students showed no behavioral problems.[93] In this sense, expectations of a lower-class position directly influenced school performance and delinquency.

Many criminologists have reported that students who reject school in opposition to mainstream culture face a host of problems. Timothy Brezina and his colleagues found that students who harbor excessive anger against teachers, students, and school generally are at risk for delinquency and victimization in school.[94] Students who resist the social reproduction that occurs in schools face higher risks of social exclusion and isolation. When Derek Kreager studied a national sample of youths, he found that students who were socially isolated often had negative peer relationships and were prone to delinquency. Children who engage in school refusal, which is reluctance or refusal to attend school, have significant school attendance problems and often experience serious anxiety and depression. Although these types of children are usually at lower risk for delinquency, they are at higher risk for internalizing problems that are conducive

to drug use.[95] Priscilla Coleman and Caroline Byrd explored the correlates of school victimization and discovered that the most popular students—who were often those individuals who were the wealthiest and most socially advantaged—had the lowest likelihood of being victimized at school. Consistent with social reproduction theory, affluent students could afford a comfortable and safe school experience, whereas disadvantaged students could not.[96]

Preventing School Crime and Violence

In the wake of the highly publicized school shootings and other school-associated violence in the late 20th and early 21st centuries, schools have implemented a variety of strategies to prevent crime on their grounds. No particular strategy has emerged as the best option; rather, each approach has both strengths and weaknesses. One popular strategy for reducing school violence is called *zero tolerance*.

Zero Tolerance

The purpose of zero-tolerance policies is to send a strong message to students that weapons, drugs, fistfights, and other violent disruptions will not be tolerated. Many schools take a zero-tolerance approach to *any* threatening behavior, including sexual harassment, cigarette smoking, and possession of over-the-counter medications. For instance, any student attending Ocean View High School in Huntington Beach, California, who is involved in possession, sale, exchange, trafficking, or use of controlled substances, narcotics, paraphernalia, or alcohol faces the threat of immediate suspension, parent conference, and referral to the Huntington Beach Police for possible legal action, in addition to a possible recommendation for expulsion from the school district.[97]

In West Monroe, Louisiana, a third-grade boy who drew a picture of a soldier holding a canteen and a knife was suspended from school. The third grader also drew a fort, listing its inventory as guns, knives, and first-aid kits. When asked to comment on the incident, the principal of Lenwill Elementary School said the school would not tolerate anything having to do with guns or knives.[98] In Dayton, Ohio, school officials suspended a 5-year-old student for 10 days and threatened to expel him for bringing a pocketknife to school. In Wyoming, two junior high school girls who threw french fries at each other during lunchtime were cited by police for "hurling missiles." A growing number of schools have dropped dodge ball from their gymnasiums and playgrounds after the game came under attack by various women's groups, who argued that it fosters aggression and future violence among players.[99]

In Colorado, 8-year-old Eathan Harris was suspended from school for sniffing his marker in writing class. The school principal said the boy was punished for smelling the Sharpie marker to send a message to students about inhaling solvents. The school has since removed every Sharpie marker in the building, even though toxicologists say Sharpies are nontoxic and cannot be used to get high. The boy said he sniffed the marker only because it smelled good.[100]

Increasing evidence suggests that zero-tolerance policies are backfiring. In other words, the one-size-fits-all solution to school disciplinary problems is not working. Bringing an aspirin to school is not the same as bringing cocaine; a plastic knife is not the same as a handgun. Research has found that children attending schools with zero-tolerance policies feel less safe and perform worse academically. Finally, a mounting body of data indicates that zero-tolerance policies are pushing more children into the juvenile justice system.

Zero-tolerance policies take away a school administrator's option of using common sense to distinguish between genuine threats to school safety and innocent mistakes. The National School Boards Association urged local school boards to give principals more discretion. In addition, the American Psychological Association has recommended implementing more violence prevention programs to reduce problem behaviors. If students are being suspended needlessly, then the policies appear to be counterproductive. Research examining the effectiveness of zero-tolerance policies reported that schools with zero-tolerance policies are no more orderly and secure than are schools that evaluate behavior problems on a case-by-case basis.[101] (See **Box 10.11**, the "Delinquency Prevention" feature.)

Reducing School-Related Risk Factors

Some school anticrime and antiviolence programs attempt to reduce school-related risk factors for

Schools in several states have banned students from having items such as purses in classrooms because the bags could hold firearms and thus compromise school safety.

© Sean Locke/iStock/Getty.

BOX 10.11

Delinquency Prevention

Zero Tolerance in Public Schools

Several horrific juvenile crimes have heightened the public's concern about how juveniles should be treated by authorities. In response to such crimes, many public schools in the United States have created "zero-tolerance" policies with respect to questionable student behavior, including possession and use of guns and possession and use of drugs. Under zero-tolerance policies, when school authorities perceive a child to be violating a school rule or law, they remove that individual from school by suspension or expulsion. In essence, these policies allow for no margin of error—even the most minor student infraction is subject to immediate school discipline. Many of these policies apply harsh penalties to relatively innocuous conduct.

Some critics of zero-tolerance policies believe they are the result of an attitude of "hypervigilance." Many of the decisions made by local school boards in this regard have been criticized for being "by-the-book," rote measures that fail to take into account the particular circumstances of individual students or incidents. These "one-size-fits-all" approaches may severely punish students for violating the letter—but not the spirit—of such policies.

Nationally, several prominent incidents highlighted extreme decisions by school officials, including students who were subject to disciplinary action for bringing Advil to school, bringing a water pistol to school, or taking a slurp of Listerine (which is 22% alcohol) during school hours. Other cases highlight the extreme nature of zero-tolerance policies:

- A Florida eighth-grade student was suspended for 3 days for repeatedly farting on the school bus.
- A junior high school student from Belle, West Virginia, gave a zinc cough lozenge to a classmate and was suspended for 3 days.
- A kindergarten boy in Newport News, Virginia, was suspended for bringing a beeper on a class trip.
- A 9-year-old boy from Manassas, Virginia, was suspended for 1 day for giving breath mints to a classmate.
- A 13-year-old honor student from Fairborn, Ohio, received an 80-day suspension for bringing ibuprofen to class, a disciplinary action that later was reduced to 3 days.

- A 6-year-old boy from Madison, North Carolina, who kissed a girl on the cheek was given a 1-day suspension.
- An 11-year-old girl from Columbia, South Carolina, was arrested and suspended for having a steak knife in her lunchbox to cut chicken she had brought to school to eat.
- Also in South Carolina, a 10-year-old boy who was in possession of a broken pencil sharpener was spotted by a teacher wielding the sharpener's detached blade. He was suspended for 2 days even though it was clear he just was trying to sharpen a pencil.
- A 10-year-old boy was expelled for bringing a 1-inch plastic knife to school.
- An 8-year-old girl from Alexandria, Louisiana, was expelled for bringing to school a 1-inch pocketknife that was attached to her grandfather's pocket watch chain.

A study by the Vera Institute of Justice found that two million students are suspended from secondary schools annually, with African American and Hispanic children four and two times more likely to be suspended or expelled than whites, respectively. Among suspensions lasting 1 week or longer, only 5% involved possession of a weapon, but 43% were for insubordination. They concluded that zero-tolerance policies do not make schools more orderly or safe and can have lifelong negative effects on affected youth. Based on data from a national sample of young people, Aaron Kupchik and Thomas Catlaw found that suspended youth were less likely to vote and engage in civic activities in adulthood. The many stories of excessive and inappropriate use of suspension and expulsion, as well as concerns about disparate impact of school discipline on youths of color, have led to a national backlash against zero-tolerance policies. For example, the American Bar Association recently voted to oppose zero-tolerance policies that have a discriminatory effect or that mandate either expulsion or referral of students to juvenile or criminal court, without regard to the circumstances or nature of the offense or the student's history. Similar resolutions have been approved by bar associations in a number of states. Although created with honest intentions, zero-tolerance policies have in many ways created more problems than they have solved.

Christopher Boccansufo and Megan Kuhfeld, *Multiple Responses, Promising Results: Evidence-Based, Nonpunitive Alternatives to Zero Tolerance* (New York: Child Trends, 2011); Erin Hickey, "Zero Tolerance for Policies Depriving Children of Education: A Comment on Zero Tolerance Policies," *Children's Legal Rights Journal* 24:18–25 (2004); Jeanne Stinchcomb, Gordon Bazemore, and Nancy Riestenberg, "Beyond Zero Tolerance: Restoring Justice in Secondary Schools," *Youth Violence and Juvenile Justice* 4:123–147 (2006); Jacob Kang-Brown, Jennifer Trone, Jennifer Fratello, and Tarika Daftary-Kapur, *A Generation Later: What We've Learned About Zero Tolerance in Schools*, (New York: Vera Institute of Justice, 2014); Aaron Kupchik and Thomas Catlaw, "Discipline and Participation: The Long-Term Effects of Suspension and School Security on the Political and Civic Engagement of Youth," *Youth & Society* 47:95–124 (2015).

delinquency, such as academic failure, low self-esteem, low commitment to school, and problematic peer relationships, by targeting classroom organization, management practices, and instructional strategies. Many of the more promising programs include reductions in class size, the elimination of grades in elementary schools, tutoring, computer-assisted instruction, interactive teaching, and cooperative learning.[102]

For school-based interventions to be most effective, they must start early in a child's school career—for example, in elementary school. Many schools have implemented early truancy initiatives that aim to reduce chronic absenteeism among children in the first through sixth grades. Cynthia McCluskey and her colleagues evaluated such an initiative in three elementary schools that were located in a lower income area and where a significant proportion of students missed more than 30 days of school per year. The program consisted of a letter sent to parents and a home visit from a school attendance officer. These simple procedures reduced absenteeism at the schools even among students who had been chronically absent.[103] If children are spending more time in school, it stands to reason that other educational outcomes will also improve.

Other programs target chronic truants by using police–school partnerships. An evaluation by Michael White and his colleagues found that these partnerships produce modest academic benefits for chronic truants; however, they do reduce school behavioral problems. Also, the partnerships help connect at-risk youths with appropriate social service and juvenile justice agencies.[104]

Counseling and Behavior Modification

Some school programs focus primarily on in-school counseling and behavior modification in an attempt to thwart juvenile delinquency. This approach involves group counseling, the use of time-out rooms, training in interpersonal and problem-solving skills, moral education, value clarification, peer counseling, and intervention in the opening moves of escalating conflicts.[105] The National Resource Center for Safe Schools recommends a number of components be considered in planning for safe schools: developing emergency response planning, creating a positive school climate and culture, ensuring high-quality facilities and technology, and instituting links with mental health social services.[106]

Still other programs place an emphasis on control. Control-oriented programs typically use measures such as closing off isolated areas, increasing staff supervision, installing electronic monitoring for weapons detection, removing tempting vandalism targets, requiring students to carry only see-through backpacks, and using police or private security personnel for patrol, crowd control, investigation of criminal activities, and intelligence gathering.[107]

One promising control-based program is the **School Resource Officer Program**, in which a police officer works within the school to perform a variety of specialized duties. According to Peter Finn, school resource officer programs provide five important benefits for police:[108]

- They reduce the workload of traditional patrol officers.
- They improve adolescent and student perceptions of law enforcement officers.
- They create and maintain positive relationships between law enforcement agencies and schools.
- They enhance the law enforcement agency's reputation in the community.
- They benefit schools by engendering improved school safety, improved police response time to problems, and improved perceptions of school safety.

Preventing Targeted Violence

Targeted violence, or incidents where an attacker targets a particular person or group, may not be amenable to general prevention programs. An intensive study of 37 school shootings involving 41 attackers conducted by the U.S. Secret Service National Threat Assessment Center reported the following findings:

- Incidents of targeted violence at school are rarely impulsive. Rather, the attacks are typically the end result of an understandable and often discernible process of thinking and behavior.
- Before most incidents, the attacker told someone about his or her idea or plan.
- There is no accurate or useful profile of "the school shooter."
- Most attackers had previously used guns and had ready access to these weapons.
- Most shooting incidents were not resolved by law enforcement intervention.
- In many cases, other students were involved in some capacity.
- Most attackers engaged in some behavior before the incident that caused others concern or indicated a need for help.

These findings have some important implications for prevention of targeted school violence. For example, because the typical student engaging in school violence did not "just snap," it may be possible to

KEY TERMS

School resource officer program
A control-based policy under which a police officer works within the school to perform a variety of specialized duties.

gather information about intent and planning before the incident. It is also helpful to distinguish between *making* a threat and *posing* a threat; adults should attend to concerns that someone poses a threat. Because profiling is not effective for identifying those students who may pose a risk of targeted violence, school officials should focus instead on a student's behaviors and communications to determine whether the student appears to be planning or preparing for an attack. It is important to discover if a student is on a path toward a violent attack. In addition, because other students often know about incidents in advance, it is wrong to assume shooters are "loners"; instead, it is important to gather information from a potential attacker's friends and schoolmates.[109]

How might schools gather this information? In 2005, the Houston County (Georgia) school board became one of the first school districts to enroll in the national Student Crime Stoppers program, which pays students as much as $100 for information about thefts, drug violations, or weapons possession on school property. Many schools use revenues from vending machines to pay student "tattlers" or "snitches" who report on the crimes and illegal transgressions of their peers. Critics argue that such a policy sends the wrong message to children—namely, that civic duty should be performed for payment. Proponents of this approach suggest that gathering information from students is a proactive way to prevent violence in schools.[110]

The "Stay-In" Problem and School Dropouts

A more controversial approach for addressing school violence is recommended by Jackson Toby, who thinks schools are unsafe because they have a *stay-in* problem—not a dropout problem. Toby believes there are too many students in school who disrupt teaching and learning. Stay-in students earn bad grades (Fs and Ds), disrupt classes, and interfere with the education of those students who go to school to be educated. For example, in an interview with one of his subjects named Joe, Jackson Toby tells us about the type of student responsible for the stay-in problem in schools today:

> "I like school" Joe said. I was surprised. Most delinquents I had known hated school and did poorly in their schoolwork. "What did you like about it?" I asked. He told me about sitting in the lunchroom with his gang and having food fights, about "making out" in the halls with his girlfriends . . . about harassing a young, inexperienced teacher. . . . "What about your classes?" I asked. "Did you like them?" "Yeah," he replied. "I liked gym." Did he like English, math, or anything else in the curriculum? "No," he replied, smiling. "They weren't in my curriculum."[111]

Although Toby is unique in making an argument about the stay-in problem, other criminologists have documented the extensive misbehavior of students like Joe. Many times, those students with the most school problems are also the most serious delinquents. Xia Wang and his colleagues compared the school careers of 5187 nondelinquent students to the same number of delinquents in Florida. Other than their delinquency status, the study groups were matched by demographic and school-based characteristics. On every measure, delinquents had worse school problems than nondelinquents. Compared to nondelinquent students, delinquents had lower GPAs, higher absenteeism and truancy rates, and greater and more serious behavioral problems; they were more likely to repeat a grade, and they received more and harsher disciplinary actions. Moreover, the delinquency and other behavioral problems of the delinquents worsened after they were expelled or received an out-of-school suspension. Anthony Peguero and Nicole Bracy examined data from 11,800 students as part of the Educational Longitudinal Study of 2002 and found that students who had lower educational achievement, weaker school involvement, and greater behavioral problems (including delinquency) were more likely not only to receive serious school discipline, such as suspension and juvenile justice intervention, but also more likely to drop out.[112]

Does dropping out of school lead to delinquency? Can dropping out turn a law-abiding juvenile into a delinquent? Although dropouts do have higher crime rates than juveniles who continue their schooling, the former group's offending rates were also higher *before* they left school. Research examining whether dropping out of school increases or decreases the likelihood of future criminality has also produced mixed results.

To investigate this issue, Delbert Elliott and Harwin Voss conducted a longitudinal study of 2617 students from eight schools in California. They compared rates of police contacts and self-reported delinquency for both dropouts and high school graduates. Rates of delinquency were higher for the dropouts and increased more while they were in school than did the rates of delinquency for the high school graduates. Once the students dropped out of school, however, their rates of delinquency declined. The decrease in their offending rates took place regardless of the student's age at the time he or she dropped out and could not be explained by social class or gender. The delinquency rate among dropouts was highest just before leaving school and dropped sharply after they quit, leading Elliott and Voss to reason that these individuals' delinquency represented a response to the frustration of negative school experiences. By dropping out of school, students reduced their frustration; in turn, their involvement in delinquency declined.[113]

The fact that dropping out of school *reduced* delinquency rates in this study has attracted attention from other criminologists. In an attempt to replicate Elliott and Voss's study, Terence Thornberry and his colleagues analyzed longitudinal data from a sample of 975 people from the Philadelphia birth cohort of 1945 (males born that year who lived in Philadelphia from ages 10 to 18). The researchers reviewed arrest records and interviewed 567 members (62%) of the sample. They found that youths who dropped out of school at 16 and 18 years of age had significantly more arrests following the dropout event than during the previous year when they were still in school.[114]

David Farrington and his associates extended the analysis of dropping out to include unemployment and delinquency. These researchers also found evidence that criminal involvement increased after dropping out of school. They reported that adolescents in school committed fewer delinquencies than (1) those who had dropped out and were fully employed or (2) those dropouts who were unemployed.[115]

These conflicting findings led Roger Jarjoura to hypothesize that the reasons juveniles drop out of school are related to their future delinquency. Jarjoura found that students who dropped out because they disliked school and students who were expelled from school had the highest rates of involvement in criminal activities after dropping out. By comparison, students who dropped out of school for personal reasons, family problems, financial reasons, or poor grades were not any more involved in delinquency after leaving school than before. Put differently, sometimes dropping out leads to more delinquency; at other times it does not.

In a follow-up study, Jarjoura found that dropping out is associated with greater involvement in delinquency for middle-class youths than for lower-class juveniles. For lower-class juveniles, dropping out of high school does not increase their involvement in violent offenses. By comparison, for middle-class students, dropping out of high school for school-related or personal reasons significantly increases their involvement in violent offenses compared with high school graduates. For middle-class students who drop out for economic reasons, dropping out does not increase their involvement in violent offenses. The importance of Jarjoura's research is its revelation that dropouts are not a homogenous group: They differ by social class, reason for dropping out, and participation in criminal activities after dropping out. His findings suggest that schools may need to develop alternative dropout prevention programs because the reason a student drops out of school affects the likelihood of whether he or she will become involved in criminal activities after leaving school.[116]

Delinquency is only one negative feature of life for many high school dropouts. Brandy Maynard and her colleagues studied 19,312 emerging adults selected from the 2010 National Survey on Drug Use and Health to see the effects of high school dropout on various life outcomes. After controlling for many demographic factors, they found that males, Hispanics, those receiving government aid, and persons living in households earning less than $20,000 per year were more likely to drop out. After dropping out, these young adults were more likely to smoke, use marijuana, attempt suicide, and have arrests for diverse crimes including larceny, assault, and drug possession or sale.[117]

When a youth drops out of school is crucial to understanding how dropping out relates to delinquency. For instance, truancy has been referred to as the "kindergarten of crime" because it often serves as a forerunner of delinquency and other problems such as unemployment, alcoholism, substance use, and adult criminality.[118] Thus children who frequently miss school early in life are in trouble.[119] Jane Sprott and her colleagues argue that attending school is one of the most important protective factors against delinquency. Coincidentally, Sprott also argues against zero-tolerance policies precisely because they remove children from school.[120]

Finally, delinquency also sets into motion the likelihood of juvenile justice involvement, and that too has negative implications for school functioning. Stephanie Wiley examined a survey of middle schoolers and found that getting arrested in seventh grade is a particularly troubling event. Youth who were arrested as seventh graders saw a 132% increase in their delinquency following the arrest, in addition to weakened school commitment, reduced attendance, and greater associations with delinquent peers.[121] Of course, it is also likely that a youth who is delinquent to the extent that he or she to accumulates arrests at such a young age is unlikely to fare well in prosocial institutions in the first place.

WRAP UP

THINKING ABOUT JUVENILE DELINQUENCY: CONCLUSIONS

Anxiety over schools is a relatively recent phenomenon in this country, following on the heels of a long period of time when education was thought to be one of the nation's greatest strengths. Today, however, there is growing concern about school violence and shootings, bullying, and teacher victimization. These fears have inspired a spate of prevention strategies such as zero-tolerance policies and have led to U.S. Supreme Court decisions regulating which clothes students may wear, how searches and seizures of their personal belongings may be conducted, and how students may express themselves.

Different theories have been advanced to explain the link between schools and delinquency. Paul Copperman, for example, points to loss of teacher authority as a key factor; he says this trend is caused primarily by open classrooms that lead to less control and lower academic standards. Lack of control, in turn, makes it easier for students to get away with behaviors such as drug use, violence, and vandalism.

In contrast, the tracking theory contends that students placed in noncollege-preparatory tracks are stigmatized by such placement and react in many negative ways, including delinquency. Finally, according to social reproduction theory, the purpose of public schools is to serve the economic elite. In other words, their primary function is to reproduce the existing class structure in society. When they succeed in doing so, the resulting inequalities cause lower-class students to become disruptive.

Numerous strategies have been put in place to prevent students from dropping out of school. What is clear from the existing research is that no single dropout prevention strategy is best: One size does *not* fit all. A program that prevents one student from dropping out may not influence the decision of another student to stay in school. Given this inescapable fact, schools must implement multiple dropout prevention programs if they are to retain the greatest number of students.

CHAPTER SPOTLIGHT

- The United States has a long history of free public education. In 1851, Massachusetts passed the nation's first compulsory school attendance law requiring all children between the ages of 8 and 14 to attend school for a minimum of 3 months each year.
- A school-associated violent death is a tragic event. In the United States, youths killed at school account for less than 2% of the total number of youth homicides overall. Young people are more than *50 times* more likely to be murdered when they are away from school than while they are at school.
- Most school crime and violence is nonfatal. However, even nonfatal crimes such as theft and drug use can lead to a disruptive and threatening school environment.
- Students are not the only victims of crime and violence at schools: Teachers may also be the targets of threats and physical attacks. In the past year, approximately 260,000 teachers have been threatened with injury by a student from their school; fewer teachers (approximately 115,000) have been physically attacked.
- Schools today are struggling to create an atmosphere that fosters learning and teaching. To achieve these goals, schools have put in place many rules and regulations. Many schools' rules have been challenged in lawsuits, and rulings regarding their legality have been made by the U.S. Supreme Court.
- Three broad explanations of school violence have been proposed: the loss of teacher authority, the advent of tracking programs, and social reproduction and resistance.
- In reaction to highly publicized school shootings and violence in the late 20th and early 21st centuries, many schools have put in place numerous strategies to curb school violence. Among the measures schools have implemented are zero-tolerance policies, reduction of school-risk factors, counseling and behavior modification, and prevention programs for targeted violence.

CRITICAL THINKING

1. In some states, schools have banned items such as purses from classrooms because the bags could hold illegal drugs or firearms and, therefore, could compromise school safety. Are zero-tolerance school policies, such as banning purses, worthwhile?

2. One reason schools are characterized by crime and violence is because they may only "warehouse" people from ages 14 to 18. This age cohort is among the most criminogenic. Is a school-delinquency connection inevitable given the ages of the students who attend school?

3. Is bullying a social problem or a minor nuisance that all people experience in their lives? Why might bullying contribute to school-associated violent deaths?

4. For most students, the threat of corporal punishment is an effective means of social control. For some students, however, corporal punishment may be viewed as a status symbol of achievement. Should corporal punishment in schools be used more widely?

5. Some people are uncomfortable with reciting the Pledge of Allegiance because it mentions God. Should schools ever expose students to moral and religious ideas?

Violence, Drug Use, and Delinquency

Of all the types of delinquency that children and adolescents commit, two general forms generate the most public concern, grab the majority of news headlines, and serve as a barometer for how the United States is doing as a nation—namely, youth violence and drug use. There is no shortage of shocking incidents in which children and adolescents have planned and committed severe forms of violence. Consider the following examples:

- In Waycross, Georgia, a group of nine third graders plotted to attack their teacher and brought a broken steak knife, handcuffs, and duct tape to school to execute the plot. The children even assigned tasks such as covering the windows and cleaning up after the attack, which was supposed to be carried out by knocking the teacher out with a crystal paperweight and then stabbing her. The children were upset that the teacher had scolded one of them a few days earlier.[1]
- In West Palm Beach, Florida, a group of 10 masked teenagers, ages 14 to 17, raped and beat a 35-year-old woman and her 12-year-old son and then forced the mother—at gunpoint—to perform a sexual act on her son. Because violence is endemic to the Dunbar Village neighborhood where this incident

OBJECTIVES

- ◆ Understand the nature, prevalence, and trends in youth violence in recent U.S. history.
- ◆ Identify characteristics, behaviors, and risk factors among violent juvenile offenders and juvenile victims of violence.
- ◆ Examine trends in substance use among American youths and identify how drugs and alcohol are related to delinquency.
- ◆ Grasp theoretical explanations for the drugs–delinquency relationship.
- ◆ Explore the diverse ways that public policy and the juvenile justice system have responded to youth violence and drug use.

KEY TERMS

dynamic cascade model of violence 290
Brady Bill 293
lifetime prevalence 295
annual prevalence 296
30-day prevalence 296
comorbidity 307

Board of Education of Pottawatomie County v. Earls et al. 310
Drug Abuse Resistance Education (D.A.R.E.) 312
keepin' it REAL 313
decriminalization 314
legalization 314
harm reduction 314

occurred, local residents suggested that the sexual assault was "no big deal."[2]

- In Tyler Hill, Pennsylvania, a 10-year-old boy named Tristen Kurilla was charged as an adult for the crime of murder for killing a 90-year old woman. The child allegedly held a cane over her throat and repeatedly punched her when he became angry after she had yelled at him. The youth remains in juvenile detention.[3]

In terms of adolescent substance use and delinquency, worrisome headlines are equally impossible to avoid: "Movies inspire children to smoke," "Survey: Parents clueless on booze, drugs at teen parties," "Meth's impact on children probed," "Many more treated for meth, pot," "Prescription drugs find place in teen culture," "More kids get multiple psychiatric drugs," and "Anti-drug advertising campaign a failure, GAO report says."[4] These are just some of the thousands of news items on adolescent drug use whose messages permeate American culture. The headlines present complex and, at times, conflicting information about the current status of substance use among children and adolescents, the effectiveness of treatments for substance use, and the most appropriate ways for the juvenile justice system to respond to drugs and delinquency.

If one were to focus exclusively on the news, it would be reasonable to conclude that youth violence and drug use are at epidemic levels. In reality, youth violence and drug use are at their lowest levels in decades. Even though general trends show declines in delinquency, citizens, politicians, and the media continue to express concerns about youth violence. Although neighborhoods and schools are much safer than in recent decades, public perceptions have changed little: People continue to believe juvenile violence and drug use are serious threats that should be dealt with severely. This chapter examines youth violence and drug use, including general trends related to these issues, the ways that violence and drug use are linked to general delinquency, and steps being taken to reduce adolescent violence and drug use.

The Nature and Extent of Youth Violence

According to the Federal Bureau of Investigation, in 2014 more than 25,890 juveniles were arrested for serious violent crimes when the most current data were available. Some 14,908 youths were arrested for aggravated assault, 9150 youths were arrested for robbery, 1501 youths were arrested for rape, and 331 youths were arrested for murder in that year. Although these figures at first appear very troubling, in the decade between 2005 and 2014, violent delinquency among juveniles, as measured by police contacts or arrests, actually declined by 43% and serious property delinquency declined by 46%.[5]

Juveniles are both perpetrators of violence and victims of violence, and their violence occurs at home, at school, and on the streets. Children are frequently victims of violence in the home, with more than 670,000 reported cases of child abuse and neglect validated each year and more than 1460 child fatalities resulting from abuse. Although children are more likely to be victimized in the home, they sometimes engage in violence toward other family members, often as a response to their own maltreatment. Violence exposure takes a heavy toll. Lynn Langton and Jennifer Truman analyzed data from the National Crime Victimization Survey and found that 66% of adolescents reported significant socioemotional problems that negatively affected their school performance, family relationships, and peer relationships in the wake of being victimized by or exposed to violence. Violent delinquency produces a range of symptoms including anxiety, anger, depression, vulnerability, distrust, sadness, and feeling unsafe. In addition, exposure to violence results in fatigue, headaches, insomnia, muscle tension, high blood pressure, and eating problems.[6]

Youth violence devastates communities and the children living in those communities. In a landmark study, Patrick Sharkey examined the effect of exposure to local homicide on the cognitive performance of children ages 5 to 17 in the Project on Human Development in Chicago Neighborhoods. Sharkey found that exposure to a local homicide significantly reduces performance on vocabulary and reading assessments among children in school by up to one standard deviation. To put this effect in perspective, about 15% of African American children in the sample spend at least 1 month out of a year functioning at a lower cognitive level entirely because of the environmental effects of local homicides. And in the most violent neighborhoods, children spend 1 week of every month—or 25% of their life—functioning at a lower level because of the murders occurring around them. It is common for about 20 Chicago public school students to be fatally shot during a school year. Many of the killings were gang related, and they involved offenders and victims as young as age 15. Approximately 40 to 70% of Chicago youths have witnessed a shooting during their childhood or adolescence.[7]

Exposure to violence is not limited to major cities such as Chicago. In a review of 15 years of research on youth violence and exposure to youth violence, Daniel Flannery and his colleagues reached the following conclusions:[8]

- Youth in community samples report high rates of exposure to violence, with rates of witnessing violence generally being higher than rates of actual victimization from violence.

- There is a strong association between violence exposure and increased risk for the perpetration of aggression and violence, even after controlling for demographic and contextual factors.
- Exposure to violence contributes to higher levels of reported mental health symptoms (e.g., anger, anxiety, depression, trauma, dissociation) in both community and clinical samples of youth.
- Rates of exposure to violence (witnessing and victimization) are generally higher for boys with the exception of sexual victimization, for which the rate of exposure is higher for girls.
- Despite overall differences in average rates of exposure, girls who report high levels of exposure to violence are at just as much risk of experiencing clinically significant mental health symptoms and perpetrating aggression and violence as boys who report high levels of violence exposure.
- Younger children report higher levels of victimization from violence than older youth, but similar levels of witnessing violence.

In short, youth violence is a pressing social problem that has severe immediate and long-term consequences for children, adolescents, and society. Recent trends in youth violence are explored next.

Patterns of Youth Violence

The United States (and other Western nations for that matter) has been enjoying unprecedented low levels of criminal violence, especially among youths, since its peak in 1993–1994. Although any amount of violence in society is too much, it is now the case that most of the time, most U.S. towns and cities are characterized by orderliness and low levels of violence especially when compared to the state of U.S. cities in the latter decades of the 20th century. This section examines youth violence perpetration and victimization from a national perspective based on recent large-scale studies.

The Developmental Victimization Survey (DVS) is a large-scale survey of victimization among more than 2000 children ages 2 to 17 years. David Finkelhor and his colleagues created the DVS around 2002. In 2008, Finkelhor and colleagues conducted an even larger survey of 4549 children ages 17 and under from across the United States. This effort is called the National Survey of Children's Exposure to Violence (NatSCEV), and it produced several important findings about youth violence. (For further discussion, see chapter 2.) For instance:

- More than 60% of children were exposed to violence at least once in the prior year.
- Violence exposure can be direct or indirect, such as witnessing a violent act.
- More than 41% of children were assaulted in the prior year.

- More than 10% of children were assaulted so severely that they incurred bodily injury.
- About 25% of children were victims of robbery.
- More than 15% suffered from child maltreatment.
- About 6% of children were sexually victimized.
- More than 22% of children witnessed a violent act, and 10% saw a family member assault another family member.
- Some children suffer from chronic exposure to violence. Approximately 11% of children experienced five or more direct victimizations in the previous year, and less than 2% experienced 10 or more direct victimizations in the prior year.

Finkelhor and his collaborators recently compared youth violence exposure in the Developmental Victimization Survey based on data from 2003 to the National Survey of Children's Exposure to Violence based on data from 2008. These two data sets show less youth violence in more recent times. The largest areas of decline are for peer–sibling assaults, bullying, witnessing weapon assaults, and witnessing nonweapon assaults. Other crimes that showed significant reductions during this time period included sexual assault, theft, and emotional maltreatment from caregivers.[9]

Similar promising news about patterns of youth violence is found in other nationally representative surveys. For example, the National Survey of Adolescents is a study of 3614 youths ages 12 to 17 that examines various forms of delinquency and exposure to violence. A recent study compared the prevalence of violence across two waves of data collection and reported impressive declines. At wave 1, 20% of youths had been delinquent. By wave 2, the prevalence declined to less than 9%. Victimization also declined in a variety of contexts. Sexual abuse declined from a prevalence of 8% to 2.2%. Physical abuse and assault declined from nearly 20% to about 6%. Witnessing community violence was reduced by half, from a

African American males are six times more likely than white males to be homicide victims. The child in this coffin was the victim of a drive-by shooting. What factors may contribute to racial differences in violent victimization among youths?

© davidford/David Reimche/iStock/Getty.

prevalence of 39% to 19%. In addition, witnessing domestic violence declined from a prevalence of nearly 8% to just over 1%. In fact, youth with continued involvement in and exposure to violence were disproportionately those who were engaged in high-risk lifestyles characterized by alcohol and drug use.[10]

In terms of trends in the most serious form of youth violence—homicide—Terance Miethe and Wendy Regoeczi suggest that if any noticeable change in youth homicides has occurred, it is that these crimes are becoming increasingly "characterized by young, African American male offenders, instrumental motives, multiple offenders, guns, and strangers."[11] To illustrate their point, African Americans account for approximately 14% of the population between the ages of 15 and 29 years, yet account for about 75% of all murder victims between the ages of 15 and 29 years. Drawing on data from the Northwestern Juvenile Project, Linda Teplin and her colleagues studied causes of death among formerly delinquent youth 16 years after their release from the juvenile justice system. African American adolescents were nearly *10 times* more likely than those in the general population to have been murdered. Among delinquent males in the sample, the majority of whom were African American, 91% of the causes of mortality were homicide.[12] In fact, the African American involvement in serious youth violence is so pronounced that it skews statistics about the involvement in violence among American youth generally. For example, Alexander Vazsonyi and his colleagues compared racial and social class differences in youth violence among adolescents in the United States, Switzerland, the Netherlands, Japan, and Hungary and found very similar rates of violence. The exception was high school-age African Americans living in rural areas—their involvement in violence was dramatically higher than that for all other groups.[13] For a closer look at youth violence around the world, see **Box 11.1**, the "Delinquency Around the Globe" feature.

Although it does not receive the same attention as violent delinquency, suicide is another important form of violence affecting the lives of children and adolescents. According to researchers, nearly one in five high-school-age youths make a plan to attempt suicide during the year, and about half actually attempt suicide. Many risk factors that contribute to violent delinquency, such as family trouble, delinquent peers, and bullying, also contribute to suicide among adolescents. For instance, Ann Burgess and her colleagues suggest that chronic bullying in schools produces students who are susceptible to suicide, school shootings, or both.[14] In the past decade, more than 20,000 juveniles have committed suicide in the United States. Suicide is the third leading cause of death of adolescents after accidents and homicide—and who knows what percentage of "accidents" are actually suicides. Although females are more likely to attempt suicide, males are four times more likely to die from suicide (i.e., males have a higher suicide *completion* rate).[15]

Why the Decline in Youth Violence?

In 1997, in the third edition of *Delinquency in Society*, we wrote that "If there is no significant change in the tendency of youths to become involved in violence, juvenile violent-crime arrests will double in just 18 years."[16] We were looking at the most current data available at the time, but such data are always out of date by the time a book is published. Thus, in 1997, the most current arrest statistics were from 1994. The 1-year decline between 1993 and 1994 did not appear to be much more than an anomaly, especially after so many years of increasing youth violence. Howard Snyder and Melissa Sickmund had recently calculated estimates of juvenile violent crime for the year 2010 based on juvenile arrests for 1992 and available projections of population growth. They stated, "If current trends continue, by 2010 the number of juvenile arrests for murder is expected to increase by 145% over the 1992 level."[17] They also projected increases of 129% for the aggravated assault rate and 66% for the rape rate. Louis Freeh, Director of the FBI, stated, "The ominous increase in juvenile crime, coupled with population trends, portends future crime and violence at nearly unprecedented levels."[18] Of course, these estimates and predictions were all wrong. Why were we and so many other criminologists so mistaken about the direction of violent youth crime, and why did juvenile violence and crime in general decline so much and so quickly?

Frank Zimring said, "Criminologists are like weathermen without a satellite. We can only tell you about yesterday's crime rates."[19] However, there is also a good deal of disagreement among criminologists as they offer interpretations and explanations of the last decade's violent youth crime rates. Indeed, a variety of hypotheses have been proposed for why youth violence declined rather than increased. Several reasons for the general decline in juvenile arrests include an improving economy, legalization of abortion, increased use of incarceration, more and better policing, changes in the age distribution of the population, and the decline in the crack market. But are explanations for why youth committed fewer thefts, used certain drugs less frequently, burglarized fewer homes, and stole fewer automobiles adequate for explaining the drop in homicides, rapes, aggravated assaults, and weapons violations?

Marc Ouimet examined the drop in crime in the United States and Canada to explore what caused the drastic declines in crime. Whereas U.S. criminal justice policy included greater numbers of police, more aggressive and specialized policing tactics, and

BOX 11.1

Delinquency Around the Globe

Youth Violence in a Global Context

The United States is not the only country that struggles with juvenile violence. Research on recent trends in juvenile crime and violence in most nations suggests that the rate of juvenile violence rose sharply in the latter part of the 20th century, just as it did in the United States. Since the early to mid-1980s, an increase in youth violence has occurred in Austria, Denmark, England and Wales, France, Germany, the Netherlands (Holland), Italy, Poland, Sweden, and Switzerland. Rates of youth violence rose in most of these countries even though overall youth crime rates appeared to be stable and even though crime rates were not increasing among older people. In some countries, the official figures increased between 50 and 250%. In England and Wales in 1986, for example, approximately 360 of every 100,000 youths ages 14 to 16 were "convicted or cautioned by the police" for violent crimes; by 1994, that figure had climbed to approximately 580 per 100,000. Increases in youth violence in Germany were even higher. Rates in the former East Germany were between 60 and 80% higher. Even Sweden, a country that forbids parental use of physical force against children and prohibits professional boxing, reports dramatic increases in the number of juveniles sentenced for assault in recent decades.

A study of 33 countries has shown that bullying is a worldwide problem and that globally, about one-third of children experience bullying among youth ages 11, 13, and 15. However, between 2001 and 2010, bullying has significantly decreased in most countries in Europe and Asia and increased in only two nations, Belgium and Finland. Frank Elgar and his colleagues studied youth bullying and fighting in 79 countries spanning Africa, Asia, Europe, North America, and South America and found a global prevalence of about 30% for bullying. The prevalence for physical assault was nearly 11% for males and nearly 3% for females, worldwide.

According to official records, victim surveys, and self-report studies, the victims of violent crimes committed by juveniles were typically other juveniles. In the Netherlands, young people were four times more likely than adults to be the victims of assault. Juveniles in Germany were also more likely to be the victims of violent crime than members of other age groups. In every country, young males were far more likely than young females to be violent crime victims. However, in Bulgaria, Croatia, Czech Republic,

Hungary, Poland, Romania, Slovakia, and Slovenia, homicide victims were more likely to be middle-aged persons as opposed to adolescents or young adults.

Explanations for the growth in juvenile violent crime rates generally parallel the explanations proposed for youth violence in the United States: unemployment, alcohol, drugs, availability of guns, and domestic abuse. In some countries—France and Germany, for example—the problem of unemployment was exacerbated in the early 1990s by an influx of immigrants from countries that had formerly been under Communist rule. Immigrants who could not overcome language and culture barriers to find employment were more likely to engage in violent crimes than those who found jobs and became integrated into society. In Albania and Macedonia—both countries marked by political instability and ethnic conflict—violence rates have not declined, however. German officials have noted an increase in the use of alcohol and other drugs among youths there in the last decade, and firearms became somewhat more available after the fall of the Berlin Wall than they had been in the past. Although many of the German males arrested for violent crimes were found to come from low-income households, the most common thread in their life histories is that they came from families where violence was common: They were beaten, their siblings were beaten, or one of their parents was beaten.

Violent delinquency even occurs in one of the nations with the most repressive social control: China. David Pyrooz and Scott Decker studied a sample of 2245 youth in China and found that 11% reported carrying weapons, 8% hit someone with the idea of hurting them, 6% attacked someone with a weapon, 3% committed armed robbery, and nearly 14% had been involved in a gang fight.

Ultimately, a major cause of youth violence outside the United States appears to be that life in many countries is shifting toward a winner–loser culture, in which many disadvantaged youth appear fated to be losers. Countries vary considerably in the mix of law enforcement and prevention efforts they have undertaken to deal with the problem of increased youth violence. Education and higher incomes will help reduce the violent delinquency problem worldwide. Elgar and colleagues' study found that a one standard deviation increase in per capita income was associated with a 4% decline in bullying and 3% less fighting among males and 1% less fighting among girls.

James Lynch and William Alex Pridemore, "Crime in International Perspective," pages 5–52 in James Q. Wilson and Joan Petersilia (eds.), *Crime and Public Policy* (New York: Oxford University Press, 2011); Kayleigh Chester, Mary Callaghan, Alina Cosma, Peter Donnelly, Wendy Craig, Sophie Walsh, and Michal Molcho, "Cross-National Time Trends in Bullying Victimization in 33 Countries among Children Ages 11, 13, and 15 from 2002 to 2010," *European Journal of Public Health* 25:61–64 (2015); David Pyrooz and Scott Decker, "Delinquent Behavior, Violence, and Gang Involvement in China," *Journal of Quantitative Criminology* 29:251–272 (2013); Frank Elgar, Britt McKinnon, Sophie Walsh, John Freeman, Peter Donnelly, Margarida Gaspar de Matos, Geneviève Gariepy, et al., "Structural Determinants of Youth Bullying and Fighting in 79 Countries." *Journal of Adolescent Health* 57:643–650 (2015); Janet Stamatel, "Using Mortality Data to Refine Our Understanding of Homicide Patterns in Select Postcommunist Countries," *Homicide Studies* 12:117–135 (2008).

increased use of prison, Canada's criminal justice policy did not. Yet, both nations enjoyed similar reductions in crime. Given this fact, Ouimet believes that the causes of the crime decline in both countries lay in demographic shifts, improved work opportunities, and changes in cultural values.[20]

According to John Conklin, "Whatever caused crime rates to fall in the 1990s saved tens of thousands of lives and millions of dollars' worth of property." Because nearly all categories of crime dropped after the early 1990s, Conklin argues that no single factor led to the decline. In fact, he suggests, increases in the number of police officers on the streets or police patrol practices, less use of crack but greater use of marijuana, more rigorous and more enforced gun laws, lower divorce rates, and even the shrinkage in the relative size of the adolescent population cannot explain the decline in violent crime *and* nonviolent crime during this period. Rather, some common forces were at work, which acted synergistically to push all the rates down.

Conklin argues that the force common to the large declines in both violent and nonviolent youth crime was essentially the harsher sentencing laws passed in the late 1980s and early 1990s; the "get-tough" attitude of the courts; the greater use of waivers, in which serious violent juveniles were transferred to adult criminal court; and the burgeoning correctional population. According to Conklin, "At least 10,800 murders, 2,176,000 robberies, 738,000 burglaries, and 748,000 motor vehicle thefts were prevented over the course of the decade by the incarceration of additional offenders. . . . The increase in the incarceration rate can account for the decreases in all four crime indicators."[21]

Alfred Blumstein has proposed another explanation for the decline in youth violence. He believes this trend largely resulted from the decline in demand for crack cocaine, which reduced the need for street markets to recruit large numbers of young drug sellers. This trend, in turn, led to a reduced need for street sellers to be armed.[22] In addition, Blumstein says that police were more effective in enforcing gun laws and disrupting gun markets and that the economy improved so young people were able to get legitimate jobs.[23]

Other criminologists contend that the focus on crack markets and lethal violence among minority youths leads to inaccurate conclusions. To illustrate, Callie Rennison and Mike Planty used National Crime Victimization Survey data for the crimes of rape, sexual assault, robbery, and aggravated assault between 1994 and 2001—the era of the greatest declines in serious youth violence. Contradicting previous findings, Rennison and Planty found that for *nonfatal* crimes, reductions in crime rates among African American and urban males were relatively modest. In contrast, major reductions in the nonfatal crime rates occurred among white, nonurban males. In other words, contrary to many media accounts that focus on delinquency among inner-city, minority youths, the trend of rural and suburban white youths "cleaning up their act" actually made the most impressive contributions to declines in serious youth violence excluding homicide.[24]

Frank Zimring says that upward and downward trends in youth violence are cyclical in unpredictable ways because "there are not uniform trends in the recent history of youth arrests for violent crime. Instead, juvenile arrest rates for homicide, robbery, rape, and assault are cyclical and the cycles for the four offense categories are different. For example, Zimring notes that although the number of gun assaults increased after 1983, the number of nongun aggravated assault cases increased even faster; although the number of gun homicides increased, the number of killings with knives remained relatively stable. Finally, there might be a more mundane reason for the decline in delinquency since its peak: cell phones. Erin Orrick and Alex Piquero studied national-level crime data spanning 1984 to 2009 and found that cell phone ownership rates were significantly associated with lower property crime, but only slightly associated with violent crime. The logic is that cell phones provide a deterrent effect with the use of cameras and video, and the ability to immediately contact the police in the event of a crime.[25]

Characteristics of Violent Juvenile Offenders and Victims

Children and adolescents who display the greatest number of risk factors for becoming violent juvenile offenders are the same children who are at greatest risk for being the victims of violence. In this respect, serious violent delinquency and victimization represent two sides of the same coin that characterize the most antisocial youth. Although there are scores of theories to explain the development of serious and violent delinquency, one of the most influential approaches is more of a conceptual model that borrows elements from multiple theories and multiple developmental phases to explain violent development. This approach is known as the **dynamic cascade model of violence**.

Kenneth Dodge and his colleagues in the Conduct Problems Research Group developed the dynamic cascade model of violence to account for the small number of youth who display problem behaviors in

KEY TERMS

dynamic cascade model of violence
A conceptual model that shows how antisocial traits and processes interact in the development of youth violence and victimization.

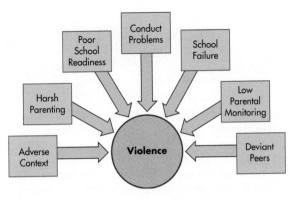

Figure 11.1 Dynamic Cascade Model of Violence

© Jones & Bartlett Learning.

multiple areas of life across developmental stages (see **Figure 11.1**).

These developmental stepping stones are as follows:

- *Adverse Context.* Youth who become perpetrators and victims of violence are disproportionately raised in impoverished, adverse contexts that feature the negative characteristics of socially disorganized neighborhoods.

- *Harsh Parenting.* Youth who become perpetrators and victims of violence are disproportionately exposed to harsh, erratic, and inconsistent parenting. Children are poorly disciplined and instead exposed to inconsistently applied corporal punishment. The parent–child relationship is also lacking in warmth and support.

- *Poor School Readiness.* Youth who become perpetrators and victims of violence are disproportionately poorly equipped for school success. They are exposed to fewer reading materials and often display deficits in social cognitive functioning. They have lower problem-solving skills and often lower intelligence, especially verbal intelligence. To compensate for their social cognitive deficits, children often must rely on aggression during interpersonal conflicts.

- *Conduct Problems*: Youth who become perpetrators and victims of violence are disproportionately likely to display serious conduct problems from very early in childhood. These deficits in self-regulation complicate virtually every aspect of development and impair social functioning.

- *School Failure*: Youth who become perpetrators and victims of violence disproportionately have a cognitive style that is dominated by aggression. It is rooted partially in their greater likelihood of child abuse victimization and overall exposure to violence. These experiences creative cognitive "scripts" whereby children encode and interpret social cues, social interactions, and social dynamics in generally confrontational, negative terms that warrant a commensurately negative,

aggressive response. This leads to impaired social and academic performance and school failure.

- *Low Parental Monitoring.* Youth who become perpetrators and victims of violence are disproportionately raised by parents who inconsistently monitor their children. Parents devote little time toward participating in the activities of their children, offer little in the way of supervision, and are generally disengaged from them. Consequently, children are often left to their own devices and have increased opportunities for delinquency and potentially violent disputes.

- *Deviant Peers.* Youth who become perpetrators and victims of violence are disproportionately rejected by conventional peers, and sooner or later become mostly acquainted with other youth who share their psychopathology. This leads to deviant peer associations, which are a potent predictor of violence.

The appeal of the dynamic cascade model of violence is that it incorporates constructs that relate both to individual-level propensities and context-based

Comparable to abuse in its negative long-term effects, parental neglect is an important predictor of youth violence and adolescent drug use.

© fasphotographic/Shutterstock.

BOX 11.2

The Face of Delinquency

The Murder of Very Young Children

Homicide accounts for more than 20% of all infant deaths in the United States. Newborns are most likely to be murdered by their mother during the first week of life, but are more likely to be killed by a male—usually the father or stepfather—thereafter. Among infants murdered on the first day of life, fully 95% were not born in a hospital. More very young children (those younger than age 6) die from homicide than from infectious diseases or cancer. Girls younger than age 6 are much more likely than girls ages 12 to 17 to be murdered, and white children younger than age 6 are nearly as likely as their teenage counterparts to be victims of homicide.

In United States, the infant homicide rate is 8.0 deaths per 100,000 children. However, the actual homicide rate for very young children is likely to be much higher than official statistics suggest, because these violent crimes are among the most difficult to document. The deaths of very young children from homicide often resemble deaths resulting from accidents and other causes. For example, a child who dies from *sudden infant death syndrome* (SIDS) is fairly indistinguishable from a child who has been smothered. A child who has been thrown or intentionally dropped is likely to have injuries quite similar to those of a child who died from an accidental fall.

Two characteristics distinguish homicides of very young children from other juvenile victims. First, such homicides are committed primarily by family members, with half of such crimes involving the use of "personal weapons,"

such as hands and feet, to batter, strangle, or suffocate victims. Second, young boys are somewhat more likely than young girls to be victims of homicide.

Among very young children, those at highest risk of homicide are infants younger than age 1 year. Homicides of children in this group include a certain number appropriately classified as *infanticide* (homicides in which recently born children are killed by relatives who do not want the child or who are suffering from a childbirth-related psychiatric disturbance). As mentioned earlier, infants are most likely to be murdered by their mothers during the first week of life; after that time, males—typically a stepfather or boyfriend of the mother—are more likely to be the culprits. Half of all infanticides occur before the fourth month of life, and the greatest risk of being murdered is on the day of birth.

A still more specific form of filicide is *neonaticide*, which is the killing of a child in the infant's first 24 hours of life. Women who commit neonaticide are often characterized by a troubled psychiatric profile. Most women who commit neonaticide engaged in denial of their pregnancy, have dissociative thoughts, and/or are experiencing psychosis. The prevalence of sexual abuse victimization among women who commit neonaticide is high.

African American infants are about three times more likely than white infants and Hispanic infants to be victims of homicide. In this regard, the risks of violent victimization in the first years of life are consistent with rates during adolescence.

Emily Douglas and Jennifer Vanderminden, "A Longitudinal, Multilevel Analysis of Homicide Against Children Aged 0–9 Years Using State-Level Characteristics: 1979–2009," *Violence and Victims* 29:757–770 (2014); David Finkelhor and Richard Ormrod, *Homicides of Children and Youth* (Washington, DC: Office of Juvenile Justice and Delinquency Prevention, 2001); Child Trends, *Infant Homicide*, retrieved March 8, 2016 from http://www.childtrends.org/?indicators=infant-homicide; Federal Bureau of Investigation, *Infant Victims: An Exploratory Study* (Washington, DC: U.S. Department of Justice, 2005), pp. 359–366; Theresa Porter and Helen Gavin, "Infanticide and Neonaticide: A Review of 40 Years of Research Literature on Incidence and Causes," *Trauma, Violence, & Abuse* 11:99–112 (2010); Matt DeLisi, *Homicide* (Dubuque, IA: Kendall/Hunt, 2015).

processes that interact during child and adolescent development. The model also shows how and why violence develops in the lives of serious offenders and victims.[26] (See **Box 11.2**, the "The Face of Delinquency" feature.)

The Role of Firearms in Youth Violence

The majority of juvenile homicide and suicide victims are killed with firearms. Although it is not the intent of this chapter to resolve the gun control debate,[27] there is no question that juveniles have significantly greater access to guns today than in past decades, guns are available through often illegal means, and the guns to which juveniles have access are much more deadly than in the past.[28] Although the number of

arrests of juveniles for weapons violations *increased* by more than 400% between 1960 and 1990, they have *decreased* significantly (dropping nearly 50%) since 1993. Today, juveniles account for slightly more than 20% of all persons arrested for weapons violations. Of those juveniles arrested and victimized in firearm-related cases, most were males, two-thirds were white, and slightly less than one-third were African American. Among all age and sex groups, males at age 18 have the highest per capita arrest rates for weapons violations, followed by males at age 17.[29]

How many youths carry guns and other weapons? Pamela Wilcox and Richard Clayton surveyed more than 6000 6th- through 12th-grade students in 21 schools in Kentucky. They found males were approximately 30% more likely than females to carry weapons to school, and that nonwhites were nearly 50% more likely than whites to bring weapons to school. In addition, students of lower socioeconomic status, students who had been threatened at school, students who reported a variety of other problem behaviors, and students whose parents owned guns were all significantly more likely to carry weapons to school.[30]

Surveys of only students may not provide the most accurate estimate of how many youths possess or carry guns on a regular basis. By the age they are most likely to carry guns, many youths have dropped out of school, and substantial numbers are confined in correctional institutions. For instance, Joseph Sheley and James Wright surveyed students as well as 835 male juvenile inmates in six different correctional facilities. Students were asked if they currently owned a gun, and inmates were asked if they had owned a gun at the time they were arrested. Approximately 22% of the students and 83% of the incarcerated youths reported ownership of a gun at the time in question.[31]

The media have often pointed to gang violence involving semiautomatic assault rifles as proof of youths' propensity to carry guns and report that some police officers believe that they are "outgunned" by many of the weapons used by violent youth. Indeed, much gang violence in recent years has been characterized by the use of more sophisticated weapons. But in reality, most youth violence is *not* gang-related violence, and the evidence suggests that the general sophistication of firearms used by juveniles has not changed significantly in recent years. When Rick Ruddell and Larry Mays examined data involving the confiscation of 1055 firearms from juveniles in St. Louis, they found that handguns were the most likely kind of firearm to be confiscated. Most often, these handguns were of the "Saturday night special" variety—cheap, easily concealed, and small caliber. Only 10 assault weapons were confiscated from juveniles over the 8-year period, compared to

Children with ready access to firearms are at an increased risk for violent offending and victimization. For child safety, guns should be kept unloaded and locked in a safe place. Does the balance of child safety and protection against criminals depend on the neighborhood in which you live?

© tlorna/Shutterstock.

134 nonpowder firearms (BB or pellet guns). According to Ruddell and Mays, "[Y]ouths are more likely to have pellet guns, .22 caliber firearms, and Saturday night specials confiscated by the police. . . . Overall, most firearms seized from juveniles by the police have a low threat level."[32]

Congress has passed a variety of laws affecting juveniles' right to use and possess weapons in recent decades. The **Brady Bill** mandated a 5-day waiting period for the purchase of handguns, whereas the *Violent Crime Control and Law Enforcement Act of 1994* made it a federal crime for anyone to sell or transfer a handgun, or ammunition for a handgun, to a person younger than age 18.[33] The act also made it a crime for juveniles to possess a handgun or ammunition for a handgun, although there are certain exceptions: A youth may possess a handgun when it is used for farming, ranching, target shooting, or safety instruction, provided the youth has his or her parent's written permission to have the handgun. However, most states already prohibit the sale of handguns to persons younger than age 21 and the sale of rifles and shotguns to persons younger than age 18.

If it is clearly illegal for youths to obtain guns through legitimate channels, how do they get these weapons? One-third of children in the United States are believed to live in homes where firearms are kept.[34] If there is no firearm available in the home, a youth is likely to have little difficulty in obtaining one from friends, on the street, through theft, or through an illegal purchase from a gun dealer.

In their research, Sheley and Wright asked students and juvenile inmates how they had obtained the guns they possessed. More than half the students said they borrowed their guns from a family member or friend, whereas most of the juvenile inmates said they had gotten their guns from friends and street sources. Both students and inmates indicated that they could obtain guns with little trouble: There was little need to steal guns or to go through normal retail outlets where a friend or family member could legally purchase a gun.[35] This finding is fairly consistent with the results of a survey of firearm use by adult offenders. In this study, approximately 40% of state prison inmates age 24 or younger obtained the gun used in their current offense from a family member or friend; only 7% obtained the gun from a retail store.[36]

Many young people live in social worlds characterized by crime and violence. Of the juvenile inmates who participated in Sheley and Wright's study, 40% had siblings who had been incarcerated, 62% had male family members who routinely carried guns,

KEY TERMS

Brady Bill
Federal legislation that mandated a 5-day waiting period for the purchase of handguns.

and 84% had been threatened with a gun or shot at during their lives. Half had been stabbed with a knife and more than 80% had been beaten up by someone. Students were only slightly less exposed to violent environments. Nearly half the students reported that male members of their households regularly carried guns, 45% reported having been threatened with a gun or shot at, and one-third of the students had been beaten up either at school or on the way to or from school.[37]

Philip Cook and Jens Ludwig believe that higher gun prevalence at the local level—that is, greater ownership of guns by adults—is associated with a greater likelihood of youths carrying both guns and other types of weapons. However, they argue that although gun prevalence does not affect the decision of a youth whether to carry a weapon, it does affect the decision of which kind of weapon the youth will carry. In other words, "the availability of guns clearly increases the likelihood that those teens that do carry weapons choose guns."[38]

Of course, guns are only one part of the equation of serious youth violence. Many youths who carry and use these weapons do so because they are also actively involved in the use and sale of drugs (which is the focus of the rest of this chapter). In other words, there is diversity in weapons carrying among youth (see "The Face of Delinquency" feature in **Box 11.3**).

BOX 11.3

The Face of Delinquency

Armed Juveniles: Subtypes of Youth Who Carry Handguns in the United States

Adolescents can possess weapons for a variety of reasons, and many of them are not related to problem behaviors. Some youth hunt, farm, or are raised in homes where weapons and guns are a hobby. The situation is less innocent when handguns are the consideration, given the ease with which they can be hidden on one's body and their instrumental link to violent delinquency.

Are there types of youth who carry handguns? Michael Vaughn and his colleagues recently attempted to answer this question using data from 7872 youth ages 12 to 17 years selected from the National Survey on Drug Use and Health. They found four general categories of youth who carried handguns. About 48% were low-risk youth and had little involvement in delinquency and very low involvement in substance use. About 20% were alcohol and marijuana users who had moderate involvement in various delinquency including serious fights, group fights, violent attacks, drug selling, and theft. Slightly more than 19% were fighters who had little drug usage but frequently engaged in assaults. Finally, a severe-risk group of about 13% of the sample was severe in all forms of substance use, violence, and delinquency. The latter group engaged in the highest levels of drug use, violent conduct, and diverse delinquent acts.

Several features differentiated the groups. Compared to low-risk youth, the other three classes had higher risk propensity, enjoyed participating in dangerous activities, and had poorer relationships with their parents. These youth had lower school engagement and disliked attending school. There were also large differences in chronic carrying of handguns. Severe-risk youth were greater than two times more likely to carry a handgun on 10 or more occasions. More than 48% of the severe-risk youth

were arrested in the past year, compared to just 3% of the low-risk group.

Youth who carry handguns, and do so frequently, are at significant risk for committing homicide. A study of serious delinquent youth in the Pathways to Desistance study found that frequent gun carrying was one of the few risk factors associated with homicide offending. Norair Khachatryan and colleagues conducted a 30-year follow-up of youth who perpetrated aggravated homicides during adolescence and found that several had continued a life of serious violence. For example, Donnell was 17 when arrested for murder, rape, and armed robbery. His juvenile career began at age 14 and included four prior arrests. He received a 22-year prison sentence. During his confinement he committed multiple violent acts including sexual battery, aggravated assault, and assault and battery. He served 7.5 years and was returned to the community for one year and three months. He was arrested three times, including twice for violent crimes (robbery), and is back in prison. Andrew was 17 when arrested for murder, rape, armed robbery, and auto theft. He was first arrested at age 7 and had a staggering 14 juvenile arrests, including several violent crimes, such as robbery, battery, and aggravated assault. He was sentenced to 22 years in prison. During confinement, he committed arson, and served 7.5 years. Although he was in the community for a mere 4 months, Andrews was arrested five times for multiple violent, property, drug, and weapons offenses. He has since been returned to prison.

In short, some youth who carry handguns are relatively low-risk in terms of delinquency; indeed the majority are in this camp. However, for others, it is a marker for serious antisocial conduct and violence.

Michael Vaughn, Christopher Salas-Wright, Brian Boutwell, Matt DeLisi, and Mary Curtis, "Handgun Carrying among Youth in the United States: An Analysis of Subtypes from a National Sample," *Youth Violence and Juvenile Justice*, in press (2016); Norair Khachatryan, Kathleen Heide, Erich Hummel, and Heng Choon (Oliver) Chan, "Juvenile Sexual Homicide Offenders Thirty-Year Follow-Up Investigation," *International Journal of Offender Therapy and Comparative Criminology* 60:247–264 (2016); Matt DeLisi, Alex Piquero, and Stephanie Cardwell, "The Unpredictability of Murder: Juvenile Homicide in the Pathways to Desistance Study," *Youth Violence and Juvenile Justice* 14:26–42 (2016).

Finally, guns are attractive to the most serious types of delinquents, such as those who commit homicide and other violent crimes. Frank DiCataldo and Meghan Everett compared adolescents who were adjudicated delinquent or awaiting trial for murder to adolescents who committed violent, nonhomicidal offenses to determine whether the two groups differed significantly on family history, early development, delinquency history, mental health, and weapons possession variables. Violent youths who did not commit homicide often began their delinquent careers earlier, had significantly greater numbers of total offenses, and had more violent offenses. They also had less stable childhood histories, more frequent placements out of the home, and more frequent sibling delinquency. They reported being more likely to use knives; had greater problems with anger control, hostility, and antisocial thinking patterns; and had more negative early memories of their parents. Compared to these nonhomicidal violent youths, juvenile homicide offenders had greater availability of guns in their homes and were more likely to report having taken guns from their homes in the past.[39]

Adolescent Drug Use

Before the 1960s, adolescent drug use was relatively rare. That situation changed when the "drug culture" burst upon the scene in the early sixties. Marijuana, LSD, "uppers," and "downers"—all of which were initially used by college students and those in the hippie counterculture—eventually spread to the high school and junior high levels. Whether it was an attraction to the lifestyle of the hippies, a simple interest in "getting high," or a growing alienation from the norms and values of conventional society, more youths began to turn on with an ever-increasing variety of drugs. The drug of choice among youths changes over time, and there is a continuous flow of new drugs and rediscovery of older drugs by each generation.

It is difficult to obtain an accurate estimate of the incidence and prevalence of delinquency. Consequently, different measures (arrest data, self-report surveys, and victim surveys) are used to gauge the most reliable estimates possible. Drug use is equally difficult to measure. Because illicit drug use is considered a "victimless crime," the NCVS does not inquire into drug violations. One estimate of adolescent drug use comes from *Uniform Crime Reports* (*UCR*) data on people arrested for drug violations. Other estimates are produced from three key self-report surveys on drug use: the University of Michigan's *Monitoring the Future* survey of high school students, the U.S. Department of Health and Human Services' *National Survey on Drug Use and Health*, and the *National Youth Risk Behavior Survey* conducted by the Centers for Disease Control and Prevention (CDC).[40]

According to these sources, the past six decades have witnessed major shifts in juvenile drug use. Among both boys and girls, illicit drug use increased at an alarming rate during the 1960s and 1970s during an era where crime, delinquency, and violence reached previously unseen levels. The escalation of drug use and delinquency continued during the 1980s and then sharply increased again during the crack cocaine era of the late 1980s and early 1990s. This period coincided with record highs in juvenile homicides and gang homicides. From the peak of juvenile violence in 1993–1994, juvenile arrests for drug abuse violations have declined sharply. After the juvenile arrest rate for drug abuse violations increased by approximately 150% during the first half of the 1990s, it declined sharply thereafter. In the first decade of the 21st century, juvenile drug abuse violations declined nearly 40%. Other forms of substance use related to delinquency have also dramatically declined over the past decade. From 2005 to 2014, juvenile drunk driving arrests were down 66%, liquor law violations were down 59%, and drunkenness was down 59%. Trend data for adolescent drug use by drug type are examined later in this chapter.

Although *UCR* data are frequently used to construct these kinds of estimates of drug use, they are far from perfect. First, with respect to drug arrests, they do not distinguish between arrests for specific kinds of drugs—for example, marijuana versus crack. Second, *UCR* data include only those juveniles arrested for drug violations. As with most other victimless crimes, however, most people who use drugs do so out of sight of police and with others who are not likely to report their drug use to authorities. As a consequence, *UCR* data do not reflect *hidden* or secret drug use. Thus arrest data grossly underestimate the amount of drug use by adolescents today.

Each year, the Institute for Social Research at the University of Michigan examines patterns of drug use and attitudes about illicit drugs in its survey of 8th-, 10th-, and 12th-grade students; this study includes nearly 50,000 students in more than 400 secondary schools. The annual survey conducted by the U.S. Department of Health and Human Services and funded by the National Institute on Drug Abuse measures the prevalence of illicit drug use throughout the U.S. civilian, noninstitutionalized population age 12 and older. Both of these national self-report surveys provide three different measures of drug use—**lifetime prevalence** (use of a drug at least once during the

KEY TERMS

lifetime prevalence
The use of a drug at least once during the respondent's lifetime.

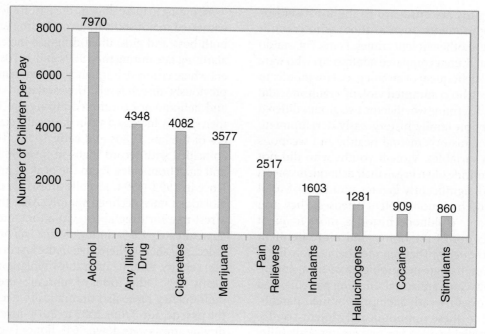

Figure 11.2 Approximate Daily Onset of Adolescent Substance Use on an Average Day

Data from *The OAS Report, A Day in the Life of American Adolescents* (Rockville, MD: Center for Behavioral Health Statistics and Quality, Substance Abuse and Mental Health Services Administration, 2013).

respondent's lifetime); **annual prevalence** (use of a drug at least once during the prior year); and **30-day prevalence** (use of a drug at least once during the previous month)—as well as a measure of frequency of use. The CDC's self-report survey monitors six categories of health-risk behaviors, including alcohol and other drug use. Each year the CDC surveys students in grades 9 through 12 throughout the United States, then combines these data with the results from an additional 32 state surveys and 18 local surveys. Unlike the *UCR*, all of these self-report surveys provide information on the use of specific drugs.

As various studies have illustrated, substantial numbers of juveniles are initiated into drug use each year. As shown in **Figure 11.2**, on an average day 7639 adolescents between ages 12 and 17 use alcohol for the first time. Some 4594 youths use any illicit drug, more than 3701 smoke their first cigarette, and about 4000 first experiment with marijuana. Still other youths first experiment with more dangerous substances, such as inhalants, hallucinogens, cocaine, stimulants, methamphetamine, and heroin.[41] Daily prevalence estimates (see **Figure 11.3**) show that more than 861,684 adolescents smoke cigarettes, more than 457,672 drink alcohol, and nearly 646,702 smoke

marijuana each day. More than 38,540 youths use inhalants, 21,775 use hallucinogens, nearly 6,747 ingest cocaine, and about 5,602 youths use heroin each day.

Adolescent males are significantly more likely than females to be arrested for drug offenses, with males accounting for more than 80% of all juvenile drug arrests. Although boys are arrested for drug offenses more than four times as often as girls, the difference in arrest rates, according to Joan McCord and her colleagues, may reflect the fact that boys use drugs more frequently than girls in public places, thereby increasing their likelihood of being arrested.[42]

None of the eventual outcomes of hardcore drug use are positive. Given this, why are drugs relatively prevalent in the United States? Why do many Americans express tolerance toward illegal drugs?

© ejwhite/Shutterstock.

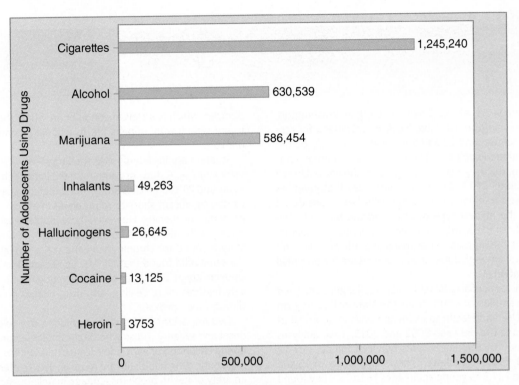

Figure 11.3 Approximate Daily Prevalence of Adolescent Substance Use

Data from *The OAS Report, A Day in the Life of American Adolescents* (Rockville, MD: Center for Behavioral Health Statistics and Quality, Substance Abuse and Mental Health Services Administration, 2013).

Alcohol-related arrests follow a significantly different pattern, and one not consistent with self-report surveys or other studies of adolescent drinking patterns. Whites account for more than 90% of all juvenile arrests for liquor law violations and public drunkenness. These arrest figures are interesting in that white and African American high school seniors report much more similar frequencies of alcohol use. Six percent of white seniors reported heavy monthly alcohol consumption, compared to 5% of African American seniors. White seniors are more likely to be "binge" drinkers, however. Approximately 36% of white seniors reported consuming five or more drinks in a row on one or more occasions during the 2-week period before one survey, compared to 12% of African American seniors.[43]

Trends in Drug Use

During the last third of the 20th century, U.S. adolescents were using illicit drugs at rates never before seen in this country. By 1975, the majority of youths (55%) had used an illicit drug by the time they left high school. By 1981, this figure had increased to 66%. It then gradually declined to 41% in 1992—which was the lowest point ever—but had again risen to 55% in 1999 and 51% in 2003. It declined to just 47% for a 3-year period from 2007 through 2009, before rising again to 50% in 2011. It has fluctuated from 48 to 50% between 2011 and 2015. In 2015, 49% of youth had used an illicit drug by the time they left high school. Drug use trends vary somewhat depending on the specific illicit drug, and recent increases are mostly connected to increases in marijuana usage. These drug-specific details are explored next.[44]

Marijuana Use

The percentage of high school seniors reporting that they had ever tried marijuana rose during the last half of the 1970s and reached a peak in 1980, when 60% of these youths admitted having tried the drug at least once in their lifetime. Since 1980, marijuana use by seniors has steadily and significantly declined, with the ever-use rate dropping to slightly more than 40% in 1990. As with adolescent drug use generally, marijuana use rose during the 1990s. By 2007, 42% of U.S. high school seniors reported having used marijuana at some point in their lifetime. Today, 45% of teens have used marijuana. Unlike other substances, the legal status of marijuana has changed since 2011, and that has produced interesting changes in viewpoints about the drug (see **Box 11.4**, the "A Window on Delinquency" feature).

Synthetic Marijuana

A new addition to the Monitoring the Future Survey is synthetic marijuana, which has traditionally been legally sold but recently has been banned because of deaths associated with its usage. More than 11% of

BOX 11.4

A Window on Delinquency

Legal Marijuana, Marijuana Smoking, and Its Effects

In recent years, Alaska, Colorado, Oregon, Washington, and Washington, DC have legalized marijuana for recreational use, and 23 additional states currently permit medical marijuana use. This is a dramatic change, considering the drug was criminalized for the entire United States until 2012. Of all the substances that juveniles can use, marijuana has traditionally been considered to be the mildest type of drug and the one with the lowest risk for delinquency and maladaptive behaviors. But has the legalization of marijuana affected use and approval among adolescents, and what are the potential implications?

Christopher Salas-Wright and his colleagues analyzed large samples of youth from the National Survey on Drug Use and Health to examine trends in approval of marijuana use between 2002 and 2013. Their analyses included 105,903 adolescents between the ages of 12 and 14, 110,949 adolescents between the ages of 15 and 17, and 221,976 young adults ages 18 to 25. They found that among 12 to 14 year olds, the proportion reporting strong disapproval of marijuana use initiation significantly increased from 74% to nearly 79%. In addition, marijuana use declined for younger and middle adolescents while marijuana use slightly increased among young adults. Adults also were less likely to strongly disapprove of marijuana use with the proportion responding with strong disapproval declining from 41% to 23%.

Trend analyses of the National Epidemiologic Survey on Alcohol and Related Conditions revealed that the prevalence of marijuana use disorder more than doubled from 2001 to 2013 among adults in the United States, increasing from 4.1% to 9.5%. It was also reported that about 30% of marijuana users develop marijuana use

disorder, which is a clinical condition in which the drug usage significantly impairs life functioning in multiple domains.

Studies vary in determining the long-term effects of marijuana use. A study of youth from the Pittsburgh Youth Study and Pittsburgh Girls Study found that marijuana use caused significant short-term problems in attention and academic functioning. However, these problems remitted once youths stopped smoking marijuana. A different story is found for chronic marijuana users. Analyses of the same data found that chronic adolescent marijuana smokers are at significant risk for psychopathic personality features, drug dealing, and drug-related problems through their mid-30s.

Two important issues with marijuana use relate to onset and severity. Those who begin smoking marijuana during childhood or early adolescence and/or those who smoke the drug habitually are more likely to suffer from an array of health problems, engage in delinquency and other problem behaviors, and even produce long-term effects on their brains. Adolescent drug use including marijuana has been shown to be an early indicator of chronic delinquency, and it negatively affects brain regions that are responsible for executive functioning and thus compromises academic potential. Indeed, Terrie Moffitt and her colleagues showed that persistent marijuana use resulted in neuropsychological decline from childhood to midlife even after controlling for important potential confounding factors.

In sum, marijuana is likely not as harmless as it is portrayed in many media outlets. However, whether it has criminological effects often depends on when it was first used and for how long.

Christopher Salas-Wright, Michael Vaughn, Jelena Todic, David Córdova, and Brian Perron, "Trends in the Disapproval and Use of Marijuana among Adolescents and Young Adults in the United States: 2002–2013," *The American Journal of Drug and Alcohol Abuse* 41:392–404 (2015); Deborah Hasin, Tulshi Saha, Bradley Kerridge, Risë Goldstein, S. Patricia Chou, Haitao Zhang, Jeesun Jung, et al., "Prevalence of Marijuana Use Disorders in the United States Between 2001–2002 and 2012–2013," *JAMA Psychiatry* 72:1235–1242 (2015); Dustin Pardini, Helene White, Shuangyan Xiong, Jordan Bechtold, Tammy Chung, Rolf Loeber, and Alison Hipwell, "Unfazed or Dazed and Confused: Does Early Adolescent Marijuana Use Cause Sustained Impairments in Attention and Academic Functioning?" *Journal of Abnormal Child Psychology* 43:1203–1217 (2015); Dustin Pardini, Jordan Bechtold, Rolf Loeber, and Helene White, "Developmental Trajectories of Marijuana Use among Men Examining Linkages with Criminal Behavior and Psychopathic Features into the Mid-30s," *Journal of Research in Crime and Delinquency* 52:797–828 (2015); Matt DeLisi, Alexia Angton, Monic Behnken, and Abdi Kusow, "Do Adolescent Drug Users Fare the Worst? Onset Type, Juvenile Delinquency, and Criminal Careers," *International Journal of Offender Therapy and Comparative Criminology* 59:180–195 (2015); Giovanni Battistella, Eleonora Fornari, Jean-Marie Annoni, Haithem Chtioui, Kim Dao, Marie Fabritius, Bernard Favrat, Jean-Frédéric Mall, Philippe Maeder, and Christian Giroud, "Long-Term Effects of Cannabis on Brain Structure," *Neuropsychopharmacology* 39:2041–2048 (2014); Madeline Meier, Avshalom Caspi, Antony Ambler, HonaLee Harrington, Renate Houts, Richard Keefe, Kay McDonald, Aimee Ward, Richie Poulton, and Terrie Moffitt, "Persistent Cannabis Users Show Neuropsychological Decline from Childhood to Midlife." *Proceedings of the National Academy of Sciences* 109:E2657–E2664 (2012).

high school seniors reported using synthetic marijuana (popularly called K2 or spice) in the previous year. In 2015, 6% of high school seniors reported using synthetic marijuana.

Cocaine Use

The percentage of high school seniors who reported having ever tried cocaine nearly doubled between

1975 and 1985, when 17% of seniors reported having tried cocaine. Cocaine use declined over the next two decades, with the drug use rate reaching a low of only 8% in 2003. Today, only 8% of high school seniors report ever using cocaine. Perhaps more importantly, the percentage of seniors reporting use of cocaine during the prior 12-month period dropped noticeably from 13% in 1985 to only 3% in 1992, but then rose again to 5% in 2007. In 2015, 4% of high school seniors had ever tried cocaine. The rate of use of crack cocaine by seniors during the prior year—a figure that was never very high—dropped from nearly 4% in 1987 to 2% in 2007. In 2015, less than 2% of high school seniors had ever tried crack cocaine.

Today cocaine use is very low for all age groups and has been in decline for years. The prevalence of powder cocaine use among 8th graders is just 1.6%, among 10th graders is 2.7%, and among high school seniors is 4%. The prevalence of crack cocaine is 1% among 8th and 10th graders and 1.7% among high school seniors.

Other Drug Use

The use of other drugs by high school seniors has largely followed the broad trends in adolescent drug use. In particular, drug use rates generally declined between the mid-1970s and the late 1980s. The use of drugs such as LSD and amphetamines, both of which were popular in the late 1960s and early 1970s, fluctuated during the period between 1980 and 1995, but has fallen sharply in recent years. Ecstasy (MDMA) use was first measured among high school students in 1996, when fewer than 5% of respondents reported having used the drug during the past year. After increasing to 9% in 2000, the rate of ecstasy use among seniors declined to only 4% in 2007. Today, the prevalence of ecstasy use is 2.3%, 3.8%, and 5.9% for 8th-, 10th-, and 12th-grade students, respectively. Heroin use by seniors has never been widespread, but it steadily increased during the 1990s, with the rate of ever-use rising from less than 1% in 1991 to nearly 3% in 2000 and declining again to 1% in 2007. Today, the prevalence of heroin use is less than 1% for 8th, 10th, and 12th graders.[45]

Sometimes adolescents discover that over-the-counter, nonprescription medicines can produce a desired "high." One of the latest drug fads involves cough and cold medicines containing dextromethorphan (DXM). More than 120 such medicines, including Robitussin, can be purchased at grocery, drug, and discount stores throughout the United States. When taken in large doses, they can produce loss of motor control and hallucinations similar to the effects of PCP. The misuse of these substances was first measured in the 2006 Monitoring the Future Survey. Today, the prevalence is 1.6, 3.3, and 4.6% for 8th, 10th, and 12th graders, respectively. There is also evidence of abuse of energy drinks, which are used by 30 to 40% of youths across grades. Time will tell if these drinks become so problematic that they will be legally regulated.[46]

Alcohol and Cigarette Use

Although use of illicit drugs has broadly declined, alcohol use by high school seniors remained fairly steady between 1975 and 1990, but then declined over the next 25 years. In 2015, 64% of high school seniors had ever used alcohol, which is down considerably from the 80% who used alcohol in 2000. Lifetime prevalence of cigarette smoking by seniors is 31%. The respective prevalence for 10th graders is 20% and 8th graders is 13%. At all grade levels, smoking is down more than 50% from the levels in 2000.

A word of caution is warranted when considering findings from these surveys, however. The school survey (including 8th, 10th, and 12th graders) does not provide information on youths who are absent from school (estimated to be about 18% of the enrolled students) or youths who have dropped out of high school (estimated to be about 15% for this survey). These two groups of students are likely to be among the most vulnerable to serious drug use. The National Household Survey of 12- to 17-year-olds also underestimates serious drug use by adolescents. It does not include institutionalized youths (those incarcerated in juvenile facilities), transients (including the growing number of homeless children), and people unable to be identified through normal census identification procedures.

It is also important to recognize that adolescent drug use is not confined to the United States. **Box 11.5**, the "Delinquency Around the Globe" feature, discusses drug use by juveniles in a variety of countries.

Causes of Adolescent Drug Use

Theories of juvenile delinquency, ranging from early classical and neoclassical theories that emphasize free will and choice to deterministic theories that attribute crime to biological, psychological, and sociological factors, have been discussed earlier. Although all of these perspectives provide good, strong explanations for why youths use illicit drugs or legal drugs inappropriately, in this section our focus is on five approaches based on the sociological perspective as they apply to the causes of adolescent drug use.

Double Failure by the Individual

In formulating strain theory, Robert Merton argued that in a competitive and materialistic society in which success through legitimate avenues is attainable by relatively few individuals, those individuals who are unable to achieve success may choose deviant modes of adaptation to deal with their failure.[47] An individual who chooses *retreatism* as an adaptation rejects both the cultural goal of success and the approved means to achieve success. Merton suggests that moral scruples might also prevent the individual from choosing criminal means to achieve success. Richard Cloward and Lloyd Ohlin believe otherwise: They suggest that the avoidance of illegitimate means is due not to the constraints applied by the person's

BOX 11.5

Delinquency Around the Globe

Adolescent Drug Use Around the World

The use of illicit drugs by adolescents is not unique to the United States. Indeed, youths around the world experiment with and use a variety of drugs in ways not too dissimilar to their American counterparts. The International Self-Reported Delinquency Project (ISRD) has examined drug use and delinquency among respondents in Belgium, England and Wales, Finland, Germany, Greece, the Netherlands, Italy, Northern Ireland, Portugal, Spain, Switzerland, and the United States. According to the researchers behind this study, like American youths, adolescents from around the globe demonstrate a multifaceted involvement in drug use and delinquency. For example, a survey of 21,000 Spanish adolescents found that the use of cocaine has increased dramatically in recent years. Only 5% of 18-year-olds had used cocaine at least once in 1994, compared to 9% in 1998. A threefold increase in cocaine use by 16-year-olds occurred during the same period: 2% reported having used cocaine at least once in 1994 compared to 5% in 1998.

When more than 1700 students in 10th grade in Bogota, Colombia, were surveyed in 1997, nearly 90% reported having used alcohol at least once during their lifetime, and 54% reported they started drinking before age 12. Some 77% of the youths reported having used tobacco at least once during their lifetime, with 60% reporting tobacco use during the 30 days before the survey. Eleven percent of the youths reported having used marijuana at least once during their lifetime.

After administering a survey to nearly 1600 Australian adolescents ages 14 to 19, researchers reported that 45% of the respondents had used marijuana at least once in their lifetime, and 78% of that group had used marijuana during the year before the survey. The use of marijuana significantly increased with age. Although many Australian youths who had tried marijuana eventually stopped using the drug, approximately 21% of those who continued

to smoke marijuana reported using it on a weekly basis and 7% smoked it daily.

In Canada (as in all nations), youths with more risk factors are more likely not only to use drugs, but also to use more dangerous drugs. For instance, a study of street youths in Vancouver found that 71% used crystal methamphetamine, a highly addictive and potentially lethal stimulant.

Although the rates of both licit and illicit drug use by youths in Taiwan are substantially lower than the rates found among American youths, the Taiwanese government is concerned about the apparent increase in drug use and its related social and health problems. A survey of approximately 2200 13- to 18-year-olds was conducted in a rural county in Taiwan. Seven percent of the youths reported tobacco use, 2% reported chewing betel gum, nearly 2% currently drank alcohol, and 1% reported illicit drug use. Males ages 13 to 15 were much more likely than females to use tobacco (9% versus 3%), but only slightly more likely to use alcohol (4% versus 2%) or illicit drugs (0.7% versus 0.4%). Research on Saudi Arabian youth indicates similarly low levels of adolescent substance use. A study of 500 adolescents in Jeddah, Saudi Arabia revealed that nearly 13% of youth had ever smoked, 2.6% had ever used alcohol, and 3% had ever used illegal drugs. These prevalence estimates are much lower than those of their American peers.

Smoking is considered to be the greatest substance abuse problem among adolescents in China. Almost all of the 320 million smokers in China began smoking as teenagers, with the average age of first use being before age 15. Most youths initially experimented with smoking out of curiosity. Chinese youths also achieve a degree of status by smoking foreign-brand cigarettes, especially Marlboros. The Chinese government is attempting to counter the "cool" image of the teenage smoker by initiating advertising campaigns designed to portray adolescent smokers as social misfits.

Kevin Beaver, Mohammed Said Al-Ghamdi, Ahmed Nezar Kobeisy, Fathiyah Alqurashi, Joseph Schwartz, Eric Connolly, and Jamie Gajos, "The Effects of Low Self-Control and Delinquent Peers on Alcohol, Tobacco, and Drug Use in a Sample of Saudi Arabian Youth," *International Journal of Offender Therapy and Comparative Criminology*, in press (2016); Xavier Bosch, "Survey Shows Cocaine Use by Spanish Adolescents on the Rise," *Lancet* 355:2230 (2000); Kow-Tong Chen, Chien-Jen Chen, Anne Fagot-Campagna, and K. M. V. Narayan, "Tobacco, Betel Quid, Alcohol, and Illicit Drug Use among 13- to 35-Year-Olds in I-Lan, Rural Taiwan: Prevalence and Risk Factors," *American Journal of Public Health* 91:1130–1134 (2001); Tsung Cheng, "Teenage Smoking in China," *Journal of Adolescence* 22:607–620 (1999); Miguel Prez and Helda Pinon-Prez, "Alcohol, Tobacco, and Other Psychoactive Drug Use among High School Students in Bogota, Colombia," *Journal of School Health* 70:377–380 (2000); Martin Killias and Denis Ribeaud, "Drug Use and Crime among Juveniles: An International Perspective," *Studies on Crime and Crime Prevention* 8:189–209 (1999); Alex Mason, Stacy-Ann January, Mary Chmelka, Gilbert Parra, Jukka Savolainen, Jouko Miettunen, Marjo-Riitta Järvelin, Anja Taanila, and Irma Moilanen, "Cumulative Contextual Risk at Birth in Relation to Adolescent Substance Use, Conduct Problems, and Risky Sex: General and Specific Predictive Associations in a Finnish Birth Cohort." *Addictive Behaviors* 58:161–166 (2016); Marie Claire Van Hout and Sean Conner, "A Qualitative Study of Irish Teachers' Perspective of Student Substance Use," *Journal of Alcohol and Drug Education* 52:80–91 (2008).

scruples but rather reflects the lack of opportunity to use such means in the pursuit of success.[48] Regardless of who is right, drug use is seen as deriving from failure to "make it" in conventional society as well as failure to achieve success in the criminal world. The

person has failed twice and, consequently, retreats into a world of drugs.

More than 55 years after Cloward and Ohlin developed their theory, Stephen Baron and Timothy Hartnagel interviewed 200 homeless adolescents living in a large western Canadian city. They found that perceived lack of opportunities for viable employment contributed to delinquency and drug use among these youths. Moreover, the effects of consorting with other young people who were similarly disaffected by their job prospects contributed to worsening drug involvement.[49] Similarly, Robert Agnew's *general strain theory* extends the "double failure" idea by suggesting that various sources of strain contribute to depression and an escapist withdrawal from society into drug use. For instance, a study by Nicole Leeper Piquero and Miriam Sealock found that social strain contributed to feelings of depression, especially among young females. Depression, in turn, is an important factor that can plunge adolescents into serious drug abuse.[50]

Not all research has confirmed this theory, however. Specifically, a number of ethnographic studies have not supported the "double failure" theory of drug use. Instead, this research suggests that many persons—at least among those who use expensive drugs and heroin—simply choose to live outside the boundaries of mainstream society and freely dabble in various forms of crime. For instance, Bill Sanders and his colleagues found that nomadic adolescents travel the country for a variety of leisurely reasons and use serious and multiple types of drugs along the way. In fact, more than 1.5 million "traveling" youth in the United States do not necessarily fit the double failure idea as it was conceptualized.[51] According to Charles Faupel and his colleagues, the theoretical notion that drug users are "double failures" is a seductive one because people who are not part of the drug culture cannot understand why a person would use drugs in the first place: "Why else would anyone use drugs or become addicted? Surely, they would prefer another lifestyle! The evidence suggests, however, that, indeed, many addicts *do* freely choose a drug-using lifestyle, indeed preferring it to nine-to-five routines." Finally, many adolescent drug users are not double failures per se, but instead are youth with considerable psychological and emotional problems, and diverse involvement in other forms of delinquency. In this regard, they are not rejected by segments of society, but instead display many highly correlated problem behaviors relating to drug use, alcohol use, and delinquency.[52]

Learning to Use Drugs

Edwin Sutherland was among the first criminologists to suggest that delinquent behavior is learned. The idea that a youth learns delinquent behavior through an interactive process has been extended by integrating Sutherland's principles of differential association with theories of operant conditioning drawn from the field of psychology. *Social learning theory* argues that a person's behavior is the result of group-based reinforced learning situations. According to Erich Goode, adolescents learn to define behaviors as good or bad through their intimate interactions with other youths in certain groups. Different groups express different norms regarding illicit drugs and differentially reward or punish the use or distribution of drugs by members of the group.[53]

Often, social groups that condone substance use engage in other forms of risky behavior. For example, Angela Gover explored the social learning approach to adolescent drug use using data from 5545 high school students. She found that teens tended to associate with other peers who use drugs and alcohol, were sexually promiscuous, and committed crimes, such as drunk driving. Moreover, youths in these social groups were significantly likely to be victimized in romantic relationships.[54] In short, the group processes that encouraged drug use similarly influenced delinquency and victimization.

Adolescent drug use, then, is positively reinforced by exposure to drug-using role models, approval of drug use by peers, and the perceived positive or pleasurable effects of the drug itself. To the extent that an individual's drug use is also not negatively reinforced either by bad effects of the drug or by statements or actions by parents, peers, or authorities, the drug use will persist. Strong empirical support exists for the idea that social learning processes form a causal basis for adolescent substance use.[55] For instance, when Jacquelyn Monroe examined the effects of social learning and teen smoking using data from the National Center for Health Statistics, she found that associating with delinquent peers, identifying with delinquent peers, holding delinquent definitions, and imitation significantly predicted tobacco use.[56]

Might this learning process involve something as simple as watching people use drugs in movies? Although Sutherland argued that learning needed to occur in face-to-face, intimate interactions, he did not anticipate the impact of the media culture in the late 20th and early 21st centuries. One study that examined the effect of viewing smoking in movies on adolescent smoking initiation was conducted by Madeline Dalton and her colleagues using a surveyed sample of 3547 children between the ages 10 and 14 who had never tried cigarettes. Follow-up of the youths occurred 13 to 26 months later, in the form of a survey inquiring about their current use of cigarettes and which of 50 popular movies they had watched during the study period. Findings from the study strongly suggest that youth who watched the most movies judged to have the greatest portrayal of smoking were approximately "three times more likely to initiate smoking than those with the least amount of exposure."[57] Moreover, children with parents who *did not* smoke were significantly *more* susceptible to the impact of watching smoking in movies.

Subcultural Socialization into Drug Use

Another explanation for adolescent drug use is that youths begin to use drugs and continue to do so because of their involvement in social groups in which drug use is reinforced. A variety of drug subcultures exist. For many adolescents, membership in one drug subculture may bring involvement in other drug subcultures—for instance, alcohol-using, marijuana-using, cocaine-using, heroin-using, or multiple-drug-using subcultures. As an adolescent's involvement in a drug-using subculture deepens, he or she becomes increasingly socialized into the values and norms of the group, and drug-using behavior is likely to ensue.

Howard Becker described the process of becoming a marijuana user through interaction with a marijuana-using subculture. According to Becker, for an individual to become a marijuana user, three events must occur. First, one must *learn the proper technique* for smoking marijuana to produce the desired effects. Second, one must *learn to perceive the effects and connect them* with marijuana. Third, one must *define the effects of marijuana smoking as pleasurable*. The smoker "has learned, in short, to answer 'Yes' to the question: 'Is it fun?'"[58]

Of course, learning to smoke marijuana by itself is not enough to make someone become a regular user. A juvenile must also establish a reliable means of supply, keep his or her drug use secret from others who may disapprove, and neutralize moral objections to marijuana use held by conventional society. Becker suggests that fulfilling these conditions requires involvement in a group whose members regularly use marijuana. Erich Goode believes that the socialization process within a drug subculture involves much convincing of new users that they have nothing to fear from the drug. He also found that heavy users of marijuana are more involved with friends who also used marijuana, as well as other drugs, and who were generally more involved in the drug subculture.[59] Brian Kelly studied the marijuana subculture among relatively affluent youths in the New York City vicinity. He found that a rather intricate culture, complete with a specific sense of style, clothing, music, and language, was devoted to marijuana use among these teens. Moreover, important normative differences existed between using marijuana from a "bong" versus from a "blunt."[60]

Denise Kandel contends that the process of socialization into drug use is selective.[61] Among early adolescents, drug and alcohol use tends to be more situational or even accidental. The specific activities of the immediate peer group greatly influence the behavior of the individual: If the youth has friends who drink, he or she will be more likely to drink; if the youth has close peers who are drug users, he or she will be more inclined to try drugs; and if the youth hangs out with friends who disapprove of alcohol and drug use, he or she will not be inclined to use either. In later adolescence, youths who have begun to use drugs or alcohol will gradually break away from nondrug-using peers and move toward peers who do use them. Andy Hochstetler has chronicled the drug-fueled lives of young adult offenders. Almost all of their offending careers began during early adolescence, when they socialized entirely with other drug-abusing peers. Over time, their decisions to engage in various forms of delinquency often simply reflected a need to obtain more drugs and continue partying. Adolescent drug users are not only at greater risk for delinquency, but also for victimization. Drawing on a subculture of violence perspective, Heith Copes and his associates have shown that drug users are viewed with disdain by active street criminals and are often targeted for their addiction.[62]

Finally, it is important to recognize that the effects of subcultural socialization on substance use are not always negative. Some social cliques exist among young people that serve to promote healthy, prosocial forms of behavior and that exert peer pressure to avoid drug use and delinquency. One example is the *Straight Edge* movement, an identifiable group characterized by vigilantly antidrug attitudes, vegetarianism, and affinity for hard-core or punk music.[63] Thus some subcultures can effectively insulate adolescents from substance use and delinquent behavior.

Weakening of Social Controls

Social control theory argues that delinquency is the result of an absence or weakening of the social control mechanisms that ensure conformity. Without established social controls, so the theory goes, people will pursue their self-interests, including pleasure. A strong social bond to conventional social institutions reduces the likelihood of deviation from normative expectations, whereas weakening of the bond releases the individual from the constraints of the norms.[64]

To the extent that a youth is strongly *attached* to conventional others (parents, peers, or teachers), is strongly *committed* to conventional institutions, is heavily *involved* in conventional activities, and strongly *believes* in conventional norms, that individual is unlikely to violate society's laws and use drugs. Conversely, if any of these elements of the social bond are weakened, the juvenile becomes more likely to pursue deviant behavior, and drug use becomes more probable. To test this idea, Michael Maume and his colleagues examined the effects of marital attachment and delinquent peer association on marijuana use. They found that young persons with strong attachments to their spouses were significantly more likely to stop using marijuana regardless of the number of drug-using peers whom they had. This finding suggests that "cutting the grass" is likely among young people who forge strong bonds to society through marriage.[65]

Adolescents are more likely to develop substance abuse problems if they were raised in homes characterized by parental conflict. Does family conflict lead to delinquency and drug use generally, or are youths who use drugs also more likely to argue with their parents?

© Don Hammond/Design Pics, Inc./age fotostock.

Recent analysis of data from the National Survey on Drug Use and Health provides support for the idea that social controls reduce the likelihood of a youth getting involved in drug use. For example, according to the survey, adolescents who participated in one or more school-based, community-based, or church- or faith-based activities during the prior year were less likely to have used cigarettes, alcohol, or illicit drugs in the past month than youths who did not participate in such activities in the past year. In addition, youth who attended religious services 25 times or more during the prior year were less likely to use alcohol, cigarettes, or illicit drugs than youths who attended fewer than 25 times; similarly, youths who reported that religious beliefs were a very important part of their lives were less likely to use drugs than were youths who reported that religious beliefs were unimportant to their lives. Finally, more than 3 million youths were considered to be school dropouts. More than half of these dropouts smoked cigarettes during the 6 months before the survey, although dropouts did not appear to be any more likely than nondropouts to use illicit drugs.

Religion is a robust buffer against adolescent drug use. Elizabeth Kelly and her colleagues conducted a meta-analysis of 62 studies that encompassed 193,656 adolescents and found that religiosity and church attendance were negatively associated with alcohol use, illicit drug use, and nondrug-related delinquency.[66] Similarly, youths with a stronger self-concept and high self-esteem are insulated from drugs and delinquency and also less likely to develop mental health problems, such as anxiety and depression.[67]

Family Conflict and Poor Parenting

Delinquency frequently occurs as a reaction to dysfunctional dynamics within the home, most often in homes characterized by poverty, disruption, and conflict. It should come as no surprise that the same conditions promote drug use among children. Parental failures, fighting, extreme or inconsistent discipline of children, lack of communication, physical and sexual abuse, emotional distance, and disrupted marriages all take their toll on children. Drug use may help ease the pain of criticism and serve as a means of escaping the fear of the next assault by an abusive parent.

It has been reported, for example, that adolescent drug use is associated with abusive and/or inconsistent parental discipline. Anthony Jurich and his colleagues found that adolescents who use illegal drugs daily are more likely to have parents who employ *laissez-faire* or authoritarian patterns of discipline rather than democratic ones or to have parents who apply discipline inconsistently.[68] Recently, Angela Robertson and her colleagues found that parents who rarely monitor their children's behavior are often drug users themselves, a factor that further contributes to the development of more drug and delinquency problems in their children.[69] In addition, a number of studies report that parental conflict in child-rearing philosophy and inconsistent or restrictive discipline are associated with both marijuana and alcohol use among children.[70]

Other family factors, such as greater emotional distance, perceived lack of love and outright conflict with parents have also been associated with adolescent drug use. Studies have found higher rates of adolescent drug use among children who perceived lower levels of parental love or negative parental attitudes expressed toward them.[71] Rick Kosterman and his colleagues reported that the likelihood of adolescent initiation into marijuana and alcohol use was reduced by proactive family management practices, such as monitoring, application of rules and discipline, and reward practices; in contrast, bonding to the mother appeared to have little or no effect on drug use.[72]

Broken homes, divorce, separation, and abandonment by the father have also been correlated with adolescent drug use.[73] In one study, Stephan Quensel and his colleagues examined the relationship between family structure and adolescent drug use among more than 3300 15-year-olds. These researchers found that rates of cigarette smoking and marijuana and alcohol use were significantly higher among youths living in single-mother families than among those living in traditional two-parent families, a relationship that held true for both boys and girls.[74]

Research has also suggested that lack of supervision by parents when children come home from school influences the likelihood of adolescent drug use. In their study, Peter Mulhall and his associates reported that *latchkey children* (middle school youth who were home alone after school 2 or more days per week) were significantly more likely to have used alcohol during the prior month, to consume more alcohol,

and to drink to intoxication than were nonlatchkey children. Furthermore, latchkey youth were more likely to have used marijuana and to have smoked cigarettes during the prior month.[75]

The relationship between child maltreatment and the child's ensuing drug use has been explored as well. Ann Burgess and her colleagues compared a group of youngsters who had been sexually abused as children with a group of non-abused youths. They found a strong connection between the childhood experience of sexual abuse and later drug use.[76] When Richard Dembo and his associates studied 145 youths confined in a detention center in a southeastern state, they found that both male and female youths who had been sexually abused were much more likely to be current drug users.[77] More recent studies using more sophisticated methodologies have also examined this relationship.[78] In addition, Timothy Ireland and his colleagues reported that maltreatment of children from childhood through adolescence significantly increases the likelihood of drug use. They note, however, that if the maltreatment is limited to childhood and does not continue into adolescence, it presents only a minimal risk of subsequent drug use.[79]

In the United States, surveys have found that nearly 10 million children live with at least one parent who abused or was dependent on alcohol or an illicit drug during the previous year. Moreover, parental use of drugs and alcohol has been found to have a direct effect on the child's likelihood of using drugs. In one study, researchers found that 78% of parents who used marijuana also had children who were drug users; other studies have confirmed that children imitate their parents' drinking habits.[80] Parents who drink are likely to have children who also drink, whereas parents who abstain from alcohol are likely to have abstaining children.

Denise Kandel and her colleagues examined parental influences on marijuana use by comparing the behaviors of the *baby boom generation* and their children. These researchers found that children of parents who had *ever used* marijuana were three times as likely to have ever used marijuana as the children of parents who had *never* used the drug. The influence was similar for mothers and fathers and sons and daughters. In addition, parents who perceived little risk associated with marijuana use had children with similar beliefs, and adolescent attitudes had the strongest association with adolescent marijuana use of any of the adolescent characteristics examined in the study.[81]

Drug Use and Delinquency

Does illegal drug use lead to acts of delinquency? Or does delinquency lead to drug use? Is the drug use-delinquency relationship spurious—that is, are the two related only because both are caused by some other factors? Or is there a reciprocal relationship between drugs and delinquency, such that drug use leads to delinquent behavior and delinquency leads to drug use? What exactly is the relationship between adolescent drug use and delinquent behavior? These questions have puzzled criminologists for some time. The reason that the drugs-delinquency relationship appears to be multifaceted is that two general, but largely distinct groups exist within the population: *adolescence-limited* and *life-course persistent offenders*.

How are Drugs and Delinquency Related?

Although many studies have led criminologists and policymakers to believe there is a causal link between drug use and delinquency, the exact nature of the relationship has not been established (see **Box 11.6**, the "A Window on Delinquency" feature).[82] Scott Menard and his colleagues explored the relationship between drugs and crime from adolescence into adulthood and reported that "the drug-crime relationship is different for different ages and for different stages of involvement in crime and drug use" and that "initiation of substance use apparently is preceded by initiation of crime for most individuals." However, these authors note that in later stages of involvement, the relationship becomes reciprocal. That is, adolescent involvement in serious illicit drug use appears to "contribute to continuity in serious crime, and serious crime contributes to continuity in serious illicit drug use."[83]

The issue of causality in the drugs–delinquency link also depends on which offenses a delinquent commits. Using data from a sample of adolescents in Finland, Richard Felson and his colleagues found that alcohol use was unrelated to crimes such as shoplifting and stealing things from one's home. Youths committed these offenses whether sober or intoxicated.

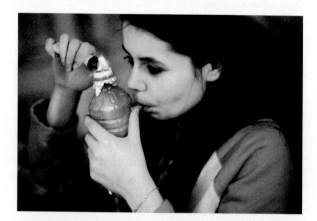

Drug use by girls does not appear to be as likely to lead to delinquency as it does for boys. However, are girls likely to experience different kinds of problems than boys who use drugs? If so, what might these problems be?

© Mikhail Zahranichny/Shutterstock.

BOX 11.6

A Window on Delinquency

Drug Use, Drug Selling, and Delinquency

Although the exact relationship between drugs and delinquency, whether it is causal, correlational, or reciprocal is still debated in the research literature, there is little question that drug use, drug selling, and delinquency are often related to serious problems among youth. Michael Vaughn and his colleagues studied 5373 youth who had reported selling drugs in the past year based on data from the National Survey on Drug Use and Health. They found four general types of drug sellers among youth in the United States. About 50% of youth and young adults were characterized as normative drug sellers. These youth had little involvement in crime generally and were likely to sell drugs just once or twice. They displayed the lowest behavioral risk for delinquency and crime. About 24% were club drug users who also sold drugs. They had much higher substance abuse problems. Sixteen percent of youth were polysubstance users who also sold drugs. They often chronically sold drugs and had extensive drug problems and moderate juvenile and criminal justice system involvement. Finally, about 10% were serious criminal offenders who had extensive and versatile delinquency, criminal justice system involvement, and sporadic drug use. Criminal offenders also frequently sold drugs. In other words, the risk profile for youth who sell drugs is quite varied.

In recent years, the Office of Juvenile Justice and Delinquency Prevention has sponsored the Pathways to Desistance Study, which follows 1354 young offenders from Philadelphia and Phoenix over a 7-year period. The goal of the project is to identify factors and events that help serious delinquents change and become productive citizens as well as to understand the characteristics of youth who continue to be antisocial. In recent years, the project has focused specifically on the nexus between delinquency and drugs, and has produced some important findings:

- Serious and chronic delinquents are more likely than less serious delinquents to not only use various drugs but also to meet diagnostic criteria for substance abuse disorders.
- There is strong evidence of continuity in drug use and delinquency across time.
- A variety of dispositional factors increase the likelihood of drug use and delinquency. These include behavioral disinhibition, sensation seeking, poor affect regulation, depression, and stress.
- Substance use and delinquency tend to fluctuate over time in the same way. This suggests there is likely less of a causal connection between the two, and suggests that both are likely the outcome of criminal propensity.

The Pathways project demonstrates the many ways that youth get into serious trouble once they initiate drug involvement. Drug abuse impairs coping and competence, contributes to school problems and academic failure, leads to more associations with delinquent peers, drives a need for fast money, and of course, increases delinquency. Over time, all of these risk factors also predict failure in conventional adult responsibilities and further criminal activity. Although the logic of "Just Say No" to drugs is often criticized for being too simplistic, it is rooted in the idea that drugs engender many other problems.

Michael Vaughn, Christopher Salas-Wright, Matt DeLisi, Jeffrey Shook, and Lauren Terzis, "A Typology of Drug Selling among Young Adults in the United States," *Substance Use & Misuse* 50:403–413 (2015); Edward Mulvey, Carol Schubert, and Laurie Chassin, *Substance Use and Delinquent Behavior among Serious Adolescent Offenders* (Washington, DC: U.S. Department of Justice, 2010); Carol Schubert, Edward Mulvey, and Cristie Glasheen, "Influence of Mental Health and Substance Use Problems and Criminogenic Risk on Outcomes in Serious Juvenile Offenders," *Journal of the American Academy of Child and Adolescent Psychiatry* 50:925–937 (2011); Glenn Walters, "Mediating the Distal Crime-Drug Relationship with Proximal Reactive Criminal Thinking," *Psychology of Addictive Behaviors* 30:128–137 (2016).

Conversely, for delinquent offenses including assault, vandalism, car theft, and graffiti writing, there was a direct causal relationship between alcohol intoxication and delinquency.[84] In other words, the context of the delinquent act is important to know when considering whether drugs/alcohol and delinquency are causally related.

Many studies confirm an association between alcohol and drug use and general patterns of delinquency yet fail to definitively establish a causal relationship. For instance, when John Welte and his colleagues studied the drugs–delinquency connection, they found that a general deviant syndrome *did not* explain specific problem behaviors, such as drug use. Although drugs and delinquency were correlated, their ultimate causes seemed to be distinct. In other words, adolescent substance abuse was not simply part of a teen's larger involvement in crime.[85]

David Altschuler and Paul Brounstein found that although drug use and drug trafficking were correlated with other delinquent activities, "still, for every type of crime reported in the past year, only a minority of offenders reported ever using drugs while committing the crime. . . . Most youths appear to commit crime for reasons completely independent of drugs."[86] Although most serious delinquents were found to be regular users of alcohol and drugs, the vast majority of their instances of drug and alcohol use occurred without crimes, and most crimes occurred without prior substance abuse.

Indeed, Scott Jacques and Richard Wright found that some youths who sell drugs go to considerable lengths to avoid violence and other serious forms of delinquency. For instance, rather than use violence to retaliate against customers or other drug dealers, they found that some drug-involved youths will engage in fraud and theft to "get back" at rivals. Thus, although they are extensively involved in the drug scene, these individuals tend to shy away from violence.[87]

Other criminologists has reached slightly different conclusions. Colleen McLaughlin and her colleagues discovered in a study of 25 male juveniles committed to Virginia juvenile correctional facilities for murder or voluntary manslaughter that more than half of the murderers were known drug dealers, compared to fewer than 10% of all juveniles incarcerated in the state. In addition, 28% of the murder incidents were regarded as drug related. Perhaps more important, these researchers found that none of the drug-related murders involved offenders who did not have some history of illicit drug use. Drug use by homicide victims was also a significant factor contributing to murder incidents: More individuals who had recently used drugs were killed in a drug-related incident than individuals who did not use drugs.[88]

David Huizinga and his colleagues reported on findings from research on the causes and correlates of delinquency conducted in Denver, Pittsburgh, and Rochester, New York. More than 4000 youths were surveyed in the three cities. In each city, the researchers found a statistically significant relationship between persistent delinquency and persistent drug use and this was true for both males and females. Huizinga and his associates note that "for males, the majority of persistent serious delinquents were not drug users, but the majority of drug users were serious delinquents. . . . [and that] among females, delinquency is a stronger indicator of drug use than drug use is an indicator of delinquency."[89] In the final analysis, it is prudent to conclude that there is a co-occurrence between drug use and delinquency.

Drugs, Delinquent Friends, and Delinquency

Research suggests that associating with peers who are delinquent, who use drugs, or both is strongly related to both delinquency and drug use. Criminologists who have examined self-report responses from a national sample of 1725 youths have concluded that a causal relationship exists between prior delinquency and involvement in delinquent peer groups and subsequent drug use.[90] For example, Helen Garnier and Judith Stein found that the most significant predictor of both drug use and delinquency is having peers who engaged in the behaviors. They also noted that youths select friends who are more like themselves—that is, who share similar values, backgrounds, *and* behaviors, including drug use.[91] Andrea Hussong reported that the strongest predictor for adolescent drug use is the extent of drug use by the youth's best friend.[92] Thus it seems that having strong bonds to delinquent peers increases the risk of both delinquency and drug use for all youths.

Juveniles who belong to gangs are significantly more likely to engage in drug use than are adolescents who are not members of gangs. Similarly, joining a gang is often a precursor to drug use. In addition, juvenile gang members, and even gangs themselves, are often explicitly organized for the purpose of drug trafficking. Research has consistently confirmed that gang members are extensively involved in drug sales, especially marijuana and cocaine.[93]

In addition, as youths become more deeply involved in delinquency and drug use, they become significantly more likely to follow long-term life trajectories involving a variety of precocious transitions. Marvin Krohn and his colleagues report that alcohol and drug use during early adolescence increases the risk of becoming pregnant or impregnating someone, dropping out of school, becoming a teenage parent, and living independently from parents. These consequences, in turn, increase the likelihood of drug and alcohol use as the youths become young adults. Krohn and his colleagues conclude that these youths are then greatly disadvantaged in their ability to establish stable adult lives and are more likely to pursue deviant lifestyles.[94]

As mentioned previously, the drugs–delinquency relationship appears to be multifaceted because it applies to two distinct groups within the population: adolescence-limited offenders and life-course persistent offenders. As the label implies, adolescence-limited offenders engage in drug use and delinquency during middle to late adolescence, largely in response to the ambiguities that arise during the transition from child to adult status. Most youths fit into this category. Among members of this group, delinquent involvement often includes less serious forms of conduct and is short lived. In terms of drug use, the "normal" adolescence-limited delinquent will experiment with marijuana, alcohol, and tobacco but will typically abstain from trying more illicit narcotics, such as heroin, cocaine, and methamphetamine. The popular notion of the high school student drinking beer on weekends or occasionally smoking marijuana meshes with the idea of the adolescence-limited offender. For most, the brief period of experimentation does not become problematic or lead to larger problems with substance abuse or antisocial behavior.[95]

In contrast to adolescence-limited offenders, youths on the life-course persistent pathway engage in drug use as part of a larger behavioral pattern of delinquency. Even during adolescence, life-course persistent or chronic delinquents experience an array of overlapping behavioral problems that mutually reinforce one another but ultimately stem from some other cause, a phenomenon called comorbidity. According to this theory, youngsters on the life-course persistent pathway suffer from several neurocognitive deficits that interact with early life disadvantages, such as abusive, erratic, or antisocial parenting, to propel them down an antisocial pathway. Experimentation with alcohol and other substances occurs very early in life, often during childhood, and at times is even introduced and promoted by parents.

Early use of drugs and alcohol is very harmful for healthy human development. According to the National Epidemiologic Survey on Alcohol and Related Conditions, 47% of persons who begin drinking alcohol before age 14 will be dependent on alcohol at some point during their lifetime—a prevalence rate that is five times greater than that for persons whose onset of alcohol use occurs at age 21.[96] When Grace Barnes and her colleagues studied the drugs–delinquency link among nearly 20,000 students in middle and high school, they found that children who experimented with alcohol very early in life were significantly likely to have further alcohol problems and higher levels of drug use and delinquency.[97]

Not all criminologists support the developmental taxonomy discussed here. Nevertheless, most social and medical scientists distinguish between drug use that appears to be normative, experimental, and unproblematic and drug use that appears to be part of a larger antisocial behavioral syndrome.[98] A host of "global explanations" have been offered to explain the antisocial behavioral syndrome.[99] One of the most popular is low self-control. Denis Ribeaud and Manuel Eisner found that low self-control, and particularly its subcomponents of risk seeking and impulsivity, accounted for involvement in delinquency and substance abuse among a large sample of ninth graders in Switzerland.[100] Other criminologists suggest that aggression and impulsivity, gang membership, and societal–poverty factors primarily explain the syndrome approach to drugs and delinquency.[101] Finally, Richard Felson and his colleagues studied whether a relationship exists between adolescent drinking and violence by comparing drinkers and nondrinkers in a national sample of American youths. Whether they were intoxicated or sober, youths who were drinkers committed more violence than nondrinkers, suggesting that it is not necessarily the presence of alcohol that contributes to youth violence, but rather some underlying delinquent propensity that comes to the fore.[102]

drug use in a variety of ways, including controlling the availability of guns; using a blended approach that balances treatment and more punitive approaches; implementing education, prevention, and treatment; and even decriminalizing marijuana. Each of these approaches is examined next.

Controlling Availability of Guns

A variety of innovative policing initiatives have been designed to reduce the availability of guns to juveniles. For instance, beginning in 1994, the New York City Police Department installed its computer statistics "Compstat" approach, which stressed zero tolerance for nuisance types of offending, such as loitering, turnstile jumping, vandalism, and prostitution. By refusing to tolerate even the most trivial violations, the police sent a message to offenders that any type of criminal behavior would not be permitted. Not coincidentally, youth who committed serious crimes and carried firearms also committed minor forms of delinquency; thus they were often arrested before their nuisance offending could escalate to more serious acts. This policing approach (popularly referred to as "broken windows" policing) was responsible for dramatic reductions in violence, homicides, and gun crimes in New York City.[103] In fact, even the harshest critics of the program acknowledge that controlling offenders who use guns and the subsequent availability of guns resulted in declines in crime rates.[104]

Similarly, the Richmond, Virginia Police Department developed a coordinated antigun program with the U.S. Attorney's Office, known as Project Exile, to aggressively prosecute all gun arrests as federal offenses. The primary advantage of this local-federal approach is that authorities are able to use existing stricter federal gun laws and the more severe penalties available in the federal courts to punish offenders. Although Project Exile does not directly target youth, gun violence in the Richmond area did appear to decline after its implementation. Critics of Project Exile argue that the decline in gun violence was simply a continuation of the more general decline in gun violence observed in large cities around the United States, rather than being an outcome of the new program. A recent reevaluation by Richard Rosenfeld, Robert Fornango, and Eric Baumer found strong violence-reduction effects resulting from Project Exile.[105]

Franklin Zimring suggests an alternative to banning firearms as a means to control youth violence. He notes that adolescents possess their own unique

Responding to Youth Violence and Drug Use

Policymakers and the juvenile justice system have responded to the problems of youth violence and

KEY TERMS

comorbidity
The overlapping of behavioral problems that mutually reinforce one another but ultimately stem from some other cause.

political economy. Youths have less monetary capital, lower regard for property as capital assets, and shorter monetary attention spans than adults. Adolescents with many economic wants, therefore, can be more easily distracted from investing their capital in guns. According to Zimring, raising the price of guns and creating a scarcity of ammunition for those who possess guns would have a significant negative impact on juveniles' (especially younger juveniles') decisions to spend money on guns.[106]

Policies aimed solely at reducing the total number of firearms in circulation in communities may not be adequate. As Marc Riedel and Wayne Welsh note, it is not the total number of guns available that leads to higher levels of violence but rather "the carrying of guns in high-risk places at high-risk times."[107] If this is true, the creation of new laws designed to reduce gun and ammunition availability may not be as effective as stricter enforcement of existing laws that prohibit persons from carrying concealed weapons.

Law enforcement agencies have been attempting to reduce the availability of guns through a variety of strategies, such as targeted enforcement operations (including focusing on hot spots of gun crime and implementing gun sweeps), community-supported "silent witness" programs that encourage residents to report the presence of illegal guns, cooperation with the Bureau of Alcohol, Tobacco, and Firearms (ATF) to trace illegal guns, safe gun storage programs, and the creation of juvenile gun courts.[108]

Blended Treatment and "Get-Tough" Approaches

There is a serious dilemma facing both criminologists and policymakers when attempting to determine the "best" treatment approach or the "most effective" punishment approach for dealing with serious, violent juveniles. Unfortunately, it is difficult to distinguish the causes of the behaviors of violent youths from those associated with nonviolent delinquent youths. To select primarily violent youths for participation in a particular treatment program or for transfer to criminal court for prosecution based on assumptions about the ability to bring about rehabilitation or deterrence might be flawed. As researcher Dewey Cornell points out, even very violent juveniles can be subdivided into smaller subgroups based on their prior adjustment problems. Cornell states, "Among violent offenders, youths convicted of the most serious violent crime, homicide, actually have less history of prior violence than do offenders convicted of less serious assaults."[109]

Regrettably, it is often the case that serious, violent, and chronic delinquents were themselves exposed to severe abuses and deprivation from very early in life. Indeed, some public sentiment is characterized by a "what did we expect" belief about the effects of early life abuses on subsequent violence and criminal

behavior. This leads many observers to wring their hands in resignation and despair, convinced that nothing can be done to stem the actions of the serious delinquents.[110] Fortunately, this is not the case. For example, Mark Lipsey recently reviewed the literature on programs that target serious delinquents and concluded:

> [T]he average effect on the recidivism of serious juvenile offender of those interventions that I studied are positive, statistically significant, and, though modest, not trivial . . . this evidence shows that optimal combinations of program elements have the capability to reduce recidivism by 40 to 50 percent, that is, to cut recidivism rates to nearly half of what they would be without such programming.[111]

Most treatment programs for violent youths occur within locked, secure correctional facilities, although they continue to emphasize rehabilitation and early reintegration into the community. One such treatment program is the Violent Juvenile Offender (VJO) program, which is designed to target chronic violent male juvenile offenders in four urban areas (Boston, Detroit, Memphis, and Newark). Youths selected for the VJO program must have been adjudicated for a Part I Index felony (a *UCR* Crime Index offense) and have at least one prior felony adjudication. The program involves efforts aimed at "strengthening youths' bonds to prosocial people and institutions, providing realistic opportunities for achievement, employing a system of rewards for appropriate behavior and sanctions for inappropriate behavior, and individualized treatment." To accomplish these goals, VJO youths are initially placed in small, secure treatment facilities and then gradually reintegrated into the community in a stepwise manner. The second phase involves treatment in a community-based residential program, after which youths progress to the third phase, involving intensive supervision in the neighborhood.

Darin Haerle evaluated a therapeutic Violent Offender Treatment Program designed to provide treatment for the most violent delinquents, including those adjudicated for murder, armed robbery, and other violent delinquent acts. The youth are placed in cottages away from other delinquents and receive extensive counseling and therapy. Youth received differential levels of counseling or different dosages of treatment. Haerle found that youth who participated in the program were less likely to recidivate (although recidivism was still rather high). Among those who received a strong dose of the program, 54% recidivated, while among those who received a weak dose, 70% recidivated.

Another treatment program for violent juvenile offenders is the Capital Offender Program (COP) in Texas. For a youth to be eligible for placement in

COP, he or she must have committed a homicide and must not have been diagnosed as having a severe psychological disorder. COP is designed to promote verbal expression of feelings, to foster empathy for victims, to create a sense of personal responsibility, and to decrease feelings of hostility and aggression. Treatment includes group psychotherapy emphasizing role-playing in which youths act out their life stories and reenact their crimes from their own perspectives and from the perspectives of their victims.[112]

Other approaches for dealing with violent youths strengthen punishments for them. Many states have lowered the age for waiver of violent youths to criminal (adult) court or are making it less difficult to transfer such youths, have established determinate sentences for youths who commit serious violent crimes that are adjudicated in the juvenile courts, and have permitted a juvenile's arrest and court record to be made available to schools and to adult criminal courts once a youth is prosecuted as an adult. In addition, some states have passed parental-liability laws whereby juveniles' parents are held in contempt of court for missing their children's court hearings.

Law enforcement, prosecutors, and the courts in a number of jurisdictions are coordinating their efforts to develop new strategies for targeting violent juveniles. For example, the Salinas (California) Police Department created a Violence Suppression Unit consisting of 15 officers who perform aggressive patrols focusing on violent and gun-related crimes. The Seattle Police Department established a system for tracking violent offenders and disseminating information through the department and other social services agencies to reduce the anonymity of the juveniles and refer the offenders to intervention services. A list of the 50 most violent juveniles was developed; through increased communication between police and probation officers, the jurisdiction aims to increase surveillance of these youths and to provide for greater enforcement of their conditions of probation. In addition, enhanced prosecution for serious, violent juvenile offenders was instituted with the addition of a new full-time position in the prosecutor's Office. At the same time, Seattle's Juvenile Firearms Prosecution Project provided for vertical prosecution of all juvenile firearms offenses, with a deputy prosecutor specializing in firearm prosecutions being assigned to handle all juvenile firearms offenses from initial filing of the case through juvenile sentencing. In Baltimore, the Police Department's Youth Violence Task Force, works closely with the U.S. Attorney's office, ATF, FBI, and school police, to identify and target gang members and violent offenders and then aggressively seeks their apprehension, adjudication or conviction, and incarceration.[113]

Conventional wisdom and much academic scholarship hold that U.S. drug policy is almost entirely based on drug interdiction and law enforcement, excessive prosecution of drug offenders, and overall a punishment-based approach in responding to substance abuse.[114] Although the United States does take a punitive stance toward substance use compared to some other countries, its drug policy blends a variety of methods to address the drug problem. For example, beginning with former President George W. Bush and continuing with President Barack Obama, the President's National Drug Control Strategy advocates a three-pronged strategy, comprising prevention, treatment, and interdiction. First, an integral part of drug prevention was the *Above the Influence* initiative, which consists of multiple media educational programs to promote drug-free living among children and adolescents. Second, drug treatment was highlighted by the *Access to Recovery* program, which expands treatment options and the use of drug courts, instead of traditional criminal prosecution, in an effort to rehabilitate offenders with substance abuse problems. Third, the Bush administration sought to disrupt drug markets using the resources of federal, state, and local criminal justice systems. In the next section, we examine four ways of responding to adolescent drug use.

Control Response

The control response to adolescent drug use emphasizes the arrest and prosecution of drug dealers and drug users. When the *Anti-Drug Abuse Act of 1988* was created, it was believed that a mostly control-based response to substance abuse would create a drug-free America within 10 years—a goal that obviously was not achieved. Legislation and guidelines were established to provide greater support for federal, state, and local law enforcement agencies and to allocate funds for the expansion of the U.S. prison system. Of course, the Anti-Drug Abuse Act has had only modest success in reducing adolescent drug use in recent years.

Each year, in an attempt to strengthen federal efforts in attacking the problem of illicit drugs in the lives of juveniles, the White House Office of National Drug Control Policy produces a *National Drug Control Strategy*. The National Drug Control Strategy budget request for 2009 was $14.2 billion, including appropriations for student drug-testing programs, continuation of the National Youth Anti-Drug Media Campaign (begun in 2001), and money to fund approximately 100 new local community antidrug coalitions working to prevent substance abuse among young people.[115]

Juvenile Drug Courts

The drug court movement is simultaneously an outgrowth of the early crackdown on drugs in the 1970s and 1980s and a reflection of the emerging interest in developing community-oriented diversionary alternatives to the traditional criminal and juvenile courts for handling drug cases. Drug courts aim to integrate a variety of alcohol and drug treatment services

with justice system case processing and to provide continued monitoring and testing of participants. Juvenile drug courts, although modeled on adult drug courts, place greater emphasis on coordinating treatment for juveniles involving the courts, the youths' families, and schools in a community—rather than institutional—environment.[116]

According to the National Association of Drug Court Professionals, more than 1600 drug courts currently operate in the United States, of which nearly 200 are devoted exclusively to adolescents. Unfortunately, there are few published evaluations of the effectiveness of juvenile drug courts. Whereas initial studies suggest the courts have had some positive effects in reducing drug use and other forms of delinquency, more recent research raises questions about the ability of drug courts to accomplish their goals. For example, Nancy Rodriguez and Vincent Webb examined data from the first 3 years of the Maricopa County (Phoenix) juvenile drug court program and compared the outcomes for 114 youths placed in the drug court with 204 juveniles placed on standard probation. They found:

> "[N]o significant difference in marijuana use between youths in drug court and those on standard probation.... [and] youths in drug court were 2.7 times more likely to test positive for cocaine than youths in the comparison group." Moreover, only 15 juveniles (30%) of the youths successfully completed and graduated from the drug court program.[117]

One problem with this control-based approach could be the somewhat arbitrary way that youths are admitted to drug courts instead of traditional juvenile justice methods. For instance, Mitchell Miller and his colleagues found that youths with an unfavorable demeanor or having the appearance of a bad attitude were 50% less likely to be admitted to drug court than youths with favorable dispositions.[118] Nevertheless, it is probable that even more juvenile drug courts will be developed to meet the demand imposed by the nearly 194,000 delinquency cases involving a drug offense in U.S. juvenile courts.[119]

Drug Testing in Schools

Efforts to control the youth-related drug problem have also involved a call for more extensive drug testing. The issue of drug testing remains highly controversial, however. Who should be tested? How accurate are the tests? Are tests for all illicit drugs equally accurate? Are such tests a violation of the tested individual's constitutional rights ensuring protection against self-incrimination and the right to privacy?

Many school districts have begun to require drug tests for high school athletes, and a New Jersey school district mandated that all high school students submit to drug tests. Failure to submit to the tests could result in suspension from school.[120] The Supreme Court, in *Vernonia School District 47J v. Acton*, held that schools could require all students participating in interscholastic athletics to sign a form consenting to a urinalysis drug test at the beginning of the season for their sport.[121] The Court's position in *Vernonia* raised several new questions. For example, should students participating in other extracurricular activities, such as debate, marching band, or school government also be tested? Should teachers and school administrators be required to take similar drug tests? If there is a legitimate concern about possible injury caused by the student's activity, then should students enrolled in certain science or vocational courses where potential danger exists with chemicals and hazardous machinery be tested? Also, because studies have found that first drug use often occurs before entering high school, should drug testing begin in middle school—or even earlier?

The Supreme Court answered some of these questions in 2002, when it decided a case brought by 16-year-old Lindsay Earls. When Earls began her sophomore year at Tecumseh High School in Oklahoma, she was confronted by a new school drug policy that required mandatory drug testing of all students participating in *any* extracurricular activity. This policy included participants in athletics, the band, choir, academic team, color guard, and Future Farmers of America. Earls was a member of the school's choir, marching band, and academic team, and she objected to what she regarded as an intrusive testing process. Earls said that she had been pulled out of class three times and sent to the vice principal's Office to fill out forms and then taken to a bathroom where a teacher would stand outside the stall while she produced her urine sample. Earls believed that if students were not using drugs, then they should not have to prove their innocence. Lindsay and her family contacted the American Civil Liberties Union (ACLU), which accepted the case. The case wended its way through the courts, eventually ending up in the U.S. Supreme Court. The Court held, in *Board of Education of Pottawatomie County v. Earls et al.*, that such testing was not an unconstitutional intrusion on the students' privacy rights.[122] See **Box 11.7**, the "From the Bench" feature, for a brief discussion of the Court's ruling.

The Court's decisions in the *Vernonia* and *Earls* cases were based on the belief that drug testing of students would likely help reduce the drug problems believed to exist in U.S. schools. By the early 21st century, drug testing of high school athletes was a policy in only 5% of schools; but testing of students in any extracurricular activities was practiced in about 25% of

KEY TERMS

Board of Education of Pottawatomie County v. Earls et al.
Supreme Court ruling that mandatory drug testing of students involved in any extracurricular activity is constitutional.

BOX 11.7

From the Bench

Board of Education of Pottawatomie County v. Earls et al.

Lindsay Earls, a 16-year-old girl, objected to her school's policy requiring warrantless random drug testing as a condition for any student to participate in any school-sponsored extracurricular activity. The school board believed that a drug problem existed in the school and that it was not limited to students involved in athletics. The U.S. Supreme Court, in a 5-to-4 decision following its earlier ruling in *Vernonia* in 1995, cited the "special needs" of public schools that permit school searches without the traditional Fourth Amendment requirement of individualized suspicion before a search. The Court ruled that:

A student's privacy interest is limited in a public school environment where the State is responsible for maintaining discipline, health, and safety. Schoolchildren are routinely required to submit to physical examinations and vaccinations against disease. . . . Students who participate in competitive extracurricular activities voluntarily subject themselves to many of the same intrusions on their privacy as do athletes. Some of these clubs and activities require occasional off-campus travel and communal undress. All of them have their own rules and requirements for participating students that

do not apply to the student body as a whole. . . . We therefore conclude that the students affected by this Policy have a limited expectation of privacy.

The court went on to say that:

In this context, the Fourth Amendment does not require a finding of individualized suspicion and we decline to impose such a requirement on schools attempting to prevent and detect drug use by students. Moreover, we question whether testing based on individualized suspicion in fact would be less intrusive. Such a regime would place an additional burden on public school teachers who are already tasked with the difficult job of maintaining order and discipline. A program of individualized suspicion might unfairly target members of unpopular groups. The fear of lawsuits resulting from such targeted searches may chill enforcement of the program, rendering it ineffective in combating drug use. . . . Finally, we find that testing students who participate in extracurricular activities is a reasonably effective means of addressing the School District's legitimate concerns in preventing, deterring, and detecting drug use.

Board of Education of Pottawatomoie County v. Earls et al., 536 U.S. 822 (2002).

schools. But does drug testing of students reduce the likelihood that students will use illicit drugs? Ryoko Yamaguchi and his colleagues found that it does not. They concluded that for adolescent students, a school drug testing policy was not significantly related to the prevalence or the frequency of student use of marijuana or other illicit drugs. Furthermore, drug testing of student athletes was not related to their use of marijuana or other illicit drug use.[123]

Police Crackdowns

A rather different approach to control adolescent drug use has been taken by the Vallejo Community Consortium in Vallejo, California, which worked with the Fighting Back Partnership of Vallejo to pass the Teen Party Ordinance in 1999. This ordinance authorizes the city's police department to recoup any costs associated with calls for service involving teenage parties where alcohol and illegal substances are used. Parents of teens are asked to repay the costs of the service calls for each reported incident. Copies of the ordinance and a pledge are mailed to the parents of all middle and high school students in the district. Parents are asked to sign the pledge, signifying that they will make their home a safe place for teens.[124]

Other jurisdictions have employed *police crackdowns*—that is, short-term periods of intensive law enforcement—to target substance use, drug dealing, and delinquency among adolescents and young adults in some of the nation's most impoverished, crime-plagued neighborhoods. For example, the Philadelphia Police Department's *Operation Safe Streets* deployed 214 officers to rigorously enforce the law in the highest drug-activity street corners spanning the summers of 2000 and 2002. An evaluation by Brian Lawton and his colleagues reported that the crackdown did significantly reduce violent and drug crimes at the target sites.[125] Despite the Philadelphia success story, police crackdowns on drugs *do not* always have the expected effects. For instance, Samuel Nunn and his colleagues reported that a crackdown in the Brightwood neighborhood in Indianapolis resulted in reductions in all types of crime except drug-related calls for service.[126]

Education, Prevention, and Treatment

In 1884, New York passed legislation to make anti-alcohol teaching compulsory in the public schools. Forty years later, Richmond Hobson, a leading

Prohibitionist, warned of "demonic drug pushers" who sought to seduce young children into drug addiction by nefarious practices such as hiding heroin in snow cones. Hobson eventually founded a number of national organizations for educating the public about the evils of drugs. Lectures and brochures were prepared and provided to hundreds of school systems for use during a week set aside in February as "Narcotics Week."[127]

In 1937, Henry Anslinger, director of the Federal Bureau of Narcotics, published a widely read article titled "Marijuana: Assassin of Youth," in which he described murders, debauchery, and the seduction of innocent girls as a consequence of marijuana smoking. In 1936, the movie *Reefer Madness*, depicting many of the same marijuana-induced behaviors, was produced under the bureau's guidance. These efforts were directed at "educating" the public, especially the young, about the dangers of drug use. In retrospect, they proved to be little more than scare tactics, misinforming rather than informing the public.

Education and Prevention in School

Today, alongside law enforcement strategies, rational and informed education about the nature and effects of drugs is finding wide acceptance. Media campaigns—including cartoon characters, popular songs, and costumed actors who appear as talking brain cells—are aimed at young children. One example is the *Protecting You/Protecting Me* prevention program sponsored by Mothers Against Drunk Driving, which targets children in grades 1 through 5. This program is intended to reach children before they have fully shaped their attitudes and opinions about alcohol use and by extension drug use. Students learn what commercials do and do not communicate about alcohol use, how to resist peer pressure, how to talk to parents and friends about alcohol, how to make informed decisions, how to manage stress without alcohol, and other important life lessons about healthy, substance-free living. Evaluation studies have indicated that children who participate in Protecting Youth/Protecting Me benefit across a variety of outcome measures; as a consequence, this effort is considered a model program by the U.S. Department of Health and Human Services and Center for Substance Abuse Prevention.[128]

Like the anti-alcohol provision of the 1884 New York law, antidrug education has become a standard part of school curricula. Many schools offer "refusal-skill training" or "resistance training" to students through such programs as **Drug Abuse Resistance Education (D.A.R.E.)**, which was begun in 1983. The D.A.R.E. program is aimed at children in kindergarten through 12th grade and is designed to equip students with appropriate skills to resist substance abuse and gangs. D.A.R.E. has the following objectives:[129]

- Acquiring the knowledge and skills to recognize and resist peer pressure to experiment with tobacco, alcohol, and other drugs
- Enhancing self-esteem
- Learning assertiveness techniques
- Learning about positive alternatives to substance use
- Learning anger management and conflict resolution skills
- Developing risk assessment and decision-making skills
- Reducing violence
- Building interpersonal and communication skills
- Resisting gang involvement

School-based prevention programs often combine teaching about the negative consequences of drug use with clearly stated policies on use, possession, and distribution of drugs. The Anne Arundel County schools in Maryland claim to have reduced the number of school drug offenses by more than 80% since 1980 after implementing their antidrug program.

Other critics are less enchanted with these programs, claiming that they reduce the school drug problem by adding to the already high dropout problem. Numerous studies have found D.A.R.E. to have *no* significant effects on reducing drug use among students exposed to the program. For example, Dennis Rosenbaum and Gordon Hanson conducted a 6-year evaluation of D.A.R.E. and found it had no long-term effects in reducing drug use.[130] Susan Ennett and her colleagues also evaluated the D.A.R.E. program and concluded that, although modest positive short-term effects were achieved, overall the program appeared to have no effect on reducing alcohol or tobacco use in D.A.R.E. participants compared to a control group.[131] When Richard Clayton and his colleagues examined the impact of the D.A.R.E. program over a 5-year period, they likewise reported no significant difference in drug use between students in the D.A.R.E. program and a control group of students.[132]

Finally, Donald Lynam and his associates conducted a 10-year follow-up study of more than 1000 sixth-grade students who participated in Project D.A.R.E. during 1987–1988. These students were surveyed again 10 years later. The results showed no differences at age 20 between D.A.R.E. participants and students who *did not* participate in the program in terms of their use of cigarettes, alcohol, marijuana, and other illicit drugs. In addition, the program did not have any effect on participants' attitudes toward drug use. The only significant finding of difference was that youths at age 20 who had participated in the D.A.R.E.

program had lower self-esteem scores than students who did not participate in D.A.R.E.[133]

D.A.R.E. officials eventually admitted the program needed to be revised. With nearly $14 million in support from the Robert Wood Johnson Foundation, a revised program was launched in six cities in 2001. Major changes included reducing the use of local police as instructors, while increasing the number of lectures to students and involving youths in more active ways. In 2007, Dennis Rosenbaum reviewed evidence related to the revised D.A.R.E. program and concluded it should be terminated in favor of programs that work.[134] Indeed it was. In 2009, D.A.R.E. was discontinued and replaced with *keepin' it REAL*, which is an intervention aimed toward middle school students and designed to equip students with decision-making skills to resist substance use. The acronym REAL stands for the following successful refusal strategies when youth are offered drugs:

- Refuse: a simple no is the best response when drugs are offered.
- Explain: offer an explanation such as fear of consequences, fear of getting into trouble, or feelings that using drugs would disappoint one's family.
- Avoid: stop attending parties or social events where drugs and alcohol are used and where use is expected.
- Leave: leave the drug-involved situation altogether.

Drug Treatment Programs

Not all communities have adequate drug treatment programs. Where programs do exist, the access for juveniles to existing drug treatment may depend on community sociodemographics and local public perceptions toward drug treatment. Yvonne Terry-McElrath and Duane McBride report that communities with higher than average median income are less likely to use juvenile drug courts than less affluent communities and that more affluent communities were more likely to provide drug treatment for juvenile offenders as a part of traditional probation.[135] Today, more than 5000 drug treatment programs are in operation in the United States. These programs fall into one of five categories:

1. *Detoxification programs,* which are usually conducted on an inpatient basis and are designed to end the user's addiction to drugs.
2. *Chemical dependency units,* which are generally inpatient programs, lasting 3 to 4 weeks.
3. *Outpatient clinics,* which offer counseling and support.
4. *Methadone maintenance programs,* in which heroin addicts are treated by means of methadone, a prescribed drug that "blocks" the craving for heroin.
5. *Residential therapeutic communities,* in which drug users may spend as long as 18 months participating in a highly structured program.

In providing effective drug or alcohol treatment for juveniles, programs face an additional problem that stems from the issues of consent and parental notification. Most states allow treatment for drug-abusing youths without parental consent, although some states restrict services to treatment for either drug or alcohol abuse but not both. Furthermore, a few states require that a youth's parents be notified before services are provided. Such requirements can interfere with a youth's perception of the acceptability of treatment: He or she may simply find it easier to avoid seeking care.[136]

Despite these problems, some drug treatment programs produce outstanding outcomes. For example, the Life Skills Training program targets middle and high school students and consists of general self-management skills, social skills, and information and skills specifically related to drug use. Life Skills Training costs only $7 per student and has resulted in reductions in tobacco, alcohol, and marijuana usage rates ranging from 50 to 75%. Other long-term evaluations have indicated that the program can reduce polydrug use by 66% and pack-a-day smoking by 25%.[137]

The Bridge is a residential therapeutic center in Philadelphia. Its primary goal is to create an atmosphere in which clients will feel comfortable, develop peer relationships for support, take responsibility for their actions, and learn problem-solving skills that are relevant in their personal lives. Although nearly 50% of the Bridge's clients are referred by the juvenile court, self-referrals, family and school referrals, and referrals by other community agencies are also common. Clients receive a minimum of 10 hours of therapy per week, with emphasis on developing awareness and life skills. Counseling is combined with an educational program that offers nearly 30 hours of classroom experience per week, as well as vocational guidance and job placement. The staff at the Bridge believe that adolescent drug users, with proper motivation and development of skills, can develop an appreciation of their personal worth, learn how to make good decisions, set goals and accept consequences, and learn how to cope, behave responsibly in difficult situations, communicate more effectively with their families, and develop honest, positive, and supportive friends."[138] Overall, drug treatment programs that address the multiple needs (e.g., psychiatric problems, family problems, poverty) of youths offer the best chance for rehabilitation.[139]

KEY TERMS

keepin' it REAL
A program aimed at children in middle school designed to equip students with appropriate decision-making skills to resist substance use.

Decriminalization

Critics of current drug control strategies argue that punitive measures will fail because profits from the sale of illegal drugs are too great and the pleasurable reinforcements that come from using drugs are too strong. Lester Thurow has stated, "If our goal is to deprive criminals of large profits from selling drugs, economic theory and history teaches us that legalization is the only answer."[140] Others have called for a national 10-year experiment in which marijuana, heroin, and cocaine would be *decriminalized*. If the experiment fails, the country could return to its present policies, which are viewed as being relatively ineffective.[141]

Essentially, **decriminalization** of some drugs involves relaxing enforcement of existing laws. For example, decriminalizing marijuana might mean that police would not make arrests for simple possession of small amounts of the drug. Possession of marijuana would still be technically illegal; however, the law would not be enforced—an approach that is already practiced in some drug "sanctuary" cities. **Legalization**, in contrast, involves eliminating many of the laws currently prohibiting the distribution and possession of drugs, but not necessarily eliminating all regulation. For example, alcohol is legal, but regulated in terms of who may sell it, where it may be sold, and how old a person must be to buy it.

Advocates of decriminalization or legalization contend that an immediate consequence of the reform would be the introduction of less-expensive drugs, produced and sold under government regulations and control and in accordance with standardized quality control. In other words, decriminalized drugs would contain no surprise additives or contaminants, and their lower cost would reduce potential black market profits. As a consequence, the economic attractions of importing and dealing would be eliminated. As another point in their favor, advocates of decriminalization or legalization argue that many drugs currently criminalized are not as harmful as some legal prescription drugs that are widely available.

Critics of decriminalization or legalization are quick to point out that either decriminalizing or legalizing particular drugs would increase their use and abuse. If drugs such as marijuana and cocaine were inexpensive and readily available, adolescents who currently refrain from drug use would be drawn to drugs in large numbers. Evidence for this position may be found in the Alaskan experience after the Alaska Supreme Court in *Ravin v. State* decriminalized small amounts of marijuana for personal use in 1975.[142] Even though marijuana remained illegal for children, the perception that marijuana was harmful decreased, and marijuana use rates among Alaskan youths soared.

Erich Goode believes that it may not be possible to eliminate marijuana use through legal controls such as those implemented in the Netherlands. Furthermore, Goode argues against any decriminalization or legalization of drugs such as cocaine and crack. He claims that both drugs are immensely pleasurable and, therefore, are strongly reinforcing drugs that have devastating personal consequences for the user. In another line of argument, James Inciardi and Duane McBride contend that policies to decriminalize drugs are elitist and racist because they would result in increasing levels of drug dependence in low-income and minority communities: Decriminalization represents a program of social management and control that would serve to legitimize the chemical destruction of an urban generation and culture.[143]

For the first nine editions of this book, talk about legalization of drugs was pure speculation, and wide-ranging opinions were offered about the likely positive and negative ramifications of legalizing drugs. Since 2011, marijuana has been legalized in a handful of states and medical marijuana is used in about half of the states. During this era, the prevalence of marijuana use disorder has more than doubled. It is difficult to determine whether drug legalization has had much effect on delinquency, because crime and delinquency have been in free fall since their 1993–1994 peak. At this writing, it is not in the public discourse that more serious substances, such as cocaine, methamphetamine, or heroin, should be legalized or decriminalized. Time, and public opinion, will tell.

Other critics of current drug policies argue for a harm reduction approach to the problem. **Harm reduction** involves using a public health model to reduce the risks and negative consequences of illicit drug use. Such an approach is guided by the idea that it is more appropriate to *manage* drug abuse than to attempt to stop it entirely. Minimizing harm can include changing national drug policies and laws (for example, ending drug prohibition, reducing sanctions for drug violations, and changing drug paraphernalia laws), establishing needle and syringe exchange programs, expanding methadone treatment programs and establishing treatment on demand, and offering counseling programs that promote safer and more responsible drug use.[144] But if punitive measures do not work, if education, prevention, and treatment programs are only marginally effective, and if decriminalization might possibly add to the drug problem, how should society respond to adolescent drug use?

KEY TERMS

decriminalization
Relaxing of the enforcement of certain laws—for example, drug laws.

legalization
The elimination of many laws currently prohibiting drugs, but not necessarily eliminating all regulation.

harm reduction
Use of a public health model to reduce the risks and negative consequences of drug use.

WRAP UP

THINKING ABOUT JUVENILE DELINQUENCY: CONCLUSIONS

The rate of youth violence had been declining dramatically for more than a decade before it began to increase again in 2004, only to then slightly decline in 2008 and remain low through 2015. Although youth violence continues to be a serious threat, it remains a lesser problem today than it was in the 1980s and early 1990s. Some criminologists think the current lower level of youth violence is primarily because of the decline in the crack market and associated lethal violence with firearms. Other criminologists, however, believe that the decrease in violence stems from a policy of placing more police officers on the street and the "get-tough" attitude adopted by the courts, both of which have resulted in more youths being incarcerated.

The vast majority of violent youths are males, disproportionately minorities, and from urban, lower-income neighborhoods where a variety of stressors and strains predominate. Juvenile victims of violence have similar characteristics: Older, male, and minority youths are significantly more likely to be victimized than are younger, female, and white youths. Guns—especially handguns—are used in most violent incidents involving juveniles.

Is it possible to prevent youth violence? Criminologists, legislators, and policymakers differ in their opinions of the root causes of youth violence and their preferred means of responding to this violence. Proposals include getting guns out of the hands of juveniles, reducing violence in the media, strengthening families, assisting schools to teach alternatives to violence, providing treatment for offenders, and getting tough on violent offenders. None of these approaches appears terribly promising on its own, but a comprehensive strategy that combines the best features of each strategy might potentially control youth violence more effectively.

Drugs are widely used in the United States—in fact, around the world. Although most drug use is legal (e.g., over-the-counter drugs, prescription drugs, tobacco products, and alcohol), many adolescents are involved in the use of illicit drugs. Adolescent drug use is one of the most important problems facing children today. In spite of declines in reported drug use during much of the 1980s, juvenile drug use increased in the early 1990s, then began to decline, and once again has increased in recent years, at least for certain drugs.

Sociological theories suggest that a variety of root causes of adolescent drug use exist. Strain theory blames drug use on youths' failure to make it in either the legitimate world or the illegitimate world. Social learning theory argues that adolescents learn to use drugs from peers, much as they learn other forms of social behavior. According to social control theory, the weakening of social controls allows an adolescent to become involved with drugs. Subcultural socialization theories hold that involvement in a delinquent subculture in which drugs are used is likely to result in drug use by the youth.

How should society respond to adolescent drug use? A punitive, or control, response is a hallmark of the "War on Drugs" mentality, as are policies emphasizing extensive antidrug advertising campaigns and drug testing in schools. Education, prevention, and treatment responses have become very popular. Unfortunately, few school-based education and prevention programs, such as D.A.R.E., are effective, and the treatment programs that do effectively reduce drug use cannot meet the demands posed by a growing number of clients. Proposals for decriminalization or legalization of drugs raise many questions: Should all drugs be made legal and subject to regulation, or should only certain drugs be legalized? If the latter, which drugs? Would decriminalization or legalization of some drugs lead to greater use of those drugs by adolescents? Finally, attempts to change the lives and environments of children assume that drug use is merely one facet of a larger, more complex milieu of social problems facing today's youth. Poverty, unemployment, homelessness, abuse, and lack of hope create an environment in which drug use, as well as other forms of delinquency, is likely to occur.

CHAPTER SPOTLIGHT

- Youth violence escalated sharply in the last three decades of the 20th century, peaked in 1993, and then declined to historically low levels.
- Involvement in gangs, carrying and using firearms, and participation in the illicit drug trade are major factors contributing to serious youth violence (e.g., juvenile homicide).
- Alcohol and drug use are related to delinquency in multiple ways. In some cases, drugs lead directly to delinquency; in other ways, both

drugs and delinquency represent the outcomes of delinquent propensity.

- A variety of theoretical explanations for drug use have been offered, including cultural deviance, social learning, social control, and family-based theories of delinquency.

- The responses to youth violence and drug use encompass a combination of tough control-oriented measures, education, prevention, and treatment.

CRITICAL THINKING

1. Violence is pervasive on the Internet and in video games, poverty rates have not changed significantly over the years, unemployment continues to be of concern, and two-parent families are in decline. Yet the rate of youth violence has declined significantly in the United States in recent years. Is it possible that violent behavior is more easily deterred by swifter and more severe punishments after all?

2. American culture seems to be pro drug. Indeed, the large baby boom cohort is notorious for its liberal attitudes toward drug use, and large percentages of Americans have experimented with a variety of illicit drugs. Because of these attitudes and behaviors, is the United States "reaping what it has sown" regarding drugs?

3. Should violent juvenile offenders be viewed as adults, given the severity of their delinquent conduct? Use contextual information about youth violence to support your answer.

4. "Peer pressure"—particularly as it applies to adolescent drug use—has a negative connotation. This does not have to be the case, however. Can positive, strong-willed teens (e.g., scholars, athletes, students with vocational skills, or cheerleaders) also be role models for their peers and provide healthy pressure?

5. Emile Durkheim viewed punishment as highly moral. How would Durkheim assess acquiescence in the drug war? Does society have an obligation to combat drug use and vice generally?

6. How does American drug use compare to other nations around the globe? Provide support for your answer using the United Nations 2015 World Drug Report (http://www.unodc.org/wdr2015/).

CHAPTER 12

Peer Group and Gang Delinquency

People are social beings who are naturally group oriented. Adolescents are possibly more social than adults because adolescents spend proportionately more time with peers than adults do, and they are certainly attracted to social groups, including play groups, cliques, peer groups, and delinquent gangs. In thinking about the effects of peers on adolescent behavior, it is important to consider *which* type of peer effect and *which* type of delinquent is the focus. For example, virtually everyone is affected by peers, and these peer effects influence a child's beliefs, attitudes, and behaviors in powerful ways. This is the very process that Terrie Moffitt used to explain delinquency among *adolescence-limited offenders*. However, most youths are never involved in delinquent gangs. Instead, youths who have multiple risk factors for delinquency and those who are already delinquent are most susceptible to gang membership. In other words, normal peer groups influence everyday delinquencies, just as delinquent gangs influence more serious delinquencies. This chapter looks closely at the nature of group delinquency, with a special focus on the role of peers and involvement in gangs.

OBJECTIVES

- Understand the ways that peer groups influence adolescent behavior and delinquency.

- Identify characteristics of gangs and ways that gang youth differ from non-gang youth.

- Evaluate the extent of the gang problem in the United States in terms of gangs' involvement in violent and drug delinquency.

- Know the extent to which female delinquents are involved in gangs and identify the characteristics of those females.

- Explore how the juvenile justice system responds to gang delinquency in terms of suppression, injunction/abatements, interventions, and prevention.

KEY TERMS

peer group   318
co-offenders   318
homophily   319
peer rejection   321
esprit de corps   322
youth gang   322
member-based
    definition   323
motive-based
    definition   323
selection model   326
facilitation model   326

enhancement
    model   326
klikas   328
turf   328
suppression   341
injunction
    (abatement)   343
Gang Reduction
    Program   344
Homeboy
    Industries   344

Group Delinquency

For many juveniles, the most important social institution—the one they spend most of their time with and are closest to emotionally—is the family. For many others, however, it is their **peer group** (youths of similar ages and interests) that empowers them in their sense of feeling worthwhile and important. The social world of some adolescents revolves around their closest friends. They search for acceptance, status, identity, and meaning through interactions with others. As part of this quest, they often adopt the same style of dress, language, and music as their peers. Peer group activities often comprise behaviors that are symbolic of adulthood and are viewed as signs that the person is no longer a child. These behaviors often have to do with drugs, sexuality, and autonomy. Wanting to be accepted and to feel worthwhile and more grown up, many youngsters engage in delinquent activities because of peer influence.

The period of adolescence and intense peer-group activity is viewed by many as the time in a youth's life that is most likely to lead to conflict with adults, conventional institutions, and the law. As young people increasingly perceive a social (and perhaps moral) distance between themselves and adults, they look to the peer group for camaraderie, acceptance, and a sense of purpose. Without close parental supervision and guidance, youths may be highly susceptible to the pulls and pushes of their peers, which may lead to minor or even major forms of deviance and delinquency. Youths who "hang out" on their own or with others, with "no place to go" and "nothing to do," often become bored.[1]

If nothing else is absolutely known about juvenile delinquency, it is that delinquency is a group activity. In fact, "no characteristic of individuals known to criminologists is a better predictor of criminal behavior than the number of delinquent friends an individual has."[2] As early as 1931, Clifford Shaw and Henry McKay reported that 80% of Chicago juvenile delinquents were arrested with co-offenders.[3] **Co-offenders** are friends or acquaintances who participate in delinquency with another peer. Few children commit their delinquencies alone. Although early research into the causal direction of the relationship between delinquency and delinquent friends suggested that delinquents are most likely to develop delinquent friendships *after* they become involved in delinquency,

KEY TERMS

peer group
A group of youths of similar ages and interests.

co-offenders
Friends or acquaintances who participate in delinquency with another peer.

For many adolescents, drug use is a *rite of passage*—and a gateway to a delinquent career. It is normal to experiment with drugs, such as tobacco, alcohol, and marijuana, yet most people do not develop substance abuse problems from this experimentation. Why?

© BananaStock/Thinkstock/Getty.

more recent studies consistently find that associating with delinquent friends leads to increased delinquent activity. Laura Bui and her colleagues examined risk factors for delinquency among a sample of female adolescents in Osaka, Japan. They found that having delinquent (referred to as troubled) peers was the best predictor of serious delinquency, and the effect increased the likelihood of serious offending nearly six-fold. Moreover, the large effect withstood controls for risk-taking, uninhibited beliefs, school bonding, school ability, and several parenting factors.[4] As noted by Albert Reiss, "most young offenders have co-offenders in their offending and associate in other group activities with still other young offenders."[5]

Studies in the early part of the 20th century probably overestimated the amount of delinquency that could be attributed to groups. These studies relied on official data, such as the *UCR*. It is known, however, that police are more likely to arrest and refer youths to court if they congregate in packs; thus official data may present a less than fair picture. To counter this bias, Michael Hindelang turned to self-reported data to estimate group delinquency rates. He found that some offenses are more likely than others to be committed with associates. Smoking marijuana and getting drunk, for instance, are primarily social activities. A few crimes are more often engaged in alone, such as carrying a weapon.[6] Based on self-reported data from the National Youth Survey Family Study, Andy Hochstetler and his colleagues reported similar findings in relation to crimes such as assault, theft, and vandalism. Although the influence of delinquent peers was an important predictor of delinquency, the *presence* of other people was not always required for youths to engage in these forms of delinquency.[7] For example, as discussed in **Box 12.1**, the "Delinquency Around the Globe" feature, delinquency in the Netherlands also involves a great deal of group activity.

BOX 12.1

Delinquency Around the Globe

Group Delinquency in the Netherlands

For many Dutch youths, hanging around—street loitering—is a preferred leisure activity. Many youths hang out in small groups and engage in troublemaking, nuisance, or intimidating behavior. More often than not, these youths are not terribly involved in crime, but when they are, they commit their crimes in groups rather than alone.

Recent surveys in the Netherlands indicate the majority of delinquencies involve co-offenders. The delinquencies most often committed with others include vandalism, followed by drug violations, intimidation, aggression, shoplifting, bicycle theft, and other thefts. Younger adolescents are more likely to commit crimes with co-offenders than are older youths. Girls are more likely than boys to commit crimes with others, especially when it comes to such crimes as shoplifting and bicycle theft. Youths who commit crimes together are most likely to be friends, followed by classmates and neighborhood youths. If not engaging in delinquencies with friends, girls are most likely to co-offend with classmates, whereas boys tend to co-offend with neighborhood youths.

As in other nations, youth in the Netherlands also engage in delinquency with peers as a result of biosocial changes. Using data from the Social Network Analyses of Risk Behaviors in Early Adolescence (SNARE) study, Jan Dijkstra and colleagues found that the maturity gap—where youths were physically transitioning from adolescents to adults but still lagging socially and emotionally—was

responsible for discord with parents, gravitation to peers, and delinquency. Other research using the SNARE data found that Dutch youth who have lower self-control and who have peers who engage in delinquency and other externalizing behaviors are particularly likely to become delinquent and engage in group delinquency as well.

More criminally involved youth groups also hang out (loiter), so it is understandable that the public and authorities often lump all street youth groups together. Nevertheless, there are some important differences between them, according to Alfred Hakkert. Hakkert has divided local youth groups into "nuisance groups," "trouble-making groups," "criminal groups," and "gangs." All of these groups engage in a variety of similar behaviors, including hanging out in groups in doorways or sidewalks, getting in the way of passersby, playing loud music, and making impudent remarks.

Nuisance groups are the least problematic, tending to simply annoy or intimidate people, especially older people, by their mere presence or incivility in encounters on the street. *Trouble-making groups* often engage in minor delinquencies, such as bicycle theft, vandalism, shoplifting, and drug use. *Criminal youth groups*, by comparison, are likely to participate in more serious offenses, such as robberies, burglaries, auto theft, and drug dealing. Finally, *youth gangs*, which are organized expressly to engage in criminal activities, tend to be involved in extortion, serious property crimes, violent thefts, and drug dealing.

Alfred Hakkert, "Group Delinquency in the Netherlands: Some Findings from an Exploratory Study," *International Review of Law Computers & Technology* 12:453–474 (1998); Finn-Aage Esbensen and Frank Weerman, "Youth Gangs and Troublesome Youth Gangs in the United States and the Netherlands: A Cross-National Comparison," *European Journal of Criminology* 2:5–37 (2005); Martin Bouchard and Andrea Spindler, "Groups, Gangs, and Delinquency: Does Organization Matter?," *Journal of Criminal Justice* 38:921–933 (2010); Jan Kornelis Dijkstra, Tina Kretschmer, Kim Pattiselanno, Aart Franken, Zeena Harakeh, Wilma Vollebergh, and René Veenstra, "Explaining Adolescents' Delinquency and Substance Use: A Test of the Maturity Gap: The SNARE Study," *Journal of Research in Crime and Delinquency* 52:747–767 (2015); Aart Franken, Terrie Moffitt, Christian Steglich, Jan Kornelis Dijkstra, Zeena Harakeh, and Wilma Vollebergh, "The Role of Self-Control and Early Adolescents' Friendships in the Development of Externalizing Behavior: The SNARE Study." *Journal of Youth and Adolescence*, in press (2016).

Helen Garnier and Judith Stein conducted an 18-year longitudinal study of juveniles. They observed that youth usually select friends who are more like themselves, and are typically selected as friends by other youths who seem to share similar backgrounds and values, a concept known as **homophily** (which means "love of the same"; see **Box 12.2**, the "A Window on Delinquency" feature). Delinquency and adolescent drug use are typically social activities, and youths tend to participate in the same behavior as their friends. Thus, as a result of social selection and peer pressure, an adolescent's likelihood of using drugs or participating in other types of delinquency increases if his or her friends engage in this conduct. Homophily is not limited to face-to-face behavior, but is also seen online. Timothy McCuddy and Matt Vogel surveyed

583 undergraduates and found that self-reported delinquency was associated with exposure to criminal behavior in online networks. This suggests that the processes underlying social interaction also tend to characterize online interaction.[8] Studies have found that close or best friends have an especially strong influence on teen behavior. A youth is about twice as likely to engage in delinquency if a close friend is already engaged in crime, and the strongest predictor

KEY TERMS

homophily
"Love of the same"; the process by which people select to associate with those persons who are most similar to them.

BOX 12.2

A Window on Delinquency

Why Are People Group Oriented?

For centuries, criminologists have observed the tendency for people to seek out others. This tendency is especially strong during childhood and adolescence. The link between antisocial peers and misconduct is so well established and consistently replicated that Mark Warr contended that "[F]ew, if any, empirical regularities in criminology have been documented as often or over as long a period of time as the association between delinquency and delinquent friends." Associating with delinquent peers is another example of homophily ("love of the same"). Put simply, people often associate with others who are similar to them in terms of age, social class, race, appearance, belief system, and other factors. Homophily is even seen in the world of pets. A recent study found that owners of vicious, highly aggressive dogs scored higher on psychopathic personality and higher on sensation seeking than individuals who owned large dogs, small dogs, and a control group. This suggests that more antisocial people gravitate toward, select, and own pets that are similarly aggressive and antisocial.

Youths are so influenced by their peers that friendship networks are substantially more important than parents in determining human behavior. In her controversial and best-selling book *The Nurture Assumption*, Judith Rich Harris argues that the socialization effects of parents on children are overrated and that friendship and peer networks during the school years are who *really* socialize them. Behavioral scientists present compelling evidence that Harris is correct—namely, that peers are the most powerful socializing agents. For instance, behavioral

genetics research indicates that genetic and nonshared environmental factors (for example, peer groups) account for nearly 100% of variation in delinquency. Shared environmental factors, such as home environment, explain little to no variation in delinquency.

The reason that sociologically oriented criminologists have noted the universal tendency for adolescents to be group oriented and seek others like them is that homophily appears to be intrinsic to human nature. Neuroscientists are discovering the genetic bases of homophily and social factors, such as associating with delinquent peers. According to Anthony Walsh, "[T]he biological events that are taking place during the teenage years should be incorporated into theories of adolescent offending. These kinds of data may go a long way to explaining the range of adolescent behaviors that [criminologists have historically] described solely in social terms."

Scientists around the world have heeded Walsh's advice, and several research teams have linked various genetic factors to processes relating to group formation, and specifically, to delinquent peer associations. Youth with specific variants of genes, for example, have been shown to gravitate toward antisocial peers, engage in gang-related delinquency, and select environments where delinquency is likely to occur. In addition, delinquent peer associations have been shown to amplify the expression of genetic dispositions toward delinquency among adolescents. Overall, these studies are shedding new light on the dynamic ways that peers influence behavior and in understanding the group orientation of people.

Mark Warr, *Companions in Crime: The Social Aspects of Criminal Conduct* (New York: Cambridge University Press, 2002), p. 40; Anthony Walsh, "Companions in Crime: A Biosocial Perspective," *Human Nature Review* 2:169–178 (2002), p. 174; Judith Rich Harris, *The Nurture Assumption: Why Children Turn Out the Way They Do* (New York: Free Press, 1999); Alessandra Iervolino, Alison Pike, Beth Manke, David Reiss, Mavis Hetherington, and Robert Plomin, "Genetic and Environmental influences in Adolescent Peer Socialization: Evidence from Two Genetically Sensitive Designs," *Child Development* 73:162–174 (2002); H. Harrington Cleveland, Richard Wiebe, and David Rowe, "Sources of Exposure to Smoking and Drinking Friends among Adolescents: A Behavioral–Genetic Evaluation," *Journal of Genetic Psychology* 166:153–169 (2005); Laurie Ragatz, William Fremouw, Tracy Thomas, and Katrina McCoy, "Vicious Dogs: The Antisocial Behaviors and Psychological Characteristics of Owners," *Journal of Forensic Sciences* 54:699–703 (2009); Frank Vitaro, Mara Brendgen, and Eric Lacourse, "Peers and Delinquency: A Genetically Informed Developmentally Sensitive Perspective," pages 221–236 in Julien Morizot and Lila Kazemian (eds.), *The Development of Criminal and Antisocial Behavior: Theory, Research and Practical Applications* (New York: Springer, 2015); Jamie Vaske, "The Integration of Biological and Genetic Factors into Social Learning Theory," pages 125–142 in Kevin Beaver, J. C. Barnes, and Brian Boutwell (eds.), *The Nurture Versus Biosocial Debate in Criminology: On the Origins of Criminal Behavior and Criminality* (Thousand Oaks, CA: Sage, 2015).

of adolescent drug use is the extent of drug use by the youth's best friend.

There is also the issue of popularity. Recall that, other than abstainers, it is normative for adolescents to engage in some form of delinquent behavior, and indeed, some commit delinquency or behave in ways where they *seem* to be delinquent in order to enhance their social standing. Owen Gallupe and his colleagues examined the delinquency–social status link using data from the National Longitudinal Study of Adolescent

to Adult Health. They found that youth who seem to have delinquency potential because they have peers who engage in delinquency are more popular and benefit from higher social status. However, they also found that youth who actually engage in delinquent acts suffer from it and have lower social status. In other words, adolescents are socially "turned off" by those who commit delinquency, but "turned on" by the prospect that someone could commit delinquency because of their friendship networks.[9]

How Do Delinquent Groups Form?

What is the origin of delinquent peer groups? Children do not generally begin their school careers belonging to or hoping to become part of a delinquent peer group. Instead, these groups often come together as part of a process of specific individuals' own antisocial development. The first step of this process typically involves **peer rejection**—that is, the rejection of a child perceived to be antisocial by conventional peers. Although children can be rejected by their peers for a variety of reasons, research has consistently found that children who are rejected are more aggressive, less sociable, less cognitively skilled, and more withdrawn than other children. However, aggressive behavior is the dominant predictor of a youth being rejected by his or her peers.[10]

Rejected children are shunned and many times ridiculed by conventional peers because of their poor social and school skills; they are also feared by conventional peers for their aggressive behaviors. This practice often leads to feelings of loneliness, isolation, and anger among rejected children. In part because of the concept of homophily—where people select to associate with those who are most similar to them—and in part because of their lack of other options, rejected children befriend other rejected children. Research has shown the tendency for aggressive children to associate with other aggressive peers as early as the preschool years. In addition, peer rejection has been found to predict involvement with antisocial peers even after controlling for the youth's personality and other traits.

Even at the preschool ages, there are different trajectories of peer victimization and rejection already in place. Children who are exposed to high levels of harsh, inconsistent, and erratic parenting and who are highly aggressive are particularly at risk to be targeted by their peers.[11]

The process of peer rejection and the selection of similarly rejected (and aggressive) children as associates provide the basis for delinquent groups. Once peer-rejected children are enmeshed in a social network with similarly aggressive and poorly skilled children, peer rejection stops. This occurs because they are no longer judged by conventional peers. Instead, these children become part of a clique that exists outside of the mainstream of conventional peers. The short-term and long-term consequences of this isolation are severe. As young as kindergarten and the first grades of elementary school, peer-rejected children who associate with aggressive peers are more likely to lie, steal, run away from home, and have conduct problems. These children are also at increased risk of joining delinquent gangs, behaving in violent ways, and being otherwise delinquent.

Although the study of delinquent group formation has traditionally focused on social dynamics and social interaction, there are more ingredients at hand. Biosocial research in recent years has articulated how genetic factors are associated with the various social processes that give rise to group formation, peer effects, and delinquency. Tina Kretschmer and her colleagues conducted a study using data from 3081 adolescents from the Avon Longitudinal Study of Parents and Children and found that a specific variant of the BDNF gene (brain-derived neurotrophic factor) was associated with affiliation with aggressive peers at age 10 and the youth's own increased aggression at age 15. For youth who had other variants of the gene, there was not an association between peer aggression and their own aggression. A study using data from the Dutch Tracking Adolescents' Individual Lives Survey (TRAILS) found that the dopamine D4 receptor gene moderated the effects of peer victimization and social well-being on delinquency. However, only carriers of the 4-repeat variant of the gene displayed these effects. Eric Connolly and Kevin Beaver analyzed data from the National Longitudinal Survey of Youth 1997 to examine the genetic and environmental underpinnings of gang involvement and carrying a handgun. They found that genetic factors explained 77% of the variance in gang membership, 27% of the variance in carrying a handgun, and 66% of the covariance between gang membership and handgun carrying. Taken together, it is clear that genetic factors moderate social experiences in the production of delinquent peer groups.[12]

To the extent that peers and their behaviors can have serious negative influence on adolescents, what may be done to reduce their impact? Which policies or practical recommendations to parents might prevent peer-related delinquency? For many decades, the policy implications of Edwin Sutherland's *theory of differential association* led parents and schools to create opportunities for children to spend greater amounts of time in supervised, productive activities. After-school, weekend, and summer recreational programs involving youth in such activities as music, sports, art, scouts, computers, and church have been regarded as the best mechanisms for preventing children from spending time hanging out with "bad kids" or the "wrong crowd." Parents have also been encouraged to provide more "quality" or family time with their children.

Although some critics of this policy argue that only weak evidence supports the hypothesis that teen involvement in after-school programs or jobs reduces youths' likelihood of becoming delinquent, other studies provide positive support for the notion

KEY TERMS

peer rejection
The rejection of a child perceived to be antisocial by conventional peers.

that youths who spend more time with their families are less likely to become delinquent. Mark Warr, for example, reports that, in his research, children who spent a great deal of time with their families every week "had low rates of delinquency *even when they had delinquent friends*."[13] In addition, youths who report having a close relationship with their parents are less likely to have any delinquent friends.

Of course, youth cannot be totally isolated from friendships, and it is difficult—if not impossible—for parents to identify or separate out the "good" children from the "bad" ones. Consequently, parents should closely monitor their children's associations, establish and maintain contact with the parents of their children's friends, and work to develop trust and open, frequent communication with their children.

Gangs and Gang Delinquency

For people working in the juvenile justice system and for criminologists, concerns about juvenile delinquency have historically centered more on gangs than on peer groups. Even so, the notion of "gang" itself has been poorly understood, defined, and measured. In reality, how gangs are defined has significant implications for police, policymakers, and criminologists who study gangs. Differences in how gangs are defined may lead to inaccurate estimates of the extent of the problem, misunderstanding of the primary activities of gang members, and incorrect identification of the demographic composition of gangs.[14] This section reviews the different ways of defining gangs and the diversity of characteristics associated with gangs and gang members.

Problems in Defining Gangs

In the early 20th century, the term "gang" was associated with groups in socially disorganized and deteriorated inner-city neighborhoods: It was applied to juveniles who engaged in a variety of delinquencies ranging from truancy, street brawls, and beer running to race riots, robberies, and other serious crimes. Frederic Thrasher, in his 1927 study of 1313 delinquent gangs in Chicago, reported that although no two gangs were exactly alike, delinquent gangs possessed a number of qualities that set them apart from other social groups. These qualities include meeting face to face, milling about, going places as a group, experiencing conflict with other gangs and adults, and planning of activities. Such collective behavior produces gang traditions, unreflective internal organizational structure, *esprit de corps* (a sense of solidarity and awareness of being a distinct group), and claims to a local territory.

This image of gangs stressed youth groups as being localized and territory based, with social organization and traditions and with group awareness and morale fostered through conflict with authorities and other gangs. Although Thrasher's work set the tone for much of the subsequent writing on gangs for many decades, it is important to note that he did not include law-violating behavior in his definition of a gang delinquent. For Thrasher, delinquent gangs were simply one type of youth group.[15]

By the 1950s, the image of the gang increasingly focused on large groups of urban boys engaged primarily in violent conflict, fighting one another in battles or "rumbles" over territory or status, much like the Sharks and the Jets in *West Side Story*. The gang, from this perspective, suggests a slightly broader definition:

[The gang is] a friendship group of adolescents who share common interests, with a more or less clearly defined territory, in which most of the members live. They are committed to defending one another, the territory, and the gang name in the status-setting fights that occur in school and on the streets.[16]

By the 1980s, police, politicians, and criminologists began to emphasize the organization and illegal activities of gangs. Walter Miller defined a **youth gang** as follows:

[A] self-forming association of peers, bound together by mutual interests, with identifiable leadership, well-developed lines of authority, and other organizational features, who act in concert to achieve a specific purpose or purposes which generally include the conduct of illegal activity and control over a particular territory, facility, or type of enterprise.[17]

But the characteristics in Miller's definition do not fit all youth groups identified as gangs by either the police or criminologists. Some groups are involved in illegal activities; some are not. Some claim territory; others do not. Some use and/or sell drugs; many do not. Some engage in drive-by shootings; most do not. And some are highly organized with identifiable leadership, whereas others are not.[18]

Such variations have not prevented state legislatures and police agencies from developing very narrow and specific definitions of gangs. For example, the *Street Terrorism Enforcement and Prevention Act* (STEP) of the California penal code defines the "criminal street gang" as follows:

KEY TERMS

esprit de corps
A sense of solidarity and awareness of being a distinct group.

youth gang
A group of youths who are willing to use deadly violence to claim and protect territory, to attack rival gangs, or to engage in criminal activity.

[A]ny ongoing organization, association, or group of three or more persons, whether formal or informal, having as one of its primary activities the commission of one or more of the criminal acts enumerated in paragraphs (1) to (8), inclusive, of subdivision (e), which has a common name or common identifying sign or symbol, whose members individually or collectively engage in or have engaged in a pattern of criminal gang activity.[19]

The criminal acts specifically included in the code include aggravated assault, robbery, homicide or manslaughter, drug trafficking, arson, victim or witness intimidation, and shooting into an inhabited dwelling. This definition gives police and prosecutors a basis for arresting any youth who actively participates in a criminal street gang, regardless of whether the individual holds formal membership in the gang, so long as the youth knows that the gang is involved in illegal activities and willfully promotes, furthers, or assists in any felonious criminal conduct by members of that gang.

Unlike California, most states do not have legislatively determined definitions of juvenile gangs. Consequently, law enforcement agencies (and criminologists) generally select their own criteria for defining a gang—which inevitably means there is a lack of consensus on just what exactly, qualifies as a "gang." The National Youth Gang Survey included the following instruction in its survey to guide law enforcement agencies. For the purposes of the survey, a "youth gang" was defined this way:

A group of youths or young adults in your jurisdiction that you or other responsible persons in your agency or community are willing to identify or classify as a "gang." DO NOT include motorcycle gangs, hate or ideology groups, prison gangs, or other exclusively adult gangs.[20]

In addition, many police agencies have developed definitions of gang members reflecting the need to document youths identified as being involved in gangs. These definitions typically distinguish between *associate* or *"wanna be," member,* or *hardcore member.* Associate or "wanna be" members are peripheral or fringe members; while they associate with full-fledged members, they may not be recognized by others as a regular member of the gang. Members form the core of the gang and are likely to have frequent contact with one another and to regularly engage in gang activities. Hardcore members are viewed by police as the most dangerous and most likely to be involved in serious, violent gang activity.

As Charles Katz notes, some law enforcement agencies require that at least one of the following characteristics must be documented to identify an individual as a gang member.

- Wears gang colors and uses gang hand signals
- Has gang tattoos
- Sprays gang graffiti
- Arrested with known gang members
- Past or current delinquency as a gang member
- High-level drug dealing or other gang-related felonies
- Involved in gang retaliations or drive-by shootings
- Identified as gang member by reliable informant
- Self identifies as a gang member

With all of these definitions, how many gang members are there? David Pyrooz and Gary Sweeten analyzed data from the National Longitudinal Survey of Youth 1997 and found there were 7335 self-reported gang members in the data. From these data, they produced national estimates of the prevalence of gang members. Pyrooz and Sweeten estimate there are 1,059,000 gang youth in the United States, which is a prevalence of 2% of all American youth. The prevalence of gang membership peaks at age 14 years at 5%. Annually, there is a 36% turnover in gang membership as about 401,000 youth join gangs while approximately 378,000 youth exit gangs.[21]

Similar to the problems of defining a gang and gang member is the problem of defining "gang-related" activity. The spread of gang violence has complicated the problem of determining those activities that are truly gang related. Malcolm Klein and Cheryl Maxson report that different urban police and sheriffs' departments use different definitions of what constitutes a gang-related crime. More than half of the law enforcement agencies responding to a recent National Youth Gang Survey indicated that they use a **member-based definition**, consisting of a crime in which a gang member or members are either the perpetrators or victims of the crime, regardless of the motive. Nearly one-third use a **motive-based definition**, consisting of a crime committed by a gang member or members in which the underlying reason is to further the interests and activities of the gang. Approximately 11% of the agents said they use some other definition.

A related problem centers on defining whether a youth has left a gang or desisted from gang involvement. Most gang members are rather loosely affiliated with the gang, and there is often little in the way of formal organization. Dena Carson and her colleagues

KEY TERMS

member-based definition
Defining a crime as "gang related" when a gang member or members are either the perpetrators or the victims, regardless of the motive.

motive-based definition
Defining a crime as "gang related" when it is committed by a gang member or members, and the underlying reason for the crime is to further the interests and activities of the gang.

examined three distinct definitions or operationalizations of gang desistance to examine the motivations, methods, and consequences of leaving gang life. They found there was a nearly 39% overlap in three distinct ways to define leaving a gang. Moreover, youth desisted from gangs for rather mundane reasons, such as they felt like doing so, moved, made new friends, just left, or got into legal trouble. Between 80 and 90% of youth were not violently assaulted by their own gang or another gang after leaving.[22]

Are Gang Members More Delinquent Than Non-Gang Youth?

When gang membership is a known factor in group offending, clear differences in delinquency rates between gang and non-gang members have been found (see **Box 12.3**, the "A Window on Delinquency" feature). Prevalence rates of delinquency and individual offending are greater for both male and female gang

BOX 12.3

A Window on Delinquency

Comparing Gang and Non-Gang Youths

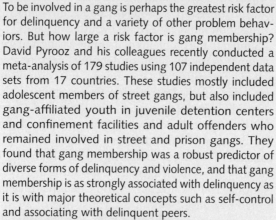

To be involved in a gang is perhaps the greatest risk factor for delinquency and a variety of other problem behaviors. But how large a risk factor is gang membership? David Pyrooz and his colleagues recently conducted a meta-analysis of 179 studies using 107 independent data sets from 17 countries. These studies mostly included adolescent members of street gangs, but also included gang-affiliated youth in juvenile detention centers and confinement facilities and adult offenders who remained involved in street and prison gangs. They found that gang membership was a robust predictor of diverse forms of delinquency and violence, and that gang membership is as strongly associated with delinquency as it is with major theoretical concepts such as self-control and associating with delinquent peers.

Children and adolescents with antisocial traits and behaviors tend to gravitate toward gangs, and once they do, their behavioral problems worsen. Youth in gangs were characterized as the most aggressive, most oppositional, most hyperactive, and least helpful based on data from the Montreal Longitudinal-Experimental Study. In a study of serious delinquents from the Pathways to Desistance study, Julia Dmitrieva and her colleagues found that gang youth had a variety of psychological, emotional, cognitive, and behavioral deficits compared to non-gang youth. In addition, once youth joined gangs, their antisocial traits worsened and their scores on a psychopathic personality measure increased the longer they were in the gang. In a study of 17,366 high school students, gang youth were shown to have significantly more risk factors than non-gang youth at the individual level, in the peer context, in the school context, and in the neighborhood context. The cumulative effect of these risk factors helps to explain

the significantly greater involvement in delinquency and violence among gang youth.

George Knox and other researchers from the National Gang Crime Research Center completed one of the largest, most comprehensive studies of gangs in the United States. Knox and his colleagues collected data in 17 states from 85 different correctional facilities (e.g., prisons, boot camps, juvenile institutions) on a national sample of 10,166 confined offenders, of whom 4140 were self-reported gang members.

Compared to youths who were not in gangs, gang members were significantly *more likely* to have the following characteristics:

- Have a parent who had served time in prison
- Have psychopathic personality traits
- Have been bullies in school
- Have sold narcotics, especially crack cocaine
- Have fired a gun at a police officer
- Have been shot, stabbed, or seriously assaulted
- Have engaged in violent, weapons-related, and drug misconduct while incarcerated

Gang members were significantly *less likely* to have these characteristics:

- Finish high school or have a GED
- Attend church
- Avoid situations involving the risk of arrest or personal injury
- Report that the juvenile or criminal justice system deterred them
- Report that they had adequate parental supervision as a child
- Believe in conventional morality

David Pyrooz, Jillian Turanovic, Scott Decker, and Jun Wu, "Taking Stock of the Relationship between Gang Membership and Offending: A Meta-Analysis," *Criminal Justice and Behavior* 43:365–397 (2016); Nathalie Fontaine, Mara Brendgen, Frank Vitaro, and Richard Tremblay, "Compensatory and Protective Factors against Violent Delinquency in Late Adolescence: Results from the Montreal Longitudinal and Experimental Study," *Journal of Criminal Justice*, 45:54–62 (2016); Julia Dmitrieva, Lauren Gibson, Laurence Steinberg, Alex Piquero, and Jeffrey Fagan, "Predictors and Consequences of Gang Membership: Comparing Gang Members, Gang Leaders, and Non-Gang-Affiliated Adjudicated Youth," *Journal of Research on Adolescence* 24:220–234 (2014); Gabriel Merrin, Jun Sung Hong, and Dorothy Espelage, "Are the Risk and Protective Factors Similar for Gang-Involved, Pressured-to-Join, and Non-Gang-Involved Youth? A Social-Ecological Analysis," *American Journal of Orthopsychiatry* 85:522–525 (2015); George Knox et al., *The Facts about Gang Life in America Today: A National Study of Over 4,000 Gang Members* (Peotone, IL: National Gang Crime Research Center, 2004).

members than for their non-gang counterparts.[23] Other researchers report that although gang members *do not* appear to have higher rates of delinquency or drug use *before* entering the gang, once they are members their rates become significantly greater than those found among non-gang youths.[24] Sara Battin and her colleagues report that gang members have higher rates of offending compared to non-gang adolescents and that belonging to a gang predicts court-reported and self-reported delinquency above and beyond the contribution of having delinquent peers and above and beyond the rate of prior delinquency. Richard Moule and his associates study of 621 youth selected from five cities found that gang members were twice as likely as non-gang youth to not only commit violent delinquency, but also to be violently victimized. In addition, these effects withstood controls for self-control, adherence to the street code, and routine activities.[25]

The opposite side of delinquency is, of course, victimization. Research indicates that gang members are much more likely to be victimized than other, non-gang youths. For instance, Dana Peterson and her colleagues explored the gang-victimization relationship among a longitudinal study of 3500 students and a cross-sectional study of 5935 students. While controlling for a variety of other social characteristics that have been shown to be correlates of victimization, these investigators found that youths who had ever been in a gang were more likely to be the victim of a serious violent crime. In addition, the increased risk of victimization among gang youths existed before, during, and after their gang involvement.[26]

In another study, using data from several thousand eighth graders selected from 11 U.S. cities, Terrance Taylor and his colleagues found that adolescents who were involved in gangs were more likely to be violently victimized during the previous year and also experienced more total victimizations than youths not involved with gangs. For instance, 70% of gang youths reported being the victims of assault, aggravated assault, or robbery. In contrast, 46% of non-gang youths reported these types of victimization, but almost all of their violence was limited to simple assaults. In other words, the more serious forms of violent victimization—aggravated assaults and robberies—were more characteristic of gang youths.[27]

In part, gang youths face a higher likelihood of being victimized because they associate and interact with other gang youths, generally engage in risky lifestyles, and put themselves in risky settings that enable delinquency and victimization. For instance, Jun Wu and David Pyrooz studied a large sample of American adolescents and found that gang members had much higher victimization than non-gang youth, and the increased victimization was due almost entirely to their greater involvement in delinquency. In addition, entering gang life significantly increased a host of

risk factors that contribute to delinquency, including risk taking, temper, self-centeredness, negative peer commitment, neutralization of violence, aggressive conflict resolution, unstructured socializing, and delinquency. Positive features, such as empathy and association with prosocial peers were reduced upon joining a gang. In his review of the links between youth gangs and violent victimization, Taylor concluded that gangs are often havens for violence in terms of both violent perpetration and victimization. And although many youths join gangs for protection or a desire for safety, violent victimization increases once they join these groups. For both boys and girls, the greatest amount of violent victimization occurs in the year following their entry into the gang.[28]

The Rochester (New York) Youth Development Study examined how much delinquency in the community could be attributed to gang members compared to non-gang youths. Approximately 30% of the youths in this study reported being members of a street gang at some time before the end of high school. Those youths who belonged to gangs, however, accounted for the bulk of delinquent acts, especially the more serious crimes. Gang members were responsible for 86% of the serious delinquent acts, 69% of the violent delinquent acts, and 70% of the drug sales. The researchers concluded that involvement in gangs substantially increases the likelihood of involvement in delinquency, particularly serious delinquency.[29]

Very similar patterns have been identified among gang youths in other major cities. In Seattle, for example, gang members made up 15% of a large sample of adolescents, but accounted for 85% of the total robberies carried out by members of the sample. Similarly, in Denver, gang members constituted 14% of a sample but accounted for 79% of all serious, violent adolescent offenses. In Montreal, gang members appeared in juvenile and criminal courts between 400 and 700% more frequently than non-gang youths.[30]

The disproportionately violent toll of gang delinquency has also been noticed in medical settings. For instance, over a 29-month period, gang members accounted for one-third of the gunshot injuries treated in hospitals in Los Angeles County. During the peak of gang violence in the early 1990s, more than 1500 people were injured in drive-by shootings in Los Angeles (about 4 persons per day), and more than 70% of the injured individuals were gang members.[31]

A slightly cautionary note about the findings just reported is suggested by Tom Winfree and his associates. They conclude that having a pro-gang attitude and a predisposition toward violence, especially group-context violence, may be a more important delinquency factor among youths than actual gang membership. In Winfree and his colleagues' work, no difference was found between gang and non-gang youths in terms of theft crimes, other property crimes, and even drug

crimes, although gang members were more likely to be involved in violent offenses.[32]

The research by Winfree and his colleagues is the exception, however, not the rule. Most research shows that gang involved adolescents are at significantly greater risk for delinquency than non-gang youth even before joining the gang. For instance, a recent study of more than 3500 adolescents living in Canada found that youths with preexisting psychopathic tendencies were particularly vulnerable to gang activity even among youths living in disadvantaged neighborhoods.[33]

Joining and Getting Out of Gangs

Although delinquent peer groups and gangs exist in virtually all types of communities in the United States, the most violent and serious gang threats are concentrated in the most impoverished neighborhood of major cities. This relationship points out a sobering fact: Socioeconomic disadvantage and family problems form the root conditions that lead adolescents to join gangs. Some youths grow up in families in which older brothers, sisters, fathers, and sometimes grandfathers are or were gang members; in these families, entry into gang life is essentially just a part of adolescent socialization. From a very young age, it is expected that they will eventually become a gang member. Rachel Gordon and her colleagues report that the same risk factors that propel youths into serious delinquent careers, such as poverty, school failures, and family dysfunction, also precede gang membership. David Eitle and his colleagues have noted that racial minority status, family financial problems, and the cumulative exposure to stressful life events during childhood also contribute to gang membership.[34]

Many of the risk factors that have been identified as correlates of delinquency are also forerunners of gang

membership. Researchers have distinguished seven general types of risk factors for gang membership:

1. *Area characteristics* include community and neighborhood measures of poverty, arrest rates, and disorganization.
2. *Family characteristics* include race, ethnicity, family structure, and family educational attainment.
3. *Parent–child relations* include the degree of attachment, involvement, and commitment between parents and children, parenting measures, abuse, neglect, and maltreatment.
4. *School factors* include the child's attachment and commitment to school, college aspirations, and test scores.
5. *Peer relationships* include delinquent peers, early dating, and sexual activity.
6. *Individual characteristics* include negative life events, psychiatric diagnoses, self-esteem, and delinquent beliefs.
7. *Prior delinquency* includes onset of delinquency, prior drug use, prior violence, and prior delinquency.

Several criminologists have found that gang members in Canada, Norway, Seattle, Rochester, and in numerous other cities often have most of these risk factors *before* their initiation into gang life. The more risk factors that an adolescent has, the greater the likelihood that he or she will become involved in a gang.[35]

Terence Thornberry, Marvin Krohn, and their colleagues described three general ways that youths join street gangs. The first is a "kind of person" model known as the **selection model**, which argues that adolescents with a strong propensity for delinquency seek out gangs. These youths are already involved in antisocial behavior and will commit crimes whether in a gang or acting alone. The **facilitation model** is a "kind of group" model; it suggests that the normative structure of the gang, working in tandem with group processes and dynamics, increases delinquency among youth. According to the facilitation model, a youth's delinquency will increase during periods of gang membership, but will be lower both before and after that period. The third model, known as the **enhancement model**, combines elements of the selection and facilitation models. According to the enhancement model, adolescents who are already involved in delinquency are most apt to join a gang (selection) but, after joining, their delinquency is likely to increase significantly (facilitation).[36] Today, the selection, facilitation, and enhancement models are the primary way that criminologists conceptualize gang entry.

Martin Sanchez Jankowski has identified six reasons for joining a gang:[37]

1. *Material incentives:* Gang membership increases the likelihood of making money.
2. *Recreation:* Gangs provide entertainment and a chance to meet girls.
3. *Refuge or camouflage:* The gang offers anonymity.

KEY TERMS

selection model
A "kind of person" explanation of gang initiation that argues adolescents with a strong propensity for delinquency seek out gangs.

facilitation model
A "kind of group" explanation that suggests the normative structure of a gang, along with group processes and dynamics, increase delinquency among youth.

enhancement model
The idea that adolescents who are already involved in delinquency are most apt to join a gang (selection) but, after joining, their delinquency is likely to increase significantly (facilitation).

4. *Physical protection:* Gangs provide personal protection from predatory elements, including other gangs, in high-crime neighborhoods.
5. *A time to resist:* The gang provides opportunities to resist living a life similar to that of one's parents.
6. *Commitment to community:* Gang membership provides the opportunity to demonstrate a form of local patriotism and dedication to protecting the neighborhood. Making money also appears to be related to gaining the social "respect" that having money produces. Whether a youth first joins a gang to gain respect or to make money, the two goals often quickly become intertwined with each other.

Motivations for joining gangs sometimes vary by sex. Boys are more likely to join gangs for excitement, to have a territory of their own, for protection, for money, and for a sense of belonging. Girls, by contrast, tend to join gangs for social or associational reasons—for example, because family members or friends were involved in gangs, to enhance their reputation, and for protection. There are also important commonalities between boys and girls who join gangs. For instance, Jody Miller, Jenna St. Cyr, and Scott Decker found that family and neighborhood problems push both girls and boys into gangs.[38]

Many youths remain in the gang into early or even middle adulthood, although most drift in and out of gangs over the years. Some join other organizations, such as social clubs or organized crime groups; some go to prison; some die from gang violence or drug use; and others get jobs, get married, have children, and find the demands of gang membership incompatible with the new demands of family and job. Although gang mythology maintains the belief that once a youth joins a gang, he or she is in for life, the reality is quite different.

Leaving a gang may be risky, especially for youths who have special knowledge of serious crimes committed by gang members. It is not uncommon after a member announces his or her decision to leave the gang that a "beating out" ceremony occurs. Leaving the gang carries two other risks: The police and courts may continue to treat the youth as a gang member, and rival gangs may not be aware the youth quit the gang. In these instances, continued gang association might provide protection from rival gangs. However, most youths ultimately age out of gangs, and many peripheral and fringe members quit gangs without being required to give a reason for their decisions. For example, David Pyrooz and Scott Decker found that only 20% of gang members are met with hostility or violence when they decide to leave the gang. The other 80% are simply permitted to disengage from it. When the motives for wanting to leave the gang are external life circumstances, gang members are surprisingly understanding. In many ways, it is not surprising that joining and getting out of gangs is relatively easy and unceremonious. Andrea Spindler and Martin Bouchard studied youth gangs in Canada and found that less than 50% of gangs even had a gang name. In addition, less than half had specified leadership, hierarchy, a gang meeting place, or any rules. With so little organization, gang youth are usually free to come and go.[39]

Characteristics of Gangs

When Walter Miller asked police, juvenile officers, social workers, and other experts to define gangs, they agreed that gangs had the following traits: organization, leadership, turf, cohesiveness, and purpose.[40] But do all gangs exhibit these characteristics and, if so, do they possess them to the same degree? Decades of research have produced mixed answers to these questions.

Organization

The organizational structures of gangs have varied widely over time, from city to city, and even within cities. An example of a highly organized gang was the *Vice Lords* in Chicago in the 1960s.

Pastor Kenneth Hammond of Durham, North Carolina, helps relocate adolescents who want out of gangs. As a social institution, has the church been overlooked as an insulator against gang delinquency?

The most important element in the new organizational scheme was the creation of an administrative body called the "board" to deal with matters affecting the entire Vice Lord Nation. Further, regular weekly meetings were instituted with representatives from all the subgroups present. Finally, membership cards were printed with the Vice Lords' insignia—a top hat, cane, and white gloves.[41]

The Vice Lords, however, may be atypical. James Short suggests that most gangs fall somewhere in the middle between crowds and mobs on the one hand and ordinary organizations on the other.[42]

Gene Muehlbauer and Laura Dodder's analysis of a suburban gang, *The Losers*, noted that its structure centered on a core group of approximately 10 to 12 members. These members formed the nucleus of the gang, and all other members were defined in relationship to this core. Alternatively, some gangs become so large they are unable to function effectively as a total unit; consequently, they divide into groupings called "cliques."[43]

In their study of Hispanic gangs in California, Robert Jackson and Wesley McBride report that cliques are based primarily on age but sometimes on a specialty. In some gangs, for instance, one clique specializes in violence and most of the "shooters" (gunmen) in the gang belong to that clique. Often, such cliques have a number of members who are not only capable of violence but actually seek it out.[44] Joan Moore has also noted age grading in Hispanic youth gangs in barrios in Los Angeles, El Paso, and San Antonio. The age cohorts, or *klikas*, appear to form every 2 years or so and become "salient lifelong membership and reference groups for some, but not all, members of the gang."[45]

Julie Amato and Dewey Cornell have reported that the different names youths use to describe gangs, such as "crew," "clique," "posse," or "mob," influence the reasoning they provide for joining the group and the type of delinquency in which they engage. In their study, students involved in groups referred to as "gangs" had the highest delinquency rates. However, students also engaged in delinquency, albeit at lower levels, when involved in other groups, such as "crews." Additionally, youths often become involved in groups such as crews or cliques for social reasons— that is, to create new friendships. Conversely, gang involvement is often expressly intended to engage in delinquency.[46]

Leadership

Many gangs have clearly established leaders, although, like any organizational structure, the form of leadership has varied over time and location. For example, in the militaristic, or Mafia-style, model of gang leadership, the top authority position "is analogous to that of the highest ranking Officer in a military unit; below him are lieutenants, sub-lieutenants, and so on. Decisions originating in higher echelons are transmitted through the ranks by a chain-of-command system."[47]

In contrast, charismatic leaders rule by force of their personalities. This type of leader is usually older, stronger, and revered by the gang's members. In the violent gangs studied by Lewis Yablonsky, leaders seemed to be self-appointed and often emotionally unstable. They would occasionally manipulate other gang members into aggressive or violent actions just to satisfy their own emotional needs. By a combination of charisma and intimidation, the leaders of violent gangs tended to be more permanent in their positions, even as turnover among the general membership of the gang remained high.[48] Leadership varied greatly among the gangs John Hagedorn studied in Milwaukee. In most cases, the youth's "reputation or ability to fight was the main criterion for a leader . . . [while in other cases] someone was the leader because they knew most about gangs. . . . Some even disputed there ever was a leader."[49] In gangs whose leaders were identified, "titles" were rarely used.

Turf

Turf or territoriality involves two components: identification and control. Many urban gangs identify with particular neighborhoods, parks, housing projects, or schools. At one time, crossing turf boundaries and entering another gang's territory, which was often clearly marked by graffiti, meant taking serious risks. However, automobiles have increased the mobility of teenagers, and slum districts have been sliced up by highways and urban renewal, blurring the old dividing lines. Identification with specific turf has been drastically altered for many gang members, largely because of frequent relocation of gang members' family residences.[50] Furthermore, according to Sanchez Jankowski "gangs operate in a given area because that location is the only place they are strong enough to feel secure and in control, not because that particular territory is fundamental to their self-definition."[51]

Cohesiveness

Are gangs very close, tight-knit organizations with loyal members bound to one another by mutual friendship and common interests? Early scholars thought so. Thrasher, for instance, depicted gangs as filled with happy-go-lucky youngsters, with the gang performing positive functions such as providing status for members. Modern criminologists

KEY TERMS

klikas
Age cohorts within Hispanic gangs.

turf
A gang's sense of territoriality.

sometimes take an equally romantic view of these groups' cohesiveness. Others disagree. Malcolm Klein, for example, says that the gang members he observed were "dissatisfied, deprived, and making the best of an essentially unhappy situation."[52] Klein adds that there are good reasons why gangs are not cohesive: The gang has few, if any, group goals; the membership is constantly in a state of flux, turning over rapidly; and group norms are practically nonexistent. James Short and Fred Strodtbeck say that gang members often fail at school, on the job, and elsewhere. These failures, along with other social disabilities, make gang members anxious and insecure about their status, and such insecurities are heightened by constant challenges and insults by other gang members.[53] Contemporary criminologists similarly note that most gangs are, at best, loosely organized and are most cohesive when committing delinquency. In short, while there is some evidence of organizational features to gangs, most studies suggest little formal organization to gang life. That there is little structure and influence to gangs is understandable and even expected when the deficits of gang members are considered. Gang members lack the wherewithal and overall functioning to maintain formal gang involvement in many respects because of the deficits that similarly impair their home, school, and work functioning.[54]

Purpose

Delinquent gangs have been often thought to exist for the purpose of committing offenses. Purpose is a state of mind that is difficult for gang researchers to measure. It is easier to study behavior, such as the extent to which gangs commit crime. Jacqueline Schneider's study of gangs in Columbus, Ohio, found that gangs often specialize in certain offenses. By looking at the arrest offense patterns of gang leaders, she discovered that gangs tend to operate within particular crime niches. For instance, members of the Crips gang were primarily involved in violent offenses, whereas the Freeze Crew accounted for a disproportionate number of property crimes.[55]

Researchers have found that gang members spend most of their time on pursuits other than crime—mostly just whiling away their time. For many, this involves little more than "partying and hanging out." Geoffrey Hunt and his colleagues' study of ethnic youth gangs in Northern California also found that "hanging around," "kicking back" and especially drinking were "commonplace and integral part[s] of everyday life among gang members." Fighting was seen as an activity more typical of one stage in the development of the gang. Constant fighting with other gangs happened early and helped structure the gang. As gang members grew older, however, their inclination was to decrease the fighting and increase the partying.[56]

The Contemporary Gang Problem

In the 1970s, few states reported gang problems and those with the largest number of gang-problem cities were California, Florida, Illinois, and Texas. Overwhelmingly, gangs were concentrated in the largest cities, such as Chicago, Houston, Los Angeles, and Miami. More recently, however, all 50 states, Washington, DC, and over 3000 cities, towns, villages, and counties have indicated they are experiencing some form of gang problem.[57]

Estimating the number of gang members is problematic, with the tally depending on how criminologists and law enforcement define gangs. As indicated earlier in this chapter, David Pyrooz and Gary Sweeten estimate there are 1,059,000 gang youth in the United States, which is a prevalence of 2% of American youth. The prevalence of gang membership peaks at age 14 years at 5%. Annually, there is a 36% turnover in gang membership each year with youth joining and leaving gangs. Given that limitation, the National Youth Gang Survey of law enforcement agencies across the country reported that there were approximately 850,000 gang members in the United States in 2012, which are the most recent available data. These 850,000 gang members belonged to 30,700 gangs that are active in more than 3100 jurisdictions. Although gangs are found in all types of communities, approximately 85% of all gang members lived in larger cities and suburban counties. According to the most recent National Youth Gang Survey:[58]

- 15% of rural counties reported gang problems.
- 25% of smaller cities reported gang problems.
- 50% of suburban counties reported gang problems.
- 85% of large cities reported gang problems.

In some ways, gangs reflect the current trends found within the broader American society. Like the youth culture, which emphasizes immediate gratification and entertainment via cell phones; Instagram, Snapchat, and other social networking sites; and video games, gangs are able to spread using these same technologies. Gangs also take advantage of social networking sites, such as Facebook, for recruitment and organization. Even gang-related video games, such as the *Grand Theft Auto* series, glorify gang life for adolescents of all walks of life.

According to police reports, 65% of gang members are adults and 35% are juveniles. This is a point worth repeating: Two-thirds of gang members nationally are adults and one-third are adolescents. This empirical point conflicts with the popular notion that youth gangs are entirely an adolescent problem. The overall age of the gang population has increased in recent years as gang problems in smaller communities have declined; these areas typically report very young gang members. In addition, increased police attention has focused on older, more criminally active gang members.

Nationally, approximately 46% of the gang population is Hispanic. African Americans account for 35% of the U.S. gang population, and whites account for nearly 12%. Approximately 25% of gangs are multiethnic. More than 90% of all gang members are male although about 22% of gangs also include female members. Approximately 66% of law enforcement agencies have reported that the return of gang members from jail or prison confinement to their jurisdiction has created several worrisome problems, such as increased violence and drug trafficking.[59]

As mentioned earlier, it can be difficult to estimate the gang population because gang members often migrate to other jurisdictions. For instance, 71% of the police agencies participating in the National Youth Gang Survey where gangs were an ongoing problem reported that gang members in their jurisdiction had recently migrated from other areas. Gang members move for a variety of reasons. According to the 2012 National Youth Gang Survey (the most current data available), 47% moved for legitimate reasons pertaining to family obligations or employment opportunities. However, 14% moved to take advantage of drug market opportunities, 13% moved to avoid law enforcement, and 10% moved to pursue other illegal ventures. Just 6% moved to escape gang life.[60]

The expansion of the gang problem throughout the United States has prompted a debate about its fundamental nature. Some in law enforcement believe the *migration* of gang members from community to community reflects the franchising of gangs' criminal activities. An alternative perspective focuses on the *proliferation* of the gang problem. This view suggests the increase in the number of communities reporting gang problems reflects the changing definitions of "gang" and "gang member," the desire of local police to obtain increased funding to respond to the gang problem, or the movement of youth who are gang members to new communities although the reasons for the move are unrelated to gang membership.

Although criminologists continue to debate the migration versus proliferation theories for gangs, one point not subject to debate is that gangs negatively affect communities. James Howell has identified several ways that delinquent gangs harm young people and communities:

1. Gang members commit a disproportionate amount of crime.
2. Gang members are most criminally active while they are in gangs; their delinquency is lower both before and after leaving the gang.
3. Gang members commit more serious crimes, such as robberies and assaults.
4. There is overlap between gang membership and chronic offending; thus members' delinquency is long-lasting.

5. Gang delinquency creates enormous costs. For instance, each assault-related gunshot injury has been estimated to bring $1 million in public costs; the criminal career of a single serious gang member can inflict costs on society between $1.7 million and $2.3 million.

Finally, all of these issues take an enormous social toll on the communities in which gangs operate, as these communities must deal with the delinquency, victimization, social costs, and fear generated by gangs.[61]

The Spread of Gangs

Walter Miller identified seven reasons offered by law enforcement, criminologists, and policymakers to explain the dramatic proliferation of gangs over the past decades. Some of these reasons suggest a pattern of gang migration.[62]

1. *Drugs.* Police believe the expansion of illegal drug markets has increased the solidarity of existing gangs, offered incentives for the creation of new gangs, and promoted the development of widespread networks of drug-trafficking gangs.
2. *Immigration.* Major waves of immigration during the past 40 years have brought into the United States many Asian, Southeast Asian, and Latin American immigrants, whose children have formed gangs in the tradition of Irish, Jewish, and Slavic immigrant groups during the late 19th and early 20th centuries.
3. *Gang Names and Alliances.* In the 1980s, the pattern of adopting a common name and claiming a federated relationship with other gangs became increasingly common. Hundreds of small local gangs adopted the names or claimed alliance with well-known gangs such as the Crips, Bloods, Latin Kings, and Gangster Disciples.
4. *Migration.* Some experts believe gangs may have exhausted drug markets or faced violent competition from other drug-dealing gangs in a particular community; to deal with this issue, they simply left their old home and transferred their operations to new markets in towns and cities with little existing gang presence.
5. *Government Policies.* During the 1960s, some policymakers viewed urban youth gangs as representing an untapped reservoir of potential leadership for improving the quality of life for residents in low-income communities. These officials advocated recognizing gangs as legitimate community groups and enlisting them in social reform efforts. In fact, more than $1 million in federal funds was allocated to urban gangs in Chicago and New York by the Office of Economic Opportunity as part of the federal war on poverty.

6. *Female-Headed Households.* This explanation suggests that the increase in female-headed households and the absence of stable adult male role models have created identity problems for male adolescents, who then turned to gangs for their sense of place and values.

7. *Gang Subculture and the Media.* Gangs have become "hot" market items in movies, novels, television, and music. The media have portrayed gang members as macho, hip, cool, and victims of racism, police brutality, and government oppression; in turn, the gang subculture has been viewed as a glamorous and rewarding lifestyle.

In contrast to Miller's suppositions, Cheryl Maxson believes the most common reason for the incursion of gangs into smaller communities is that gang members often move with their families to suburbs or other, traditionally safer areas to improve their quality of life and to be near relatives and friends.[63] For instance, Karen Wilson recently reviewed the problem of youth gangs in rural areas and found that the primary way that gangs "appear" in rural areas is by formerly urban gang members relocating to the country. What is particularly problematic about youth gang problems in emerging areas is that local law enforcement, social service networks, and community residents often persist in disbelief that rural America could have a gang presence or gang problem. Yet, gang members can quickly bring more serious delinquencies that rural communities must ultimately confront.[64] Other research suggests the recent appearance of gangs in communities that have not previously had gang problems is not the result of "migrated" gang members, but rather the result of the development of loosely organized cliques of age-graded neighborhood adolescents who are growing up in areas characterized by declining local economic conditions and growing poverty. In his systematic review of the gang literature, Chris Melde suggests that the spread of gangs and gang factors generally should best be understood from a life-course perspective that tracks the social development and delinquent career of at-risk youth. The various "spreading out" of gangs into new jurisdictions is less a function of gang organization and more a function of delinquent youth who either move to or are transferred to another state as part of their juvenile justice involvement.[65]

Racial and Ethnic Variations in Gangs

Gangs differ significantly in their organization and structure, leadership, cohesiveness, purpose, and sense of turf. Older perceptions of gangs as comprising similar kinds of youth groups must be reconsidered in light of the ethnic and racial diversity of modern-day gangs.

African American Gangs

The most notable and widespread of the contemporary African American gangs are the Bloods and the Crips. These gangs have become essentially confederations of smaller sets or subsets. The sets are generally organized around neighborhoods and typically have between 20 and 30 members, although a few of the larger sets may have more than 100 members.

African American gangs have little, if any, formal structure. What these gangs lack in organizational structure, however, they make up in violence. Much of the violence stems from traditional rivalry and competition over turf, although fights may start from something as minor as wearing a red hat in a Crips neighborhood or showing the wrong hand sign in the wrong place. Violence between the Bloods and the Crips also often results from both gangs' involvement in the drug trade. The large amounts of money that flow from narcotic sales allow the gangs' members to purchase high-powered, military-style automatic weapons. Unfortunately, many of those affected by the violence of the Bloods and the Crips are innocent victims caught in the crossfire of a gang fight or in random drive-by shootings.[66] Specific cities have additional African American gangs. In Chicago, for instance, the Black P-Stone Nation and the Black Gangster Disciple Nation are the two main delinquent street gangs. These gangs have merged with prison gangs and currently the gangs are referred to as the People Nation and Folk Nation, respectively.

Hispanic Gangs

Hispanic gangs are composed of youths whose ethnic backgrounds include Mexican, Mexican American, Cuban, and Puerto Rican, among others. (For a look at what has been called the most violent gang in the country, see **Box 12.4**, the "Delinquency Around the Globe" feature.) Hispanic gangs such as the Latin Kings, Mexican Mafia, MS-13, and Sureños have shown a remarkable longevity over the decades, with multiple

Gang violence between the Bloods and Crips in Los Angeles County and later nationwide exemplified African American gangs.

© manley099/Vetta/Getty.

BOX 12.4

Delinquency Around the Globe

MS-13 (The Mara Salvatrucha Gang)

A growing security threat to the United States, Mexico, and Central America is the Mara Salvatrucha (a rough translation is "mob of El Salvadoran youths on guard"), or MS-13 gang. In the course of El Salvador's civil war, children as young as 11 and 12 years old were trained and served as soldiers. The war devastated the small nation and displaced approximately 1 million Salvadorians, most of whom emigrated to the United States. Many of these youths had received military training in El Salvador, including training in explosives, booby traps, small arms, and hand-to-hand combat. When they arrived in the United States, however, the El Salvadorian youths were not accepted by many of the Hispanic groups in Los Angeles and other American cities. As they became marginalized, they banded together for protection and formed what is known as MS-13.

Because El Salvador's weak state created a breeding ground for criminal violence, MS-13 engages in some of the most extreme forms of terror and violence of any gang. These acts include machine-gun killings, home-invasion robberies, and machete attacks. Much of the gang violence that MS-13 commits is directed toward the Latin Kings, its chief rival among street gangs. Although originally organized in cliques, MS-13 is creating alliances to better organize its criminal activity, which included human smuggling, drug trafficking, and an array of other crimes. MS-13 chapters can be found in 33 states, and the gang has more than 250,000 members in the United States. Members are distinguished by heavy tattooing covering the body and face.

Although MS-13 is notorious for the severity of its violence, the causal roots of its gang members are consistent with the social backgrounds of gang youth and serious delinquents in the United States. Studies of El Salvadorian youth indicate an array of social risk factors and antisocial traits that are associated with gang activity and serious violence. However, youth who have powerful protective factors, such as religious involvement and belief, are able to avoid the potential allures of gang life. In addition to delinquency and violence, MS-13 poses a threat to national security. Al-Qaeda and other Islamic terrorist groups are creating relationships with MS-13 because of the gang's involvement in human trafficking across the United States and Mexican border. This liaison has the potential to create a major security concern for Americans. Ultimately, Mara Salvatrucha and other similar gangs pose a serious threat to border security for Mexico, Central America, and the United States.

Mara Salvatrucha recruits and manipulates vulnerable youth. These youths then provide fresh blood—and are expendable assets—for the gang. The question is how the United States, Mexico, and Central American governments will react to this critical and increasing threat.

Jeffrey Wenner, "MS-13 in Montgomery County Maryland," *Journal of Gang Research* 11:23–28 (2004); Andrew Grascia, "Gang Violence: Mara Salvatrucha—Forever Salvador," *Journal of Gang Research* 11:29–36 (2004); Shelly Domash, "America's Most Dangerous Gang," *Police: The Law Enforcement Magazine* 29:30–34 (2005); G. V. Corbiscello, "Border Crossings: A Look at the Very Real Threat of Cross Border Gangs in the U.S.," *Journal of Gang Research* 15:33–52 (2008); Christopher Salas-Wright, René Olate, and Michael Vaughn, "The Protective Effects of Religious Coping and Spirituality on Delinquency Results among High-Risk and Gang-Involved Salvadoran Youth." *Criminal Justice and Behavior* 40:988–1008 (2013); René Olate, Christopher Salas-Wright, Michael Vaughn, and Mansoo Yu, "Preventing Violence among Gang-Involved and High-Risk Youth in El Salvador: The Role of School Motivation and Self-Control," *Deviant Behavior* 36:259–275 (2015); Christopher Salas-Wright, René Olate, and Michael Vaughn, "Substance Use, Violence, and HIV Risk Behavior in El Salvador and the United States: Cross-National Profiles of the SAVA Syndemic," *Victims & Offenders* 10:95–116 (2015); Federal Bureau of Investigation, "They Poison Our Streets with Drugs, Violence, and All Manner of Crime," retrieved from https://www.fbi.gov/about-us/investigate/vc_majorthefts/gangs; National Gang Intelligence Center, *National Gang Report*, 2015, retrieved from https://www.fbi.gov/stats-services/publications/national-gang-report-2015.pdf.

generations of family members being affiliated with the same gangs. Today, Hispanic gangs make up nearly half of the known gangs in southern California, although only a small percentage of Hispanic youths have any gang affiliation. Nationally, 50% of all gang members are Hispanic.

Most Hispanic gangs are organized around age cohorts, or *klikas*, separated in age by 2 or 3 years, and are territorially based: "For gang members the word for gang and for neighborhood is identical. '*Mi barrio*' refers equally to 'my gang' and 'my neighborhood.'" The fierce loyalty to one's barrio is the basis for much intergang violence. "Gang members feel obliged to respond with violence in defense of their barrio. This often involves repelling intruders—especially those from rival barrios—from the territory claimed by the gang." Like all racial and ethnic groups, most Hispanic gang violence is *intraracial*—that is, directed against other Hispanics. For instance, Alison Rhyne and Douglas Yearwood found 80% of Hispanic gang violence is directed against other Hispanics.[67]

Membership in Hispanic gangs is achieved through initiation rituals designed to establish a member's loyalty to the gang. The ritual typically consists of a beating at the hands of three or four members of the gang. Serious beatings in the initiation are rare, because the intent is to see if and how the would-be member stands up and defends himself or herself. The ritual is also intended to solidify the new member's integration into the gang.[68]

Members of Hispanic gangs tend to spend much of their time partying and drinking in casual settings or

Based on their involvement in the drug trade and the use of extremely violent means to protect their interests, the El Salvadorian gang MS-13 (Mara Salvatrucha) is considered one of the most dangerous gangs in the United States.

© ES James/Shutterstock.

in more structured settings, ranging from residences, public parks, or isolated streets. There are typically two categories of partying. The first involves more conventional family-oriented gatherings, such as weddings, birthday parties, baptisms, and barbecues. Both male and female gang members attend such parties, where beer and marijuana are casually consumed. The second type of party is more spontaneous, likely to include only male gang members, and often involves heavy alcohol and polydrug use.[69] As Alice Cepeda and Avelardo Valdez note, "The primary objective, according to several respondents, is to get 'loaded and high.'"[70]

Asian American Gangs

Asian juvenile gangs are a relatively new development in the United States. According to Kolin Chin, the first Asian youth gangs formed in the Chinese section of San Francisco in the 1950s; they were composed almost exclusively of American-born Chinese.[71] With the arrival of large numbers of Hong Kong–born Chinese in the 1960s, however, gangs such as the Wah Ching (Youth of China) were formed as rivals to American-born Chinese gangs. These gangs soon became involved in prostitution, drugs, gambling, and extortion. The accumulation of money—rather than fighting with other gangs over turf—dominated gang activity.[72]

Indochinese gangs, predominantly Vietnamese, are the most numerous among Asian gangs today. It has been estimated that there are more than 100 Indochinese gangs in the United States, with thousands of members. The city of Westminster in Orange County, California, for example, has a population of 86,000, of which approximately 25% are Asian, and most of whom are Vietnamese refugees.[73] Unlike Hispanic gangs, Vietnamese gangs are weakly connected to the local community and its institutions. Rather, gangs are organized around personal friendships. Consequently, members "are more likely to attack local

citizens and exploit the organizations that remain in the community."[74] Although the Asian American gangs are dominated by Vietnamese youths, Cambodians, Hmong, Thais, and Laotians are also found in independent ethnic gangs or in mixed gangs. In addition to Indochinese gangs, there are Pacific Islander gangs composed of Filipino, Samoan, Tongan, Fijian, and Hawaiian youths, as well as Japanese and Korean gangs.

In a study of Southeast Asian gangs, Geoffrey Hunt and his colleagues reported that these gangs have little internal hierarchy or clearly defined leadership and a minimal concept of territory, although they do have tattoos, colors, and patterned cigarette burns as symbols. Gang initiations are more informal than those found in Hispanic gangs. Instead of "jumping in" ceremonies, Southeast Asian gangs were more likely to evaluate potential members through a process of "kicking back" or "hanging around" that could last from a few months to a year. Hunt and his colleagues concluded the everyday life of Southeast Asian gang members is rather similar to that of other California gangs; these gang members, like the members of the other groups, make a variety of attempts to deal with and transcend the mundane. Some Southeast Asian gangs operating in the United States have developed relatively unique patterns of violent crime, such as bank robbery and murders in which victims are bludgeoned to death.[75]

Box 12.5, the "A Window on Delinquency" feature describes the violent crime of rape engaged in by some Hmong gangs.

Native American Gangs

Until recently, little attention had been paid to Native American or American Indian youth gangs. Only in the 1990s did criminologists and police notice the emergence of these gangs. Attempting to estimate the number of Native American gangs and gang members is no less problematic than the task posed in general gang research. Nevertheless, Janice Joseph and Dorothy Taylor report that the number of Native American gangs more than doubled between 1994 and 2002. Today, there are at least 113 Native American gangs around the country. There are 55 gangs including 900 members on the Navajo Reservation in the "Four Corners" area of Arizona, Colorado, New Mexico, and Utah. Gang activity has been reported on all nine South Dakota reservations, as well as in cities ranging from Seattle and Rapid City (North Dakota) to Tulsa and Albuquerque.[76] Joseph Donnermeyer and his colleagues surveyed a sample of junior and senior high Native American youth in reservation and urban schools in several Western states and found that 6% of males and 1% of females reported gang membership.[77] In their survey of 212 middle school students on reservations in the upper Midwest, Les Whitbeck and his colleagues found that 6% of males and 4% of females indicated that they were in gangs.[78]

BOX 12.5

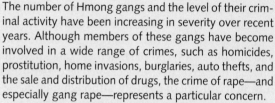

A Window on Delinquency

Hmong Gangs and Rape

The number of Hmong gangs and the level of their criminal activity have been increasing in severity over recent years. Although members of these gangs have become involved in a wide range of crimes, such as homicides, prostitution, home invasions, burglaries, auto thefts, and the sale and distribution of drugs, the crime of rape—and especially gang rape—represents a particular concern.

Following the Vietnam War, many Hmong families immigrated to the United States, first settling in California, Minnesota, and Wisconsin. Today, at least 36 states have Hmong populations. According to Richard Straka, a street Officer and investigator who has worked with the Hmong community for more than 10 years, Hmong gangs began to appear in the St. Paul and Ramsey County, Minnesota, area in the mid-1980s. The first Hmong gang in Minnesota, the Cobras, began as a group of teenage friend who played on a soccer team. By 1988, a number of 10- and 11-year-old Hmong youths wanted to join the Cobras but were told they were too young. As a result, they started their own gang, the White Tigers. Their early crimes included breaking into gun shops to obtain weapons. By the late 1990s, Hmong gangs were identified as major players in local gang violence. In the summer of 1999, at least 22 reported shootings and the deaths of two were attributed to Hmong gangs. Most of the shootings occurred among four rival gangs: the White Tigers, the Oroville Mono Boys, the Purple Brothers, and the Oriental Ruthless Boys.

But Hmong gangs represent a violent threat to non-gang members as well. The most frequent and violent crimes against non-Hmong gang members is rape. The majority of victims in the sexual assaults are juvenile Hmong females. In one case that occurred in 1977, a number of girls 12 to 15 years old had arranged to meet gang members through a message service. The victims went willingly with the boys, thinking they were going for a ride or to a party. Instead, gang members took them to the attic of a garage or a house, turned off the lights or put a blanket over their heads, and raped them. The gang members called this "doing the Ninja," as the victims could not identify who had sexually assaulted them.

Violent rape by Hmong gang members is not limited to Minnesota. In Warren, Michigan, several members of a Hmong gang were arrested for repeatedly raping teenage girls whom they had held prisoners for nearly 3 weeks. Authorities in Fresno, California, reported a similar case in which at least 33 victims had been raped and held by gang members for periods ranging from 2 days to 3 months.

Hmong girls who have been sexually assaulted are hesitant to report the crimes. After being raped, they fear being shunned by family members who might consider them "damaged" or having "shamed" them. Gang members use this cultural factor to their advantage, telling the victims that "they were no good to their families and that the gang was now their family." Some of the victims stayed with the gang members even after they were raped. They felt that they had nowhere else to go, because they feared their own families more than the gang members.

Richard Straka, "The Violence of Hmong Gangs and the Crime of Rape," *FBI Law Enforcement Bulletin* February 2003:12–16; John Wang, "A Preliminary Profile of Laotian/Hmong Gangs: A California Perspective," *Journal of Gang Research* 9:1–14 (2002); Associated Press, "9 Reputed Gang Members Charged in Rape of St. Paul Girl, 14," retrieved March 11, 2016 from http://www.twincities.com/2012/03/22/9-reputed-gang-members-charged-in-rape-of-st-paul-girl-14/; James Howell, *The History of Street Gangs in the United States: Their Origins and Transformations* (Lanham, MD: Lexington Books, 2015).

Native American gangs generally do not reflect traditional native culture; instead, they identify with nationally recognized African American and Hispanic gangs. Native American gangs account in large part for the increasing trend of serious and violent crime on reservations, including homicide, assault, rape, drug dealing, drive-by and walk-by shootings, and extortion. Marijuana is easily cultivated in these areas, and remote sections of reservations provide many locations for setting up methamphetamine labs.

According to Joseph and Taylor, "Current trends indicate that Indian gangs are mirroring the gang activity occurring in the communities surrounding Indian Country."[79] Liz Martinez notes that Native American authorities are concentrating their resources on arresting and prosecuting gang members primarily because of their disproportionate involvement in crime on reservations.[80]

Gang Violence

Gang members pose a significant danger to American society in terms of their involvement in the most violent forms of delinquency. Using data from the 1993–2003 National Crime Victimization Survey, Erika Harrell discovered that between 6 and 10% of all violent victimizations were reported by victims to be committed by gang members.[81] This rate equated to nearly 400,000 rapes, sexual assaults, robberies, aggravated assaults, and simple assaults committed by gang members. At the height of gang violence in 1994, gang members accounted for more than 1.1 million violent victimizations annually. Aggravated assaults and robberies are the violent crimes most commonly committed by gang members; however, they also commit a disproportionate number of murders. Based on the FBI's Supplemental Homicide Reports, gang youths commit 5 to 7% of total murders and 8 to 10% of firearm-perpetrated murders each year (see **Box 12.6**, the "The Face of Delinquency" feature). Even in the current era of historically low levels of delinquency, gangs exact a considerable toll. In the 2012 National Youth Gang Survey, there were 2363 gang-related homicides, which equates to more than six per day in the United States.

Although gang violence is a national problem, it is often more destructive within certain communities (see **Box 12.7**, the "A Window on Delinquency" feature). For instance, police departments in some major cities often underreport crime, many of which are crimes committed by gang members.[82] Unfortunately, police underreporting of gang-related crimes found in small cities throughout the United States is also rampant. Even if law enforcement agencies underreport gang violence, the prevalence of anti-gang measures by police departments suggests that gang violence is widespread and must be addressed each day. For example, in the 2012 National Youth Gang Survey, the percentage of agencies that use specific anti-gang measures is as follows:

- 76% have targeted patrols.
- 64% have a dedicated gang unit or gang officer.
- 52% have participated in a multiagency gang task force.
- 51% conduct coordinated probation searches of gang offenders.
- 47% employ a curfew ordinance to combat gang activity.
- 30% have participated in a multiagency community-based anti-gang strategy.
- 26% have targeted firearms initiatives for gang members.[83]

Comparing matched samples of gang members and at-risk youths from four high-crime neighborhoods, Ronald Huff found that gang members were 20 times more likely than at-risk adolescents to participate in a drive-by shooting, 10 times more likely to commit murder, 8 times more likely to commit robbery, and 3 times more likely to commit assault of someone in public. Lisa Kort-Butler studied gang youth in a national panel of American adolescents and found that their

BOX 12.6

The Face of Delinquency

Who Will Grow Up to Murder?

In many respects, gang members embody the behavioral outcome of multiple risk factors for delinquency. Even when compared to serious delinquents, gang-affiliated youth generally score much worse on a variety of family background, cognitive, and conduct-related factors. To what extent do various risk factors among youth at risk for gang involvement predict the most serious form of delinquency: murder? Mark Berg and his colleagues studied this question using data from the Pittsburgh Youth Study, a prospective, longitudinal study of at-risk boys some of whom engage in gang delinquency. They found that several childhood risk factors significantly increase the likelihood that the individual will perpetrate homicide during adolescence or early adulthood. For instance:

- Boys who had been in gang fights before age 14 were 2.3 times more likely to be convicted of homicide later in their delinquent career.
- Boys who carried weapons before age 14 were 4.8 times more likely to be convicted of murder.
- Boys who committed multiple violent acts were 4.2 times more likely to later murder.

Other risk factors also predicted subsequent homicide offending. For instance, peer delinquency increased the risk of murder by a factor of three and delinquent peers increased it by a factor of two.

- Gang-involved youth are often convicted of serious felonies during adolescence.
- Conviction status had dramatic effects on later homicide offending. Weapons convictions increased the likelihood of murder more than 13-fold and robbery convictions increased it 10-fold.

With these sorts of serious convictions, serious delinquents often are committed to confinement facilities. But even that process carries with it a risk for homicide. Matt DeLisi and his colleagues found that juvenile confinement independently predicted homicide offending during adulthood even when other important factors were considered. In sum, the risk factors of gang-involved youth, and the juvenile justice system responses to it can collectively contribute to murder later in life.

David Farrington, Rolf Loeber, and Mark Berg, "Young Men Who Kill: A Prospective Longitudinal Examination from Childhood," *Homicide Studies* 16:99–128 (2012); Matt DeLisi, Andy Hochstetler, Gloria Jones-Johnson, Jonathan Caudill, and James Marquart, "The Road to Murder: The Enduring Criminogenic Effects of Juvenile confinement among a Sample of Adult Career Criminals," *Youth Violence and Juvenile Justice* 9:207–221 (2011); Matt DeLisi, Alex Piquero, and Stephanie Cardwell, "The Unpredictability of Murder: Juvenile Homicide in the Pathways to Desistance Study," *Youth Violence and Juvenile Justice* 14:26–42 (2016).

BOX 12.7

A Window on Delinquency

The Criminology of Gang Homicide

In many U.S. cities, gangs are responsible for a disproportionate number of homicides. During the late 20th century, gang homicides in Chicago increased almost 500% and accounted for 25% of all murders in that city. In Los Angeles, nearly 50% of homicides in Los Angeles County were gang related. In Boston, the approximately 1300 gang members, who represented less than 1% of their age group in terms of population, were collectively responsible for 60% of all youth homicides in the city.

According to Scott Decker, the quick rise and fall of gang homicide rates are consistent with the inconsistent organization of gangs and its generally weak leadership. Most gangs are loosely organized and seemingly waiting for something to unite them. The uniting element is a real or perceived threat from an "outgroup" usually a similarly disorganized set of youths from another neighborhood or ethnic group. Very quickly, the threat is framed as an enemy to the gang. This perception serves to increase the cohesion of the gang and justify the use of violence to "respond" to the real or perceived threat posed by the gang's enemy. Some short-lived act of violence, such as a drive-by shooting, occurs; the violence then rapidly deescalates until the process begins again. Decker described this process as occurring in seven steps:

1. Loose bonds to the gang
2. Collective identification of a threat from a rival gang, which reinforces the use of violence, expands the number of gang members, and increases cohesion
3. A mobilizing event (possibly, but not necessarily, violence)
4. Escalation of activity
5. A violent event (e.g., homicide)
6. Rapid deescalation
7. Retaliation

Subsequent research has supported this model of gang homicides. In fact, Jesenia Pizarro and Jean McGloin found it was a better explanation of gang homicide patterns than social disorganization theory. Qualitative research shows even more clearly—and more shockingly—how disorganized violent delinquency often sets into motion a cycle of homicide and retaliatory homicide. In many respects, homicide is portrayed as the necessary and appropriate response to violence and perceived affronts from other gang members and even members within one's own gang. Timothy Laugher conducted ethnographic research of gang members in Indianapolis and documented the centrality of homicide or attempted homicide in gang life:

"Of the five individuals who I routinely observed, one (Shawn) has been murdered, one (Layboy) has been the victim of two shootings and has been imprisoned for both robbery and burglary, and another (TJ) was shot but not mortally wounded since the conclusion of my study. Shawn and Layboy's younger brother Dre, who was member of the gang and a less central figure in the study, was also murdered after the conclusion of the study."

Given the haphazard nature of gang organization and violence, it is clear that controlling gang access to lethal weapons and encouraging youth involvement in structured activities can significantly reduce lethal violence among adolescents.

Scott Decker, "Collective and Normative Features of Gang Violence," *Justice Quarterly* 13: 242–264 (1996); Jesenia Pizarro, Kristen Zgoba, and Wesley Jennings, "Assessing the Interaction between Offender and Victim Criminal Lifestyles and Homicide Type," *Journal of Criminal Justice* 39:367–377 (2011); Anthony Braga, "Serious Youth Gun Offenders and the Epidemic of Youth Violence in Boston," *Journal of Quantitative Criminology* 19:33–54 (2003); George Tita and Allan Abrahamse, *Gang Homicide in Los Angeles, 1981–2001* (Sacramento: California Attorney General's Office, 2004); Jesenia Pizarro and Jean McGloin, "Explaining Gang Homicides in Newark, New Jersey: Collective Behavior or Social Disorganization?" *Journal of Criminal Justice* 34:195–207 (2006); Lisa Bell Holleran and Donna Vandiver, "U.S. Homicides: Multi-Offenders and the Presence of Female Offenders," *Violence and Gender*, 3:27–35 (2016); Timothy Laugher, "Violent Stories: Personal Narratives, Street Socialization, and the Negotiation of Street Culture among Street-Oriented Youth," *Criminal Justice Review* 39:182–200 (2014), page 187.

behavioral world was characterized by high levels of general delinquency, violent delinquency, experienced victimization, witnessed victimization, negative emotions, group fights with peers, and low socioeconomic status. About 14% of youth in her sample indicated that they expected to be murdered by age 21. The criminality of gang members is so pronounced that Matt DeLisi and his colleagues concluded:

In addition to various forms of violence, gang members commit antisocial acts such as randomly intimidating or assaulting patrons in shopping centers and grocery stores, using and selling drugs in school, and assaulting their teachers during class.

Even among samples of youths characterized by multiple risk factors for delinquency and violence, gang members are noteworthy for their strident criminality.[84]

Two significant differences between contemporary youth gangs and those of earlier decades are that many of today's gangs are exceptionally violent and much of that violence occurs within school settings. In some instances, gangs have effectively taken control of urban high schools. By the 1970s, for example, gang violence and other gang activities in public schools had reached startling levels. Gang operations have been identified at all three levels of

Gang homicides are commonplace in major U.S. cities. What is the allure of the gang lifestyle for adolescents? Why are gang youth seemingly unafraid of its violent subculture?

© kilukilu/Shutterstock.

schools: elementary school, junior high or middle school, and senior high school. Serious assaults have been directed by gang members against other gang members, teachers, and fellow students.

However, most gang violence occurs *outside* school settings. Violence perpetrated by members of youth gangs in major U.S. cities began to rise dramatically in the late 20th century. Walter Miller attributes the growth of gang violence during this period largely to a single factor—guns. By the mid-1970s, many youth gangs were giving up their traditional zip guns, chains, and knives and turning to revolvers, shotguns, and semiautomatic rifles. Miller predicted that the problem would become worse, more violent, and more confrontational with law enforcement agencies. His prediction was correct: Youth gang homicides clearly increased. Whereas 633 gang-related killings occurred in major gang cities in 1980, Chicago and Los Angeles alone accounted for more than 1000 gang homicides in 1994. With more weapons available, with more gang members carrying guns as a matter of course, and with the reality that gangs often attract young males who enjoy violence, the increased levels of serious violence came as no surprise.[85]

Gang homicides appeared to decline significantly after 1995 in most large cities that had been reporting large numbers of gang homicides. More recently, gang-related homicides have doubled in southern California's Orange County, and increases in gang violence have been reported in other cities in the early 21st century. For instance, more than half of the 1000-plus homicides in Los Angeles and Chicago since 2000 were gang related. In 171 other major U.S. cities, approximately 25% of homicides since 2000 were gang related. In 2004, U.S. cities experienced an 11% increase in gang homicides over the previous 8-year average.[86] Very recent research adds some complexity to the nexus between gangs, victimization, and weapons. Richard Spano and his colleagues have studied these factors using data from the Mobile (Alabama) Youth Survey, which included adolescents living in extreme poverty in the Deep South. They found that gang membership was not significantly related to violent victimization once poverty and lifestyle variables were considered. Similarly, Lorraine McKelvey and her colleagues studied more than 700 families living in violent neighborhoods in Little Rock, Arkansas; Bronx, New York; Cambridge, Massachusetts; Miami, Florida; Philadelphia, Pennsylvania; Dallas, Texas; Seattle, Washington; and New Haven, Connecticut, who were interviewed as part of a project serving families who had low birth weight, preterm infants. They found that males living in these neighborhoods who had high family cohesion and bonding to parents displayed far fewer externalizing problems and were less likely to join gangs.[87] This conclusion suggests that gang violence is a complex outcome of a variety of risk factors faced by adolescents living in disadvantaged neighborhoods.

Drugs and Drug Dealing by Gangs

In the summer of 2006, police in three states arrested more than 30 people with ties to the Mickey Cobras, a street gang based in the Dearborn Homes Apartments in Chicago. The gang had been selling a deadly type of heroin that was mixed with the powerful (and often lethal) painkiller *fentanyl*. The drug concoction killed nearly 150 people and resulted in several hundred nonfatal drug overdoses.[88] This incident underscored the public belief that gang members are extensively involved in drugs and drug dealing.

Are gang members more likely than non-gang members to use drugs? The answer is yes, and they are more likely to do so in conjunction with other delinquent activity. Arielle Baskin-Sommers and Ira Sommers' study of methamphetamine users found that 35% of regular drug users committed a violent crime while under the influence. Of these violent offenders, nearly 30% were either active gang members or actively involved in the drug trade.[89] Gang members are several times more likely than non-gang youth to use drugs and to use them more often than youths who are not involved in gangs. Dana Peterson and her colleagues found gang-related youths to be

Research indicates that gang members are often extensively involved in drug trafficking in addition to their general involvement in delinquency. Ultimately, do youths join gangs to make large sums of money without investing in conventional pursuits like legitimate work? Because of the allure of drug money, is the gang-drug link likely to be broken?

© monkeybusinessimages/iStockphoto/Getty.

disproportionately involved in drug use; for many of the gang members in this study, their initiation into the gang was a precursor to their use of drugs. Alice Cepeda and her colleagues reported extensive drug use, drug dealing, and diverse other forms of delinquency in their study of male Mexican American gang members. Even those who had positive connections to family and school nevertheless were actively involved in drugs as user, dealer, or both.[90] Gang members not only are more likely to use and sell serious drugs, such as cocaine, but also are more likely than non-gang adolescents to commit homicides primarily during the course of drug activity. Indeed, the drug activity of gang members, with all of the negative consequences that it produces, has been likened to a public health epidemic.[91]

Are juvenile gangs extensively involved in drug trafficking? Ronald Huff reported in his study of four communities in Colorado, Florida, and Ohio that gang members were extensively involved in drug sales, especially sales of cocaine and marijuana, and that gang members sold significantly more cocaine than do non-gang youths.[92] In George Knox and his colleagues' study of more than 4000 gang members from 17 states, 82% of gang members reported that their gang had sold crack cocaine. In addition, drug trafficking for profit was one of the primary reasons for their gangs' existence.[93]

The actual level of gang involvement in the drug trade appears to vary by ethnicity and locale. African American gangs are more heavily involved in drug trafficking than are Hispanic, Asian, or white gangs. Jeffrey Fagan notes that in Los Angeles, whereas Hispanic gangs sell small quantities of marijuana, the crack and cocaine trade is dominated by African American gangs. In New York, the crack trade is not controlled or dominated by any particular group of street gangs.[94]

There also appear to be variations in the relationship between gang status, ethnicity, and drug use. When Mitchell Miller and his colleagues surveyed more than 3000 Hispanic youths living in south Texas, they found that those individuals who reported greater use of English at home and at school—that is, language acculturation—were more likely to use marijuana. In contrast, Hispanic youths who preferred to socialize with white youths as opposed to other Hispanics were less likely to use marijuana. Youths with greater language acculturation had greater cocaine use. Regardless of language skills, Hispanic youths who were involved in gangs also reported greater drug usage.[95]

The National Youth Gang Center surveyed more than 1000 police and sheriffs' departments and reported that drug sales in their jurisdictions involved gang members, although the degree of involvement varied extensively. For instance, only 25% of gang members selling drugs were seen as doing so at a "high" level; nearly half were involved at a "low" level. Although gangs are involved in drug dealing, respondents indicated that gangs did not control or manage most of the drug distribution in their jurisdictions. Overall, however, nearly 75% of survey respondents felt that drug-related factors push youth into gang membership.[96]

Some take issue with police, criminologists, and members of the media who overemphasize the gang–drug connection. Malcolm Klein argues that drug gangs and *street gangs* are not the same. More important, most street gangs simply do not have the necessary leadership, cohesiveness, sense of loyalty and secretiveness, or narrow focus on the mechanics of drug sales. Rather, Klein says, typical street gangs have shifting leadership, intermediate levels of cohesiveness, frequently broken codes of honor, and very versatile and independent criminal involvements. For all these reasons, Klein believes that gangs are lousy mechanisms for drug distribution.[97] Similarly, James Inciardi and his colleagues' study of drug use and serious delinquency found that only 5% of the street youths in their sample had ever been involved in gangs. Most youths involved in drug distribution saw little reason to belong to gangs.[98]

Of course, criminological studies often rely on small samples and are not necessarily reflective of national trends in gang activity. The assessment of the threats posed by gangs from criminal justice practitioners is often more stark than the assessments made by academics (see **Box 12.8**, the "A Window on Delinquency" feature). For example, each year the National Alliance of Gang Investigators Associations (NAGIA—a consortium of more than 10,000 gang investigators in the law enforcement and intelligence communities) produces a national gang threat assessment. In its national assessment, the NAGIA reported that gangs

BOX 12.8

A Window on Delinquency

The National Gang Threat Assessment

The National Alliance of Gang Investigators Alliances (NAGIA) includes 15 state and regional gang investigators associations, representing more than 10,000 gang investigators across the United States and gang-focused practitioners from the Federal Bureau of Investigation; Bureau of Alcohol, Tobacco, Firearms, and Explosives; National Drug Intelligence Center; and other agencies. The NAGIA conducts a national survey to produce a national gang threat assessment. Highlights of the 2011 survey include the following findings:

- Gangs are the primary distributors of drugs throughout the United States.
- Gangs are increasingly associating with organized crime organizations from Mexico, Russia, and several nations in Asia.
- Few gangs have been found to associate with domestic terrorist organizations, although gang members are most susceptible to these influences while in prison.
- There is increased fluidity between delinquent street gangs and prison gangs.
- Hispanic gang membership is increasing and spreading throughout the United States.
- Indian Country is reporting escalating levels of gang activity and crime.

- Approximately 31% of communities refuse to acknowledge that they have a gang problem despite evidence to the contrary.
- Gang activity around schools and college campuses has increased.
- Depending on the region of the country, gangs are disproportionately responsible for the trafficking of marijuana, cocaine, crack cocaine, and methamphetamine.
- Organized motorcycle gangs, including the Mongols, Pagans, Outlaws, Vagos, and Wheels of Soul, are an increasing criminal threat.

Another multiagency group called the National Gang Intelligence Center also produces a National Gang Threat Assessment. Their most recent report estimated there are approximately 1.4 million gang members belonging to more than 33,000 gangs in every state in the United States (notice the different estimates from the National Youth Gang Survey). It is estimated that gang members account for as much as 90% of the crime in many communities and they are the primary retail-level distributor of narcotics in the United States. On average, across all jurisdictions, gangs are responsible for 48% of violent crime and delinquency. Although relatively small in number, gang members impose a disproportionately heavy burden on society.

National Alliance of Gang Investigators Associations, *2005 National Gang Threat Assessment* (Washington, DC: Bureau of Justice Assistance, 2006); National Gang Intelligence Center, *National Gang Threat Assessment, 2011* (Washington, DC: U.S. Department of Justice, 2011).

are the primary distributors of drugs throughout the United States and that many of the fastest-growing gang-related problems pertain to drug trafficking.[99]

Female Gang Delinquency

It is difficult to obtain reliable estimates of the number of female gang members. Research suggests that girls may account for as many as 38% of all gang members and most gangs have at least one female member.[100] The National Youth Gang Survey, however, reports that about 7% of gang members identified by law enforcement are female. Such a wide range of estimates likely reflects the type of data being used, with the lower estimates generally based on official data and higher estimates using self-report measures.[101]

Although the majority of gang boys are in all-male gangs, most girls join gangs with mixed gender composition. For instance, the National Youth Gang Survey reports that 85% of all youth gangs have some female members and that only 2% of gangs

are identified as predominantly female.[102] At times, female gang members are very antisocial. For instance, in recent years, a female gang known as the Sixth Street Bandits attracted police attention when they targeted intoxicated males exiting bars in Austin, Texas. After drugging their victims, the Sixth Street Bandits forced their victims to withdraw money from ATMs.[103]

Overall, gang girls are much more likely to be involved in delinquency, and especially serious delinquency, than are non-gang females. In general, gang-associated girls commit fewer violent crimes than gang-associated boys and are more inclined to commit property crime and status offenses. Based on in-depth interviews with 27 female gang members in St. Louis, Jody Miller and Scott Decker noted that although girls are less often involved in violent crime than are boys, fully 85% of the girls reported having hit someone with the idea of hurting them.[104] Finn-Aage Esbensen and his colleagues surveyed nearly 6000 eighth graders in 42 different schools. Whereas gang boys reported more delinquencies than the girls, 39% of the gang girls reported attacking someone with a weapon, 21% indicated that they had shot at

someone, 78% had been involved in gang fights, and 65% had carried hidden weapons.[105]

Gang girls are also more likely to be heavier and more frequent users of drugs than are non-gang girls. In one study, Geoffrey Hunt and his colleagues conducted interviews with 168 females who were currently gang members. Nearly two-thirds of the females reported using marijuana more than 50 times, with about one-fifth using marijuana on a daily basis. In addition, more than 80% of the female gang members reported regular or somewhat regular use of such drugs as cocaine, crack, LSD, heroin, and methamphetamine.[106]

Girl gang members have traditionally been exploited and have often been brutalized at the hands of male gang members. For instance, recently several gang members in Fort Worth, Texas, were arrested for forcing teenage girls—some as young as age 12—into prostitution rings. Gang members targeted runways and other girls with unstable home lives, befriended them, provided drugs to them, and generally made them feel part of the group. After the initial overtures, the girls were forced into prostitution, which served as one source of the gang's profits. Girls who refused were beaten and raped, and their families were threatened. In many respects, the brutality that girls face in gangs is consistent with their victimization histories before joining. The preponderance of seriously delinquent and gang-affiliated girls have been sexually, physically, or emotionally abused.[107]

Jody Miller suggests that violence against African American girls in gang-infested neighborhoods is the result of gender, race, and class disadvantage. According to Miller, young African American girls face widespread gendered violence as a systematic and overlapping feature of neighborhoods, communities, and schools and have few social supports to protect them. For example, *gendered dangers* include public spaces in disadvantaged communities where gang-involved males congregate and perpetrate violence against women in open-air drug markets. Miller found extremely high rates of violent victimization among young women in gang- and drug-infested neighborhoods; for example, approximately 30% of girls in these areas had been sexually assaulted or raped multiple times over their lifetimes. When girls associate overtly with gang members, they become vulnerable to even more victimization and exploitation.[108]

Similarly, gang girl criminality can reflect the gender structure of the gang. Girls in sex-balanced gangs are significantly less likely than their male counterparts to engage in violent offenses, carrying of weapons, drug sales, and serious property offenses. Offending by girls in majority-male gangs is more likely to reflect similar levels of involvement in delinquent activities as male members. Finally, girls in majority-female or all-female gangs report significantly less delinquency than males in all-male gangs.

Gang girls are much less likely to be victims of violence than are gang boys, although they are much more likely than non-gang females to be targets. Their lower rates of violent victimization are attributed to a number of factors: Gang boys tend to exclude them from potentially violent activities; girls' peripheral status as gang members reduces the likelihood of their being targets of violence by rival gang members, and girls are protected by male gang members against predatory males in the community.

Females, like their male counterparts, are generally initiated into gangs through a process of being "beaten in" or being required to assault a rival gang member or participate in a serious crime. Some girls are tattooed with gang symbols; others may be "blessed in" by gang members praying over the girl.

More problematic are initiations where a girl is "sexed in," meaning the girl is required to have intercourse with multiple male gang members. Girls who are sexed into a gang are at much greater risk for continued sexual mistreatment and exploitation and are generally viewed by male and female gang members as weak, promiscuous, and subject to contempt and disrespect.

Girls join gangs for many reasons. Sadly, many of these young females see the gang as an escape from family problems. In the Hispanic gangs that Joan Moore and John Hagedorn studied, girls were more likely than boys to come from abusive families. The parents of gang girls were also more likely to be alcoholics or heroin users.[109] Jody Miller also reports that gang girls are more likely to come from *very* dysfunctional families: 71% of the gang girls in her study reported serious family problems, such as violence, drug addiction, and drug or alcohol abuse, compared to only 26% of non-gang girls.[110] Anne Campbell's study of mixed-sex gangs in New York City suggests that girls generally join gangs to escape the isolation they experienced in their families while growing up. The girls she studied looked to the gang for a sense of belonging, for loyalty in relationships, and for unconditional acceptance.[111]

Other research suggests a rather different relationship between gang girls and their families. Geoffrey Hunt and his colleagues report that gang girls maintain strong ties to family members, especially mothers, sisters, and other female relatives, and that these family connections are significant elements of social support. In many ways, gangs are viewed as extensions of their families. These girls have often grown up around gangs and gang activities, so that gangs are simply part of their daily lives. Fully 96% of the girls interviewed by Hunt and colleagues said they had family members who had been, or were currently, members of gangs.[112]

Some girls may "choose" to join gangs because they believe they have no other choice. According to Alan Turley, who studied female gang members in the six largest cities in Texas:

Girls feel they have no choice; that eventually the male gang members will have them (sexually), so it makes sense to the girls to submit to the gang, rather than becoming female prey for the gang.[113]

In contrast, in her study of Hispanic gangs in California, Mary Harris found that girls become members of gangs in a manner similar to joining other teenage groups. They are not pressured or coerced into membership, but rather enter gangs through friendships and family ties. Once in the gang, the girl soon takes on the attitudes of other gang members, including the willingness to fight, to be "bad," to be "tough," and to use drugs. Although she might have entered the gang through family ties, the gang soon becomes the girl's primary reference group, demanding stronger loyalty than either family or school. However, fighting or engaging in potentially violent confrontations is not the dominant activity of gang girls, any more than it is the focus of gang boys. Rather, most gang girls (and boys) spend the greater part of their time together simply hanging out—watching television; listening to the radio; playing music, video games, or cards; drinking beer; or smoking marijuana.[114]

Gangs and Juvenile Justice

Several strategies for responding to the problem of youth gangs have been developed. These strategies include *neighborhood mobilization* approaches, which were popular in the 1920s and 1930s; *social intervention* programs, which were prevalent in the 1940s and 1950s; programs aimed at *creating social and economic opportunities* for inner-city and at-risk youths, which were used in the 1960s; the emergence of *suppression efforts* in the 1970s and 1980s; and *intervention and prevention* strategies, which have been given more emphasis in recent years. Although suppression strategies continue to dominate the field today, many intervention and prevention programs are being pursued in schools and communities. To many gang experts, suppression strategies combined with intervention programs appear to be the most promising approaches. Currently, the best approach to reducing gangs is through prevention. In 2013, the National Institute of Justice and Centers for Disease Control and Prevention partnered to publish a book called *Changing Course: Preventing Gang Membership*. The book was an invitation to policymakers and practitioners to employ a comprehensive prevention strategy that addresses the multiple domains of problem areas in the family, in schools, and among peers. It is hoped that by reducing risk factors and boosting protective factors, fewer youth will gravitate toward gangs and the litany of problems that cascade from gang life.[115]

Many law enforcement agencies have created special gang units in response to the growing gang problem. Today, there are more than 500 police gang units in the United States, more than 85% of which have been established in the past decade. Across the United States, 64% of law enforcement agencies have specialized units primarily assigned to combat delinquent gangs.

Almost 30% of national law enforcement agencies use firearm suppression initiatives to address gang violence.[116] Police gang suppression strategies involve a variety of activities. According to a Bureau of Justice Assistance report on urban street gang enforcement, the key elements in police gang suppression involve understanding the nature and scope of the community gang problem, gathering information and intelligence and compiling it into a comprehensive database, and developing strategies that will ultimately incapacitate gang leaders and the most violent and criminally involved members and associates.[117]

Suppression

Suppression is a police response to gangs that includes selective surveillance, arrest, and prosecution of gang members. A number of states have attempted to tamp down the growing gang problem by revising existing laws or by establishing entirely new legislation aimed at both gang members and gang behaviors. These laws make it possible for police to charge gang youths with basic criminal offenses as well as to use conspiracy laws to target gang members who may not have been physically present during the commission of a crime. In some states, conviction for a gang-related crime may limit the range of possible sentences or may carry an automatic maximum sentence (see **Box 12.9**, the "Delinquency Prevention" feature). At the federal level, the *Violent Crime Control and Law Enforcement Act of 1994* included provisions allowing federal prosecutors to try juvenile gang members as adults if the juvenile played a leadership role in an organization or otherwise influenced other persons to take part in criminal activities involving the use or distribution of controlled substances or firearms.[118]

One of the most commonly employed suppression strategies is the neighborhood "sweep," in which a large number of officers sweep through a neighborhood, arresting and detaining known or suspected gang members. Another strategy involves "hot spot targeting" of known gang members and their hideouts. With this approach, police select certain gangs for intensive or saturated surveillance and harassment in an effort to apply pressure and send a message of deterrence. For instance, the Dallas

KEY TERMS

suppression
A police response to gang activity that includes selective surveillance, arrest, and prosecution of gang members.

BOX 12.9

Delinquency Prevention

Using the Law to Get Tough on Gangs

As the gang problem continues to grow, an increasing number of states and local communities are forging new anti-gang legislation or seeking new interpretations of existing statutes in an attempt to crack down on gangs and gang members. Included in these efforts are the use of the federal *Racketeer Influenced and Corrupt Organizations Act* (RICO); the California *Street Terrorism Enforcement and Prevention Act of 1988* (STEP Act), which is based on the RICO model; the creation of Safe School Zones; and the use of civil gang injunctions and public congregation ordinances.

The RICO Act was signed into law in 1970 and was used for nearly two decades to fight the Mafia and other adult organized-crime groups. Today, however, prosecutors see the RICO laws as a weapon to be used against entrenched youth gangs, partly because these laws allow prosecutors to charge gang members for simply being part of a criminal enterprise. As a consequence, the more insulated, better protected higher level leaders of gangs can be prosecuted for the criminal activities of street-level members.

The STEP Act uses a pattern of specified crimes as the basis for increasing sentences of youths convicted of gang-related crimes and mandating the forfeiture of a street gang's assets. Typically, they link definitions of "criminal street gang," "pattern of criminal gang activity," and "participation in a criminal street gang." Under the California STEP Act, for example, "criminal gang activity" is defined as the commission of one or more of seven predicate offenses on two or more separate occasions; a "criminal street gang" is defined as an ongoing group that has as one of its primary activities the commission of one or more of the predicate crimes and that has a common name or common identifying sign or symbol. Participation in a criminal street gang is considered a separate offense, which allows law enforcement agencies to avoid violating members' constitutional right to free association. By keeping precise records pertaining to

gang incidents, the police assist prosecutors in targeting gang participants.

Some states, such as Illinois, have enacted Safe School Zone laws that enhance penalties for certain weapons violations that occur within 1000 feet of a school, public housing property, or a public park. Violations include possessing a silencer or machine gun or carrying a pistol, revolver, stun gun, firearm, or ballistic knife when hooded, robed, or masked. However, a federal Safe School Zone law prohibiting the mere possession of a gun within 1000 feet of a school was deemed unconstitutional.

Local governments also have begun to wage a turf war against gangs using a variety of ordinances, including curfew laws, antiloitering laws, and civil gang injunctions. In addition, some courts have issued nuisance-abatement injunctions against street activities of gang members, effectively prohibiting their congregating in public space. For example, the San Fernando, California, city council passed an ordinance prohibiting active gang members with recent histories of violent crime from entering Las Palmas Park. Violation of the ordinance could result in a citation and a fine of as much as $250. However, the Supreme Court, in *Chicago v. Morales*, held that a Chicago antiloitering law targeting gang members by prohibiting the gathering of two or more people in any public place was unconstitutional and vague. The court stated that "in this instance the city has enacted an ordinance that affords too much discretion to the police and too little notice to citizens who wish to use the public streets."

Today, many jurisdictions use civil gang injunctions as a means to hinder gang activities. Fully half of those jurisdictions are located in southern California, with another four being found in northern California. The city of Los Angeles has obtained 17 such injunctions. Injunctions prohibit a variety of behaviors, including association with known gang members; using public pay phones, cell phones, or pagers; engaging in vandalism; drug dealing; or trespassing on private property.

Jamilah Owens and Robert Boehmer, *New Anti-gang Laws in Effect* (Chicago: Illinois Criminal Justice Information Authority, 1993); Claire Johnson, Barbara Webster, and Edward Connors, *Prosecuting Gangs: A National Assessment* (Washington, DC: National Institute of Justices, 1995); Malcolm Klein, *The American Street Gang: Its Nature, Prevention and Control* (New York: Oxford University Press, 1995), p. 184; *U.S. v. Lopez*, 514 U.S. 549 (1995); *Chicago v. Morales*, 527 U.S. 41 (1999); Cheryl Maxson, "Civil Gang Injunctions: The Ambiguous Case of the National Migration of a Gang Enforcement Strategy," pages 375–389 in Finn-Aage Esbensen, Stephen Tibbetts, and Larry Gaines (eds.), *American Youth Gangs at the Millennium* (Long Grove, IL: Waveland Press, 2004); Cheryl Maxson, Karen Hennigan, and David Sloane, "It's Getting Crazy Out There: Can a Civil Gang Injunction Change a Community," *Criminology & Public Policy* 4:577–606 (2005); Arlen Egley, James Howell, and Meena Harris, *Highlights of the 2012 National Youth Gang Survey* (Washington, DC: U.S. Department of Justice, 2014).

Police Department's Anti-Gang Initiative targeted five areas of the city that were home to seven of the city's most violent gangs. The suppression strategy included saturation/high-visibility patrols in target areas; as part of this monitoring, suspected gang members were stopped and frisked, aggressive curfew enforcement was applied whenever suspected gang members were encountered, and truancy laws and

regulations were strictly enforced. An evaluation of the program conducted by Eric Fritsch and his colleagues found that gang-related violence decreased in both targeted and control areas, although the decrease was more substantial in targeted areas (57% versus 37%).[119] Neighborhood sweep programs produced similarly positive outcomes in Boston, Indianapolis, and Minneapolis.[120]

Sometimes suppression efforts produce unexpected outcomes. Susan Popkin evaluated an antidrug initiative in the Chicago Housing Authority. Although the program reduced drug sales and disorder, residents felt more vulnerable to gang members who lived in the projects because they retaliated against residents who cooperated with police. Another unintended consequence was that power vacuums were created after gang leaders were arrested and detained, which in turn contributed to *more* violence and disorder.[121] Suppression efforts alone often cannot reduce gang problems; however, when paired with prevention, this strategy is more effective. Arresting gang youths is merely one part of the equation: Prosocial alternatives and other programs need to be provided as alternatives to gang life. Indeed, Anthony Braga and his colleagues report that anti-gang initiatives that balance crime control and social services produce the strongest and most enduring effects. For example, Anthony Braga and David Weisburd reported that suppression policies such as focused deterrence programs can produce huge declines in homicide and juvenile homicide. Among their findings, *Operation Ceasefire* in Boston produced a 63% reduction in youth homicides, the *Indianapolis Violence Reduction Partnership* produced a 34% reduction in total homicides, *Operation Peacekeeper* in Stockton, California, yielded a 42% reduction in gun homicides, *Project Safe Neighborhoods* in Lowell, Massachusetts, contributed to a 44% reduction in gun assaults, and the *Cincinnati Initiative to Reduce Violence* produced a 35% reduction in homicides.[122]

Another suppression strategy involves establishing specialized prosecution programs to target gangs.

Police departments have initiated street sweeps of suspected gang members in an effort to combat delinquency. Will such programs be effective? Do these policies aggravate or enhance police–community relations?

© ES James/Shutterstock.

Responsibilities of these specialized prosecutors include coordinating their efforts with law enforcement, creating and managing databases designed to track gangs and gang members, and pursuing vertical prosecution of gang members. Vertical prosecutions involve a process by which an attorney or a small group of attorneys is assigned to gang cases and is responsible for handling them from inception to sentencing.[123] For example, in Orange County, California, a gang reduction program brought together the police, probation department, and prosecutor's Office to create the Tri-Agency Resource/Gang Enforcement Team (TARGET). This approach permitted the participants to merge gang member Identification, field interviews, enforcement, case preparation, witness support, vertical prosecution, sentencing and probation into a single collaborative effort.

Other gang prosecution programs around the United States include the following:[124]

- Transfers to adult court for juvenile gang members
- Forfeiture of cars used in drive-by shootings
- Enhanced penalties for crimes committed near schools
- Enhanced penalties for graffiti writing
- Prosecution for gang recruitment
- Prosecution for criminal conspiracy under the federal *Racketeer Influenced and Corrupt Organizations Act* (RICO) and similar state laws in cases of drug sales and other applicable crimes

Suppression efforts may also target a small number of identified gang members. For instance, the work of a task force in Lowell, Massachusetts, which advertised to gang members the certainty and severity of punishment for committing crimes, resulted in declines in murders and aggravated assaults committed with handguns.[125]

Injunction/Abatement

An **injunction** or **abatement** is a civil process in which gang members are prohibited from engaging in mundane activities, such as loitering at schools or hanging out on street corners. If they violate these mandates, gang members face arrest. Basically, gangs are defined as a "public nuisance"—that is, something injurious to health, indecent or offensive, or an obstruction of free use of property that interferes with the enjoyment of life. If gang members violate the civil injunction, they are issued a temporary restraining order (much like defendants in domestic violence cases). If they

KEY TERMS

injunction (abatement)
A civil process in which gang members are prohibited from engaging in mundane activities, such as loitering at schools or hanging out on street corners; if they violate these mandates, they face arrest.

then violate the temporary restraining order, they can be legally held in contempt of court and charged in civil or criminal court. Nationally, approximately 8% of U.S. law enforcement agencies use abatement ordinances and 6% use civil gang injunctions.[126]

Sometimes, injunctions creatively attempt to reduce gang delinquency. For example, in Cicero, Illinois, police had the vehicles of gang members towed to remove them from town. According to officials, the city could seek injunctive relief to abate the public nuisance (gangs). When the American Civil Liberties Union challenged the towing policy, however, it was voluntarily suspended by the city.[127]

Do gang injunctions work? Cheryl Maxson and her colleagues evaluated a gang injunction in five neighborhoods in San Bernardino, California. Residents were surveyed about their perceptions and experiences with gangs 18 months before and 6 months after the gang injunction. In the most gang-ridden areas, the injunction resulted in less gang presence, fewer reports of gang intimidation, and less fear of confrontation with gang members. However, areas that previously had less gang problems reported more gang presence, presumably caused by the gang members fleeing the injunction area. Even with these mixed findings, total fear of crime was reduced in all neighborhoods.[128]

Intervention and Prevention

Not all gang experts believe the gang problem should be viewed in an "us versus them" context or that policy responses should focus exclusively on suppression. Some criminologists suggest that gangs and the problems they present are best considered within their social, economic, and cultural context.

For example, John Hagedorn argues that the growth of gangs in "Rustbelt cities," such as Milwaukee, is largely the product of the emerging African American urban underclass. Growing unemployment, poverty, and the fight from the cities by both whites and upwardly mobile blacks have left the underclass behind in the inner city. As the poverty of the minority underclass increases, old gangs reposition themselves, new gangs emerge, and gangs generally get stronger, drawing from the increasing number of school dropouts and underemployed or unemployed youths looking for the only jobs in town. Moreover,

the social organization of the community, the social cohesion, friendship ties, and willingness to establish and participate in informal social controls are negatively affected by joblessness. Solutions to this problem will require creating jobs that pay adequate wages and improving educational opportunities for the urban underclass.[129]

The federal Office of Juvenile Justice and Delinquency Prevention created the **Gang Reduction Program**, which includes a framework for coordinating a wide range of activities that have demonstrated effectiveness in reducing gang activity and delinquency. Activities center on the following five goals:[130]

- *Primary prevention*—focusing on the entire population in high-crime and high-risk communities
- *Secondary prevention*—focusing on high-risk youths ages 7 to 14 to provide appropriate services for prevention of onset of gang membership and related problem behaviors
- *Intervention*—focusing on active gang members and their close associates to provide a combination of services and opportunities while holding these youths accountable for their actions
- *Reentry*—focusing on gang-involved and other serious offenders who face multiple challenges to reentering their communities after confinement
- *Suppression*—focusing on gang leaders to undertake aggressive prosecution efforts

The Gang Reduction Program has been credited for partially reducing crime in places such as Richmond (Virginia), Milwaukee, North Miami Beach, and Los Angeles, where gangs are responsible for nearly 60% of all homicides and 70% of all shootings citywide.

Another example is the Boys & Girls Clubs of America Gang Intervention Through Targeted Outreach program. The program is sponsored by the Office of Juvenile Justice and Delinquency Prevention and has four components: (1) community assessment and mobilization, where city leaders examine community resources and develop a strategy to prevent youth from joining gangs; (2) recruitment, where schools, foster care, juvenile justice organizations, and social service providers recruit gang-affiliated youth to join the local Boys & Girls Club; (3) programming, where gang awareness, conflict resolution, bullying prevention, and educational programs are created; and (4) case management, where the youths' response to the programs is evaluated. To date, the Boys & Girls Clubs of America Gang Intervention Through Targeted Outreach has shown positive strides toward reducing gang delinquency and gang membership and is classified as a promising prevention program.[130]

One of the most successful anti-gang programs is **Homeboy Industries** in Los Angeles. This job-training program educates, trains, and finds jobs for at-risk youths and gang members. Among the training and jobs that Homeboy Industries provides are those

KEY TERMS

Gang Reduction Program
An initiative within the federal Office of Juvenile Justice and Delinquency Prevention that includes a framework for coordinating a wide range of activities that have demonstrated effectiveness in reducing gang activity and delinquency.

Homeboy Industries
A Los Angeles–based program that educates, trains, and finds jobs for at-risk youths and gang members.

related to silk screening (e.g., of T-shirts), maintenance, food service, car detailing, restaurants, and bakeries. Several free services, such as tattoo removal, counseling, job referrals, and life-skills training, are provided. The program is so successful that former First Lady Laura Bush visited Homeboy Industries as part of her Helping America's Youth Initiative.[131]

Many communities have implemented intervention and prevention programs that target youths before they join gangs. Contemporary approaches evolved out of programs developed during the late 1960s and early 1970s, in which street workers (also known as "detached workers") were assigned by social service agencies to work directly with gang members. Current programs target at-risk youths in the community who have not yet joined gangs; they are intended to help youths develop positive social relationships and find alternatives to gang participation. These programs typically use combinations of the following community-, school-, and family-based strategies:

- Youth outreach programs
- Establishment of community centers
- Employment and training assistance
- School dropout services
- Multicultural training for teachers
- Family intervention and training
- Substance abuse counseling
- conflict mediation programs
- Recreational activities

According to Ronald Huff, intervention and prevention programs should be multilevel and multifaceted,

reflecting the fact that serious adolescent gang behavior typically is the result of multiple factors. Programs should address family and peer issues, the child's psychological needs, school adjustment problems, and any ecological or neighborhood disorganization factors that affect the child. Huff believes that if these programs are to bring about "significant and sustainable change in youth behavior," they must also be systematic in nature and long term, lasting a minimum of 2 years.[132] One anti-gang program that has received considerable attention is Gang Resistance Education and Training (G.R.E.A.T.), a curriculum taught by police officers to elementary and middle school students. G.R.E.A.T. students are given the opportunity to discover for themselves the ramifications of gang violence through structured exercises and interactive approaches to learning. Police officers and teachers work together to teach students to set goals for themselves, resist peer pressure, reduce impulsive behavior, enhance self-esteem, and learn to make better choices, thereby leading to reduced gang affiliation and delinquent activity. Recent evaluations of G.R.E.A.T suggest that the program is working: Students who go through the G.R.E.A.T. program are less likely than peers who did not go through the program to become involved in gangs or to engage in most indicators of delinquency, including drug use, property crimes, and crimes against the person. These studies also indicate that G.R.E.A.T. is more effective for youths who are at higher risk for gang affiliation and delinquency—specifically, young minority males.[133]

WRAP UP

THINKING ABOUT JUVENILE DELINQUENCY: CONCLUSIONS

For many youths, next to the family, the peer group contains the people with whom they spend most of their time. Put differently, their social world often revolves around their peers. Through peers, youths search for identity, acceptance, and meaning. Although peer groups are important in the socialization of adolescents, they also provide opportunities for youths to develop values, attitudes, and behaviors contrary to those of many adults. Many behaviors engaged in by peer groups involve delinquency. Adolescents who have delinquent friends will also be more likely to become delinquent.

Most of the criminological research on the relationship between peers and delinquency has centered on gangs. The mythology about gangs often depicts them as organized and cohesive, with strong leadership and an orientation to protecting their turf. Criminologists

have found that, by and large, these perceptions *do not* accurately describe what most gangs are or do. Gangs do appeal to minorities and lower-class youths in large cities. Gang members often have important problems as adolescents, and they learn to cope by being aggressive, even against other members in the gang. Recent studies suggest that gang violence is increasing at a worrisome rate and that much of the current gang violence is related to competition in drug markets.

Although legislative, law enforcement, and community strategies to combat gangs have varied greatly over the past century, little evidence suggests that they have been successful at stemming the tide of gangs. Like delinquency in general, gang delinquency ultimately brings youths into contact with the police, the juvenile and criminal courts, and the correctional system.

CHAPTER SPOTLIGHT

- Research shows convincingly that peer groups exert influence over behavior, such that having delinquent peers is among the strongest correlates of delinquency.
- Youths involved in delinquent gangs have greater and more intense risk factors for violence, delinquency, and victimization.
- Facilitation, selection, and enhancement are three models that have been advanced to explain how delinquency increases and why it increases after youths become involved in gangs.
- Although they can be diverse, gangs are organized by neighborhood, race, and ethnicity, and all gangs are disproportionately involved in violence and drug dealing.
- The juvenile justice system has developed policies that specifically target gang members and the presence of gangs within communities.

CRITICAL THINKING

1. Scholars frequently disagree over the appropriate definition of gangs. Is this only a semantic issue? Are gangs, by implicit definition, a negative, criminal phenomenon?
2. Are the rationales youths provide for joining gangs merely excuses? Why do the majority of youth in gang-infested neighborhoods choose not to join these groups? How does the idiom "birds of a feather flock together" apply to delinquent gangs?
3. At the height of gang activity in the 1990s, gangs were responsible for hundreds of homicides each year. In cities such as Chicago and Los Angeles, gang members murdered one to two fellow youths every day. How might the media or academic portrayal of gang-affiliated youths contribute to the problems they pose?
4. To avoid gang violence, should prison populations be segregated based on gang affiliation? Would such a policy be construed as acquiescence to the criminal element?
5. Fraternities and sororities on university campuses meet many of the criteria for gangs. Which sorts of deviance and crime do Greek organizations engage in at your college? Why do criminologists not call fraternities "gangs"? Do class and ethnic characteristics influence the manner in which we conceptualize gangs?

SECTION 4

Special Topics

During most of the 20th century, actions related to juvenile offenders typically came under the exclusive domain of the juvenile justice system. There, offenders were treated according to a more protective philosophy than would have applied had they been cast into the adult system. Because the overwhelming majority of delinquents are low-risk, adolescence-limited offenders, the juvenile justice system employs many diversionary mechanisms intended to correct their behavior without getting the youth formally involved in the criminal justice system. A different approach is being taken for serious, violent, and chronic juvenile delinquents, however. These youths are being transferred into adult courts and, if convicted, face some of the same punishments faced by adults. Chapter 13 explores characteristics of juvenile offenders and outlines the juvenile justice process from arrest to disposition. It also investigates those cases in which juveniles are transferred to the adult criminal justice system and the demise of life without parole for juvenile offenders and the juvenile death penalty.

Chapter 14, Delinquency Prevention, explores approaches, policies, and programs intended to prevent juvenile delinquency from occurring in the first place, to prevent its recurrence among first-time offenders, or at least to reduce recidivism among juvenile offenders who have already moved into the juvenile justice system. Prevention approaches target individuals and groups in family, school, and community settings at the front end, before delinquency becomes a patterned reality. Control or management of delinquency occurs *after* the fact and is essentially what the juvenile justice system was designed to accomplish.

SECTION OUTLINE

Chapter 13: The Juvenile Justice System

Chapter 14: Delinquency Prevention

The Juvenile Justice System

OBJECTIVES

- Know the laws constraining police in searches and seizures of juvenile suspects.
- Understand the nature of police discretion, including how legal and extralegal factors influence the decision to make an arrest.
- Be familiar with the different stages of the juvenile court process.
- Describe the alternative dispositions available to the juvenile court.
- Explain the means by which a juvenile may be waived from juvenile to criminal court for prosecution as an adult.

KEY TERMS

In 1964, then FBI Director J. Edgar Hoover commented on what he saw as the arrogant attitude of youth toward the criminal justice system, noting that many delinquents believed that because they were minors, the full force of the law could not touch them.[1] Most often, they were right. Many arrested offenders who are *juveniles* (typically defined as persons younger than age 18, although this age varies across states, as shown in **Table 13.1**) go through a separate juvenile justice system in which they receive lenient treatment and, at most, brief confinement in a detention or juvenile correctional facility. Today, most juvenile offenders have very limited contact with the adult criminal justice system, except for temporary detention in adult jails.

A major reason why so few adolescents have contact with the adult criminal justice system is that most juvenile offenders are unremarkable in their delinquency and do not warrant such legally serious treatment. In the 21st century, states have increasingly attempted to remove the vast majority of juvenile delinquents from various stages of the criminal justice system. Seven broad trends have occurred to overhaul American juvenile justice systems:

- Several states, including Arkansas, Georgia, Hawaii, Indiana, Kansas, Kentucky, Nebraska, New Hampshire, South Dakota, Utah, and West Virginia, have legislated

Table 13.1 Minimum Age at Which a Child Can Be Tried as an Adult

No minimum age specified	Alaska, Arizona, Delaware, District of Columbia, Hawaii, Idaho, Indiana, Maine, Maryland, Oklahoma, Oregon, Rhode Island, South Carolina, South Dakota, Tennessee, Washington, West Virginia
10 years	Kansas, Vermont
12 years	Colorado, Missouri
13 years	Georgia, Illinois, Mississippi, New Hampshire, North Carolina, Wyoming
14 years	Alabama, Arkansas, California, Connecticut, Florida, Iowa, Kentucky, Louisiana, Michigan, Minnesota, Nevada, New Jersey, North Dakota, Ohio, Pennsylvania, Texas, Utah, Virginia, Wisconsin

OJJDP Statistical Briefing Book. [Online]. Available at: http://www.ojjdp.gov/ojstatbb/structure_process/qa04105.asp?qaDate=2009. Released on March 17, 2016. Material originally compiled by P. Griffin for the National Center for Juvenile Justice's State Juvenile Justice Profiles website.

comprehensive juvenile justice reforms that divert lower-risk youth from the system, invest in effective, evidence-based, community-based programming, and preserve public safety.

- Nearly half of states have returned jurisdiction of juvenile offenders to the juvenile justice system. This is accomplished in a variety of ways. Arizona, Indiana, Nevada, Missouri, Ohio, Vermont, and Wisconsin reformed their transfer, waiver, and direct file laws to give more discretion to juvenile courts in sentencing matters. Missouri amended the "once an adult, always an adult" statute to allow a juvenile offender to return to the juvenile justice system if he or she was found not guilty in criminal court. Other states, including Connecticut, Illinois, Massachusetts, and New Hampshire, expanded their juvenile court jurisdictions to include older youth who previously would have been automatically prosecuted as adults.

- About half of states have enacted laws that address delinquency prevention and early interventions, including the reform of detention, diversion of nonviolent youth, diversion of status offenders, and the realignment of state funds from state institutions to evidence-based community alternatives. Ohio and Texas, for instance, reinvested savings from closed youth prisons into community-based rehabilitation programs. California, Indiana, Kansas, Kentucky, Louisiana, Massachusetts, Nebraska, Rhode Island, Texas, and Washington have reformed laws on status offenders that basically transfer them from juvenile justice facilities to child welfare agencies that provide services that the youth need, such as drug treatment.

- Many states have expanded the due process protections of juvenile delinquents. Twenty-three states and the District of Columbia have enacted juvenile competency statutes that potentially allow a juvenile to be found incompetent to stand trial on the basis of developmental immaturity, mental illness, or intellectual disability. Other areas of due process protections include access to counsel for indigent juveniles, reduction in the use of shackling (placement in handcuffs and/or leg irons), and greater restriction of the use of solitary confinement.

- There is increasing focus on the mental health needs of serious delinquents. Approximately 70% of youth who are taken into custody each year have a diagnosable mental health condition. Arkansas, Idaho, Louisiana, Michigan, Mississippi, Montana, Texas, and Washington have enacted laws that divert delinquents with serious mental health problems, require mental health screening and assessment of juvenile offenders, authorize law enforcement to bring juveniles to evaluation and treatment facilities when they were contacted for non-serious offenses, or prohibit juvenile statements made during mental health screenings from being used in court.

- In an effort to reduce racial and ethnic disparities in juvenile justice system contact and involvement, 31 states have laws that define and prohibit racial profiling. Connecticut, Iowa, and Oregon established racial impact statements that require legislation be screened for language that might result in unequal targeting or treatment of minority youth. Georgia requires probation staff to use race-neutral risk assessments to eliminate racial and ethnic bias in detention screening.

- There is greater focus on aftercare and the lives that delinquents will lead after release from custody. Florida, Illinois, Louisiana, Oregon, and Washington have enhanced aftercare support through work release programs, transitional housing, and wraparound treatment programs. Thirty-three states allow juvenile court records to be sealed or expunged. In Iowa, North Carolina, Oklahoma, and Washington, juvenile records are automatically sealed or expunged without any action on the part of the juvenile.

These progressive changes in juvenile justice policy are consistent with the position of the general public, which tends to be pragmatic and prefers less restrictive responses to juvenile delinquents. For example, Riane Miller and Brandon Applegate analyzed data from the Florida Survey on Today's Youth and found that respondents preferred nonincarceration as a punishment for juvenile offenders in 88% of cases. Public approval of use of incarceration was just 17% for violent delinquents, 9% for property delinquents, and 18% for drug delinquents. This means that the public has a general understanding that most delinquents can be saved and rehabilitated. However, the public also recognizes there are more severe offenders who must be dealt with more punitively.

The legislative changes help to ensure that adolescence-limited and otherwise non-serious delinquent youths are not processed in the adult criminal justice system. Of these recent trends, one of the most important rationales centers on the developmental differences between adolescents and adults in terms of their decision making, their ability to cognitively control behavioral impulses, and their overall maturity.[2] The developmental differences between children and adolescents—particularly that based upon new neuroscience research findings—is finding its way into juvenile justice policy that is explored later in this chapter.

It is important to note that there is another subgroup of delinquents in the larger offender population. Studies have consistently shown that most serious juvenile crime is committed by a relatively small number of youths—as few as 2 to 10% of juvenile offenders have been shown to be responsible for half of all juvenile crime and nearly 70 to 90% of serious crimes such as homicide, rape, robbery, and aggravated assault committed by juveniles. Using nationally representative sources of data, Michael Vaughn and his colleagues documented the existence of a "severe 5%" of serious, violent, and chronic juvenile offenders that has previously been shown in localized samples. In addition to engaging in delinquency at much higher rates, starting their delinquent career earlier, and engaging in the most violent of offenses, these youth also had many antisocial personality traits and were weakly bonded to school, conventional peers, parents, and church.[3] Even though juvenile crime constitutes a minor part of the larger crime problem, the fact that many juveniles commit very serious crimes—and the fact that some offenders commit such crimes frequently—is a reality that prompts us to explore how society responds to juvenile crime, how the juvenile justice system operates, and how we should deal with the most serious of juvenile offenders. Many of these more serious offenders will grow up to be adult offenders who subsequently engage with the criminal justice system.

The U.S. juvenile justice system is composed of unique judicial and correctional agencies that specialize in dealing with juvenile offenders and operate with specific policies and procedures that are intended to protect youths from the potentially stigmatizing effects of criminal courts (see **Figure 13.1**). Historically (at least until the early 1970s), juvenile justice systems dealt with three types of cases:

1. Delinquents
2. Status offenders
3. Neglected, abused, or dependent (i.e., destitute, homeless, or abandoned) youths

In recent years, many states have established family courts to deal with status offenders and cases of neglect, abuse, or dependency. In these jurisdictions, specialized juvenile courts focus on cases of delinquency.

The terminology used to describe the various stages and procedures associated with the juvenile justice system differs from that employed in the adult criminal justice system (see **Table 13.2**). These differences are not meant to be merely semantic; rather, they reflect the desire of the juvenile system to avoid unnecessary stigmatization of juvenile offenders.

Law Enforcement

There has always been tension between police and adolescents. Many criminologists believe that this conflict stems from the beliefs held by police that separate these officers from the public and especially from younger citizens. Many police officers are secretive, defensive, and distrustful of outsiders and see themselves as "the pragmatic guardians of the morals of the community . . . the 'thin blue line' against the forces of evil."[4] Indeed, many police view delinquent juveniles as part of that evil force. Conversely, many youths see the police as intrusive, intimidating, and anxious to find fault. For these reasons, any encounter between police and juveniles can be problematic.

Search and Seizure

Every crime is like a jigsaw puzzle, with a few missing pieces to be filled in by investigators. Police *search* for the missing pieces by canvassing the premises or looking for suspects they believe are linked to the crime. Related to the search process is *seizure*, where people or objects relating to the crime are taken into custody.[5] Speaking practically, seizure means that the police have taken legal control over those individuals or items. People are legally seized when they are not free to leave a scene, but not when police merely detain them for a very short time to ask them a few questions.

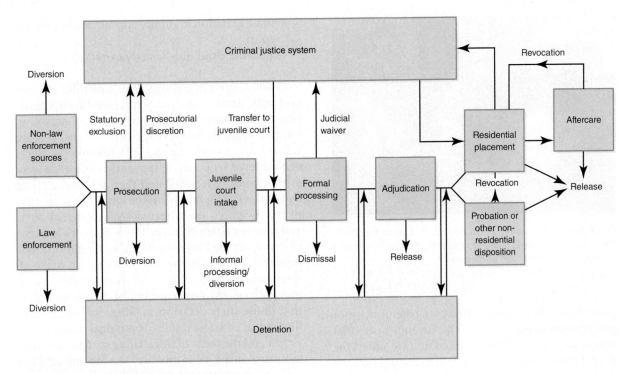

Figure 13.1 The U.S. Juvenile Justice System

Data from Melissa Sickmund and Charles Puzzanchera, *Juvenile Offenders and Victims: 2014 National Report* (Pittsburgh, PA: National Center for Juvenile Justice, 2014), p. 95.

Table 13.2 Differences in Terminology Used in Adult and Juvenile Justice Systems

Adult Criminal Justice System	Juvenile Justice System
Crime	Delinquent act
Criminal	Delinquent
Arrest	Take into custody
Arraignment	Intake hearing
Indictment	Petition
Not guilty plea	Deny the petition
Guilty plea	Agree to an adjudication finding
Plea bargain	Adjustment
Jail	Detention facility
Trial	Adjudication hearing
Conviction	Adjudication
Presentence investigation	Social history
Sentencing	Disposition hearing
Sentence	Disposition
Incarceration	Commitment
Prison	Training or reform school, youth center
Parole	Aftercare

Data from Howard Snyder and Melissa Sickmund, *Juvenile Offenders and Victims: 2006 National Report* (Washington, DC: National Center for Juvenile Justice, 2006), p. 105.

The **exclusionary rule**, which is derived from the Fourth Amendment to the U.S. Constitution, protects people from unreasonable search and seizure. This protection applies to juveniles in the same way as it does to adults: Based on the Supreme Court ruling in *Mapp v. Ohio*, evidence that is obtained illegally may not be admissible in a criminal prosecution or in a juvenile court adjudication hearing.[6] However, juveniles do not have *exactly* the same Fourth Amendment protections *if* searches are conducted in schools. Furthermore, school officials need only reasonable suspicion—not probable cause—to conduct a search of a student. In contrast, when juveniles are outside school, in the public arena, police are held to the same standards that apply when they are searching adults.

Juveniles also *do not* have the same Fourth Amendment protections regarding privacy and searches at home. Courts have held that parents may give third-party consent for officers to search their child's room based on their "common authority" over the premises. In other words, parents may allow police to search the home and their child's bedroom based on either parent's right to control their child or their exercise of

KEY TERMS

exclusionary rule
Rule stating that illegally obtained evidence may not be admissible in a criminal prosecution or in a juvenile court adjudication hearing.

Police and juveniles often find it difficult to trust one another. What programs could law enforcement agencies implement to improve relations with adolescents?

© Peter Casolino/Alamy.

control over the premises.[7] However, parents may not give consent to police to search a juvenile's personal effects, such as a toolbox or locked suitcase, unless the parent claims an established right to control over the items.[8] Parents may also conduct their own searches of a child's room and possessions because the Fourth Amendment protection applies only to government agents, such as law enforcement or probation officers (see **Box 13.1**, the "Delinquency Around the Globe" feature).

Police Discretion

Although the idea of policing is grounded in the legal order and its rules, police officers have vast discretionary powers regarding when and how to apply the law. The contact between a police officer and a juvenile is a form of social interaction, and like all social interaction, its "quality" depends on different factors, including the youth's attitude, personality, and demeanor. **Police discretion** is the authority of police to choose one course of action over another.

When police suspect a juvenile of a crime, they can handle the matter informally or take the child into custody and refer the child to juvenile court, criminal court, or a welfare agency. Specifically, police have discretionary authority to take the following actions:

- Release the child with or without a lecture
- Release the child with or without a lecture but write a report describing the contact
- Release the child but file a more formal report referring the matter to a juvenile bureau or an intake unit for possible action
- Interrogate or search the child

- Issue a citation for future appearance in juvenile court
- Take the child into custody (arrest)

Most police encounters with juveniles do not end with arrests. In fact, Stephanie Myers's analysis of data from Indianapolis and St. Petersburg, Florida, suggests that very few juvenile suspects are taken into custody. Of the 654 juvenile suspects encountered by police in her study, only 13% were arrested. Police lectured and then released 22% of suspects, wrote a report on the situation with 15% of the juveniles, interrogated 48%, searched 20%, and issued a citation to 3%. Heidi Bonner's analysis of data from the Project on Policing Neighborhoods found that officers generally prefer to not make an arrest when contacting youth. Bonner also found that officers employ a variety of "working rules" that guide their decision making, such as greater likelihood of arrest if there is physical injury to the victim and the tactic of threatening to make an arrest to ensure suspect compliance. Lee Slocum and her colleagues found that how police officers interact with youth in terms of their professionalism and legitimacy affects how juveniles respond to them and can even impact future delinquency. Given that the majority of police–juvenile contacts do not result in arrest and are instead handled informally, is it possible that both legal and extralegal factors might affect the arrest decision of police?[9]

Legal Factors

Although a number of legally relevant factors may influence police decisions to arrest, four appear to be most common and important: offense seriousness, prior arrest record or police contacts, presence of evidence, and suspicious behavior.

Offense Seriousness. Juveniles who commit serious crimes are more likely to be arrested than youths who commit minor offenses. Studies consistently show that more serious forms of delinquency such as murder, armed robbery, and burglary are much more likely to result in arrest than less serious offenses, including shoplifting and disorderly conduct. This is the conclusion reached by Robert Terry based on a study of police dispositions of more than 9000 juvenile offenses. In a related study, Donald Black and Albert Reiss divided offenses into four types and found that the likelihood of being arrested increased with offense seriousness. Moreover, as Stephanie Myers found in her analysis of data from Indianapolis and St. Petersburg, juveniles are more likely to be arrested not just for serious offenses but also for crimes involving a weapon.

Offense seriousness not only affects the likelihood of arrest, but also police authority. Robert Brown and his colleagues examined predictors of police

BOX 13.1

Delinquency Around the Globe

Punishing Juvenile Offenders in Russia and the Netherlands

Although juvenile crime rates have declined significantly in the United States during the past decade, Russia and the Netherlands have experienced increases in juvenile delinquency during the same period. Juvenile offenders in these countries, as in the United States, tend to be male (92% in Russia and 80% in the Netherlands) and to have more likely committed property crimes and social order offenses rather than violent offenses.

In Russia, local prosecutors determine what will happen to youths aged 14 to 18 who are arrested by police. A youth may have the case dismissed, be referred to a citizen's juvenile court for informal disposition, or be sent to a People's Court for formal adjudication. Approximately 60% of juvenile offenders in Russia are convicted in the People's Courts. Before 1996, 40% of convicted youths received suspended sentences, and 50 to 60% received incarceration sentences. Since 1996, in response to a rising rate of serious delinquency, closer to three-fourths of convicted youths have been sentenced to confinement in a *reformatory colony* or youth correctional facility for no more than 10 years. Juveniles are confined separately from adult offenders. First-time male offenders are typically incarcerated in a labor colony, whereas first-time female offenders more often are placed in re-educational colonies.

The Netherlands takes a more liberal approach in dealing with delinquent youths. Youths who are younger than age 12 cannot be held criminally responsible for an offense and may not be criminally prosecuted. Instead, they are sent home with a caution. However, if the youth committed a serious crime, then he or she may be referred to a civil court with the option of psychological counseling. Juveniles aged 12 to 17 are diverted out of the justice system whenever possible at each stage of the process. In recent years, nearly half of all juveniles dealt with by the Dutch police have been referred for HALT sanctions, which are similar to many police and court diversion programs in the United States. The youth must first admit committing the offense, and the case is then handled informally with an emphasis on cautioning. If the case is sent to the court and the youth is found guilty, a nonpunitive sentence is most often imposed. Such a sentence may include fines, community sentence (either service or education), detention, and possibly placement in a juvenile institution for a maximum of 12 months if the youth is younger than age 16 and for a maximum of 24 months if the youth is 16 to 18 years old. Approximately half of adjudicated juveniles receive community sentences.

As in Russia, rising rates of serious youth crime have led to a more punitive attitude toward juvenile delinquents in the Netherlands in recent years. The Ministry of Justice is increasing the number of juvenile institutions and bed space in current institutions. Between 1995 and 2001, the Netherlands increased the total number of custodial beds from 900 to 2100.

These countries provide two perspectives in dealing with serious delinquency, one characterized by punitive control and enforcement and the other more progressive. The United States has traditionally engaged in both approaches, although it favored a punitive approach to respond to the historically high levels of delinquency, crime, and violence in the latter three decades of the 20th century. But the current era is also historically significant—for relatively low delinquency—and the U.S. juvenile justice system now looks more like the Netherlands than ever before.

James Williams and Daniel Rodeheaver, "Punishing Juvenile Offenders in Russia," *International Criminal Justice Review* 12:93–110 (2002); Dmitry Shestakov and Natalia Shestakova, "An Overview of Juvenile Justice and Juvenile Crime in Russia," pages 411–440 in John Winterdyk (ed.), *Juvenile Justice Systems: International Perspectives* (Toronto: Canadian Scholars' Press, 2002); Henk Ferwerda, "Youth Crime and Juvenile Justice in the Netherlands," pages 435–453 in John Winterdyk (ed.), *Juvenile Justice Systems: International Perspectives* (Toronto: Canadian Scholars' Press, 2002); Karin Wittebrood, "Juvenile Crime and Sanctions in the Netherlands," *Journal of Contemporary Criminal Justice* 19:435–453 (2003); James Howell, Mark Lipsey, and John Wilson, *A Handbook for Evidence-Based Juvenile Justice Systems* (Lanham, MD: Lexington Books, 2014).

behavior among officers in Cincinnati and found that offense seriousness was a strong predictor of arrest. In addition, offense seriousness increased the likelihood of a juvenile being questioned by police, being commanded to comply, being searched, and other coercive police responses.[10]

Prior Arrest Record. Police are more likely to arrest children who have a prior arrest record. Terry found that a juvenile's prior arrest record was a strong predictor of police action. In his study, first-time offenders accounted for 38% of all juveniles arrested but only 7% of the juveniles referred to juvenile court. At the other extreme were juveniles with five or more

previous arrests, who accounted for 20% of arrests but more than 66% of juvenile court referrals. Cindy Cottle and her colleagues published a meta-analysis of 23 studies that included 15,265 juveniles and found that prior arrest record was the strongest predictor of juvenile recidivism, or continued delinquency. Thus, the police recurrently contact youth with a prior record, not because they are labeled, but because they continually commit crime.[11]

Based on his observations of police–juvenile encounters in two cities, Aaron Cicourel concluded that having a prior arrest record often turned an otherwise trivial event into a serious one. He also discovered that a youth's prior arrest record became a more important factor when decisions were made at the police station rather than on the street. Patrol officers often lack the necessary information to take an individual's prior arrest record into account. They may also view past-offense history as irrelevant, because their primary concern is handling the situation they face in the least troublesome manner.[12]

Presence of Evidence. Suspects are typically connected with a crime in one of two ways: (1) police see the suspect commit the crime or (2) a citizen informs the police about a crime and the person(s) who did it. When Kenneth Novak and his colleagues analyzed data collected in Hamilton County, Ohio, they found the presence of evidence to be positively related to arrest: In cases where a greater number of evidence criteria were present (ranging from the officer hearing a confession from the suspect and hearing claims from others about the suspect to the officer observing physical evidence and seeing the suspect commit the act), suspects were significantly more likely to be arrested.

Kerrin Wolf's study of school resource officers in Delaware found that quality of evidence was the number one reason for the arrest decision. In addition, just like patrol officers in the community, school resource officers sometimes decline to make an arrest despite evidence of delinquency. David May and his colleagues similarly found that evidence was a primary determinant of arrest among school resource officers. In addition, school resource officers were less likely than law enforcement outside of school to take youth into custody for minor offenses even when there was evidence of delinquency.[13]

Suspicious Behavior. A police officer's discretionary decision to stop and then possibly arrest a juvenile generally begins when the officer observes a youth engaging in what he or she believes to be suspicious behavior. Suspicious behavior is more than presenting a disrespectful demeanor or "attitude" (discussed later in this chapter); it includes acts that appear out of place given the particular circumstances. In 1968, the Supreme Court held in *Terry v. Ohio* that if the police observe behavior that leads them to conclude criminal activity may be in progress and that the suspect is likely armed, they may stop and frisk the individual.[14] However, merely acting suspiciously does not provide a legal justification for an arrest.

Unfortunately, some research suggests that police perceptions of youths acting suspiciously may be related to both the sex and the race of the youths. Terrence Allen found that police officers are overwhelming (84%) more likely to agree with the statement that, "If two or more males are together, they are probably committing a delinquent act."[15] Moreover, Geoffrey Alpert and his colleagues suggest that minority status influences whether a police officer initially perceives a youth as suspicious. Specifically, African Americans are more likely to be viewed by police as suspicious based on nonbehavioral indicators (for example, the individual's appearance, race, and time and place where he or she is observed).[16]

Extralegal Factors

Extralegal factors are those elements of an encounter or characteristics of a juvenile suspect or the officer that have nothing to do with the actual crime but may still influence the decision police make. The most significant of the many extralegal factors are discussed next.

Race and Ethnicity. Race has received more attention than any other extralegal factor. Research on the influence of race on police use of discretion has produced mixed results (see **Box 13.2**, the "Delinquency Controversy" feature). Some studies have concluded that race matters; others have found it does not matter very much. In at least one recent study it was reported that police are actually more lenient with minority suspects. Criminologists, however, generally believe police do treat African American and white children differently for comparable offenses or when holding prior record and presence of evidence constant. However, these differences in police behavior are subtle and complex and pale when compared to race differences in delinquent behavior.[17]

Proportionally more African American than white juveniles are arrested. There are several reasons for this discrepancy in arrest rates, but the primary reason is that African American youths commit proportionally more delinquency than white youth, particularly for the most serious offenses (e.g., murder and armed robbery) that are most likely to result in arrest. The different delinquent rates by race reinforce police perceptions that African American juveniles are more likely to be involved in serious criminal activity than are whites. Robert Sampson reports that police tend to be suspicious of minority youth and that this suspicion leads them to stop African American and Hispanic juveniles more frequently and to make a record of these encounters. Later, when police stop and question these youths again, they are already "known" to the police and their "prior contact" with the police becomes a basis for more severe treatment.[18]

Not surprisingly, police officers' nearly automatic suspicion of minority youth, coupled with discriminatory practices and beliefs on the part of police, tend to generate feelings of hostility among African American children. In turn, African American juveniles are more likely than white youths to interact with police in a more antagonistic or disrespectful manner, which may lead to their being arrested more often.

Although race appears to play a role in the arrest decision, Robert Brown believes that African Americans are not simply arrested because of their

BOX 13.2

Delinquency Controversy

Race and the Police Revisited

Early policing research largely expected for there to be widespread differential enforcement of the public by race. Although evidence for police bias has been found, and indeed appears in the news media on a frequent basis, biased policing is not the main reason why African American and Hispanic youth are overrepresented in arrest data. The primary reason for race differences in police data relates to behavioral differences. For instance, research has found that:

- Nonwhites are more likely than whites to be disrespectful toward police.
- Nonwhites hold more negative attitudes about police than whites.
- Nonwhites are more likely than whites to behave in suspicious ways toward the police.
- Nonwhites are more likely to perceive that the police behaved improperly toward them during traffic stops.
- Nonwhites are less likely to report crime to the police than whites.
- Nonwhites who have a stronger sense of ethnic identity are more likely than their same-race peers with a neutral ethnic identity to perceive that the police discriminate against them.

It is important to note that use of force by police is extremely rare. Data from the Bureau of Justice Statistics' Police-Public Contact Survey indicated 43.9 million face-to-face contacts between the police and the public. Of these, just 1.6% or 715,500 incidents involved the threat or use of force (in most cases, force was verbally warned

or threatened). About 1.4% of white contacts, 3.5% of black contacts, and 2.1% of Hispanic contacts involved threatened or used force. Put another way, 98.6% of white contacts, 96.5% of black contacts, and 97.9% of Hispanic contacts are smooth and force-free. Even though most police–citizen interactions are routine and professional, there remain sharp racial and ethnic differences in views about police. Jennifer Peck conducted a meta-review of 92 studies and found that regardless of the measures that were used, African Americans and Hispanics had significantly more negative views of police than whites.

In the wake of controversial police shootings of African American youth, a concern is that police may pull back from interacting with racial minorities or patrolling their neighborhoods in response to negative events in places such as Ferguson, Missouri. In their survey of 567 deputies at a law enforcement agency in the southwest United States, Scott Wolfe and Justin Nix found there was a "Ferguson effect," in that officers were less likely to engage in community partnerships. However, once organizational justice and self-legitimacy were accounted for, the Ferguson effect disappeared. This means that officers who are confident in their authority and perceive their department to be fair are willing to engage all communities irrespective of the negative publicity that could ensue.

In other words, the race–police relationship is complex. It is framed by a troubled history of bias, discrimination, perceptions, and dramatic race differences in delinquency. Because of this, it will likely remain a controversy in the study of delinquency.

Shelley Hyland, Lynn Langton, and Elizabeth Davis, *Police Use of Nonfatal Force, 2002–2011* (Washington, DC: U.S. Department of Justice, 2015); Ronald Weitzer and Rod Brunson, "Strategic Responses to the Police among Inner-City Youth," *The Sociological Quarterly* 50:235–256 (2009); Matt DeLisi, "Where Is the Evidence for Racial Profiling?" *Journal of Criminal Justice* 39:461–462 (2011); Jennifer Peck, "Minority Perceptions of the Police: A State-of-the-Art Review," *Policing: An International Journal of Police Strategies & Management* 38:173–203 (2015); James Unnever, Shaun Gabbidon, and George Higgins, "The Election of Barack Obama and Perceptions of Criminal Injustice," *Justice Quarterly* 28:23–45 (2011); Scott Wolfe and Justin Nix, "The Alleged 'Ferguson Effect' and Police Willingness to Engage in Community Partnership," *Law & Human Behavior*, 40:1–10 (2016).

race, although race does appear to factor into this decision. According to Brown, extralegal factors appear to have little effect on arrest decisions for white suspects, whereas all of the extralegal factors measured do significantly affect arrest decisions for African American suspects. Moreover, both legal and extralegal factors increase the likelihood of arrest for African Americans. Daniel Lytle's meta-analysis of the effects of suspect characteristics on arrest found that African Americans and Hispanics are more likely than whites to be arrested.[19]

Attitude and Disrespect. Police suspiciousness of juveniles may be prompted by how youths portray themselves to police, including their demeanor, dress, and attitudes suggestive of disrespect. Piliavin and

Briar's study of police–juvenile encounters was among the first that reported that police decisions were based on character cues that emerged from interactions with juveniles. Among the cues police observed were the juvenile's age, race, grooming, dress, and demeanor. A juvenile's demeanor was a principal predictor of outcome in 50 to 60% of the cases.[20]

In a related study, Black and Reiss classified juveniles' demeanor as "very deferential," "civil" (expressing moderate and realistic amounts of respect), or "antagonistic."[21] Black and Reiss reported 18% of the "antagonistic juveniles" were arrested, whereas Piliavin and Briar found nearly four times that many arrests for "uncooperative juveniles." Only 4% of the "cooperative juveniles" in Piliavin and Briar's study were arrested, compared with 13% of the combined "civil and deferential suspects" in the Black and Reiss sample.

Social Class. Several criminologists have examined the impact of social class on police disposition of juveniles. George Bodine divided more than 3000 records of police dispositions of juveniles into five income-level categories. After comparing dispositions and income levels, he concluded that juveniles from lower-class areas had higher court referral rates than juveniles from upper-class neighborhoods. Bodine offered two explanations for this finding:[22]

- Lower-income youths were more likely to be repeat offenders.
- Juveniles from lower-class areas tended to account for a larger proportion of offenses that generally had high court referral rates, such as petty theft.

Terence Thornberry analyzed data from a large Philadelphia birth cohort. He found that social class had a strong effect on police dispositions that could not be explained when controlling for offense seriousness or prior record. Thornberry also found that lower-class youth were less likely than higher-class juveniles to receive a remedial disposition; this difference was most pronounced for serious offenses.[23]

Sex. Males are arrested in much larger numbers than females, and males generally commit more serious crimes and commit crimes more frequently compared to females. Do these differences simply reflect differences in delinquent behavior of boys and girls, or does their sex influence police decision making? Conventional wisdom tells us that a suspect's sex is likely to make a difference in police dispositions, and a good deal of research appears to support this notion. It is generally believed that female juveniles are treated in distinct, opposite ways. On one hand, the police treat female suspects more leniently and on the other hand are more likely to arrest girls than boys for sex offenses. Subsequent research has investigated one or the other of these findings. For example, Delbert Elliott and Harwin Voss concluded that girls were treated more leniently even in serious cases. They believe that these differences were not because of differential involvement in delinquency, but rather that official records reflect a bias in favor of girls in serious cases.[24] Their findings have been confirmed by separate studies by Gail Armstrong and Meda Chesney-Lind.[25] In contrast, Katherine Teilman and Pierre Landry found that police responded more harshly to girls who committed relatively minor status offenses, such as running away and incorrigibility. Similarly, Ruth Horowitz and Ann Pottiger found that girls who committed serious felonies were less likely to be arrested than boys but were more likely than males to be arrested for less serious crimes.

Finally, Christy Visher observed that "police officers adopt a more paternalistic and harsher attitude toward young females to deter any further violation of appropriate sex-role behavior." More recent research found that the police generally treat girls and boys more similarly than different based on nationally representative data and large delinquent samples. It is also important to note that apparent sex differences in police responses to male and female delinquents are also a function of who is involved in serious delinquency. Because delinquent offenses such as murder, rape, armed robbery, aggravated assault, and others are far more prevalent among boys than girls, there will always be the appearance of differential police response.[26]

Age. Criminologists have studied the association between an offender's age and police disposition. In a classic study, Nathan Goldman found that older youths were more likely to be referred to juvenile court. Juveniles younger than age 10 were referred to court 21% of the time; those between ages 10 and 15, 30% of the time; and adolescents 15 to 18 years old, 46% of the time. In accounting for this referral pattern, Goldman proposed two possibilities:[27]

- The offenses of very young children were typically less serious.
- Some police officers considered the offenses of young children as normal childhood escapades requiring informal rather than formal actions; others thought that formal system processing would do more harm than good; still other officers were too embarrassed to assume a police role in cases where the offender did not fit the stereotypical mold of a criminal menace to society.

George Bodine's analysis of more than 3000 juvenile dispositions showed that for both first-time and repeat offenders, the percentages of children referred to court were smaller for younger juveniles than for older ones.[28] Being young was more likely to reduce the possibility of referral for first-time offenders, though not for recidivists. Police apparently will give young children a break if they do not have a prior record of delinquency.

Arrest

Although the police have a great deal of discretion in deciding when to arrest juvenile offenders, most state statutes provide some guidance for arrest procedures. In general, the laws that govern juvenile arrests are similar to the laws that apply to adults. There is one significant difference, however: Delinquency cases do not require probable cause (a set of facts and circumstances that would lead a reasonable person to believe that a crime has been committed and that the accused committed it) before the juvenile's arrest. Instead, police may take any juvenile into custody if the officer has reasonable suspicion (a suspicion that creates a reasonable belief that the youth committed a delinquent act).

In *misdemeanor cases*, police can arrest a person *only* if the crime is committed in their presence (called the *in-presence requirement*). In *felony cases*, police may make an arrest (1) if they observe the crime in progress or (2) if they have knowledge that a felony crime has occurred and have probable cause for believing a particular person committed it. But these are the rules for arresting adults—many jurisdictions allow police to take a juvenile into custody if the officer has reasonable suspicion to believe the youth is delinquent. In addition, most states require that juveniles taken into custody be transported to a juvenile detention facility rather than to a jail and that parents be notified of the arrest.

Once an officer arrests a juvenile, some states require the officer to notify a probation officer (or other designated official), who will then inform the youth's parents. In some jurisdictions, a juvenile who is taken into police custody goes to the police station for initial screening. Other jurisdictions give officers discretion to choose another course of action:

- Investigate the offense and the juvenile's background
- Decide to terminate the case
- Refer the offender to a community diversion program
- Send the offender to the juvenile court system

Booking

The procedure used when booking juveniles who have been arrested is essentially the same as in adult cases, with one notable exception: Some states forbid routine fingerprinting and photographing of juvenile suspects unless specifically ordered by the juvenile court. When these identification techniques are used, they are intended only for temporary use and should not become part of a permanent criminal record. Advocates of fingerprinting and photographing all youth argue that these techniques provide complete records of young offenders, which are necessary for dealing with youths who refuse to reveal their identity, such as runaways, gang members, and serious offenders. Critics, however, contend that such permanent records make it more difficult for youths to be accepted by teachers or to find employment.

A juvenile's record may also be sealed or destroyed when a case is closed. *Sealing* a record means that it is removed from the main police files and secured in a separate file to be made available only to selected persons with designated authority. *Expunging* a juvenile's arrest record actually physically destroys the record. Some states, such as Massachusetts, allow a juvenile record to be sealed only after the child has reached the age of majority and served his or her sentence

Generally speaking, the laws that govern arrests of juveniles are the same as those that apply to adults. Do you think adults and juveniles should be treated the same?

© Doug Menuez/Photodisc/Getty.

for a crime. Judges in later criminal cases against the same person may still use sealed records, even after the person becomes an adult.

Interrogation

In 1966, the New Jersey Supreme Court, in *In re Carlo*, held that the ultimate objective of the juvenile justice process was to arrive at the truth of a case so as to further the rehabilitation of the juvenile.[29] That same year, the U.S. Supreme Court decided the *Miranda v. Arizona* case.[30] One year later, in 1967, in the case of *In re Gault* (discussed later in this chapter), the Court directed police to change their practices with respect to how juvenile suspects were treated.[31] In *Gault*, the Court extended to juveniles many of the same protections that had been established for adults in *Miranda*, including the right against self-incrimination and the right to counsel. The standard *Miranda* advisement states:

> You have the right to remain silent. Anything you say can and will be used against you in a court of law. You have the right to speak to an attorney, and to have an attorney present during any questioning. If you cannot afford a lawyer, one will be provided for you at government expense.

A number of states believe that juveniles, especially younger children, need to be provided with a *Miranda*-style warning that is more age appropriate. For example, Missouri has established the *McMillian* warning as an alternative to *Miranda* for use when interrogating juveniles:[32]

> I am a police officer, your adversary, and not your friend.

> You have the right to remain silent.

> Anything you say can and will be used against you in a court of law.

> You have the right to talk to a lawyer and have him present with you while you are being questioned.

If you cannot afford to hire a lawyer, one will be appointed to represent you before any questioning, if you wish.

You have the right to have a parent, guardian, or custodian present during questioning.

Any statement you make can be used against you if you are certified for trial in adult court.

Another issue that may become important when police interrogate juveniles is whether children can waive their rights to an attorney, as can adults. The validity of such a waiver may depend on numerous factors, such as the child's age, education, intelligence, knowledge about the substance of the charge, and experience with previous interrogations; the methods of interrogation used; and the length of police questioning.[33] For example, the Wisconsin Supreme Court held that a confession made by a 14-year-old boy with an IQ of only 84, who had limited prior experience with police, had been interrogated by the police for a total of nearly 6 hours, and had repeatedly asked if he could call his mother or father and was told that he could not, was unconstitutional.[34]

In 1979, in *Fare v. Michael C.*, the U.S. Supreme Court ruled that there was no need for courts to impose special protections for minors during interrogation.[35] The Court held that the same standards for adults could be used to assess the constitutionality of a waiver of a juvenile's rights during questioning. As long as the waiver is done "knowingly and intelligently" under the "totality of the circumstances," it is a valid waiver. However, a child asking police to speak to a probation officer is not viewed as being equivalent to his or her requesting to speak to an attorney; only a request to speak to an attorney is considered to invoke the juvenile's *Miranda* rights.

Unfortunately, the interrogation process for juveniles is an area where there is much speculation about what occurs and little in the way of empirical data. An important recent exception is a study of videotaped police interrogations with nearly 60 juveniles who were taken into custody. Hayley Cleary and Sarah Vidal transcribed the language that police used to advise youth of their *Miranda* rights. They found that police officers delivered the *Miranda* advisement in a neutral manner immediately at the beginning of the interview with police. The police presented the

Miranda information verbally and in written format that was rated at a seventh-grade level of reading comprehension. The juveniles readily understood their *Miranda* rights, and 90% agreed to waive their rights and talk with officers.

Some states, such as New Mexico, require that the *Miranda* warning be triggered even when a child is not under custodial interrogation, but simply "suspected" or "imagined" to be engaged in some wrongdoing. In 2001, the New Mexico Supreme Court ruled that before questioning, a child who is detained or seized and suspected of wrongdoing must be advised that he or she has the right to remain silent and that anything said can be used in court.[36] If a child is not advised of the right to remain silent and warned of the consequence of waiving that right, any statement or confession obtained as a result of the detention or seizure is inadmissible in any delinquency proceeding. Officers are not required to give the warning before asking questions about a child's age or identity, when asking general on-the-scene questions, or when a child volunteers statements. Moreover, New Mexico law prohibits the admission of any statements made by a child younger than the age of 13 *in any circumstance*, and imposes a legal presumption that any statements made by children age 13 or 14 are inadmissible.

In 2004, the U.S. Supreme Court reinforced the notion that juveniles do not require special consideration when being questioned by police. In a 5-to-4 decision in *Yarborough v. Alvarado*, the Court held that police do not need to factor in the youth and inexperience of a suspect in their decision of whether to read a juvenile his or her *Miranda* rights if the youth is *not* believed to be "in custody."[37] The *Miranda* warning applies only to persons who are under arrest or who, under the circumstances, reasonably believe they are not free to leave.

Courts

Nearly 1.1 million youths are handled by the juvenile courts in the United States each year. Several key features distinguish these courts from their adult counterparts:

- Absence of legal guilt
- Nonadversarial, nonconfrontational interactions
- Focus on treatment rather than punishment
- Emphasis on the offender's background (e.g., social history, prior behavior, and clinical diagnosis)
- Absence of public scrutiny (private proceedings)
- Speed in processing cases
- Flexibility with sentencing options
- Short-term incarceration

Intake

Courts with juvenile jurisdiction handle an estimated 1.1 million delinquency cases each year in the United States. Just as arrest rates for juveniles have fallen

KEY TERMS

Yarborough v. Alvarado
Case in which the U.S. Supreme Court ruled that police do not need to factor in the age and inexperience of a suspect in their decision about whether to read a juvenile his or her *Miranda* rights if the youth is not believed to be "in custody."

dramatically since the mid-1990s, similar declines in court cases have also occurred. Between 1997 and 2013, delinquency cases in juvenile courts declined by 44%. In the 10 years between 2004 and 2013, total delinquency cases in juvenile courts fell 37%. From 2009 to 2013, the decline was 29% and the 1-year change in delinquency cases in juvenile courts reflected a 7% decrease. Over the past 5 years of data on delinquency filings in juvenile courts, homicides were down 33%, robbery was down 25%, aggravated assault was down 32%, burglary was down 32%, and drug-law violations were down 14%[38] These delinquency cases were referred to the courts by a variety of sources, including law enforcement agencies, social services agencies, schools, parents, probation officers, and victims.

Intake screening procedures are designed to screen out those cases that do not warrant a formal court hearing. Typically, cases that are dismissed meet one of the following criteria:

- Lack of sufficient evidence
- Minor law violations that could be handled informally (i.e., through counseling by a probation officer)
- Compensation already made to the victim
- Jurisdiction inappropriate for juvenile courts (i.e., suspects found to be younger or older than the legal age for juvenile court jurisdiction)
- Circumstances that make the case more appropriate for criminal prosecution (i.e., the serious nature of the crime, the extensive criminal history of the juvenile, or a determination that the juvenile is not amenable to treatment in the juvenile system)

To help make this determination, intake officers may order social background investigations or medical or psychological diagnoses of juvenile suspects. Intake officers are typically given broad discretion in determining which cases warrant formal handling. In an effort to reduce the court's caseload, they may advocate for informal hearings, adjudications, or probation supervision rather than referral to a judge.

If intake does result in the decision for a formal hearing (which happens in approximately 60% of delinquency cases), the intake officer files a **petition**, which states that a delinquent act has been committed by the youth (equivalent to an indictment in criminal prosecutions).[39] The prosecutor at this stage evaluates the case in terms of its legal adequacy. In any case in which a juvenile is alleged to qualify for prosecution in the juvenile court, the prosecutor submits a petition to the court. If the prosecutor decides not to file the petition, that decision is regarded as final and the case is dismissed. If the prosecutor does file the petition, it is usually followed by a report by the intake officer on the behavior patterns and social history of the juvenile.

Bail and Detention

Once a juvenile has been arrested, he or she may be temporarily placed in detention while the court decides how to proceed. If a juvenile was placed in detention, then a petition must be filed in the case and a hearing held within 48 to 72 hours. The primary goal of detention is to ensure that the youth appears at the necessary court hearings.

Most adults are afforded the right to post bail if they are arrested. **Bail** is money or a cash bond deposited with the court or bail bondsman that allows the arrestee to be released after assuring he or she will appear in court at the proper time. In contrast, if a child is not released immediately to his or her parents after being taken into custody, the child must be taken to a local or regional juvenile detention facility. When no bail or bond is available for juveniles, the detention hearing is typically used when the court considers whether to release the juvenile.

Juvenile **detention** is the temporary confinement of a child within a physically restricting facility pending filing of a petition, while the child is awaiting adjudication or disposition hearings, or while the child is awaiting the implementation of disposition. The primary purpose behind detention is twofold: (1) to ensure that the youth will appear for all court hearings and (2) to protect the community from future offending by the youth.

These purposes reflect the perspective of the juvenile justice system, but for serious delinquents, there is another purpose of detention—escape. Elizabeth Barnert and her colleagues interviewed serious delinquents in juvenile detention in Los Angeles and found that youth perceived the path to jail as being easy to achieve and as a form of sanctuary from their home, school, and neighborhood environments, which were chaotic, unsupportive, and violent. Thus, even

KEY TERMS

intake
The initial screening process in the juvenile court to determine whether a case should be processed further.

petition
Similar to an indictment; a written statement setting forth the specific charge that a delinquent act has been committed or that a child is dependent or neglected or needs supervision.

bail
Money or a cash bond deposited with the court or bail bondsman allowing the person to be released on the assurance he or she will appear in court at the proper time.

detention
The temporary custody and care of juveniles pending adjudication, disposition, or implementation of disposition.

as detention protects the community from youthful offending and violence, it also paradoxically provides youth with respite from the same crime and violence to which they contribute.[40]

If a youth is brought to the detention facility by the police after having been taken into custody, intake probation officers must then determine whether the youth should be released or detained. If the juvenile is to be detained, then a petition must be filed and a detention hearing scheduled within 48 to 72 hours. For example, Alabama requires that a child taken into custody be released except in the following situations:

- The child has no parent, guardian, custodian, or other suitable person able and willing to provide supervision and care for such child.
- The release of the child would present a clear and substantial threat of a serious nature to the person or property of others where the child is alleged to be delinquent.
- The release of such child would present a serious threat of substantial harm to such child.
- The child has a history of failing to appear for hearings before the court.

Juveniles also may be detained for evaluation purposes and while awaiting placement in a long-term correctional or treatment facility. As with adults who are detained in jail, the mere fact of being detained increases the likelihood that the youth will be adjudicated delinquent and receive a more severe disposition. The reason for this is two-fold. First, many more serious, chronic, and violent juveniles are placed into detention compared with their less-delinquent peers, which makes them more dangerous settings. Second, there appear to be labeling and criminogenic effects of having been in detention that stay with youth even after they leave the facility (see **Box 13.3** the "A Window on Delinquency" feature).[41]

Approximately 21% of all delinquents are detained at some point in the criminal justice process—either immediately after arrest, while awaiting a hearing, after sentencing, or before incarceration. In 2005, nearly 354,000 juveniles were held in detention for some period of time. Of these cases, 31% involved crimes against a person, 27% involved property crimes,

10% were related to drugs, and 32% involved public order offenses.[42]

Because the juvenile courts view children as more vulnerable than adults, a number of states have established limits on how long youths may be held in detention before a hearing takes place—generally within 30 days. In *Schall v. Martin* (1984), however, the U.S. Supreme Court ruled that juveniles who pose a serious risk of committing additional crimes could be held without determination of probable cause.[43] In this case, the court reasoned that the protection of society was a sufficiently important goal in itself to justify preventive detention of juveniles.

Diversion

Even after a petition has been filed, efforts may still be taken to avoid formal hearings. Similar to plea bargaining in adult cases, the process of **diversion**— the early suspension or termination of the official processing of a juvenile—favors informal or unofficial alternatives. Officials may implement diversion at any of several points along the juvenile justice process in an effort to avoid the negative stigma associated with formal processing in the justice system. For example, police officers may handle delinquents informally by

Detention is used for juveniles, like jails for adults, to ensure the youths' appearance at required court hearings.

© Mikael Karlsson/Alamy.

KEY TERMS

Schall v. Martin
Case in which the U.S. Supreme Court ruled authorizing the preventive detention of juveniles who are identified as "serious risks" to the community if released.

diversion
The early suspension or termination of the official processing of a juvenile in favor of an informal or unofficial alternative.

BOX 13.3

A Window on Delinquency

The Perils of Detention: Findings from the Northwestern Juvenile Project

The Northwestern Juvenile Project is a longitudinal study of 1829 juveniles at intake to the Cook County Juvenile Temporary Detention Center in Chicago, Illinois, who were followed-up on at various points up to 5 years later. The project has been critical in describing the assorted behavioral and psychiatric problems of delinquents in detention and in tracing the effects of detention on their subsequent development. Among the many findings from the Northwestern Juvenile Project:

- Youth in detention are significantly more likely than nondelinquents and diverted youth to exhibit any psychiatric disorder, mania, depression, dysthymia, any anxiety disorder, behavioral disorders such as oppositional defiant disorder and conduct disorder, ADHD, and substance use disorders.
- Youth who have any disorder are three times more likely to be arrested for a violent offense between 3 and 5 years after detention.
- Of youth in detention, 10% have contemplated suicide in the past 6 months and 11% have attempted suicide.
- About 35% of boys in detention and 50% of girls in detention report feelings of hopelessness and consider suicide.
- Fewer than half of detainees with recent thoughts of suicide told anyone, such as a counselor, parent, psychologist, or doctor about their suicidal thoughts.

- The standardized death rate for delinquent youth after detention is four times higher than youth in the general population.
- The primary cause of death among delinquent youth is homicide.

Of course, juveniles who are placed into detention, even temporarily, are more antisocial than youth who are not placed in detention. However, the experience is traumatic for many juveniles and often fails to address the overlapping emotional, behavioral, and substance use problems that afflict this population. For these reasons, juvenile justice systems are eager to divert delinquent youth to more community-based, treatment-oriented placements so that their comorbid problems can be addressed. A recent innovation to replace detention is juvenile evening reporting centers where juveniles report to a juvenile justice facility that also provides treatment, services, and educational materials. Evening reporting centers are modeled on day reporting centers to which various adults report in the criminal justice system. The logic of evening reporting centers is that youth are in school during the day and would also have a structured environment in the evening. This allows them to remain in the community and receive services while avoiding the stigma and potentially negative consequences of detention.

Katherine Elkington, Linda Teplin, Karen Abram, Jessica Jakubowski, Mina Dulcan, and Leah Welty, "Psychiatric Disorders and Violence: A Study of Delinquent Youth after Detention," *Journal of the American Academy of Child & Adolescent Psychiatry* 54:302–312 (2015); Karen Abram, Jeanne Choe, Jason Washburn, Linda Teplin, Devon King, Mina Dulcan, and Elena Bassett, *Suicidal Thoughts and Behaviors among Detained Youth* (Washington, DC: U.S. Department of Justice, 2014); Jason Washburn, Linda Teplin, Laurie Voss, Clarissa Simon, Karen Abram, Gary McClelland, and Nichole Olson, *Detained Youth Processed in Juvenile and Adult Court: Psychiatric Disorders and Mental Health Needs* (Washington, DC: U.S. Department of Justice, 2015); Linda Teplin, Gary McClelland, Karen Abram, Darinka Mileusnic-Polchan, Nichole Olson, and Anna Harrison, *Violent Death in Delinquent Youth after Detention* (Washington, DC: U.S. Department of Justice, 2015); Brett Garland, Sara Moore, Mary Stohrn, and Michael Kyle, "Juvenile Evening Reporting Centers: A Research Note on an Emerging Practice," *Youth Violence and Juvenile Justice* 14:164–174 (2016).

communicating an expectation of participation in a community recreation program, probation officers may choose to require restitution rather than recommend a formal hearing, or judges may choose to delay sentencing while the youths are supervised on informal probation.

Good candidates for diversion programs include individuals with the following characteristics:

- First-time offenders charged with less serious offenses
- Repeat status offenders
- Offenders already participating in community-based treatment programs

These youths may be given an opportunity to participate in a variety of diversion efforts, including mediation—meetings that bring the complainant,

the juvenile, and a neutral hearing officer together to reach a mutually acceptable solution.

Diversion is very popular because it allows juveniles the opportunity to avoid formal juvenile justice system contact in favor of another disposition. There is mixed anecdotal evidence about the effectiveness of diversion. For many youths, being diverted from the juvenile justice process is a golden opportunity to avoid the negative consequences that stem from delinquency and desist from offending. For others, diversion simply provides additional opportunities to keep offending until the next delinquent offense and juvenile court involvement. This mixed bag of effectiveness is also shown in scholarly reviews of diversion. Craig Schwalbe and his colleagues conducted a meta-analysis of 28 studies involved 57 experimental comparisons of diversion/nondiversion programs that included more than 19,000 juveniles. Overall, they found no significant relationship between diversion programs and lower recidivism among juveniles who received them compared to other legal interventions. Among five types of diversion programs, including case management, individual treatment, family treatment, youth court, and restorative justice, only family treatment produced significant reductions in recidivism. This suggests that refinement of diversion programs is needed to warrant their use.[44]

Adjudication

The **adjudication** stage in the juvenile justice system parallels the prosecution and trial phase in adult criminal courts. The purpose of the **adjudication hearing** is to determine whether the juvenile is responsible for the charges outlined in the petition.

Hearings in a juvenile court have traditionally been based more on civil—rather than criminal—proceedings. In addition, juvenile court proceedings have historically been nonadversarial in nature. However, the public has become increasingly disillusioned with the ability of the courts to reduce serious juvenile crime through informal proceedings, and a series of Supreme Court decisions have determined that juveniles have many of the same due process rights as adults in criminal proceedings. For these reasons, in recent decades juvenile courts have taken on many of the same characteristics as criminal courts. For example, juveniles may be represented by counsel, cross-examine witnesses, and invoke their Fifth Amendment protection against self-incrimination, largely as a result of the 1967 Supreme Court decision in *In re Gault* (see **Box 13.4**, the "From the Bench" feature). In 1970, in *In re Winship*,[45] the Supreme Court held that juveniles have the constitutional right to be found delinquent only when there is proof beyond a reasonable doubt. The court reasoned that even though juvenile proceedings are civil and not criminal in nature, the juvenile still faces the risk of losing his or her individual freedom and, therefore, there should not be a reasonable doubt of the juvenile's guilt when such sentence is imposed.

In 1971, the Supreme Court ruled in *McKeiver v. Pennsylvania* that juveniles are not constitutionally entitled to a trial by jury (although 12 states allow jury trials in serious cases if juveniles request them).[46] Four years later, in *Breed v. Jones*, the Court ruled that the Fifth Amendment's prohibition against **double jeopardy** forbids criminal prosecution of a juvenile after he or she has been tried in juvenile court for the same offense.[47] The Court reasoned that a juvenile runs the risk of losing his or her freedom in a juvenile court for many years and, therefore, is put in jeopardy, making the criminal trial "double jeopardy."

Disposition

At the conclusion of the adjudication hearing, the judge may either dismiss the case (equivalent to an acquittal) or sustain the petition (equivalent to a conviction). If the petition is sustained (which happens in approximately two-thirds of cases brought before the court), the judge may either immediately determine an appropriate disposition (equivalent to a sentence) or set a date for a disposition hearing.

The **disposition hearing** is the equivalent of the sentencing stage in the adult criminal court process. At this hearing, the court decides which disposition is best both for the child and for the community. In the early years of the juvenile court, dispositions were held to be in the "best interests of the child." Thus disposition hearings were informal, approached on a case-by-case basis, and intended to provide for the most appropriate treatment or rehabilitative strategy as a means to improve the lives of the children. Early dispositions were noncriminal (civil) in nature and almost entirely indeterminate. That is, a judge could send a child to a state institution for an undetermined amount of time, often until the age of maturity.

What happens at the adjudication and disposition stages in many respects reflects the same factors that influence police discretion. Juvenile courts

KEY TERMS

adjudication
The stage in the juvenile justice system that parallels prosecution and trial in adult criminal courts.

adjudication hearing
A hearing to determine whether a juvenile committed the offense of which he or she is accused.

In re Gault
Case in which the U.S. Supreme Court ruled that juveniles could not be denied basic due process rights in juvenile hearings.

In re Winship
Case in which the U.S. Supreme Court ruled that, in delinquency cases, juveniles should be convicted only if proof of their guilt beyond a reasonable doubt exists.

McKeiver v. Pennsylvania
Case in which the U.S. Supreme Court ruled that juveniles do not have a constitutional right to a jury trial in juvenile court.

Breed v. Jones
Case in which the U.S. Supreme Court ruled that a criminal prosecution of a child following a juvenile court hearing constitutes double jeopardy.

double jeopardy
Rule that forbids criminal prosecution of a juvenile after he or she has been tried in juvenile court for the same offense.

disposition hearing
A hearing to determine the most appropriate placement of a juvenile adjudicated to be delinquent.

BOX 13.4

From the Bench

In re Gault

From its inception until the mid-1960s, the U.S. juvenile court system tolerated wide differences between the procedural rights accorded to adults and those accorded to juveniles. In practically all jurisdictions, rights granted to adults were withheld from juveniles. It was believed that juvenile court proceedings should not be adversarial or criminal. Rather, the right of the state as *parens patriae* permitted the juvenile court to act informally in the best interests of children. Consequently, juvenile proceedings were described as "civil" and, therefore, were not subject to the requirements that restrict the state when it seeks to deprive a person of his or her liberty. All of this changed in 1967, when the U.S. Supreme Court handed down its decision in what has been considered the leading constitutional case in juvenile law: *In re Gault*.

On June 8, 1964, 15-year-old Gerald Gault was arrested and taken to the Children's Detention Home in Gila County, Arizona, as a result of a verbal complaint by a neighbor, Mrs. Cook, that he had made lewd phone calls to her. No notice was given to Gault's parents that he had been taken into custody, and neither Gault nor his parents were given copies of the petition charging delinquency. At the initial hearing, Mrs. Cook did not appear and no transcript or record of the hearing was made. At a second hearing, Mrs. Cook was still not present. After this hearing, Gault was found to be delinquent and was committed to the state training school for 5 years.

The State of Arizona did not permit appeals by juveniles in delinquency cases, so the defense filed a writ of *habeas corpus* with the Arizona Supreme Court, which referred

it to the Superior Court for a hearing. The Superior Court dismissed the writ. The defense then sought review in the Arizona Supreme Court, which ruled that the juvenile court had acted appropriately. Gault appealed to the U.S. Supreme Court, arguing that the juvenile court had violated his rights of due process guaranteed by the Fourteenth Amendment.

Justice Abe Fortas, delivering the opinion of the U.S. Supreme Court, challenged the very essence of the juvenile court's operation with his assertion that the basic requirements of due process and fairness must be satisfied in juvenile proceedings and that "neither the Fourteenth Amendment nor the Bill of Rights is for adults only." The court's position that its activities worked for the good of the child was shown to be suspect, and its procedure, in fact, violated juveniles' fundamental rights. According to Justice Fortas, "Under our Constitution, the condition of being a boy does not justify a kangaroo court." He further argued that the proper goal of the juvenile court would not be impaired by constitutional requirements and expressed his belief that the essentials of due process would reflect a fair and responsive attitude toward juveniles. Justice Fortas then set out the essentials of due process that should apply in juvenile delinquency proceedings, including the right to counsel, the right to confront and cross-examine one's accuser, the right against self-incrimination, and the right to timely notice of the charges.

As a result of the *Gault* decision, the operation of the juvenile court was significantly altered, making it more formal and adversarial in nature.

In re Gault, 387 U.S. 1 (1967).

overwhelmingly rely on legal factors, such as offense seriousness, evidence, and the youth's prior history of delinquency, to determine case outcomes. However, extralegal factors play a role as well. Jennifer Peck and her colleagues have examined the role of gender, race, and the type of attorney a youth has in determining case outcomes. Using court data from jurisdictions in the Midwest and Northeast, Peck found that African Americans were treated more harshly than whites at the adjudication and disposition in one jurisdiction, but received more leniency than whites at adjudications in another jurisdiction. The effects of type of counsel were also mixed. Black youth who had private attorneys generally received more severe outcomes than white youth at adjudication and disposition, whereas white youth who had public defenders received more severe outcomes at adjudication and disposition than African American youth. Similarly differential effects

at referral, detention, adjudication, and disposition were also shown, with some circumstances favoring white youth and others favoring minority youth. Whereas most legal outcomes favored girls, others did not, depending on the type of offense for which the youth was petitioned. Despite the mixed effects of extralegal factors, legal factors were consistently and robustly associated with referral, detention, adjudication, and disposition. A study of more than 8300 youth referred to a juvenile probation office reported similar findings. Jonathan Caudill and his colleagues found that African American youth were 26% more likely to be referred at a first referral, but by the sixth referral, they were 41% less likely to be referred. In comparison, the effect of a felony offense (indicating high offense seriousness) on a first referral was 1019% greater likelihood and at sixth referral was 712% greater likelihood. These findings show how strongly legal criteria trump extralegal characteristics.

Today, an increasing number of states are using offense-based sentencing guidelines to determine appropriate sanctions for juvenile offenders. For example, in Washington State, the guidelines consider the seriousness of the offense and the juvenile's age, with younger, less serious offenders receiving more lenient sanctions.[48] In traditional disposition hearings, the judge, the probation officer, the prosecutor, the defense attorney, and the child's parents typically discuss available options. Hearsay evidence and opinions are admissible at this stage.

At this hearing, the judge may, in an effort to obtain more information, withhold the final disposition and continue the case; alternatively, the court may release the child into the custody of his or her parents or place the child on probation. Judges have a great deal of discretion at disposition. Although the most common disposition is probation, they may sentence a youth to a correctional facility or other "out-of-home" placement. In addition, judges have a wide variety of alternative dispositions available, such as restitution, home detention, fines, and community service. If probation is selected as the disposition for the case, the juvenile may be referred to the probation department for formal or informal supervision. A child may also be removed from the custody of his or her parents, placed under the court's authority, and placed in a public or private facility or foster home.

Disposition decisions are made in regard to a relatively small number of juveniles, and youths who are evaluated for various disposition outcomes have already been processed through several decision points. As noted earlier, nearly 1.1 million juveniles are eligible for referral to the juvenile court each year. Of these cases, 55% are petitioned to the juvenile court for an adjudication hearing (**Figure 13.2**). Roughly 4000 (less than 1%) of the petitioned cases are waived to criminal court.

Corrections

The juvenile corrections system involves two main components: probation and institutional placement. An aftercare phase often follows release from corrections facilities.

Probation

Probation is the conditional freedom granted by the court to an alleged or adjudicated offender as long as he or she avoids further misbehavior and meets certain conditions. The majority of youths on probation have been ordered by the court to supervision at disposition after having been formally adjudicated. Approximately 64% of all adjudicated delinquents receive probation. However, many youths who are not adjudicated delinquent voluntarily agree to abide by certain probation conditions with the understanding that if they successfully complete their probationary period, their case will be terminated without any formal processing.

Probation is based on the belief that misbehavior may be better corrected by trying to rehabilitate the juvenile in the community than in an institution. The major goals of probation are rehabilitation and reintegration, and the principal figure in accomplishing these objectives is the probation officer. Some juvenile courts have no probation services at all. Those courts that do have this option available usually have large caseloads in which counseling and supervision take the form of occasional phone calls and perfunctory visits rather than careful, individualized services.

Probation may be used at the front end of the juvenile justice system for first-time, low-risk offenders or at the back end as an alternative to institutional confinement for offenders who commit more serious crimes. The official duties of probation officers can differ between states and even between jurisdictions within a single state. In any case, the basic set of juvenile probation functions includes intake screening of cases referred to juvenile and family courts, predisposition or social history investigation of juveniles, and court-ordered supervision of juvenile offenders. Probation orders imposed by the court related to supervision of juveniles usually require that the youths obey all laws, attend school regularly, periodically visit the probation officer, remain within the community, and be at home at night by a set hour. The judge has the statutory authority to frame these conditions. Some probation departments also provide aftercare for youths who have been released from institutions; others may administer detention or manage local residential facilities or special programs.

Probation is also commonly used as a way to supervise children with major family problems that often accompany delinquent youth. Unfortunately, these family problems often contribute to the youth being unsuccessful on probation. Amy Cook and Jill Gordon surveyed 88 parents of adolescents on probation and found that low parental monitoring, parental anger toward the child, and negative home behaviors were associated with continued juvenile offending while on probation. It is also important to recognize that juvenile delinquents are a heterogeneous population that often has varied, and at times, wildly different needs. Sarah Walker and her colleagues conducted a

KEY TERMS

probation
The conditional freedom granted by the court to an alleged or adjudicated offender, who must adhere to certain conditions and is generally supervised by a probation officer.

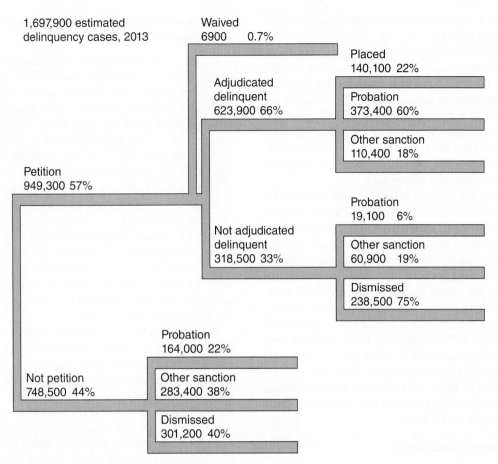

Figure 13.2 Processing of Juvenile Court Cases

Data from Julie Furdella and Charles Puzzanchera, *Delinquency Cases in Juvenile Court, 2013* (Washington, DC: U.S. Department of Justice, 2015).

latent class analysis of 1731 female delinquents and found four classes or "types" of delinquent girls. One group is characterized by high family conflict and trauma that includes neglect, sexual abuse, physical abuse, and mental health problems. The second group has complex treatment needs but extensive antisocial peers, and it is these delinquent friendships that are the root cause of their problems. The third group has better social backgrounds with few adverse experiences but high substance abuse problems. The fourth group has acute mental health needs with otherwise strong social supports. Given these differences, it is clear that a one-size-fits-all type of probation supervision will not be effective at reducing delinquency among all youth.[49]

It is not only parents who contribute to a youth's success on probation, but also probation officers. Craig Schwalbe and Tina Maschi surveyed over 300 probation officers and found that they were more likely to use client-centered approaches when the youth was considered honest and with youth with greater prior use of social services. Probation officers were admittedly more confrontational with clients who were younger and had more extensive substance abuse problems. This suggests that the general approach a

juvenile probation officer uses can have an effect on the compliance likelihood of their clients.[50]

Home Confinement and Electronic Monitoring

Home confinement, sometimes called *house arrest* or *home detention*, is the intensive supervision and monitoring of a person in his or her home environment. Juvenile court probation departments usually administer home confinement programs. Surveillance consists of personal daily contacts with the youth and daily contacts with parents, teachers, and employers. Juveniles are typically confined to their homes unless attending school, work, or other previously agreed-upon activities. At any other time when the youths are not at home, both parents and probation department supervisors must closely monitor them. Advocates of home confinement programs contend that these programs cost less than

KEY TERMS

home confinement
The intensive supervision and monitoring of an offending youth within his or her home environment.

one-fourth as much as confinement of youths in jail or detention centers.

A variation on home confinement is **electronic monitoring**. Electronic monitoring or tracking systems are generally of two types: passive and active. In *passive* systems, the youth sends electronic signals via phone in response to computer-activated calls. The juvenile may respond either by inserting a special plug worn on the wrist into the transmitter or by speaking on the phone (his or her voice is matched to a voiceprint programmed into the computer).

Active systems are used when constant surveillance of the juvenile is desired. Traditional active systems require the youth to wear a transmitter on the ankle, neck, or wrist. The transmitter sends a constant signal (allowing for movement to a distance of 100 to 150 feet) to a receiver connected to the home telephone. The signal is then sent to a central computer, which matches it to patterns preprogrammed for arranged absences such as school and work. The newest type of active monitoring is the satellite-based GPS (global positioning system) unit. Such a unit allows for real-time tracking of the wearer: It can plot a subject's path, retrace his or her movement over several days, and even determine if the youth was walking or in a vehicle.

Institutional Placement

In general, placement in correctional facilities (known as residential placements) is reserved for those juveniles who have committed serious, violent, or property crimes. The United States has approximately 2259 public and private correctional facilities used for the placement of juvenile delinquents. More than 79,166 juveniles were housed in such facilities according to the most recent data. This is the fewest youth in residential placements since 1997 and the number of residential placement facilities in the United States has declined 21% since 1997.[51] These institutions include the following types of facilities:

- Training schools, reform schools, boot camps, and youth centers (secure residential facilities)
- Confinement facilities (juvenile prisons)
- Shelter-care facilities (nonsecure housing for temporary placement of status offenders or dependent or neglected youths)
- Jails (secure facilities for holding persons who are awaiting trial or who have been convicted of misdemeanors)
- Ranches, forestry camps, and farms (nonsecure facilities for delinquents who have committed

less serious crimes and that provide outdoor environments)

It takes a considerable delinquent career of chronic police contacts, numerous violations of probation sentences, and/or involvement in extremely violent offenses including murder, rape, armed robbery, kidnapping, carjacking, and home invasion to be committed to a confinement facility. Chad Trulson and his associates have studied multiple samples of serious delinquents who have been placed in training schools, reform schools, and confinement facilities in Texas. These "deep end" placements have dozens of arrests and probation violations as juveniles and have been adjudicated for the most serious forms of crime including murder, rape, and gun assaults. Many youth who receive institutional placements were arrested before age 10 years and their severe delinquency history embodies Moffitt's concept of the life-course persistent offender.

The severe social and behavioral profile of youths in confinement is not limited to the United States. Lauren Freedman and her colleagues' study of confined child and adolescent offenders in Canada found extensive social histories of maternal and paternal substance use; maternal and paternal criminal history; physical, sexual, and emotional abuse; traumatic experiences; and a host of psychiatric problems. Pedro Pechorro and his associates analyzed data from juvenile offenders in confinement facilities in Portugal and found that most have extensive delinquency histories and highly psychopathic personalities. Catherine Shaffer and her collaborators similarly showed that Canadian youth in prison were often acutely psychopathic and had violent and chronic delinquency histories. Moreover, the most psychopathic youth also engaged in misconduct and violence even while in confinement.[52]

Nearly all juvenile correctional facilities are organized around the following major programming areas: treatment and counseling, education, vocational training, and recreation. Whereas some institutions emphasize treatment, others focus greater attention on security issues. Although the emphasis may differ, all such facilities attend to each of the programming areas.

Treatment and Counseling

The juvenile court was founded on the belief that juvenile delinquency was only a reflection or symptom of a deeper or more serious individual disorder. By taking an individualized, nonpunitive, treatment approach built on the *medical model*, which views delinquency as a disease, it was thought that juvenile delinquents could be "cured" of their problems. Recent surveys of mental health disorders among institutionalized delinquents report a significant portion of institutionalized youths meet current psychiatric definitions of disorders. For example, Steven Pliszka and his colleagues found between 15 and 40% of

KEY TERMS

electronic monitoring
An active or passive computer-based tracking system in which electronic signals are used to verify that the youth is where he or she is supposed to be.

detained youths have affective disorders, such as bipolar disorder and depression. Similarly, a recent multistate study reported that more than 70% of youths in the juvenile justice system meet criteria for at least one mental health disorder, such as disruptive disorders, substance use disorders, and anxiety and mood disorders.[53]

The fields of psychology and psychiatry dominated the treatment of institutionalized juveniles during most of the 20th century, and a variety of approaches have been used as part of this strategy. These techniques include *behavior modification, milieu therapy, reality therapy*, and many different kinds of individual and group counseling.[54]

Two very popular group treatment approaches, *guided group interaction* and *positive peer culture*, attempt to create prosocial group environments in which groups control members' antisocial actions and support conventional behaviors. As part of these techniques, group, or peer, leaders facilitate, encourage, and reinforce conventional values and interactions in a supportive environment.

Education

Most incarcerated youths are at least 2 years behind their peers in basic academic skills and have had higher rates of absenteeism, suspension, or expulsion from school. Approximately one-third of all institutionalized youths read at or below the fourth-grade level, and only one-fifth read at or above the ninth-grade level. Whereas only 10% of youths in U.S. public schools are identified as academically disabled and in need of special education, between 30 and 50% of incarcerated youths have learning disabilities.[55] Because the majority of youths placed in correctional facilities have educational deficiencies, nearly all juvenile facilities maintain some type of remedial and basic educational programming.

Institutions have to attend to the academic needs of children in a broad range of grades, provide basic literacy classes, and prepare youths for a traditional high school diploma or a GED certificate. Although school in a juvenile correctional facility differs from traditional school in many ways, one of the most significant differences is tied to the constant arrival and departure of youths throughout the year. As a consequence, there is no "semester plan." In many of these institutions, youths are grouped according to their academic level rather than their age. Teachers then individualize learning plans for each youth based on the child's educational evaluation. Most institutions provide the normal range of subjects, including math, science, history, and English.

Vocational Training

Vocational training in juvenile correctional facilities reflects the early reference to such institutions as "industrial schools" or "training schools." Most youths sent to institutions by juvenile courts have not yet developed job skills, even though many have already dropped out of school and are looking for work. It is not uncommon for vocational programs to reflect sex stereotyping. In other words, programs at boys' facilities typically include auto repair, woodworking, drafting, small-engine repair, computer programming and repair, printing, and metalworking, whereas programs in girls' facilities are more likely to include secretarial training, cosmetology, library services, and data entry. The relative lack of vocational programs designed to give girls the most current, in-demand skills has long been a complaint and may reflect a lower level of commitment to female corrections more generally.

Recreation

Most juvenile institutions provide a wide range of recreational activities, such as basketball, Softball, volleyball, billiards, art, music, table games, and sometimes swimming. Although physical activity itself is seen as useful for avoiding problems of boredom and using up excessive adolescent energy, many social scientists and penologists view recreation as an important element in the institution's rehabilitative efforts. Recreation can assist with alleviating stress; identify activities that can serve as alternatives to drug and alcohol use; foster interpersonal skills such as trust, cooperation, and teamwork; enhance self-esteem; foster new interests; and develop decision-making and problem-solving skills.[56]

Aftercare

After release from juvenile correctional facilities, delinquent youths typically enter the **aftercare** phase (equivalent to parole in the adult system)—that is, the release and subsequent community supervision of an individual from a correctional facility to ensure a more positive and effective transition back into the community. Delinquents in aftercare are subject to conditions and supervision requirements similar to those imposed on youths who receive probation. Youths who violate the law or any condition of their supervision may face revocation of their aftercare release (removal from parole) and return to a correctional facility.

Nearly 100,000 juveniles enter aftercare each year.[57] These youths share several common characteristics:[58]

- Multiple previous commitments (40% of juveniles in aftercare have been held five or more times)

KEY TERMS

aftercare
The release and subsequent community supervision of an individual from a correctional facility, intended to ensure a more positive and effective transition back into the community.

Juvenile boot camps frequently use a military-style approach and strenuous physical activities in an attempt to reduce recidivism.

© Mike Powell/Digital Vision/Getty.

In many jurisdictions, adolescents accused of serious crimes such as murder and aggravated robbery are waived automatically to the adult criminal justice system for prosecution.

© Bob Ingelhart/E+/Getty.

- History of nonviolent offenses
- Residence in a single-parent home or dysfunctional family unit
- Relatives who have been incarcerated
- Educational setbacks when compared to peers
- Extensive time in some form of institutional placement

For serious violent offenders, **intensive aftercare programs (IAP)**—equivalent to intensive parole supervision—may be used to provide closer supervision. IAP officers have much smaller caseloads and are expected to conduct a number of face-to-face meetings with their parolees each week. They are also expected to establish and maintain contact with the juvenile's parents or guardians, school authorities, and, if applicable, employer on a regular basis.

These relationships are also the focus of **wraparound programs**, which are designed to build positive relationships and support networks between youths and their families, teachers, and community agencies. Such programs typically entail a centralized coordination of services through the juvenile court, including clinical therapy, drug and alcohol treatment, special

education, medical services, caregiver support, mental health care, and transportation.

Similar in philosophy to wraparound programs, there are interventions for seriously delinquent youth who have been or are at risk for out-of-home placements because of their delinquency. Multisystemic therapy is designed for chronic and serious delinquents and is designed to restructure the youth's environment across multiple systems, including the family, the peer network, and capacity for employment. The program is applied at least once per week for 3 to 5 months and has been shown to improve delinquents' communication skills, problem-solving, and job-related skills. Another intervention is Multidimensional Treatment Foster Care, which places highly delinquent youth with supervised foster families that implement a behavior management program. Youth receive at least 1 hour of individual and family therapy per week for 6 to 9 months, and the program has been shown to improve their interpersonal skills, prosocial behavior, problem-solving, and family management skills.[59]

Juvenile Offenders in the Adult Criminal Justice System

In response to public and legislative perceptions of judicial leniency and the inability of the juvenile justice system to deal adequately with serious or repeat adolescent offenders, some delinquents—owing to their age, prior delinquent record, or seriousness of their offense—may face prosecution in criminal court and the possibility of sentencing to adult prisons.

Transfer to Criminal Courts

The **waiver of jurisdiction** is the judicial mechanism by which a juvenile may be transferred from juvenile

KEY TERMS

intensive aftercare program (IAP)
Equivalent to intensive parole supervision; a monitoring approach used to provide greater supervision of youths after their release from official institutions.

wraparound programs
Programs designed to build positive relationships and support networks between youths and their families, teachers, and community agencies through coordination of services.

waiver of jurisdiction
A legal process to transfer a juvenile from juvenile to criminal court.

court to criminal court. Waivers are usually filed in cases involving two types of delinquents:

1. *Serious violent offenders*. Criminal courts can impose harsher punishments for serious violent offenders.
2. *Chronic offenders*. The criminal justice system is believed to provide more appropriate (e.g., punitive) treatment for offenders with long criminal records who have not responded positively to treatment programs.

To be eligible for transfer to the adult criminal system, juvenile offenders in many states must be older than a minimum age (see Table 13.1). In reality, most offenders who are waived to criminal courts are older than age 16.[60]

Research has shown that youth who are waived to adult court are deserving of it, based on their delinquent involvement and other risk factors for antisocial conduct. Serious and chronic offenders have already failed multiple opportunities in the juvenile justice system and routinely continued to commit serious felonies, even while under court supervision or while serving a probation sentence. A study of youth from the Northwestern Juvenile Project found that those who were processed in adult court and sentenced to prison were much more likely to have conduct disorder, oppositional defiant disorder, any substance use disorder, or any psychiatric disorder.[61]

In ***Kent v. United States*** (1966), the U.S. Supreme Court held that the differences between juvenile and adult courts were so great that the transfer decision must be based on clearly established procedures designed to protect the rights of juveniles. Although the court ruled that the practice of trying juveniles in criminal courts was constitutional, the juvenile may not be deprived of his or her constitutional rights. The decision to transfer offenders must include the following elements:

- A waiver hearing
- Effective counsel
- A statement of the reasons behind the decision to transfer

In its *Kent* decision, the Supreme Court also enumerated several criteria to guide judges in making transfer decisions, including the seriousness of the offense, the presence of violence, and the sophistication and maturity of the youth.[62]

Despite the existence of these guidelines, the transfer of juveniles to criminal courts remains controversial. Many citizens and correctional experts are unsure about the appropriateness of harsher punishments for youths or the possibility of rehabilitation for juveniles in the adult correctional system. At the same time, long-term incarceration is possible only within the adult system and may be necessary to keep chronic or serious offenders off the streets. Approximately 4000 juvenile offenders are transferred to adult criminal courts in the United States each year; this equates to less than 1% of all petitioned cases.

Several procedures (or remands) are used to transfer youths between juvenile and criminal courts, though they are not all employed in all states:

Judicial waiver: the most common form of transfer to the criminal system. It involves a formal decision by the judge after careful consideration of the relevant issues at a transfer hearing.

Statutory exclusion: the automatic transfer to the criminal system of certain juvenile offenders based on age, seriousness of offense, or prior criminal record.

Prosecutorial waiver: (or *direct file*): a situation in which there is concurrent jurisdiction; the prosecutor then has the authority to decide whether to file the case in either juvenile or criminal court.

Demand waiver: a request by a juvenile offender to be transferred to criminal court. Although rare, such waivers are filed by delinquents who are seeking acquittal by jury or shorter sentences.

Reverse waiver: a request by a juvenile who is being prosecuted in criminal court to be transferred back to the juvenile system.

Prosecution in Criminal Courts

Some juvenile cases that are transferred to criminal court (approximately 16%) are dropped before charges are formally filed. Even when charges are filed, some

KEY TERMS

Kent v. United States
Case in which the U.S. Supreme Court ruled that requiring a formal waiver hearing before transfer of a juvenile to criminal court.

judicial waiver
Most common waiver procedure for transferring youths to criminal court, in which the judge is the primary decision maker.

statutory exclusion
Process established by statute that excludes certain juveniles, because of either age or offense, from juvenile court jurisdiction; charges are initially filed in criminal court.

prosecutorial waiver
Process in which the prosecutor determines whether a charge against a juvenile should be filed in criminal or juvenile court.

demand waiver
Process by which a juvenile may request to have his or her case transferred to criminal court.

reverse waiver
Process in which a juvenile contests a statutory exclusion or prosecutorial transfer.

cases (about 11%) are terminated by the prosecutor's *nolle prosequi* (decision not to prosecute). If the prosecutor decides to proceed with the case, a trial may still be avoided by the process of plea bargaining.[63]

If the case does go to trial, a juvenile offender is significantly more likely than an adult to be convicted. Researchers have suggested various reasons for this high conviction rate, including impaired competence to stand trial because of immature judgment and decision-making ability. Other studies, however, have shown no significant differences between those youths who are tried in criminal courts and similar peers who are tried in the juvenile system, other than the seriousness of their charges.[64]

Sentencing the Convicted Juvenile

Juveniles subject to criminal convictions have several advantages over adult criminals in obtaining lenient sentencing. First, age is a mitigating factor that is taken into consideration in determining the appropriate sentence. Second, most juveniles do not have adult criminal records, and prior juvenile records are sometimes prohibited from being introduced in criminal hearings (primarily because the courts have traditionally believed that juvenile misbehavior reflects immaturity and should not be held against juveniles once they became adults). Prior criminal records are important because many states' sentencing laws require incarceration of the offender when he or she is convicted of a second felony. Despite these considerations, research has demonstrated inconclusive findings about lenient sentencing of juveniles in general.[65]

Juvenile Offenders in Prison

Only a small number of juveniles are incarcerated in state prisons, where they account for less than 0.2% of the total incarcerated population. Nevertheless, this population presents serious challenges for both offenders and correctional administrators.[66]

Life in adult prisons is significantly different from life in juvenile institutions, and juvenile offenders often have difficulty adjusting to prison subculture. A youth's reputation as being tough, which might have afforded him or her elevated status on the streets or in a juvenile institution, carries little weight among older inmates. Juvenile offenders find themselves at the bottom of the status ladder, subject to both the formal authority of guards and the informal power of other inmates. They may merely resent the authority or, worse, be subject to victimization. Indeed, juveniles in adult prisons are significantly more likely to become victims of violent crime or sexual assault than youths in juvenile institutions.[67]

Daily survival becomes the primary concern for youths in prison. For many, survival means adapting to the inmate subculture. Although this adaptation may improve their daily life in prison, it may also distract or discourage juveniles from pursuing activities that would improve their chances of getting out of prison earlier, such as participating in counseling and educational programs and conforming to institutional expectations.[68] Survival may also include forging an alliance with an older inmate who will provide protection, which all too often comes at the cost of sexual exploitation.

The characteristics of juvenile inmates also create difficulties for prison administrators. In states with very small numbers of juvenile inmates, the cost of building special housing for these juveniles (rather than integrating them into the general inmate population) becomes a serious budgetary concern. Furthermore, because juvenile inmates are younger and proportionately more violent than adult inmates, they may have greater difficulty in adapting to institutional rules and consequently require greater supervision by institutional staff. Unlike juvenile correctional facilities, which try to foster resident and staff interactions that promote the social and personal development of youthful offenders, most adult prisons emphasize custody and control. Adult correctional facilities are not intended to cater to, nor are they typically equipped to provide for, the educational or psychological needs of juveniles. Because most states have only a handful of juvenile inmates, legislatures hesitate to allocate additional expenditures for programs or staff to give these youths specialized treatment.

The recidivism rate among juveniles released from prison also poses a challenge for criminal justice professionals. Juveniles who are paroled from prison fare no better than their adult counterparts, with approximately 60% returning to prison for a new offense or violation of probation in less than 3 years. The length of time served appears to make little difference in the recidivism rate. In addition, prison exposure significantly increases the mental health problems of juveniles, especially depression, which is a major risk factor for antisocial conduct as well.[69]

Life Imprisonment for Juveniles

Given the many negative consequences of prison confinement for juveniles, critics began to question the effectiveness of life imprisonment sanctions for juveniles convicted of the most serious crimes. Discussion about life imprisonment for juveniles reached a boiling point in the case of Terrence Graham in Florida. Graham was a serious, violent, and chronic juvenile delinquent who at age 16 committed a home invasion and was later convicted of armed robbery and armed burglary and sentenced to life imprisonment. This sentence was delivered 1 month shy of his 18th birthday.

The case was appealed on the grounds that such a sentence is a violation of the Eighth Amendment's proscription of cruel and unusual punishment. In *Graham v. Florida* (2010), the U.S. Supreme Court held in a 5-to-4 decision that juveniles cannot receive a life sentence without the possibility of parole upon convictions for a nonhomicide offense. Because Graham was not convicted of murder, his sentence was viewed unconstitutional and thus he could not receive a life sentence. Because his most recent crimes were not murders, he could not receive a life sentence. To do so, as the Supreme Court reasoned, would violate the Eight Amendment's prohibition of cruel and unusual punishment.[70]

The changing juvenile justice viewpoint on life imprisonment does not end there. In 2012, the American Bar Association filed an amicus brief in *Miller v. Alabama* (2012) and *Jackson v. Hobbs* (2012) that the U. S. Supreme Court should rule that life sentences without parole are also unconstitutional for juveniles convicted of murder. The cases were consolidated in *Miller v. Alabama*, where the Supreme Court held that mandatory sentences of life in prison without the possibility of parole are unconstitutional for juveniles. After the decision in *Miller*, the 28 states that had mandatory life imprisonment without parole statutes had to amend their laws. Several states, including California, Hawaii, Massachusetts, Nevada, Texas, Utah, Vermont, West Virginia, and Wyoming, eliminated life without parole as a sentence. Other states, including Delaware, Iowa, Louisiana, Michigan, Nebraska, and Washington, retained life without parole as a possible sentence. However, states vary considerably in terms of the length of sentence that constitutes a "life sentence." Nebraska and Texas require youth to serve 40 years in prison before parole review, whereas Louisiana, Massachusetts, and Pennsylvania require 35 years. Seven states, including Arkansas, Delaware, Michigan, North Carolina, Utah, Washington, and Wyoming, require that youth serve 25 to 30 years. Other states require 15 years, 15 to 20 years, or an unspecified amount of time.

An unresolved question in *Miller* was whether the ruling would apply retroactively to offenders who were sentenced to life imprisonment without parole as juveniles. In *Montgomery v. Louisiana* (2016), the Supreme Court held in a 6-3 ruling that the ruling in *Miller v. Alabama* would apply retroactively and potentially affect nearly 2500 cases nationwide.[71]

Abolition of the Death Penalty for Juveniles

Although juveniles have rarely been executed in the United States, at least 366 have been legally put to death since 1642. Since the 1890s, juvenile have accounted for less than 2% of all people executed. From the 1890s to 1930, fewer than 30 juveniles were executed in any given decade. In the 1930s and 1940s, however, an unusual increase in juvenile executions occurred, with 40 and 50 executions taking place in those two decades, respectively. Between 1965 and 1984, no juveniles were executed. However, with the execution of Charles Rumbaugh in Texas on September 11, 1985, juveniles once again faced the prospect of execution. Between 1985 and April 2003, 22 persons who were juveniles at the time when they committed their crimes were executed.

Beginning in 1982, it became clear that the U.S. Supreme Court had taken an interest in the death penalty as it applied to juveniles when it held that the youthfulness of an offender must be considered as a mitigating circumstance at sentencing, reflecting a growing ambivalence about juvenile executions among policymakers and the public alike.[72] Six years later, in *Thompson v. Oklahoma*, the Court held that the execution of a person who was younger than age 16 at the time of the commission of his or her crime was unconstitutional.[73] The next year, in *Stanford v. Kentucky*, the Supreme Court rejected an appeal that could have prohibited the execution of anyone younger than 18 at the time of his or her crime.[74]

A total of eighteen 17-year-olds and one 16-year-old were executed after the *Stanford* decision. Then, on March 1, 2005, the Supreme Court, in a divided 5-to-4 decision in *Roper v. Simmons*, ruled that "the death penalty is disproportionate punishment for offenders under the age of 18" and, therefore, is a violation of the Eighth Amendment's prohibition against cruel and unusual punishment.[75] Although the court and the country remained deeply divided over application of the death penalty to juveniles, the debate had finally come to an end. Interestingly, a recent study found that the *Roper* decision has had no effect on juvenile homicide rates.[76]

KEY TERMS

Graham v. Florida
Case in which U.S. Supreme Court ruled that life without parole for nonhomicide convictions is unconstitutional for juveniles.

Miller v. Alabama
Case in which U.S. Supreme Court ruled that life without parole for any offense is unconstitutional for juveniles.

Montgomery v. Louisiana
Case in which U.S. Supreme Court ruled that life without parole for any offense is unconstitutional and would apply retroactively.

Roper v. Simmons
Case in which the U.S. Supreme Court ruled that the death penalty for anyone who was younger than age 18 at the time of his or her crime is unconstitutional.

WRAP UP

THINKING ABOUT JUVENILE DELINQUENCY: CONCLUSIONS

Although most modern-day encounters between police and juveniles are constrained by the same rules and court decisions governing police–adult interactions, this has not always been the case, and the courts and state legislatures continue to provide for some differences in treatment. For example, juveniles are typically taken into custody, not arrested; booking procedures in most states prohibit fingerprinting and photographing juveniles; and youths are not given the same latitude in waiving their right to remain silent or to have an attorney present as are adults.

The police officer's discretionary decision to arrest a juvenile suspected of a crime is based on many factors—some legal, others extralegal. The seriousness of the offense, a youth's prior record, the presence of evidence, the suspiciousness of the youth's behavior, and characteristics of the juvenile such as race, sex, age, and attitude—all affect how an officer responds to the situation at hand. Such discretionary decisions by the police, especially decisions appearing to be arbitrary or discriminatory, often lead to relational problems between youth and police.

The U.S. juvenile court system was changed dramatically in the mid-1960s, when the U.S. Supreme Court, in a series of cases, recognized the due process rights of juveniles and established guidelines as well as legal constraints under which the juvenile courts must operate. Other court decisions and statutes established by state legislatures have placed constraints on the public nature of juvenile court hearings, although public access to court proceedings and information has increased in recent years.

A very important issue today involves the transfer of serious juvenile offenders to criminal court for prosecution as adults. In most states, juveniles who are charged with serious violent crimes and who meet the minimum-age standard for waiver may be transferred. Once transferred, they face the same prosecution process that adult defendants must navigate. Some states rely exclusively on judicial waivers, but an increasing number of states permit the prosecutorial transfer of youths. Most youths tried in criminal court, however, are there as a result of legislatively mandated transfers. Given the growing liberal sentiment among the public and politicians, it is reasonable to expect that a decreasing number of youths will be tried in criminal courts for their crimes in the coming years.

CHAPTER SPOTLIGHT

- Despite the tensions that often emerge in encounters between police and juveniles, officers are required to accord juveniles the full due process protections given to adults, with a very few exceptions.
- Given the amount of discretion officers have, most of their encounters with juveniles do not end up with arrests. Police are more likely to release a child with or without a lecture, interrogate the child and then release him or her, or issue a citation for future appearance in juvenile court.
- The discretionary decision to release or arrest is affected by both legal factors, such as seriousness of the offense and prior record, and extralegal factors, such as a youth's race, sex, and demeanor.
- Delinquency cases do not require probable cause for arrest; rather, only reasonable suspicion is necessary for an officer to take a juvenile into custody.
- Because juveniles may not fully grasp the meaning of the *Miranda* warning, courts consider the totality of the circumstances to determine whether statements made by youths in custody may be used in a delinquency hearing.
- Juvenile courts differ from adult courts in a number of ways, including the absence of guilt, a greater focus on treatment, the emphasis on the offender's background, the absence of public scrutiny, and the use of short-term incarceration.
- The adjudication hearing for juveniles is similar to a trial in adult criminal court, while the disposition hearing is the same as the sentencing stage. Except for the right to a jury trial, juveniles have the same due process rights as adults in these hearings.
- The majority of juveniles adjudicated delinquent are placed on probation, with many being required to wear electronic monitoring devices.
- Institutional corrections for juveniles include reform schools, boot camps, ranches, forestry camps, and farms, as well as temporary shelter-care facilities.
- Juveniles who commit particularly serious crimes or who are considered not amenable to treatment

in the juvenile justice system may be transferred to the criminal court for prosecution as adults.

- Most states use one or more of the following procedures for transferring juveniles: judicial waiver, statutory exclusion, and prosecutorial waiver (direct file).

- Juveniles convicted in criminal court face the same sentencing alternatives as adults, with the exception of the death penalty. As in the juvenile system, most juveniles are placed on probation, with those sentenced to prison accounting for only 0.2% of all inmates.

CRITICAL THINKING

1. Policing is a largely reactive endeavor. Allegations that the police discriminate against African Americans by actively patrolling minority neighborhoods are largely anecdotal. How do the offender–victim relationship and official and victimization data address the issue of police bias against African Americans?

2. Extralegal factors influence the treatment that individuals receive from criminal justice personnel. Is the justice system held to an unrealistic ideal of equality that other social institutions are not? If not, why?

3. Most people would agree that juvenile offenders who repeatedly commit serious violent crimes are the real concern—not youths who are involved

in petty delinquency. Should the juvenile justice system be used exclusively for youths who engage in minor offenses? Should serious violent juvenile delinquents always be prosecuted and punished as adults?

4. Electronic monitoring allows many youths opportunities to remain in the community. Monitoring also permits closer surveillance than traditional probation. Are juveniles advantaged or disadvantaged during electronic monitoring?

5. Juveniles who commit serious crimes often face adult sanctions. Is this an appropriate response to youth crime? Does the criminal justice system effectively "wash its hands" of juvenile delinquents who engage in serious criminal offending?

Delinquency Prevention

OBJECTIVES

◆ Understand how society has attempted to control and manage juvenile delinquency over the past two centuries.

◆ Distinguish between primary, secondary, and tertiary prevention.

◆ Know the risk factors present in very early childhood and adolescence.

◆ Explain the key features of model and promising prevention programs.

◆ Understand the recent research into the effectiveness of prevention programs.

KEY TERMS

Previously we explored how the juvenile justice system responds to delinquent youth. Police investigate crimes and take youths into custody; those juveniles may then be placed in detention and go through the intake process. If their crimes are serious, a petition is filed and an adjudication hearing is held. If they are found guilty, a disposition hearing is held. Although probation is the typical disposition, some youths may face the prospect of placement in a correctional institution. All of this activity takes place under the aegis of the juvenile justice system—from the police and courts to probation, institutionalization, and parole. In the United States, police arrest approximately 1.6 million juveniles every year, 582,800 juveniles are formally petitioned to the juvenile court, and about 323,300 are adjudicated delinquent. More than 205,300 of those youths are placed on probation, and 118,000 juveniles are sent to correctional institutions or receive some other sanction. Nearly 4000 youth are waived to criminal court to face prosecution as adults.[1] These numbers reflect the juvenile justice system's failure to *prevent* juvenile delinquency as these youth have already usually committed multiple crimes.

The Control and Management of Delinquency

During the 19th century, the Child Savers and Reverend Charles Loring Brace made a concerted effort to help the poor, orphaned, runaway, and throwaway children who were living on the streets in big cities of the United States, particularly New York City. These children were not necessarily engaged in criminal activities, but rather were seen as "bad seeds"—that is, prime candidates for becoming delinquent if nothing was done to improve their general life conditions. Poor, orphaned, neglected, and modestly delinquent children were all handled by the same agencies and typically placed in similar institutions, such as the Houses of Refuge, because all of the children were seen as products of the same social forces: poverty, lack of education, disrupted families, poor nutrition, and deteriorated housing conditions. By the latter half of the 19th century, reformers came to believe that children could be saved from a life of delinquency, and eventually criminality, by establishing programs to improve the life chances of even the youngest children. This was, essentially, the earliest form of primary prevention of delinquency in America.

Dependency, neglect, and status offending behaviors were identified separately from juvenile criminal behavior, although the juvenile courts had jurisdiction over all such cases. Moreover, both status offenses and criminal acts were treated as delinquencies and carried similar disposition alternatives, including probation and out-of-home placement in a correctional institution. At this time, the goal of the juvenile court was to serve the needs of the child (dependent, neglected, or delinquent) who was at risk of becoming a more serious problem to the community. According to Barry Feld, for delinquents, "the juvenile court's treatment ideology attributed young people's misdeeds to their environment or flawed developmental process rather than to a vicious free will."[2] Such treatment, which was intended to serve the "best interests" of the child, also became a means to control the disobedient or disapproved behavior of children.

It was not long before the pragmatic functioning of the juvenile court reflected a greater concern with the control and management of delinquents. As Feld notes, "The juvenile court functioned as a coercive treatment agency, equipoised between the social casework treatment model, on the one hand, and criminal court's punishment paradigm, on the other."[3] Early intervention to thwart protocriminal behavior in youth "allowed juvenile courts to become roving commissions to seek out and 'treat' errant youth under their *parens patriae* power."[4]

By separating juvenile offenders from adult offenders, the juvenile court reinforced the rehabilitative ideal and the social welfare model of civil (rather than criminal) proceedings. However, this rehabilitative model of treatment came at a significant cost to youths: "[The] juvenile courts operated free from the due process and adversarial legal proceedings that characterized the adult criminal courts."[5] The increase in juvenile crime and violence beginning in the early 1960s led lawmakers, as well as the public, to seek means to exert greater, and more formal and uniform, control over youthful offenders—control that could not be provided by a civil, social work model of treatment. As a consequence of a series of U.S. Supreme Court decisions in the mid-1960s and early 1970s, the juvenile court, as well as the larger juvenile justice system, was significantly transformed during this period. Although juveniles were accorded most due process rights given to adults, they were also subject to a system organized around the identification, interrogation, and adjudication of youthful criminal offenders. The focus of the juvenile justice system on early delinquency prevention was essentially abandoned, with the system instead responding after the fact to juveniles who became involved in acts ranging from youthful misbehavior to serious violent crime. Its purpose was to control and manage delinquency as best it could.

When criminologists speak of **delinquency control**, this references a reaction to the problem of juvenile delinquency *after* it has occurred. To *control* means to restrain, limit, reduce the incidence or severity of, or prevent the spread of something—in this case, delinquency. Control is a reactive approach, which represents an attempt to deal with juvenile delinquency in the present, directly with those children who have been identified as a delinquent. The concept is essentially the same as that underlying crime control: A crime problem exists, and the function of the criminal justice system is to limit or reduce crime as much as possible, but with little hope of eradicating crime. So it is with delinquency. The problem of delinquency cannot be eliminated, goes the theory, so the juvenile justice system should simply do its best to limit its severity and prevent its spread.

The **management of delinquency** has a slightly different meaning. It suggests that juvenile delinquency is a social problem to be worked on or altered for a purpose, an issue to come to terms with. This view is

KEY TERMS

delinquency control
An approach that emphasizes dealing with the problem of juvenile delinquency after the fact.

management of delinquency
An approach that emphasizes delinquency is a problem to be worked on or altered for a purpose, or come to terms with.

very similar to the notion of **regulating delinquency**, or maintaining with respect to a desired condition, degree, or rate. In *The Rules of Sociological Method* (1895), the French sociologist Émile Durkheim wrote that "crime is normal" and that it "is completely impossible for any society entirely free of it to exist."[6] Thus, since crime cannot be eliminated, the best society can do is to possibly attempt to manage it.

In a similar vein, sociologist Kai Erikson examined crime rates in Massachusetts Bay Colony. In his book *Wayward Puritans*, Erikson theorized that the amount of behaviors defined as deviance (delinquency) will remain relatively constant or stable over time, reflecting societal perceptions of how much deviance is normal. Vigorous law enforcement will be directed against only those behaviors that exceed some "normal" level. In Erikson's view, all societies construct definitions of deviancy, which then produce problems more or less equal to the interests or ability (size and complexity) of their criminal and juvenile justice systems to handle. Erikson observed that a "community's capacity for handling deviance, let us say, can be roughly estimated by counting its prison cells and hospital beds, its policemen and psychiatrists, its courts and clinics."[7]

What Durkheim and Erikson are suggesting is that American—or any other—society will never be entirely free of juvenile delinquency. Given this understanding, the best that can be hoped for is to maintain a level of juvenile delinquency, in terms of both frequency and severity that society can afford to recognize and manage.

Later, former U.S. Senator Daniel Moynihan wrote that American society had gone beyond the levels of affordable management, to the point that "we have been redefining deviancy so as to exempt much conduct previously stigmatized, and also quietly raising the 'normal' level in categories where behavior is now abnormal by any earlier standard."[8] Moynihan believes society has lost its "outrage" over disapproved behaviors, such as drug use, divorce, and out-of-wedlock births, and is willing to cast problems of crime and delinquency in a new light so that we can live with their present levels. Again, from this perspective, delinquency cannot be prevented, only managed.

If there is a preventive approach to be found within the juvenile justice system, it takes the form of intervention efforts designed to keep juvenile offenders

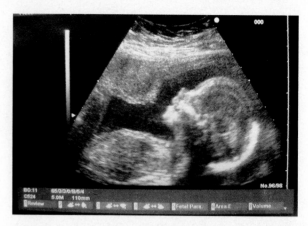

Deficiencies or problems in development at the fetal stage can put the child at risk for delinquency later in his or her life.
© Simon Pedersen/Getty.

from recidivating (repeating crimes) or becoming more serious offenders. Offending youth are subjected to treatment, correctional supervision, or punishment in an attempt to bring about positive change in the individual. Prevention within the juvenile justice system is limited to controlling or managing a child's tendency toward delinquency once he or she has come to the attention of the police and the juvenile courts. The remainder of this chapter focuses on steps being implemented to prevent delinquency *before* it takes place.

Prevention of Delinquency

The largely reactive policies for dealing with juvenile delinquency dominated the field of juvenile justice until the early 1980s, when a more proactive approach emerged as an alternative to ever-greater reliance on the law enforcement, courts, and corrections. This new approach adopted a **public health model**, which emphasized the prevention of disease before it occurs by reducing the risk of that disease and increasing resiliency against disease within the larger population. As applied to juvenile delinquency, the public health model focuses on the identification of social conditions and personal characteristics of youth that are either a *risk factor*, which statistically increases the likelihood of delinquency, or a *protective factor*, which is a condition that statistically reduces the probability of delinquency. When risk and protective factors are identified early in a child's life and are acted upon through effective programs and policies, the youth is, in short, immunized against delinquency. Prevention, from a public health model, occurs at three levels: primary, secondary, and tertiary.

Primary Prevention

Recall Durkheim's idea that a society can never be completely free of crime. That is probably very true if only the symptoms are being treated (think of

KEY TERMS

regulating delinquency
A policy that attempts to manage a desired condition, degree, or rate of delinquent behavior.

public health model
A model that emphasizes the prevention of disease before it occurs by reducing the risk of the disease and increasing resiliency against disease within the larger population.

BOX 14.1

The Face of Delinquency

Saving Children and Society from a Life of Delinquency and Crime

Cynics might assert that prevention programs are idealistic, and that it is not realistic to believe one could prevent the development of a serious delinquent career. However, this text has shown the cascade of developmental processes that result in delinquency, and thus if one or many of those developmental steps is changed, then the entire cascade of delinquency will be changed as well.

Today, most youth are exposed to some type of delinquency or violence prevention program. David Finkelhor and his colleagues' analysis of nationally representative surveys indicated that 65% of youth ages 5 to 17 years have been exposed to a prevention program with 55% having exposure in the past year. Most of these programs occur at school. Moreover, 71% of youth rate the programs as very or somewhat helpful. A program that has "life-saving" potential is the Stop Now and Plan (SNAP) program. SNAP is an intervention for boys ages 6 to 11 who already display serious antisocial behavior and delinquency, with these problems exceeding clinical levels of problem behaviors. Some children in the program have already been arrested. SNAP contains group-based modules where children are taught how to respond in specific situations, relating to theft, coping with anger, and managing group pressure. Each group session involves role play, problem solving, and feedback to evaluate prosocial and antisocial responses to each scenario. Jeffrey Burke and Rolf Loeber conducted an evaluation study and found that compared to youth who received standard services, those in SNAP had lower aggression, less rule breaking, fewer conduct problems,

and lower externalizing behaviors. At follow-up, 22% of youth in the control group had been charged in juvenile court compared to just 12% of youth who participated in SNAP. SNAP youth also had nearly three times fewer delinquent charges against them compared to controls.

Finally, a study by the Conduct Problems Prevention Research Group is revealing. Drawing on data from 979 early starting kindergarteners with serious conduct problems who participated in the Fast Track program, Kenneth Dodge and his colleagues examined the effect of a primary prevention program on their life and well-being at age 25 years. The results were wide-ranging. Compared to youth who did not receive the intervention, those who received the program in kindergarten and during early elementary school were much healthier and better behaved as adults. The intervention effects included:

- Fewer externalizing, internalizing, or substance use problems
- Fewer antisocial personality symptoms
- Fewer ADHD symptoms
- Fewer mood disorders
- Lower anxiety and depression
- Fewer alcohol or drug problems
- Better overall health
- Greater happiness and subjective well-being
- Fewer relationship problems
- Greater positive and fewer negative parenting behaviors
- 35% fewer convictions for drug-related crimes and 31% fewer convictions for violent crimes

David Finkelhor, Jennifer Vanderminden, Heather Turner, Anne Shattuck, and Sherry Hamby, "Youth Exposure to Violence Prevention Programs in a National Sample," *Child Abuse & Neglect* 38:677–686 (2014); Jeffrey Burke and Rolf Loeber, "The Effectiveness of the Stop Now and Plan (SNAP) Program for Boys at Risk for Violence and Delinquency," *Prevention Science* 16:242–253 (2015); Kenneth Dodge, Karen Bierman, John Coie, Mark Greenberg, John Lochman, Robert McMahon, Ellen Pinderhughes, and the Conduct Problems Prevention Research Group, "Impact of Early Intervention on Psychopathology, Crime, and Well-Being at Age 25," *American Journal of Psychiatry* 172:59–70 (2015).

delinquent behavior), but not addressing the underlying causes (such as low birth weight, poor nutrition in early childhood, and mental defects). That approach would be similar to doctors treating the symptoms of malaria, but officials ignoring the extensive breeding of the mosquitoes that cause the infection. A wide range of drugs is available to cure malaria, but if the source of the disease (mosquitoes) is not attended to, the disease will persist. Perhaps Durkheim is not correct. If appropriate efforts and resources are redirected to attack the underlying conditions that set young children on a path toward delinquency, it may be possible to significantly reduce the number of new delinquents. Again, using a public health model, if a new generation of infants and very young children were "inoculated" against delinquency, over time delinquency may be eradicated.

This ideal may sound "pie-in-the-sky" or unrealistic, given the contemporary social, political, and economic realities of American society. Nevertheless, it may be possible to at least reduce both the incidence and the seriousness of delinquency through primary prevention programs. **Primary prevention** policies and programs target the child at the earliest point possible. Accomplishing this type of prevention means developing and implementing programs aimed at the very first stages of life in fetal development, toddlers (persons younger than age 3), and early childhood (ages 3 to 5). As shown in **Box 14.1** in "The Face of

KEY TERMS

primary prevention
Policies and programs that target the child at the earliest point possible.

Delinquency" feature, effective prevention programs can save the life of a youth who statistically was very likely to have a sustained delinquency career and all of the hardships that accompany it.

Secondary Prevention

Secondary prevention efforts are aimed at youths or groups of youths who have already been identified as being at risk of becoming serious or chronic delinquents. These programs and policies seek to reduce the prevalence of delinquency within a community by reducing its seriousness or duration. Early identification of problem students in schools, juveniles brought to youth services agencies by their parents or guardians, and youth arrested for relatively minor delinquencies are targeted for treatment.

Tertiary Prevention

If efforts to prevent delinquency from emerging in the very beginning or to prevent the recurrence of minor delinquency have failed, juveniles become candidates for monitoring by the juvenile justice system. In the public health model, persons who have not been

For many juveniles, initial contact with the juvenile justice system is sufficient to turn them away from more serious criminal behavior.

© Trista Weibell/E+/Getty.

KEY TERMS

secondary prevention
Policies and programs aimed at children who are already identified as being at high risk of becoming serious or repeat delinquents.

tertiary prevention
Policies and programs that target existing delinquents and attempt to reduce recidivism by treating the individual with appropriate therapeutic efforts, or by incapacitating the youth to protect the community against further delinquencies.

inoculated to prevent a particular serious disease (primary prevention), and who are then exposed to the disease and show symptoms of early stages of the disease, are likely to be treated by a doctor or to make a visit to an urgent care office (secondary prevention). Unfortunately, if the person is already very ill, he or she is taken to the hospital for longer-term treatment until well or to be isolated from the public to prevent further spread of the disease (tertiary prevention). In the context of juvenile delinquency, **tertiary prevention** targets existing delinquents, with the goal being to reduce recidivism by treating the individual with appropriate therapeutic efforts or, if the child is not amenable to treatment, at least to incapacitate the youth to protect the community against further delinquencies.

Tertiary prevention is largely the responsibility of the juvenile justice system. When the police become aware of and investigate youth crimes, an arrest is often made. The child is then either warned and released by the officer or referred to the juvenile court. At intake, if the probation officer believes the case is appropriate for further processing, a petition is filed and the youth faces an adjudication hearing. If adjudicated delinquent by the court, the youth will face supervision while on probation or out-of-home placement in a correctional facility. Alternatively, if at intake the case is determined to be serious enough or the youth meets particular waiver requirements, he or she may be transferred to criminal court for prosecution as an adult and possible sentencing to incarceration.

The remainder of this chapter focuses on programs that involve primary prevention. First, however, some of the issues in early childhood development that guide primary prevention programs are examined (see **Box 14.2**, the "Delinquency Around the Globe" feature).

Early Childhood Development

Criminological theory over most of the 20th century focused on explaining juvenile crime as reflected in official delinquency statistics, which were largely based on police arrests, juvenile court appearances, and institutional placements of juveniles. In nearly all instances, these youths were already delinquent. Much theorizing approached the problem with data that examined the problem at only a single point in time, which limited researchers' scope to causal factors within the youths' current circumstances (e.g., adolescent socialization, delinquent friends, disrupted or dysfunctional families, poverty, stressors and strains, and the pushes and pulls of interpersonal and institutional relationships). It was not until the emergence of developmental theories in the late 20th and early 21st centuries that delinquency theory started

BOX 14.2

Delinquency Around the Globe

Preventing Delinquency in the People's Republic of China

Although juvenile delinquency is not as significant a problem in China as it is in the United States, it has been growing in both its prevalence and seriousness, especially since the 1980s after China opened its doors to Western nations (and their cultures). Today, youth crime is considered one of the country's most important public security problems. The government has responded by creating legislation and a specialized juvenile justice system designed to prevent delinquency before it occurs and to effectively intervene when prevention fails.

Chinese scholars and officials generally point to the following factors as causing the recent rise in delinquency: growing unemployment among youth; the disruption of the urban opportunity structure; the growing divorce rate; the increasing permissiveness of parents; and the inability of officials to control the influx and influence of harmful foreign TV, films, pornography, and customs. Many experts, however, see delinquency as the result of children's failure to see and act upon the right choices—their education has been deficient or they have been corrupted by bad influences.

In response to the "new" problem of delinquency, a specialized juvenile court was established in Shanghai in 1984, the first of its kind in China. By 2000, more than 15,000 judges were presiding over more than 3000 juvenile courts around the country. In 1991, the government established the Juvenile Protection Law, which was designed to define and protect the legal rights and interests of juveniles. This law stipulates education as the first response to delinquency, with punishment being meted out only as a last resort.

When delinquency rates continued to climb during the 1990s, in 1999 the Chinese government passed the Juvenile Delinquency Prevention Law. This law contains a number of provisions focusing on the role of parents and education, with parents defined as the primary agents in prevention of delinquency. Parents are expected to supervise their children and provide a proper moral education, which will strengthen youths' legal awareness and develop positive attitudes and values that reinforce law-abiding behavior.

The Juvenile Delinquency Prevention Law also contains a provision aimed at juvenile self-prevention. Juveniles are held responsible for developing a sense of self-respect and self-discipline, as well as enhancing their ability to resist temptations to instigate or participate in crime. They are also given the responsibility for reporting any problems of abuse or abandonment and for reporting to authorities any observed delinquent behavior by others.

If these informal measures fail and a child commits a crime, the law spells out the youth's rights and stipulates specific procedures for processing juveniles through the juvenile courts, as well as correctional measures for both minor and more serious delinquencies. Trials of youths age 14 through 16 are closed to the public. If children are found guilty, juvenile correctional treatment is administered to them separately from adult offenders. Most juveniles are treated at the community level, typically within the child's neighborhood; there, the juvenile is turned over to his or her parents, teachers, or neighborhood committee for help in better understanding correct moral values and behavior. Youths who commit more serious offenses are sent to reform schools run jointly by the bureau of education and the bureau of public security for "reform through education"—an approach that emphasizes educating the juvenile in political ideology, social and public morals, and basic knowledge of culture and production techniques in light labor.

Lening Zhang and Hianhong Liu, "China's Juvenile Delinquency Prevention Law," *International Journal of Offender Therapy and Comparative Criminology*, 51:541–554 (2007); John Hewitt, Eric Hickey, and Robert Regoli, "Dealing with Juvenile Delinquency: The Re-education of the Delinquent in the People's Republic of China," pages 67–81 in Jim Hackler (ed.), *Official Responses to Problem Juveniles: Some International Reflections* (Oñati, Spain: International Institute for the Sociology of Law, 1991); Yunjiao Gao, Dennis Wong, and Yanping Yu, "Maltreatment and Delinquency in China: Examining and Extending the Intervening Process of General Strain Theory," *International Journal of Offender Therapy and Comparative Criminology* 60:38–61 (2016); Zhenzhou Bao, Dongping Li, Wei Zhang, and Yanhui Wang, "School Climate and Delinquency among Chinese Adolescents: Analyses of Effortful Control as a Moderator and Deviant Peer Affiliation as a Mediator," *Journal of Abnormal Child Psychology* 43:81–93 (2015).

to take into account the influence of early childhood life experiences.

The extensive body of research based on developmental theories has yielded consistent findings regarding the most significant risk factors for future offending by youths. Individual factors (e.g., low intelligence and academic achievement, personality, and impulsiveness), family factors (e.g., criminal or antisocial parents, poor parental supervision, and disrupted families), and community factors (e.g., growing up in a poverty-level household, attending high-delinquency-rate schools, and living in poor and disorganized neighborhoods) have all been found to significantly increase the likelihood that an infant or young child will eventually move into delinquency and even adult criminality.[9]

Risk Factors in Very Early Childhood

Although the focus of this section is on very early childhood (from birth to age 3 years), some risk factors that increase the likelihood of a child eventually engaging in criminal behavior apply while the fetus

Table 14.1 Early Childhood Risk Factors

Child Health & Wellness	Maternal Factors	Family Factors
Low birth weight	Smoking/drinking	Child maltreatment
Lead	Substance abuse	Poor parenting
Immunizations	Prenatal checkups and care	Antisocial/incarcerated parents
Nutrition	Single, teen mother	Household violence
Sleep	Nutrition	Weak parent–child bond
Postnatal infant care	Depression	Substandard child care

© Jones & Bartlett Learning.

is still in the womb. In this section, we briefly explore three groups of risk factors: child health and wellness, maternal characteristics, and family circumstances (**Table 14.1**).

Child Health and Wellness

From the time the embryo begins to form in the womb, it may be negatively affected by the mother's poor nutritional habits; by chemicals ingested via the mother's smoking, drinking, or substance abuse; through secondhand and third-hand smoke produced by others; and by the presence of lead in the child's home (in water from lead pipes and in walls and carpet from lead paint residue).[10]

Neonatal exposure to nicotine, alcohol, marijuana, and other illicit drugs may result in neuropsychological defects affecting the child's verbal functioning, including memory, speech, reading, writing, and receptive listening, and problem-solving skills. In addition, it eventually places the child at a much greater risk of behavioral problems, including inattention, hyperactivity, and impulsivity. The primary reason prenatal and neonatal exposure to toxins produces neuropsychological and behavioral problems is that exposure to toxins impairs brain regions implicated in self-control and behavioral regulation. The primary brain self-control networks include the anterior cingulate cortex, medial prefrontal cortex, and the striatum. Unfortunately, toxins produce structural and functional deficits in these and other brain regions.[11]

Self-control, and more specifically impulsivity, are common targets of prevention programs. Richard Tremblay and his colleagues conducted a randomized controlled trial for behaviorally disordered kindergarten boys using data from the Montreal Longitudinal-Experimental Study. The 2-year intervention targeted social and problem-solving skills among the boys and provided training on effective child-rearing for their parents. Eight years after the program, boys in the experimental group had fewer drug-related delinquency problems, and a main reason was because of reductions in impulsivity. Other researchers have shown a gene x intervention interaction where children who had variants of the brain-derived neurotrophic factor

(BDNF) gene interacted with an impulsivity school-based program to produce reductions in aggression among youth.[12]

Neonatal exposure to these toxins is also related to low birth weight. Nearly 10% of infants born in the United States are low-birth-weight babies. Low-birth-weight babies are more likely to suffer from a variety of physical, emotional, and intellectual problems, as well as elevated medical expenditures during their first year of life. In addition, low-birth-weight babies have a higher incidence of deafness, blindness, epilepsy, cerebral palsy, learning disabilities, and attention-deficit disorder; when they begin school, they are more likely to be enrolled in special education and to repeat a grade in school.[13]

From birth to age 3, children's general health and wellness is also at risk from poor nutrition, inadequate sleep, and failure to have complete immunizations. Poor nutrition and lack of sleep are related to early behavioral problems, including inattention and failure to achieve normal cognitive development. Finally, very young children who do not receive postnatal medical follow-up care are at greater risk of health-related problems associated with missing school or underachieving in schoolwork during childhood. All of these health and wellness risk factors increase the likelihood of problem behaviors, conduct disorders, and delinquency.

Maternal Factors

Mothers who drink alcohol, smoke cigarettes and marijuana, or use other illegal drugs while pregnant and who maintain poor nutrition are directly affecting their fetuses. A very young child is also at risk of secondhand or thirdhand effects (the lingering smoke residue on the walls and ceilings and in the carpets) from his or her mother's smoking nicotine, marijuana, or crack cocaine while in the home or vehicle. When new mothers are unmarried and still only teenagers themselves, they are more likely to experience depression, to lack resources for helping to ensure postnatal checkups, and to fail to maintain healthy levels of nutrition necessary to manage and provide for very young children.[14]

Mothers are also the primary emotional nurturers of very young children. The emotional health of a child depends on the love, care, feeding, warming, touching, rocking, and cognitive stimulation transmitted through being read, sung, and talked to by his or her mother. Strong interactive contact between babies and adults is necessary to develop basic competence in children as well as to establish the trust in others needed to ensure healthy psychological development in both childhood and adulthood.

Although some of the health and wellness issues discussed here may be considered maternal-related factors, fathers are equally responsible for ensuring that infants receive immunizations, get adequate sleep, are fed appropriately, and receive required postnatal care. Unfortunately, a large proportion of the very young children who are at greatest risk do not have fathers involved in their lives on a regular basis. When neither parent steps up to handle these important responsibilities, risks for the child accumulate.[15]

Family Factors

Families are the source of some of the greatest risk factors to very young children: child maltreatment, single parenting, exposure to household violence, inconsistent or consistently poor parenting, antisocial or incarcerated parents, weak parent–child bonds, and substandard child care.

Stressed and dysfunctional parents are more likely to deliver abusive, harsh, or inconsistent parenting, which in turn exacerbates parent–child conflict and struggles over autonomy and control and sets the stage for further coercive exchanges in parent–child interactions during adolescence. Childhood impulsivity, hyperactivity, noncompliance, and aggression often emerge from ineffective disciplinary practices, limited warmth and involvement, and poor mother–child relationships. Parents who are antisocial, who engage in criminal behavior themselves, or who are in jail or prison or on probation or parole not only present problematic role models, but are less able to provide stable parenting and supervision. Indeed, they often must leave their children in foster care or other arrangements provided by the state.

Family factors are reciprocal in their relation to delinquency. This means that negative parenting behaviors impair a child's development, *and* a child's antisocial conduct worsens parental responses. For this reason, most prevention programs target not only the delinquent or at-risk child's problem behaviors and deficits, but also those of his or her parents. For instance, the SNAP program that serves aggressive and delinquent boys between the ages of 6 and 11 has been shown to improve boys' problem-solving skills, prosocial behavior, and emotional regulation skills. In turn, these improvements reduce parental stress and improve parenting skills, in part because the parent is responding to a more behaviorally well-regulated child rather than a fledgling delinquent.[16]

Children of incarcerated parents experience some additional stressors that compound their risks for delinquency. These stressors include separation from the parent, economic hardships, changes in caregivers, stigma and social isolation, and poor or unclear explanations of the parent's absence. Separation because of parental imprisonment leads to higher levels of emotional and psychological problems in the child, including withdrawal, depression, shame, guilt, anxiety, and antisocial behavior. Numerous studies report that children of incarcerated parents are more likely to engage in delinquent behavior, enter the juvenile justice system, and exhibit severe antisocial behavior when they reach adulthood.[17]

A mother who is a single teen parent, who did not complete high school, and who is living in poverty also often faces an absence of high-quality child care, either on an in-home basis or at child-care centers. The average cost for an infant to attend a high-quality urban child-care center usually exceeds $12,000 per year—a cost that is greater than the average tuition at many public universities.[18] Rural child-care centers are few and far between, and most are of substandard quality. For example, in Nebraska, approximately 80,000 children younger than age 6 are in the care of someone other than their parent(s) during the day. The average annual cost of center-based child care for a 4-year-old in Nebraska is more than $4,500. More important, only one-third of child-care centers are considered to be of "good quality," whereas nearly half are rated as being of "minimal or mediocre quality"; approximately 20% are rated as "poor quality."[19] When substandard child care is combined with inadequate early education programs, children are clearly at serious risk of developing problems in school, aggressiveness, and antisocial behavior (see **Box 14.3**, the "Delinquency Prevention" feature).

Childhood and Adolescence Risk Factors

If a child makes it to age 5 and has managed to avoid the risks discussed in the previous section, he or she faces an additional set of risks from childhood through adolescence. Just as risk factors associated with health and wellness, maternal circumstances, and family are related and accumulate in a general increase in likelihood of future delinquency, so risks facing children once they enter childhood and venture into their neighborhoods and schools also are related and cumulative. In this section, the four groups of factors are reviewed: school, peers, gangs, and poverty.

School

For all too many children, school is a terrifying place populated with bullies, gangs, fights, and violent

BOX 14.3

Delinquency Prevention

Can Conduct Disorder Be Prevented and Treated?

Conduct disorder is a serious behavioral disorder that is largely defined by a refusal and inability to follow rules and is strongly correlated with delinquency. It is not only a concern for American youth, but youth worldwide. In the United Kingdom, researchers and practitioners helped to launch Sure Start, which is a major social welfare program similar to Head Start in the United States. Several interventions for children at risk of conduct disorder have been performed in Sure Start settings.

Evaluations suggest that prevention programs focused primarily on parenting deficits are effective at reducing problem behaviors in children. Rhiannon Edwards and her colleagues found that it would cost $10,666 to bring a child with the highest behavioral risk score to below the clinical range in conduct problems if not for the program. This means that for every one point improvement on behavior, there is a savings of $142. In a related study, researchers found that 63% of children in Sure Start programs made a minimum behavioral improvement. About 54% made a large improvement in their behavior and 39% made a very large improvement (measured as 1.5 standard deviations). This supports the larger conclusion of prevention programs in that it saves much more money than it costs.

In their review of 26 meta-analyses of nearly 2000 studies of treatment approaches for children and adolescents with severe conduct problems, Christine Litschge, Michael Vaughn, and Cynthia McCrea found that overall there is good news. The overall effect size, which is a measure of the average effectiveness of the treatment,

was modest but significant. The most successful treatment approaches were cognitive-behavioral therapies that attempt to reshape the thinking patterns of antisocial individuals. Family therapies and multimodal therapies were also moderately effective followed by group therapy. Overall, programs that include multiple domains and multiple participants, such as parents, siblings, families, teachers, peers, and the conduct-disordered youth are generally the most successful.

Kenneth Dodge and his colleagues with the Conduct Problems Prevention Research Group have shown the precise mechanisms by which prevention programs can neutralize conduct disorder. Drawing on data from the Fast Track project, which is the largest and longest federally funded prevention intervention for high-risk, aggressive kindergarten children, Dodge and his colleagues found that the parent and social-skills trainings help conduct-disordered youth respond to their environment in new ways. Specifically, the program helps to devalue aggression as a behavioral response, increases competent responses to interpersonal problems, and reduces hostile attribution bias—the tendency to believe that others are out to get you and mean you harm. These improvements account for nearly 30% of the program's effectiveness.

In sum, although conduct disorder is a pernicious condition that often is the forerunner of a serious delinquency career, many programs in the United States and abroad have been shown to forestall it, and save children from a life of serious behavioral problems.

Rhiannon Edward, Alan Ceilleachair, Tracey Bywater, Dyfrig A. Hughes, and Judy Hutchings, "Parenting Programme for Parents of Children at Risk of Developing Conduct Disorder: Cost Effectiveness Analysis," *British Medical Journal* 334:682–685 (2007); Tracey Bywater, Judy Hutchings, David Daley, Chris Whitaker, Seow Tien Yeo, Karen Jones, Catrin Eames, and Rhiannon Edwards, "Long-Term Effectiveness of a Parenting Intervention for Children at Risk of Developing Conduct Disorder," *British Journal of Psychiatry* 195:318–324 (2009); Christine Litschge, Michael Vaughn, and Cynthia McCrea, "The Empirical Status of Treatments for Children and Youth with Conduct Problems: An Overview of Meta-Analytic Studies," *Research on Social Work Practice* 20:21–35 (2010); Jamila Reid, Carolyn Webster-Stratton, and Mary Hammond, "Follow-Up of Children Who Received the Incredible Years Intervention for Oppositional Defiant Disorder: Maintenance and Prediction of 2-Year Outcome," *Behavior Therapy* 34:471–491 (2003); Kenneth Dodge, Jennifer Godwin, and the Conduct Problems Prevention Research Group, "Social-Information-Processing Patterns Mediate the Impact of Preventive Intervention on Adolescent Antisocial Behavior," *Psychological Science* 24:456–465 (2013); Brad Bushman, Katherine Newman, Sandra Calvert, Geraldine Downey, Mark Dredze, Michael Gottfredson, et al., "Youth Violence: What We Know and What We Need to Know," *American Psychologist* 71:17–39 (2016); Phillippe Cunningham, Jeff Randall, Stacy Ryan, and Beata DaNine Fleming, "Conduct Disorder and Oppositional Defiant Disorder," pages 143–162 in Alfiee Breland-Noble, Cheryl Al-Mateen, and Nirbhay Singh (eds.), *Handbook of Mental Health in African American Youth* (New York: Springer, 2016).

attacks on students, teachers, and staff. For some children, school is a place where they try to learn, but that learning process is too frequently frustrated by disruptive students, incompetent or burned-out teachers, or out-of-date books and broken or nonexistent class equipment, such as science labs, computers, and software programs. For still other children, school is a place where drug dealing, thefts, and even sexual activities take place in the halls, rest-rooms, classrooms, locker rooms, and playgrounds.

Research shows that teachers perceive poor students less positively and tend to have lower achievement

expectations for them than for non-poor children, mostly on the basis of nonacademic considerations. Teachers of poor students are also more likely to perceive the school and classroom climate less positively.[20]

The environments of too many schools expose even bright and serious students to risks presented by the negative influences of other students, the failings of school administrators and teachers, and the perception that the larger community has neither faith in the school nor interest in providing needed resources. For students who enter school with a number of risk factors accumulated since conception, these detrimental school factors merely exacerbate the problem and increase the likelihood that these students will fail, drop out, and act out.

Peers

Peer groups are composed of youths of similar ages and interests. Peers empower one another as they help their counterparts feel worthwhile and important. For many children, peers are their closest friends and role models. The dress, language, music, and behavior of peers frequently become their own. The peer group provides adolescents with camaraderie, acceptance, and a sense of purpose. A youth's closest or "best" friends can strongly influence his or her behavior. If parental supervision and monitoring are weak or nonexistent, peers become even more influential.

If a youth's peers are law abiding, conventional, studious, and hard working, the child will likely exhibit those same characteristics. Conversely, children whose peers use alcohol or drugs and engage in other problem behaviors are more likely to also be involved in those behaviors. In fact, a child is nearly twice as likely to engage in delinquency if his or her best friend is already committing delinquencies.[21] Thus peers can—but do not necessarily—pose a significant risk factor for adolescents.

Gangs

Juvenile gangs present a number of risk factors for adolescents. Gangs are present in neighborhoods and schools where nondelinquent children are exposed to them because of parental decisions related to housing location and because of laws mandating school attendance. Sometimes gangs aggressively recruit new members, often youths calculate that they will be safer if they join a gang, and occasionally adolescents who are not yet delinquent are attracted to gangs for their social activities and sense of belonging.

Children living in impoverished neighborhoods are more likely to have lower quality child care, to attend underfunded schools, and to have fewer successful role models than children in more affluent neighborhoods.

© iStockphoto/Getty.

Risk factors posed by gangs include an increased likelihood of being victimized if not a gang member and an even greater risk of violent victimization once a member of a gang. Youths who are drawn into gangs are less likely to finish high school and more likely to use drugs and alcohol, to commit crimes, to be arrested and processed by the juvenile court, and to be placed in juvenile correctional facilities.[22]

Neighborhood and Poverty

Structural forces, such as living in a disadvantaged neighborhood, poverty, and social isolation, negatively influence parenting practices and increase the risk of delinquency. Several studies have produced evidence supporting the relationship between poverty, social isolation, and child maltreatment.[23] Because the neighborhood is the ecological niche where families function, its conditions may either compound or counteract the deficiencies and vulnerabilities of parents. Residential segregation based on socioeconomic factors presents a serious threat to family well-being because it produces concentrations of high-need, low-resource families, or families that are often exposed to "social impoverishment" and weak systems of social support.[24] Because most adults residing within impoverished neighborhoods have inadequate education and menial employment at best, they provide poor role models for achieving success through the conventional means of education and work.

Poor children are more likely than non-poor children to live in housing located in commercial and industrial areas. Often these areas lack safe outdoor places for children to play, which in turn limits their opportunities for social interaction and cognitive development. Children living in poverty are less likely to have access to stimulating materials or experiences. Those who live for long periods in impoverished conditions experience more negative life events and adverse conditions that may place demands on their coping resources that go well beyond what they can handle. Thus exposure to chronic adversity exacts a toll on children's mental, physical, and emotional health.[25]

Model and Promising Prevention Programs

The Office of Juvenile Justice and Delinquency Prevention takes prevention very seriously. In 2000, it developed a Model Programs Guide to serve as a comprehensive resource on evidence-based delinquency prevention programs. Currently, the Model Programs Guide uses CrimeSolutions.gov evidence standards and criteria to evaluate programs. This section explores a wide variety of prevention programs that have been found to be effective or show promise of eventual payoffs. First, we examine primary prevention programs that target the prenatal, postnatal, and very early childhood period.

Prenatal and Very Early Childhood Prevention Programs

The most effective programs for delinquency prevention are aimed at children in the earliest stages of life, even while they are still in the womb. This is because the health and well-being of children from conception through the first 3 years of life will have significant effects on them throughout childhood and adolescence and into adulthood.

Nurse–Family Partnership

The best-known prevention study demonstrating the long-term effects of early-life interventions on a high-risk sample is the Nurse–Family Partnership program, which was supervised by David Olds and his colleagues. The Olds study used a sample of 400 women and 315 infants born in upstate New York between April 1978 and September 1980. Women were eligible to participate if they were pregnant with their first child and either were single parents, were younger than age 19, or had a low income. Home visits focused on the health of the mother during pregnancy, fetal development, infant health, postpartum development, and strengthening of the formal and informal community support systems for the family.[26]

The women in the sample possessed a variety of risk factors that increased the likelihood of their children engaging in delinquency. All of the mothers were unmarried, 48% were younger than 15 years of age, and 59% lived in poverty. Random assignment was used to create four groups receiving various social services. The comprehensive experimental group received 9 home visits during pregnancy and 23 home visits from nurses from the child's birth until the child's second birthday. Control subjects received standard, but less comprehensive prenatal care. All groups were followed up 15 years later. The results were impressive in terms of the reduction of problem behaviors associated with chronic delinquency. Compared to controls, boys who were in the treatment groups had a lower incidence of running away, accumulated significantly fewer arrests and convictions, accrued fewer probationary sentences and subsequent violations, had fewer lifetime sexual partners, and had a lower prevalence of smoking, alcoholism, and casual alcohol use. Thus this experiment offered compelling evidence that early-life interventions, which teach parents the skills they need to raise healthy children, are helpful.[27]

The Nurse–Family Partnership program is considered to be a model prevention program. The nurse visits in the Olds study resulted in 79% fewer verified reports of child abuse and neglect; 31% fewer subsequent births and increased interval between births; a 30-month reduction in the receipt of Aid to Families with Dependent Children (a social welfare subsidy); 44% fewer maternal behavioral problems because of substance abuse; 69% fewer maternal arrests; and 56% fewer children arrests. Most impressive from a policy perspective, the costs of the program—approximately $3,200 per family annually—were recouped by the child's fourth birthday. Given the many successes of the Nurse–Family Partnership, the program has also been implemented in Australia, Canada, England, the Netherlands, Northern Ireland, and Scotland.[28]

Elmira Prenatal/Early Infancy Project

Started in the early 1970s, the Elmira Prenatal/Early Infancy Project is based on the premise that most of the more serious problems faced by high-risk children are a product of poor prenatal and very early childhood conditions, including preterm delivery and low birth weight, dysfunctional caregiving of the child, stressful environmental conditions negatively affecting family functioning, and lack of a social support network for child and family. Home visits by nurses are intended to reduce these problems by helping to improve the health and nutrition of women during pregnancy; reduce their use of nicotine, alcohol, and illegal drugs; and provide for early identification and treatment of obstetrical problems before they become too serious. The overall goal is to improve infant and child health and development by helping parents develop competencies in child care and become more responsible for their child's well-being.

The Elmira program focuses on low-income, first-time mothers. Nurses begin visiting the women in their homes during the end of the first trimester of pregnancy, with visits continuing through the child's second birthday. In their evaluation of this program, David Olds and his colleagues reported that the home visits reduced the frequency of low-birth-weight or preterm deliveries, improved diets of mothers and children, decreased smoking, increased the likelihood that mothers would make use of WIC (Women, Infants, and Children) nutritional supplementation, and led to reduction of subsequent pregnancies.[29]

Syracuse University Family Development Program

This program provides weekly home visitation, parent training, and high-quality individualized day care for children aimed at improving children's cognitive and emotional functioning, creating positive outlooks, and reducing delinquency. The program targets primarily low-income, single-parent, African American families, who are provided with a full range of education, nutrition, health and safety, and human resources support programs, beginning prenatally and lasting until the child turns 5 years old.

Evaluation studies of the Syracuse program followed the participant children through age 16. Children who were not in the program were found to be 10 times more likely to have committed a crime than

Any number of risk factors for delinquency can be reduced when nurses are able to visit expectant or new mothers in their homes.

© Dmitry Melnikov/Shutterstock.

comparable or matched children who were enrolled in the program. The crimes of nonparticipant children also were more serious, including robbery, assault, and sexual abuse.[30]

Parents as Teachers

Parents as Teachers (PAT) is one of the most widely available home-visiting programs in the United States, with more than 2300 local programs operating across the country. PAT serves families from the prenatal stage until the child reaches age 5. Home visits are conducted by trained parent educators on a monthly, biweekly, or weekly schedule, depending on the family's need and preference. Parent educators work with parents regarding principles of child development, modeling appropriate activities, and promotion of strong parent–child relationships. PAT staff arrange for group meetings to assist parents in building support networks, create opportunities for sharing successes and common challenges, and provide outside speakers to bring parents additional information and techniques for effective parenting. In addition, health, vision, hearing, and developmental screenings are conducted on an annual basis, and parents are trained to carefully observe their child's development to detect any learning difficulties or developmental delays.[31]

Edward Zigler and his colleagues conducted an evaluation of the PAT programs in Missouri. Based on their analysis of a sample of children who entered kindergarten between the 1998–1999 and 2000–2001 school years, these researchers reported that PAT significantly improved school readiness as a consequence of better parenting practices, increased parents' time spent reading to children, and increased the likelihood of PAT children enrolling in preschool programs such as Early Head Start, Head Start, or other preschool programs available in the community. Zigler and his associates noted that "poor children who received both the PAT program and quality preschool education had

school readiness scores that approximated those of more advantaged children."[32]

Yale Child Welfare Research Program

The Yale program provided services to 17 poverty-level, pregnant, African American women expecting their first child; services were continued until the children were 30 months old. As part of this program, clinical and health professionals made home visits and counseled mothers about securing adequate food and housing, and making decisions about their future goals including those related to family, education, and careers. Children were provided with pediatric services and child care, and mothers were taught about child development.

A 10-year follow-up study showed that youths enrolled in the Yale Child Welfare Program missed significantly fewer days of school, required significantly fewer remedial and supportive school services, and were rated significantly less negative, less aggressive, less likely to act out or to engage in predelinquent behavior, and were rated more socially well-adjusted by their teachers compared to controls. Almost all of the program families were self-supporting by the time the first-born children were 12 and a half years old. Mothers in the program also had fewer children and spaced their births further apart than did comparison mothers. This program is no longer deliverable, however—that is, no technical assistance is available to those who wish to implement it.[33]

Early Head Start

Designed to promote healthy prenatal outcomes for pregnant women, to enhance the development of very young children, and to promote healthy family functioning, Early Head Start (EHS) was created by the U.S. Congress in 1994 when it reauthorized funding for the Head Start Act. Today more than 700 community-based Early Head Start programs serve

The risks for delinquency can be reduced by very early focus on physical, social, emotional, and cognitive development of children.

© Jupiterimages/Polka Dot/Getty.

approximately 63,000 children throughout the United States. EHS serves pregnant women and children from the prenatal stage through age 3.[34]

Early Head Start provides services through center-based programs, home-based programs, and a combination of center-and home-based programs that are individualized to best meet the needs of children and families. Programs are aimed at supporting the physical, social, emotional, cognitive, and language development of each child through comprehensive prenatal and postpartum health care, prenatal education, and breastfeeding education; home visits with families with newborns; comprehensive health and mental health services; and high-quality child-care services.

The positive effects of Early Head Start have been reported in an evaluation study involving 3000 children and families in 17 sites. In the sample, half of participants received EHS services, whereas the other half were randomly assigned to a control group not receiving EHS. Children in EHS scored significantly higher in cognitive and language development, demonstrated lower levels of aggressive behavior, and exhibited more advanced social-emotional development compared to children in the control group. EHS parents demonstrated more emotional supportiveness to their children, provided significantly more support for language and learning, and read to their children more. EHS fathers were less likely to report using corporal punishment during the previous week and to be less intrusive, and EHS children were observed to be more able to engage their fathers and to be more attentive to their fathers than children in the control group.[35]

Early Childhood and Preschool Programs

Targeting delinquency prevention programs at children before they are old enough to enter school has produced significant positive results. Most of these programs are aimed at children under age 5 and many involve parents directly in knowledge and skill development.

Chicago Child-Parent Center Preschool Program

The Chicago Child-Parent Center Preschool program has served more than 100,000 3- and 4-year-olds since 1967. This center-based program provides educational and family support to economically disadvantaged and at-risk children from preschool to third grade. The program was initially implemented in four locations, but has since expanded to 24 centers throughout the Chicago public schools. There are five primary components to the Chicago program:

1. Placement of educational interventions before the child beginning primary school

2. Use of a child-centered structured language and basic skills learning approach
3. Linking of parents and schools through the role of parent volunteers one half-day each week
4. A continuity of educational care between preschool and primary school
5. Health and nutrition services, including speech therapy, health screening, and free breakfasts and lunches

In a study of this program, compared to the comparison group, preschool participants demonstrated a significant reduction in special education placement and grade retention, significantly higher rates of high school graduation, lower juvenile arrest rates, fewer arrests for violent crimes, and a more than 50% reduction in reports of child maltreatment. Moreover, program participants between the ages of 18 and 24 were significantly less likely to have been convicted of a violent crime in adult court or to have been incarcerated in an adult jail or prison.[36]

High/Scope Perry Preschool

The High/Scope Perry Preschool program was begun in 1962 as a high-quality, 1- to 2-year-long early educational program built around principles derived from Jean Piaget. Piaget's theory emphasized that children are active learners and learn most effectively when engaged in activities that they plan themselves, carry out, and then review. In the High/Scope Perry Preschool program, preschool classroom activities are combined with home visits by trained staff who encourage parents to observe, support, and extend their child's activities. The curriculum does not include defined subject matter for children to be taught by adults. Rather, adults and children participate in a free conversation process, allowing both to interact as thinkers and doers.

Extensive research has followed program children into middle adulthood and reports significant lifetime crime prevention effects. For example, by age 27, matched sample at-risk children who did not participate in the program were five times more likely to have been arrested than program participants. At age 40, nonparticipating children were twice as likely to have been arrested for violent crimes as were participating children. Moreover, children who were not in the program were more likely to abuse drugs and to have been arrested for drug-related felonies than those in the program. For a more extensive discussion of the High/Scope Perry Preschool Program, see **Box 14.4** the "Delinquency Prevention" feature.[37]

Head Start

The roots of Project Head Start can be traced to 1965, when this program was established as part of the "War on Poverty." Head Start is a school readiness program for low-income children that is intended

BOX 14.4

Delinquency Prevention

High/Scope Perry Preschool

The High/Scope Perry Preschool in Ypsilanti, Michigan, was established to provide high-quality early education opportunities for 3- and 4-year-old, low-income children who were identified as having low IQ scores (between 70 and 85—the range for borderline mental impairment) with no organic deficiencies (i.e., biologically based mental impairment), and who were at high risk of failing school. The program was based on an active learning model that emphasizes participants' intellectual and social development. In the study of this program, children attended the preschool Monday through Friday for 2.5 hours per day over a 2-year period. During that same period, a staff-to-child ratio of one adult for every five or six children enabled teachers to visit each child's family in their home for 1.5 hours each week. In addition, parents participated in monthly small-group meetings with other parents, with program staff acting as facilitators for the sessions.

Participants in the High/Scope Perry Preschool study were characterized by better academic performance than those in the control group, as demonstrated by higher graduation rates, better grades, higher standardized test scores, and fewer instances of placement in special education classes. In addition, members of the program group spent more time on homework and demonstrated more positive attitudes toward school at ages 15 and 19. More parents of program group members had positive attitudes toward their children's educational experiences and were hopeful that their children would obtain college degrees.

Although it was initiated as an educational intervention, the High/Scope Perry Preschool Project has demonstrated a number of other positive outcomes, including a significantly lower rate of crime and delinquency and a lower incidence of teenage pregnancy and welfare dependency among program participants. Overall, the program group has demonstrated significantly higher rates of prosocial behavior, academic achievement, employment, income, and family stability as compared with the control group.

Data collected from police and court records reveal that juvenile delinquency rates were significantly lower among the High/Scope Perry Preschool program group as compared with the control group, with the former group having fewer arrests and fewer juvenile court petitions. Only 31% of the program group had ever been arrested, compared with 51% of the control group. In addition to police and court records, data collected from respondents at age 19 were used as an overall indicator of delinquency. When study participants were 19 years old, researchers found significant differences between the program and control groups: The program group had fewer arrests overall than the control group (on average, 1.3 versus 2.3 arrests per person), fewer felony arrests (on average, 0.7 versus 2.0 arrests per person), and fewer juvenile court petitions filed (on average, 0.2 versus 0.4 petition per person).

Data collected from respondents at age 27 indicated significant differences between the program group and control group in terms of adult arrests: The control group had more than twice as many arrests as the program group (on average, 4.0 versus 1.8 arrests per person). Thirty-six percent of the control group accounted for 98 felony arrests between ages 19 and 27, whereas 27% of the program group accounted for 40 felony arrests during the same period. Thirty-five percent of the control group were considered frequent offenders (defined as five or more arrests), compared with only 7% of the program group. In addition, 25% of the control group had been arrested for drug-related offenses, compared with 7% of the program group. The control group also averaged more months on probation (6.6 versus 3.2 months) and had more than twice as many of its members placed on probation or parole for longer than 18 months (20% versus 9%).

A cost–benefit analysis of the High/Scope Perry Preschool study indicates that the program produced a savings to the public of more than seven times the initial investment per child, with a return of $7.16 for every $1 spent on the program. When adjusted for inflation and a 3% discount rate, the investment in early childhood prevention resulted in a taxpayer return of $88,433 per child from the following sources:

- Savings in welfare assistance (before welfare reform)
- Savings in special education
- Savings to the criminal justice system
- Savings to crime victims
- Increased tax revenue from higher earnings

Greg Parks, *The High/Scope Perry Preschool Project* (Washington, DC: Office of Juvenile Justice and Delinquency Prevention, 2000); W. Barnett, "Benefit–Cost Analysis of Preschool Education: Findings from a 25-Year Follow-up," *American Journal of Orthopsychiatry* 63:25–50 (1993); Lawrence Schweinhart, Helen Barnes, and David Weikart, *Significant Benefits: The High/Scope Perry Preschool Study through Age 27* (Ypsilanti, MI: High/Scope Press, 1985); Brandon Welsh, Christopher Sullivan, and David Olds, "When Early Crime Prevention Goes to Scale: A New Look at the Evidence," *Prevention Science* 11:115–125 (2010); B. K. Elizabeth Kim, Amanda Gilman, and J. David Hawkins, "School- and Community-Based Prevention Interventions during Adolescence: Preventing Delinquency through Science-Guided Collective Action," pages 447–460 in Julien Morizot and Lila Kazemian (eds.), *The Development of Criminal and Antisocial Behavior: Theory, Research and Practical Applications* (New York: Springer, 2015).

to equip those children with the tools they need to enter kindergarten at the same level as more affluent children. The program provides comprehensive services to children ages 3 to 5, including preschool education, nutrition services, medical and dental checkups, social and emotional development, parental involvement, and assistance to parents in accessing community resources. In 2007, Congress passed the Head Start Reauthorization bill, which committed the government to providing Head Start programs to homeless children, including those living in shelters, motels, cars, or shared housing with others.

Although the large number of studies evaluating Head Start have provided mixed findings, the majority suggest that the program produces small positive effects. Small to moderate positive gains have been seen among Head Start children who entered the program as 3- or 4-year-olds in the areas of prereading, prewriting, and vocabulary, as well as positive effects on the health status of children. Longer-term effects have also been demonstrated: Head Start children are significantly more likely than non-Head Start children to complete high school and attend college, and they are significantly less likely to repeat a grade, commit crimes as adults, and be arrested and charged with a crime.[38] For a more extensive discussion of a program that is consistent with the Head Start approach, see **Box 14.5**, the "Delinquency Prevention" feature.

BOX 14.5

Delinquency Prevention

The Incredible Years: Parents, Teachers, and Children Training Series

For more than 25 years, Carolyn Webster-Stratton and her colleagues at the University of Washington's Parenting Clinic have worked to develop and evaluate training programs for parents, teachers, children, and families with children ages 2 to 10 who exhibit conduct problems. The purpose of the series is to prevent delinquency, drug abuse, and violence. Its specific goals are outlined here:

Reduce Conduct Problems in Children

- Decrease negative behaviors and noncompliance with parents at home.
- Decrease peer aggression and disruptive behaviors in the classroom.

Promote Social, Emotional, and Academic Competence in Children

- Increase children's social skills.
- Increase children's understanding of feelings.
- Increase children's conflict management skills and decrease negative attributions.
- Increase academic engagement, school readiness, and cooperation with teachers.

Promote Parental Competence and Strengthen Families

- Increase parents' positive communication skills, such as the use of praise and positive feedback to children, and reduce the use of criticism and unnecessary commands.
- Improve parents' limit-setting skills by replacing spanking and other negative physical behaviors with nonviolent discipline techniques and by promoting positive strategies such as ignoring the child's behavior, allowing for logical consequences, providing redirection, and developing problem-solving and empathy skills.

- Improve parents' problem-solving skills and anger management.
- Increase family support networks and school involvement.

Promote Teacher Competence and Strengthen School–Home Connections

- Strengthen teachers' classroom management strategies by using proactive and positive teaching approaches (e.g., clearly delineated classroom rules and use of strategies such as redirection, nonverbal warning signs, proximity praise).
- Increase teachers' collaborative efforts in promoting parents' school involvement and developing plans for behavior modification that connect home and school environments.
- Increase teachers' ability to offer social skills and problem-solving training in the classroom.

The Incredible Years Series involves a number of separate training program components directed at parents, teachers, and children.

Parent Training

The Incredible Years Basic Parent Training Program includes both early-childhood and school-age components. The Incredible Years Early Childhood Basic Parent Training Program (ages 2 to 7) involves group discussion of a series of 250 video vignettes. The program teaches parents interactive play and reinforcement skills; nonviolent disciplinary techniques, including "timeout" and "ignore" logical and natural consequences; and problem-solving strategies.

The Incredible Years School-Age Basic Parent Training Program (ages 5 to 12) is a multicultural program similar to the early-childhood program in content but aimed at a somewhat older age group. It gives greater emphasis to strategies for older children, including logical consequences, monitoring, problem solving with children, and family problem solving. Approximately 40% of the people featured on the videotapes for this version of the Basic program are people of color.

The Incredible Years Advanced Parent Training Program (ages 4 to 10) is a 10- to 12-week supplement to the Basic program that addresses other family risk factors, such as depression, marital discord, poor coping skills, poor anger management, and lack of support.

The Incredible Years Education Parent Training Program (Supporting Your Child's Education) supplements either the early-childhood or school-age Basic program by focusing on ways to foster children's academic competence. It was designed to teach parents to strengthen their children's reading and academic readiness and to promote strong connections between home and school.

Teacher Training

The Incredible Years Teacher Training Program was designed to train teachers in classroom management skills such as how to encourage and motivate students, strengthen social competence, decrease inappropriate behavior, and teach social skills, anger management, and problem solving in the classroom. Teacher training is offered to groups of teachers and may be delivered in 6 daylong workshops offered monthly or in 2-hour sessions offered once a week for 24 weeks. Videotaped vignettes of teachers managing common and difficult situations in the classroom are used to stimulate group discussion and problem solving.

Child Training

The Incredible Years Child Training Program, Dina Dinosaur's Social Skills and Problem-Solving Curriculum, was designed to teach groups of children friendship skills, appropriate conflict management strategies, successful classroom behaviors, and empathy skills. In addition, it teaches children cognitive strategies to cope with negative attributions (i.e., hostile thoughts about others' intentions) and situations that incite anger. Videotaped vignettes are used to stimulate children's discussions, demonstrate problem solving, and prompt role-playing and practice activities.

Evaluations of the effectiveness of the Incredible Years program report significant positive effects from its use. Teachers who received this training showed improvement in classroom management styles, including being less harsh, critical, and inconsistent in their interactions with the children in their classrooms. Students who participated in the program displayed significant improvement in emotional self-regulation, social competence, and self-control of conduct problems. Students also displayed more prosocial solutions to problem situations than did students who did not participate in the program.

Carolyn Webster-Stratton, "The Incredible Years: Use of Play Interventions and Coaching for Children with Externalizing Difficulties," pages 137–158 in Linda Reddy, Tara Files-Hall, and Charles Schaefer (eds.), *Empirically Based Play Interventions for Children*, Second edition (Washington, DC: American Psychological Association, 2016); *The Incredible Years Training Series* (Washington, DC: Office of Juvenile Justice and Delinquency Prevention, 2000); Carolyn Webster-Stratton, M. Jamila Reid, and Mike Stoolmiller, "Preventing Conduct Problems and Improving School Readiness: Evaluation of the Incredible Years Teacher and Child Training Programs in High-Risk Schools," *Journal of Child Psychology and Psychiatry* 49:471–488 (2008); The Incredible Years, retrieved March 21, 2016 from http://www.incredibleyears.com.

School and Family Programs

The programs discussed in this section are focused on both the school and family as important social contexts for child development. Children, typically between the ages of 6 and 12, their teachers, and their families receive help in preventing and reducing problem behaviors before they become serious.

The Incredible Years Program

In addition to delinquency prevention programs that target infants, toddlers, and their families, some other approaches have proved effective at reducing antisocial behavior among children with pronounced behavioral problems. These programs offer treatments not only to the antisocial child, but also to his or her parents, other family members, and teachers they face the uphill challenge of reducing antisocial behavior that has already occurred. One program to accomplish this is the Incredible Years Parent, Teacher, and Child Training Series developed by Carolyn Webster-Stratton. The Incredible Years is a comprehensive social competence program that treats conduct problems in children between the ages of 2 and 8. In six randomized trials of this program, aggression and conduct problems have been reduced by 60% among the participating children and families. Other promising outcomes have included increased academic competence and achievement, increased sociability and friend-making skills, better anger management and problem-solving skills, and increased empathy among previously problem youth.[39]

Seattle Social Development Project

The Seattle Social Development Project (SSDP), which was first implemented in 1981 in 18 Seattle elementary schools, offers parent management training, social competence training, and support for academic skills in an attempt to increase children's attachment to school and family, reduce involvement with antisocial peers, and reduce aggressive behavior. Teachers are trained in cooperative learning, interactive teaching, and proactive classroom management. Parents take classes to develop child behavior management skills, academic support skills, and specific techniques for reducing their child's risk of drug use.

Numerous follow-up studies have been conducted examining the short- and long-term effects of the program. According to criminologist J. David Hawkins and his colleagues,[40] by the end of the second grade, participation in the program had a significant positive impact. Among males, the SSDP group exhibited less externalizing antisocial behaviors, and SSDP females were significantly less self-destructive than control group students. By completion of the sixth grade, boys in the SSDP group were rated as more socially competent by teachers and had earned significantly higher grades. By age 18, SSDP students were significantly less likely to have repeated a grade, to have engaged in drinking 10 or more times in the prior year, to have engaged in sexual intercourse, and to have been pregnant or to have caused a pregnancy than non-SSDP students.[41]

Promoting Alternative Thinking Strategies

The Promoting Alternative Thinking Strategies (PATHS) curriculum is a comprehensive program that is intended to promote emotional and social competencies and reduce aggression and behavior problems in elementary school children (kindergarten through grade 5), while enhancing the educational process in the classroom. It is taught three times per week for 20 to 30 minutes per day. PATHS seeks to improve students' emotional literacy, self-control, social competence, positive peer instructions, and interpersonal problem-solving skills. The curriculum also focuses on the ability of the students to label, understand, and manage their feelings, impulses, and stress. In program evaluations, PATHS has been shown to improve protective factors (which insulate children from delinquency) and to reduce risk factors (which propel youths toward delinquency). Other positive outcomes include increased self-control, improved understanding and recognition of emotions, more effective conflict-resolution strategies, improved thinking and planning skills, reduced depression, and fewer conduct problems. The PATHS program costs only $45 per student per year.[42]

Nurturing Parents Programs

Across cultures, parenting of infants and toddlers is the most important factor in producing healthy and functioning children versus unhealthy and antisocial children. Consequently, Nurturing Parenting Programs (NPP) have been implemented in several countries across Europe and South America, in addition to Canada, Israel, and Mexico. Within the United States, these programs have been developed to reach the potentially special needs of African American, Hispanic, and Hmong families. NPP target families considered to be at higher risk for abuse and neglect,

Bullying is a widespread problem in schools across the country. Are bullies also more likely to engage in juvenile crime?

© P_Wei/E+/Getty.

families identified by local social service providers as abusive or neglectful, families in recovery for alcohol and other drug abuse, parents incarcerated for crimes against society, and adults seeking to become adoptive or foster parents.

An evaluation conducted by the National Institute of Mental Health examined the effectiveness of NPP among 121 abusive adults and 150 abused children from several states. The researchers discovered that 93% of the adult participants successfully modified their previously abusive parenting techniques. Only 7% failed the program and committed new acts of child abuse. Overall, parents reported being more empathetic to their children's needs and development and also showed improvements on cognitive ability, enthusiasm, self-assuredness, and self-confidence. After treatment, parents reported reduced incidence of anxiety, radicalism, and poor attitude. Similarly, formerly abused children improved their self-image, happiness, and expectations of conventional parenting; that is, they learned that it is wrong to abuse children and that child abuse is not a tolerable aspect of childhood. As a whole, the families were more cohesive, expressive, organized, harmonious, and moral after participating in NPP. Undoubtedly, healthier families reduce the likelihood that early home environments will be characterized as abusive breeding grounds for multiple problem behaviors.[43]

Functional Family Therapy

Functional Family Therapy (FFT) is an outcome prevention and intervention program for children who demonstrate a broad range of antisocial behaviors, especially conduct disorder, oppositional-defiant disorder, and substance abuse. The program targets children between the ages of 11 and 18, with anywhere from 8 to 26 hours of program content being delivered. On average, FFT is administered during 12 home visits over a 3-month period, and the program costs between $1,350 and $3,750 per child. A range of professionals administer the FFT program to children and their families during home visits. The goal is to engage, motivate, and assess families and to change antisocial behavior to prosocial behavior.

In clinical trials, FFT has been shown to reduce problem behaviors, reduce social service needs, prevent future incidence of disorders, prevent younger children in the family from following antisocial pathways, divert delinquents from the criminal justice system, and enhance the effectiveness of other treatment programs.[44]

Olweus Bullying Prevention Program

The Olweus Bullying Prevention Program is a universal intervention for the reduction and prevention of bully and victim problems. The program targets students in elementary, middle, and junior high schools, with additional interventions being available for students who have a prior history of bullying and/or bullying victimization. Core components of the program are implemented at the school, class, and individual levels and comprise assistance from counselors, teachers, and mental health professionals.[45]

The Olweus Bullying Prevention Program has been found to significantly reduce bullying and victimization among boys and girls; to reduce related delinquency problems, such as vandalism, fighting, theft, and truancy; and to improve the social climate of the school. Dan Olweus and Susan Limber have shown that the intervention has proven effective in Norway and in various applications in the United States, including South Carolina, Pennsylvania, Washington, and California. Moreover, the program has been instrumental in making bullying prevention a nearly universal feature of schools in the United States and abroad. This is a far cry from when bullying was tolerated as a seemingly "normal" part of the school experience.[46]

I Can Problem Solve

I Can Problem Solve (ICPS) is a school-based prevention program developed to enhance interpersonal cognitive problem-solving skills and, consequently, to increase the probability of preventing later serious problem behaviors. The program is geared toward both younger, preschool-age children and children in elementary school. Children are taught skills for solving interpersonal problems, learn to consider the consequences of their solutions, and are encouraged to recognize the thoughts, feelings, and motives that produce problem situations. In other words, children are taught *to* think, rather than *what* to think. The goal is to change thinking styles to strengthen children's social adjustment and prosocial behavior, as well as to decrease impulsivity and inhibition. During the 3-month program, children learn a problem-solving vocabulary, discover how to identify their own and others' feelings, and come to understand that people can feel differently about the same thing. Toward the end of the program, they are given hypothetical problem situations and are asked to think about people's feelings, the consequences of their actions, and alternative ways to solve problems.[47]

Evaluation studies of ICPS report that, compared to a control group of children, children who participated in the program exhibited less impulsive and inhibited classroom behavior, better problem-solving skills, improved classroom behavior, more positive and prosocial behaviors, and healthier peer relationships.[48]

Guiding Good Choices

Guiding Good Choices (GGC) is a curriculum program designed to teach parents of children ages 9 to 14 a variety of skills to help them prevent drug and alcohol abuse and delinquency in those children; the focus is on increasing positive interactions between parents and children, reducing family conflict, and promoting more consistent family management. Parents participate in a series of five 2-hour sessions that focus on risk factors associated with adolescent substance abuse, the positive effects of social bonding, development of family guidelines and strategies for conveying expectations for children's behavior, consequences for bad behavior, techniques to resist peer influences, and ways for parents and children to express and control anger.[49]

It has been reported that GGC effectively promotes proactive parent-to-child communication and reduces negative or antagonistic behaviors by mothers toward their children. In addition, children of participating parents have reported using less alcohol when compared to a control group of students.[50]

One issue that prevention programs attempt to preclude or reduce is weapons carrying among juveniles. For legal discussion of the gun rights of school children, see **Box 14.6** the "From the Bench" feature.

Neighborhood and Community Programs

Older children, those in middle school or high school, are also at risk of becoming delinquent. Many prevention programs located within neighborhoods or the larger community are designed to help adolescents avoid becoming involved in drug and alcohol use, both highly correlated with other delinquent behavior.

Project STAR/Midwestern Prevention Project

Project STAR (formerly known as the Midwestern Prevention Project) is a comprehensive, multifaceted program geared toward prevention of drug abuse in adolescents. It involves an extended period of programming that is initiated in the schools and extends

BOX 14.6

From the Bench

United States v. Lopez

On March 10, 1992, a 12th-grade student arrived at Edison High School in San Antonio, Texas, carrying a concealed .38 caliber handgun and five bullets. Acting on a tip, school authorities confronted the student, who admitted to carrying the weapon. The student was arrested and charged by federal agents with violating the *Gun Free School Zones Act of 1990*. The student's attorney moved to dismiss the federal indictment on the grounds that it was unconstitutional for Congress to legislate control over public schools. However, the district court concluded that Congress was permitted to regulate activities of public schools that affect interstate commerce. The student was tried and found guilty;

the juvenile was subsequently sentenced to 6 months incarceration.

On appeal to the U.S. Supreme Court, the government argued that possessing a firearm in a local school zone affects interstate commerce for the following reasons: The costs of violent crime are substantial; insurance costs are spread throughout the population; and violent crime reduces the willingness of people to travel to areas within the country that are perceived to be unsafe. However, the Court disagreed, holding that "the possession of a gun in a local school zone is in no sense an economic activity that might, through repetition elsewhere, substantially affect any sort of interstate commerce."

United States v. Lopez, 514 U.S. 549 (1995).

---

to family and community contexts. The program targets sixth and seventh graders, with its goal being to prevent the onset of alcohol, tobacco, and marijuana use that could serve as a gateway to delinquency and other antisocial behaviors. The program recognizes the great social or peer pressures that exist to experiment with these substances. To counter these forces, it uses active social learning techniques—including modeling, role playing, use of student peer leaders, and homework assignments involving family members—to create a social network that works against the use of these harmful substances.

Compared to children who did not participate, the program yielded 40% reductions in smoking and marijuana use that were maintained through grade 12. The program has also reduced the use of all substances in follow-up studies into early adulthood (up to age 23) and has enhanced parent–child communication and relationships. Unfortunately, the program is expensive, requiring an investment of $175,000 over a 3-year period to train teachers, parents, community leaders, and for project-related materials.

The school-based element of the program is supported by four other elements. The media component is designed to disseminate the antidrug message to the community. In the parent component, parents are encouraged to reinforce the school program by working with their children on the homework assignments in addition to being given training opportunities for developing effective communication and substance use resistance skills. Two other components—community organization and health policy change—recruit volunteers to oversee the implementation and maintenance of the program, as well as provide a mechanism for the development

and implementation of local health policies that affect drug, alcohol, and tobacco laws.

Follow-up evaluations have reported that students who participated in this program were less likely to smoke marijuana, drink alcohol, and abuse illegal drugs than students who did not participate. Moreover, this decrease in alcohol, marijuana, and tobacco use was maintained for more than 3 years after the students went through the program.[51]

Big Brothers/Big Sisters of America

For nearly 100 years, Big Brothers/Big Sisters of America has provided mentoring, one-on-one relationships for youths between the ages of 6 and 18 from single-parent homes. The service is provided by volunteers who complete rigorous training and follow published, required procedures for youth mentoring. In a recent 18-month follow-up evaluation, children who participated in Big Brothers/Big Sisters were 46% less likely than a group of children who did not participate to begin using drugs, 27% less likely to use alcohol, and 30% less likely to hit someone; they also had better academic behavior, attitudes, school performance, and relationships with parents and peers.[52]

Motivated by the successes of mentoring programs such as Big Brothers/Big Sisters of America, the National Faith-Based Initiative for High-Risk Youth (a public/private venture of the Office of Juvenile Justice and Delinquency Prevention) uses one-on-one and group mentoring approaches to address the delinquency and mental health problems (especially depression) of high-risk juvenile offenders. Although the program has not been formally evaluated, preliminary outcomes from programs in Baton Rouge, Brooklyn, Denver, Philadelphia, and Seattle appear promising.[53] For a closer look at mentoring programs, see **Box 14.7**, the "Delinquency Prevention" feature.

Striving Together to Achieve Rewarding Tomorrows

The aim of this program is to reduce delinquency by minimizing adolescent exposure to drugs and criminal activity by alleviating individual, neighborhood, and community risk factors through effective case management services, after-school and summer activities, and increased police involvement. The children targeted by this program are ages 11 to 13 and live in severely distressed neighborhoods. Key elements of the program include increased police presence and involvement in the community and working with youth, small social service caseloads of 13 to 18 families, enhanced communication between case managers and juvenile probation departments, and family services ranging from parent programs and counseling services to organized activities and family advocacy. In addition, after-school and summer activities provide children with recreational and entertainment opportunities, an environment supportive of personal social development, and tutoring and homework assistance.

In an evaluation of this program, after 1 year, children involved in the program were less likely to report past-month, past-year, and lifetime use of drugs compared to matched control group subjects. In addition, program youths were less likely to report involvement in drug sales and engaged in lower levels of violent crimes during the past year.[54]

Do Delinquency Prevention Programs Work?

Although each of the delinquency prevention approaches described previously in this chapter has been effective in at least some settings (e.g., preschool centers, school, families, neighborhoods), for different-aged children (e.g., infants, very young, adolescent, and young adults), and for various levels of risk (e.g., youths not yet demonstrating problem behaviors, those identified as at risk, and youths already involved at some level with the juvenile justice system), not all delinquency prevention programs throughout the United States can claim similar success.

BOX 14.7

Delinquency Prevention

Mentoring Works!

A central theme of this text is the problematic ways that children are often treated by adults, and how this oppression and general negativity contributes to problem behaviors and other forms of maladaptive conduct. About 34% of youth and 37% of at-risk youth report that they never had a prosocial adult mentor of any kind during their childhood. This equates to about 16 million youth overall and 9 million at-risk youth without a mentor. Mentoring is a great way to overcome this negative trend because it involves pairing a caring, interested adult with an at-risk child to engage in prosocial activities mostly geared toward educational success. More than 3 million children participate in more than 5000 mentoring programs in the United States. Mentoring is advantageous in a variety of ways:

- Mentoring is a relationship between mentor and mentored child that is rooted in mutuality, trust, empathy, and care.
- Mentoring enhances the social-emotional development of children and adolescents.
- Mentoring enhances the cognitive development and school habits of children and adolescents.
- Mentoring bolsters the identity development of children in a positive, conventional, as opposed to antisocial, direction.
- Mentoring contributes to better school performance, higher grades, greater well-being, and fewer problem behaviors.

David DuBois and his colleagues have extensively studied mentoring programs and recently conducted a meta-analysis of 73 evaluations of mentoring programs. They found that mentoring improved outcomes in terms of behavior, social, emotional, and academic domains and that mentored children fare better than their peers who are not mentored. This research not only is promising because of its preventive value, but also serves as a public service call to get involved in mentoring programs. Patrick Tolan and his colleagues conducted a meta-analysis of 163 studies published between 1970 and 2011 and found that mentoring had significant positive effects in terms of improving academic achievement and reducing delinquency.

Mary Bruce and John Bridgeland, *The Mentoring Effect: Young People's Perspectives on the Outcomes and Availability of Mentoring* (Washington, DC: Civic Enterprises with Hart Research Associates, 2014); Patrick Tolan, David Henry, Michael Schoeny, Peter Lovegrove, and Emily Nichols, "Mentoring Programs to Affect Delinquency and Associated Outcomes of Youth at Risk: A Comprehensive Meta-Analytic Review," *Journal of Experimental Criminology* 10:179–206 (2014); David DuBois, Nelson Portillo, Jean Rhodes, Naida Silverthorn, and Jeffrey Valentine, "How Effective Are Mentoring Programs for Youth? A Systematic Assessment of the Evidence," *Psychological Science in the Public Interest* 12:57–91 (2011).

College students can have a direct impact on reducing delinquency by volunteering to be a Big Brother or Big Sister.

© Jupiterimages/Creatas/Getty.

School-based and after-school prevention programs have been widely implemented by well-intended organizations and groups. Although many of these programs are based on published "model" or "promising" programs, many others are not; instead, they are developed and implemented locally, often without a strong theoretical foundation. What may be said about these programs?

David Wilson and his colleagues examined the results from 165 school-based prevention program studies. They noted that although school-based programs appeared to be modestly effective in reducing nonattendance, the likelihood of dropping out of school, and alcohol and drug use, the effects were small, although greatest for those youth most at risk. Wilson and his colleagues also found that the effect sizes ranged widely across program approaches. For example, programs using cognitive-behavioral and behavioral instructional methods showed positive results, whereas programs using noncognitive-behavioral counseling, social work, and other therapeutic approaches resulted in consistent negative outcomes.[55] Based on an analysis of 221 studies of school-based programs, Sandra Wilson and her colleagues reported that programs using behavioral approaches and

counseling, when implemented in an intense, one-on-one format and administered by well-trained teachers, showed the greatest impact.[56] Finally, in a recent analysis of 35 after-school programs, Denise Gottfredson and her associates reported that smaller programs that had greater structure, used published curricula, hired more college graduates, and had a greater percentage of male staff produced the most significant reductions in substance use, delinquency, and victimization.[57]

In spite of their founders' best intentions, many delinquency prevention programs simply do not work. Indeed, some have even produced negative effects for youths who have participated in them. In 2001, the U.S. Surgeon General released a report on the effectiveness of youth violence prevention programs.[58] This report noted that nearly half of the most thoroughly evaluated strategies for preventing violence were ineffective, whereas a few were found to harm participants. According to the Surgeon General's report, program effectiveness depends as much on the *quality* of implementation as on the *type* of intervention. Many programs are ineffective not because their strategy is misguided, but rather because the quality of implementation is poor.

Among the ineffective prevention programs are some, such as Drug Abuse Resistance Education (D.A.R.E.) and Scared Straight, which are national in scope and generally well known to students and parents. Many of these programs are variations on approaches used in schools, neighborhoods, and juvenile correctional facilities around the country.

A number of school-based prevention programs have been evaluated and found to be ineffective in reducing delinquency or substance abuse, or in improving academic achievement, self-concept, or interpersonal relations. Peer counseling, peer mediation, and peer leader programs have all been found to have no positive effect. At least one school-based program, involving nonpromotion of youths to succeeding grades, appears to have negative effects on student achievement, attendance, behavior, and attitudes toward school. The most widely implemented school-based program is D.A.R.E. Unfortunately, evaluations of D.A.R.E. consistently have shown no significant differences in substance use by students exposed to the curriculum and those not exposed to it.

Some very popular community-based programs aimed at high-risk youths have been demonstrated to be ineffective as well. For example, gun buyback programs have no positive effect on deterring gun violence in the community, although some guns are taken off the street. However, most of the guns turned in are not functional or are turned in by the persons least likely to ever use them in criminal activity. Midnight basketball is aimed at redirecting high-risk youth toward conventional activities involving recreational, enrichment, and leisure activities.

Unfortunately, such programs have not had any positive effect on reducing youth violence, perhaps because they increase the cohesiveness of delinquent peer groups. Finally, **Scared Straight**, a program in which at-risk youth are provided with brief encounters with inmates who describe the brutality of prison life, is intended to shock, scare, and deter these youths from committing crimes. Research shows that, at best, Scared Straight programs are ineffective; at worst, they produce *higher* rates of subsequent criminal activity for youths exposed to the program than for youths not involved in the intervention.[59]

Delinquency prevention programs provided by the juvenile justice system are tertiary in nature; that is, a child has not been prevented from engaging in delinquency, but rather is now engaged in the system. In such cases, program strategies aim to prevent additional or more serious delinquencies in the future. Unfortunately, boot camps, which are modeled after military basic training and focus on physical discipline, have been shown to produce no positive significant effects; in fact, some evaluations have shown that they produce significant harmful effects, with significant increase in recidivism.[60] Juvenile offenders placed in residential correctional facilities are likely to participate in either **milieu treatment**, which is characterized by resident involvement in decision making and day-to-day interaction for psychotherapeutic discussion, or a **behavioral token economy** program, in which youths are rewarded for conforming to rules, exhibiting prosocial behavior, and not exhibiting antisocial or violent behavior.

Although both of these approaches have shown some positive effects while the youth is incarcerated and participating in the program, any positive effects disappear after youths leave the program.[61]

Many of the counseling, therapy, and social work approaches to treating delinquent youth have also proved ineffective. Individual counseling may be one of the least effective approaches for delinquent youths, although research finds that its lack of effectiveness is tied to characteristics of the targeted population and program, as well as characteristics of individual counselors. **Social casework**, which combines individual psychotherapy or counseling with close supervision of youths and a coordination of social services, has failed to demonstrate any positive effects on recidivism.[62]

In recent years, programs such as D.A.R.E. and Scared Straight have fallen out of favor in the public eye and are openly maligned by the criminological community. However, it should be noted that even culturally popular types of tertiary prevention and other delinquency interventions have been shown to be questionably effective. Several examples are revealing. Sema Taheri and Brandon Welsh conducted a meta-analysis of after-school programs for delinquency prevention and found a trivial and nonsignificant effect on delinquency reduction. That is, children who attend after-school programs are no more or less likely to engage in delinquency than youth who do not participate in such programs. Kristen Kremer and her colleagues' meta-analysis of studies of after-school programs that target school attendance and externalizing behaviors similarly found very small, nonsignificant effect sizes. Even the relationship of sports participation to juvenile delinquency has been challenged. Anouk Spruit and his collaborators examined 51 studies of sports participation as a protective factor against delinquency among 132,366 adolescents and found there was no relationship. Although teachers, administrators, and parents believe that sports involvement keeps children out of trouble or shields them from delinquency, the empirical reality is that the programs have zero effect.[63]

Clearly, much that is done to address juvenile delinquency (both effort and expense) is reactive, after the fact, and ineffective. A significant reduction in delinquency in the United States will likely require a more proactive approach, with a shift in emphasis from the juvenile justice system to early and even very early intervention strategies. Prevention programs designed to provide interventions at the prenatal stage, infancy, and preschool stage, as well as in school or at home when children are in the early elementary grades, are not likely to be effectively run by federal- or state-level administrators.

Rather, early intervention is likely to be most effective when programs are managed by local government, community groups, local schools, and individual citizens.[64] Equally important, prevention strategies must be built on programs that have already been demonstrated to be effective at reducing those risk factors associated with later delinquency. As shown in **Box 14.8** in the "A Window on Delinquency" feature, prevention programs not only reduce delinquency, but also they are cost-effective.

KEY TERMS

Scared Straight
A program in which at-risk children are provided with brief encounters with inmates who describe the brutality of prison life.

milieu treatment
A treatment approach in which residents are involved in decision making and day-to-day interactions for psychotherapeutic discussion.

behavioral token economy
A treatment program in which youths are rewarded for conforming to rules, exhibiting prosocial behavior, and not exhibiting antisocial or violent behavior.

social casework
A treatment approach that combines individual psychotherapy or counseling with close supervision of youths and with a coordination of social services.

BOX 14.8

A Window on Delinquency

Does Prevention Save Money? "Yes"

Although the United States is enjoying historically low levels of delinquency and youth violence, far too many youth continue to ruin their lives with antisocial behavior. Delinquency and violence impose a heavy toll. For instance, each year, more youth ages 10 to 24 die from homicide than cancer, heart disease, birth defects, influenza, pneumonia, respiratory diseases, stroke, and diabetes combined!

Evidence-based prevention programs provide many benefits to the youths who are served, their families and social networks, and society at large. According to the Washington State Institute for Public Policy, for every $1 of cost invested, the following fiscal benefits are provided by these programs:

• Communities That Care	$3.69
• Functional Family Therapy	$11.50
• Good Behavior Game	$84.63
• Guiding Good Choices	$8.93
• Life Skills Training	$28.19
• Multidimensional Treatment Foster Care	$4.86
• Multisystemic Therapy	$4.54
• Nurse–Family Partnership	$2.73
• Parent–Child Interaction Therapy	$3.28
• Triple P Positive Parenting Program	$5.46

None of these prevention programs lose money. In addition, the benefits are conservatively estimated, whereas the costs of programs are estimated in full. In fact, all turn a considerable profit that is realized in the form of reduced crime and delinquency, fewer victimizations, less juvenile and criminal justice system expenditures, and greater societal well-being.

It is also important to observe that not everything can be monetized. For example, the Nurse–Family Partnership has the lowest benefit to cost ratio cited here, but it is one of the most important prevention programs substantively. David Olds and his colleagues found that two decades after enrolling in the program, women who had two nurse visits were significantly less likely to die than women in the control group. Moreover, children whose mothers received home visits during pregnancy and through age 2 years were less likely to have died from preventable causes compared to their counterparts in the control group. Thus prevention not only saves money, it saves lives.

Corinne David-Ferdon and Thomas Simon, *Preventing Youth Violence: Opportunities for Action* (Atlanta, GA: National Center for Injury Prevention and Control, Division of Violence Prevention, Centers for Disease Control and Prevention, 2014); Washington State Institute for Public Policy, *Cost-Benefits of Prevention Programs* (Olympia, WA: Washington State Institute for Public Policy, 2014); Brandon Welsh, David Farrington, and Raffan Gowar, "Benefit-Cost Analysis of Crime Prevention Programs," *Crime & Justice* 44:447–557 (2015); David Olds, Harriet Kitzman, Michael Knudtson, Elizabeth Anson, Joyce Smith, and Robert Cole, "Effect of Home Visiting by Nurses on Maternal and Child Mortality: Results of a 2-Decade Follow-Up of a Randomized Clinical Trial," *JAMA Pediatrics* 168:800–806 (2014).

WRAP UP

THINKING ABOUT JUVENILE DELINQUENCY: CONCLUSIONS

How should the United States allocate limited funding and resources to best respond to the problem of juvenile delinquency? Should it attempt to control and manage the amount and seriousness of juvenile delinquency as best it can, or should it take more aggressive steps to prevent it from occurring in the first place? Controlling and managing delinquency is what the juvenile justice system does: It keeps delinquency and the costs associated with juvenile courts and corrections at a level with which the larger society feels marginally comfortable. But the juvenile justice system does not prevent young children from becoming delinquent. Instead, it focuses on dealing with children who already are delinquent and is sometimes able to reduce the probabilities that these youths will commit new crimes.

Primary prevention programs have not been as popular as a reliance on secondary and tertiary approaches, in part because the effects of primary-oriented strategies are typically not seen for many years. Prenatal programs can immediately affect the well-being of the fetus and later the infant, and nurse–family programs can ensure that very young children receive proper nutrition and achieve closer bonding with their parents. Nevertheless, these programs' effects on delinquency will not be seen until the child reaches late elementary or middle school or even later. The same is true for preschool programs, such as Head Start, and school- and family-based programs such as the Incredible Years. These programs touch the lives of children typically between the ages of 3 and 8, yet their effects in reducing the risk of delinquency and adult crime will not be seen for a decade or more.

Secondary and tertiary programs, by comparison, demonstrate immediate or at least short-term effects. Juveniles engaged in delinquency are brought into the juvenile justice system and subsequently placed on probation or in a correctional institution. The success of this approach is often measured in terms of successful completion of probation or a reduction in recidivism within the first few years of release from an institution. Both are short-term effects, however, and the general conclusions of research evaluating the ability of the juvenile justice system to curtail delinquency are not very encouraging.

In the final analysis, reliance on the juvenile justice system will at best help to keep juvenile crime from growing into a greater problem. To accomplish significant reductions in juvenile delinquency, increasing attention and resources focused on primary prevention may be required.

CHAPTER SPOTLIGHT

- In the 19th century, the Child Savers viewed street children as "bad seeds" who were in need of special attention by well-intended religious and social service agencies.
- In the early 20th century, the new juvenile courts and juvenile justice system functioned largely as coercive treatment agencies; that is, the court attempted to accomplish what parents appeared unable to do—control their children.
- Throughout much of the 20th century, the juvenile justice system functioned to intervene in the lives of children already identified as delinquent and place them in programs or institutions designed to prevent further, more serious delinquencies.
- In the 1980s, a public health model emerged as a significant alternative to the juvenile justice system; it focused on primary prevention approaches aimed at preventing delinquency before it occurs.
- Using a public health model, criminologists identified a number of risk factors that increase the likelihood of a child exhibiting problem behaviors and eventually moving into delinquency.

Risk factors associated with a child's health and wellness, as well as maternal and family circumstances from the prenatal period through the youth's early childhood, are early predictors of delinquency and adult criminality.

- In childhood and adolescence, the quality of schools, association with peers, exposure to gangs, and neighborhood conditions are among the most important risk factors for delinquency.
- Many primary prevention programs have been shown to significantly reduce childhood risk factors. Among the more successful are nurse–family partnerships, prenatal and early infancy wellness programs, preschool programs, school- and family-based programs, and programs developed to provide community-level interventions.
- Not all prevention programs have proved equally effective at delinquency prevention. Many programs and approaches—such as D.A.R.E., peer counseling in school, midnight basketball, boot camps, and social casework—have been largely ineffective; in some cases, they have actually been counterproductive by increasing recidivism.

CRITICAL THINKING

1. Were Durkheim and Erikson correct that the best that can be hoped to accomplish is to keep delinquency under control—that it can never be fully eliminated? Explain your answer.
2. If the health and wellness of children at the prenatal stage are consequences of actions of the mother (and father), which may sometimes put the child at increased risk for problem behaviors, should the parent(s) be held responsible for any subsequent delinquencies by the child?
3. Does targeting at-risk children for special intervention in hopes of reducing later delinquency run the risk of negatively labeling these children and their families, thereby possibly producing the very problems the programs are designed to prevent?
4. Which of the early childhood delinquency prevention programs do you believe can be most effective for the greatest number of children?
5. Why does the United States continue to fund and administer programs involving children when research has demonstrated they have no positive effect and possibly a negative impact on delinquency?

Glossary

abstainers

Youth who do not commit delinquency.

achieved status

A status that is earned.

adjudication

The stage in the juvenile justice system that parallels prosecution and trial in adult criminal courts.

adjudication hearing

A hearing to determine whether a juvenile committed the offense of which he or she is accused.

adolescence-limited offenders

A term applied to the overwhelming majority of children who commit a few minor acts of delinquency on an inconsistent basis during their teenage years.

aftercare

The release and subsequent community supervision of an individual from a correctional facility, intended to ensure a more positive and effective transition back into the community.

age–crime curve

The empirical trend that crime rates increase during preadolescence, peak in late adolescence, and steadily decline thereafter.

aging-out phenomenon

The gradual decline of participation in crime after the teenage years.

Allen v. United States

The U.S. Supreme Court ruling stating that a child younger than age 7 cannot be guilty of a felony or punished for a capital offense because he or she is presumed incapable of forming criminal intent.

annual prevalence

The use of a drug at least once during the prior year.

anomie

Normlessness leading to social disorganization.

antisocial personality

The set of characteristics that describe a person's deviant beliefs, deviant ways of thinking, deviant motivations, and antisocial behaviors.

ascribed status

A status that is received at birth; it partly determines what opportunities are available and, thus, what can be achieved.

assortative mating

The concept that people tend to choose mates who are similar to themselves.

atavistic beings

The idea that criminals are a throwback to a more primitive stage of development.

attachment theory

Theory stating that the enduring affective bond between child and caregiver (usually parents) is importantly related to child development because it provides a variety of benefits that serve as buffers or protective factors against the development of antisocial behavior.

attention-deficit/hyperactivity disorder (ADHD)

The most common neurobehavioral childhood disorder, which is characterized by the following symptoms: inattention and hyperactivity that cause difficulty in school, poor relationships with family and peers, and low self-esteem.

authoritarian parents

Parents who place a high value on obedience and conformity, tending to favor more punitive, absolute, and forceful disciplinary measures.

authoritative parents

Parents who are warm but firm; they set standards of behavior for their child and highly value the development of autonomy and self-direction.

baby boomers

People born between 1946 and 1964.

bail

Money or a cash bond deposited with the court or bail bondsman allowing the person to be released on the assurance he or she will appear in court at the proper time.

Baker v. Owen

U.S. Supreme Court decision stating that teachers can administer reasonable corporal punishment for disciplinary purposes.

behavioral theory

Theory suggesting that behavior reflects our interactions with others throughout our lifetime.

behavioral token economy

A treatment program in which youths are rewarded for conforming to rules, exhibiting prosocial behavior, and not exhibiting antisocial or violent behavior.

Bethel School District No. 403 v. Fraser

U.S. Supreme Court decision stating that schools may prohibit vulgar and offensive language.

Board of Education of Independent School District No. 92 of Pottawatomie County et al. v. Earls et al.

U.S. Supreme Court decision that expanded the *Acton* ruling; it stated that schools may require students to submit to a urinalysis for illegal drugs prior to participating in all competitive extracurricular activities.

Board of Education of Pottawatomie County v. Earls et al.

Supreme Court ruling that mandatory drug testing of students involved in any extracurricular activity is constitutional.

bond

The glue that connects a child to society.

bootstrapping

A practice in which a chronic status offender who commits a new status offense while on probation is charged with the criminal offense of violating a formal court order that specified the conditions of that child's probation.

Brady Bill

Federal legislation that mandated a 5-day waiting period for the purchase of handguns.

Breed v. Jones

Case in which the U.S. Supreme Court ruled that a criminal prosecution of a child following a juvenile court hearing constitutes double jeopardy.

bullying

Negative acts by students carried out against other students repeatedly over time.

Child Savers

Reformers in the 19th century who believed children were basically good and blamed delinquency on a bad environment.

chivalry hypothesis

The notion that the lower crime rates for females reflect men's deference and protective attitude toward women, whereby female offenses are generally overlooked or excused by males.

choice theories

Theories that claim delinquency is an outcome of rational thought.

chronic offenders

Youths who continue to engage in law-breaking behavior as adults. They are responsible for the most serious forms of delinquency and violent crime.

chronic status offender

Children who continue to commit status offenses despite repeated interventions by the family, school, social service, and law enforcement agencies.

classical school

A school of thought that blames delinquency on the choices people make.

co-offenders

Friends or acquaintances who participate in delinquency with another peer.

Code of Hammurabi

One of the oldest known sets of written laws.

coercive exchange

A test of wills, in which a child uses misbehavior to extort a desired outcome from his or her parents.

collective efficacy

Mutual trust among neighbors, combined with willingness to intervene on behalf of the common good—specifically, to supervise children and maintain public order.

communal school organization

A partnership of teachers who have shared values and expectations of student learning and appropriate student behavior.

comorbidity

The overlapping of behavioral problems that mutually reinforce one another but ultimately stem from some other cause.

compulsory school attendance law

A legislative act that requires students to attend school between specific ages (e.g., 6–16 years old).

concentrated disadvantage

Economically impoverished, racially segregated neighborhoods with high-crime rates.

conduct disorder

A repetitive and persistent pattern of behavior in which the basic rights of others or major age-appropriate societal norms or rules are violated.

conduct norms

Rules that reflect the values, expectations, and actual behaviors of groups in everyday life. They are not necessarily the norms found in the criminal law.

conflict theory

Theory arguing that society is held together by force, coercion, and intimidation and that the law represents the interests of those in power.

continuity of crime

The idea that chronic offenders are unlikely to age-out of crime and more likely to continue their law-violating behavior into their adult lives.

corporal punishment

The infliction of physical pain as a penalty for violating a school rule.

Crime Index

A statistical indicator consisting of eight offenses that was used to gauge the amount of crime reported to the police. The Index was discontinued in 2004.

crime norms

Criminal laws that prohibit specific conduct and provide punishments for violations.

crimes of interest

The crimes that are the focus of the National Crime Victimization Survey.

cultural transmission

The process through which criminal values are transmitted from one generation to the next.

cumulative disadvantage

The process by which successive misbehavior leads to a serious detriment for an individual's life chances.

dark figure of crime

The gap between the actual amount of crime committed and the amount of crime reported to the police.

decriminalization

Relaxing of the enforcement of certain laws—for example, drug laws.

delinquency control

An approach that emphasizes dealing with the problem of juvenile delinquency after the fact.

delinquent career

The pattern of delinquent behavior that an individual exhibits over the course of his or her life.

delinquent propensity

The likelihood of committing delinquency and other antisocial acts; it is a trait that is largely set in early childhood.

demand waiver

Process by which a juvenile may request to have his or her case transferred to criminal court.

detention

The temporary custody and care of juveniles pending adjudication, disposition, or implementation of disposition.

determinate sentence

A prison sentence of a fixed amount of time, such as 5 years.

developmental theories

Theories that focus on an individual's entire life course, rather than one discrete point in time.

Developmental Victimization Survey (DVS)

A telephone interview survey of a nationally representative sample of 2030 children ages 2 to 17 years that examines 34 types of victimization.

differential coercion theory

Theory stating that children who are exposed to coercive environments are more likely to develop social–psychological deficits that increase the possibility of their committing crimes.

differential oppression theory

Theory stating that delinquency is the culmination of a process that begins at conception and evolves through adolescence; the more a child is oppressed, the greater the likelihood he or she will become delinquent.

differential social organization

Neighborhoods are differentially organized based on a combination of prosocial and antisocial characteristics.

direct aggression

Aggression that is typically physical and overt; it includes behaviors such as hitting, kicking, punching, and biting.

disintegrative shaming

A form of negative labeling by the juvenile justice system that stigmatizes and excludes targeted youths, tossing them into a class of outcasts.

disposition hearing

A hearing to determine the most appropriate placement of a juvenile adjudicated to be delinquent.

diversion

The early suspension or termination of the official processing of a juvenile

in favor of an informal or unofficial alternative.

dizygotic twins (DZ)

Fraternal twins who develop from two eggs fertilized at the same time.

double jeopardy

Rule that forbids criminal prosecution of a juvenile after he or she has been tried in juvenile court for the same offense.

doubly oppressed

Description of adolescent girls as being oppressed both as children and as females.

Drug Abuse Resistance Education (D.A.R.E.)

A program aimed at children in kindergarten through 12th grade, designed to equip students with appropriate skills to resist substance abuse and gangs.

dualistic fallacy

The mistaken notion that delinquents and nondelinquents are two fundamentally different types of people.

dynamic cascade model of violence

A conceptual model that shows how antisocial traits and processes interact in the development of youth violence and victimization.

ecological fallacy

The mistake of assuming relationships found at the neighborhood level mean those factors are related at the individual level.

ecological–transactional model of community violence

Cicchetti and Lynch's theory, which suggests that broad exposure to violence in the community stresses the ability of parents to protect their children from the pernicious effects of violence.

educational neglect

Acts of omission and commission that include permitting chronic truancy, failure to enroll a child in school, and inattention to the child's specific education needs.

egocentric bias

A condition in which the primary motivation of thought and behavior is related to satisfying one's self-interest.

electronic monitoring

An active or passive computer-based tracking system in which electronic signals are used to verify that the youth is where he or she is supposed to be.

emotional abuse

Acts of commission that include confinement, verbal or emotional abuse, and other types of abuse, such as withholding sleep, food, or shelter.

emotional neglect

Acts of omission that involve failing to meet the nurturing and affection needs of a child, exposing a child to chronic or severe spouse abuse, allowing or permitting a child to use drugs or alcohol, encouraging the child to engage in maladaptive behaviors, refusing to provide psychological care, and other inattention to the child's developmental needs.

enhancement model

The idea that adolescents who are already involved in delinquency are most apt to join a gang (selection) but, after joining, their delinquency is likely to increase significantly (facilitation).

esprit de corps

A sense of solidarity and awareness of being a distinct group.

etiological

Relating to the cause of a behavior.

evolutionary psychology

A branch of psychology that examines the ways that evolutionary forces shape patterns of human cognition and behavior.

exclusionary rule

Rule stating that illegally obtained evidence may not be admissible in a criminal prosecution or in a juvenile court adjudication hearing.

facilitation model

A "kind of group" explanation that suggests the normative structure of a gang, along with group processes and dynamics, increase delinquency among youth.

Family Dependency Treatment Courts

Family courts that specifically adjudicate child welfare cases involving child abuse and neglect and parental substance abuse.

Five Factor Model of Personality

The major model of personality, in which the determinants of personality include neuroticism, extraversion, openness to experiences, agreeableness, and conscientiousness.

focal concerns

The primary values that monopolize lower-class consciousness.

free will

The idea that people can and do choose one course of action over another.

Gang Reduction Program

An initiative within the federal Office of Juvenile Justice and Delinquency Prevention that includes a framework for coordinating a wide range of activities that have demonstrated effectiveness in reducing gang activity and delinquency.

Garcia v. Miera

U.S. Supreme Court decision stating that school authorities who use excessive or extreme punishment against a child may be sued for damages suffered by the student and must pay attorney fees if they lose the lawsuit.

gender-role identities

Individual identities based on sexual stereotypes.

gendered juvenile justice system

The existence of double standards regarding how female delinquents and male delinquents are treated and supervised within the justice system.

genotype

A person's genetic composition.

Goss v. Lopez

U.S. Supreme Court decision stating that students who are to be suspended for 10 or fewer days must receive a hearing.

Graham v. Florida

Case in which U.S. Supreme Court ruled that life without parole for nonhomicide convictions is unconstitutional for juveniles.

Hall v. Tawney

U.S. Supreme Court decision stating that parents do not have a constitutional right to exempt their children from corporal punishment in public schools.

harm reduction

Use of a public health model to reduce the risks and negative consequences of drug use.

Hazelwood School District v. Kuhlmeier

U.S. Supreme Court decision stating that school administrators can regulate the content of student publications in public schools for educational purposes.

hierarchy rule

The guideline for reporting data in the *Uniform Crime Reports*, in which police record only the most serious crime incident.

home confinement

The intensive supervision and monitoring of an offending youth within his or her home environment.

Homeboy Industries

A Los Angeles–based program that educates, trains, and finds jobs for at-risk youths and gang members.

homophily

"Love of the same"; the process by which people select to associate with those persons who are most similar to them.

Honig v. Doe

U.S. Supreme Court decision stating that before school officials may expel a disabled student, the school must first determine whether the offending behavior was caused by the student's disability.

In re Gault

Case in which the U.S. Supreme Court ruled that juveniles could not be denied basic due process rights in juvenile hearings.

In re Winship

Case in which the U.S. Supreme Court ruled that, in delinquency cases, juveniles should be convicted only if proof of their guilt beyond a reasonable doubt exists.

incidence

The number of delinquent acts committed.

indeterminate sentence

A prison sentence of varying time length, such as 5 to 10 years.

indifferent parents

Parents who are unresponsive to their child and may, in extreme cases, be neglectful.

indirect aggression

Aggression that is usually verbal and covert; it includes actions such as gossiping and ostracism.

individual justice

The idea that criminal law must reflect differences among people and their circumstances.

indulgent parents

Parents who are relatively more responsive, accepting, benign, and passive in matters of discipline and place few demands on their child.

Ingraham v. Wright

U.S. Supreme Court decision stating that corporal punishment does not violate the cruel and unusual punishment clause of the Eighth Amendment.

injunction (abatement)

A civil process in which gang members are prohibited from engaging in mundane activities, such as loitering at schools or hanging out on street corners; if they violate these mandates, they face arrest.

intake

The initial screening process in the juvenile court to determine whether a case should be processed further.

integrated structural-Marxist theory

Theory suggesting that serious delinquency is the result of the reproduction of coercive control patterns tied to the relationship between production and class structure in capitalist societies.

intelligence

The ability to learn, exercise judgment, and be imaginative.

intensive aftercare program (IAP)

Equivalent to intensive parole supervision; a monitoring approach used to provide greater supervision of youths after their release from official institutions.

IQ score

A person's intelligence quotient, defined as the ratio of one's mental age multiplied by 100 and divided by one's chronological age.

judicial waiver

Most common waiver procedure for transferring youths to criminal court, in which the judge is the primary decision maker.

justice model

A corrections philosophy that promotes flat or fixed-time sentences, abolishment of parole, and use of prison to punish offenders.

juvenile

A person younger than age 18.

juvenile delinquency

Behavior that violates the criminal code and is committed by a youth who has not reached the specified adult age.

juvenile delinquent

Usually a person younger than age 18 who commits an illegal act and is officially processed through the juvenile or family court.

keepin' it REAL

A program aimed at children in middle school designed to equip students with appropriate decision-making skills to resist substance use.

Kent v. United States

Case in which the U.S. Supreme Court ruled that requiring a formal waiver hearing before transfer of a juvenile to criminal court.

klikas

Age cohorts within Hispanic gangs.

labeling theory

Theory assuming that social control leads to deviance; how behavior is reacted to determines whether it is defined as deviant.

latchkey children

Children who regularly care for themselves without adult supervision after school or on weekends.

legalization

The elimination of many laws currently prohibiting drugs, but not necessarily eliminating all regulation.

liberation hypothesis

The notion that changes brought about by the women's movement triggered a wave of female crime.

life-course persistent offenders

The most serious juvenile delinquents; a small group of children who engage in antisocial behavior of one sort or another at every stage of life.

lifetime prevalence

The use of a drug at least once during the respondent's lifetime.

maltreatment

Severe mistreatment of children, involving several types of abuse and neglect.

management of delinquency

An approach that emphasizes delinquency is a problem to be worked on or altered for a purpose, or come to terms with.

master status

The primary perceived status of an individual; it determines how other people initially react when they see or meet the person for the first time.

maturational reform

The idea that nearly all children who participate in delinquency reduce or stop such activity as they grow older.

McKeiver v. Pennsylvania

Case in which the U.S. Supreme Court ruled that juveniles do not have a constitutional right to a jury trial in juvenile court.

member-based definition

Defining a crime as "gang related" when a gang member or members are either the perpetrators or the victims, regardless of the motive.

middle-class measuring rod

The standards used by teachers to assign status to students.

milieu treatment

A treatment approach in which residents are involved in decision making and day-to-day interactions for psychotherapeutic discussion

Miller v. Alabama

Case in which U.S. Supreme Court ruled that life without parole for any offense is unconstitutional for juveniles.

mitigating circumstances

Factors that may be responsible for an individual's behavior, such as age, insanity, and incompetence.

monozygotic twins (MZ)

Identical twins who develop from one fertilized egg. MZ twins have identical DNA.

Montgomery v. Louisiana

Case in which U.S. Supreme Court ruled that life without parole for any offense is unconstitutional and would apply retroactively.

moral disengagement

An individual's tendency to use mechanisms conducive to a selective disengagement from moral censure.

morality of constraint

In Piaget's theory, the stage of development where children think rigidly about moral concepts and believe that people who break rules must be punished.

morality of cooperation

In Piaget's theory, the stage of development where children employ greater moral flexibility and learn that there are no absolute moral standards about behavior.

Morse v. Frederick

U.S. Supreme Court decision that further clarified juveniles' right to free speech at school and in public areas.

motive-based definition

Defining a crime as "gang related" when it is committed by a gang member or members, and the underlying reason for the crime is to further the interests and activities of the gang.

National Crime Victimization Survey (NCVS)

An annual nationwide survey of criminal victimization conducted by the U.S. Bureau of Justice Statistics.

National Opinion Research Center (NORC)

The organization that conducted the first nationwide victimization survey in the United States.

National Survey of Children's Exposure to Violence (NatSCEV I and NatSCEV II)

A telephone interview survey of a nationally representative sample of 4503 children ages 1 month to 17 years that examines 54 types of victimization and offenses against youth.

National Youth Survey Family Study (NYSFS)

A nationwide self-report survey of approximately 1700 people who were between the ages of 11 and 17 in 1976.

neoclassical school

A school of thought that considers mitigating circumstances when determining culpability for delinquency.

New Jersey v. T.L.O.

U.S. Supreme Court decision stating that school officials can conduct warrantless searches of individuals at school on the basis of reasonable suspicion.

Oedipus complex

A condition in which a child has an unconscious desire for the exclusive love of the parent of the opposite sex, which includes jealousy toward the parent of the same sex and the unconscious wish for that parent's death.

oppositional defiant disorder (ODD)

A clinical disorder characterized by a pattern of negativistic, hostile, and defiant behavior.

parens patriae

A doctrine that defines the state as the ultimate guardian of every child.

patriarchy

A social system that enforces masculine control of the sexuality and labor power of women.

peer group

A group of youths of similar ages and interests.

peer rejection

The rejection of a child perceived to be antisocial by conventional peers.

personal competence

The combination of generally high individual levels of self-esteem, self-efficacy, perceived popularity with peers, school attachment, future educational expectations, and perceived future opportunities in life.

personality

The set of characteristics that describe a person's beliefs, ways of thinking, motivations, and behaviors.

petition

Similar to an indictment; a written statement setting forth the specific charge that a delinquent act has been committed or that a child is dependent or neglected or needs supervision.

physical abuse

Acts that cause physical harm, including death.

physical neglect

Acts of omission that involve refusal to provide health care, delay in providing health care, abandonment, expulsion of a child from a home, inadequate supervision, failure to meet food and clothing needs, and conspicuous failure to protect a child from danger.

police discretion

The authority of police to choose one course of action over another.

positive school

A school of thought that blames delinquency on factors that are in place before a crime is committed.

power-control theory

Theory that emphasizes the consequences of the power relations of husbands and wives in the workplace on the lives of their children.

precocious transitions

An important life event (e.g., pregnancy) that is experienced unusually early in life.

prevalence

The number of juveniles committing delinquent acts.

primary deviation

Deviant behavior that everyone engages in occasionally.

primary prevention

Policies and programs that target the child at the earliest point possible.

proactive aggression

Aggression that includes a premeditated means of obtaining some instrumental goal in addition to harming the victim.

probation

The conditional freedom granted by the court to an alleged or adjudicated offender, who must adhere to certain conditions and is generally supervised by a probation officer.

prodrome

A precursor of early symptoms; a warning sign of another disease or disorder.

Project on Human Development in Chicago Neighborhoods

A study designed to investigate the development of delinquency and violence in children and adolescents; it has yielded primary data for examinations of collective efficacy.

prosecutorial waiver

Process in which the prosecutor determines whether a charge against a juvenile should be filed in criminal or juvenile court.

prosocial behavior

The combination of behaviors such as good grades and involvement in sports, religious, and family activities.

prosocial competence

The combination of generally high individual levels of personal efficacy, educational expectations, grades, commitment to conventionality, and involvement in conventional activity.

protective factors

Situations, settings, events, or characteristics that decrease the likelihood that one will be delinquent.

psychodynamic theory

Theory stating that unconscious mental processes that develop in early childhood control an individual's personality.

psychopathology

The set of behaviors and attitudes that show clinical evidence of a psychological impairment.

psychopathy

A personality disorder that impairs interpersonal, affective, and behavioral functions and is closely linked to serious antisocial behavior.

public health model

A model that emphasizes the prevention of disease before it occurs by reducing the risk of the disease and increasing resiliency against disease within the larger population.

racial profiling

A practice in which police use race as an explicit factor to create "profiles" that then guide their decision making.

radical nonintervention

An approach to juvenile justice whereby police and the courts would, whenever possible, "leave kids alone."

rational choice theory

Theory stating that delinquents are rational people who make calculated choices regarding what they are going to do before they act.

reactive aggression

Aggression that is impulsive, thoughtless or unplanned, driven by anger, and occurring as a reaction to some perceived provocation.

regulating delinquency

A policy that attempts to manage a desired condition, degree, or rate of delinquent behavior.

reintegrative shaming

The expression of community disapproval of delinquency, followed by indications of forgiveness and reacceptance into the community.

relational aggression

Behaviors that employ damage to relationships, or the threat of damage to relationships, as a means to harm another person.

resilience

The ability to withstand environmental stressors and general forms of adversity.

retribution

A punishment philosophy based on society's moral outrage or disapproval of a crime.

reverse waiver

Process in which a juvenile contests a statutory exclusion or prosecutorial transfer.

risk factors

Situations, settings, events, or characteristics that increase the likelihood that one will be delinquent.

Roper v. Simmons

Case in which the U.S. Supreme Court ruled that the death penalty for anyone who was younger than age 18 at the time of his or her crime is unconstitutional.

routine activities theory

Theory arguing that motivated offenders, suitable targets, and absence of capable guardians produce delinquency.

Scared Straight

A program in which at-risk children are provided with brief encounters with inmates who describe the brutality of prison life.

Schall v. Martin

Case in which the U.S. Supreme Court ruled authorizing the preventive detention of juveniles who are identified as "serious risks" to the community if released.

School Resource Officer Program

A control-based policy under which a police officer works within the school to perform a variety of specialized duties.

school-associated violent death

A homicide, suicide, legal intervention (involving a law enforcement officer), or unintentional firearm-related death where the fatal injury occurred on the campus of a functioning elementary or secondary school.

school-to-prison pipeline

The cycle of disproportionate suspension and serious disciplining of African American children that is consistent with disparities seen in the juvenile and criminal justice systems.

Seattle Social Development Project

A leading study in the creation and application of developmental theory.

secondary deviation

Deviant behavior based on the youth's taking on and accepting the deviant role as part of his or her identity.

secondary prevention

Policies and programs aimed at children who are already identified as being at high risk of becoming serious or repeat delinquents.

secular law

A body of legal statutes developed separately from church or canon law.

selection model

A "kind of person" explanation of gang initiation that argues adolescents with a strong propensity for delinquency seek out gangs.

self-report study

A study that yields an unofficial measure of crime, and in which juveniles are asked about their law-breaking behavior.

sexual abuse

Acts of commission of sexual acts against children that are used to provide sexual gratification to the perpetrator.

single-parent families

Families composed of children and one parent who is divorced or widowed or who was never married.

social casework

A treatment approach that combines individual psychotherapy or counseling with close supervision of youths and with a coordination of social services.

social cognition

A discipline that focuses on how people perceive, think, learn, and come to behave in particular ways as a result of the interactions with their social world. The social world includes observations of and participation in real social interactions, such as with parents and peers, and fictional social interactions, such as with the media.

social support

The perceived and actual amount of instrumental and expressive or emotional supports that one receives from primary relationships, social networks, and communities.

socialization

The process through which children learn the norms and values of a particular society or social group so that they can function within it.

sociopath

A person who shows psychopathic characteristics that are largely the result of early-life abuse and neglect.

somatotype

The idea that criminals can be identified by physical appearance.

status offense

An act considered illegal *only* for children, such as drinking alcohol, running away, truancy, curfew violations, and smoking cigarettes.

status
A socially defined position within a group.

statutory exclusion
Process established by statute that excludes certain juveniles, because of either age or offense, from juvenile court jurisdiction; charges are initially fled in criminal court.

stigmata
Distinctive physical features of born criminals.

street efficacy
The perceived ability to avoid violent confrontations and be safe even in negative, violent environments.

Stubborn Child Law
A law passed in 1641 stating that children who disobeyed their parents could be put to death.

suppression
A police response to gang activity that includes selective surveillance, arrest, and prosecution of gang members.

sweep search
A search of all students' lockers.

techniques of neutralization
Rationalizations used to justify delinquent activities.

tertiary prevention
Policies and programs that target existing delinquents and attempt to reduce recidivism by treating the individual with appropriate therapeutic efforts, or by incapacitating the youth to protect the community against further delinquencies.

theory
An integrated set of ideas that explain and predict *when* and *why* children commit crime.

30-day prevalence
The use of a drug at least once during the previous month.

Thompson v. Carthage School District
U.S. Supreme Court decision stating that school officials may legally search students and their lockers without consent.

Tinker v. Des Moines Independent Community School District
U.S. Supreme Court decision stating that students have the right of free expression, as long as their behavior does not interrupt school activities or intrude in school affairs or the lives of others.

tracking
The grouping of students into curricular categories, such as the college-preparatory, general, vocational, business, agricultural, and remedial tracks.

truant officers
Individuals whose job is to check for student absences from school.

turf
A gang's sense of territoriality.

turning points
Key life events that can either drive someone toward delinquent behavior or initiate the process of desisting from it.

Uniform Crime Reports (UCR)
The annual publication from the Federal Bureau of Investigation that provides data on crimes reported to the police, number of arrests, and number of persons arrested in the United States.

utilitarian principles
A set of ideas that assume behavior is calculated and that people gather and make sense of information before they act.

utilitarian punishment model
The idea that offenders must be punished to protect society.

Vernonia School District 47J v. Acton
U.S. Supreme Court decision stating that students participating in school athletic activities must submit upon request, to a drug test (urinalysis).

victimization survey
A method of producing crime data in which people are asked about their experiences as crime victims.

waiver of jurisdiction
A legal process to transfer a juvenile from juvenile to criminal court.

West Virginia State Board of Education v. Barnette
U.S. Supreme Court decision stating that students do not have to salute the flag while reciting the Pledge of Allegiance.

wraparound programs
Programs designed to build positive relationships and support networks between youths and their families, teachers, and community agencies through coordination of services.

Yarborough v. Alvarado
Case in which the U.S. Supreme Court ruled that police do not need to factor in the age and inexperience of a suspect in their decision about whether to read a juvenile his or her *Miranda* rights if the youth is not believed to be "in custody."

youth gang
A group of youths who are willing to use deadly violence to claim and protect territory, to attack rival gangs, or to engage in criminal activity.

INDEX

Boxes are noted with b, figures with f, tables with t.

JUVENILE DELINQUENCY TIMELINE

500s

500s CE: Age 7 was established under Roman Law as the minimum age at which youthful offenders could be prosecuted for their crimes.

1500s

1535: "Poor laws" were established to compel poor and neglected children into servitude.

1600s

1601: Elizabethan poor laws were enacted and became the model for the treatment of poor offenders.

1641: General Court of Massachusetts Bay Colony passed the Stubborn Child Law, which stated that children who disobey their parents could be put to death.

1642: The Massachusetts School Law was passed, which required parents (and masters of apprenticed children) to provide children with basic education and literacy.

1642: Thomas Graunger, age 16, became the first juvenile to be executed in the United States.

1700s

1764: Cesare Beccaria published *On Crimes and Punishments*.

1800s

1800s: Gangs became an unwanted fixture in urban areas.

1825: The first house of refuge for wayward children opened in New York.

1831: The Pennsylvania Supreme Court ruling, *Ex parte Crouse*, established the doctrine of *parens patriae*, whereby the state can act as the ultimate parent of a child.

1841: John Augustus became the first probation officer in the United States.

1851: The New York Juvenile Asylum was opened to house delinquents and orphans until they could be placed with rural families.

1852: Massachusetts passed the nation's first compulsory school attendance law.

1853: Charles Loring Brace established the Children's Aid Society.

1854: The "orphan trains" began carrying orphaned or destitute children from urban slums to rural areas to be placed with families.

1856: The first state institution in the United States built exclusively for girls opened in Massachusetts.

1859: Charles Darwin published *On the Origin of Species*.

1867: Karl Marx and Friedrich Engels published *Capital*.

1871: Charles Darwin published *The Descent of Man*.

1871: The first child abuse case was unsuccessfully brought before the courts when Emily Thompson, age 8, was returned to her abusive foster mother.

1874: Ten-year-old Mary Ellen Wilson became the first child to be protected from abuse after being removed from her home because of abuse suffered at the hands of her stepmother.

1876: Cesare Lombroso published *On Criminal Man*.

1893: The U.S. Supreme Court ruled in *Allen v. United States* that children younger than age 7 could not be guilty of a felony or punished for a capital offense because they are presumed incapable of forming criminal intent.

1893: Emile Durkheim published *The Division of Labor in Society*.

1895: Emile Durkheim published *The Rules of Sociological Method*.

1899: Cesare Lombroso and William Ferrero published *The Female Offender*.

1899: The first juvenile court was established in Cook County (Chicago), Illinois.

1900s

1902: Charles Horton Cooley published *Human Nature and the Social Order*.

1905: Alfred Binet and Theophile Simon developed the first standardized IQ test.

1905: Portland, Oregon, hired the first female police officer, Lola Baldwin.

1908: In *Commonwealth v. Fisher*, the state court upheld the right of the state to intervene in the lives of children without ensuring that their constitutional rights were protected.

1910s

1912: President Taft signed into law an act establishing the U.S. Children's Bureau.

1916: The widely used Stanford-Binet intelligence was developed.

1916: Willem Bonger published *Criminality and Economic Conditions*.

1920s

1923: W.I. Thomas published *The Unadjusted Girl*.

1924: Many urban police departments had established juvenile bureaus.

1927: In *Buck v. Bell*, the U.S. Supreme Court ruled that sterilization laws were constitutional.

1929: The orphan train made its last run. From 1854 to 1929, approximately 200,000 children were transported from urban slums to rural homes.

1929: All states and territories had passed compulsory school attendance laws.

1930s

1930: Sheldon Glueck and Eleanor Glueck published *500 Criminal Careers*, the first study of chronic juvenile offenders.

1930: The Federal Bureau of Investigation launched the Uniform Crime Reporting Program.

1931: The Chicago Area Project was established to address adolescent crime.

1932: Jean Piaget published *The Moral Judgment of the Child*.

1934: George Herbert Mead published *Mind, Self, and Society*.

1938: B.F. Skinner published *The Behavior of Organisms*.

1938: Frank Tannenbaum published *Crime and the Community*.

1938: Thorsten Sellin published *Culture and Conflict in Crime*.

1938: Robert Merton introduced strain theory to the literature on sociology of deviance.

1940s

1942: In *Skinner v. Oklahoma*, the U.S. Supreme Court ruled that the sterilization of criminals was unconstitutional.

1942: Clifford Shaw and Henry McKay published *Juvenile Delinquency in Urban Areas*.

1943: In *West Virginia State Board of Education v. Barnette*, the U.S. Supreme Court ruled that the free speech rights of students had been violated when they were required to salute the flag while reciting the Pledge of Allegiance.

1945: All U.S. states had established juvenile courts.

1946: Austin Porterfield conducted the first self-report study of juvenile delinquency.

1947: Edwin Sutherland published the theory of differential association in the fourth edition of *Principles of Criminology*.

1950s

1950: George Homans published *The Human Group*.

1950: Otto Pollak published *The Criminality of Women*.

1951: Edwin Lemert published *Social Pathology*.

1955: Albert Cohen published *Delinquent Boys*.

1960s

1960: Richard Cloward and Lloyd Ohlin published *Delinquency and Opportunity*.

1961: In *Mapp v. Ohio*, the U.S. Supreme Court extended the exclusionary rule to prohibit illegally obtained evidence in state criminal proceedings.

1963: Howard Becker published *Outsiders*.

1964: David Matza published *Delinquency and Drift*.

1965: The Head Start program was launched.

1965: James F. Short, Jr. and Fred Strodtbeck published *Group Process and Gang Delinquency*.

1966: In *Miranda v. Arizona*, the U.S. Supreme Court ruled that suspects in police custody have the right to remain silent and the right to counsel if they cannot afford one.

1966: In *Kent v. United States*, the U.S. Supreme Court ruled that a formal waiver hearing was necessary before a case in juvenile court could be transferred to criminal court.

1966: Kai Erikson published *Wayward Puritans*.

1967: In *In re Gault*, the U.S. Supreme Court established that juveniles could not be denied basic due process rights in juvenile adjudicatory hearings.

1967: The National Opinion Research Center conducted the first nationwide victimization survey.

1968: The U.S. Congress passed the *Juvenile Delinquency Prevention and Control Act*, which recommended that children charged with noncriminal (status offenses) be handled outside the court system.

1969: In *Chimel v. California*, the U.S. Supreme Court limited the extent of police searches.

1969: Travis Hirschi published *Causes of Delinquency*.

1970s

1970: In *In re Winship*, the U.S. Supreme Court ruled that in delinquency cases the state must prove its case beyond a reasonable doubt.

1971: In *McKeiver v. Pennsylvania*, the U.S. Supreme Court ruled that jury trials are not required in juvenile court hearings.

1972: The National Crime Victimization Survey (NCVS) was launched.

1972: Marvin Wolfgang, Robert Figlio, and Thorsten Sellin published *Delinquency in a Birth Cohort*.

1973: Edwin Schur published *Radical Nonintervention*.

1974: The U.S. Congress enacted the *Juvenile Justice and Delinquency Prevention Act*.

1974: Richard Quinney published *Critique of Legal Order*.

1975: James Q. Wilson published *Thinking about Crime*.

1975: In *Baker v. Owen*, the U.S. Supreme Court ruled that teachers could administer reasonable corporal punishment for disciplinary purposes.

1975: In *Goss v. Lopez*, the U.S. Supreme Court ruled that students facing suspension have specific legal rights.

1975: In *Breed v. Jones*, the U.S. Supreme Court ruled that the waiver of a juvenile to criminal court following adjudication in juvenile court constituted double jeopardy.

1976: Delbert Elliott launched the National Youth Survey.

1977: Albert Bandura published *Social Learning Theory*.

1977: In *Ingraham v. Wright*, the U.S. Supreme Court ruled that corporal punishment of students *does not* violate the cruel and unusual punishment clause of the Eighth Amendment.

1980s

1982: In *Eddings v. Oklahoma*, the U.S. Supreme Court ruled that a court must consider a juvenile's age as a mitigating circumstance during a capital sentence.

1985: James Q. Wilson and Richard Herrnstein published *Crime and Human Nature*.

1985: In *New Jersey v. T.L.O.*, the U.S. Supreme Court ruled that school officials may conduct warrantless searches of individuals at school on the basis of reasonable suspicion.

1986: James Messerschmidt published *Capitalism, Patriarchy, and Crime*.

1986: In *Bethel School District No. 403 v. Fraser*, the U.S. Supreme Court ruled that schools may ban vulgar and offensive language.

1987: William Julius Wilson published *The Truly Disadvantaged*.

1987: In *Garcia v. Miera*, the U.S. Supreme Court ruled that school officials may use corporal punishment, although it must not be excessive.

1987: Marvin Wolfgang, Terrence Thornberry, and Robert Figlio published *From Boy to Man, from Delinquency to Crime*.

1987: Francis Cullen published *Rethinking Crime and Deviance Theory*.

1988: In *Hazelwood v. Kuhlmeier*, the U.S. Supreme Court ruled that schools could regulate the content of student publications.

1988: The U.S. Congress passed the *Uniform Federal Crime Reporting Act*, which mandated that all federal law enforcement agencies submit crime data to the *UCR* program.

1988: In *Honig v. Doe*, the U.S. Supreme Court ruled that before schools can expel a disabled student, the school must first determine whether the offending behavior was caused by the student's disability

1989: In *Stanford v. Kentucky* and in *Wilkins v. Missouri*, the U.S. Supreme Court ruled that the execution of persons age 16 or 17 at the time of their crime was permissible.

1989: The Federal Bureau of Investigation launched the National Incident-Based Reporting System.

1990s

1990: The U.S. Congress passed the *Crime Awareness and Campus Security Act*, which required colleges to tally and report campus crime data to the *UCR* program.

1990: Michael Gottfredson and Travis Hirschi published *A General Theory of Crime*.

1990: The U.S. Congress passed the *Hate Crime Statistics Act*.

1991: Youth violence was recorded to be at an all-time high.

1993: Terrie Moffitt introduced the ideas of life-course persistent and adolescence-limited offenders.

1993: Adrian Raine published *The Psychopathology of Crime*.

1994: The U.S. Congress passed the *Violent Crime Control and Law Enforcement Act*.

1995: In *Vernonia School District 47J v. Acton*, the U.S. Supreme Court ruled that students participating in school athletic activities *must* submit upon request to an involuntary drug test.

1998: Mark Fleisher published *Dead End Kids*.

1999: Montana abolished its juvenile death penalty law.

2000s

2000: Mark Colvin published *Crime and Coercion*.

2001: Jody Miller published *One of the Guys*.

2001: President George W. Bush signed into law the *USA PATRIOT Act*.

2002: In *Board of Education v. Earls*, the U.S. Supreme Court ruled that schools could require drug testing before allowing students to participate in extracurricular activities.

2004: South Dakota and Wyoming abolished their juvenile death penalty laws.

2004: The Federal Bureau of Investigation discontinued use of the Crime Index.

2005: In *Roper v. Simmons*, the U.S. Supreme Court ruled that it was unconstitutional to execute persons who were under age 18 at the time of their crime.

2006: Florida Governor Jeb Bush closed all juvenile boot camps and replaced them with facilities focusing on education and training.

2009: President Barack Obama signed into law the *American Recovery and Reinvestment Act*, which provided law enforcement agencies with $400 million to purchase improved equipment and hire additional personnel.

2010s

2010: In *Graham v. Florida*, the U.S. Supreme Court ruled that juvenile offenders could not be sentenced to life imprisonment without parole for nonhomicide offenses.

2011: The Campaign for Youth Justice published a report on legislative changes in 15 states that have removed adolescents from the adult criminal justice system since 2005.

2012: The U.S. Department of Justice announced that it would expand the conceptualization and definition of forcible rape in the Uniform Crime Reporting Program to include nonfemale victims and other forms of sexual assault.

2012: In *Miller v. Alabama* and in *Jackson v. Hobbs*, the U.S. Supreme Court ruled that life imprisonment for juveniles convicted of murder is a violation of the Eighth Amendment

2014: Matt DeLisi and Michael Vaughn published their temperament-based theory of antisocial behavior and criminal justice system involvement.

2016: Chad Trulson and colleagues published *Lost Causes: Blended Sentencing, Second Chances, and the Texas Youth Commission*.

2016: In *Montgomery v. Louisiana*, the U.S. Supreme Court ruled that a sentence of life without parole for any juvenile offense is unconstitutional and would apply retroactively.